MORE PRAIS
STAND UP ST

This former Congresswoman from Colorado feels a little silly recommending a book by the husband of one of Congress's greatest progressive current representatives, Congresswoman Jan Schakowsky from Chicago! The real political experience of Robert Creamer makes *Listen to Your Mother, Stand Up Straight!* one of the best "how to do it" books around. Progressives are always accused of being policy wonks with no real political experience on how to deliver. Not the case here, you get the policy and but also how to make that policy a reality!
—**Pat Schroeder, President Association of American Publishers**
   Former Member of Congress

Stand Up Straight! is a straight up shot in the arm for progressives. Robert Creamer has successfully turned decades of campaign and organizing skills into an essential handbook for understanding political power, activism, and progressive values. Creamer rightly argues that progressives should embrace their core principles and fight for the real political center in American politics today -- issues like universal health care and pre-k, energy independence, redeployment from Iraq, and a return to sane and sensible national security policies.
—**John Podesta, President and CEO, Center for American Progress**
   Former Chief of Staff to President William J. Clinton

A stand-up book from a stand-up guy, showing us how to put progress back into "progressive." From broad vision to minute details, Creamer offers an invaluable manual for those who want to reassert our country's historic egalitarian values of fairness, justice, and opportunity for all.
—**Jim Hightower, Best selling author**
   Radio commentator and editor of the Hightower Lowdown

Progress takes more than passion, it requires planning. This book is a blueprint for victory.
—**Congressman Lloyd Doggett**

Well worth the read because it focuses the mind on an unusual subject for progressives—winning.
—**Tom Hayden, California state senate [ret.], author,** *Ending the War in Iraq*

This book is one stop shopping for progressive activists who want to keep their values and win. It combines vision, program, strategy, political context, tactics, organizing and election techniques and is infused with an optimistic spirit. It is 1/2 organizing training manual, 1/2 manifesto, 1/2 values to live by. It is so chock full of insights and good sense as well as personal stories that it is more than one whole. Bob Creamer is a treasure.

—**Heather Booth, Founder Midwest Academy**
  Former Training Director Democratic National Committee
  Democratic Political Consultant

A truism: those who can, do; those who can't... teach and write books. So when someone who can, and does, like Bob Creamer, takes the time to stop and write a book, everyone who cares about the art of activism should seize the chance to learn from that rarest of rarities: a teacher who actually knows what he's talking about and who has successfully put into practice what he preaches.

—**Doug Phelps, President Public Interest Research Group (PIRG)**

There are lots of people who are smart and sophisticated about political strategy, and there are lots of people who are passionate and committed about progressive causes. There are very few people who combine those qualities as well as Bob Creamer, a fact which readers of his book will quickly come to appreciate.

—**Geoffrey Garin, President (and Democratic pollster)**
  Peter D. Hart Research Associates

In *Stand Up Straight!*, Bob Creamer gives citizens an owners manual for Democracy. With a practical eye from his decades of experience, Bob shows how to do the real work of political organizing and win, by promoting deep progressive values. With hundreds of real world examples and step-by-step advice, *Stand Up Straight!* is both inspirational and a serious tool. Thanks, Bob.

—**Wes Boyd, Founder of MoveOn.org**

One of the great progressive strategists of our time insightfully explains how to conduct successful issue campaigns and the challenges we face in moving forward on a social justice agenda.

—**Chuck Loveless, National Legislative Director, AFSCME**

In *Stand Up Straight!*, Bob Creamer brings together the best of both worlds: years of old-school experience combined with a fresh new approach to politics. A must-read for anyone attempting to navigate the ever-changing political environment.

—**Will Robinson, Founder and Partner, The New Media Firm**

Finally, a comprehensive manual for progressive victory. Politics is not just about right and wrong. It's about results, and building a better world for our children.

—**Bill Zimmerman, political and media consultant, Zimmerman and Markman**

This book lays out a play book for the blocking and tackling of politics: understanding self interest, nuts and bolts execution, and refusing to give the other side any quarter. That kind of winning attitude is exactly how we're reviving the Democratic Party in the State of Virginia. A must-read for state Democratic Party chairs.
—Dick Cranwell, Chairman, Virginia Democratic Party

Bob Creamer's forty years of organizing has made him a master organizer. This book, *Stand Up Straight!*, more than any other I have read, combines values, passion, methodology, nuts and bolts and a will to win. I run an organizing institute that trains hundreds of organizers and thousands of leaders. I will put this book on the must read list for all those who choose to make organizing their path.
—Greg Galluzzo, Director, Gamaliel Foundation

By articulating a strategy which incisively combines passion and pragmatism, Creamer not only shows how progressives can achieve electoral victories but, more crucially, how we can imagine and build a different nation, based on integrity and justice.
—Ariel Dorfman, author of play and movie *Death and the Maiden*
  Professor, Duke University

Invigorating, insightful, inspiring and battle-tested. Creamer provides a 'how-to' manual for progressive victory in 2008 as well as a thoughtful guide for turning around America and meeting the challenges of our global future. A must-read for serious progressives, whether they are grassroots activists or candidates for elected office.
—John Cameron, Illinois Political Director, AFSCME

In *Stand Up Straight!*, Bob Creamer puts on paper the *'where'* we need to go as a nation, and the *'how'* we can get there by making 'Democracy' and 'Justice' mean something real in the United States of America.
—Josh Hoyt, Executive Director
  Illinois Coalition for Immigrant & Refugee Rights

Everyone who wants the inside scoop on how progressives can win on the important issues of our time must read this book. Bob Creamer knows because he is at the center of it all.
—Alan Charney, Program Director, USAction

Both an inspirational and practical guide to show progressives how to organize successfully, and play to win.
—Saul Shorr, Democratic Media Consultant, Shorr, Johnson Magnus

This is an important handbook for all of us. Bob Creamer has turned a lifetime of progressive leadership into an interesting and essential treatise for longtime activists, politicians and aspiring politicians, and the growing numbers of concerned young people. This book outlines not only what we need to accomplish to achieve a just society and personal fulfillment, but also shows us in chapter after chapter how, why and with whom progressives will accomplish those goals.
—**Robert M. Brandon, Public Affairs Consultant**

Robert Creamer has written an indispensable resource for Progressives--organizers, strategists, electoral and issue activists. It's user-friendly and filled with important how-to's, strategy and tactics, insights and wisdom from a long and distinguished career. It combines serious discussion of broad concepts and vision with meticulous attention to campaigning details. Your copy is bound to be dog-eared in no time.
—**Ira Arlook, Managing Director, Fenton Communications, Washington, DC**

Bob Creamer has been doing the Lord's work all his life, organizing people for decades that no one else cared about or fought for to work together to fight for themselves. Now he has poured all that knowledge and passion into a political primer for our times, giving us a strategy for building a progressive political majority that will last.
—**Mike Lux, Progressive Strategies, Blogger on Openleft.com**
  Former Special Assistant to President Clinton

Encyclopedic! A tour-de-force! Peppered with stories, case studies, field-tested tactics, and complex concepts simplified, this is a must read book for all progressive organizers!
—**Jackie Kendall, Executive Director, Midwest Academy**

Stand Up Straight! is different from the recent slew of mostly superficial books by political consultants and observers telling Democrats how to win elections. Long time organizer Bob Creamer fills this exceptionally useful book with in-depth, essential information built on perceptive analysis of human behavior. He includes the nuts and bolts essentials – who to target, how to plan, how to mobilize. But also he also analyzes the "vision thing" – what are progressive values and how progressives can and must communicate a vision of a truly democratic society in order to create one.
—**Gene Guerrero, Public Interest Lobbyist**

Perhaps the most comprehensive treatment available of how to build political support for progressive policies that would chart a new course. Creamer's book belongs on the bookshelf of those who are, or aspire to be, progressive activists.
—**Bob Greenstein, Director Center on Budget and Policy Priorities**

Bob Creamer offers a must read blueprint for reclaiming progressive values and power at the grassroots and the ballot box. It perfectly blends his streetwise organizing sense and strategic and tactical lessons -- with his informed optimism for the progressive possibilities of U.S. politics. Read *Listen To Your Mother Stand Up Straight!* NOW –and let's get to work!
—**Chuck Collins, Institute for Policy Studies**
 Author of *The Moral Measure of the Economy*

Bob Creamer is one of the best in the country at synthesizing message research, earned and paid media, grassroots organizing and other components of a political or issues campaign into one powerful, integrated voice. This book is a how-to manual for everyone who wants to beat the Karl Roves of the world at their own game.
—**Pete Giangreco, Democratic Political Consultant**
 Partner, The Strategy Group

As an organizer and strategist, Bob Creamer has won all kinds of improbable victories for progressive causes. This book is must-reading for his fellow progressives who seek to do the same, and to build a more decent world.
—**Harold Meyerson, Executive Editor, The American Prospect**

Long one of the nation's most brilliant and creative strategists, Bob Creamer has written a compelling and timely book that is must reading for those who want the progressive movement to achieve sustainable success.
—**Ralph G. Neas, President Emeritus, People For the American Way**

Robert Creamer's book comes along just as the activist "netroots" are firing up a new generation of progressive activists -- and just as average Americans are rejecting the radical conservatives who have weakened our country and undermined the middle class. It lays out a blueprint -- and an optimistic attitude -- for taking our country back. Everyone who cares about America's future should buy this book.
—**Roger Hickey, Co-Director, Campaign for America's Future**

If you care about economic and social justice, read this book. If you want to act in the name of economic and social justice, read this book. Creamer has lived the fight and learned from the fight. There are few with his experience or expertise.
—**Paul Tewes, Democratic Political Consultant**
 Partner, Hildebrand-Tewes Consulting

Bob Creamer has devoted his life to progressive causes. Here he provides a fascinating narrative of how progressives have won in the past and provides a blueprint for future victories.
—**David Axelrod, Democratic Political Consultant**

Thank goodness for Bob Creamer's call to courage, to principle, and to faith in our history of progressive action. Represent what you truly believe in, find common ground whenever and wherever you can, use the arrows in your quiver wisely and sparingly, be outraged by, and oppose policies (not people). Whatever happens do NOT compromise what you believe in; you not only won't prevail, you will cease to exist in many important ways. Bob has my admiration, my appreciation, and my "vote".
—**Peter Yarrow of Peter, Paul and Mary**

Bob Creamer has managed to summarize a strategy for progressive politics while presenting an inspiring moral vision for this country. He argues that the future of America can, and must, rest on a society that values diversity over monoculturalism, peace over war, economic justice over greed, and consensus over divisiveness. As eager as many of us in" the values business" are to capitalize on the building momentum for a progressive values message, it will all come to naught without Creamer's insistence on good organizing, solid community-building, smart politics, and sophisticated messaging.
—**Rev Ron Stief, Director of Organizing Strategy, Faith in Public Life,**
  A Resource Center for Justice and the Common Good

Bob Creamer has inspired and taught our movement for over 30 years. Read this book and act accordingly.
—**Jeff Blum, Executive Director USAction**

Bob Creamer's welcome book rightly instructs progressives to say and fight for what they believe. To Hell with the politics of timidity - a long-term progressive majority is within our reach.
—**Congressman Jim McGovern**

Bob Creamer's message to progressives, to Stand Up Straight, is one that must be heeded by all who are willing to fight for a truly equitable American society. Those of us whose daily work consists of opening doors for the underserved, realigning the priorities of our country's governing bodies, and fostering a long term vision of prosperity for generations to come, cannot afford to miss this book. Bob's messages of hope and optimism, combined with strategies for how to build campaigns that successfully intersect vision and action, could not be delivered during a more critical time in our country's history.
—**Wade Henderson, Esq.**
  President and CEO, Leadership Conference on Civil Rights

Creamer's book connects the dots from the grass-roots to the Democratic Party structure--and through the blogosphere. Listen to Creamer and stand up straight for a progressive victory!
—**Mitchell J. Freedman, MF Blog, author,** *A Disturbance of Fate*
  (Finalist, Sidewise Awards, 2004)

Listen to Bob Creamer. One of America's best organizers has written one of the best books on how progressives can stand up, fight back, and win for a change. This book is filled with proven, practical advice about how to out-work, out-organize, and out-argue the other side.
—**David Kusnet, Chief speechwriter for former President Bill Clinton**
 1992-1994, author, *Speaking American: How the Democrats Can Win*

Bob Creamer is a creative and bold visionary who has written a valuable resource guide that progressives can refer to time and again not only to win elections, but to also secure a more just society for us all. With his moral clarity, clear vision and good-old common sense, Creamer's book provides the "shot in the arm" that the progressive movement needs. Guaranteed to turn "whining" progressives into "winning" progressives.
—**William McNary, President, USAction**

This book is an invaluable toolkit for any campaign local or national -- and a tremendous tool for training. This is a must have for any progressive organization or effort.
—**Celinda Lake, Democratic Pollster, Lake Research Partners**

In this book Creamer not only lays out a plan for progressives to win, he also describes a progressive vision for the future that recognizes the interconnection of people all over the globe. That vision requires that the world address the most critical issue of our time: the structural violence visited on billions of people in the developing world by powerlessness and poverty.
—**Dr. Paul Farmer, Presley Professor at Harvard Medical School**
 Partners in Health, author *Pathologies of Power*

This book is so important because it focuses like a laser on the one element that is essential to progressive victory: courage. Without exception, all of our historic victories have required that people had the courage to act -- and stand up straight. The lessons in *Stand Up Straight!* were learned the hard way by generations of Americans fighting for civil rights, women's rights and important social change. It's a must read for anyone who is passionate about changing America – now.
—**Rev. Jesse L. Jackson, President, Rainbow/PUSH Coalition**

In *Stand Up Straight!*, Robert Creamer gives progressives practical insights, tools, and analysis to work smarter. It will hopefully inspire more people to act and help more people to act effectively.
—**Andy Stern, President, SEIU**

When I was in college, this is the book that I always looked for ... and never could find. *Stand Up Straight!* is definitive—a guide for serious political organizers. This should be standard material in every classroom!
—**David (Dino) Martino, Political Director, SEIU Local 1**

In Ruth McKenney's famous 1938 play, *My Sister Eileen*, the breakthrough moment is when Ruth decides to "write what you know." In *Stand Up Straight!*, Bob Creamer has done exactly that. For over thirty years, since we worked together in Chicago, Bob Creamer has stood up straight, and has won. From door to door organizing, to legislative issue victories, to winning political campaigns, Bob Creamer has done it all. This book-- a distillation of a lifetime of incredible work-- contains invaluable advice for progressives, and any one else smart enough to listen.

—**Miles Rapoport**
   President, Demos: A Network of Ideas and Action
   Former Connecticut Secretary of the State

Bob Creamer has written a book both brilliant in its analysis and inspiring in its vision. It's a guide for all of us on how to create the kind country and society that many of us have talked about and worked for all our lives. It's a candidate's roadmap on how to win and win as a strong progressive....a strategist cogent analysis of what it will take to gain power based principles we can be proud of....a organizer's guide to success in their campaign next week and for a major policy victory three years away...and a leader's manual for the principles and vision to inspire everyday citizens to rally to their side. Bob has is brought 40 years of on-the-front-lines experience to produce what will be shortly become the manual that all progressive leaders and activists alike will keep close at hand.

—**Marc Caplan, Program Officer, Proteus Fund**

Robert Creamer is a scarce national resource -- a progressive organizer with an astute sense of strategy and tactics. This book is replete with insight, common sense, and vision. Organizers will find it an invaluable resource.

—**Robert L. Borosage, Co-Director, Campaign for America's Future**

Creamer's classroom has been the frontlines and trenches of progressive organizing, from the Civil Rights Movement to the battle for children's health care. Here, he shows us how to replace fear with hope, to renew the call to commitment, and to create our society's next historical movement.

—**Congressman John Lewis (D-Georgia)**

Listen to Your Mother

STAND UP STRAIGHT!

★ ★ ★ ★ ★ ★ ★ ★

HOW PROGRESSIVES CAN WIN

★ ★ ★ ★ ★ ★ ★ ★

ROBERT CREAMER

SEVEN LOCKS PRESS

SANTA ANA, CALIFORNIA

Seven Locks Press
P.O. Box 25689
Santa Ana, CA 92799
(800) 354-5348

Individual sales: This book is available through most bookstores or can be ordered directly from Seven Locks Press at the address above.

Quantity Sales: Special discounts are available on quantity purchases by corporations, associations and others. For details, contact the "Special Sales Department" at the publisher's address above.

Cover & Interior Design by Kira Fulks • www.kirafulks.com

Printed in the United States of America

Library of Congress Cataloging-in-Publication Data is available from the publisher

ISBN: 0-9795852-9-5
        978-0-9795852-9-6

DEDICATION

This book is dedicated to my late parents,
Robert W. Creamer, whose optimism never flagged,
and my mother, Adelaide Boggs Creamer,
who always taught me to stand up straight.

ACKNOWLEDGEMENTS

Many thanks to all of those who made this book possible, in particular Jim Riordan and the people at Seven Locks Press, my editor John Seiler, and designer Kira Fulks.

For help on the book and everything else in my professional life, I am deeply indebted to my colleagues at the Strategic Consulting Group, in particular Cheri Whiteman who put in hours and hours preparing the book for publication; Linda Saucedo who is the soul of our firm and manages its day to day operations; Jill Beckwith who is an invaluable member of our staff; and the remarkable Christine Carr who recently left our firm to attend medical school.

I learn an enormous amount everyday from the wonderful clients our firm is privileged to serve including Americans United for Change, Americans Against Escalation in Iraq, the Emergency Campaign for America's Priorities, American Federation of State County and Municipal Employees, Coalition for Comprehensive Immigration Reform, Illinois Coalition for Immigrant and Refugee Rights, and many other organizations and candidates for public office.

Much in this book I have learned from the many great political professionals, organizers and leaders with whom I have had the privilege of working closely over the last four decades, especially my former partners at SCG, Jerry Morrison and John Hennelly.

The analysis in this book has been heavily influenced by the work of a number of important writers and thinkers including Jared Diamond, Malcomb Gladwell, George Lakoff, Tom Peters, Robert Waterman, Saul Alinsky, Ariel Dorfman, David Grinspoon, Paul Krugman, Clayton Christensen, Neil Smelser, Kevin Phillips, George Packer, Seymour Hersh, Daniel Goleman, Donald Phillips, George MacGregor Burns, Nolan McCarty, Keith Poole, Howard Rosenthal, E.J. Dionne, Al Gore, Paul Farmer and many others. I sincerely hope that they would approve of my application of their ideas, but I bear sole responsibility for the characterizations, descriptions and interpretations in this volume.

I did much of the preliminary work on this book while spending five months on a forced sabbatical at the Federal Prison Camp at Terre Haute, Indiana. I want to thank the men who were my colleagues there for their support and friendship.

Finally, I want to thank my family for their lifelong support and inspiration: my daughter Lauren McLaughlin and her husband Michael McLaughlin; step son Ian Schakowsky and his late wife Fiona Schakowsky; step daughter Mary Hart and her husband Dan Hart; brother Steve Creamer and his wife Lena Creamer; sister Nancy Nix and her husband Collins Nix; Sister-in-law Deborah Danoff; and for their unconditional approval, my Golden Retrievers Lucky and Buddy.

Most of all I am deeply indebted to my wife Jan Schakowsky, who has been my personal and professional partner, my inspiration and supporter for almost thirty years. In addition to being an extraordinary Member of Congress she is also the best political strategist I know, and the love of my life.

TABLE OF CONTENTS

SECTION THREE
TARGETS FOR COMMUNICATION

SECTION FOUR
THE PRINCIPLES OF POLITICAL COMMUNICATION

SECTION SEVEN
THE BATTLE OVER VALUES-THE RIGHT IS WRONG

SECTION NINE
BUILDING A DEMOCRATIC SOCIETY

FOREWORD

TAKE RESPONSIBILITY FOR WINNING
BY
TOM MATZZIE, MoveOn.org

As in life, on every issue and in every campaign there are at minimum two groups of people—the people who get it done and the people who watch the folks who get it done.

Understanding which one you are is the first step towards changing the world. A key hallmark of the first group—those who get it done—is that they take personal responsibility for the job and the larger mission.

Progressives today need to take direct responsibility for winning.

The time is past for being happy if we hold a good event or have a pretty website. The goal is to build and use political power to change the world. That is a big task and progressives must match the task with a vision and plan just as grand.

This is what we did at MoveOn.org during the 2006 election—we took responsibility for winning. By the time the polls had closed we had worked in 57 races—contributing to 33 of the 36 election wins. More than six million phone calls to voters. TV ad campaigns in 15 congressional districts. And, MoveOn members contributed over $28 million to the cause.

This win started in a three-part plan for winning the election that the MoveOn leadership, including myself, hatched in early 2006. What was unique was that in the planning process we asked the hard question: what do we need to do to win? We weren't content to ask what we could do. The question was, what could we do with our efforts that would create a dynamic to help win? The answer was MoveOn's big plan to win the election.

There were three steps for MoveOn driven by the world we lived in and a belief that we could build a campaign big enough to meet the enormity of the task. Faith in a big plan—is something more Progressives need to embrace.

First, we knew early on that there weren't enough competitive House races—so we made a plan to make more races competitive with significant TV advertising buys. Dozens of races had to be competitive to make winning a majority possible—and in early 2006 they weren't. It took about $2 million—a large sum (not really a lot of money in politics) but certainly something on the scale MoveOn members could support. This strategy worked with great success—opening a second and third-tier of races.

Second, we knew no other groups were working to get out the vote in enough congressional districts to win the 15 seats Democrats needed to throw the Republicans out. So, we made a plan and built a revolutionary phone-based GOTV program to mobilize voters. More than 200,000 volunteers joined in the effort making millions of phone calls. The technology for this effort didn't exist when we started the effort but through imagination and hard work we were able to get it done.

Third, we knew having a lot of competitive races meant a lot of candidates would need resources to run their campaigns—so we fundraised for these candidates from hundreds of thousands of MoveOn members in small credit card gifts. The average donation was $43 during 2006.

There were some key moments in the race—like five days before the election when we got word that Senate candidate Jon Tester was almost out of money. At that moment, MoveOn was the only organization in America who could raise hard-money fast enough to keep Tester's campaign going. In less than 24 hours—and by the time the banks opened in Montana—we had raised over $240,000 online.

I'm not sharing the story of the MoveOn election program to brag about a political war story. The moral of the story is that MoveOn took responsibility for doing everything possible to win the 2006 election—and it worked.

If we hadn't cooked up such a comprehensive plan to win, would Democrats have taken the House and Senate? Maybe. But our plan was aimed at success regardless of their actions—we took responsibility for winning. That is exactly what progressives need to do today. It is our country and we need to lead it into the future.

To do this sort of work you need to start with a fundamental trust and belief in the American public. The voting public in America isn't stupid. Every now and then you hear some patronizing person insult the intelligence of the American people complaining about how people get snookered and voted against their interests. I'm not convinced.

In my experience, the public trusts in leaders like George W. Bush early on because they trust in all people. Their naiveté is a symptom of healthy honesty. The public doesn't want to walk around assuming everybody is a liar. What a terrible place that would be. We want to trust our neighbors and hope our leaders aren't scoundrels.

Progressives need to have faith in the American people and ask them to trust us. We earn that trust by showing leadership. Nobody is entitled to the levers of power because we have good ideas. All of us have to earn the opportunity to lead and the first step is to take responsibility for winning.

Strategic insights about how progressives win—and not merely show up—is what this book, and Bob Creamer's life, is all about. I have benefited from Bob Creamer's sage advice and guidance more than once. This book should be read by anybody and everybody working for change through advocacy, politics or organizing. From strategy to tactics—grand vision to nuts-and-bolts—Bob Creamer has a roadmap for all of us.

For those of us who spend time targeting politicians to try to get them to vote specific ways, this book has probably the first comprehensive set of strategies and tactics ever assembled. At the core of it is an analysis of the psychology of members of Congress—all their soft spots and how to affect them. Every progressive lobbyist should commit to memory "The Six Categories of Self Interest" and use them to effect change and win.

But in the end, the key to successful organizing runs through the entire book. It is a lesson every new and old organizer should internalize like a religious creed. Progressives must take responsibility for winning

INTRODUCTION

In November of 2004, progressive political power in the United States reached a fifty-year low. Our Presidential candidate had been rejected. Both houses of Congress and the Presidency were in the hands of radical conservatives. The Supreme Court was on the brink of being lost for a generation. The Labor movement was fracturing. Progressives were demoralized.

Yet today, less than three years later, we have an historic opportunity to create a progressive political realignment that could reshape American and world politics for years to come.

This book is about how—together—we can make that realignment a reality. How progressives can win.

Its thesis is simple. In order to win, Progressives need to proudly and self-confidently talk to Americans about our values and our vision of the future. We need to listen to our mothers and stand up straight.

The book is addressed to progressive political activists. It's addressed to long-time activists, brand-new activists and those who are considering dipping a toe into the political stream for the very first time.

It's intended for young people who are considering a life-long commitment to the progressive cause, and for anyone who is curious about how voters make political decisions and what is involved in organizing for change.

This book lays out a broad strategy for victory, but it also analyzes the tactics needed to win real world political battles one at a time.

It is about the critical importance of political vision, the subtleties of political communication and the nuts and bolts of executing political action.

It's about progressive values, the future of human society, the self-interests of Members of Congress, and the techniques of a good precinct captain.

Most of all, this book is aimed at people who are serious about transforming an historic opportunity into long-term progressive political realignment in the United States; people who want to see their children grow up in a peaceful, prosperous, democratic world—and are willing to fight to make it happen.

SECTION ONE

AN HISTORIC OPPORTUNITY

CHAPTER ONE

2004 — What Were They Thinking?

I sat on the hotel room bed staring at the TV in disbelief. Like many others who had worked so hard to bring out the progressive vote in 2004, I was devastated that America would have to endure four more years of George W. Bush. To make matters worse, the Republicans had actually increased their majorities in both the House and the Senate.

All afternoon, exit polls had buoyed our spirits. Our political consulting firm – the Strategic Consulting Group (SGC) had worked hard to put thousands of Election Day Get-Out-the-Vote volunteers on the streets in Florida, Michigan and Arizona. Those volunteers had joined hundreds of thousands of others across the country who had poured megawatts of energy into an attempt to end the greatest resurgence of conservatism in America since the Gilded Age.

We had lost—and things in America looked bleak.

His victory would give George Bush, and the conservative movement, unprecedented control of the levers of governmental power. It would allow him to shape the Supreme Court and judiciary for a generation, and to embed conservatives at every level of government.

The odds were high that he could reshape the basic structures of American political economy. Once made those changes would be very hard to undo. The conservatives planned to use their "mandate" to privatize Social Security and Medicare, to remake the tax code and to create what they called the "ownership society." (Illinois Senator Dick Durbin says that really means: "We're all in this alone.")

They planned to gut environmental laws, and viewed the election results as a vote of confidence in their disastrous foreign policy. The religious right saw the ensuing four years as an opportunity to impose its understanding of "moral values" on everyone.

In the afternoon of Election Day, dismal exit polls had settled like a pall on the Bush headquarters. But by early in the morning on November 3rd, as I stared blankly at the TV screen, they were once again riding high.

To many Progressives it just didn't add up. The tax breaks for the rich that lay at the center of the Bush economic policy had done nothing for middle-class incomes. While Paris Hilton jetted around the world spending her tax cuts, most families were having a harder and harder time. By Election Day, it was clear to everyone that Bush had stampeded the country into the Iraqi quagmire with arguments about Weapons of Mass Destruction that were patently untrue. More soldiers were being killed by the day and there was no end in sight. Voters across America felt that the country was on the wrong track. How in the world could they elect him to a second term? *What were they thinking?*

Of course there are many serious investigators—including Robert F. Kennedy, Jr.—who believe that Bush didn't really win at all. They make a compelling case that the Ohio Secretary of State and local election authorities disenfranchised over 300,000 predominantly Democratic voters, costing Kerry Ohio's decisive electoral votes.[1] No one contests, however, that Bush did in fact win the popular vote in 2004. And besides, given Bush's record, it shouldn't have even been close. What went wrong?

In the weeks that followed, pundits turned out a blizzard of paper analyzing the Kerry defeat. But in all the analysis, one key symbolic mystery stood out: Why did the poorest counties in Ohio vote Republican? In the economically depressed counties of Meigs or Adams or Vinton, very few people received part of the hundreds of billions of dollars in tax breaks that had flowed to the wealthiest people in America. The economic prospects of small towns like Pomeroy and West Union had seriously declined during the Bush presidency. Why would these people seemingly vote against their own self-interest?

And why, just two years later, did many of these same people cast their votes against the Republicans in the Midterm Elections—and turn their backs on George Bush in the opinion polls? Meigs County had gone 58% to 41% for Bush in 2004, yet it gave Democrat Sherrod Brown almost 52% in 2006. Vinton, the poorest county in Ohio, had supported Bush 55% to 45%, but when the votes were counted in 2006 it gave Brown 55%.

Unraveling that mystery is the key to long-term progressive success.

Some might answer that these voters were simply uninformed or under-educated, or duped by the Republican propaganda in 2004, and finally "woke up" in 2006.

But voters like those in Vinton County did not vote contrary to their *perception* of their own self-interest in 2004, nor did they simply wake up one day and recognize their "real" self-interest in 2006. In fact, voters have an understanding of their self-interests that involves a much more complex spectrum of needs than simply their economic well-being.

This book will make the case that to effectively contest for these and other swing voters—to effectively contest for the future of our society—Progressives need to understand that entire, complex matrix of self-interests. And we have to address the full range of those self-interests head-on.

To win elections and create a long-term progressive realignment of American politics, Progressives have to understand and address the patterns of needs and desires that define how people think about their *core identities. We need to address their need for meaning and purpose.* The size of a person's paycheck has to be understood in the context of how he views his *overall relationship to the world.*

There are "moderate" or "pragmatic" Democrats who argue that in order to win, Democrats should adopt many conservative assumptions. They believe that attracting swing voters involves "splitting the difference" between Progressives and conservatives.

Nothing could be further from the truth.

In order to consistently win—in order to successfully contest for the power to chart the course for the future of our world—Progressives must offer a clear progressive vision for that future.

We need to offer a world view—a coherent set of values that provides Americans a sense of meaning and purpose.

In the past, congressional Democrats have often been criticized for their failure to provide "positive" alternatives to right-wing policy. But it's not the proposals and policies that were lacking—there have been hundreds of proposals. What has often been lacking is the progressive vision that gives broader meaning to those proposals. We have failed to frame the American political debate in terms of progressive values.

In 2004 Democrats didn't lose the presidential election because we lacked policies and programs. The Kerry Campaign trotted out new policies and proposals every other day. We lost because our campaign talked about policies and programs while Bush talked about right and wrong—about values. He talked about his vision of the future.

As he created a master plan for the city of Chicago, after the Great Chicago Fire, architect Daniel Burnham said: "Make no small plans; they have no power to stir men's blood." Neither do "10-point" programs.

By the 2006 Midterm Elections, it had become clear to many Americans that the Bush vision was a mirage. Now it is up to us to provide America with a clear progressive alternative—a vision that confronts the challenges presented by the future, and describes how we can realize its possibilities.

To beat the right—to fundamentally realign politics in America for many generations—Progressives need to consistently, proudly, self-confidently articulate that progressive vision.

People want and need meaning in their lives. They want something to be committed to. Tepid, moderate, incremental policies and programs do nothing to address that need. An inspiring progressive vision for the future does.

The right characterizes progressive values as "soft," "utopian" and "naïve." But the hard fact is that progressive values *must* prevail if human beings are to survive and prosper in the world of the future. Far from being "pie in the sky," "utopian" or "softheaded," progressive values are the most precious, adaptive possessions of humanity—and they have provided the moral foundation for the unfolding story of American democracy.

The future of our society and our planet depends on our ability to create a world that reflects those values. And the growing power of our technology—our new ability to destroy human civilization, and alter our climate—means that we don't have forever to get ourselves on the right track.

In this book we will discuss the many ingredients that are necessary to assemble winning electoral and issue campaigns—and a winning Progressive Movement. But the one ingredient necessary to bring all of the others together—the one ingredient without which long-term victory is impossible—is the clear elaboration of our values and our vision.

If we do it proudly and self confidently—and if we plan and execute well-run electoral and issue campaigns—we can win.

Progressives have what it takes to win the battle for our future, if only we will listen to our mothers and *stand up straight.*

CHAPTER TWO

An Historic Opportunity
for Political Realignment

EMERGING FROM OUR DEFENSIVE CROUCH

Since the mid-1970s, American Progressives have been on the ideological defensive. For 70% of the years since 1968, America has had a Republican president. Even during the Clinton years, conservatives controlled the broad value frame for the nation's political debate.

The Clinton presidency provided major pushback and achieved important successes—but only in the face of the dominant conservative values.

When Clinton was President, at least there were two teams on the ideological field. But even then, Progressives always played the role of the underdog. By completely consolidating power from 2000 to 2006, Republicans had virtual free rein to implement their neocon foreign policies and trickle-down economics.

As a result, most Americans know a lot more about what Progressives are against, than what we are for. The polling confirms that twice as many people say they know what conservatives stand for than what Progressives stand for.

It's no wonder. For the twelve years before the Midterm Elections, Progressives were forced to spend most of our time running campaigns to stop right-wing assaults. Republicans had the only team at bat. Progressives played nothing but defense.

Finally, in the 2006 Midterm Elections, Progressives began to emerge from our defensive crouch.

We won a major battle with the right.

Many American voters rejected the war in Iraq, trickle-down economics, the incompetence of the response to Hurricane Katrina and the culture of corruption.

They responded to the message: Had enough? *Vote Democratic.*

But most Americans voted *against* conservatives, not *for* Progressives. That was enough in the 2006 Midterms. To fundamentally realign politics over the long haul, Americans need to know—and come to believe in—what we are for, not just what we are against.

THE TWO COMPONENTS OF POLITICAL REALIGNMENT

Real long-term political realignment has two components:

- Democrats must forge a solid working majority in the electorate that can translate into repeated electoral victories—especially at the Federal level.
- Progressives need to change the fundamental frame for political and economic debate. We must re-establish the dominance of progressive values in mainstream political and economic dialogue and project a clear, compelling, progressive vision for the future of America and all of human society.

Our success at achieving either of these two goals will heavily influence our ability to achieve the other. The new Democratic control of Congress greatly enhances our ability to reframe political debate.

But it is equally true that by proudly reasserting our progressive values we greatly increase our chances of repeated electoral victory.

What's needed in this regard is not just a list of progressive policies and programs—what is needed is a reassertion of our *fundamental values.*

We have to provide a clear contrast to the right's belief in unbridled pursuit of individual interest with our commitment to the common good; selfishness versus commitment to others; division versus unity; fear versus hope; that we're all in this together, not "all in this alone."

In a period of realignment—when political allegiances are in flux—we need to give people something to *believe in.* We have to redefine "common sense." And we need to place the political dialogue in its historic frame. We have to give the voters a sense of important historical consequences, a sense that we are at a crossroads in history, and a sense of the challenges we face and the possibilities we might realize.

In fact today human society is passing through a gauntlet where we will determine if our values and our political structures can keep pace with our exploding technological power. We entered that gauntlet, about 60 years ago, when we first became capable of destroying the planet and changing our own climate. The next several generations will determine if we pass through and create a truly democratic, sustainable society of unparalleled possibility—or, like our cousins the Neanderthals, become evolutionary dead ends. Those are high stakes.

WHEN YOU HAVE THEM ON THE RUN— THAT'S THE TIME TO CHASE THEM

After his momentous defeat at Gettysburg on July 4, 1863, Confederate General Robert E. Lee retreated toward the Potomac River and the relative safety of the South. President Lincoln desperately wanted the Union general, George Meade, to pursue Lee and deliver a mortal blow to the remains of his army.

It rained heavily for several days after the Battle of Gettysburg. That made movements difficult for both armies—but it also flooded the Potomac.

By July 7, Lee was stalled waiting for the Potomac's water to recede. But much to Lincoln's distress, Meade was still in Pennsylvania.

By July 14, the river's level had dropped, and all of Lee's remaining army had escaped into Virginia. That afternoon, Lincoln wrote to Meade:

"My dear general, I do not believe you appreciate the magnitude of the misfortune involved in Lee's escape. He was within your easy grasp, and to have closed upon him would, in connection with our other late successes, have ended the war."

"As it is the war will be prolonged indefinitely," Lincoln wrote. "Your golden opportunity is gone, and I am distressed immeasurably because of it."

The letter went on to compare Meade to the cautious General George McClellan, who had previously refused to pursue the enemy.

Lee had his back against a swollen, impassable river and Meade had not moved to crush the retreating army of Confederates. As it turned out, his failure to pursue Lee permitted the South to continue the war for almost two more years.

Lincoln never sent that letter to Meade, assuming it would have caused Meade to resign. Lincoln had not yet made his critical decision to make Ulysses S. Grant the senior Union commander—a general who would pursue the Confederates *relentlessly*—all the way to Appomattox Courthouse.

When you have them on the run—that's the time to chase them.

Much like Gettysburg, the Democratic victory in the mid-term elections represents a major turning point in our war for progressive values. But, like Gettysburg, its significance will be determined by *how we follow up*.

THE 2006 VICTORY—
BUILDING THE ELECTORAL FOUNDATION FOR REALIGNMENT

In 2004, Karl Rove claimed that he was on the verge of making the Republican Party a "permanent majority." Wrong. When "The Architect" as he was called, resigned his position at the White House in August of 2007, the Bush Presidency was in shambles.

In 2006, Democrats, led by Democratic Congressional Campaign

Committee Chair Rahm Emanuel and Democratic Senate Campaign Committee Chair Charles Schumer, mounted a major, successful counter-attack. We gave Republicans what President Bush himself referred to as "a thumpin'."

For the first time since 1922, Democrats made major inroads without losing a single Democratic incumbent. In the 2006 Midterms Democrats picked up 30 House seats and 6 Senate seats. Fifty-eight percent of the total national Congressional vote went to Democrats, as did 55% of the Senate vote.

The Democratic House victory extended into the special election in Texas where former Congressman Ciro Rodriguez defeated Republican incumbent Henry Bonilla in a newly- drawn district that resulted from a court challenge to former Republican Leader Tom Delay's redistricting of Texas.

The 2006 Democratic majority includes House seats that have been in Republican hands for decades. In the Northeast, voters that have increasingly supported Democrats in presidential races ousted a number of Republican "moderates." In fact, New England now has only one Republican Member of the House. Republicans will have a hard time winning back those seats.

We took House seats in 11 districts where Kerry won less than 45% of the vote, 19 districts where Kerry won less than 50% and 4 seats where the Kerry margin was less than 3%.

WINNING EVERYWHERE

Democratic gains were spread throughout the country—five in the South and Border States, nine in the Midwest, as well as 11 in the East. Perhaps most significantly, we made gains in the West and Southwest—two in Arizona, one in Colorado and one in California. In the Senate, John Tester's victory over Senator Conrad Burns in Montana was key.

The election also marked another first. This is the first time Democrats have held a majority in Congress without holding a majority in the South. In fact, the election isolated Republican strength increasingly in the South, rooted in its strong support by conservative Evangelicals.

But even in the South there were clear signs of a shift. The victory of challenger Jim Webb in the Virginia Senate race, Harold Ford's narrow loss in Tennessee and newly elected Members of Congress John Yarmuth of Kentucky and Heath Schuler of North Carolina pointed the way to victory in Dixie.

Among suburbanites—who account for 47% of the electorate—Democratic candidates won 50% to 48%. That was a gain of 4% over 2004.

Among rural voters, Democrats ran almost even—48% to 52%. We won urban voters by a whopping 61%-37%. Democrats carried small towns 49% to 48%, small cities by 57% to 41% and large cities by 68% to 30%.

Progress with Every Demographic Group

In the 2006 Midterms, self-identified Democrats voted for the Democratic candidate 93% of the time. We won 57% of Independents and 8% of Republicans. Our vote among Independents increased by 8% from 2004.

African-Americans continued to vote solidly for Democrats and support grew substantially among Hispanics (69%) and Asians (62%).

Republicans had made decent inroads with Hispanics in 2004 –Bush captured 40%. But the immigration battle brought Hispanics decisively back to the Democratic column in the Midterms. That was especially important in races like those in Phoenix, Tucson and Denver—all critical Democratic pickups.

In 2006 we made gains among white men and women and won all age groups—making 5% gains among the critical voters 18-29 and voters over 60.

Overcoming Structural Challenges

The 2006 Democratic House victories were all the more impressive because of the structural barriers thrown up by Republicans through redistricting. Compared to other turning-point elections, 2006 featured far fewer open seats or evenly balanced districts. Democrats were successful because we won *so many* of the available open seats. Democrats won eight open seats—the best showing since 1974 when Democrats won 11. Six of the eight were in districts where Kerry won no more than 46.7% of the vote. [1]

State Races

The 2006 Midterm victories weren't limited to Congress. Democrats picked up 350 seats in state legislatures. Democrats now control 23 state legislatures to 17 for Republicans. Nine have split control.

In 15 states Democrats control both the Governor's mansion and both houses of the Legislature. That is a good starting point for the critical 2008 and 2010 elections that will control post-2010 redistricting.

Ohio is a particularly good example. The Democratic wave swept out the Republican Governor, a US Senator and a Republican Congressman. Potentially most importantly, Republicans in Ohio no longer control the state's electoral apparatus since the Republican Secretary of State Ken Blackwell, who helped manipulate the results of the decisive 2004

Ohio Presidential vote, was replaced by a Democrat. Blackwell was also trounced in his bid for the Governor's mansion.

THE POTENTIAL FOR REALIGNMENT

The stage is set.

The massively unpopular War in Iraq galvanizes broader and broader opposition to Bush and the Republicans in Congress who stubbornly continue to support his policies.

The period leading up to and immediately following the 2008 Presidential Election could very well trigger a major long-term progressive realignment in American politics. But we have to remember that in 2006 voters mainly voted for change—they voted *against* Republicans much more than they voted *for* Democrats.

Realignment is possible, but it is far from inevitable. Whether it happens will depend entirely on our ability to build on our electoral victory and reassert the dominance of progressive values at the center of American political debate.

Whether it happens is entirely up to us.

This book is about how we succeed in turning this historic opportunity into long-term progressive political realignment—how Progressives can win.

OUR PLAN OF ATTACK

In the following pages, we'll examine the complex question of voter self-interest—how to understand it, and how to address it in order to make realignment a reality. We'll talk about broad concepts—but we'll also explore practical applied politics.

- The last chapter of this section describes the successful battle to defeat the privatization of Social Security, which was the first turning point on the road that led from the 2004 electoral disaster to the 2006 Democratic victory.

- Section 2 addresses the concept of self-interest in politics and analyzes the six major categories of self-interest that motivate voters.

- Section 3 discusses the key audiences whose self-interests we must address—the groups whose attitudes and behavior we need to change in order to win.

- Section 4 presents the principles of political messaging that we need to use to successfully address these self-interests.

- In Section 5 we get down to the concrete task of how to plan and execute successful, progressive electoral and issue campaigns.

- Section 6 describes the culture of winning political organizations, and factors that allow us to effectively organize for victory.

- Section 7 describes what we mean by "progressive values" and how traditional progressive values contrast with the radical conservative values of the right.

- Section 8 explores the challenges and possibilities facing us in the 21st century, the progressive vision for the future — and how we can talk about it.

- Section 9 argues that to realize that vision, we need to focus on structural change — on changing the relations of power — to build a truly democratic society.

- The Conclusion summarizes some of the key lessons that I believe we need to incorporate into our strategy to make political realignment a reality.

CHAPTER THREE

Getting Up Off the Floor—The Battle to Stop the Privatization of Social Security

Before we look forward, let's get back to the period immediately following the 2004 elections.

The right wing was ecstatic. Visions of fundamental change in the American political economy danced in their heads.

Late in 2004, Bush began to drop hints that he would propose a plan to privatize Social Security. It was to be the underpinning of his "ownership society"—the central domestic initiative of his second term.

Along with my wife, Jan Schakowsky, who is a Democratic Member of Congress, I had worked closely for many years with Roger Hickey, Co-Director of the Campaign for America's future, and Jeff Blum, Executive Director of USAction. Just before Christmas, I got a call from Roger. He and Jeff asked if I would prepare a preliminary campaign plan to organize the opposition to the Bush privatization effort. I jumped at the chance.

THE DEFINING BATTLE

It was clear from the beginning that the fight over the proposal to privatize Social Security would be the defining battle of Bush's second term domestic policy.

The Washington Post reported on January 1, 2005:

President Bush's political allies are raising millions of dollars for an election-style campaign to promote private Social Security accounts, as Democrats and Republicans prepare for what they predict will be the most expensive and extensive public policy debate since the 1993 fight over the Clinton administration's failed health care plan.

With Bush planning to unveil the details of his Social Security plan this month, several GOP groups close to the White House are asking the same donors who helped reelect Bush to fund an extensive campaign to convince Americans—and skeptical lawmakers—that Social Security is in crisis and that private accounts are the only cure.

U.S. News and World Report wrote on January 10, 2005:

President Bush's bid to win Social Security reform will likely cost $40 million in TV and radio advertising. And that's just the pro side. GOP message developer Frank Lutz tells us to expect the ads to feature senior citizens worrying that their grandkids will be left out in the cold if Bush doesn't win.

Gannett News Service reported on November 26, 2004:

The Club for Growth, another conservative advocacy organization, plans to spend $10 million pushing Social Security private accounts next year....

Interest groups on the other side of the Social Security war are shouting just as loudly. Those groups also boast nationwide memberships and deep pockets. "This is the final showdown," said Roger Hickey, Co- Director of the Campaign for America's Future, backed by the AFL-CIO and other organizations opposed to private Social Security savings accounts. Just this week, Hickey's group sent e-mails to hundreds of thousands of individuals, asking them to pressure their representatives in Congress to oppose the accounts....

In addition to its massive impact on the welfare of retirees, children, people with disabilities and surviving spouses, the battle over the future of Social Security represented a critical turning point in the broader historic struggle between progressive and right wing values in American society.

The success and popularity of Social Security is a monument to the fact that our progressive values lie at the foundation of America's 200-year-long struggle to create a truly democratic society. Together with Medicare, Social Security, as much as any other program of our government, embodies progressive principles: that we are responsible for each other; that everyone deserves the opportunity to live in health and dignity; and that the most efficient way to provide these things is through the only truly democratic institution we have—our government.

Social Security's success—and its very existence—fundamentally contradicts the principles of right-wing orthodoxy. It stands in stark contrast to the vision of a society where everyone must fend for themselves—must sink or swim—and where those who succeed are considered morally superior to those who do not. And Social Security's efficiency makes clear that the private sector is not always the most economical way to distribute the fruits of our economy.

The right wing viewed the battle to stop the 1993 Clinton health-care reform package as a historic "make or break" challenge to prevent the spread of progressive values into a massive new sector of American life. We viewed the defense of Social Security as a similarly historic moment.

The administration and their conservative backers were clear from the beginning that they intended to make the privatization of Social Security the cornerstone of their second-term domestic policy. To successfully counter the initiative it was clear that an effort was needed that was far more formidable than any mounted previously to counter Bush initiatives.

The American Federation of State County and Municipal Employees (AFSCME) took the leading role to assemble the financial resources. They were joined by the AFL-CIO and various other unions, USAction, the Campaign for America's Future, the Alliance for Retired Americans, the National Committee to Preserve Social Security and Medicare and MoveOn.org. AARP supported our position but did not directly support the coalition.

Several critical decisions were made at the outset. First, a new entity was organized to spearhead the campaign—Americans United to Protect Social Security.

Second, Americans United hired an experienced campaign manager, Paul Tewes, to conduct the effort like an election campaign. Our plan was to merge the urgency and focus of the campaign culture with the ability to leverage resources that come with coalition politics.

Tewes had served as Political Director of the Democratic Senatorial Campaign Committee with a reputation as a political street fighter. He'd managed a number of important campaigns and had the trust of the Senate Democratic leadership. Tewes was a brilliant strategist and had a "crash through the walls to win" attitude.

He had recently founded a consulting firm with Steve Hildebrand, who also had a lengthy history managing Senate campaigns. Hildebrand consulted regularly with the new effort.

Tewes assembled a large crack campaign team. He brought in Brad Woodhouse to be Communications Director. Woodhouse was a smart, tough North Carolina guy who had headed press at the Democratic Senate Campaign Committee. He is the best press guy I have ever met.

Tewes also hired Kim Molstre, a young veteran of the Kerry campaign and the Capitol Hill staff of Minority Leader Richard Gephardt. Molstre had more presence of command than any 29-year-old I know. She was Deputy Director and also Political Director of the campaign.

In a critical early decision, Tewes decided to ramp up rapidly. He knew that the first month and a half would frame the entire campaign. We had to be in every critical state and have an overwhelming presence in the press immediately.

The ability of Americans United to move fast from a standing start was made possible because of the participation of USAction. USAction had state affiliates in 25 of our 37 target states. The USAction Political Director

Alan Charney, and Field Director Cassandra McKee, mobilized the buy-in of these operations.

Oliver Gottfried—another Senate campaign alum—became AU's Field Director and hired experienced organizers in the additional 12 states.

Early on, I was a general consultant to Americans United and worked with Tewes on strategic and organizational questions. Gottfried ultimately left to take a key position at the DSCC and I then took over the role of National Field Director as well.

The administration couched its proposal to privatize Social Security as an effort to deal with what it called the program's "impending crisis of solvency." Bush argued that Social Security was going bankrupt, and that "personal accounts" must be created as part of a broader solution to the problem of solvency. Not even the most pessimistic prognosticators thought Social Security would be bankrupt anytime soon. But Bush contended that every day Congress refused to act would increase the severity and imminence of the crisis.

Job # 1
Develop a Unified Message

Americans United's first challenge was to develop a unified message that could be echoed by all of the progressive forces—including Democrats on Capitol Hill. So the AFL-CIO hired Hart Research to do a poll. The poll found that close to half of the voters supported privatization at first blush. But it also found that if we communicated our message in a disciplined way, the bottom fell out of the support for privatization.

The 1993 Parallel

In 1993, Republican conservatives were confronted with a similar situation. Bill Clinton had proposed a sweeping health-care reform package. Even Senator Bob Dole—then Senate Minority Leader—agreed with the administration that the country faced a "health-care crisis." Conventional wisdom held that some form of health care reform was certain to pass Congress. The Republicans did not control the House, Senate or the Presidency.

Yet in the face of this tidal wave of elite and public opinion, the right wing mobilized the campaign with three goals:

- To undercut the notion that there was a "health-care crisis."
- To argue that the American healthcare system was the "best in the world."

- To convince elite and public opinion that the Clinton cure was worse than the "healthcare disease"—that it would put in jeopardy the "best health care system in the world."

Bill Kristol, who had been Chief of Staff to Vice-President Dan Quayle and then headed the "Project for the Republican Future," launched a simple counter-slogan: "there is no health-care crisis." This ultimately became the Republican mantra.

They rolled out spots featuring a couple called "Harry and Louise" to skewer the Clinton health-care plan. An army of insurance industry lobbyists descended on Capitol Hill. The right held onto most Republicans and managed to shave off a number of Democrats. In the end the Clinton health-care plan was dead in its tracks.

The Republicans *never* offered their own systematic health-care reform initiative. Instead, they insisted (contrary to all evidence) that the American healthcare system was the best in the world and that whatever problems there were could be solved by modest reforms.

There were some differences between the situation that confronted the right in 1993, and the one Progressives faced in 2005. Chief among them was that the most powerful economic interests had lined up against the health-care reform in 1993—but Wall Street stood to benefit a great deal if Bush successfully privatized Social Security in 2005.

On the other hand, there was a massive constituency of highly vested voters who had very personal stakes in the Social Security system.

The other similarities were clear:

- The right-wing opposition to health-care reform in 1993 did not control Congress—neither did we in 2005.

- In both cases elite & public opinion began with the presumption that a "crisis" existed in the current system and that fundamental change was necessary.

Three Strategic Message Objectives

Like the right in 1993, we, too, had to accomplish three strategic-message objectives in order to succeed:

Objective # 1. We had to undermine the presumption that there was a Social Security "crisis." We knew that the Republicans controlled the entire apparatus of Congress and the Executive branch and that "crises" required fundamental overhauls. The moment we conceded the existence of a crisis, we set the stage for our defeat since anything "fundamental" that was done to Social Security would be done on their terms.

For years, voters had heard a drumbeat of skepticism about the financial solvency of Social Security. As a consequence, the Hart Research poll found that 28% of the voters believed Social Security faced a "major crisis," while 39% believed it had "major troubles."

That meant we could not afford to dismiss the concern that Social Security had long-range problems. That issue had to be addressed. But we did not need to deny that Social Security needed to be bolstered in order to argue that there was no "crisis." People believed that Social Security had long-term problems, but not because they had personally experienced problems with the program. After all, Social Security had faithfully paid checks every month for 70 years. They believe it had problems, because they had been repeatedly *told* it was so.

It was up to us to clarify that there was no "crisis" — that Social Security could be strengthened by modest changes in the program that would continue to guarantee that it paid the benefits that were due to retirees who had faithfully paid into the system.

The Hart Research poll indicated that the most effective messaging (especially with younger voters) was to argue that:

While we must take action to guarantee Social Security is secure over the long run, the Bush plan to privatize Social Security would only make matters worse by siphoning $2 trillion from the Social Security Trust Fund.

The "modest changes" message was also persuasive with swing voters, but not as compelling to young voters. It ran:

Modest changes could be made in Social Security to ensure that the system was secure for several generations.

To be completely persuasive, arguing that the right wing had fabricated the Social Security crisis, we also needed to explain to the public why the right would do so. Was the problem simply an honest difference of actuarial opinion? Our answer was a resounding *no.*

In fact, of course, there were at least two real motivations that were heavily intertwined. One was the ideological opposition of the right to the progressive values underlying the system. After all, Republicans opposed Social Security at its inception. The other was the desire of Wall Street to get its hands on the Social Security Trust Fund.

Objective # 2. We had to repeatedly assert that Social Security was a spectacular success. We had to focus a spotlight on the things people liked about Social Security—things that would be put at risk under the Republican plan.

Objective # 3. We had to persuade elite, public and swing congressional opinion that the right wing "cure" to the problems of Social Security was a lot worse than the disease. We contended that they intended to kill the patient—that they would place in jeopardy all the things that made Social Security such a huge success. As Paul Krugman of the *New York Times* said, "They come to bury Social Security, not to save it."

In this regard, the Hart Research poll found two general categories of arguments were the most compelling with persuadable voters:

- The president's privatization plan would cut benefits.
  - The plan would throw large numbers of seniors into poverty.

  - The plan would cut guaranteed benefits for workers under 50-years-old from 30% to 50%. It would cut benefits by 30% even if you decided not to invest in a private account.

  - The average retiree would lose $134,000 in benefits if they lived for 20 years after retirement.

- The president's privatization plan would massively increase the deficit.
  - The plan would increase the deficit by $2 trillion over the next 10 years alone—much of it borrowed form China and Japan.

This message was especially powerful with young voters and college-educated men. It was also compelling to many swing members of Congress. The Republican plan required that the government borrow $2 trillion of new debt over the next decade to finance the "transition" to this program. There would be another $3 trillion needed over the next decade, and $5 trillion more in the decade after that. As Paul Krugman noted, "By the time privatization started to save money, if it ever did, the federal government would have run up around $15 trillion of extra debt."

The polling resulted in a simple narrative that ran like this:

The Bush privatization plan undermines retirement security by cutting guaranteed benefits 30% to 50%, and the risky privatized accounts would fail to make up the difference for millions of Americans. Working people should get the benefits they paid for.

The Bush plan would hurt the economy and pass huge bills on to future generations by borrowing an additional $2 trillion.

Social Security faces challenges, not a crisis, and Bush's privatization plan actually makes things worse by draining $2 trillion of the Social Security Trust Fund.

We should require Congress to pay back the money it diverted from the Social Security Trust Fund in order to give tax breaks to the wealthy and give Americans new opportunities to have tax-free savings for their retirement, in addition to their Social Security.

The AARP began an advertising campaign that picked up on these themes:
"There are places in your retirement planning for risk, but Social Security isn't one of them."
"If we feel like gambling, we'll play the slots. Winners and losers are stock market terms. Do you really want them to become retirement terms?"

Poll briefings were held throughout the progressive community and on Capitol Hill. Most organizational leaders and the House and Senate Democratic leadership agreed to adhere to this message.

Job # 2
Prevent Democrats from Proposing, Their Own "Solution"

Our second problem was to prevent Democrats from buying into a so-called "bi- partisan" approach to Social Security. The reason was simple: our goal was to prevent privatization. Any legislation that involved Social Security during the Republican Congress and Bush presidency would necessarily involve privatization.

The Senate had only 55 Republicans—and the Republican leadership couldn't count on all of them to support privatization. To overcome an inevitable Democratic filibuster, the Republican leadership required 60 votes. Majority Leader Bill Frist had to have Democratic support.

As the campaign developed, and the proposal's popularity declined, Republicans also realized that they needed to craft a "bipartisan" proposal to protect themselves from paying the electoral price.

Senate Democratic Leader Harry Reid dealt with the freelancing problem by recruiting Senator Max Baucus (D-MT) to lead the Senate Democratic efforts. Baucus, who frequently engineered compromises with Republican Senate finance Chair Charles Grassley (R-IA), was the ranking Democrat on the committee. His refusal to buy into privatization—and any form of negotiation—was a critical element necessary for Democratic success.

In the House, Democratic leader Nancy Pelosi (D-CA) tapped senior Ways and Means member Sandy Levin (D-MI) to lead the Democratic effort. When several Democratic members came out early for "personal accounts," they were immediately politically isolated.

JOB # 3
TAKE ON THE PRESIDENTIAL ROAD-SHOW

The president formally announced his plan in his State of the Union message in February 2005. He also announced an extensive tour to sell the plan. Over the next four months he held 60 events throughout the country, focused on target congressional districts.

At every one of these 60 stops, Americans United organized an event to counter his message. Each time, our formula was similar. The day before the president arrived, we held a press event of our own to frame the debate and attack his plan. Whenever a president comes to visit a community, the TV news runs a story the night before about the impending visit. Our events the day before he arrived provided a hook for the press that made that story more interesting. They were always widely covered.

Then on the day of the president's visit, we would put on a mass turnout event as close to the president's event as possible. These featured lots of people holding large black and yellow Day-Glo signs with a message like "Hands off my Social Security." Any picture of our protest would therefore deliver our message with or without written copy. The visual of hundreds of signs was always widely covered, and often our spokespeople would give a counterpoint to the president on television as well.

These events were aimed at the local media, because the national media was generally traveling in the presidential "bubble" and didn't see anything outside of the staged events themselves. But Woodhouse and his press gang bombarded the national press corps with our local clippings and used them as a demonstration of our claim that there was a grassroots revolt against the president's plan.

Of course, the president's events were notoriously scripted. Tickets were distributed by local Republican operatives and congressional offices. As taxpayer funds were used to pay for these road shows, we decided to attack the president's credibility by focusing on the nature of the events themselves.

One day in Denver, a group of Republican "volunteers" representing themselves as Secret Service agents threw several potential "troublemakers" out of the event. MoveOn.org dubbed them the "Denver Three". Now the "Denver Three" were not thrown out of the event because they had caused disruption, but because they had simply been observed putting on shirts that covered T-shirts with anti-Bush slogans and arriving in a car with an anti-Bush bumper sticker.

After the event, they went to the press and demanded the identities of the personnel who had thrown them out of this taxpayer-financed forum. The Secret Service denied that their people were involved, although the volunteers looked and acted like agents—with earphone radios, lapel pins, etc.

The "Denver Three" filed Freedom of Information Requests, came to DC for press conferences and meetings with members of Congress—and generally became the symbol for the staged road shows that the president was conducting across the country.

It didn't take long to see the validation of our polling. We stuck to our message, both in DC and in the local press, and the president stuck to his. It turned out that the more he went on the road, the higher the visibility of the issue. And the higher the visibility of the issue, the greater our opportunity to frame it with our message in the earned media.

In fact, the issue had such high visibility that it didn't require large quantities of paid advertising to get our message out.

Woodhouse's press operation was everywhere—especially in target congressional districts—churning out releases by the boatload, ginning up op-eds and editorials, framing the issue for reporters on background, responding to any comment or charge from the other side.

Tewes' decision to ramp up quickly—both in the field and in DC—was critical to our ability to frame the terms of the debate in the early phases.

Job # 4
Naming the Battle

We also succeeded early in naming the president's proposal, as his attempt to "**privatize**" Social Security. Our research showed that people were much more prone to consider a proposal to create "personal accounts"—which the administration tried desperately to name the proposal. They claimed they didn't want to "privatize Social Security," just create "personal accounts." The fact that we were able to name the issue was critical.

Job # 5
Taking Them on At Home

We organized angry groups of seniors to confront target members of Congress at town meetings and public appearances.

Republican targets waffled, so we ran a month-long "Take A Stand" campaign, demanding that they go on record as either for privatization or against it.

We conducted a drive to get local and state elected officials to sign anti-privatization pledges and put indirect pressure on Congress.

We released reports in local media markets.

These events were not organized haphazardly, but in fights that were coordinated across the country. In the end, Americans United held over 1,200 events in our 37 target states over the privatization campaign.

We also got state legislatures and city councils to pass resolutions against privatization, and generated tens of thousands of phone calls to congressional offices through "patch through" calls and e-mail alerts.

In each state, we devised targeted strategies to engage the friends, political supporters and business associates of congressional targets. In other words, we did "bank-shots" that put pressure on people who would in turn put pressure on the members of Congress.

THE TURNING POINT

The first Senate Finance Committee hearing on privatization was scheduled for April 27, 2005. We thought a while about how we would handle testimony. Then we realized that we would answer their hearing with a show of ironclad opposition. We planned a 4,000- person rally to coincide with the first day of hearings. Just as importantly, 140 members of the House and Senate, including the Democratic leadership of both houses, marched onto bleachers at the front of the crowd and pledged not to privatize Social Security.

To the other side, the rally said: our opposition is a stone wall. The spirit, confidence and sense of mutual support flowing from that event solidified opposition to privatization among congressional Democrats. It also contributed to achieving one of our major goals: making any member who did business with the Republicans on privatization feel that he or she would be *persona non grata*—off the team.

By early summer, we had them on the run. The polls had turned against privatization, and there was no legislative movement. Of course, when you have them on the run—that's the time to chase them.

The closing act in the privatization battle was a celebration of the 70th anniversary of Social Security, held in August, 2005. The event gave us the opportunity to highlight the importance of Social Security's guaranteed benefits. AU organized 70th anniversary celebrations around the country, especially in targeted districts. We also organized a ceremony at the Roosevelt Memorial that was widely covered nationally.

By early fall, the pundits began writing the obits—Bush's plan to privatize Social Security was dead. In the spring of 2006, *Washington Post* columnist E.J. Dionne wrote:

> *The collapse of the Social Security initiative was thus more than a policy failure. It was a decisive political defeat that left Bush and Rove with no fallback ideas around which to organize domestic policy.* [1]

In defeating the president's plan to privatize Social Security, Progressives had repelled a right-wing assault on a major portion of the American political economy. But the battle was also a critical turning point in the war between progressive and conservative values and helped set the stage for the precipitous decline in the public's approval of Bush's performance that followed over the next year and a half.

After the 2006 Midterm Election victory, Rick Klein of the *Boston Globe* wrote:

> *Democrats made huge gains in the mid-term elections for a variety of factors—an unpopular war in Iraq, congressional scandals, frustration with Bush's style of leadership.*
>
> *But the victory had its roots in that early and successful battle against Social Security reform, which gave Democrats crucial unity and momentum at a time when many pundits were predicting a permanent Republican majority, according to party strategists and veteran Democratic lawmakers.* [2]

Due to a navigational error, the U.S. 4th Infantry Division landed on the wrong inlet on Utah Beach in Normandy on D-Day in 1944. For some time they were disoriented and pinned down by German defenders. Then the only general to accompany the amphibious assault, General Ted Roosevelt (son of President Teddy Roosevelt), personally rallied troops from the beach, over the seawall and established a beachhead.

The successful battle to defeat privatization did the same for Progressives. It allowed Progressives to pick themselves off the floor after the terrible 2004 defeat.

The Social Security battle allowed Progressives to stand up straight and be proud.

The Democratic congressional leadership held a disciplined line against the Republicans' domestic policy assault. The Republicans' failure to breach that line was the beginning of a political retreat that continues to this day.

The battle to defend Social Security did one other thing. It provided a model for Progressive success.

It showed how if we proudly defend our values—if we stand up straight—we can beat the right and fundamentally realign American politics.

(Endnotes)

SECTION TWO

ADDRESSING THEIR SELF-INTEREST

CHAPTER FOUR

The Six Categories of Self-Interest

If you want a solid strategy to win any battle, you start with the basics. The great Green Bay Packers coach Vince Lombardi was blessed with some of the best football players in America. But he is said to have started each season by raising a football in his hand and saying: "Gentlemen, this is a football." Lombardi believed that victory began with blocking and tackling.

The blocking and tackling of politics begins with understanding self-interest.

Economic self-interest is critical, but it's not the end of the story. Whether it's the poorest counties in Ohio voting for Bush, or white working-class men who oppose unions, you don't have to look far to find people who seem to act contrary to their own economic self-interest.

In his book *What's the Matter With Kansas?: How Conservatives Won the Heart of America*, Tom Frank describes a conservative movement that is rooted among working-class whites.[1] They rail against what they see as the destruction of their values and way of life—the deteriorating economies of their small towns, and the intrusion of sex and violence into the mass media. At the same time they support the Republican Party, which is dominated by the multinational corporations that ship jobs from their communities to Third World countries, breaks the unions that would raise their wages, and owns the very media they decry.

There are four possible explanations for this phenomenon:

1) These people are stupid.
2) They are willing to sacrifice their economic well-being for something else that is more important.
3) Conservatives leaders divert these people's attention from their economic well-being by inflaming their concerns about other self-interests that come to monopolize their political agenda.
4) Something more fundamental is going on here.

We will dismiss out of hand the notion that working-class conservatives are simply "stupid," uninformed and unsophisticated, or are too benighted to understand what is in their own interests.

In my 38 years of progressive organizing—much of it together with white working-class people the one thing I can say for *sure* is that working–class people are not stupid. They understand what matters to them. The problem for Progressives is not "educating" working-class people about what they *should* want. It is providing them candidates, and a political movement, that offer them what they *really* want.

Before you put this book down and curse out loud that I'm just one of those guys who want Democrats to be more moderate or accommodating on questions like reproductive choice or gay marriage, let me just say clearly—you would be wrong.

Make no mistake; there will always be working-class voters for whom questions like these are overriding. But for most, these kinds of concerns do not lie at the core of their own perceived self-interest.

Reason number two is also a nonstarter. Working-class people who vote for social conservatives don't consciously say, "I know the people I'm voting for will take my job or lower my wages, but abortion or gay marriage or fighting pornography are so important that I'll just have to sacrifice." They don't make a conscious trade-off between their economic interests and other things that matter to them.

Reason number three comes much closer to the truth. There is little doubt that President Bush's former chief operative Karl Rove's reputation as a "genius" lay more in his skill as a magician than anything else. Rove was brilliant at focusing the voters' attention on symbolically powerful issues like gay marriage with one hand while he gave tax breaks to the wealthy with the other. *New York Times* columnist Paul Krugman wrote in June 2006, "... why have the last three elections been dominated by talk of terrorism with a lot of religion on the side? Because a party whose economic policies favor a narrow elite needs to focus the public's attention elsewhere. And there is no better way to do that than accusing the other party of being unpatriotic and godless. Thus in 2004, President Bush basically ran as America's defender against gay married terrorists. He waited until after the election to reveal that what he really wanted to do was privatize Social Security."[2]

There is no doubt the Republicans have proven over and over that the hand is quicker than the eye. But the fact that they are great magicians is not the whole story.

Something else *is* going on here and our ability to understand and address that something else will—more than any single factor—determine whether we are successful in this critical period that lies ahead.

To understand what is really going on, let me tell you about an experience that helped shape my own understanding of self-interest.

Like Martha Stewart, I too spent five months in a Federal Prison Camp. Unfortunately, my commitment to the progressive organization I led in the late 1990s led me to make serious errors in judgment and violate the law. I floated checks between accounts to assure the organization's program could continue. No bank ever lost any money, and I didn't personally benefit, but that mistake certainly had a major consequence on my life and was a big burden to my wife Jan, both personally and as a Member of Congress.

But from my point of view, one good thing did result. My time in the Federal Prison camp at Terre Haute, Indiana, helped crystallize my understanding of the things people want and need.

Like all new inmates, when I reported to the camp, I was given a TB scratch test before I was allowed to mix with the rest of the prison population. It takes two days to read the test, so I was held in what is known as the "hole." The "hole" is where inmates are sent to be disciplined. Basically, I spent 60 hours with another new inmate in a cell that was about 10-foot by eight-foot. In one corner was a shower. The toilet was in the middle of the cell. There were two bunks (upper and lower). There was one small slit for a window and a small window in the massive steel door.

Food was brought to the cell three times a day and slid through the slit in the door. The second day we had "recreation" for 45 minutes in a 25-foot by 15-foot room with a handball, a pull-up bar and five other guys.

No one would tell us how long we would stay in the "hole" before going to the minimum security prison camp. For some people it was two days. For others it was five days or two weeks. It depended partially on the availability of beds at the camp.

Shortly after I got to the camp another inmate returned from the "hole" after spending 87 days locked in a cell for a disciplinary infraction.

We were lucky. After just two-and-a-half days in the "hole," we were moved to a minimum security prison camp where we could move with much greater freedom within the camp and socialize freely with other inmates.

During and right after my own stay at the "hole" it occurred to me that all of my physical needs were in fact being cared for there. I was given three meals a day, and a place to sleep, kept out of the weather, and could see to my sanitary needs. So what was so bad? Why was the "hole" so horrible—both in relation to my normal life, and to the relative freedom of the prison camp?

The answer, of course, is that people's physical needs represent only one subset of their overall needs—or self-interests.

There is no doubt that physical needs are critical. There is very little a person will not do to provide food for himself or his family. Every human being has a primary, basic, hardwired self-interest in seeing to it that these physical needs are met. They are, after all, the needs that allow people to sustain their lives. But there are other self-interests as well.

In his historical novel, *The Killer Angels,* Michael Shaara describes the thoughts of Confederate General Lew Armistead as he helped lead George Pickett's famous charge at the Battle of Gettysburg.

"Garrett's boys had reached the road. They were slowing, taking down rails. Musket fire was beginning to reach them. The great noise increased, beating of wings in the air. More dead men: along the line of dead, like a shattered fence. And now the canister, oh God, he shuddered, millions of metal balls whirring through the air like startled quail, murderous quail, and now for the first time there was screaming, very bad sounds to hear. He began to move past wounded struggling to the rear, men falling out to help, hearing the sergeants ordering the men back into line, saw gray faces as he passed, eyes sick with fear, but the line moved on...

Armistead moved on, expecting to die, but was not hit. He moved to the wall up there, past mounds of bodies, no line anymore, just men moving forward at different speeds, stopping to fire, stopping to die, drifting back like leaves blown from the fire ahead."[3]

Sixty-percent of the soldiers in Pickett's charge were lost—the charge failed. What self-interest could possibly have motivated men to behave like that?

There are obviously categories of self-interest, other than physical needs, or even self-preservation, that are of enormous importance to human beings. Otherwise why would a soldier risk his life for his country or his religion? Why would a fireman risk his life to run into a burning building to save a child? And what could you possibly say about a suicide bomber?

THE SIX CATEGORIES OF SELF-INTEREST

In addition to physical needs, there are non-physical needs that I divide into five additional categories of self-interest. It was the absence of these that made the "hole" in the Federal Prison Camp so unbearable.

Overall then the six categories of self-interest that we must address in politics are:

- Physical needs
- The need for control over one's life
- The need for structure
- The need for community, human interaction and affirmation
- The need for intellectual stimulation
- The need for meaning and purpose in life

Picture yourself locked in a tiny cell for an indeterminate period of time. You have little to do but pace the cell, sleep, gaze from a small window that looks out on a razor wire fence, and read books from a cart with a small selection of Western potboilers. You can't get anyone's attention, unless they happened to walk by. You have no idea when it will end. You have no control, only a vague and indeterminate structure to the day, little intellectual stimulation, hardly anyone to talk to, and no purpose to your life.

Is there any doubt that would be a horrible existence?

According to a blue-ribbon report by the Vera Foundation called "Confronting Confinement," "… in 1997 psychologists Craig Haney and Mona Lynch reviewed dozens of studies conducted since the 1970's and concluded that there was not a single study of non-voluntary solitary confinement for more than 10 days that did not document negative psychiatric symptoms in its subjects."[4]

Human beings desperately need, desire and seek to achieve the five nonphysical goals as much as the physical ones. Our pursuit of them has defined much of the course of human history. Social psychologists and philosophers like Abraham Maslow and Victor Frankel have analyzed these human needs and motivations for decades.

Just like physical needs, the desire to achieve the five nonphysical goals is hardwired in genetics and in the culture of human beings. And they are hardwired for the same reason as physical needs—they're all adaptive traits. Striving to maximize these goals has historically helped human beings survive and prosper.

Let's briefly review each category of self-interest starting with the physical.

Chapter Five

Physical Needs

Human beings are programmed genetically to do just about anything in order to meet the most basic physical needs. Adrenaline courses through our veins to prepare us for fight or flight. Hunger pangs wrack us to remind us to eat. Pain is a signal that the body has been violated. And, of course, our society deals constantly with the critical, problematic, yet marvelous consequences of the sex drive.

Society addresses physical needs mainly through our economic system and the systems we've developed to provide physical security — police, fire departments, healthcare systems and the military. There are two subcategories of physical needs: basic economic needs — especially for economic necessities like food, water, shelter and clothing; the need for physical security — including the need to protect one's physical health.

Economic Self-Interest

Someone's economic activity is first and foremost about meeting his or her physical needs and those of the family.

Of course, income and economic status can also have a great deal to do with one's ability to address other nonphysical self-interests. Fundamentally, income gives people the ability to select and achieve goals of whatever sort.

The more income you have, the greater your ability to control your life, order your life, find social approval and intellectual stimulation. Greater income frees people from economic necessity and allows them to pursue whatever work they consider most fulfilling and important.

But income and the pursuit of wealth only enhance one's ability to fulfill nonphysical needs — they do not guarantee their fulfillment. Higher income does not necessarily provide people with a greater sense of community or meaning in life. It might help, but it is certainly not the only factor — or even the main factor — in determining whether many nonphysical needs are met.

Higher income is, however, very closely related to the ability to meet most physical needs — especially those most basic needs like food, water, decent housing, medical care, protection from the hot summer and cold winters. It was no coincidence that most of those who died in the aftermath of Hurricane Katrina were poor.

Much political behavior—especially voting behavior—is a direct consequence of economic self-interest, perhaps more than any other factor.

In their fascinating book *Polarized America: The Dance of Ideology and Unequal Riches,* political scientists Nolan McCarty, Keith Poole and Howard Rosenthal make a convincing case that *most* voting behavior and ideological orientation is in fact related to income. That is especially true for the great mass of *partisan* voters, those who self-identify with a party and cast partisan votes on a regular basis. [1]

In the presidential election years of 1992, 1996 and 2000, survey respondents in the highest quintile of income were more than twice as likely to identify as Republicans as were those at the lowest quintile. And stratification of partisanship by income has risen steadily over the last 40 years.[1]

But in fact, as the example of Ohio's poorest counties makes clear, a variety of other self-interests also play a powerful role. This is particularly true on the margins among the persuadable voters that influence the outcome of elections, legislative battles, and other potential struggles that will determine the future of our society. Those other self-interests are also critically important in motivating chronic nonvoters to participate in elections. Economically downscale voters are much more likely to vote for progressives—for Democratic candidates. But their economic self-interest alone will not motivate them to vote. In fact, low-income voters are *less likely to vote.* The principal factor that keeps people from voting is their view that little they ever do will affect the quality of their lives.

In the last 20 years there has been an increasing polarization of incomes in America between the wealthiest 1% of the population and everyone else. From 1990 to 2004, the income of the top 1% of the population has increased 57%. The richest Americans—the top one-tenth of 1%—have experienced income growth of 85%. Yet the median income of the bottom 90% has increased only 2%.[2] If incomes were the only determinant of voting, Democrats would have won Ohio in the 2004 presidential election and had a landslide nationwide vote.

And within the two parties' hard-core bases, there are major exceptions to the general relationship between income and party affiliation. You can find them among the culturally conservative, working class people of Kansas and in places like my own hometown of Evanston, Illinois. In Evanston, many high-income people are hard-core Democrats.

Obviously something else is going on in addition to economic self-interest.

PHYSICAL SECURITY

People's self-interest in protecting their physical security is also obviously an incredibly compelling factor in all politics. The political world changed after 9/11. Throughout history, one of the first priorities of government has always been the protection of the political unit from invasion and extermination — and often the extension of political power through wars of conquest. Fears of death and illness from disease are obviously also a deep-rooted human concern.

History shows why physical security *should* be such a compelling interest. Take the fate of Native Americans. The Native American population of the New World as a whole declined by 95% in two centuries following Columbus' arrival. Between 1492, when Columbus arrived at Hispaniola, and 1535, the Native American population of Hispaniola declined from 8 million to zero. The population was systematically destroyed by Old World germs to which many of the conquered people had never been exposed and against which they had therefore developed no immunity. Many also died as a result of imprisonment, forced labor and murder. [3]

More recently, World War II cost the lives of 40 million people. And the flu pandemic at the end of the First World War killed 21 million. [4]

Self-interest in physical security is and should be a deeply rooted human concern.

The right wing has been extremely effective at using physical fear — terrorism and crime — as a rationale to justify their own power, particularly in their attempts to limit personal freedom. But their effectiveness has nothing to do with the superiority of their policies as the fiasco in Iraq makes ever so clear.

Physical security includes the need to protect yourself from illness and disease. People care enormously about their health because it is fundamental to everything else they do or want in life.

The availability and quality of health care — and issues like stem cell research and end-of-life care — drives politics more today than ever before. After all, human society's ability to deliver health care really developed for the first time over the last several centuries and exponentially expanded over the last several decades.

The physical needs — economic security, physical and health security — must all be major focuses for the progressive movement. In an age of international conflict, economic insecurity, nuclear arms, terrorist attacks, global warming and bird flu, Progressives must effectively deliver on these issues if voters are to support us.

But focusing on these issues is not really our problem. Empirically, progressive policies are much better suited to achieve these goals than their conservative counterparts. Our framing of the debate regarding these issues is a problem. And that, in turn has to do with our ability to address the five nonphysical self-interests. Over the last 30 years the right has not been more successful at defending America from terrorists, natural disasters, hunger, epidemics or at generating economic growth. During the Clinton years America experienced the most prosperous period of any group in human history. That did not stop the right from dominating the political dialogue. The reason is that the right has been more successful at meeting the five nonphysical needs. Those needs are the keys that will enable us to have the political power to put our policies into practice—and to stay in power by fundamentally realigning American politics.

These five nonphysical self-interests are incredibly powerful. They're especially important for swing or persuadable voters, the switch-hitters that have so much impact on the outcome of elections in todays closely divided America. Let's turn to these factors now.

CHAPTER SIX

Control Over Your Life

In general, people want to have a sense that they can exercise some measure of control over their lives.

In fact, in many ways human history is the story of human beings striving to constantly broaden their ability to select and achieve goals.

This desire plays itself out in the historic struggle to expand the realm of human freedom—freedom from oppression and tyranny. It can be seen in the endless progress of technology—of our insatiable desire to understand the universe and make it the instrument of our will. It can be seen in any number of psychological studies that show that even the illusion of choice makes us perform better.

In the 1980s, Tom Peters and Robert Waterman, Jr. looked at the qualities that characterize the most successful companies. The result was a classic book on management called *In Search of Excellence*.

Peters and Waterman found that employees desperately need to have a sense that they have some control over their work lives. They cite an experiment where adult subjects were given some complex puzzles to solve on a proofreading chore:

> In the background was a loud, randomly occurring distracting noise; "to be specific it was a combination of two people speaking Spanish, one speaking Armenian, a mimeograph machine running, a desk calculator a typewrite, and street noise—producing a composite non-distinguishable roar." The subjects were split into two groups. Individuals in one set were just told to work at the task. Individuals in the other were provided with a button to push to turn off the noise, "a modern analogue of control—the off switch." The group with the off switch solved five times the number of puzzles as the their cohorts and made but a tiny fraction of the number of proofreading errors. Now for the kicker: "… none of the subjects in the off switch groups ever used the switch. The mere knowledge that one can exert control made the difference'." [1]

In another experiment, when subjects were given four cans of unmarked soft drinks to taste and choose their favorite, they were more likely to choose their first choice than if the choice had been restricted to two cans (the drinks are all the same beverage in all cans). The fact, again, that we *think* we have *a bit* more discretion leads to much greater commitment. [2]

One important caveat to the findings about the soft drinks is also instructive. There are limits to which the degree of choice offers a sense of control. *Too many choices or too much information* seem to result in a sense of being overwhelmed, and as a consequence being out of control.

The desire for control plays itself out in the desire for political power and military conquest. It plays itself out in the desire to be the CEO. It plays itself out in the desire to obtain massive fortunes. After all, past the point where one's physical needs are met—or, we have "economic security"— the accumulation of money is often more about accumulating power and status than it is about consumption.

The bottom line is that people don't want to be corks bobbing around in a stream with little ability to control their direction or the outcome of life's journey. They want to be able to come and go as they please, choose what they'll have for dinner, control the TV remote, have some control over their work day. The desire for control is weaker among people who are conditioned to subservience or socialized institutional settings, but it persists at some level in almost everyone.

CHAPTER SEVEN

The Need for Structure

People want to have a sense of structure in their lives. At first blush this desire may seem to conflict with the desire for control, and on occasion it certainly does. But it is also true that if life were in fact an undifferentiated span of time with no formal rules, exercising control would be impossible. To control your life, it has to have some structure. If the rhythm of life were entirely random and unpredictable, no one could plan or control their existence.

To control the physical universe, we have to understand its structure and laws. The same goes for our lives and social relationships. A sense of structure in your life provides the latticework on which you can build decisions about life's direction. It gives you handles to grab onto life and manipulate it.

People fear randomness. They hate the idea that they could be shot at random while they are out shopping, or that terrorists could suddenly destroy the World Trade Center. Randomness makes them feel vulnerable and out of control. That's why random acts of violence are magnified in their importance well beyond the actual odds of pure physical harm. Polling by Lake Research after 9/11 showed that married women in Montana and Indiana worried a great deal about the danger terrorism posed to their families, even though the real odds of terrorists attacking the Terre Haute Stuckey's were pretty remote. Random terrorist acts made them feel vulnerable and out of control.

So in many ways, the desire for control and the desire for structure are corollary needs that go hand in hand.

But in other contexts they conflict.

The more people feel at loose ends—that life has lost its structure and grounding—the more they are willing to sacrifice another form of control—their personal freedom—in exchange for structure and order.

Civil liberties are most at risk in any society when people feel things have lost their structure and predictability. Whenever tyranny, dictatorship or totalitarianism takes root, they do so on the pretext of grave threats to security—either internal disorder or an external threat. *Their premise is always the perceived need for more order and structure in the society.*

Whether it is the internment of Japanese-Americans during World War II, or the suspension of due process rights in cases involving Islamic fundamentalists, or the creation of secret prisons, or wholesale spying on Americans, or Soviet gulags, or the 1973 Chilean military coup, or the unspeakable horrors of the Holocaust, they were all justified—and all made politically possible -- by "extraordinary" circumstances arising from "threats to security."

The conflict between individual freedom and public order has extended throughout history, and especially the history of the United States. Here the progressive tradition is firmly rooted in Benjamin Franklin's admonishment: "Those who would sacrifice liberty for security deserve neither."

The need for structure has another critical implication. It translates directly into the need for a framework or narrative around which to organize our understanding of the world.

Conservatives have done a brilliant job of providing small-town Kansas with that kind of narrative. They do it proudly and repeat it often. In *What's the Matter With Kansas?*, Frank explains that in Kansas, social conservatives have two critical understandings that color every fact they hear or article they read:

1) They believe that they—and their values—are under attack in the broader society
2) They believe that the enemies attacking them are the professional elites—the actors in Hollywood, the lawyers, the politicians, the academics—the "intellectuals." In other words, they see the world through the lens of class struggle. But the classes are not the workers on the one side and big business on the other. They're the ordinary, God-fearing Americans who play by the rules and believe in America, versus the professional elites with secular values, who live lives of decadence and self-indulgence.

Everyone receives thousands of inputs of information every day, whether from ads for McDonald's or newscasts about Darfur. To make sense of the world we have to fit these inputs into some framework or structure—into some set of assumptions about how the world works. We do this every day in our own interactions with the physical world. For instance, we take for granted that if we drop a ball, it will fall. Gravity is an unconscious assumption that allows us to function in every day life. The same is true of broad assumptions about our role in the social and political world.

Later we will discuss the driving human desire for meaning in life— or purpose. The word meaning, of course, can both indicate the concept

of "purpose" and the concept of "understanding a set of relationships."
It is not accidental that the word has both connotations. To understand
your meaning, or identity, or purpose in life, you have to find meaning—
structure and organization—in the world around you.

Human beings are always seeking to bring order out of chaos to find
meaning or structure in their surroundings, and to understand how
they fit in. That is the only way we can determine our own identity and
trajectory in life.

Cognitive linguist George Lakoff explains this process in more detail.
He argues that all thought uses conceptual frames, which are mental
structures of limited scope with systematic internal organization. The
repetition of these frames over long periods creates physical neural circuits
in the brain, which provide the structure through which we interpret the
inputs of information that our senses provide us about reality.[1]

Neurological science is making enormous strides understanding the
physical basis for these frames and the neuro-pathways that define them.
A study reported in the December 18, 2006 issue of *Nature Neuroscience* by
Dr. Matthew Wilson and Daoyun Ji of MIT shed new light on the way the
brain processes recent memories of sensory stimuli, consolidates them as
long-term memories, and uses the new data to create and modify frames
for understanding the world.

Researchers have known for some time that new memories are laid
down in the hippocampus section of the brain and later transferred to
the neocortex, the sheet of neurons on the outer surface of the brain that
mediates conscious thought and contains long-term memories. But it turns
out that the process doesn't simply involve a transfer of memories, but a
processing of data.

"The neocortex is essentially asking the hippocampus to replay events
that contain a certain image, place or sound," said Dr. Wilson. "The
neocortex is trying to make sense of what is going on in the hippocampus
and to build models of the world, to understand how and why things
happen," he said. These models are then presumably used to direct
behavior. The research indicates that much of this activity occurs during
nondreaming sleep.[2]

Most thought is unconscious—a fact that has important implications
for all political communication. Many frames reside at the unconscious
level and are not instantaneously available to conscious introspection.

Lakoff categorizes frames as "deep" or "surface." Deep frames structure your moral system or worldview. Surface frames have a smaller scope
and apply to any number of ideas or concepts. We use these surface frames
every day in politics. Bush reframed the Iraq war as a "front in the war on
terror." That's a surface frame.[3]

In general, Lakoff points out, *whoever frames the debate about a controversial issue, wins.*[4]

Deep frames are especially critical because they structure how we view the basic organization of the world and our own place within it—our meaning or identity. Lakoff puts it this way: *"Deep framing is the conceptual infrastructure of the mind: the foundation, walls, and beams of that edifice. Without deep frames there is nothing for the surface message to hang on to."* [5]

Frames provide the broad symbolic structure that allows us to understand reality. Most cognition is accomplished through symbols that also allow us to interpret the meaning of information.

In addition to frames, Lakoff focuses heavily on another important form of symbol—the metaphor. He argues that metaphorical thought is especially important when we think about moral or political questions. For instance, we use spatial images to discuss the much more abstract notion of time: "I'm looking forward to that event." We talk about the abstract concept of knowing as seeing: "Do you see what I mean?" Or: "That was an eye-opening event."

In general, Lakoff says, "metaphorical thought is tied to the embodied experience... it links abstract ideas to visceral, bodily experience." In other words, it is used to make abstract concepts into concrete experiences that we can see, hear, touch, smell or taste with our senses. [6]

It is the frames and metaphors in our brains that define what we think of as "common sense." As a consequence, frames generally trump facts that don't fit into the frame. If we hear or see a fact that is not consistent with our frame, we will generally ignore the fact and keep the frame. After all, for us, the fact must not be so, because it "defies common sense." [7]

Frames themselves are changed only through experience and repetition, not through simple argument.

People want structure—and they want frames to allow them to understand the world. That's why when it comes to the moral and political world, they want to know right from wrong.

Chapter Eight

Community, Human Interaction
and Affirmation

Human beings are pack animals—they travel in packs. They are social, herding animals. They are programmed to want interaction with other people and approval from those with status in the group. Among human beings, loners are the exception, just as they are among most other herding animals.

As an aside, it's worth noting that all of the other large mammals that we have managed to domesticate are herding animals (there are 15), save two: the cat and the ferret. Every other domesticated creature—dogs, hogs, cattle, horses, water buffalo, sheep, goats, you name it –are all herding animals. Domestication requires a creature's willingness to associate with others of its kind and imprint on leaders.

Cats, by the way, "sort of domesticated themselves," says Carlos A. Driscoll, a molecular genetics graduate student who was involved in a study of cat genetics. When large-scale grain agriculture began in the Fertile Crescent in the Near East about 13,000 years ago, the storage of grain attracted mice. Wildcats came out of the woods and grasslands to exploit this new ecological niche and ultimately adapted to their close relationship to humans. Most other domesticated creatures were intentionally domesticated by humans from their wild cousins.[1]

If people feel isolated from each other—if they don't have an opportunity for human contact and interaction in their lives, if they are lonely—they are unhappy. And the desire for affirmation or validation from others is endless. People may vary by the degree that they need validation from others and interaction with others, but on average this need is an extremely powerful interest in most human beings.

Of course the power of this need is massively magnified by the power of the sex drive, and the innate and socially amplified power of sexual attraction.

If you put someone into solitary confinement, you deprive them of a critical need and deny them the ability to fulfill one of their most powerful self-interests.

The desire to be part of the group, the desire for validation, the desire to avoid loneliness—are all powerful factors in people's political decision-making.

In making voting decisions and adopting their political views, people rely heavily on the views of the group and its opinion leaders. Our job as Progressives is to create a bandwagon effect for progressive points of view, to surround people with our view of the world, to repeat our values over and over; to make our values "mainstream."

That requires conscious strategy. It also requires self-confidence and pride.

Just as important, we need to take seriously people's need for community. Large chunks of the religious right respond to this need. The right's constant emphasis on family is right on point.

Progressives cannot afford to be caricatured as single urbanites who don't believe in community.

Of course nothing could be further from the truth, either. It is Progressives who are dedicated to community values. It's the right wing that promotes radical individualism—the "ownership society" where "you're on your own, buddy."

People desperately want a sense of community—and Progressives need to proudly and confidently assert that we offer it to them. Deep in our genetic material, people understand that life is about how we take care of each other, not just how well we take care of ourselves. *They want to hear us say that it is right for us to look out for each other and wrong not to.* They need to know that we are the political movement truly looking after families—families that are destroyed not by allowing people of the same sex to marry but by hopelessness and unemployment and alcoholism and a value system that places emphasis on what you can do for yourself instead of what you can do for each other.

They want us to help create progressive institutions to bring community into their lives—real and personal relationships not mediated through a TV. One method is grassroots campaigns themselves. By mobilizing people to communicate with voters, we create communities—fighters for the progressive cause—that directly address the need for community.

CHAPTER NINE

Intellectual Stimulation

To varying degrees people all need some level of intellectual stimulation. They hate boredom.

Human intellectual curiosity is obviously one of our most selective traits. Our desire to learn and explore the unknown—to discover, to find adventure—has served us as the principal engines of human progress.

People risk their lives to avoid boredom. They need new intellectual inputs almost as much as they need food and drink. This trait is not unique to human beings, as anyone who has lived with a dog or cat knows. Higher mammals succeed because they are curious.

John F. Kennedy's challenge to America in 1962 to land on the moon by the end of the decade captured the imagination of Americans for many reasons. One of them was simply the challenge to learn and explore—to go where no man had gone before—sharing the adventure of learning and discovery.

You don't have to go far to convince most Americans of the importance of education or scientific inquiry.

As a political organizer, I advocate that political communication must use powerful symbols and must be clear and concise without insulting the intelligence of the voters.

Political communication must never talk down to voters but it also shouldn't overestimate how much they care, at least at the outset. In fact, the innate need that people have for intellectual stimulation means that our political communication competes with myriad other communications and cannot be boring or predictable. It must be interesting and entertaining. People love to be engaged in a lively fight or debate if it involves something they care about.

In our political activity, it is our job to address people's need for intellectual stimulation. It is our job to be interesting and engaging. It is not *their* job to look past a boring and uninteresting campaign and become engaged regardless. If you talk in boring "policy speak," people's eyes glaze over. Their eyes don't glaze over because they're stupid or uninterested. They glaze over because "policy speak" is boring and uninteresting.

It's *our* job as progressive organizers to engage people's innate curiosity and interest—to understand all of their self-interests and engage them.

CHAPTER TEN

Meaning, Purpose and Identity

More than anything else, people want meaning in life. They want purpose. They want to know that their lives have some significance; that they matter. They want an identity.

In the book *In Search of Excellence,* Peters and Waterman argue that the desire for meaning has two parts.

On the one hand, people want to be part of something bigger than themselves—a movement, an organization, a club, a religion, a company.

On the other hand, they want to stick out. They want to be an especially significant part of this larger enterprise, to make a special contribution.

Our need for meaning and significance manifests itself in our insatiable desire for affirmation, approval and status. It plays itself out in the ways we dress, the wedding parties we throw for our kids, the pride we feel when we receive recognition, the pleasure we take from a compliment.

But the most important way people find meaning in their lives is by making commitments to something outside of themselves. They get meaning from the commitments they make to their family, their company, their country, their religion, a project, a team, their art, a campaign, a cause, a lover. When we commit to something, we tell ourselves that we are needed, that we are important.

When someone says his life is empty, it's often because he hasn't found something or someone to which he can commit.

The fact that we, as human beings, desperately seek meaning drives us to support each other, to explore and discover, to invent, to create things of beauty, and to care about one another.

Since meaning demands commitment, it often demands action to change the status quo, and it is that human action that is at the root of all human progress. Our search for meaning is our species' most priceless selective trait.

In managing organizations, the most powerful tool to guarantee concerted action is the realization that if we want people to be self-motivated—so that they energetically do things on their own without having to be told—they must be inspired by their own understanding of the significance of what we want them to do.

Self-motivation comes from inspiration and inspiration comes from a sense of meaningfulness.

That is why President Kennedy's call to "ask not what your country can do for you, ask what you can do for your country," is such a critical element of the progressive vision. People want to be motivated with a call to commitment. They want to be called upon to sacrifice. They don't want to hear calls for sacrifice that imply failure or surrender. Jimmy Carter's reflection on the "malaise" of American society and his call for Americans to get used to living with less were viewed as a demand to sacrifice in the face of failure—to simply settle for a lower quality of life. (Although he didn't use the word "malaise," the July 15, 1979 speech quickly was branded his "Malaise Speech").

In contrast, Kennedy called on Americans to "lift any burden, fight any foe" in order to defend liberty; to sacrifice for the higher goals of human progress. People want to be called upon to sacrifice their time, their effort—even their lives—for a better future. That kind of sacrifice isn't about defeat, it is about empowerment.

To be inspired is to feel empowered. When you hear Jesse Jackson speak, you may not remember what he says, but you can remember how he made you feel. When you are inspired, you are called upon to be more than you are, to overcome an obstacle, to be stronger, to fight harder, to sacrifice for something to which you are committed.

Human beings want to be called upon to make a commitment—to sacrifice—in order to make a difference with their lives.

George Bush called on military families to sacrifice to fight terrorism. At the same time, he called for the wealthiest Americans to take billions of dollars in tax breaks. His hypocrisy provides the perfect pivot for an inspiring progressive message that asks Americans to make a real commitment—a real sacrifice—for the future of hope and possibility.

My wife, Jan, often says that the greatest tragedy of the Bush years is not what he's done, but the opportunities he has squandered.

On June 28, 2006 The New York Times ran a front-page story by Celia Dugger about the lack of progress defeating malaria in Africa:

> The mosquito nets arrived too late for 18-month-old Philip Odug.
>
> The roly-poly boy came down with his fourth bout of malaria the same day the nets were handed out on March 16 at the makeshift camp where he lived in northern Uganda. "It was because of poverty that we could not afford one," his mother, Jackeline Ato, recalled recently seated in rags beneath a mango tree·
>
> The morning after his fever spiked, she took him to a clinic, but because it did not have the medicines that might have saved him, he died four days later, crying, "mommy, mommy" before losing consciousness.

It is no secret that mosquitoes carry the parasite that causes malaria. More mystifying is why 800,000 young African children a year still die of malaria—more than from any other disease—when there are medicines that cure for $.55 a dose, mosquito nets that shield a child for a dollar a year, and indoor insecticide spraying that cost about $10 annually for a household.[1]

Rather than invading other countries, our technology gives us the ability to lead the world in eliminating hunger and desperate poverty. It affords us the opportunity to lay the foundation for the creation of a truly democratic world by assuring that everyone can live a prosperous life, every child can get a good education, and no child dies of preventable disease.

It's not just that we could do some good here or there—our superpower status could enable America to help transform the world in our lifetimes.

Later, we'll explore in more detail what it means to have progressive values in modern America and the historic role that Americans could fulfill.

That historic role can help fulfill our powerful need for meaning. Meaning is the greatest motivator—the pre-eminent self-interest. Providing people the opportunity to have meaning in life, to make a real difference in the world—is the cornerstone of successful political strategy.

CHAPTER ELEVEN

From Garbage Cans
to the Meaning of Life

When I moved to Chicago in 1969 I had my first encounter with the legendary Regular Democratic Organization of Cook County—the Democratic "Machine."

As a progressive anti-Vietnam War activist my view of the "machine" was symbolized by Mayor Richard J. Daley and his treatment of the anti-war protesters at the Democratic Convention in 1968. When I thought of the Democratic Machine, I saw Chicago police swinging batons at unarmed anti-war protesters.

I assumed that the same repressive tactics must certainly have been behind Daley's ability to deliver the vote. The vaunted precinct captains surely must threaten, intimidate, or pay off voters to deliver those huge electoral margins.

Most of my early Chicago political experience was for candidates who opposed the "machine," but I gradually began to see that it was much more complex than I originally believed. Of course, most of those captains worked their precincts because they had patronage jobs—an issue that is still being fought out in Chicago. But the really interesting question had to do with the relationship between the precinct captain and the voters. Precinct captains did all of what any precinct worker does in politics. They identified the "plus" voters who supported their candidates, and they mobilized them on Election Day.

But they did something more. They could deliver a "controlled" vote. In other words, they had a core of voters that they could persuade to do pretty much whatever they asked. Most of the time the reason was *not* that the voter lived in fear that if he didn't do the precinct captain's bidding, his city services would go away or he would experience some form of retaliation. After all, he voted by secret ballot.

No, the precinct captain did something much more sophisticated. He would develop a personal relationship to the voter. He would analyze his self-interests, and then try to address them.

When someone new moved into the neighborhood, the good precinct captain was a veritable Welcome Wagon. He came to meet the new family, and would ask if he could be of any assistance. He could tell you about available city services and programs for the kids at the local park, and answer questions about the local school. And maybe he would provide a garbage can for the alley emblazoned with something like "Ed Jones, Committeeman, 47th Ward Regular Democratic Organization."

If you were a senior and needed a step on your porch fixed, he might get the local lumberyard to donate some lumber and bring some guys over to fix the step.

He would mention that the Ward Committeeman had office hours, every Monday night, at the Democratic headquarters where you could come and ask for his help. If you had a problem with city services, or needed a summer job for your son, or a real job for your son-in-law, or a liquor license for your new tap—just walk in and ask.

He would leave his card so you could call any time if you had a problem with your city services—or anything else for that matter. "Make sure to put this card on your refrigerator," he would say.

If you were older he might ask if you wanted to come to the committeeman's monthly senior citizen Bingo, where you could win a prize or meet your neighbors, or at least get out of the house.

Or maybe—if you're interested—you might want to come to a political rally where you might meet some of the politicians that you see on TV.

Whether it was your physical needs, your social needs, your aspirations in life, the excitement of seeing a "famous" person—the precinct captain was there for you. In addition to which he was your friend; a personal relationship developed. So when he asked you to vote for the people on his palm card on Election Day, you were happy to help.

After all, he might explain, the better he did in his precinct, the better he was able to look out for you and the services for the neighborhood like new curbs and sidewalks. He showed you respect. And he wasn't just there when election time came. He was there year-round. You became part of his team, and he was "on your side."

Of course the reason the precinct captain did all his work was that his government job or promotion was contingent upon his precinct's performance on Election Day.

I'm not suggesting that Progressives should attempt to re-create great patronage armies. Government services should be provided by employees who have the protections of civil service and union contracts.

But for years, many Progressives and Democratic operatives thought that television had made great precinct operations obsolete. That was dead wrong. That was a huge strategic error that cost us dearly.

And the rank-and-file precinct captain understood something else that has been forgotten by many high-priced "political operatives" as well. To win, you have to understand and address the full range of a voter's self-interests, from garbage cans to the meaning of life.

SECTION THREE

TARGETS FOR COMMUNICATION

CHAPTER TWELVE

Whom Do We Have to Move In Order to Convert This Historic Opportunity Into Progressive Realignment?

To recap:

- The results of the 2006 Midterm Elections and the failures of the Bush presidency have given us an opportunity to create a fundamental, long-lasting realignment in American politics.

- Even though the American electorate has been evenly divided for the last quarter-century, conservative assumptions and values have dominated political dialogue and political decision making since the mid 1970's.

- Remember that in the 2006 Midterm Elections, many swing voters were convinced to vote *against* conservative candidates and policies, but they often did not vote *for* progressive candidates, values or policies.

- A progressive realignment will not flow automatically from that victory. Bill Clinton vanquished the Republicans twice during the 1990s, yet the Republicans came back to win control of all three branches of Government.

I said earlier that progressive realignment must include two critical components:

1) It requires creating a substantial enduring majority in the American electorate. That means we have to change the American electorate, either by expanding the number of people who always vote, or by persuading critical segments of voters who do regularly vote that it is in their interests to support progressive candidates over the long-haul.

2) It requires a shift in the fundamental assumptions and values—the terms that frame the debate in American Politics. We need to reactivate the traditional progressive value frame that has always been central to the growth of American democracy.

Both of these goals require that we change people's behavior—their ways of thinking and their actions as voters. That may sound obvious, but that simple fact often gets lost in day-to-day political activity.

The fact that our goal is to change people's behavior becomes especially important as we decide whom we target for political communication. The threshold questions are: whose behavior do we need to change, whose behavior can we change—and how?

Whom Do We Talk To – And How Do We Change Their Behavior

The goal of any political movement—or political campaign—is to change people's behavior, to get them to behave differently than they would behave if our movement or campaign did not exist.

If the targets of our communication vote the same way, believe the same things and express the same opinions as they would if we didn't communicate with them at all, we should quit doing political work and all go to the beach.

But many electoral and issue campaigns—and movements—fail to adhere to this basic principle when they allocate their resources or plan their activities.

To realign American politics—to defeat the right—we need to carefully evaluate who the targets of our communication should be based on whose behavior we need to change in order to succeed. Then we need to determine whose behavior actually can be changed by evaluating their self-interests and formulating a communications program that engages those self-interests.

The Self-Interest Spectrum

For three decades the Midwest Academy, which trains progressive organizers, has used a simple tool to analyze the actors with whom we should communicate in a particular situation.

It's called the "Self-Interest Spectrum."

The Midwest Academy was founded by an extraordinary person named Heather Booth. She's been involved in pretty much every major progressive struggle of the last 35 years. She participated in the famous "Mississippi Freedom Summer" during the civil rights movement and was one of the early activists in the Feminist Movement while she was a graduate student at the University of Chicago.

Her husband, Paul Booth, helped to begin the so-called New Left in the 1960s and was the National Secretary of the Students for a Democratic Society (SDS) in its early years. He worked with me at Chicago's Citizens Action Program (CAP) as the organization's chair in the 1970s. He's now one of two chief deputies to Jerry McEntee, President of the American Federation of State County and Municipal Employees (AFSCME) — among the nation's largest unions.

Heather met Paul at a sit-in at the University of Chicago. Five days later they moved in together. They've been a team for over 35 years.

Heather went on to serve as the architect of the NAACP Voter Fund's massive voter registration and get-out-the-vote campaign in 2000. She was training director of the Democratic National Committee. She also founded the Citizen Labor Energy Coalition (CLEC) in the 1970s. CLEC was organized to fight rising gas and oil prices, and Big Oil. It was the first major coalition between organized labor and the young people who came out of the 1960s since the rift in the progressive movement caused by the Vietnam War.

Now Heather is one of the most sought-after progressive consultants in Washington.

She founded the Midwest Academy in the early 1970s to address the critical need to train a new generation of progressive organizers. Since then thousands of people have graduated from its many training programs.

Since Heather left in the mid-1970s, Jackie Kendall and Steve Max have led the Midwest Academy — both are brilliant organizers and trainers.

The idea of the "self-interest spectrum" is simple. Our slightly modified version divides any of the actors involved in any issue or electoral campaign into six groups along the spectrum:

- They share our self-interest and know it
- They share our self-interest and don't know it
- Our allies
- Their allies
- They share our opponent's self-interest and don't know it
- They share our opponent's self-interest and know it

The first group includes those actors who self-interests are completely and unequivocally aligned with our side of any particular issue or contest — and know that this is true. These people don't have to be persuaded. Instead they must be mobilized — set in motion to win the battle. Some people mobilize themselves. Others must be spurred to action. Messages for mobilization require that we engage their emotions, that we inspire them to action, that we give them self-confidence, that we break their inertia. Our message to them is very different message than a persuasion message.

The second group includes people who share our self-interest completely—but don't recognize it. For them the message is to wake up and smell the coffee. Sometimes this requires a loud alarm. Our first job when communicating with this group is to make them realize that they share our interest and that we share theirs.

The third group, our allies, includes people who have a mixed set of interests. Some of those interests would lead them to support us, and others would lead them to support our opponents. Our job when communicating with this group is to highlight those interests that they share with us, and minimize those that they share with the other side. In other words, our job is to prevent them from becoming "their allies" instead of "our allies."

This group is always one of our principal targets for communication.

Our second primary target is "their allies." They are the mirror opposite of "our allies," but our goal is the same: to emphasize their interests in being with us, and minimize their interests in siding with our opponents. Our first task is to determine who among them is the most persuadable and which arguments are most resonant.

With the next group—people who share our opponents' self-interest but don't recognize it—our job is to keep them uninterested in the fight. Our messages to them are lullabies.

The final group—those who share our opponent's' self-interest and recognize it—cannot be persuaded. It is generally counterproductive to even try, because it will agitate them into action. Our job is to keep them uninterested, demobilized, divided and demoralized. In the end, of course, sweet persuasion will not work with them. We must overpower them.

During a campaign, the occupants of the categories of "our allies" and "their allies" can move back and forth. And those who share each side's self-interests, and don't know it, can come to recognize they have skin in the game.

But the actors who are aware that they "share our self interest" or that they "share our opponents' self interest," do not move from one category to another unless the structure of the situation entirely changes so that altogether new self-interests emerge.

Fundamentally then, we have **five tasks** in any issue or electoral campaign:

- To awaken those who in fact share our self-interests, but don't yet realize it, to the true facts of life

- To move "their allies" to become "our allies"

- To lull both those who "share their self-interest and know it and those who "share their self-interest and don't know it" into inactivity so we can more easily defeat them

- To prevent our opponent's attempts to do these same things from their point of view

- To mobilize those who "share our self-interests" and "our allies" into action on our behalf

By placing actors in any particular situation into these categories, and understanding their constellation of interests, we are able to communicate the right messages to the right targets.

CHAPTER THIRTEEN

Categories of Message Targets

In both election and issue campaigns our primary targets are always the actual decision-makers. In elections, these are the voters. In issue campaigns they are sometimes voters (referenda), but they are usually public officeholders or private officials.

ELECTIONS—PERSUADABLES AND MOBILIZABLES

In election campaigns our goal is to change the behavior of the voters, since they are the actual decision-makers. Sometimes there are secondary targets as well, but the secondary targets are only important insofar as they can help us impact the primary targets—voters.

And our primary targets are not just any voters. They are the only two categories of voters whose electoral behavior can be changed by a campaign.

We call them persuadable voters and mobilizable voters.

Persuadable voters have two characteristics:
- They generally vote.
- They are undecided.

Mobilizable voters also have two characteristics:
- They would support our candidate.
- They are unlikely to vote unless they are mobilized to do so·

These are only two groups that are primary message targets in an electoral campaign, because they are the only two groups of direct decision-makers whose behavior can be changed.

In terms of the "self-interest spectrum," mobilizable voters always "share our self-interest and know it" or they are *firmly* committed allies. They are always solidly in our camp. But they may not be willing to act, to go to the polls. Our job is therefore entirely about motivating them to act.

Persuadable voters include those who "share our self-interest and don't know it" and any group of allies whose support for our candidate is not certain.

In many political campaigns, massive amounts of political resources are wasted because they are used to communicate with voters who are not part of one of these two groups. They are spent trying to convince voters who always vote Democratic to vote for a Democrat, or they are spent trying to convince people who always vote Republican to vote Democratic. They may also be spent trying to convince voters who never vote, but would vote Republican if they did, to vote Democratic. All of these are wastes of campaign resources, since the behavior of these target voters will not likely change.

Democrats are particularly prone to target voters who always vote Democratic—and always go out to vote—with resources that should go elsewhere.

Of course, base Democrats who always vote are critically important to campaigns as potential sources of volunteers and contributors. But they are not primary targets for the campaign's message since we don't want their voting behavior to change. They always vote Democratic, and always go out to vote. They behave that way no matter what is done by the campaign.

In Sections Four and Five we'll discuss the rules for messaging to persuadable and mobilizable voters—and how we find them.

ISSUE CAMPAIGNS—THE DECISION-MAKERS

The primary message targets of the issue campaigns are obviously the decision-makers, who can make the decision we desire. While in referenda they are also voters, in most issue campaigns, they are Members of Congress, state legislators, elements of the Executive branch, or officials of corporations or other private sector organizations.

In Section Six, we'll analyze the self-interest of members of legislatures, bureaucrats, governors, mayors and presidents—and how they can be addressed in issue campaigns. We'll also discuss campaigns aimed at private-sector decision-makers.

ADDITIONAL PROGRESSIVE MESSAGE TARGETS

Aside from the primary decision-makers of electoral or issue campaigns, Progressives must systematically focus on a number of secondary targets that are critical to both long- and short-term success.

There are six key categories:

- Activists
- Contributors

- Opinion Molders (including Mavens, Connectors & Salesmen)

- Leaders

- Organized Constituencies

- The Press

Each of these categories of actors includes people who lie in every sector of the self-interest of spectrum. We can affect the behavior of some more than others, but we can affect all of them to some degree.

A particular actor may fit in any of a number of these categories. Understanding the multiple roles targets play enables us to develop the most appropriate strategy for each.

Chapter Fourteen

Activists

I include in this category anyone who takes an active role in political or voluntary association of any type. Activists include people who make phone calls for a candidate, people who are active in the PTA or in a bowling league. The category includes people who are ardent bloggers and people who lead political organizations. Activists share one thing in common: they have demonstrated their willingness to engage in group activity over and above that which is required by their jobs or family.

In a real sense, activists are the cornerstones of American democracy. When we send an organizer to put together a volunteer political organization for a candidate, we send him to look for these activists. Often we would rather find an activist in a Holy Name Society or a block club than a person who is very interested in politics, but never engages in group activity. The willingness to be involved in common, voluntary activity is the key characteristic that distinguishes an activist from everyone else.

PROGRESSIVE ACTIVISTS

We need to create an army of progressive activists across America.

Obviously, our over-arching strategic goal, with respect to progressive activists, is to get them increasingly engaged in activity in some way that allows them to make a real contribution. Cheering at the TV set is fine, but it is not making a real contribution.

To do this, we need to create and motivate activists on the one hand, and on the other we need to structure opportunities for individuals to make that contribution. We need to create ways to tap into their energy.

WHEREWITHAL AND WILL

Whenever you want someone to do something—whether it's canvass door-to-door, make phone calls, give money, or buy a product—two elements are always involved. The person to be motivated needs both *will* and *wherewhithal*.

You can use any combination of the self-interests we have discussed to give people the *will* to get active in politics. You can pay them, or give them a job, or get them a garbage can. But in the end, self-motivation comes from inspiration.

The best way to give an activist the will to become involved is by inspiring her—convincing her that the goal is important and meaningful *in and of itself*—and that she herself can play an important role in achieving the goal.

Both of these elements are critical to motivation: being part of something important, and the ability to play a role personally to make a contribution.

In some sense, then, providing the *wherewithal* for someone to make a contribution is actually an important part of giving him the will to act. After all, more than anything else, to be inspired is about feeling personally empowered.

Once motivated, there are two ways to give an activist the wherewithal to do whatever it is you have motivated them to do:

CREATING DIFFERENT ROLES

First, you have to be able to accommodate different levels of potential involvement. You need to find ways to use the energies of people who can pitch in a few hours around election day, as well as find ways to use people who are able to devote their all to the effort.

Different people have different amounts of time, energy and skill, and the more of them you can accommodate with roles in the effort the more energy you can harvest. We need to engage a person who can make one phone call to their Member of Congress each month; the person who can do online research; the student who can organize a MeetUp; and the senior who can make political calls every day.

The Internet and new phone technology have created an infrastructure, a latticework, around which we can organize more and more opportunities for activist involvement. This reduces the transaction costs associated with getting someone involved.

Twenty years ago, it was very expensive to get someone who expressed an interest in an issue to make a phone call to her Member of Congress. We had to mail to her, or a living, breathing person had to call her. Today an e-mail alert or robo-patch-through call that automatically connects the respondent to her Senator's office does the trick at very little cost.

INVEST IN TRAINING

The second way to give them the wherewithal is to provide activists with training and skill development that upgrade the quality of their contributions—and, in turn, the depth of their commitment.

I've found that the time invested in training and skill development for activists and organizers always provides returns many times what is invested. In campaigns, there never seems to be the time to do training. But in reality, it is almost always a good investment when you tally up total volunteer activity that good training programs ultimately generate.

TAKE THEM TO 95TH STREET

In addition to providing will and wherewithal, our third strategic goal is to take them to 95th Street. Let me explain.

When I first got into organizing, I worked for a guy named Peter Martinez. We would often work late at night at an office that was located on Chicago's North Side in a church on Fullerton Avenue. Frequently, as we were about to leave for the night at nine or 10 o'clock, he would ask if I would mind dropping him at the "El" train downtown on my way to my apartment in the Hyde Park neighborhood on Chicago's Near South side. He lived on the Far South side.

I would always agree.

When we got downtown, he'd ask if I would mind going a little out of my way down the Dan Ryan Expressway and drop him at the train at 55th Street. Then, he said, I could cut over to my apartment in Hyde Park. I would agree again.

Finally, when we got to 55th Street on the expressway, he'd say, "Gee, we're only 10 minutes from my house on 95th Street—can you just drop me there?" And I would say yes, again.

I fell for this deal over and over again. I would never have agreed to take him to 95th Street if he had asked me at the office, but he took me there one step at a time.

We need to take progressive activists to 95th Street. We need to get them involved in one thing, and then another, until they do commit their lives, fortunes and sacred honor to progressive activism—or at least until we get them as far as they will go.

Here's why "one step at a time" works so well at getting people to 95th Street.

In the words of Harvard psychologist, Jerome Bruner, "you're more likely to act yourself into feeling than feel yourself into action."[1]

In their book *In Search of Excellence*, Peters and Waterman cite an example of this from an experiment in Palo Alto, California. Subjects who initially agreed to put a small yard sign in their front window supporting a cause (traffic safety) subsequently agreed to display a billboard in their front yards, which required letting outsiders dig sizable holes in the lawn. Those who were not asked to take the first step (the small sign) turned down the larger sign in 95 cases out of a hundred. [2]

"The implications of this line of reasoning are clear. Only if you get people acting, even in small ways, the way you want them to, will they come to believe in what they're doing. Moreover, the process of enlistment is enhanced by explicit management of the after-the-fact labeling process—in other words, publicly and ceaselessly lauding the small wins along the way. 'Doing things' (lots of experiments, tries) leads to rapid and effective learning, adaptations, diffusion, and commitment." [3]

One final note on inspiring progressive activists. My wife recently made a speech to a conference of the Campaign for America's Future, an organization dedicated to the creation of a progressive majority in the United States. She warned Progressives not to spend so much time complaining about other Democrats:

> ... we all need to resist, as hard as I know it is at times, griping about the Democrats, because it takes time away from the real work of defeating Republicans, and because it's counterproductive, demoralizing to the very people we need to be engaged and enthusiastic.

In fact, it is critical that our activists have self-confidence. This requires that they hear our assumptions and values constantly repeated with confidence. That's why talk radio like Air America and Nova M, and progressive publications like *The American Prospect* and *The Nation* are so important. They help build a progressive echo chamber. Most persuadable voters don't listen to Air America or read *The Nation*. But the media are critical in providing self-confidence and clarity to progressive activists.

Get 'Em While They're Young

During high school, college and early adult life, most activists firmly settle on their understandings of their relationship to society and their self-interests—including their sense of meaning in life. Once that happens, these commitments are very hard to change. That is why it is so important for Progressives to contest actively for the allegiance of young people.

In general core partisanship in the electorate changes by generational replacement. Once someone has voted Democrat or Republican several times, they are much less likely to change party affiliation.

The good news is that young people have made a sharp turn toward Democrats. The Washington Post's E. J. Dionne reports:

> In 1984 three exit polls pegged Ronald Reagan's share of the ballots cast by Americans under 30 at between 57 and 60 percent. Reagan-style conservatism seemed fresh, optimistic and innovative. In 2006, voters under 30 gave 60 percent of their votes to Democratic House candidates, according to the shared media exit poll. Conservatism now looks old, tired and ineffectual. [4]

In fact, young people in Generation Y appear to be substantially more progressive and tolerant than their immediate generational predecessor— Generation X.

A summer, 2007 study by Anna Greenberg and Democracy Corps found that 57% of the voters under 30 years old expected to vote Democratic for Congress in the next election and only 39% for Republicans. Forty five percent said they had a positive view of the Democratic Party compared with 31% unfavorable. While 31% said they had a favorable view of the Republican Party and 45% were unfavorable. Strong majorities of this group also said the government should play a major role in solving America's problems. [5]

That certainly bodes well, not only for the pool of future voters, but for future activists. Young people are particularly important source of activists. They have the wherewithal of activism in abundance: time and energy.

But the Greenberg study also uncovered findings that once again reinforce our need to clearly articulate the progressive value frame. Notwithstanding their support for many progressive views, under 30 year old voters were still very disconnected from politics. Many of their concerns involved their own individual difficulty in attaining some level of economic security. But they didn't exhibit a keen sense that their economic insecurity had anything to do with politics or the behavior of corporations. In fact even though they supported government action in general, they were less anti-corporate, less populist and less hostile to privatization of government services than other groups in the population. In other words their political views didn't hang together or reference a coherent set of values.

As much as anything, I believe that can be traced to the fact that during the years when many of this group politically matured, progressive values were marginalized in national political dialogue. That has to change.

The Howard Dean phenomenon, and online groups like Democracy for America and MoveOn.org, have helped a great deal in recruiting and training young activists. The same is true for the Public Interest Research Group (PIRG) and other door-to-door canvass operations that provide a systematic means for young people to take concrete progressive action, and assume more and more responsibility quickly on the job.

The events that led me to a life-long commitment to progressive politics involved a collision between the social values I learned in church, and everyday life in the Deep South of the 1960s.

It Just Didn't Square

I was born in Tulsa, Oklahoma but moved to Shreveport, Louisiana at the age of 11. My first real political "action" came when I was President of the Student Council at Broadmoor Junior High School. The big complaint among my "constituents" was simple—the food in the school cafeteria was crummy. So about midway through the school year, I led the student body in a boycott of the cafeteria, demanding that the quality of the food improve. Everybody simply brought his or her lunch. The school principal—who had been my friend and mentor—was not amused. The school cafeteria received funds based on the number of meals it served each day. I was called in to the principal's office and my old mentor looked at me across the desk and said, "You are behaving like a revolutionary." It was meant as a real dressing down, but it didn't sound so bad. I guess I kind of liked being a revolutionary.

We persisted with the boycott for several weeks, and finally were presented with a package of improvements. The boycott ended in a victory.

I was also active in the Presbyterian Church. It was some of the people I met at that church, coupled with the social restlessness of the early 1960s, that increasingly convinced me that the racism of my community simply didn't square with the social implications of my religious beliefs.

One day, shortly after the cafeteria boycott ended, I did some more building on my new "revolutionary tradition." I shocked many of my classmates, teachers and my mother by making a speech to a pre-school-day Chapel service advocating an end of racial segregation in my all-white public junior high school. You didn't have to do much to shake things up in the mid-1960s South.

At the time it seemed to me that the best way to resolve the conflicts I saw in society was libertarianism. My experience in the South led me to believe that the power of the state—and of the status quo—were linked so completely that the only way to end racial oppression was through the limitation of state power and massive increases in individual liberty. In 1964 I even represented Barry Goldwater in a mock presidential debate before the C.E. Byrd High School student body.

But in 1965 I went off to Duke University, and within three months had decided that the imperatives of racial and social justice—and the principles of my religious beliefs—compelled me to become a progressive activist.

The summer after my sophomore year I returned home to Shreveport to a job managing logistics for the new summer Head Start program. But before the program got started, the governor held up the funds. I joined several African-American ministers who decided to organize a silent vigil outside of the parish courthouse to protest. Accompanied by a local reporter, we went to City Hall to apply for a permit to hold a demonstration. The Public Safety Commissioner, a man who very much resembled the famous Bull Connor of Birmingham, told the group, "If you boys protest, I'll throw you all in jail. I don't care if it's peaceful or not."

We consulted with the New Orleans Chapter of the American Civil Liberties Union and were prepared to proceed, but then we were struck by the fact that many of the teachers who would be out of summer work without Head Start were white. White teachers would never come to a protest—especially if they were going to be thrown in jail. But they might come to meetings about their jobs.

So instead of a protest vigil, we decided to organize something that was pretty rare in Shreveport: a series of racially integrated protest meetings— to which we also invited the press. My most vivid memory of those meetings was the sight of police writing down the license numbers of the cars of everyone in attendance. But surprisingly, that kind of intimidation didn't have much effect. The meetings launched a barrage of phone calls, letters and legislative visits that shortly forced the governor to relent. We got our Head Start Program—and I learned a lot about coalition politics.

Later that summer, my friends and I decided to continue our newly-found program of racial collaboration by launching a series of weekly racially integrated discussion groups at homes throughout the city. They weren't very popular with white parents, but they were a big hit with their kids. The discussion groups began with 10 or 15 people and by summer's end, 100 young people, black and white, were meeting each week to discuss world events and experiencing, many for the first time, the excitement of mixing freely and socially with each other.

These discussion groups also spawned political action. We became active in voter registration drives sponsored by African-American churches, and signed onto a campaign for an all-black slate of candidates for the all-white Parish School board. My first experience running a political phone bank was in the "casket show room" of a black funeral home. By day it was used to show caskets; by night 15 phone lines were plugged into phone jacks. Volunteers called through voter lists while surrounded by caskets of every size and shape.

April 1968

On the night of April 4, 1968, I was studying in my dorm room at Duke. I was a political science major, and the Assistant Housemaster of a freshman dormitory. In mid-evening a freshman raced down the hall to my room, in tears. He blurted out words that were being repeated all over the country: "Martin Luther King has been shot."

I left my dormitory room to search out my colleagues among the growing cadre of Duke's progressive community. We believed that King's assassination compelled us to take action and worked until early morning developing our plan.

THE DUKE VIGIL

The next afternoon, hundreds of students joined a march of civil rights activists in downtown Durham, North Carolina. Then the racially mixed group marched to the "University House"—home of the president of the University, Douglas Knight. In many ways Knight was a visionary, a liberal leader. As he spoke to about half of the students and the press in front of his house, the other half took up positions inside.

When he was done, a group of us greeted him at the door. We said, "Mr. President, we appreciate your speech, but we have several demands. We'd like to sit down and negotiate, and we're not leaving until our demands are met." There were now riots in cities nationwide, and a machine gun mounted on the steps of the U.S. Capitol. We believed that we had a responsibility to take action—to make change.

Our demands included:

- An increase in the $1.15 per hour wage for many of the mostly black, non-academic employees
- Recognition of the American Federation of State County and Municipal Employees (AFSCME), who had been organizing a union for non-academic employees
- Withdrawal of the president from an all-white Hope Valley Country Club.

Three days later, we were still sitting in the house when the head of student activities came to tell us that the president of the University had had a nervous breakdown. The Chairman of the Board of Trustees would fly in from Detroit to take interim control of the situation; he was the Vice President of Ford Motor Company. Our leadership met, and after several hours of deliberation, we decided to shift tactics. We would move our protest to the quadrangle of the University in front of the massive Duke University Chapel. There we would maintain a silent vigil until our demands were met.

We marched to the quadrangle and were joined by representatives of AFSCME, who announced they had called a strike.

Over the next two days, the "Duke Vigil," as it came to be called, grew from several hundred students to thousands. Sororities prepared food for the demonstrators. A group of faculty members called their own work stoppage. Threats were made by the North Carolina Ku Klux Klan to attack the students. The state police were called out to protect the campus. Joan Baez and Pete Seeger came to sing. Senator Robert Kennedy sent a telegram of support. Dr. King's funeral was broadcast live to the crowd. News came pouring in about riots and unrest all across America.

Negotiations finally began. About a week after it all had started, the administration signed an agreement with the student leadership, meeting our demands. Wages were to be increased, the union was on its way to formal recognition, the President quit the all-white country club. We had won.

I suppose that "vigil" was the decisive event in my life. I was hooked. I knew that for me, the most empowering and fulfilling calling to which I could possibly commit my life was the struggle for justice.

On the 25th anniversary of the "Duke Vigil," I received a call from a young reporter at the Duke Chronicle. She asked me—as an established middle-aged, middle-class person—if I still believed in the kind of organizing that I'd done in the 1960s. She asked if I would do it again. "Do it again? That's what I do for a living," I said.

TRAINING A NEW GENERATION OF PROGRESSIVE ORGANIZERS

My firm, the Strategic Consulting Group (SCG), has focused heavily on recruiting and training young people to be political activists.

When my wife, Jan Schakowsky, first ran for Congress in 1998, she needed to develop a field operation that could compete with the regular Democratic Party of Cook County—the vaunted Democratic Machine— that was backing one of her opponents, a state senator and Democratic Ward Committeeman. Her other opponent was the heir to the Hyatt Hotel fortune.

We decided to recruit 15 organizers by creating the "1998 Chicago Campaign School." We advertised for applicants from around the country to come to Chicago this winter, where we do real "in the trenches" politics.

We said we'd pay a small stipend, put them up in a supporter's home, give them training from some of the best political professionals around, and work them 14 hours a day, seven days a week. They had to have a car. Each organizer was assigned a turf to organize, and got constant training and supervision. They also got to work for a great candidate. We received 200 applications, and took the 15 we thought were the best.

Job One was to build a volunteer organization that could identify enough Schakowsky voters ("plus" voters) to win the primary (about 31,000 votes), and then to get them out to the polls.

Election Day was cold and rainy, a "precinct captain's" Election Day, but our organizers had accumulated and trained 1,500 volunteers to hit the streets. They delivered the 31,000 votes—and Jan won, 45% to 35% to 20%.

After the election, our firm began using the same model to recruit and train organizers for other electoral field operations. Since then, 800 organizers have been through 17- week training programs and electoral campaigns. Many have gone on to important careers in progressive political organizations, campaign management, work on Capitol Hill, progressive think tanks, unions and advocacy organizations.

SCG's Campaign Management Program is just another example of getting them while they're young.

Of course, some activists are "activated" by some other experience later in life—work on political campaigns, union or church activity, or some other life-transforming events.

But once activated, few change their political spots. There are of course notable exceptions. David Brock writes about his sojourn from conservative to progressive activist in his fascinating book, *Blinded by the Right,* and of course there is the famous evolution of Arianna Huffington.

But in general get them while they're young.

SWING CONSTITUENCY ACTIVISTS

In terms of the self-interest spectrum, swing constituencies include people and groups who share our self-interest but don't recognize it, and those in the "Allies" category.

Our strategic goals here are much the same as for progressive activists. We want to engage these activists to work for progressive causes and elections.

But there is one big difference. Before we can mobilize them to work for a progressive cause, we have to convince them that they share all or part of our self-interests.

In all cases, this involves using the rules of symbolically powerful message communication that we'll discuss in Section Four. We need to describe the issue, election or cause to the activist in a palpable, personal way.

There are two additional rules for swing activists.

WE NEED TO BE AGITATORS

First, we need to be *agitators.* Some people think that calling someone an "agitator" is an insult. Personally, I think it's a great compliment.

The definition of an agitator is simple: in Saul Alinski's terms, an agitator "rubs raw the sores of discontent." An agitator brings the real self-interests of the person being "agitated" into focus and makes it tangible by putting it at the top of the mental agenda. Whether a person entirely or partially shares the self-interest that would make him a Progressive, an agitator converts that portion of his constellation of interests that would lead that person in a progressive direction into an overarching concern in the person's consciousness.

Back when I worked for Peter Martinez at the Citizens Action Program, I was assigned to organize a community around the U.S. Steel South Works that used to be on the far south side of Chicago. We were demanding that the plant clean up the pollution it spewed into the air and water.

Back then a lot of people in the neighborhood still didn't have clothes dryers and hung out their wash to dry. I would go visit people like Ms. Persanski of the St. Peter and Paul Holy Name Society. If Ms. Persanski had her laundry out on the line, I would say, "Gee, I bet it's a problem keeping the sheets white, since you have to hang them in the polluted air the steel mill puts out."

Now Ms. Persanski may have never thought about whether her sheets stayed white before, but after we talked it's likely that, as she got into bed each night, she might ask herself if her sheets really were white. What if the pollution made them—or maybe her lungs—gray?

The same goes if someone tells you that you have a spot on your pants. Maybe when you put them on you saw it, but assumed no one would notice. But once it's pointed out, you are self-conscious about it for the rest of the day. That's being an agitator.

THE COALITION RULE

The second rule we have to use with swing activists you might call the "coalition rule." The "coalition rule" goes like this: an activist or leader will happily forgive their disagreement with many of your positions on issues if you support them when it comes to the things that matter most to them.

Illinois Public Action, the progressive coalition which I directed for many years, took positions on a wide array of issues. Its board included a broad group of leaders from various constituencies whose self-interests generally placed them in the progressive camp. But members didn't necessarily agree with the organization's positions on everything.

A farm leader from downstate Illinois would forgive the organization for supporting gay rights or choice (even if neither was popular with his members) if it also supported increased farm prices.

Of course, the corollary of the "coalition rule" is also true. *A coalition member never forgives or forgets if you abandon them with respect to their principal self-interest*—even though they may agree with everything else you stand for.

If you oppose disability rights, it's hard to keep disability rights organizations in the fold even if they agree with the rest of the coalition's positions.

MAKING ALLIES FEEL COMFORTABLE

A special word about more conservative allies. The use of agitation and the coalition rule are just as appropriate to conservative allies as they are with other swing constituencies. But peer pressure and the bandwagon effect are particularly important with this group. When we're trying to recruit potential allies, we need to make them feel comfortable that working with us in a particular situation will not make them feel marginal, outside the mainstream.

Our communications to this group has to emphasize how many "people like them" are on our side.

The corollary is true in preventing "raids" intended to pick off our allies and entice them to join the other side. Here our job is to make "our allies" feel very uncomfortable with their potential new friends—out of place—outside of the mainstream.

In both cases, using symbolically powerful people with whom they can identify is key. In the campaign to stop the repeal of the Estate Tax, it helped a great deal to have Bill Gates, Sr., the father of the richest man in the world, on our side. His message, as much as anything, was that it was safe and reputable to oppose Estate Tax repeal, even if you were a wealthy member of the business community.

CONSERVATIVE ACTIVISTS

If the self-interest of conservative activists are in fact congruent with conservative ideology, most will be unmoved by any argument. It doesn't do much good to debate or argue with them. Generally, that will have the counterproductive effect of stimulating their activism.

DEACTIVATE THEM

In general our strategic goal with people who have become conservative activists is not to convert them—that isn't going to happen. It is to *demoralize* them—to "deactivate" them.

We need to deflate their enthusiasm, to make them lose their ardor, and above all their self-confidence. Conservatives were very successful at doing these things to us in the past.

There are basically two ways to achieve this goal:

- *One is to defeat them—even in small battles or skirmishes.* There's nothing like defeat to knock the wind out of your sails. The gang from the Cato Institute and other conservative think tanks, who fought so hard to privatize Social Security, are not so gung-ho after the initiative fell flat on its face.

One caveat here. The religious and social conservative movement has developed a good antidote to the poison of progressive victory. Their view of the world virtually requires that they think of themselves as victims under attack. Of course it has been quite a trick to pull off a *"we're under attack"* world view when your people controlled the White House, Congress and the Supreme Court. But they did it quite successfully.

The recent conservative "red herring" that Christmas is under attack was one of the latest absurd examples. Here we are in a country where this religious holiday practically defines popular culture at the end of the year. Walking through just about any shopping area in America in December, it's hard to convince yourself that Christmas is under attack.

But the "we're under attack" mindset has served conservatives well. The modern conservative movement is a coalition of two groups with very different self-interests. Big Business and upper-income conservatives who mainly want economic benefit are on one side; on the other are cultural conservatives interested in defending their social and cultural customs and values.

It has been said that the Republican Party is a coalition of rich people who hate the AFL-CIO, and poor people who hate the ACLU, and that the Democratic Party is a coalition of rich people who hate the Moral Majority and poor people who hate Mutual of Omaha.

In fact, the conservative government of Bush and the Republican Congress have delivered big-time for the pro-business wing of their party and only barely for the cultural conservatives. The rich got massive tax breaks, deregulation, and relaxed environmental laws, have had markets opened abroad, while getting literally trillions in special legislative benefits and contracts.

The cultural right has gotten a lot of lip service. But the media is still loaded with sex and violence, abortion is still legal, and the gay community is considered more mainstream than ever before. Rather than blaming the conservative political leadership, they frame their entire narrative with the notion that the culprits are the "elite" media, academics, lawyers, actors, etc.—the "liberal culture." Rather than demoralizing the activists of the cultural right, these defeats are used to demonstrate the correctness of their world view.

Even with the cultural right, however, there is a limit. Defeat, even when used as a rationalization for world view, is innately demoralizing. It always hurts to lose.

- A second way to demoralize conservative activists is to surround them with the echo chamber of our positions and assumptions. We need to make them feel that they are *not mainstream*, to make them feel isolated. We need to use the bandwagon effect in reverse. This comes with repeated, confident restatement of our values, our frame of reference, our positions—and our simultaneous, poll-tested attacks on their positions, policies, values and candidates. We must isolate them ideologically. Later we will discuss how we use the progressive echo chamber in more detail.

  By defeating them and isolating them ideologically, we demoralize conservative activists directly. Then they begin to quarrel among themselves or blame each other for defeat in isolation, and that demoralizes them further. We've seen precisely that kind of demoralization and isolation since the Midterm elections.

I know that this works. They did it to progressives for many years. Never again.

CHAPTER FIFTEEN

Contributors

In many respects, contributors are simply a subset of activists. As a consequence, all of the rules we have just described apply directly to contributors as well across the self-interest spectrum.

But contributors are such an important group to the political struggle in modern America that several special points should be made.

It goes without saying that the twin concepts of wherewithal and will are critical here. To be useful to the battle, contributors need both the will to give and the wherewithal to do so. That's why, in order to maximize the dollars raised by a campaign organization, we have to create a wide array of different mechanisms to recruit funds at various levels of giving.

The biggest problem here is that the cost of raising money often does not vary directly with the amount raised. As a percentage of a gift, it costs a great deal more to raise small contributions than large ones.

There are many high-income, progressive contributors who support our cause. But let's face it, there are a whole lot more high-income conservatives—and that used to put us at a major fund-raising disadvantage. We had fewer high-end fundraising targets, and it cost us a great deal more per dollar to raise funds from low-end donors who were more prone to support our causes.

In the past when Democrats have been in the majority in Congress, one approach to solving this problem has sometimes been to sell our souls to the many special interests with business before Congress. Even when Democrats have been in the minority, many members consider "Exclusive Committees" like Ways and Means and Energy and Commerce to be great assignments not only because they have jurisdiction over important issues, but because they can raise lots of campaign money from the interests with business before those committees.

This approach to the progressive fundraising problem leads inevitably to the defection of Democrats who vote for bills like the draconian changes in the bankruptcy law proposed by the credit card industry and passed in 2005. The motivation of many of these members had very little to do with the popularity of this issue with the voters. In fact, it wasn't popular at all. But it was a top priority of the banks that gave out oodles of campaign contributions.

Luckily, a new force has arrived on the scene that is revolutionizing the recruitment of small donations –the Internet.

One reason the Internet is so important is because it massively reduces the cost of raising small donations. Once someone is on the e-mail donor list, they can be resolicited at virtually no cost. There is no need for an expensive fundraising letter or phone call.

MoveOn.org and the 2004 Dean campaign were the first to understand and tap the full potential of this medium. The emergence of the Internet means that Progressives can turn to small donors—who share our progressive commitments—for a much greater proportion of the funds needed to win.

In 2006, MoveOn.org directly raised $27 million for Democratic candidates. And an analysis of all 2006 Democratic campaign contributions showed, over $180 million came from MoveOn.org members.

As important as it is, there are two things the Internet does not mean:

- Progressives should put no less emphasis on raising funds from large donors who share our self-interest. We need resources to win the battle. The Internet should add to our resource base, but not replace old sources.

- Internet fundraising does not eliminate the critical necessity of publicly financing elections. As long as a great deal of campaign money for candidates must come from wealthy people and PACs, such donors will have a disproportionate, undemocratic, effect on American politics. The late Senator Paul Simon used to say, "Let's face it. If I get to my hotel room and I have five phone messages and one of them is from a big donor, and it's too late to return more than one call, he is the one who will get the call. That's human nature. And that's why we need campaign finance reform."

No Way to Run a Political System

By campaign finance reform, I don't mean reforms that place major limits on the ability of campaigns to communicate with the voters. America spends a lot more on the marketing of fast food than it does discussing candidates or political views. The problem isn't too much political communication. The problem is who pays for it. In the end, there are really only two choices: either private interests pay, or the public pays.

"Clean Elections" systems are now in place in a number of state and local jurisdictions. A simple, elegant form of campaign finance reform that I personally favor would provide high-leverage matching from public funds for every qualifying contributor the candidate recruits. For instance, the fund would match every contribution of $200 or less on an eight-to-one basis.

This system would put a premium on real political organizing and set the qualifying contribution level high enough so that the cost of raising it is not so high that it is prohibitive to do so. If a campaign raised $100,000 in contributions of under $200, it would receive $800,000 in matching funds.

The system would also automatically distinguish between "fringe" candidates and "real" candidates. Candidates who can organize themselves a large enough political base to raise a lot of qualifying contributions would define themselves as "real" candidates. Those who had big mouths but no supporters would receive less support from the public fund.

Finally, the system would stop forcing candidates to spend huge chunks of their time as telemarketers.

Today, a new candidate for Congress must spend at least half of his time on the phone raising money in what we call "call time." This activity is so important to most campaigns (except wealthy "self-funders") that our firm insists that most new candidates spend no fewer than five hours per day on the phone raising money.

In today's campaign world, if you can't raise the money to communicate to persuadable and mobilizable voters, it doesn't much matter what views you have or values you hold. You'll be a proverbial tree falling in the forest that no one hears, if you can't communicate to the voters.

We think "call time" is so important in a campaign that it takes on an almost religious dimension. If something comes up that requires that it be substituted for a scheduled hour of "call time," that hour must first be replaced on the schedule with another hour during the week. In other words, "call time" is the first priority for the scheduling of candidate time.

I've thought seriously about writing a novel in which the chair of the Democratic Congressional Campaign Committee wins by recruiting challenge candidates from the ranks of the best telemarketing firms in America.

Even many sitting Members of Congress spend a quarter of their time raising money.

This is no way to run a political system, but as with everything else, you start where things are, not where you wish they were.

To Get Public Financing of Elections, We Need Candidates Willing to Raise Money

It may sound counter-intuitive, but the campaign to get public financing of elections must be led by political leaders who are willing to raise lots of money under the current system. To get public financing of elections at the federal level, we have to have a solid progressive majority in Congress and a progressive Democratic President. To get that, we have to have winning candidates who can raise a great deal of money under the current rules.

So if you are considering running for Congress, don't even think about it unless you're willing to spend five hours a day on the phone raising money (or can dip into the family fortune).

I don't mean to discourage people from running for Congress. I do want to encourage people to run who are serious about winning. Even under the current rules, hard-working progressive candidates manage to raise the funds necessary to win.

It simply requires discipline and commitment—a willingness to work your rear off. It requires that you have what it takes—and what it takes at the very least is guts, grit and an absolute determination to win.

If you think it might be "fun" to dip your toe into the pond of electoral politics, but aren't willing to do the hard work necessary—don't waste everyone else's time. If you think that you have good ideas and make good speeches, but aren't willing to do what it takes to raise the money—do us all a favor and make your speeches into the mirror, because you won't win.

Politics is, in fact, war without bloodshed, because it involves a battle over the allocation of our resources and the future of our society. We don't need dilettantes as our candidates. We need warriors who will do what it takes to win.

Make It Personal

All of the other rules that apply to activists across the self-interest spectrum also pertain to contributors. That goes especially for three rules that I want to highlight.

First, like any other activist, you have to convince donors that by giving they will personally play a significant role in something important. Usually a donor needs to believe that the outcome of the race itself will impact some self-interest that he cares about (whether ideological, personal or business).

Usually, this requires that the donor believe that the candidate can win—but that his victory is not such a slam dunk that his contribution won't matter. Of course, sometimes other currents of self-interest enter the picture:

- The desire of the donor to meet or have access to the candidate or officeholder

- The desire of the donor to spend face time with someone famous (the President, Barbara Streisand, the local mayor, or the friend he wants to impress)

- The desire to please someone who asked him to give

Like anything else in politics, fundraising is very personal. The more personal the "ask" can be, the more effective it will be. That's why a call from the candidate is so much more effective than a call from anyone else, unless that someone else has a personal relationship that makes her or him more effective.

That's also why the more intimate the fundraising event, the more money you can ask the donor to give.

INSPIRE THEM

Second, like any other activist, the more inspired and self-confident we can make the progressive donor base, the more we can get them to give— and the more campaigns will be able to attract swing constituency donors. That is particularly true of our low-end and Internet donor base, but it is also true of high-end donors, at least those who give for ideological reasons.

In standing firmly for progressive principles, we do in fact risk alienating some donors who give money to assure access or favorable action on measures that affect them or their industries. But you would be surprised at how many even in this group redirected more of their resources to progressive candidates when they began to realize that we might actually win control of Congress.

Hard-right donors will never support our candidates, but swing constituency donors will. Generally, they are looking for winners; at the very least, they want to hedge their bets.

So even when it comes to fundraising, I would argue that the same strong, clear statement of progressive principles that is so necessary to persuade and mobilize voters, and energize activists, will actually help us raise more money, not less. Of course, this assertion flies in the face of those who argue that Democrats should be, in essence, "Republicans-lite" in order to raise more money and win elections.

In my view, not only are they wrong when it comes to fundraising, they are wrong because voters who want Republicans-lite are much more prone to vote for the genuine article than they are to vote for a pale imitation.

CHAPTER SIXTEEN

Opinion Molders

In his brilliant book *The Tipping Point*, Malcolm Gladwell analyzes social movements, ads and marketing programs using the model of epidemiology—the study of the spread of contagious diseases. Both *The Tipping Point* and Gladwell's more recent book, *Blink*,[1] contain important insights that I believe are critical to understanding how Progressives can beat the right in modern America.

Among other things, Gladwell analyzes the vectors—or media—used to communicate messages from one person to the next. He contends that three groups of people are particularly important to the message diffusion process: Connectors, Mavens and Salesmen.

Taken together these three groups constitute a category I refer to as opinion molders. Each is critical both in moving voters, and in diffusing progressive assumptions throughout our society.

Gladwell argues in *The Tipping Point* that even in the age of mass communications and multimillion-dollar media ad campaigns, word-of-mouth is still the most important form of human communication. That is certainly true in politics. When people in politics talk about the buzz around a candidate, they're talking about things other political people say, over lunch, over the fence, or in e-mails.

It is that word-of-mouth communication that is picked up and repeated by political reporters, columnists, editorial writers and pundits. Of course, what the media say and write in turn impacts the word-of-mouth networks in a never-ending dialogue. And if one columnist writes something, the odds are good it will trigger another columnist and so on.

But what goes on in the media is ultimately important mainly insofar as it impacts the content of person-to-person communication among everyday people—not just the political "chattering class." It is in that person-to-person communication that opinions, attitudes and values are formed and reinforced in the broader public.

In our efforts to spread political messages to average people, we use both the mass media and direct contact programs aimed at the relatively small group of opinion molders who communicate directly by word-of-mouth (including e-mail).

The opinion molders we must target have a rare set of social gifts.

Most of us don't have a particularly broad or diverse group of friends. Gladwell cites one study of the residents of the Dykman public housing project in Manhattan that showed that, when asked to name their friends, 88% lived in the same building and half lived on the same floor.

Mostly, we know and communicate with people of the same race and age. We choose our friends from those who occupy the same small, physical spaces we do—the people with whom we share common activities.

On the other hand, Gladwell cites psychologist Stanley Milgram's famous study addressing the question of how individual human beings connect to each other.

Milgram got the names of 160 people who lived in Omaha, Nebraska and mailed each of them a packet. Gladwell tells the story:

> In each packet was the name and address of a stockbroker who worked in Boston and lived in Sharon, Massachusetts. Each person was instructed to write his or her name on the packet and send it to a friend or acquaintance, who he or she thought would get the packet closer to the stockbroker.... The idea was that when the packet finally arrived at the stockbroker's house, Milgram could look at the list of all those whose hands it went through to get there and establish how closely connected someone chosen at random from one part of the country was to another person in another part of the country. Milgram found that most of the letters reached the stockbrokers in five or six steps. This experiment is where we get the concept of six degrees of separation. [2]

How is it that we can be so closely connected, if we typically have such a limited group of acquaintances or friends? The answer is that some people act as connectors for the rest of us.

CONNECTORS

Connectors seem to know everyone. They are very social. Whereas most people may have dozens or even hundreds of friends or acquaintances, connectors have thousands.

It's not only that connectors know lots of people, they know different kinds of people—people who have a different kinds of interests or preferences—or live in different geographic locations.

Connectors ".... are people who all of us can reach in only a few steps, because, for one reason or another, they manage to occupy many different worlds in subcultures or niches." [3]

As an example of the consummate connector, Gladwell cites a woman named Lois Weisberg who is currently Commissioner of Cultural Affairs for the city of Chicago. My wife and I—like apparently everyone else—

know Lois. In fact, we have beach houses near each other in Michigan City, Indiana.

Lois is not just a "cultural" person. We know her mainly from politics. But she also belongs to at least eight worlds—actors, writers, doctors, lawyers, park lovers, politicians, railroad buffs and flea market aficionados.[4]

Lois loves people. "When Weisberg looks out at the world... She sees possibility, and while most of us are busily choosing whom we would like to know, and rejecting the people who don't look right or live out near the airport, or whom we haven't seen in 65 years, Lois likes them all."

When I spent five months at Terre Haute Federal Prison Camp, I had a unique opportunity to see the concept of Connectors in action. The prison camp is populated entirely by nonviolent offenders. About 60% were drug offenders and the balance were white-collar. There was quite a variety of different types of people: executives who were owners of companies, political people, professionals and antiwar protesters. You also had young people who sold drugs as part of gangs. I would have never met many of these people had it not been for this experience. I would have never been in the same space. Having been in that space, I now know many of them and their life stories. But like anywhere, the various groups in the prison tended to hang together.

There was one guy at Terre Haute who was the perfect example of a Connector. His name is Jeff, a former lawyer and portfolio manager who got involved in a business deal and made errors in judgment that landed him in prison. People in all the different networks in the prison sought Jeff out for free advice on their cases. He would spend hours helping people draw up their pro se briefs and doing their research.

But that wasn't all. Jeff was "Commissioner" of the camp basketball league. He played on a softball team. He played soccer (which made him part of a group of Hispanics and Middle Easterners who mainly played soccer). He ran the camp library. And he taught weekly adult education business courses. Finally, he was active in the life of his own housing unit (we had eight).

As result, Jeff was the guy who knew everyone. And everyone knew him. He was the classic Connector.

One more note on Connectors. Most people have a core set of strong social ties. But you can only have a limited number of strong ties. We are limited by the available time and emotional energy to maintain a fairly limited number of strong social ties—with people we see and talk to regularly. What makes Connectors so important is that they have many, many weak social ties—people they see or communicate with only periodically.

Gladwell refers to a study on job searches that shows that most people in the study got their job through a personal connection, but in most cases by referral of people they rarely saw.

He argues that when it comes to finding out about new jobs, or any new information, weak ties are always more important than strong ones—because friends already occupy the same world you do.

Connectors have long lists of weak ties.

The first job of a progressive organizer is to locate the Connectors. Connectors must always be one of our top targets when it comes to building an organization or promoting an idea or candidate.

MAVENS

Gladwell's second category of special communicators he calls Mavens. Connectors connect people with people. A maven (from the Yiddish—one who accumulates knowledge) is a person upon whom people rely to connect them with new *information*.

Mavens have two essential qualities. First they are obsessed by learning all they can about one or more subject areas. Second, they are eager to share what they know, to be *helpful*. They collect information and want to tell you about it.

A Maven may be a person who knows everything about the best new restaurants and is eager to give you a recommendation. He may be obsessed by baseball. Want an update on the latest trades of the off-season? He's your guy.

There are many, many Mavens who focus on politics. They may constantly watch C-SPAN. They may read every blog. They may be a blogger. In fact bloggers and some journalists are the consummate Mavens. For them success and failure in life is defined by their possession of the latest hot gossip or political news.

Mavens may not know *everyone*, but they know *everything*. They are sought after for their recommendations and views.

The same person can be both a Connector and a Maven. My friend Jeff was the consummate Connector, but he was also a Maven about developments in sentencing, appeals, congressional action on parole—all of the things most important to the inmates at a Federal Prison Camp.

Mavens exist everywhere. They may blog to hundreds of thousands. Some are sought-after by interest groups. Most go to work at regular jobs or frequent the senior center or the local tap.

When we organize issue or electoral campaigns we need to find them at both the local and national level. They are important to us both as sources of information and transmitters of information to others. *They are major sources of political intel.* They help us understand the self-interest of actors, and help to scout our opponent's moves.

They are also information distribution points. We need to systematically provide them with our talking points, our framing and our facts.

Mavens are constantly narrowcasting information on politics and political values. We need to make sure they have plenty of progressive material for their daily rounds of narrowcasting. When we plan an issue or electoral campaign, they must be targeted systematically.

We find these people by *asking*. In a community, it won't take long to find the local political or issue maven. Ask someone, "Who knows about local politics around here?" and you'll get pointed in the right direction in just a few tries.

Mavens can also be found through what Gladwell refers to as "maven traps"—institutional settings that attract and concentrate Mavens. Interactive blogs attract political mavens. But traditional local political organizations do as well. In almost every electoral political organization there is someone who is obsessed with the political information and all too eager to tell you about it if you ask.

Some professions attract and encourage Maven-like activity. Barbers, hair stylists, teachers, and the more obvious: political staffers, reporters, and PR types are often Mavens. To target our resources we need to find those for whom the collection and distribution of political information is an end in itself. They are the Mavens who can heavily impact the distribution of our political messages.

SALESMEN

Mavens are not persuaders. They think of themselves more as teachers who are eager to share the information they collect. They are databanks, information brokers.

There is a select group of opinion molders that specializes in persuasion. As Gladwell puts it: they have the skills to "persuade us when we are unconvinced of what we are hearing, and they are as critical to the tipping of the word-of-mouth epidemics as the other two groups." [5]

What makes someone persuasive is a lot less straightforward than it seems. But the mystery of persuasion haunts politicians. After all, though we most certainly look for Salesmen for the progressive cause throughout the broader community, our "A" team should be the cadre of progressive elected officials. Every politician wants to be persuasive. Some are fair— some are unbelievable. Think Bill Clinton. What makes Bill Clinton so persuasive? What makes anyone persuasive—a salesman?

Gladwell cites a study where a group of students were recruited for what they were told was market research on headphones. They were given headphones and told that the marketer wanted to see how well the headphones worked when the listener moved—say, with his head in motion.

Each listened to Linda Ronstadt and Eagles songs, and then heard an editorial arguing that tuition at the University should be increased from $587 to $750.

A third were told that as they listened they should nod their heads up and down. A third were to shake their heads from side to side. And a third were told to hold their heads still.

Afterwards, they were given a short questionnaire on the quality of the music. Slipped in at the end, they were asked, "What do you feel would be an appropriate dollar amount for undergraduate tuition per year?"

You guessed it. Those who shook their heads from side to side as they listened to the editorial (even though they thought they were testing for headphone quality) disagreed strongly with the proposed increase. They wanted tuition to fall to $467 per year. Those who nodded their heads up and down agreed that tuition should rise to an average of $646. Those who kept their heads still settled on $582—approximately the current tuition.[6]

This, of course, seems completely remarkable. That the act of moving your head as if in agreement or disagreement could impact the persuadablity of an argument seems absurd. But the subtleties of physical and psychological buy-in have a lot to do with persuasion.

When it comes to persuasion, Gladwell argues that:

1) Little things apparently make as much difference as big things.
2) Nonverbal cues are as important as verbal ones.
3) Persuasion often works *very subtly.*

Great salespeople engage the subject of their persuasion in an elaborate "dance." They synchronize their movements and the rhythm of their speech to the target individual or audience, and they "lead" the dance.

Gladwell presents studies that show how two people arrive at a conversation with very different conversation patterns, but almost instantly reach a common ground. They forge a bond using their movements and speech.

"Part of what it means to have a powerful or persuasive personality, then, is that you can draw others into your own rhythms and dictate the terms of the interaction," says Gladwell. [7]

Bill Clinton is spectacular at eye contact– at making you believe you were the only person in the room.

The eyes are an extremely important part of persuasion—the emotional connection, the dance. Eyes are the windows into the soul. Human beings are massively affected by eye contact. In some cultures it is entirely inappropriate for a man to look a woman in the eye.

Jan was part of the Congressional delegation that accompanied President Clinton's presidential trip to India in 2000. The briefer gave the delegation one key word of warning before they left. If you see, monkeys don't look them in the eye—it will make them angry. Most primates are hardwired to respond to eye contact.

Gladwell's second book, *Blink*, he discusses at length why this is true. It's because when you look in someone's eyes, you can literally read their mind.

It turns out that the facial expressions of human beings are not, as previously thought, culturally determined by social convention. They don't vary from one culture to the next. Their meanings are apparently hardwired genetically.

Silvan Tomkins and Paul Ekman have devoted their careers to the study of facial expressions. They have found that there are some 3,000 different facial expressions that mean the same thing to the most sophisticated jet setter as they do to the most isolated tribesmen in the Amazon basin.

These expressions are composed of 43 "Action Units" of facial muscles.

Gladwell describes a conversation with Ekman, where he explains that, "happiness, for instance, is essentially A.U. (Action Unit) six and twelve—contracting the muscles that raise the cheek *(orbicularis oculi, pars orbitalis)* in combination with the zygomatic major, which pulls up the corners of the lips. Fear is A.U. one, two, and four or more fully, one, two, four, five and twenty with or without action units twenty-five, twenty-six, and twenty-seven." Ekman and his associates have assembled these combinations and the rules for interpreting them in the Facial Action Coding System, or FACS.

Getting back to Bill Clinton, Gladwell quotes Eckman commenting on one of Clinton's expressions: "It's that-hand-in-the-cookie-jar, love-me-mommy-because-I-am-a-rascal look. It's A.U. twelve, fifteen, seventeen and twenty-four, with an eye roll." [8]

Not only does the face express emotions directly, the expressions themselves can change the emotional state of the individual.

Eckman indicates that he and his colleagues have discovered the expressions alone are sufficient to create marked changes in the autonomic nervous system. By smiling, you can be happier. By frowning, you can make yourself sadder.

Gladwell cites a study by a German team of psychologists that had a group of students look at cartoons. One group held a pencil clenched between their teeth, forcing them to smile. One held a pencil in their lips—

preventing them from smiling. The first group found the cartoons much funnier.

Facial expressions are not simply billboards for inner feelings. They work in the opposite direction. They create feelings. That's one of the reasons people can "act themselves" into beliefs and commitments. If you get someone to come to a rally, and he cheers for a candidate or cause in order to go along with everyone else, he will feel excited simply because he is cheering. If you smile at a candidate's jokes, you will actually feel happier in the presence of the candidate.

Great salesman read expressions and set a rhythm that causes you to follow along, to mimic his expressions. That in turn directly changes your emotional state. Great salesmen engage in "motor mimicry." If you show people pictures of a smiling face or a frowning face, they will smile or frown back involuntarily, if even for a fraction of a second.

At one level or another human beings are hardwired with some level of empathy. Gladwell points out that, "If I hit my thumb with a hammer, most people watching will grimace; they'll mimic the emotional state."

In other words, the emotions are contagious. Great salesmen are terrific at using words, facial expressions and body movements to communicate emotions. They seduce you into their emotional state (whether it is about a product, a political belief or a candidate) the same way a lover is seduced. They use the full range of voice tones, facial expressions, speech rhythms and postures—and make you mimic them. Bill Clinton is a great persuader because he can lead the dance of the interaction. He transports you from wherever it is you were at the beginning of the interaction to where it is he wants you to go.

Most importantly, great salesmen do all of this on a level that does not focus solely on the content of their argument, but by changing your emotional disposition toward the subject of persuasion—the candidate, the idea, or the product.

You don't just think positive or negative thoughts, you *feel* positively or negatively toward an idea or candidate. Not only does this make the argument more convincing, it makes it more *memorable* as well. It is much easier to remember a feeling than a thought.

THE FUNCTION OF CONNECTORS, MAVENS AND SALESMEN

To understand the importance of Connectors, Mavens and Salesmen, Gladwell explores what sociologists refer to as a diffusion model that analyzes the spread of a contagious idea, product or innovation.

One diffusion model divides the population into five categories of actors:

- Innovators
- Early Adopters
- Early Majority
- Late Majority
- Laggards

Gladwell illustrates with a study by Bruce Ryan and Neal Gross on the spread of hybrid seed corn in Greene County, Iowa in the 1930s:

> *The new corn seed was introduced in Iowa in 1928, and it was superior in every respect to the seed that had been used by farmers for decades before. But it wasn't adopted all at once. Of the 259 farmers studied by Ryan and Gross, only a handful had started planting the new seed by 1932 and 1933. In 1934, 16 took the plunge. In 1935, 21 followed, then 36 and the year after that a whopping 61 and 46, 36, 14, and 3 until by 1941, all but two of the 259 farmers studied were using the new seeds. In the language of diffusion research, a handful of farmers who started trying hybrid seeds at the very beginning of the 1930s were the Innovators, the adventurous ones. The slightly larger group who were infected by them were the Early Adopters. They were the opinion leaders in the community, the respected, thoughtful people who watched and analyzed what those wild Innovators were doing and followed suit. Then came the big bulge of farmers in 1936, 1937, and 1938, the Early Majority and the Late Majority, the deliberate and skeptical mass, who would never try anything until the most respected of the farmers had tried at first. They caught the seed virus and passed it on, finally to the Laggards, the most traditional of all, who saw no urgent reason to change. If you plot the progression on a graph, it forms a perfect epidemic curve—starting slowly, tipping just as the Early Adopters start using the seed, then rising sharply as the majority catches on, and falling away at the end when the Laggard comes strolling in."* [9]

The first two groups, Innovators and Early Adopters, were visionaries and they are generally willing to take risks—with their behavior or their ideas. The Early Majority, by contrast, is typically much more *risk averse.*

Gladwell argues that the key to spreading an idea or product throughout the society is bridging the great chasm of self-interest between the Early Adopters and the Early Majority.

In American politics, of course, support for a candidate or progressive values does not always spread to the entire population, any more than the use of a new technology or product spreads to everyone. But in politics, like anywhere else, there is a *Tipping Point,* where support for a candidate, or policy position, or set of values "tips" and becomes mainstream.

Part of the role of Connectors, Mavens and Salesmen is to transmit these ideas from the Early Adopters to the Early Majority. In the act of transmission, they also legitimate the ideas for the more cautious, risk averse, Early Majority. That depends heavily on peer legitimation for cues to the ideas they should accept or believe.

In politics, Innovators and Early Adopters are typically political activists. Connectors, Mavens and Salesman are generally a subset of these activists. They are the ones who translate political ideas to the majority of the population—and especially to Persuadable and Mobilizable voters who are generally not political activists (though they may be activists in the broader sense within the community).

A look at the Howard Dean presidential campaign in 2003-2004 is illustrative. Dean's political popularity began with a narrow set of Innovators in his campaign and spread to a wide group of Early Adopters, often through the Internet. The phenomena tipped when a variety of Connectors, Political Mavens, and Salesmen began to communicate about Dean to the wider community of the Early Majority. Some of these came from within the ranks of the Early Adopters. Some were bloggers and political pundits, Mavens who began to put Dean on everyone's political "radar screen."

The "meetup" phenomena also played an important role. "Meetups" were organized over the Internet. Invitations were extended by those who declared themselves a "meetup" leader to convene Dean supporters in a particular area. "Meetups" became places where individual Dean supporters could reinforce each other's commitments to Dean, and where simple "spread the word" tasks could be parceled out. Since they were organized somewhat randomly over the Internet, their ability to spread support for Dean depended on the likelihood that they had attracted Connectors, Mavens and Salesman. When they didn't, they were stuck reinforcing each other's commitments and doing simple tasks, e.g., sending letters to voters in other states, or getting canvass assignments. These were important tasks. But when meetups attracted Connectors, Mavens and Salesman, their potential expanded exponentially.

The Dean campaign was also one of the first national political campaigns to demonstrate fully the "viral" nature of the Internet. The Internet provides a latticework that allows "viral" transmission of ideas better than any previous medium. It does so by amplifying the communications ability of Connectors, Mavens, and Salesmen. In a traditional word-of-mouth context, a Connector may talk to a few people in a particular group or communication loop, who then talk to their acquaintances and exponentially expand the circle of connection. One person talks to another, who talks to three others. Each of them then talks to three more. With every new layer of connection, the web of transmission grows exponentially. In just six layers of transmission, one becomes three becomes nine becomes 27 becomes 81 becomes 243, and so on.

The Internet allows this viral transmission to happen much more rapidly and without respect for geographic boundaries. Once an information epidemic tips, it can spread like wildfire. On the other hand, the Dean campaign's ultimate problem, at least in the Iowa caucuses, had a lot to do with the failure of the campaign to organize more deliberately through traditional means.

The Kerry campaign in Iowa was conducted along more traditional lines. It sent its organizers out to find and enlist local activists who became their Early Adopters and out of this pool they recruited many *local* Connectors, Mavens and Salesmen.

As the primary election approached, swarms of orange-hatted Dean activists from all over America flooded Iowa. But Kerry had locked up many of the local, legitimate Connectors, Mavens and Salespeople that could bridge the chasm of risk aversion that stood between Dean's activists and the majority of the voters. Dean needed to make the majority comfortable with his candidacy. He needed to convince them it was safe to support him. More than anything else people needed to see their neighbors, people they knew and trusted, supporting Dean. What they often got instead were people with orange hats from other states.

In politics, Connectors, Mavens and Salesmen translate the message of innovation into terms that are safe and familiar to voters. They bridge the gap between the Innovators and Early Adopters who are willing to take risks—who favor change—to the risk-averse, traditional majority that is more concerned about being part of the mainstream, part of the pack.

WHAT CAUSES TIPPING POINTS?

Gladwell argues that there are two distinct factors that can make an epidemic "tip." First is the extent to which the message is "contagious"—how easily can it be transmitted? In the epidemiology of actual disease, the common cold is easy to communicate, to pass from one person to the next. It is transmitted through the air. HIV is more difficult to transmit, since it must move from one host to the next through bodily fluids.

The second factor is "stickiness." Once communicated, how easy is it to infect a person and for how long? A cold is not very "sticky." The immune system rids the body of the typical cold virus quickly. HIV is very "sticky." Once infected, left to its own devices, it is extremely difficult if not impossible for the body to rid itself of HIV.

Ebola virus, like HIV, is very "sticky." It kills a huge proportion of those it infects. But unlike HIV, its incubation period is very short. It infects and kills very rapidly, so it leaves little time for the victim to infect others. That is why HIV is so much more prevalent than Ebola. Its incubation period is measured in years during which the victim may not have any clue he or she is infected—plenty of time to infect others.

When a communication epidemic tips, it jumps the barrier of Early Adopters to the Early Majority. The number of interactions where the communication is transmitted also expands geometrically.

Gladwell argues that whether an epidemic tips or not depends on subtle factors, little things that affect both the contagiousness of the message and its stickiness. The "law of the few" says that if the *right kinds* of people communicate the message—Connectors, Mavens and Salesmen—its contagiousness will increase exponentially.

We'll examine *"stickiness,"* or what makes a political message break through or stick with us, later.

But there is one other factor that is key to tipping a social message epidemic. In the 1960s, sociologist Neil Smelser wrote a classic book called *The Theory of Collective Behavior.*[10] In it, he argued that a "precipitating event" is almost always necessarily associated with the point where social movements are qualitatively transformed. These, though he didn't use the term, are "tipping points."

Precipitating events are symbolic occurrences that legitimate for the majority the views of some group of Early Adopters. Precipitating events are important, whether the type of social communication or movement is an election, an issue campaign, a riot or a revolution.

The Hutu president of Rwanda was returning to that country when he was killed in a plane crash. That was the precipitating event that turned smoldering anti-Tutsi sentiment in Rwanda's Hutu community into a massive genocide that killed tens of thousands.

The acquittal of a Los Angeles police officer in the videotaped beating of Rodney King was the precipitating event that set off riots in the South Central neighborhood of Los Angeles in 1992.

Howard Dean's scream at the rally following his caucus loss in Iowa—replayed over and over on the news—was the precipitating event in a substantial decline in his support. It crystallized for many Democratic Primary Voters their discomfort that he was out of the mainstream and helped to amplify the impact of his Iowa loss on their evaluation of whether he could beat George Bush.

The images surrounding Hurricane Katrina were the precipitating event for a major decline in support for President Bush. They convinced millions of voters that his administration was incompetent.

Many major qualitative "tips" in public opinion require a precipitating event. Examples abound—the Dubai ports deal, the Abu Ghraib photos, Pearl Harbor, the Boston Tea Party, the burning of the Reichstag, the shelling of Fort Sumter, the 9/11 attacks.

For an event to precipitate a major shift or tip a message epidemic, it must have at least three qualities:

- It must be powerfully symbolic.
- It must address some unmet self-interest of the previously unconvinced "Majority." It must, in other words, "rub raw some sore of discontent" that already exists.
- It must legitimate a solution or means of addressing the unmet self interest that is being promoted by some set of Early Adopters. That solution or message can be anything from passing a bill, to voting for a candidate, to going to rally, to supporting a revolution, to burning down your neighborhood in a riot, , to declaring war.

One of the best contemporary examples of a precipitating event was the House passage of Congressman Sensenbrenner's Immigration Bill that made felons out of all 12 million illegal immigrants in the United States and anyone who knowingly helped them. That included the local priest or the volunteer who operates a soup kitchen.

My friend and client Josh Hoyt is the Director of the Illinois Coalition for Immigrant and Refugee Rights (ICIRR). ICIRR has toiled in the trenches for decades to empower immigrants and promote passage of legislation that would provide a pathway to citizenship for many illegal immigrant families. He says that the Sensenbrenner bill "kicked the sleeping giant" — and awakened millions of undocumented immigrants, their family and friends, especially the entire Hispanic community.

After the Sensenbrenner bill passed, I remember talking to Juan Carlos Ruiz, who was with the D.C. Area Coalition for Immigrant Rights. He was organizing a rally on Capitol Hill to protest the bill. He expected 6,000 to 7,000 people—a very large crowd. The day of the rally, Senator Dick Durbin relates being in his Capitol office that overlooks the West Front where the rally was to be held. He says he glanced out of his window and saw a big crowd. Later, he looked again and saw a bigger crowd. And not too much later, the crowd had swelled to fill the entire West Front.

Thirty thousand people came to the Capitol that day—more than four times what was expected.

Now if you've ever put together a rally, you'll find that almost unbelievable. Normally you would apply the 25% Rule: 25% percent of the people who said they will be at your event won't show. It doesn't matter if it's the Second Coming. Normally you recruit people to events in clusters, on buses, in a very precise way. You sign people up in advance, and still a quarter of them won't show up. You plan for that.

But sometimes social movements achieve a "tipping point" where they spontaneously combust—where people talk to people who talk to people—and create a chain reaction explosion. These are the times you encounter a true social mobilization.

The next weekend in Chicago, 100,000 people marched from mainly Hispanic communities to the "Loop"—downtown Chicago.

The next weekend, 500,000 people marched in Los Angeles—and hundreds of thousands more around the country.

Several weeks after that, over 400,000 once again came out in Chicago.

The passage of the Sensenbrenner bill rubbed raw the years of discontent in immigrant, and especially Hispanic, communities. The image of 12 million people being rounded up as felons, along with their pastors, was clear and palpable. It became an impetus for two actions already being promoted by groups of Early Adopters: joining mass demonstrations and promoting the passage of comprehensive immigration reform legislation that gave a path to citizenship for the undocumented.

In 2003-2004, our firm was hired by a group that became known as the Coalition for Comprehensive Immigration Reform to help them develop a campaign plan for the upcoming and inevitable fight over immigration reform. The new coalition involved many of the major players in the Immigration Rights movement. But none of us could have imagined the level of mobilization—the social explosion—that the passage of the Sensenbrenner bill would provide.

A MOMENT OF HISPANIC REALIGNMENT

When movements "tip" and become major social mobilizations, they create moments of political realignment that can impact political loyalties and perceptions, and understandings of self-interest, for generations to come. The civil rights movement caused a major realignment both of African-American voters and Southern whites. In 1994, the campaign by California Governor Pete Wilson to pass Proposition 187 that would limit the rights of undocumented aliens in California caused a major shift of Latino support for the Democratic Party.

Karl Rove understood how central it was for the Republican Party to avoid making this mistake again. That, coupled with support from the business community, is why he and President Bush supported a comprehensive immigration bill that did indeed give undocumented workers a pathway to citizenship. But the recalcitrance of Republican social conservatives has nonetheless created a moment of realignment that will benefit Democrats for years and undermine much of the recent progress Republicans have made with Hispanic voters. We have already seen big payoffs. In 2004, 40% of Hispanic voters cast their votes for

Bush. In the 2006 Midterm elections, 69% of Hispanics cast their votes for Democrats. And a number of Republican anti-immigration hard-liners lost their seats.

The increasingly Democratic Hispanic vote was especially important in Democratic victories in Denver, Phoenix and Tucson. If Democrats continue to stand unequivocally with Hispanics and recent immigrants, it will benefit the party for years to come.

Of course there are complications. I was a consultant to the Coalition for Comprehensive Immigration Reform (CCIR) during the 2007 legislative battle over immigration reform that ended in a stalemate.

The anti-amnesty crowd preyed upon the sense of economic insecurity that spread well beyond the tiny core of nativist true believers who so ardently opposed immigration reform. It is no accident that periods of economic dislocation have always spawned an anti-immigrant backlash. The Republican business elite—who backed the reform—actually contributed to that sense of insecurity by arguing that "there aren't enough workers in the US willing to do these jobs." The resounding response among workers was: "Raise the pay and improve the working conditions and we'll be glad to do these jobs." Middle-class Americans are easy targets for the argument that immigrant labor is undermining their own standard of living.

To help neutralize this backlash, we need to reframe the battle for immigration reform as a campaign for an *"Earned Path to Citizenship"* that will prevent employers from exploiting an undocumented work force and thereby undercut the wages of everyday Americans. As long as there are large numbers of undocumented immigrants (and we're not going to deport 12 million people) they can easily be exploited and undercut middle class wages. *We have to reframe the battle as a solution to fears of economic insecurity—not as a potential cause of future economic insecurity.*

Many in the Anglo community were amazed at the size and strength of the 2006 anti-Sensenbrenner rallies. They seemed to spring up from nowhere. That's because the Connectors, Mavens and Salesmen who spread the immigrant rights gospel to the mainstream of the Hispanic community spoke Spanish and used Hispanic churches and media. Hispanic radio DJs, who are usually very competitive, cooperated to publicize the events. At churches and jobsites, they quickly became everyone's topic of conversation. They became so "mainstream" that it was hard to imagine yourself as a Hispanic who did not go to the immigration rally, along with your kids. It was just what you did as part of the community.

I watched another similar process take place around the first victory of Harold Washington, who in 1983 became the first black mayor of Chicago. Washington was a member of Congress, and had run for mayor before and been crushed.

When leaders of the black community in Chicago approached him to run again in 1983, he told them he would only run if they would provide him with the wherewithal he needed to win. They needed to raise $250,000 and register 100,000 new black voters.

The leadership of the African-American community in Chicago took up the challenge and succeeded. The highly public success of the community in meeting Washington's challenge was the precipitating event that caused the campaign to tip. The moment he appeared truly viable, the campaign took off like wildfire.

If an African-American walked down the streets of Chicago in the winter of 1983 without a Herald Washington button, someone would put one on him. People began to believe that a black man could actually win, and not only because of the success of fundraising and voter registration. He was running in a three-way race, where a united black community could band together with a growing number of Hispanic voters, and progressive whites, to get more votes than either white candidate.

The Connectors, Mavens, and Salesmen could be found among black pastors, professors at increasingly black community colleges, black radio, and civil rights organizations like PUSH, the Rev. Jesse Jackson's People United to Save Humanity coalition.

The weekend before the election my friend, the late Sid Ordower—a community activist and gospel music producer—put on a huge rally at the University of Illinois at Chicago Campus Pavilion. People saw each other, both in person and over TV, and were thrilled.

Over 80% of the black vote turned out in a municipal election—where turnouts normally run half of that—and Washington became Chicago's first black mayor.

A recent poll conducted by our firm showed that to this day, almost 20 years after his death, Washington is still the single most powerful icon in Chicago's African-American community.

CHAPTER SEVENTEEN

Leaders

Thirty-five years ago, I participated in a training seminar for organizers that was run by my mentor, Pete Martinez. One particular exercise made a huge impression.

"Tell me the qualities that make someone a leader," he said. Students in the seminar began to list qualities like self-confident, articulate, empathetic and charismatic. Martinez focused in. "No," he said, "tell me the *one* quality that makes someone a leader." The students struggled to rank the "qualities of leadership" as best they could.

"No, no, no," he finally said. "There is only one quality that makes someone a leader—a leader has *followers*."

A leader may be a Connector, Maven or Salesman—or he may be none of the above. A leader may take on this role because of his family lineage, or because she is promoted by the boss, or because she's the smartest person in the class, or because he's the quarterback of the football team. Leaders have only one thing in common: other people follow them; people do what they ask, or emulate their behavior.

The category of leaders may overlap many of our other target groups. They are often a special brand of activist, though not always. They can be writers, broadcasting personalities, actors, or supervisors at work who have very little to do with the kinds of political or voluntary organizations normally associated with activists.

However they become leaders, the quality they share—having followers—makes them critical targets for the progressive movement. Let's analyze our strategic goals with each segment of leaders on the self-interest spectrum.

PROGRESSIVE LEADERS

Our number one strategic goal with progressive leaders is simple: we need to elect, promote, recruit, and train large numbers of progressive leaders who have the skills and project the qualities necessary to make Americans follow them.

More than any other factor, the number and quality of progressive leaders will determine the success of the progressive movement. The reason is simple. Most people do not follow ideas or ideologies or positions, they follow *people*—living, breathing human beings.

Great ideas, the structure of economic institutions, ethnic identities— all of these are important elements in determining the dynamics and constructs of historic development. Geography and environmental factors are enormously important at determining the directions of human societies.

But when it comes to our ability to influence the course of history, to change history, human beings obviously make all the difference. Human beings are persuaded and motivated by leaders. And human decisions about courses of action are structured, and heavily impacted by leaders.

In the next section, as we analyze effective political message, we'll look at the qualities that make voters support candidates. Section Six will look at the qualities that make leaders good at organizing and motivating followers, volunteers and employees—at creating organizations. These are the qualities and skills that we must instill in new generations of potential progressive leaders.

Training and Recruiting Leaders

As we'll see, many of these leadership qualities are not the result of decisions that candidates, public officials and other potential progressive leaders make on a conscious level. Many result from attitudes and actions that emanate from a portion of our brain that Malcolm Gladwell refers to as the "adaptive unconscious:"

> The adaptive unconscious is not to be confused with the unconscious described by Sigmund Freud, which was a dark and murky place filled with desires and memories and fantasies that were too disturbing for us to think about consciously. This new notion of the adaptive unconscious is thought of, instead, as kind of a giant computer that quickly and quietly processes a list of the data we need in order to keep functioning as human beings… The only way that human beings could ever have survived as a species for as long as we have is that we've developed another kind of decision-making apparatus that's capable of making very quick judgments based on little information. [1]

Peters and Waterman point out in *In Search of Excellence* that "research on the function of the brain shows that the left and right hemispheres differ substantially. The left half is the reasoning, sequential verbal half; it is the 'logical' and rational half. The right half is the artistic half; it is the half that sees and remembers patterns, recalls melodies, waxes poetic." [2]

Peters and Waterman argued that for most behavior, our symbolic right brain is at least as important as our rational deductive left.

In fact, the thing that makes the human brain so powerful is not so much its ability to do logical or verbal analysis of a problem as its ability to discern patterns in huge volumes of information.

Herbert Simon, the Nobel prize-winning pioneer in artificial intelligence, showed that chess masters make decisions not by reviewing the countless logical options available, but by developing a massive "pattern of vocabulary." This "pattern of vocabulary" takes the form of subconsciously remembered patterns that the chess master can pick out on a chessboard based on years of past experience.

"While a Class A player has a vocabulary of around 2,000 patterns, the chess master has a vocabulary of around 50,000 patterns… They begin with the patterns: have I seen this before? In what context? What worked before?" [3]

When you think about it, our ability to pick out patterns is quite remarkable. Research shows that we can hold only six or seven pieces of data in short-term memory before we begin to forget things, but our unconscious mind holds tens of thousands of patterns available for immediate recall.

Scientists can use FMRI's (functional magnetic resonance imagery), that measure blood flow to portions of the brain, to pinpoint sections of the brain which store and process these patterns. The *fusiform gyros* is the incredibly sophisticated portion of the brain where we store and process the images of thousands of people we know. The *inferior temporal gyros* is reserved for objects.

When we walk down the street, we can pass thousands of people we don't know or recognize and pick one out of the crowd that is our friend — pretty amazing when you think about it.

Peters and Waterman argue that "the mark of a true professional in any field is the rich vocabulary of patterns, developed through years of formal education and especially through years of practical experience." [4]

When I was a graduate student in Ethics and Society at the University of Chicago, my social science specialty was economics. I remember a wonderful professor of economics said one day, "Our goal is not just to teach you the laws of supply and demand or marginal cost, it is to make you *think* like an economist."

In law school, the object is not to memorize all the cases in the case-book. It is to use the drill of doing the cases to teach you how to *think* like a lawyer. The same is true in medical school or art school. You teach someone to think a certain way through repeated practice, attempting over and over to recognize the patterns in facts. The goal is to train the unconscious mind, to provide it with a growing "pattern vocabulary."

When I first learned to fly a plane, the goal of the training was also to provide me with a growing "pattern vocabulary" of situations and feelings—experiences in the airplane—so I wouldn't have to think logically about the next move every second. Logical, conscious thinking of that sort is simply too slow for many situations you run into when flying an airplane, or for that matter, driving a car. You want to train your unconscious mind so you can automatically make the wiser choice. That ultimately is what we mean when we say someone has good judgment. He has a large pattern vocabulary, and he can evaluate the applicability of these patterns, usually unconsciously, in real time.

To successfully pursue our goal of nurturing new progressive leaders—leaders skilled at getting people to follow them and our movement—we must systematically provide opportunities for leaders and those who would be leaders to develop the "pattern vocabularies" of leadership, to instinctively make the right moves.

Books and training seminars are useful to leaders and potential leaders in understanding the principles and qualities involved in good leadership. But as every football coach knows, real-life experience on the field—playing time—is the only real way to provide people with the rich "pattern vocabularies" they need to be successful.

Just any kind of experience is not enough. My eighth-grade teacher used to say that "practice doesn't make perfect—the *right kind* of practice makes perfect."

To develop progressive leaders who are naturals at getting people to follow them, potential leaders must be mentored by others who know the way and can label, or name, patterns of experience as they happen. These are people who can help potential leaders pick out patterns and learn to commit them to unconscious memory.

There are four specific tactics that will help Progressives produce more progressive leaders.

1) Systematic Mentoring. The progressive movement must create more systematic programs to mentor progressive leaders. These mentoring situations can be embedded in formal training programs like those at the Midwest Academy or the ones we run at SCG. However, they most generally occur on-the-job –when an experienced Senate press secretary mentors and trains her assistant, or when the Democratic Congressional Campaign Committee assigns Democratic members to mentor new candidates.

Mentoring arrangements do not simply involve doing training seminars and throwing new recruits into campaigns or issue battles. To be most effective, they allow the mentor to share and observe experience with a potential leader and help him think through the experience, to decipher patterns and experience. This doesn't have to be formal, it could simply involve a "you know, that happened to me once and this is how it turned out." Or "let me tell you what we did when…"

The best way to organize experience is with stories or narratives. Stories are the clearest, most memorable means of allowing people to discern patterns in advance, because they are the least abstract. People can immediately connect and identify.

In *Mind and Nature: A Necessary Unity,* Gregory Bateson says:

> …*a man wanted to know about mind, not in nature, but in his private large computer. He asked, 'do you compute that you will ever think like a human being?' The machine then set to work to analyze its own computational habits. Finally, the machine printed its answer on a piece of paper, as such machines do. The man ran to get the answer and found, neatly typed, these words: That reminds me of a story.' A story is a little knot or complex of that species of connectedness which we call relevance. Surely the computer was right, this is indeed how people think." [5]*

The best mentors are storytellers who have been there and done that. Progressives need to shape a culture where mentoring at all levels of every type of organization is the norm.

2) Role Models and Network Development. For many years the Midwest Academy and Citizen Action cosponsored an annual "Midwest Academy Retreat" that was broadly attended by progressive leaders and activists throughout the country. Many attended primarily so that they could connect with each other. Over the last eight years this function has been taken over by the Campaign for America's Future conference in June of each year.

Other organizations and networks sponsor similar conferences, seminars and "networking" opportunities, and these are critical. They help us share experiences, find jobs where our skills can be put to use, and provide encouragement, inspiration and self-confidence to current and potential leaders.

But these events also have another critical function. They provide the opportunity for potential leaders, and up-and-coming leaders, to meet and learn from current and established leaders.

In the 1960's, when I came of age politically, the ranks of progressive leadership had been decimated and marginalized by the McCarthy years.

We looked at many Democratic leaders who would otherwise have been role models as "unworthy" because of their support for the Vietnam War.

That led many of the young leaders of the "New Left" to figure things out for themselves. And that led to some major errors in judgment.

Role modeling is different than mentoring. A role model shows you how it's done, creating a story line you can emulate. A mentor helps you interpret your own experience, helping you name the patterns in your own experience. A role model and mentor can be– and often are–the same person. That's especially true if the role model/mentor is your boss or co-worker.

Role modeling can be done person-to-person. It can also be done through the retelling of stories, anecdotes or legends that are reported by various media. Our role models can be very distant. As the first female Speaker of the House, Nancy Pelosi is a role model to many young women.

To develop more progressive leaders, our movement needs to self-consciously promote stories about progressive leaders and progressive heroes of all sorts. These stories should be systematically promoted through books, magazines, TV and radio, Internet and word-of-mouth.

Role models can also be recognized through regular awards and honors. For many years the Midwest Academy gave annual "Midwest Academy Awards" for precisely this reason. The awards focused attention on the story of the recipient. They made real the qualities that allow progressive leaders to be successful. They also impart status and importance to the accomplishments of progressive leaders. They help address that most important human self-interest—the search for meaning in life–by showing that you can have meaning in life as a progressive leader.

3) Recruitment. Researchers at Brown University did a study several years ago to determine why more women don't run for office.

When women run, they win in about the same proportion as men. So why are they less likely to run for office than men?

The answer, it turns out, is that people are substantially less prone to ask women to run than they are to ask men. Women were less prone to be asked to run both by their own peers and by political leaders.

The lesson was simple—if we want more women to run for office, we have to systematically ask them to do so. EMILY's List, the major political action committee that supports pro-choice Democratic women, and many female political leaders took up that challenge. They conduct systematic programs aimed at recruiting women candidates—*asking them.*

That would be good medicine at all levels of progressive leadership recruitment. We need to ask people. This is especially true when it comes to young people who are making life career choices. Systematic recruitment programs are in order, aimed at college campuses, workplaces, volunteer and community organizations, Internet users—even prisons.

My recent experience in the Federal Prison Camp at Terre Haute made it clear to me that many of the young African-American kids who get into trouble selling drugs are some of the most potentially talented and skilled organizers around. If progressive organizations give them opportunities to turn their lives around in service to their communities—in service to a progressive vision—there are many ready to sign up now. The problem is, of course, they need both the will and the wherewithal. There have to be jobs or roles for them to fill. Progressive organizations looking to recruit young African-American organizers would do well to talk with re-entry centers that have been set up to reintegrate young prisoners into society. That kind of recruitment has to be done carefully and with the view that while you trust—you also verify. But if it were done well—with streetwise recruiters—it could pay big dividends.

Another major avenue for recruiting young people is door-to-door canvass operations like those run by USAction, the Public Interest Research Groups (PIRG), Clean Water Action, and many others. Door-to-door canvass programs allow young people to learn management and training skills, and take on responsibility rapidly. They provide a drill in assessing self-interest and opportunities to learn political and coalition-building skills involved in issue campaigns.

Of course, entry-level campaign jobs and especially systematic campaign training programs like the ones we run at SCG are particularly geared to recruiting and inspiring young people to sign up for careers in progressive political organizing.

We should be actively making the case to young people considering their future that they should consider committing their lives to the progressive movement. We should be positively evangelical about it—with campus-based recruitment rallies for political volunteers—and opportunities to hear from role models about what is important in life.

I'm not talking here about recruitment on college campuses the way IBM or Exxon might. I'm talking about asking people to devote their lives to create a better world. I'm talking about challenging the notion that the only way to be successful in life is by getting a high-paying job or corner office. I'm talking about asking people to devote their lives to something more important than themselves by appealing to the most important self-interest of all: meaning in life.

I know that works. It sure worked for me, and much of a whole generation in the 1960s. Today's crop of young people is thirsting to hear it once again.

LEADERS WHO ARE—OR COULD BE—PROGRESSIVE ALLIES

They are many leaders in American who are, or could be, progressive allies—either over the long haul or for a specific battle or campaign.

Leaders of organizations of pharmacists may or may not be Progressives, but they certainly were allies when it comes to exposing the problems of President Bush's prescription drug program for seniors.

Leaders of physicians' organizations often are not Progressives, but they were allies in the fight to limit the power of HMOs.

The same goes for many members of Congress. Senator Olympia Snowe is no Progressive, but she was often the key vote against Bush tax cuts for the wealthy.

Of course, our goals with allied leaders are much the same as our goals with allied activists. We need to use the coalition rule and the agitation rule to bring them our way, and we need to make them comfortable working with us. Engaging Connectors, Mavens and Salesmen help to do that—to translate our messages into terms with which others are comfortable.

But what sets apart leaders is that they have followers, and that adds a key element to our strategic treatment of allied leaders. We need to engage a portion of those who follow them to help us cement their support. We need to communicate with their constituency.

ASKING FOLLOWERS TO ENLIST LEADERS AS PROGRESSIVE ALLIES

With political leaders, the tactics we employ are obvious. We generate grassroots contacts between voters and the politician. We organize constituency group leaders in the districts and contact them in support of our position. We analyze their following to determine whom we might mobilize on our behalf—which people really matter to the target.

But the same principles often apply to constituency-group leaders as well. In the early 1970s, I was organizing the campaign to stop the Crosstown Expressway in Chicago. Had it been built, the Crosstown Expressway would have been, per mile, the most expensive highway in the history of humankind. It would also have displaced 30,000 residents and 10,000 places of business. Just as importantly, CAP felt that its construction would have continued the diversion of money to urban expressways and away from mass transit.

The campaign was organized around Catholic parishes on Chicago's Northwest and Southwest sides, as well as the town of Cicero. On the South Side, African-American churches were the main building block. We brought together blacks and whites in a common battle that didn't happen often in 1970s Chicago. Many of our tactics involved "actions" where middle-class whites and blacks took on public officials with TV cameras in tow. We held mass meetings with officials. We released reports on the impact of the highway. We organized a march of 10,000 people near Midway Airport. And in the end, we conducted a voter education project that helped the Democrat Dan Walker defeat Republican Governor Dick Ogilvie. Walker had promised to kill the project if he won and transfer the funding to mass transit.

Election night 1972 ended with a declaration of victory by Walker, and his announcement that the Crosstown Expressway would not be built. Many of the decisive votes had come from the "Crosstown Corridor."

In this campaign our major constituency consisted of people who lived along the route. We were particularly keen to enlist the pastors of many of the big Catholic parishes that would be impacted. Some of them were with us immediately and signed up to help us organize the communities around their parishes. Others were more traditional, so we went to work organizing cadres in their parishes to get them out front and sweep them along. We paid special attention to leaders in the parishes that mattered to the pastor: the group that ran the Holy Name, the Altar and Rosary societies; the crew that ran the church bingo; the leaders at the church parochial school. These leaders went to the pastor and asked to have a meeting at the church hall about the Expressway and its impact on the community. At the meeting, we asked the pastor himself to say a few words. Pretty soon he was a leader in our coalition. His followers had moved him into action—and put him in a position where he "acted" himself into a commitment to our cause.

Getting Leaders and Followers to Reinforce Each Other

Sometimes the relationship between leaders and their followers can work both ways. You can set up situations where they reinforce each other.

Around 1973, CAP started to focus on the increasing problem of "redlining" of city neighborhoods by financial institutions and insurance companies. Whole areas had "red lines" drawn around them where these financial institutions would not make loans or write policies. In the early 1970s, these practices were not well known or understood.

As part of our campaign to develop the issue, CAP called a meeting at a Catholic parish on Chicago's Northwest side. We invited then-Congressmen Frank Annunzio and Dan Rostenkowski to come to the meeting and hear from constituents who were "very concerned" about redlining. Now, although CAP's leaders in the area were in fact very concerned about redlining, *unfortunately* most people in the neighborhood didn't yet have a clue what redlining was.

We put big signs on trees and poles all over the area. They said, **"Is our neighborhood redlined? Come Hear Congressmen Annunzio and Rostenkowski Report to the Community on What Can Be Done to Stop Mortgage Redlining in our Area."**

Of course, Congressmen Annunzio and Rostenkowski didn't know much about redlining either. But hundreds of people came to the meeting. Seeing so many people at the meeting on redlining, the Congressmen made strong statements about the urgent need to stop redlining in the community. Hearing their Members of Congress express such strong concerns for the issue, the people who came to the meeting were convinced it was in fact an urgent issue, and hurried to sign up as the meeting ended to do something about the problem.

At the start of the meeting only the CAP neighborhood leadership cared about redlining. At the end, the Members of Congress had been convinced of the urgency of the issue by the crowd, and the hundreds in attendance figured that if the Congressmen were concerned they should be too.

The Cockroach Theory of Lobbying

When leaders in general—and politicians in particular—experience pressure from a small set of active constituents, they assume these constituents represent many more. If the district office gets a hundred phone calls on an issue, a politician believes that thousands of others agree with them. The same is true of visits, letters and meetings.

My friend, Illinois State Representative Julie Hamos, calls this the "cockroach theory of lobbying." If you see one cockroach in your kitchen, you assume there are thousands more behind the walls or under the floorboards. It isn't the one cockroach that gets you to call the exterminator, it's the prospect that you are infested by a colony of cockroaches—that they're moving in, inviting their friends and preparing to have legions of baby cockroaches.

When segments of a leader's constituency contact them about an issue or position, he or she feels the same way.

Leaders of the Opposition

Like conservative activists, conservative leaders will not often be convinced by argument to change their views. Instead, our goal with conservative leaders, as well as all conservative activists, is to defeat and demoralize them. Once again, their positions of leadership give us a special tool: their followers.

Elected political officials are obviously most vulnerable to their followers, since their power and status as leaders is heavily dependent on their re-election. Fear of electoral defeat or other problems from constituents are huge self-interests for officeholders. While a good deal of the balance of this book will be devoted to specifics of winning the electoral and issue campaigns, it is useful to introduce two key concepts here.

Hang One in the Public Square

First, as Machiavelli made clear in *The Prince*, you don't have to hang all of your opponents. You just need to hang one in the public square. Machiavelli was of course referring to a course of action that allowed a Prince to contain opposition. But the same principle works with public officials who oppose the progressive agenda—and often other conservative leaders as well. In this case the "hanging" needs to be accomplished by a group of the particular leader's followers, or constituents, in a very public way.

One of the best examples of hanging in the public square also involved former Congressman Rostenkowski (though he was far from a conservative leader). In the late 1980s people might have thought that "the powerful chairman of the House Ways and Means Committee, Dan Rostenkowski" was his full given name. Rostenkowski was referred to that way by all of the media, and with good reason. He was one of the most powerful people in Congress. Given his position, he was also an architect of the Catastrophic Health Care Program. This program was an add-on to Medicare for seniors, and it was well-intended. Unfortunately, it was financed entirely by seniors, not by broader taxes.

The financing mechanism made middle-class seniors—your typical UAW retiree—pay a higher tax rate than Donald Trump. The Washington powers-that-be—including most senior groups—had supported this plan. But once it went into effect the grassroots were furious.

My wife, Jan Schakowsky, was not yet a member of Congress. At the time she was the Executive Director of the Illinois State Council of Senior Citizens. This organization had been demanding a meeting with Rostenkowski for some time to discuss the Catastrophic Health Plan. He had been avoiding them.

Finally, after a group visited his Northwest side Chicago office with TV cameras, he agreed to meet.

The meeting was held at the Copernicus Senior Center in the middle of his district on Milwaukee Avenue in Chicago. He had agreed to meet with a group of leaders, but several hundred additional seniors came to rally in the Center and await a report from the meeting.

After the not-very-successful conclusion of the meeting, Rostenkowski was asked to say a few words to those outside, who were mostly his constituents. The episode could have ended there, if he had agreed. But he marched right by, imperious. The seniors were not happy. They followed Rostenkowski out of the Copernicus Center to Chicago's Milwaukee Avenue, and the TV cameras started rolling.

Rostenkowski sped up his pace, and suddenly, he was being "chased" by seniors down Milwaukee Avenue in the center of his own district, and it was all being recorded for TV.

After a block, his driver pulled up the car to spirit him away. But once he got into the car, the seniors surrounded the car and refuse to move. As the driver gradually stepped on the gas, a woman named Leona Kozion lay splayed across the car hood. As the late *Chicago Tribune* columnist Mike Royko later wrote, she looked like a hood ornament on Rostenkowski's car. And she was a perfect symbol for his situation, with her slightly blue hair and heart-shaped sunglasses.

Cameras rolled, photos snapped. Once freed, Rostenkowski's car sped away.

The entire episode played at the top of the evening TV news, not only in Chicago but across the country. Kozion's face graced the front page of many newspapers. The TV anchors intoned: "The powerful chairman of the House Ways and Means Committee, Dan Rostenkowski, was chased down a street in the center of his Chicago district today by seniors angry at the Catastrophic Health Care Bill that he shepherded through Congress."

The next day a congressional delegation departed Washington by plane for the funeral of the late Congressman Mickey Leland of Texas. All the talk among the members on the trip to Houston was about the Rostenkowski chase. The consensus was simple: if it could happen to the "powerful chairman of the House Ways and Means Committee," it could happen to them.

Six months later, Congress repealed the "catastrophic healthcare plan." It had truly been a political catastrophe.

After the great chase, Rostenkowski is said to have asked one of his aides, "People will forget that soon, don't you think?" His aid is said to have replied, "Let me put it this way, Congressman, when you die, they'll play the footage of that chase."

Rostenkowski was hung in the public square.

In Americans United's campaign to stop the Bush plan to privatize Social Security, one of our tactics was to make several especially vulnerable Republican freshmen into "poster children" for the campaign. Congressmen English, Gerlach, and Fitzpatrick of Pennsylvania were chosen as especially ripe targets. Our goal was not only to make their lives miserable with town meetings, press events, neighborhood canvasses, etc. It was also to make sure that every other vulnerable Republican—especially freshmen—knew about their travails. So we circulated clips on actions and town meetings that were run against them—widely—both to the press and to the offices of other vulnerable members.

Our target lists in the Social Security campaign not only included members who might switch their votes, to oppose privatization. It also included "squealers"—members with a known history of loud complaining to the press and to the Republican leadership. Basically, "squealers" are members with low thresholds of political pain; they make particularly good victims for hanging in the public square since they "squeal" all the way to the gallows.

Former Congressman Mark Foley of Florida (before his "page familiarity" woes) was always one of our favorite "squealers." At the slightest provocation he would yelp and cry and whine; and of course, that kind of behavior is contagious. It causes demoralization among leaders in the enemy camp and it raises the subjugation costs of the Republican leadership's attempts to force members to take tough votes.

FOMENTING DIVISION BETWEEN OPPOSITION LEADERS

The second major rule when it comes to dealing with opposition leaders is to foment division. Historically, conservatives and Republicans have been particularly good at dividing Progressives.

Progressives need to get better at exploiting the rifts in the conservative coalition. These rifts revolve around many sets of divergent self-interests. They can be personal, they can be ideological, and they can be political.

The point is that we must constantly be on the lookout for opportunities to pit conservative leaders against one another. Apart from its utility in specific campaigns, it is important in and of itself. It consumes their energy, prevents coordinated action by the opposition, is unattractive to swing voters, fosters demoralization and disaffection, and sets up the possibility that competing leaders will destroy each other.

I am not suggesting Progressives engage in "dirty tricks" campaigns that are built on untrue rumor and innuendo. These generally backfire, and they undermine people's faith in us.

There is plenty of true, live ammunition available to allow us to promote conservative discord without having to invent anything. Fundamentally, the conservative coalition has a major—unstable—fault line between upper-income economic conservatives and lower-income social conservatives. The fact is that the Bush Presidency has delivered big time for the upper income economic conservatives and used the social conservatives as cannon fodder. That is a true fault line and one that we should constantly exploit.

As Bush has sought a way out of Iraq, another key fault line opened like a chasm—the division between Republican Neoconservatives like Cheney and Rumsfeld, and the "realists" like former Secretary of State Jim Baker. The "Baker-Hamilton" Commission Report in the winter of 2006 opened this fault line like a gaping wound.

Electoral and issue campaigns and research operations need to focus on ways to sow discord and division in conservative ranks at all levels. This is particularly true of progressive publications and blogs.

Many conservatives are experts at the art of sowing dissension in the ranks of their opponent. They know that embers of discord will not necessarily burst into flames of conflict unless they are fanned. We need operations intended to exploit and widen the massive personal, political and ideological rifts that exist throughout the conservative coalition.

One caveat here. In some situations—if, say, our goal is to hold five Republican senators to vote against a Bush budget—we need to exploit the rifts carefully. In a situation like this, we have to exploit the rift, while we also make the five Republicans feel comfortable enough to vote with us.

We most likely would refrain, for instance, from doing anything that would make the five senators feel that they were out there all alone— isolated from the Republican mainstream—at least before the vote. Tactically, we generally go to great lengths to get business people and Republicans to contact these members—to make them feel at home.

But we also look for any sign of disrespect from the Administration that would really frost the swing Senators. We do our best to highlight the slight: "Why are the president and his aides ignoring Senator _____," for example.

In most of the budget and tax battles while the Republicans were in charge of Congress, we sought to inflame tensions between former House Ways and Means Chairman Bill Thomas and Senate Finance Committee Chairman Chuck Grassley. They had very different economic philosophies and approaches to dealing with fellow members. Grassley was much more collegial and Thomas was domineering and strong-willed. In addition, the two didn't like each other. We didn't just let their divisions sit. We tried to fan the flames, with reporters and lobbyists and staff. The worse they got along, the better for Progressives (and the country in general). After all, the Bush tax and budget program—taking food from the mouths of poor children to give tax breaks to the rich—is the best example around and something that needed to be stopped dead in its tracks.

Chapter Eighteen

Constituency Groups

Constituency groups matter in politics for many reasons. By constituency groups, I mean groups of people for whom the characteristics they share as a group contribute to defining their personal identity, their meaning in life. In general, someone's race, ethnicity, nationality and gender help define who they are. The same can be true for occupation, marital status, sexual orientation, as well as for one's ideology or religion or "way of life."

They provide the basis around which many political organizations are fashioned, many dollars are raised, and many powerful institutions are built. Organizations and institutions of all sorts are important to Progressives, because by their very nature they give us the means of communicating with, and mobilizing, all sorts of people. But there is one major reason why constituency groups matter to a progressive strategy. They are important if and when they serve to help define the identity and meaning of the participants.

To one degree or another, anytime someone joins an organization it helps define who they are and their relationship to the world around them. But true constituency groups are more than just organizations. In fact, they might not be embodied as organizations or institutions at all.

Meaning is the key motivator, so it follows that someone's relationship to a constituency has a lot to do with their perception of their own self-interest—how they vote and whether they vote.

That's why the demographics of the country, and demographic trends, mean so much to our political strategy.

Blue Demographics

There are several central demographic facts in America:

- America is becoming a "majority minority" country. Groups that were previously "minorities"—African-Americans, Latinos and Asians—taken together will constitute a majority of Americans by the middle of this century. Texas, Hawaii, California and New Mexico are already "majority minority." These groups—especially African-Americans—have traditionally voted overwhelmingly Democratic.

- Immigrants—particularly lower-income immigrant workers—are growing as a percentage of the population. This group breaks heavily Democratic.

- Knowledge workers—those who make their living manipulating information (from data processing people to writers)—are growing as a percentage of the work force. This group also breaks heavily Democratic.

- America is becoming more cosmopolitan. More people are moving into metropolitan areas around cities that tend to be more cosmopolitan, diverse and tolerant—and less parochial and homogeneous. Democrats have historically been successful in these areas as well.

- The number of single women continues to grow as a percentage of the overall population. This group also votes overwhelmingly Democratic.

- Generation Y—current 18-to-25 year-olds—have attitudes that are considerably more tolerant and generally progressive than the cohorts that came before them. In fact they are down right "intolerant of intolerance."

The good news for Democrats is that roughly 80% of Bush voters in both elections came from whites who lived in less cosmopolitan areas, and these groups are shrinking as a percentage of the country's population. As the workforce is increasingly dominated by immigrant workers on one hand and knowledge workers on the other, the Democratic/progressive base will grow proportionately.

But there are offsetting factors. Most notable:

- American continues to be a very religious country. And, historically at least, the more frequently someone attends church, the more likely they are to be Republican.

One of the reasons why formerly Republican suburban areas have begun to be competitive for Democrats is their altered demography. Illinois' formerly solidly Republican 6th CD went Republican in 2006, but it was a toss up-to the end. The formerly Republican 8th CD went solidly Democratic. The demographic changes depicted below help explain why:

Category	6th	CD	8th	CD	Illinois	
Percent Hispanic	1990	5.2%	1990	5.5%	1990	7.9%
	2005	16.6%	2005	14.2%	2005	14.5%
Percent Black	1990	1.4%	1990	1.6%	1990	14.8%
	2005	2.9%	2005	4.0%	2005	14.5%
Percent Asian	1990	4.9%	1990	4.0%	1990	2.5%
	2005	9.8%	2005	8.2%	2005	4.1%
Ave. Household Income		$67,096		$66,165		$50,260

In other words, the Sixth CD in west suburban Chicago has gone from 11.5% minority in 1990 to 29.3% in 2005. The northwest suburban Eighth CD has gone from 11.1% minority in 1990 to 26.4% minority in 2005.[1]

That changing demography is one reason why the Sixth CD, which was formerly overwhelmingly Republican, has gone to 31% Republican, 30% Democrat and 35% independent, and the formerly heavily Republican Eighth CD has gone to 29% Republican, 29% Democrat and 38% independent.

The extent to which these and other characteristics impact someone's self-definition varies enormously depending upon the individual and the context. A couple of rules:

1) The more a particular characteristic makes someone "special" sets them apart—the more it usually matters.

For instance, sexual orientation helps define a gay man's self-identity a lot more than it does for a typical straight man. The fact that someone is South Asian in the United States helps to define his self-identity a lot more than does having an English background.

I grew up thinking I was Heinz—57 varieties—kind of a mishmash of European stock (English, Scotch Irish, German). About 10 years ago, out of the blue, my sister said, "Guess what, mom says our great-grandfather was Jewish." "What?" I said, "and she never mentioned this, even when I married a Jewish woman?"

So I asked my mother if her grandfather was indeed Jewish. She replied "Oh, yes." So I said, "Well then, I guess he must have converted, became a Methodist or something, since you never mentioned it?" She replied, "Oh no… Never converted."

Of course, I suppose it should have been obvious. I had known since childhood that my great-grandfather was named Saul Bergman, had come from Bavaria and opened a general store in Moscow, Texas.

I was elated. My wife is Jewish. Much of our family is Jewish And now I was, too, at least a small part Jewish. I was no longer a nondescript Heinz—57 varieties—kind of guy. I had an ethnic background. It changed the way I thought about myself. I became more special somehow.

2) Issues sometimes become emblematic of constituency identfition. Gun ownership is probably the best example.

The reason the "right to bear arms" has become such a defining issue for many voters is only partly a result of the specific policy concerns of gun owners. In fact, most of the measures that the NRA fights in the name of "gun owner rights" do not directly impact most gun owners. Most gun owners don't own assault weapons. Most don't hunt with handguns. Gun ownership is such a powerful issue in places like the poorest counties of Ohio, because it is emblematic of people's "way of life." It is a right that is deeply embedded in rural and small-town culture across America and especially in areas like Appalachia, the South and the non-urban West.

Conservatives use the gun control issue as code for—"those urban liberals don't respect you or your way of life—they are not like you— they're not on your side."

3) The most important technique to address a particular constituency is "showing up." In fact, showing up is indeed half of politics. I mean this both figuratively and literally.

In the next Section, I will argue that two of the most important messages in politics are: "I'm on your side" and "I respect you." There is no better symbol to communicate these messages than *paying attention*. There is no clearer way to communicate, "I'm not on your side" and "I don't respect you" than ignoring people.

Unfortunately, when it comes to many key constituencies, Democrats failed to show up during the last two presidential cycles. Steve Jarding, who helped engineer Virginia Senator Webb's victory over incumbent Senator George Allen, specializes in communicating with rural voters. He says the key for Democrats to be successful in rural America is simple: just show up. "You can't write it off," he says. "We need to quit conceding turf to the Republicans." [2]

Last presidential election, Republicans had a systematic strategy to attract Catholics. A conservative group put out voter guides in Catholic churches on what he called the five non-negotiable issues for Catholics—along with the positions of the candidates. They were: homosexual marriage, abortion, fetal stem cell research, euthanasia, and human cloning. *No mention* of the Catholic positions on poverty, war, capital punishment, worker rights, etc. Democrats had no systematic program aimed at Catholics whatsoever.

Of course, you could argue that with rural voters and Catholics we communicated our message to the same people through other means. But that misses the point. Constituency groups are important, precisely because they define people's identities, as rural people, Catholics or whatever. If we ignore that self-identification, we ignore them.

For average candidates, the rule of showing up means that they need to go to the Croatian dinner, the Chinese New Year's celebration, the Greek Summerfest, because their very presence communicates a message of respect and says "I'm on your side." We tell candidates to worry about one major thing at these events—make sure everyone knows you're there. At minimum, we want them to be introduced and to greet and schmooze with the leaders of the group. Their major message is simple: "I'm here."

4) Communicate with constituencies, using language and symbols to which they can relate.

Every constituency has its own culture—its own collection of myths and symbols that embody its common experience as a group. Using them is critical to assure that your message is understood. The very act of using someone's symbols and language communicates respect.

Members of ethnic groups love to hear political leaders use some phrase from their native language or enjoy their foods or participate in their cultural ceremonies.

Of course, that has to be done with care. If you're not part of the group, you can pretend you are and look like you pander to every one and tell everyone what they want to hear.

But knowing a group's history, understanding its culture and translating messages into stories with which a constituency can identify–all go a long way to address the core concerns of people who identify as a constituency.

The comfort with which a political figure uses the symbols and style of a constituency may be more important in determining their feelings toward a candidate—or political movement—that anything about his program or policies.

After the 2000 election there was much discussion in the consultant community and political "chattering class" about why Gore had lost many rural areas to Bush. Much of the blame was centered on his policies concerning guns and coal—since polling showed the policies were not popular in many rural areas. But often polling that focuses only on policies tends to lead us in the wrong direction. Bill Clinton had exactly the same policies on guns and coal—but did much better in these same areas.

Why did Clinton do so much better than Gore? The reason was simple. Bill Clinton was Bubba—he was your neighbor down the road. He was a guy who grew up in Hope, Arkansas, and who understood, and identified with rural and small town people. Al Gore (who had spent many summers on the family farm) looked to many rural voters like a stiff urban guy who went to St. Albans private school. Worse yet, he was running against a guy from Texas who looked at home in jeans.

Many politicos and policy types don't like to think these kinds of symbols have such a major role in determining people's votes—but they do. If we're going to win we had better accept the fact and use it to our advantage the way Clinton did in 1992 and 1996.

Of course, everyone cannot be every constituency. But every progressive organizer and leader can learn how to do their best to understand different constituencies. They can address and use the culture of constituencies, and symbols of that culture, as tools rather than impediments to communication.

5) Use Connectors, Mavens and Salesmen, who can translate our messages to the constituency.

Progressive organizers and leaders have to search out Connectors, Mavens and Salesman for our candidates and messages—people who can translate the message smoothly into symbols, stories and language that work in the constituency.

We might not be able to *be* every constituency, but we can find translators for every constituency. Just anyone won't do. We're looking for Connectors, Mavens and Salesmen.

6) Use the constituency group's own struggles to make its leaders part of our team.

We're always looking for leaders—people with followers. And we don't want to simply relate to them as leaders of constituencies that are foreign to our cause. We need to enlist them onto the team—to make our cause their cause and vice versa. Making them part of *our* team requires that we get on *their* team. They need to feel that our political leaders and organizers are honorary members of their family, and will be there when the chips are down.

In campaigns this may take the form of "ethnic councils" or "labor advisory boards" or informal groups of clergy to meet with the officeholder regularly. In all cases, it's about developing personal relationships between leaders, and making constituency leaders into progressive leaders and vice versa.

Often the relationship starts as an outgrowth of a battle over a constituency group's specific issue. Through our work on those issues, leaders and activists who were originally activated by the specific issue alone become active in the broader progressive movement as well.

In fact, that's how *most* Progressive leaders and activists are recruited. Jan became a progressive activist as a result of an early battle to put freshness dates on food. Many people in my generation were activated by the Vietnam War, or the Civil Rights Movement. Other progressive leaders got involved because of a labor struggle, or battle in their community or an electoral campaign. They get "exposed" to the "virus" of progressive politics in these battles—they are exposed to the people, the values and excitement of political struggle—and they're hooked.

7) People who identify themselves with a constituency remember who stands with them when the chips are down.

Just after the 9/11 attacks, a group of macho "patriots" marched on the Southwest side of Chicago to a mosque where they protested the presence of Muslims in their community. Chicago's Mayor Richard Daley was livid. He held a press conference immediately to denounce the marchers. Daley, who of course is Irish, said, "Just because the IRA were terrorists doesn't make all Irish terrorists, does it?"

My wife decided the next day that it was critical for the people of her congressional district to make a forceful statement that targeting Muslim Americans for revenge or discrimination was itself un-American. Her district includes large numbers of Muslim Americans and scores of other ethnic communities.

Forty percent of the people in Illinois' Ninth Congressional District speak a language other than English at home. Traveling down Devon Avenue on Chicago's North Side is like a quick tour of Karachi, Pakistan, Mumbai, India, and Jerusalem—with a quick dash of Zagreb, Croatia.

From Damen Avenue to Western Avenue along Devon, you have mainly Pakistani Muslim shops and restaurants. At Western Avenue, they become more Indian—Hindu shops and restaurants. Then at California Avenue, they gradually turn into the shops of Orthodox Jews. The Croatian cultural Center is thrown in for good measure.

Jan decided to lead a unity march down Devon Avenue. She thought that it was particularly important that the Jewish Congresswoman should march shoulder to shoulder with leaders from the Muslim and Hindu communities. The message was simple: we're in this together—we are all Americans.

The march was called on two days' notice. Over a thousand Muslims, Hindus, Jews, Catholics, Protestants, Assyrians, Croatians, and pretty much every other brand of Chicagoan turned out to stand together and make a clear statement about the true progressive values that should define what it means to be a patriotic American. The march was covered widely on TV and in the papers.

Not only did the march frame the 9/11 crisis in terms of progressive values, but the Muslim community never forgot. The Jewish Congresswoman and Muslim leadership have worked together closely ever since.

PROGRESSIVE CONSTITUENCIES

Our strategic goal with normally progressive constituencies is to assure that their members always feel that they are part of the team—that they're not abandoned or taken for granted by the progressive movement or its candidates. A number of key constituencies come to mind:

- African-Americans
- Pro-Choice Women
- True Believers
- Many Hispanics (though big subsets of Hispanics are swing constituencies)
- Muslims
- Jews (though a significant number of Jews vote Republican, three-fourths vote Democratic and identify with progressive goals)
- Union Members and Retirees
- Disability Rights Activists
- The Gay Community

Many of those in these groups do indeed define themselves at least partially in terms of these constituency characteristics.

We need to use all of the tools described above in order to generate a sense of inclusion that will assure they are enthusiastic participants in the larger progressive project.

Sometimes this requires that we take some risks. As I mentioned earlier, periods of social mobilization are also periods of political realignment. The political allegiances of the Hispanic community will be hugely impacted by the stance of Progressives and the Democratic Party in the immigration debate. As tempting as it is for some Democrats to duck and weave when it comes to resolving the immigration issue, that would represent a major strategic error over the long haul. Progressives and Democrats need to stand unequivocally with immigrants in general and Hispanics in particular in the debate over immigrant rights.

Not only will America be "majority minority" by the middle of the century, Hispanics already represent the largest minority group in America –14.5% of the entire population in 2005. The U.S. Census estimates that Hispanics now represent roughly half of all U.S. population growth each year. Many new immigrants can't vote yet. But their families and friends often can, and one day, many of them will vote as well.

The coalition rule is key. If Hispanics see Progressives standing with them on this central question that involves their identity as a people, it will forgive many disagreements on social policies like choice.

We should stand up proudly, loudly, and often for Hispanics in this battle and use every opportunity to characterize the views of people like Congressman Sensenbrenner and Tom Tancredo for what they are—anti-Hispanic extremism.

THE SECRET OF HOW TO TURN WHITE MALE GUN OWNERS INTO DEMOCRATS (HINT: IT'S A FIVE-LETTER WORD)

Sometimes participation in a group can change or solidify a person's political orientation.

If you're a white man, who is not gay, not Jewish or Muslim, and not a member of a union, you were 80% likely to vote Republican in the last presidential election. We did better with white men in the 2006 Midterms. But the fact remains that white men tend heavily to vote Republican.

But if you are a white, gun-owning union member, you are over 60% likely to vote Democrat. The five-letter word is "union."

Union organizing is the silver bullet for expanding the progressive movement among white men. Of course unions also provide the best means of persuading and mobilizing women, Hispanics, blacks, and pretty much everyone else, too.

As a consequence, one of the principal strategic goals of the progressive movement must be the massive expansion of the percentage of the workforce represented by organized labor. Of course, thanks to a long-term right-wing campaign that has been waged at every level, the percentage of the workforce represented by organized labor has sunk to a 50-year low. Progressives should view that decline as a critical warning calling for emergency action. In particular, it means that we need to crusade to pass the Employee Free Choice Act (EFCA) that would make it easier to organize unions, soon after we elect a Democratic President in 2008.

Unions are so effective because they redefine the identity of the worker vis a vis the rest of the world. They provide a structure that represents a member's self-interest. They can sort through the political landscape and make recommendations that workers trust to represent their interests—and many unions run programs that do it regularly. Unions deliver for their members who, on the average, make one-third more than their unorganized counterparts.

SWING CONSTITUENCIES—ALLIES

This category includes constituencies whose defining characteristics do not necessarily predispose one ideological view or another—but do impact the way people define themselves.

RELIGIOUS GROUPS

Mainstream religious groups are especially important here—people such as the Catholics we described earlier. It is inexcusable that Progressives and the Democratic Party have been so remiss in failing to systematically persuade, recruit and mobilize the mainstream religious community.

What is needed, in particular, is simply showing up. How hard can it be to distribute a progressive Catholic voter guide? You don't win if you don't show up for the game.

But more fundamentally, religious Progressives must reclaim the symbols of their religious traditions from the far right.

At the end of 2005, the Republican leadership and White House had to pull out all the stops to pass their budget "reconciliation" bill that cut funds for health care, student loans and services to the poor in order to give tax breaks to millionaires.

After a lengthy battle coordinated by our client, the Emergency Campaign for America's Priorities (ECAP), the Republicans eked out a House victory by one vote and had to fly Vice President Cheney in from the Middle East to cast a tie-breaking vote to pass the bill out of the Senate.

ECAP and organizations like the Center on Budget and Policy Priorities had shifted the political equation surrounding the budget and tax debate. For many years, some Democrats in marginal districts had begged the Democratic leadership to allow them to vote for Bush's tax and spending cuts because they believed that was good politics.

But by 2005 Republicans in marginal districts begged the Republican leadership to allow them to vote against the same measures because they had become bad politics. Not one Democrat in either chamber voted for the 2005 budget "Reconciliation" bill.

One of the reasons for this shift in the political equation has been ECAP's success at reframing these cuts as *morally wrong*. In other words, we shifted the debate away from "the funding levels" and "line items" — away from policies and programs—to a question of what was right and wrong.

The Reverend Jim Wallis's Call to Renewal organization made a big contribution to this effort. Through his organization, his recent book *God's Politics,* [3] and the magazine *Sojourners,* Wallis has brought together progressive evangelical Christians to reclaim the preeminence of the Gospel message of justice and community instead of the right wing religious message of fear and division.

As the vote on the budget "Reconciliation Bill" approached, Call to Renewal organized a day of civil disobedience at the Cannon House Office Building in Washington. Roughly 120 Call to Renewal members knelt on the stairs of the building and refused to leave. They were arrested and led away by the Capitol Police. This kind of prominent Christian witness—coupled with the involvement of religious people around the country—helped reframe the debate.

Former DNC chair and Clinton Campaign Manager David Wilhelm is spearheading a new effort called Faithful Democrats that has created an interactive Website to provide an online home for Democrats of Christian Faith. It's intended to let America know, "The Democratic Party is second to none when it comes to faith and values." [4]

Faithful Democrats targets three major groups that are swing or persuadable constituencies:

- **White Catholics**
  - Composed 21% of all voters in 2004
  - Bush, Sr. won by 14%, Clinton by 5% and then 7%, Bush, Jr. by 7% then 13%

- **Moderate Evangelicals**
  - 11% of all voters in 2004
  - Evangelical "centrists" voted 64% Bush; "modernists," 52% Kerry

- **Mainline Protestants**
  - 20% of all voters in 2004
  - 50%-50% Bush-Kerry; highest total ever for a Democrat
  - Mainline "centrists" voted 58% Bush

At the same time, it seeks to mobilize involvement from the four base Democratic Christian religious groups:

- **Black Protestants**
  - 13% of Kerry voters in 2004
  - Voted 83% Kerry

- **Modernist Catholics**
  - 9% of Kerry voters in 2004
  - Voted 69% Kerry

- **Modernist Mainline Protestants**
  - 9% of Kerry voters in 2004
  - Voted 78% Kerry

- **Latino Catholics**
  - 4% of Kerry voters in 2004
  - Voted 69% Kerry

Other efforts are also under way. All of them require a clear, proud, reaffirmation and commitment to progressive values expressed in the language of faith.

OTHER SWING CONSTITUENCIES

There are other swing constituencies that may or may not be in play in elections, but can be very important as allies and legislative battles. They often include trade or professional associations like:

- Pharmacists
- Artists
- Nurses
- Teachers
- Doctors
- Lawyers
- Pilots
- Farmers
- Milk Producers
- Social Workers
- Insurance Agents

There's been a tendency on the part of those who organize progressive issue campaigns to ignore these groups or write them off. They may not join our coalitions, but they are valuable allies and their participation with us can help change the political loyalties of its members over the long haul.

OPPOSITION CONSTITUENCIES

Here, traditional targeting doctrine teaches us to ignore constituencies where the cost of moving votes is especially high. Given limited campaign resources this is often sound judgment. The expenditure of every dollar and every hour of energy must be allocated so as to maximize the marginal number of new voters they produce.

But over the long haul—and in campaigns with adequate resources—it is entirely appropriate to apply resources to cut the Right's margins by small slices of percentage points—to pick up the low-hanging fruit of constituencies that are normally conservative Republican strongholds.

Often the marginal cost of each new "low-hanging fruit" vote from a traditional opposition constituency is lower than the last votes we might squeeze out of traditionally progressive constituencies. Once again, we can often pick off those "low-hanging fruit" votes simply by showing up.

Political Consultant Will Robinson handled the media for Democrat Ted Strickland's successful 2006 race for Governor in Ohio. He had lobbied Kerry-allied groups hard in 2004 to spend part of their media budgets in smaller markets with fewer swing voters. His argument was simple. With a limited number of contacts with voters in these areas—even though each contact might be more expensive than other areas—Democrats could pick up "low-hanging fruit" voters. These are voters whom we simply wouldn't get if we didn't "show up" and contest for them. If you decided not to compete for them at all, you simply handed them to the other side by default.

Robinson lost the debate in 2004. That was one additional factor in why some of the poorest counties in Ohio went Republican in 2004. While it had a lot to do with a failure to understand the full range of people's self interest, it also had to do with failing to "show up."

In 2006, he was in charge of Strickland's media buys. The Strickland campaign went after every vote, from every constituency, from every area. They went after the "low hanging fruit" that could be picked off in rural areas surrounding Zanesville, and the orchards of Democrats in Cleveland. That approach helped contribute to Strickland's victory and to that of Ohio's new junior senator, Sherrod Brown—who had formerly served as one of the most progressive members of the House.

The right has adopted a similar strategy in its attempt to shave percentages off of Democratic majorities in black and Hispanic communities.

An obvious target for this strategy is Hispanics of Cuban origin. Mainly based in Florida and New Jersey, this group has been one of the cornerstones of conservative victories in the Sunshine State. But like most constituencies, it is not monolithic, and it is in flux. It turns out that Cubans who immigrated to the US after 1980 have a very different view of themselves and their homeland than those who immigrated in the two decades immediately after Fidel Castro came to power in Cuba. They think of themselves as immigrants, not exiles, and are much more interested in open travel and economic relations with Cuba than the earlier group.

The Democrats would do well to forcefully advocate these open travel and trade policies and build on the growing cadre of increasingly progressive young Cuban-Americans. We aren't going to get the majority of the Cuban-American vote anytime soon; however, we could certainly compete for an increasing share. But we can do that only if we are clear and self-confident about our policies, and refuse to pander to the hard-line exile groups.

Sarah Stephens of the Freedom to Travel Campaign and Bill Goodfellow of the Center for International Policy have both worked for years to build a constituency among these younger Cuban immigrants.

CHAPTER NINETEEN

Earned Media—The Press

Members of the media have a unique and powerful role in shaping the political, economic and cultural dialogue in the United States—and for that matter, in affecting the outcome of elections and issue campaigns.

Our targets in the media include people who think of themselves solely as journalists, observers of political events. But the media also includes those who consider themselves active participants in political movements. It includes people who play the role of Connectors, Mavens and Salesmen. It includes leaders who have large followings (especially columnists and editorialists). And it includes the leaders and participants in many organized constituencies.

But the fact that someone is a member of the media gives them self-interests that make them unique message targets requiring special treatment.

SELF-INTERESTS OF THE MEDIA

Eight of these self-interests are especially important in shaping progressive media strategy:

1) THE DESIRE TO BUILD VIEWERSHIP OR READERSHIP.

Media executives who ultimately decide the kinds of stories that are presented in a particular medium—and their slant—are generally very focused on building the viewership or readership of that medium. This is particularly true of media owned by commercial, and advertising-based, circulation-driven media. But to one degree or another, even not-for-profit media shares this interest—if only to accomplish their mission.

This means that your news coverage and your other programming must be interesting to someone.

Many critics decry the fact that—particularly with local news shows—"If it bleeds it leads." That's not because news editors are a bunch of death-obsessed freaks, it's because someone, correctly or not, believes that such stories are interesting to potential viewers.

If we want to get our message out, Progressives need to produce *interesting* news opportunities. A bunch of old white guys at a press conference do not always satisfy the definition of "interesting." Interesting means creative, surprising, memorable, entertaining, exciting, emotive, engaging, heartwarming, funny, cute, inspiring, unexpected, moving, educational, dramatic; you get the drift. "Interesting" engages the intellect or the emotions; *it is not boring.* Generally, a man-bites-dog story is more interesting than a dog-bites-man story.

And we need to remember something else if we want to be interesting to the media. *Not for nothing* do they use the word "story." Interesting news stories are actually "stories;" they are narratives that paint a picture or tell a tale.

Many years ago, when I was coordinating the campaign to stop Chicago's Crosstown Expressway, we set a goal of creating one interesting event each week to keep the campaign in the news and drive the action. A campaign like that gave us a lot of opportunity for "interesting."

Here's an example. One day I got a call from a friend who is an architect and planner. He was between jobs and wanted to know if it would be useful to our campaign if he were to go to work for one of the firms that was part of "Crosstown Associates," the consortium planning the highway. From that vantage point, he might be able to do some behind-the-scenes "whistle blowing" and report facts concerning the Expressway that were being kept from the public.

Sounded great to me. So a few weeks later, he gave me a call to say he was on board at "Crosstown Associates."

A few weeks after that, our source called to tell us that "Crosstown Associates" had a study of the environmental impact of the proposed expressway that was devastating. It would bring pollution, congestion and massive amounts of noise to the neighborhoods through which it sliced. Giant "earth berms" and sound fences would have to be built. All of this was being withheld from the public; would I like a copy? You bet.

It wasn't long before a group of housewives from the affected neighborhoods went to the offices of "Crosstown Associates," followed by TV cameras. They charged that "Crosstown Associates" was intentionally withholding information from the public. Then they entered the "Crosstown Associates" office and bolted past the receptionist. They began to pass out leaflets to the staff that said: "Rat on Your Boss—how can you work as an engineer or design professional and withhold critical information from the public? Where are your professional ethics?"

The event offered drama, mystery and surprise. Prim and proper middle-class housewives in a surprise assault on the Expressway's design office was a very interesting story. It also set up dramatic tension for the release of the report that would come the next week. And as a side benefit, it made everyone at "Crosstown Associates" a "suspect" for leaking the report. It provided cover to our source.

A week later, we released the "secret" environmental impact study to a flurry of publicity.

If memory serves, at least three directors of "Crosstown Associates" were fired over the next year because of successive leaks to our "Anti-Crosstown Coalition." Those leaks yielded horrible publicity for the project and helped lead to its defeat. When our "whistleblower" left "Crosstown Associates" a year and a half later, he was given a party. To this day only two or three of us at the Citizens Action Program knew his identity.

2) FILLING THE NEWS HOLE

Whether you're a newspaper editor who has to fill up a certain number of column inches, or a newscast producer needing to fill a certain number of minutes of airtime, the media needs a constant flow of new stories to feed its machine.

As they try to bag their quota of news stories, we have to remember that some days and times of day present them with more fertile hunting than others. The value, or newsworthiness, of stories goes up if they occur in periods or areas of scarcity, the proverbial "slow news day."

So, for instance, Sunday afternoons are often a good time to hold a news event. The media has to fill a big "news hole" on Sunday evening. In fact, the Sunday night late news (10 p.m. Central and Mountain, 11 p.m. Eastern and West Coast) is the most widely watched newscast of the week. Yet there are not a lot of news events Sunday, because a lot of newsmakers generally aren't working. Of course, depending on which Sunday, this may not be true. If the city's football team is in the Super Bowl, or there is a major plane crash, all bets are off. In addition, there are fewer news crews and reporters on weekends than on weekdays—so one big car crash may divert the people who were on the way to cover your story. But in general, Sundays are great news days.

Monday mornings are often good times for news events as well, because a lot of the people who plan news events don't want to work over the weekend to get them ready.

Of course, most smaller regional TV markets have the same "news hole" to fill as the stations in Chicago or New York. The effect is that a less interesting, less newsworthy story is much more likely to get played in Peoria than in Los Angeles.

But smaller markets are critical to the progressive strategy. Many swing congressional districts are dominated by one or two smaller TV and newspaper markets. This should make it that much easier for us to get our message out, but it requires that we concentrate on generating lots of press there. National organizations have a tendency to release their reports and studies in D.C. and other major markets. They should also systematically do so in targeted, small markets in swing districts.

3) JOURNALISTIC STANDARDS

Many journalists are heavily driven by their own sense of the role of the journalist and journalistic ethics.

In the US, more so than in many countries, the members of the "fourth estate" view themselves as objective free agents who have no ideological ax to grind besides the pursuit of the truth. While in many cases this is far from accurate, it requires that to be effective we have to respect journalists' sense of their role.

Even if the reporter is your best friend, you never want to assume that anything you tell her is really off the record. That just puts her in a difficult position, could get you in serious media trouble, and ruin a perfectly good friendship.

4) THE VIEWS OF THE PUBLISHER OR OWNER

Much as they say that the publisher's views never influence news coverage, it's just not true. The movie, *Good Night and Good Luck,* that chronicled legendary newsman Edward R. Murrow's battle with Senator Joe McCarthy, showed clearly some of the interplay between news organizations and the corporations who own them.

I have to admit there is a great difference between the views expressed on the editorial page of the *Wall Street Journal* and the generally high quality of reporting of its news side. But when it comes to many stories, the overall strategy of news outlets—especially with big stories such as Watergate, the publication of the Pentagon Papers, the pictures from Abu Ghraib, the revelations about government programs like domestic wiretaps by the NSA or secret CIA prisons—publishers are often heavily involved.

Who would argue that the news coverage of the Reverend Sun Myung Moon's *Washington Times* is of same caliber as that of the *Washington Post*? Of course, the Reverend Moon created the Washington Times precisely because he believed in the old dictum, "the press is free to those who own them."

That's why a critical progressive goal must be the creation of more and more media outlets that are *owned* by Progressives. It's why we must also strongly oppose increased media ownership concentration.

Several years ago, Progressives won an unexpected victory on the media concentration front. The Federal Communications Commission

(FCC) had proposed that media concentration regulation be relaxed. That would allow a few large media companies to massively expand their holdings of media—and the news messages that Americans actually receive.

A lot of people thought that "media concentration" was a boring inside-the-beltway subject area. It turned out that many Americans were intensely interested, so interested that the FCC received an unprecedented volume of mail, e-mails, phone calls, etc. Once the FCC defied public opinion and loosened the rules anyway, the pressure on Congress was so great that a Republican-controlled Congress had to actually block increased concentration through Congressional action.

A few years ago, Jan and I met two Chicago area venture capitalists named Shelly and Anita Drobny. Though they had done well at traditional venture deals, they were not your run-of-the-mill entrepreneurs. They were deeply committed to progressive values, and the idea that Progressives should compete seriously with right-wing talk radio. Right-wing talk radio had been incredibly successful at achieving important conservative goals during the previous 20 years.

- It allowed Conservatives to reach more downscale audiences who responded to the message that they had been victimized by the professional elites—that their values and way of life were under attack.

- It allowed right-wing assumptions, values and symbols to be echoed and reinforced among the conservative base. And the discussion on talk radio wasn't embedded in "civil" disagreement with progressive values. Progressive values were mocked and marginalized as outside the mainstream. This gave substantial self-confidence to the conservative core.

- The influence of conservative talk radio (and its counterparts on TV, such as Fox News) ran well beyond the conservative base, because its format was presented as entertainment. It was not intended simply to inform, agitate, mobilize or persuade—it was intended to entertain. As a result, many swing voters tuned in—not for the politics—but for the entertainment value. Of course, the political message was absorbed as well. Another result of packaging politics as entertainment was its commercial, financial success.

- Finally, right-wing talk radio could create controversy that would drive coverage in the mainstream media.

The Drobnys wanted to create a venture that would go head-to-head with the Rush Limbaughs of the world. The result of their efforts, after several fits and starts, was Air America.

Our firm did a brochure to help them recruit investors. The cover featured a woman surrounded by flames and the disembodied images of various right-wing talk show hosts. It read: "Ever think you'd died and gone to right-wing talk show hell? Had enough?"

The Drobnys believed that to compete with right-wing talk radio a progressive network needed to:

- Entertain, not just inform.

- Involve a network of stations with *all-progressive* formats. They believed that Progressives wouldn't tune into a mostly conservative talk station to hear the one progressive show sandwiched between Limbaugh and Sean Hannity. Potential listeners wanted to know that if they tuned into the station anytime they would get progressive programming, whether in the car or in the kitchen. My wife says she always knows that when she turns on Air America, it will be like a refreshing breeze of progressive views flowing from the radio.

- Be a commercial venture that makes money. The Drobny's believed that there was a big progressive talk radio audience that could support commercial talk radio. They conceived of the mission of progressive talk radio much the same way as their conservative competition: politics coupled with entertainment that can attract core Progressives, as well as more nonpolitical entertainment seekers. That would create very a different sound than, say, National Public Radio, which has a critical mission in our society, but one that is very different from Air America.

Air America contracted with comedian/political satirist Al Franken to provide a major-league anchor, and secured talent like Randy Rhodes. After many, many problems Air America finally went up on the air. It has continued through several incarnations of ownership and now is hopefully on solid financial ground. The Drobnys are currently involved in the creation of yet another progressive radio venture, Nova M.

The self-interest of the publisher or owner really matters to the context of newscasts and other programming. Focus on expanding progressive media ownership at all levels and preventing the concentration of media ownership in the hands of big corporations, must be two major strategic priorities for today's progressive movement.

5) The Journalist's Own Views and Those of Their Peers

Try as they might to appear "objective," reporters bring their own views and prejudices to every story written. To be effective at message to the media, it is critical to understand those views and if possible communicate to the reporter in terms that resonate with them. It's also important to influence those views by constant communication with reporters, communication that frames the discussion of the issue or campaign in our terms.

Brad Woodhouse, now the President of Americans United for Change, absolutely surrounded reporters with our framing of the Social Security debate. His press shop peppered them with press releases, favorable articles from other outlets, and articles by our allies. The goal was to make *our* frame, *their* frame. It was also to make the views of the other side appear to be outside of the mainstream. After all, reporters are just as inclined as anyone to have the normal human herding mentality, perhaps even more so, since what they write about an issue or candidate is out there for everyone to see.

I used to observe herding mentality that always reminded me of the press every summer when vacationing on the Gulf Coast. For years, my mother rented a house on Navarre Beach on Florida's Panhandle. All of the family would gather there for a wonderful week.

The water was turquoise clear. The sand was white. And periodically you came across a big school of very little fish that swam near the shore. While they are small, nature has programmed these fish to swim in tightly regimented schools because that makes them more likely to survive an encroachment of a Big Fish. They turn and maneuver almost like one organism. When one fish turns, all of them turn, so quickly that it's impossible to tell who turned first.

Not being a fish expert, I don't have a clue how they communicate or signal their changes in direction, or how they "decide" to go one way or the other. But they move like big dark clouds underwater, in jerky motions, all in unison.

The press is exactly like that. They move in schools. If we want to influence their direction, we have to create a sense that the school is moving in the direction we want it to go.

It helps to send them clips from other press outlets that reflect our views and tell our story. It also helps to pitch stories to the opinion leaders of the press itself, perhaps the beat reporter or political reporter of the *New York Times*, *Washington Post*, *Wall Street Journal*, or *Los Angeles Times*. In the case of candidates, the views of the entire press corps are heavily influenced by the writing of political reporters in the home areas (often summarized in the Hotline), or by the top "nonpartisan" observer journalists like Charlie Cook of the "Cook Report" in D.C. that handicaps races.

Managing the direction of the press "school" is a key priority of good political press work.

6) CAREER ADVANCEMENT

Most reporters, journalists and columnists care a lot about winning a Pulitzer, getting invited to be on the Sunday panel on Meet the Press or Stephanopoulos, or getting a contract to be a commentator on a TV network (it also pays a lot more than most newspapers).

They care a lot about getting their stories on the front page, or having a regular column. Generally, like most people, they want to believe that their work is significant and meaningful.

We can help them do that by providing them exciting, newsworthy stories. We help them every time we provide a good quote or give them an exclusive. We help them when we work with them on stories that change policy or make a real difference to real people.

Great progressive press operatives are always thinking about how they can help specific reporters achieve their own goals. It should go without saying that great press people will do almost anything to prevent a reporter from being embarrassed because she gave him bad information or a bum steer.

The press operations of progressive organizations and candidates need to think of reporters' self-interests and career advancement as an opportunity—a source of energy to be tapped with clever ideas for stories, and good reliability and availability from our end. Understanding the needs of reporters is good press work.

7) MAINTAINING A GOOD SOURCE

Reporters need sources. If you can become one, you become a valuable asset to a reporter. If you're a valuable asset, you and your causes will generally get better treatment than otherwise. That's why White House reporters are so loathe to criticize the President. They risk being cut off —no more stories—no more insider interviews.

You can be a source that comes up with great leads for the reporter, great potential story ideas. You can just be a good source of quotes. In American journalism, reporters need to have quotes from the "other side" to make their stories look evenhanded. If you can provide an appropriately simple but meaty quote representing our side every time reporters call, and they'll keep calling.

When we put on our press events the day before the President came to town in the Social Security campaign, we tapped into that self-interest. The reporters all had to do "the President's coming" stories anyway. We provided them with content that allowed them to seem more balanced by covering our event, plus an interesting, dramatic press hook. Remember, great newspaper stories are just like great novels—*they need conflict.*

Or you can be an "off the record" source on background. Reporters need leads—they need the inside scoop. If you can provide it, you can develop a strong relationship.

Often you find reporters calling for a person with a specific demographic or experience set. "Gee, I need an 85-year-old Native American woman, who has a Hoover vacuum cleaner—know who I should call?" What a pain. But to the extent we can point to reporter the right way, the relationship pays off big time for the reporter, and makes them more likely to call again.

8) CONVENIENCE

Reporters and news crews have limited time. The more convenient it is for them to get the story, the more likely it will be covered. In general, this is like gravity. The likelihood of that an event will be covered is inversely related to the square of the distance from the news shop.

That's not to say that you should always sacrifice the content of the story for convenience. The venue may *be* the story. But all things being equal, if an event is held in the press room of the state capital, is more likely to be covered that if it is held "Yenervelt" (Yiddish for faraway).

When we're doing press work on taxes or Social Security that often means we do a press event at a state Capitol press room to pick up the written press all over the state. But we may have had to do separate events in different TV markets to get all the all-important TV and radio coverage.

Convenience is also a key when it comes to time. Good press times are between 9 a.m. and 3 p.m.—after that it's hard to get on the evening news, unless the event is so hot it could command a live feed.

Obviously, the hotter the event, the more some inconvenience is outweighed by the need for the media to get the story. When the President comes to town, there is never a bad place or time.

WHAT MAKES SOMETHING NEWSWORTHY?

Something is newsworthy if it addresses one or more of the self-interests of the press' decision makers.

News stories and events address these interests with a combination of one or more of the following three characteristics:

1) *Who Says or Does Something?*

Some stories are newsworthy just because of who it is who says or does something. Generally that's because the person is so powerful, interesting, or influential that press decision-makers think that people are interested in what they do or say.

The only real criterion here is the press assessment of viewer or reader interest—not whether it's true or deserved. Editors think people are interested in what the President says or does, so they cover him. They also think people are interested in Paris Hilton or Jennifer Lopez, so they cover them too. Perception of interest is all that matters.

In general, there is no such thing as overexposure for a "celebrity." One reason Jesse Jackson receives so much coverage is that he's famous. He's famous because he's on TV. The more he is on TV, the more famous he becomes.

Increasing the overall coverage of our stories depends, to some degree, on whether a progressive organization, or the progressive movement as a whole, has spokespeople whom the public has come to know and find interesting. The more familiar and interesting the person is, the better.

One of the ways people become interesting to the public is if the public comes to know interesting facts or characteristics about them. If the public knows a narrative or "legend" about them, it makes them more interesting.

Paris Hilton isn't a particularly talented actress or entertainer. She has made herself more interesting than the typical beautiful blonde because of the interesting, unusual things people know about her—about her lineage, about her early "acting" jobs, about her bratty attitude. They are all part of a carefully cultivated image to make her interesting to the public.

Of course, sometimes an event is newsworthy precisely because the people are unknown; or center on stories that evoke empathy, pathos, or inspiration in the viewers or listeners. In particular, people like stories about average people who have overcome long odds to achieve something important. They like stories about heroes.

2) *What Did They Say or Do?*

The *content* of the press event—what is said, done or revealed—is the next thing that makes something newsworthy. The content can be a policy decision by the UN Security Council, the release of a report, or a particularly good line or sound bite. Again, the key to making content newsworthy is to make it interesting. This requires that people feel a sense of relevancy to them and to their lives, or something else that they care about. The more unusual, unexpected, dramatic, suspenseful, or compelling, the more newsworthy it will be. The more symbolically powerful, the more newsworthy.

3) How or Where Was It Said and Done?

The third thing that can make something newsworthy is how or where it is done.

Is the event or action symbolic in and of itself? The visual or the unusual are especially important to TV, as is immediacy. TV viewers want a sense that they are experiencing a report from the scene. You don't learn more from a TV reporter who is standing in front of the police station or emergency room than you would from a TV anchor in the studio, but you feel more sense of immediacy.

As I mentioned earlier, I'm a pilot. I fly single-engine airplanes for business and family events. Over the years, that skill has been useful in organizing the "fly-around" press event. When I was Director of Illinois Public Action, I found I could really maximize electronic news coverage by doing a five-city fly-around press conference to release a study or a report.

The fact that it was a "fly around" was part of the attraction to the press: "In a five-city fly around to release a new report…"

The fact that we released a study was also considerably more compelling than the release of a "statement" or "position paper." A study with conclusions was more interesting and earned more credibility than simply stating our position.

When we were organizing events to protest the president's position on Social Security, the "how and where" were always huge parts of the story. They were more interesting to the press if they were visually proximate to the location where the President was speaking. We often announced that our people would be circulating petitions against privatization two or three days before the President arrived. Footage of people circulating petitions was always compelling, and created a hook for a story.

On the day the President actually made his pitch for privatization, this would of course be the lead story, so we had to create a means of communicating that was quick and clear. As I mentioned earlier, we printed thousands of 18-inch by 22-inch signs—black print on DayGlo yellow—that said simply: "Hands off my Social Security." As a consequence, pictures of the protest event were always dominated by a sea of signs that visually communicated our message even if all we got on the news was a background picture. The "message" wasn't simply the words on the sign—it was the sea of signs, and the angry tone. The message communicated was: lots of people are angry about the President's plan to attack our Social Security—you should be, too.

If the *how* and *where* of an event are clever, a small group of people can dominate the news at a big event.

In the early days of Illinois Public Action—even though Richard Nixon was still president—it was nevertheless the height of the "consumer movement." There was a proposal in Congress to create a Federal Department of Consumer Affairs. The administration opposed the proposal and came back with their own to create an Office of Consumer Affairs in the White House instead of a cabinet-level department. To drum up support for their proposal, they planned to conduct a series of town meetings around the country. The first was to be held in Evanston, Illinois in the auditorium of Northwestern University.

The town meeting was to be chaired by the controversial Secretary of Agriculture, a man named Earl Butz. He was joined by the President's Consumer Affairs Adviser, a woman named Virginia Knauer. Our Washington, D.C. colleagues were eager that we do something to counter the publicity blitz the White House hoped to get from a series of town meetings.

The problem was that we had just organized Illinois Public Action and didn't yet have many troops. Jan Schakowsky (who was not yet my wife) and Jackie Kendall (who would later be Director of the Midwest Academy training center) had just joined our organizing staff.

The Nixon Administration planned to bus in 500 or so people. Most were from Republican strongholds (a technique that the second Bush administration would refine to an art form). We decided that Jan and Jackie would recruit 20 or so friends from the area for two specific activities.

First, they would pass out a leaflet to everyone coming to the event, and to the press, inviting them to a "baloney and crumbs luncheon" immediately following the town meeting. Our event, said the flyer, symbolized that the administration was giving "crumbs" to consumers, and the fact that their proposal was "baloney." In fact, the "baloney and crumbs" invitations looked so "official" that for a while we actually got the ushers at the event to pass them out as the crowd arrived. That drove the organizers of the event crazy.

Second, we discovered that the organizers of the town meeting planned to take questions from the floor based on who was standing behind the six microphones spread throughout the audience. Each of our 20 or so people was given a question or statement and asked to position themselves next to a microphone before the event started.

After opening remarks, Butz and Knauer went to the audience for questions. Our people, who had been in line at microphones all over the auditorium, peppered them with criticism from every section of the hall. As our critical line of questioning proceeded, some in the Republican crowd began to agree with their questions and would applaud. In frustration, Butz finally said, "I know that *all* of you who are criticizing must not speak for *everyone* in the audience."

The event was a huge embarrassment for the administration. That night, the NBC Nightly News led with a story headlined, "Administration proposal runs into buzz saw in Chicago." The story played across the country with "B-roll" of the baloney and crumbs luncheon and sound bites of our 20 people incessantly confronting Butz and Knauer with critical questions.

The remaining White House town hall meetings were canceled.

WHICH MEDIA INFLUENCE THE VOTERS?

The relative importance of various media as sources that influence the opinions of voters has shifted over the last couple of decades.

A recent survey of voters in swing congressional districts found that local TV—including Spanish language TV and local Superstations—are the major sources of news for 38% of the voters. Here's how outlets ranked:

- Local TV (including Spanish language & local Superstations) 38%
- Cable News Networks 24%
- Newspapers (print and online) 14%
- Network News 8%
- Radio 5%

The importance of TV, and especially local TV, can't be overstated. Aside from being the most frequently watched medium, it is also the most powerful and immediate. It completely involves the viewer in its simultaneous visual and audio imagery. Many people put on the radio in the background but focus on other matters. That is much less true of TV. People have a natural tendency to look at the flickering TV screen the same way they have a natural tendency to watch a fire. That's why when you want to get romantic, it's OK to switch on "smooth jazz" on the radio but not OK to turn ESPN on TV. If you walk into a room with a television on, it's hard not to constantly glance at the screen. A press strategy that focuses only on print stories, and is not geared to TV, misses most communication.

On the other hand, the print medium often lays the foundation for what is covered on TV and elsewhere. Clippings are tangible and easily reproduced, and can be sent around to create a buzz or frame the debate.

Elite outlets like the *New York Times* and *Washington Post* are particularly important in creating a bandwagon effect of "conventional wisdom" in the media. If Robert Pear, the health beat reporter for the New York Times, reports that the President's prescription drug plan for seniors has serious problems, that sets the frame for many other outlets.

The same can be said of the wire services, and particularly the Associated Press (AP). Since the emergence of the Internet, it is especially important to ensure that the first AP story about an event frames the discussion properly. It may be posted within minutes of the press event and it will help frame everyone else's coverage. The same is true for the online stories posted early on newspaper websites.

In Washington, and many state capitals, the so-called "trade press" is also an important frame for other coverage, and for the debate in a legislative body. In DC, *Roll Call, Politico* and *Congressional Quarterly Daily* play this role and often run "inside the Beltway" stories that are very important to the internal dynamics of the political debate. This "trade press" is often the only target of a particular press story or event.

Finally, the ethnic press has substantial importance. It is often the major communication structure that defines ethnic communities.

Aside from the physical events, there are of course many ways to generate message through *earned* media. There are "leaks" from officials or their staffs, background briefings, phone conference press calls (very convenient), editorial board memos and conversations with columnists. There are exclusives to reporters and there are press releases that are not expected to generate an immediate story but rather to frame the subject for reporters.

Remember: members of the media are the *targets* for our communications, not simply the vessels through which we communicate to the public. They are a constituency that needs to be organized like any other with full cognizance of their self-interests and needs.

Uses of Radio

While radio may not be the primary source of news for many in swing markets, it is still very important. That's especially true in Hispanic and other immigrant communities where people depend upon outlets in their native tongues that broadcast their own music and community news.

Radio is also important as a means of distributing symbols that I call "political facts." "Political facts" are symbolically powerful pieces of information that help frame the debate and are extremely memorable—or "sticky." Once we get them in circulation, they are repeated over and over and come to define the conventional wisdom about a subject.

During the 1990s, I regularly served as a spokesperson for Citizen Action on various consumer issues. Frequently we had press conferences at the National Press Club in D.C. (a very convenient venue for the press corps) where we released studies containing key "political facts" that we intended to help define a debate. The principal medium we aimed at was network radio.

On one occasion, during a battle on rail safety legislation that was mostly about the transportation of toxic chemicals, there was a crash of a D.C. suburban MARC commuter train in which people were killed. We use the aftermath of the event to release a report that showed that the per-mile odds of being killed as a rail passenger was higher than the per-mile odds of being killed in an airplane crash.

That was a very interesting finding to the press and public because it was surprising. Everyone knows someone who is afraid to travel by air and goes everywhere by train instead.

This fact received wide coverage, first on network radio and then in other outlets. It was good for radio, because the entire finding could be expressed in about six seconds. It didn't require a visual or additional explanatory copy to communicate the full impact of the finding.

This political fact was the perfect backdrop for the discussion of legislation to increase rail safety.

The rail safety campaign also provided a good example of the importance of the "how and where" aspect of news worthiness. A freight train loaded with toxic material was involved in a major derailment on a track next to the Sacramento River. The Sacramento River in Northern California was one of America's premier trout streams, a kind of Mecca for trout fisherman throughout North America.

The derailment discharged toxic chemicals into the river and killed the trout and trout habitat for miles. It was sort of a small, river-based, Exxon Valdez disaster.

The day after, I flew to the city of Sacramento—some miles from the accident—to do a press conference. We called for the passage of tougher rail safety laws and the defeat of legislation that would have weakened incentives for safety.

The event was held on the bridge overlooking the Sacramento River. Because Sacramento is the state capital, a press corps representing most major networks and outlets was close by.

We could have said the same things from Chicago or Washington, but it wouldn't have been as interesting or newsworthy to the press. We received nationwide coverage of the report we released that day.

STAND UP STRAIGHT: HOW PROGRESSIVES CAN WIN

SECTION THREE · 141

Small Town and Rural Media

In many areas, local radio stations and weekly newspapers play the role of prominent local opinion molders. Often people may keep track of state and national stories on the TV, radio and newspapers from surrounding metropolitan areas. But for purely local news they depend on the local radio station and weekly newspaper.

In many rural areas, we organized media tours for candidates so they can systematically meet, and do interviews with, the local media outlets and set the stage for friendly coverage throughout the rest of the campaign. Here, too, showing up is half of politics.

These small outlets are also prone to use radio actualities (audio press releases that are run on the air) and photos taken by campaigns or organizations, where major media outlets do not.

Creating the Echo Chamber

One of our key strategic goals is to surround swing voters and our opponents with an echo chamber reflecting our values and positions—to create a sense that our views represent the consensus of the mainstream. Normally we build the echo chamber through a sequence of activities.

First we release a story utilizing earned media. Second, we simultaneously launch a paid media campaign to support the stories in the press. Then we follow up with communications generated through our grassroots. These include:

- Letters to the Editor
- Blogs
- Articles in neighborhood or alternative papers
- Call-ins to radio talk shows

Above all, we intentionally talk to Connectors, Mavens and Salesmen who get our message out through word-of-mouth. This can be done rapidly through e-mail lists or assignments for conversations with key opinion molders.

If our goal is to surround targeted members of Congress with our message, we follow up by generating calls using automated patch-throughs and call-in days using 800 numbers. Automated patch-throughs involve calling thousands of voters with an automated call to action and asking them to punch "1" on their touch tone phone, "...to be connected at no charge to Senator's_____ office." That can generate thousands of calls to Congress from constituents whenever we need them to give a Congressional office the sense that "everyone" is on our side.

Automated patch-through calls are supplemented with phone calls generated by calls to action to e-mail activist lists.

Finally, the word-of-mouth campaign can be reinforced with community meetings or presentations to key groups of opinion molders and leaders in the target area.

Using Base Media to Affect the Broader Political Dialogue

Rush Limbaugh and far-right talk radio were important because they fired up the conservative base and its entertainment value attracted an audience of other listeners. But it also served the function of driving the broader political dialogue in the mainstream media. The right-wing talkers made outrageous charges that in turn made headlines.

Today, Progressives use a combination of the blogosphere and YouTube to drive the mainstream political dialogue. We can reach their growing audiences and drive more mainstream media debate at the same time by systematically putting video clips on YouTube and working hard to get progressive blogs inside, firsthand information from Democratic officer holders and campaigns.

Blogs cannot be treated exactly like other forms of media. We can't just send them press releases. To engage bloggers we need to involve them in our organizations. Bloggers are not traditional journalists. They are high-tech "pamphleteers." To get maximum access to their readers, we need to engage them as part of progressive campaigns the same way the organizers of the American Revolution engaged people like Tom Paine.

The War Room

In the 1992 Clinton campaign, James Carville and Paul Begala set up their famous War Room communications center. Its goal was to ensure it was the Clinton Campaign that was always setting the frame on the conversation, that it was always on the offensive, and that every statement or charge of the opposition was answered in the same news cycle.

Recall that, in math, 100×0 = nothing, but with politics 100×0 = something. The more times something is repeated unanswered or communicated using the other side's framing, the more the opposition will define our candidate, our issue and the debate. If a charge in politics goes unanswered, people assume it is true—no matter how outrageous.

If you wait until the next news cycle, people will hear the unanswered charge of the opposition exclusively through their frame. Your response will also generate a second news story on day two that will *reiterate* their charge. Finally, if they are smart, they will respond to your answer, generating a *third* day of coverage to their charge.

The way to avoid this problem is simple. Answer today, in the same news cycle. Carville and the Begala set up a War Room to monitor the other side's communications and respond quickly, in real time.

This also enabled them to stay on the offensive, to define the debate. Clinton campaign manager David Wilhelm says that his first rule of political communication is that "whoever is on the offensive and defines the debate almost always wins." Or to put it another way, "If you're on the defense," he says, "you're losing."

One other lesson that Clinton himself learned late in his presidency: if there is negative news, get it out quickly and cauterize it. The worst thing that can happen is for bad news to dribble out. Accept responsibility for the problem. Stand tall. Never sound defensive. To the extent possible, don't repeat the charge. Get it all out, and then shut up. As soon as possible, change the subject, move forward and take the offensive when you do.

That's a good transition from this section's analysis of the targets of communication to the next section's discussion of how we use the rules of political communications to beat the right, and convert a political opportunity into political realignment.

SECTION FOUR

THE PRINCIPLES OF
POLITICAL COMMUNICATION

CHAPTER TWENTY

Persuadable and Mobilizable Voters

So far we've analyzed the concept of self-interest, and the groups of actors whose self-interests we must address.

We've also looked at some of the special approaches that the characteristics of each group require.

There are also *general* principles for political communication. To win, Progressives need to understand and systematically apply these principles in order to address the self-interests of every group of actors with whom we must communicate.

These general principles are particularly important in our communication with the two groups most critical to the battle—groups that we addressed briefly last section—*persuadable* and *mobilizable* voters.

Recall that persuadable and mobilizable voters are so central because in the context of elections they are the only two groups of voters whose voting behavior can be changed by a campaign.

Persuadable voters are voters that have two characteristics: they are likely to vote, and they are undecided.

Mobilizable voters also have two characteristics: they support our candidate, but they are unlikely to vote unless we mobilize them to go to the polls.

Section Five deals extensively with how to find these two groups. For now, we'll explore how to communicate with them once we've found them, as well as the general principles that apply to all political communication.

> *In an election, persuadable and mobilizable voters are never the same people—and our communication with these two distinct groups has two different goals.*

This is one of the most important rules of effective electoral politics— and one that is most often violated, forgotten and confused.

A person cannot be a persuadable voter and a mobilizable voter at the same time—by definition. Persuadable voters are very likely to vote and are undecided. Mobilizable voters are unlikely to vote unless we mobilize them, and they will vote for our candidates if they do. These are *mutually exclusive* qualities.

Our message to persuadables is intended to convince them to vote for our candidate when they cast their ballot.

Our message to mobilizables is not intended to convince them to vote for our candidate. By definition they are already likely to support our candidate. Our message to mobilizables is intended to convince them to go to the polls and cast a ballot—*to take action.*

These are very different goals, directed at two entirely different groups of people.

In elections, the subject of the campaign's persuasion message is the candidate. The subject of the mobilization message is the voter we are trying to motivate.

There is a lot of confusion about political messages. You constantly hear the media, the pundits and even political consultants tell us that the Democrats' message is about the economy, or the Republicans' message is about national security, or that one candidate's message is about education, and another's is about taxes.

This is *never* true in American politics. The subject of a campaign message is never an issue, or even a problem.

The subject of a persuasion message is always the same: the candidate or, in some political systems, the party. A political message is always about the subject of the decision we are asking people to make. With mobilization, the subject is not the candidate. It is the voter, because the voter's action is the subject of the decision we are asking the individual to make.

First let's deal with persuasion. Issues like prescription drugs or Social Security or tax cuts are often symbols that are used to describe the qualities of a candidate or party. But they are not the *subject* of the message in a political campaign.

With persuadables, our goal is to convince the voter to cast his ballot for our candidate. So, the *candidate* is the subject of the message.

If you want to prove to yourself that persuasion messages in elections are about candidates and not issues, reflect on some recent examples:

- In the 2000 election, all of the polls showed that a much greater percentage of the population supported Al Gore's positions on most critical issues than voted for Al Gore, the candidate.

- In 1984, Illinois voted overwhelmingly to reelect President Ronald Reagan. At the same time it elected Paul Simon, US Senator—a Democrat who espoused views directly contrary to those of Reagan on most critical issues.

• In 2002, former Senator Robert Torricelli & Senator Frank Lautenberg had virtually identical views on most major issues. New Jersey polls showed that former Senator Torricelli would lose overwhelmingly to the Republican in the New Jersey Senate race, yet when he was replaced on the ballot by Senator Lautenberg because of a campaign financing scandal, Lautenberg won easily.

• In 2004, one million Illinois voters supported Democrat Barack Obama for Senate and also cast their vote for George W. Bush in the Presidential race.

CHAPTER TWENTY-ONE

The Nine Qualities

There are *nine* major candidate qualities that stand out as most important in persuading undecided voters to support candidates.

More than anything else, communicating about these qualities is the key to persuading undecided voters to support our candidates—and becoming part of a lasting progressive majority.

These qualities are also the things people look for when they consider their allegiance to a political movement or party.

QUALITY # 1—IS THE CANDIDATE ON MY SIDE?

This is first and foremost, the central question of politics.

More than anything else, voters want to know if the candidate is on their side. Will she stick up for me, fight for me, help me achieve my goals, whatever they are? Will she, in other words, address the things that I have defined as my self-interests?

Partisan voters—voters who always vote Democrat or Republican— have often long since decided that candidates of the other party are simply not on their side. For decades after the Civil War, African-Americans identified the Republican Party as the Party that was on their side. It was the party of Lincoln that had championed their liberation from slavery. It was also the party of wealthy northern capital, but no matter what else it was—it was on their side in the battle that mattered most to them. It wasn't until Franklin D. Roosevelt's New Deal that African-Americans began to decide instead that Democratic candidates could be on their side. And it was finally the historic decision of Kennedy and the Democratic Party to back the civil rights movement that ultimately consolidated 90-plus percent support for Democratic candidates among African-Americans.

Persuadable voters are swing voters precisely because they have not come to identify one or the other party as solidly on their side. As a result it is far more critical that a compelling, symbolically powerful case be made that our candidate is on the swing voter's side (and often that the opponent is not). Far from steering clear of "who's on whose side" messages, we have to focus on them even more clearly.

What Factors Determine Who Appears to be "On My Side"?

The symbols used to communicate that a candidate is "on our side" can differ widely. It can in fact be the commitment of a candidate to a critical "litmus test" issue position, for example, whether he is pro-choice. It can be a story about a battle the candidate fought and won, or something about the candidate's background or heritage that makes people identify with him — "he's like us so he'll stand up for us."

Many persuadable voters in general elections have less overall interest in politics than partisan voters. As a result the "on our side" questions are the ones that are powerful enough to punch through the message clutter, and they play a disproportionate role in affecting those voters' decisions.

That's especially important because persuadable voters often perceive their self-interests in ways that do not mirror the complete package of positions taken by one of the major political parties.

We said earlier that in general the Republican Party is a coalition of rich people who hate the AFL-CIO and poor people who hate the ACLU, while the Democratic Party is a coalition of rich people who hate the Moral Majority and poor people who hate Mutual of Omaha.

To win, each party needs both its "economic wing" and its "social policy" wing. But individual voters often do not share the views of both wings of their respective party. A "Log Cabin Republican" may be socially liberal, but share his party's views on economic and tax policy. While a "Reagan Democrat" may hold a populist economic world view and very conservative social values.

In any given election, these "conflicted" voters will move one way or another depending on which set of their own self-interests they feel are most important at that particular time and place. That has a lot to do with who is controlling the political dialogue at the time of the election, or the events dominating the news. And it has a lot to do with how the competing candidates frame the symbols which they use to vie for voters' allegiances.

Quality # 2 — Does the Candidate Have Strongly Held Values–Is He Committed to Something Other than Himself?

Voters want leaders who want to serve in public office, who want to lead them because they believe in something other than their own personal advancement or status. When voters say that someone is a "typical politician," what they usually mean is that he really doesn't believe in anything — that he will say or do anything to get elected — that he puts his finger in the wind to decide what he believes — that he is afraid to take a tough position.

Appearing to be a leader who has strong core values, stands up for something and talks straight is not just the right thing to do. It is also good politics.

Senator John McCain's popularity was largely built on the notion that he is a straight shooter who stood up for what he believes, even when there is some cost to it.

When John Kennedy published *Profiles in Courage* in 1956, it wasn't just to celebrate the moral fiber of those that went before. He wanted to identify himself with other men who stood up for what they believed. He knew that would be good politics.

One of Al Gore's most politically damaging qualities in 2000 was that he came off as a dissembler—as if he was always dancing around the truth. That wasn't true at all but it seemed true, the way he trimmed his language and carefully choose his words.

Voters want clear straightforward language. Right-wing commentator Tucker Carlson tells a story about George Bush in the January 19, 2003 *New York Times Magazine:*

> The day I arrived, Bush held a news conference to explain his views on the war in Kosovo. He proceeded to mangle almost every word. Bush referred to 'Mylo-sovack' (commonly known as Milosevic), then talked at some length about the 'Kosovanians' and our allies 'the Grecians.' I was shocked. This may work in Texas, I thought, but the rest of the country won't tolerate this level of inarticulateness in a presidential candidate. As it turned out, the rest of the country didn't care. If anything, voters interpreted Bush's dyslexia as candor. At least he's not slick, was the idea. [1]

This critical lesson of politics, many politicians never figure out: being mealy-mouthed does not convince a single swing voter. Voters, and especially swing voters, hate politicians who weave and bob to avoid being pinned down. They want clear, committed, and unafraid. If taking a position appears to be somewhat dangerous, so much the better.

And voters don't just want commitment. They want passion. They want candidates who have deeply held beliefs that they will advocate with zeal. Lukewarm is not a politically attractive characteristic.

In 2002 lots of consultants counseled that Democrats should avoid taking a principled position opposing the Bush tax cuts—which mostly benefited the rich. They argued that then Democrats couldn't be "accused" of supporting higher taxes. The problem was that not taking on the President's tax breaks meant failing to differentiate Democratic bottom-up economic program from the Republican's top-down, trickle-down program.

In the end the Democratic Party looked like it was desperately trying not to be accused of anything. As a result, Democrats didn't stand for anything, and far from helping Democrats win, that helped guarantee our defeat.

Swing voters don't want leaders who will duck fights. They want leaders who will pick the right fights—that is, fights on their behalf. And they want leaders who will pick those fights not only because they seem to be important politically, but because they believe they are right.

Standing up for what you believe is an independent variable in voters' evaluation of a candidate. It often doesn't even matter if voters agree with you. When Ronald Reagan was President you'd hear people say: "Well, I don't agree with him, but he sure stands up for what he believes."

Swing voters—by definition—are less committed to highly partisan positions than partisan voters. If they were highly partisan, they wouldn't be swing voters in the first place. So they are heavily impacted by qualities like the degree of commitment shown by a candidate in the defense of his or her views.

Just ask John Kerry. In the 2004 presidential election, Republicans believed that they could convince a critical mass of persuadable voters that John Kerry wasn't committed to core values—that he was *a flip-flopper*. They decided that this quality would be the critical element that they would drill in on during the campaign.

They knew that Kerry was prone to "Senate speak," a disease that widely affects senators and helps explain why one had not become President since John Kennedy's election 45 years ago. "Senate speak" makes it difficult or impossible for senators to speak in short declarative sentences, to get to the point, to take clear, *unequivocal* stands. It seems to require its victims to speak in long convoluted paragraphs, replete with qualifiers. Kerry had a particularly severe case.

Karl Rove also realized that Kerry's vote for the Iraq War, and then against continued funding in 2004, could be portrayed as the symbolically powerful flip-flop. The icing on the cake was Kerry's explanation of the 2004 vote: "I voted for it before I voted against it."

After the election, Rove referred to Kerry's Iraq votes as "the gift that kept on giving."

Not long after the election, I was in a New Jersey taxicab. The driver was a typical male New Jersey cabbie. "So what do you think of Corzine?" I asked. "Oh, Corzine, tough guy. Like him," he replied about the then-Senator.

"What do you think of Bush?" I said. "Like him too. Tough guy. Stands up for what he believes," came the answer.

"What about Kerry?" I asked. "Kerry? Can't stand him. Flip-flopper."

"How about Hillary Clinton?" I asked. "Tough gal. Like her," he said.

Ideology, policy positions—none of that mattered to this cabdriver who liked Corzine, Clinton and Bush. He wanted a tough, committed leader. But the Republicans had sold him on its core message—"John Kerry is a flip-flopper."

It's generally very hard to hide or finesse your core beliefs, and because swing voters are more concerned with whether you have strong beliefs than your content, it's usually a bad idea to try.

I'm not suggesting that candidates flaunt disagreements with key constituencies—they generally shouldn't. They should lead with the things that prove the case that they are truly "on your side."

But a candidate shouldn't try to duck disagreements either. One reason, of course, is that your opponent generally won't let you. If you try, you not only highlight your position, you make it look like you're trying to hide it, or aren't sure where you stand and have no moral convictions.

I learned this lesson when I was 16 years old, and it snowed in my hometown of Shreveport, Louisiana. When it snows in Shreveport, everything stops and the schools let out. Well, this snowstorm happened right in the middle of Mardi Gras, so a friend and I set off on the train to stay with his brother in New Orleans and partake in the Mardi Gras fun.

In the course of that trip, we were naïvely—and with wide eyes—walking down Bourbon Street, when a big hawker at a strip joint said something that taught me an important lesson in life and politics. He said: "Come on in, sonny, they're going to say you did anyway."

The Republicans are going to attack Progressives for our core beliefs regardless. We are much better off proudly standing by them than we are trying to finesse them and looking like we have no commitment to our values.

This goes for tough votes for sitting members of legislative bodies as well. When members are called upon to take votes that they worry might be unpopular, it is generally better to vote your convictions, even when the outcome is not at stake.

In most circumstances, members will have to defend tough votes, to the media and to constituents one way or the other. Jan's view has always been that it is better and easier to defend a vote or position you believe in than to have to defend a position you really don't believe is right.

In 2004 the Democratic campaign talked on and on about policies and programs. Bush talked about right and wrong.

Swing voters want to know about the values of their candidates and leaders. They are much less interested in the specifics of an education or health care policy. To most voters, particularly swing voters—this just sound like "blah, blah, blah."

QUALITY # 3—IS THE CANDIDATE A STRONG, EFFECTIVE LEADER?

All things being equal, voters aren't just interested in leaders who stand up for them. They would prefer leaders who are successful at standing up for them. They want leaders who deliver—leaders who project competency—and who actually produce what they promise.

Communicating that a leader gets things done, and has a record of success, can be a critical message for swing voters.

But don't bet that a record of effectiveness alone will carry the day. Candidates who try to position themselves as competent technocrats can be blown away by candidates who communicate that they are "on your side."

Take Michael Dukakis. In 1988 he ran for President arguing that he would be the most effective candidate, that he was in fact the most competent to govern. He argued that he stood for politics that was "beyond ideology." Of course ideology, at its core, is about who is on whose side.

At the end of the Democratic Convention in 1988, Dukakis led George Bush by 18%. Bush proceeded to eviscerate Dukakis with advertisements that chose several powerful symbols to communicate that Dukakis was not on the side of average Americans and won by a landslide in the general election.

Dukakis had touted the economic "Massachusetts Miracle" and said he wanted to "Do for America what he had done for Massachusetts." Bush's campaign turned that goal on its head.

Bush ran a vicious ad attacking the Dukakis failure to clean up Boston Harbor… "And now he wants to do for America what he's done for Massachusetts… America can't afford that risk."

He said that Dukakis had failed to back legislation that would restrict drug sales near schools… "And now he wants to do for America what he's done for Massachusetts."

He ran ads that highlighted Dukakis' record of raising taxes and said: "Now he wants to do for America what he's done for Massachusetts. America can't afford that risk."

Finally, Bush ran ads that revolved around the furlough program of the Massachusetts prison system. Those furloughs included the infamous "Willie Horton," who committed a brutal rape, kidnapping and armed assault while on furlough. Horton was African-American, and the ads played on white fear of black crime. The ad ended once again: "Now he wants to do for America what he's done for Massachusetts. America can't afford that risk."

Bush convinced swing voters that no matter how "competent" Dukakis claimed to be, he wasn't on their side.

People would rather have a weak leader who is on their side than a strong leader who is against them—and they should.

People want strong, effective leadership, but they want strong, effective leaders who are working *for* their interests—not against them.

In the early stages of the George W. Bush administration, one of its major strengths was the notion that Bush and his people had strongly-held beliefs and were competent at executing them.

Then came Katrina. Hurricane Katrina in September 2005 ripped the curtain off the "Great Oz." It displayed gross incompetence for everyone to see. That included a FEMA director whose main qualifications were his Republican credentials and his history representing Arabian horse owners.

The resulting Katrina calamity shook the confidence of swing voters, not only in the ability of the administration to handle emergencies like Katrina, but its competence at everything it did. That spilled over into people's confidence in the administration's ability to run the war in Iraq and prepare for another potential terrorist attack.

Quality # 4—Is the Candidate Self-Confident?

Voters want their leaders to be self-confident. They want leaders who believe that they can be successful. And voters can sense a lack of self-confidence the way a dog senses fear.

The Republicans allegedly won the Presidency in 2000 with 500,000 fewer votes than Al Gore. All the national polling showed that the Bush program was not particularly popular. His centerpiece tax-cut proposal was low on the priority list for most Americans—and downright unpopular when they found out that most of the benefits went to the top 5% of the population.

Yet Bush and the Republicans in Congress proceeded as if they had an absolute mandate. They delivered for their core constituencies—rich people and oil companies—without any hesitation or apology. They laid out their priorities clearly and they delivered.

Voters don't like losers (or whiners). They want leaders who think of themselves as winners. They want leaders who are positive and optimistic. People want to be around winners. Part of the reason for that is that people think of themselves as winners and don't want to hang out with losers.

In a classic psychological study, a random sample was asked to rank themselves on "the ability to get along with others," all subjects, 100%, put themselves in the top half of the population. Sixty percent placed themselves in the top 10%, 25% put themselves in the top 1%. Seventy percent rated themselves in the top quartile in leadership; only 2 percent felt they were below-average leaders. Sixty percent of the males said they were in the top quartile of athletic ability; 6% said they were below average.

The minute someone believes that a politician is, or might be successful, their interest in and their attraction to that person increases, as does their willingness to follow them. If you want people to volunteer to work for your candidacy, you don't tell them how bad things are going and beg for help, you tell them how well things are going and challenge them to get involved on a winning team.

That's one reason why candidates for President pick up so much support when they win a couple of primaries. Voters who never considered supporting him before decide to jump on the bandwagon. People respond both to the notion of being part of the mainstream and also to their desire to be "winners."

Of course, none of this should come as a surprise. The bandwagon effect is well known in economics, in marketing, in high school popularity contests—in every aspect of life.

The surest indication that someone thinks of himself as a loser is his unwillingness to stand up for himself or his beliefs. In the 2002 elections, Republicans savaged Democratic Senator Max Cleland of Georgia for being "unpatriotic" since he insisted on protecting the rights of the Homeland Security Department's workers to belong to a union. Max Cleland was a wheelchair-bound veteran and war hero who had lost three limbs in Vietnam. The fact that Democrats let Republicans get away with this characterization is astonishing on its face. But it resulted from Democratic unwillingness to vigorously defend its leaders.

In a speech before the 2003 House Democratic Caucus Retreat, former President Clinton argued that a similar Republican attack on then-Senate Majority Leader Tom Daschle's patriotism in vicious South Dakota TV Commercials should have caused the rest of the Senate Democrats to halt all work in the Senate until the Republicans withdrew the outrageous spots. He was right.

Al Gore's refusal to defend and run on the eight-year record of the Clinton-Gore administration sent the message that he was not self-confident about that record—and his association with Bill Clinton; it was something to be ashamed of. Why in the world would voters want four more years of a record that someone seemed to be ashamed of?

One of the most astounding aspects of the 2004 Presidential race was the right's willingness to attack Kerry's war record and the Kerry campaign's failure to counterattack.

George Bush, let's recall, basically went AWOL during the Vietnam

War. He joined the National Guard to avoid being drafted and sent to Vietnam. Then he got himself transferred to a duty station in Alabama where he worked on a Congressional Race and never showed up for his National Guard drill.

Kerry, on the other hand, was a decorated Vietnam War hero who had returned home and made a name for himself as a warrior who had come to oppose the war that most Americans increasingly believed was a mistake.

The idea that the Bush campaign would, or could, put Kerry on the defensive about his war record was preposterous.

The Kerry campaign knew how important Kerry's war hero credentials were to the country's desire for strong, effective, self-confident leadership. As Democratic consultant David Axelrod says, they practically turned the 2004 Democratic Convention into a VFW rally.

But when a Republican front group came with the now famous "Swift Boat" ads attacking Kerry's war record, Kerry and the campaign failed to rise to the challenge.

Their decision on how to respond was complicated by the fact that the Democratic Convention was a full five weeks before the Republican Convention. That meant that Kerry's federal campaign money would have to last five weeks longer than the Republicans' money had to. It made them reluctant to go up with paid counterattack ads.

But the Kerry campaign missed the key point. At issue was not the factual basis of the attacks. The goal of the attacks was to cloud and confuse Kerry's massive advantage over Bush as a strong, effective leader with enough integrity to take his responsibilities seriously. While Kerry was serving America, Bush kicked back and hoisted a few brews as he "worked" on the campaign of one of his dad's pals.

The Republicans intended to define Kerry in August, intentionally timing it just as swing voters were beginning to focus their attention on the race. First impressions mean a lot, and the Republicans had used the August strategy successfully many times before. The attacks came as no surprise.

But what if Kerry had walked out of his house the day after the first attack and said to the press: "If George Bush wants to make our war records an issue in this campaign, I challenge him to come right here, right now and debate man-to-man over who had a war record during the Vietnam conflict that he can be proud of. Stop hiding behind little fake groups like the so-called 'Swift boat Veterans' and debate me face to face."

That kind of counterattack would have defined him as a self-confident leader, with the strength and commitment to defend his values. *A winner.*

Voters want self-confident leaders who believe they are winners.

Political campaigns or candidates who don't believe they can win, rarely do.

QUALITY # 5—DOES THE CANDIDATE RESPECT ME?

Given people's overriding need for meaning in their lives, it is no surprise that they want leaders who respect them.

Voters will forgive political leaders for momentary lapses in competency, or for taking an incorrect position here or there, but they have a hard time forgiving being disrespected. Disrespecting the voters is one of the few cardinal sins of politics.

Bill Clinton was marvelous at showing people he respected them. He never talked down to a group, or appeared to be lecturing them. He always seemed to be genuinely glad to be with people. He would speak to people using clear, understandable language but he never seemed to "dumb down" the argument or imply people wouldn't understand.

The "tough on immigration" policy of the right in the Republican Party clearly communicates to Hispanics that Republicans are "not on their side." But even more importantly, it communicates a lack of respect. The same goes for the "English only" movement.

Republican Senator Mel Martinez of Florida has been a key Republican point man in trying to move Hispanics to the Republican column. He has been frustrated by many of his Republican colleagues. "When they start saying that it's un-American to have ballots printed in Spanish, it sends a message that we're not wanted, not respected," he said in the *Washington Post*. [2]

In a 2006 vote, 181 House Republicans supported a ban on bilingual ballots, but nearly all Democrats and a minority of Republicans joined to defeat the measure.

Of course this kind of disrespect borders on contempt. People who are great political leaders never show contempt for their constituents. Contempt is, after all, the mirror opposite of respect.

Malcolm Gladwell reports that for 20 years, a psychologist named John Gottman has brought thousands of married couples to his lab at the University of Washington to measure what he calls their SPAFF (specific affect). SPAFF is a coding system that measures the emotional interactions between couples during a conversation.

He asks couples to have conversations about some aspect of their relationship. Their conversation is videotaped and emotional states are coded: disgust, for instance, is a 1, contempt 2, sadness 12 and so on.

Based on the analysis of the videotape, his SPAFF can predict with 95% certainty whether the couple will be married in 15 years. Pretty amazing.

He has found that the most important predictors are four emotions: defensiveness, stonewalling, criticism and contempt. If one of the partners in the marriage exhibits contempt for the other, that is the single most important sign the marriage is in trouble.

Gottman explains that, "Contempt is qualitatively different than criticism. With criticism, I might say to my wife, "You never listen, you're really selfish and insensitive".... But if I speak from a superior place, that's far more damaging, and contempt is any statement made from a higher level. A lot of the time it's an insult: 'You're a bitch. You're scum.' It's trying to put that person on a lower plane than you." [3]

Gottman has even found that the presence of contempt in a marriage can predict things like the number of colds someone gets. Apparently having someone you love express contempt for you is so stressful it affects the functioning of the immune system.

Expressing contempt for someone objectifies them—it makes them less than fully human.

Expressing respect has the opposite effect. It makes someone feel empowered. Jesse Jackson's trademark chant at meetings of the Rainbow PUSH coalition is "I am...*Somebody.*"

Everybody wants to be somebody. Everyone wants to have a meaningful life.

Respect for voters and subordinates is communicated in many different ways. One of them is how you approach persuasion and decision-making. In 2006 George Bush famously said that he was the "decider" and, in effect, the power of other Republicans and Democrats in Congress was simply irrelevant. People were angry because he disrespected them—he had shown contempt for them and for Congress.

In 1843, well before he was elected President, Abraham Lincoln made a speech to the Springfield Temperance society, where he clearly articulated the philosophy regarding persuasion that would follow him to the White House:

> *When the conduct of men is designed to be influenced, persuasion—kind, unassuming persuasion—should ever be adopted. It is an old and true maxim that a "drop of honey catches more flies than a gallon of gall." So with men. If you would win a man to your cause, first convince him that you are his sincere friend. Therein is a drop of honey that catches his heart, which, say what he will, is the great high road to his reason, and which when once again, you will find that little trouble in convincing his judgment of the justice of your cause, if indeed that cause really be a just one. On the contrary, assume to dictate to his judgment, or to command his action, or to mark him as one*

to be shunned and despised, and he will retreat within himself, close all the avenues to his head and his heart; and tho' your cause be the naked truth itself... you shall no more be able to reach him, than to penetrate the hard shell of a tortoise with a rye straw.

Such is man, and so must he be understood by those who would lead him, even to his own best interest.

Donald Phillips in his book on Lincoln's leadership style says, "He treated people the way you would want to be treated, the way he knew others wanted to be treated... People generally want to believe that what they are doing truly makes a difference, and more importantly, that it is their own idea." [4]

This of course is an obvious fact of human nature that the advocates of the theory of *"grab them by the balls and their hearts and minds will follow"* have gotten wrong from Vietnam in the 1960s to Iraq in 2006.

As the earlier discussion of marriage makes clear, there is a strong connection between showing people respect and whether or not they make an emotional connection with you. That is the key to the 6th quality.

Quality # 6 — Do the Voters Like or Make An Emotional Connection with the Candidate?

Ask Al Gore if this is not a critically important quality.

When he ran for president in 2000, people just couldn't seem to "connect" with him. Gore was "stiff." The chemistry was never right.

It is hard to exaggerate the importance of candidate likeability as a factor in electoral politics. It is important at every level. You can win without it, but it's a lot harder. And if you have it, it can make up for a multitude of other sins and deficits.

Of all the qualities candidates must communicate to voters, establishing an emotional connection—making people like you—is often one of the most difficult.

Campaigns can develop very straightforward strategies to communicate that a candidate is on the voter's side, or that she is committed to a set of values, or that she is a strong, effective leader. But creating "likeability," or an emotional bond with the voters, often requires changing the most fundamental and highly ingrained aspects of a candidate's personality. At the very least it can involve calling attention to certain aspects of the candidate's persona, and de-emphasizing others.

Notwithstanding this difficulty, there are a variety of rules that can substantially increase the ability of any candidate to emotionally connect with voters.

Because of the importance of this quality, for the next few pages we'll take a quick detour to discuss some of those tactics. Not surprisingly many have to do with respect. Respect and likeability are closely related. Tactics for the candidate:

• *Making an Emotional Connection with the electorate is having a love affair with the voters — a courtship*

To understand what is necessary to make an emotional connection with the electorate, you need to think about the problem the way you would think about a courtship. Making an emotional connection with voters is not about poll numbers or issue positions. It is about emotional energy exchanged between people. It's about feelings, not rational judgments. It is about how you make people feel in your presence and when they see you on TV.

And just like a love affair, it's more about how you make people feel about *themselves* than it is how they feel about *you*.

When you relate to them, do you make them feel happy, empowered, energized, uplifted, interested, respected, liked, cared about, important, meaningful, safe or loved? Or do you make them feel depressed, bored, unimportant, insignificant, disrespected, unloved, at risk — or something between these extremes?

• *People like you if you appear to like and respect them*

This is the first rule of emotional connection. You have to convince the voters that you like and respect them before you can expect them to like and respect you. If voters think you believe you are better than they are, or that you don't like to mingle with them, or that you don't like people in general, they won't connect with you.

When you speak to them, tell them how good it feels to be with a group like theirs. Tell them how much you feel at home with them, that they are like family. Mingle with them. Laugh with them. If it's your style, dance with them, and toast with them.

• *When you speak to them, talk about how you feel, not just what you think*

People are much more likely to make an emotional connection with you if they have a glimpse of your emotions. They want to know that you're not just some preprogrammed wind-up doll delivering poll-tested jargon. They want to know that you feel the things they feel. An emotional connection is about bonding between you and the voters. To bond with you, they need a sense of emotional intimacy. This is also a critical element of communicating that you are on their side. If you can feel what they feel, the voters are inclined to think you must understand them and their needs, and they believe they understand the things you truly value.

• *Half of Politics is Showing Up*

Showing up at their events, having dinner with them, and mingling with them communicates more than any single act that you like them, that you respect them enough to take the time to be there, that you think they are important, and that you identify with them. Of course, this also helps with the primary problem of convincing people that you are on *their side.*

Every little appearance at a school event, an ethnic dinner, a union function, communicates: "I like you," "I respect you," "I like to spend time with you," "You are important to me."

You don't need to stay for the entire event. And if it appears that you really went out of your way to be there, so much the better.

• *Always seem happy to be there*

No matter how much you'd rather be at home with the kids or watching a ball game, always communicate how happy you are to be there. In a love affair, the last thing you want is a lover who behaves as if it is an imposition to spend time with you, or to talk on the phone, or to be intimate with you. You don't want a lover to be with you out of a sense of *obligation.* You want your lover to be excited to see you, to look forward to being with you.

Your love affair with the voters is the same way. You don't want them to think that you are doing them a favor by showing up at their reception, or that you are with them because you feel an obligation. You want them to know that you are genuinely excited to spend time with them—that you want them as much as they want you (or as much as you want them to want you).

• *Focus on each individual you talk to as if he is the only person in the world*

When you go to an event, when you're out campaigning, or when you do the official functions of an office holder, focus on each person in a way that lets him know you think he is important. One of the greatest political skills (and it can be a learned skill) is to make the person you are talking to believe that you think they are the most important person on earth, at least for that moment. The goal of each encounter should be to establish a highly focused *connection* with the individual. The goal is *intimacy*, even if it is momentary.

The opposite of this focused connection is the politician who is always looking over his shoulder to see if there is someone more important that he should be meeting.

Bill Clinton and Barack Obama are both masters of making you feel you are the only person in the room.

• *Take Time with People*
Don't make people feel that you are in a hurry to get away from them to go do something "more important." Try to have a relaxed and focused look when you talk to them, convey that you are fully there in the moment. Don't look nervously at your watch.

It is useful to have a staffer whose job it is to get you out of overly-long conversations, or to move you to the next event by pulling you away. This way, someone else is the bad guy; you would take all the time in the world with that person....but you *can't*.

•*The key to establishing a focused connection is your eyes*
The most important, single factor in establishing an intimate, focused connection is looking people in the eye. Remember from Section Three that it allows people to "read your mind" through your facial expressions and vice versa. That's why eye contact is the key to intimacy.

If you look in other directions when you talk to someone, the message you send is that you aren't interested in them; it's as if your thoughts are elsewhere, or that you are trolling for a more important conversation. And if your eyes dart back and forth (a la Richard Nixon), you look shifty-eyed and untrustworthy.

• *Touching connects you to people—the importance of the handshake*
The first page of the novel Primary Colors puts it best:

> We shook hands. My inability to recall that particular moment more precisely is disappointing: the handshake is the threshold act, the beginning of politics. I've seen him do it two million times now, but I couldn't tell you how he does it, the right-handed part of it—the strength, quality, duration of it, the rudiments of pressing the flesh. I can, however, tell you a whole lot about what he does with his other hand. He is a genius with it. He might put it on your elbow, or up by your biceps: these are basic, reflexive moves. He is interested in you. He is honored to meet you. If he gets any higher up your shoulder—if he, say, drapes his left arm over your back, it is somehow less intimate, more casual. He'll share a laugh or a secret then—a light secret, not a real one—flattering you with the illusion of conspiracy. If he doesn't know you all that well and you've just told him something 'important,' something earnest or emotional, he will lock in and honor you with a two-hander, his left hand overwhelming your wrist and forearm. He'll flash that famous misty look of his. And he will mean it." [5]

Touching, and the handshake in particular, is important to establishing intimacy and emotional connection. Some candidates are more at ease as "touchers" than others, but to the extent a candidate can master the art of the handshake, the hand on the shoulder, holding the hand of the older constituent—these are powerful tools.

• *If you make people think they are important in your presence, they will like you*

If you want people to make an emotional connection with you as a candidate, you need to make them feel important and respected in your presence. Of course, the very act of showing up to an event or meeting with them communicates this message. But it is important to remember when you make a speech or talk to them one on one, or raise money from them, that your major goal is not to convince them that you are important, but rather, it is to make them *feel* important as a result of your interaction with them.

Here are some examples of how this principle plays out:

• **The Fundraising Message**

A candidate might leave the following message on voicemail when calling to raise money: "Joan, I'm calling you because the polls show that if I just raise an additional $100,000 for TV, I have a good shot at winning the election. I'd really appreciate your help."

This is not a bad fundraising message, but it is entirely about the *candidate*. A better message is: "I'm calling successful women like you who, I hope, are interested in helping to elect at least one woman to the Maryland delegation to Congress." Here we have a message that makes the recipient feel important and addresses the recipient's interest—not just the candidate's interest.

• **The Speech Theme**

Campaign speeches should not focus entirely on what you the candidate have done, or what you believe in. They should focus on the issues and concerns of the people you're talking to. When you talk about yourself, tell a story that makes it clear from your history that you understand the lives and concerns of the audience. Don't tell stories that celebrate how smart or effective you are. Tell stories about how important other people are.

• **Complimenting the Audience**

If you can, always compliment your audience on how effective or significant they have been. People want to know that you have noticed what they have done, that it is important to you. They need to feel empowered by their relationship with you. For example: "First, let me congratulate your organization on the extraordinary work it did to get a new park in the neighborhood."

Have your staff or advisers brief you on examples of these accomplishments before you meet with a group.

• *There is no such thing as too much flattery*

People never tire of being flattered. I am not suggesting that you make things up, but however you can find to compliment someone—no matter how small—is worth a mention. In fact the more specific you are about your compliment the better; it shows you are really paying attention.

You might fear that people will think you're just "sucking up." They won't. They will love it. This goes for people more famous and powerful than yourself; it also goes for the poorest, most marginal person you will meet. Everyone loves to be flattered, even if they think you've slightly exaggerated, because it implies that you think they are important and meaningful enough to be flattered.

• *Most People Think of Themselves as Winners. You Need to Treat Them as Winners*

Good leaders create systems designed to produce winners. They are constructed to celebrate the winning once it occurs.

Attribution Theory is the study of the way we assign cause for success or failure. The fundamental "attribution error" is that we treat success as our own, and failure as "the system's." If things go well, it is quite clear that "I made it happen," "I am talented," etc. If something bad happens, "It's them," "It's the system." People tune out if they feel they are failing, because "the system" is to blame. They tune in when the system leads them to believe they are successful. They learn that they can get things done because of skill and they are likely to try again.

Researchers studying motivation find that the prime factor is simply the self-perception among motivated subjects that they are, in fact, doing well. Whether they are or not by any absolute standard doesn't seem to matter much.

Warren Bennis: "In a study of school teachers, it turned out that when they held high expectations of their students, that alone was enough to cause an increase of 25 points in the students' IQ scores."[6]

You will be more successful making an emotional connection with a voter if the voter feels more successful (or potentially successful) in your presence—or as a result of your speech—or by virtue of the way you inspire him. You will also be more apt to inspire him to participate in your campaign and he in turn will be more enthusiastic in motivating other voters.

• *Most of your conversations with voters should involve asking them questions about themselves or their thoughts—not telling them about yourself*

People love to be asked. It is an indication that what they have to say is important. And of course it is. You won't understand people's self-interests or concerns—the things that motivate them—unless you ask them. And you will make a much more powerful connection—a much more intimate connection—if you ask them about their lives.

Too many politicians spend far too much of their time telling instead of asking.

• *Use humor if you can—especially self-effacing humor*

People love humor. They like people who are funny and interesting. They also like people who don't take themselves so seriously that they can laugh—especially at themselves.

Self-effacing humor is especially good at taking the sting out of your own personality deficits. Gore helped his cause considerably by making jokes about being boring. George W. Bush does well when he points out his own shortcomings as a speaker or when he says that he has made the world safe for "C" students. A candidate who is arrogant or aloof can do a lot to increase the level of emotional connection by laughing at his own crotchety style.

• *It's good to be tough. It's bad to be mean*

People want leaders who are tough, who fight for their interests. But they don't like leaders who are mean—just ask Newt Gingrich.

You have to be careful not to appear petty or gratuitously vengeful.

• *In fact, people prefer leaders who they consider fundamentally kind and generous, and people who empathize with the feelings of everyday people and truly care about them*

Being a tough, effective leader who is willing to make the hard decisions is important. People don't want leaders who are sappy and unwilling to make the hard calls. But if you want them to develop an emotional connection to you, they need to believe that you are a fundamentally kind, generous person who genuinely empathizes with people and cares about them.

That means you should try to be generous. Compliment your adversaries on occasion. Always give credit to the people who work with you rather than yourself. Tell stories that indicate you empathize with people's problems and feelings. Don't get a reputation for constantly being critical of other people—even your adversaries.

• *Smile*
Ronald Reagan was the master at smiling. He would say the most outrageous things that would sound "grandfatherly" because he smiled as he said them.

Remember, most communication is nonverbal. If you want people to think you like them, smile at them. A smile communicates on a very basic primordial level that you like the person who sees it. A frown communicates just the opposite. Remember, people won't like you if they do not believe that you like them.

This is particularly true of appearances on TV. Television greatly exaggerates facial expressions. Try to smile most of the time on TV, even if you are saying something tough or forceful.

And remember to smile whenever someone takes a picture, unless it is a very serious occasion.

• *Be On Time*
There aren't many things more disrespectful than being late. Every effort should be made to arrive on time for campaign events and meetings. It communicates respect. It also sends the message that you are an effective person who runs a spit and polish operation.

• *Don't Whine*
Don't ever whine. Don't whine about how tired you are, or how many events you have to go to, or how difficult your job is. People hate it. Their view is that no one begged you to run for public office in the first place. They think there would be lots of other people who would gladly do your job—so if it's too tough, don't run for office.

Whining communicates that you view yourself as a victim or a spoiled brat—not as a strong, effective leader who is in command of his or her life. And it leads people to dislike you because it communicates that you don't like the campaigning that fundamentally involves being with them.

Always maintain the appearance of a positive, winning attitude.

Because people like to think of themselves as winners, they also like to support winners. You need to communicate—even in the bleakest moments—that you expect to win. You need to communicate that winning attitude through what you say, through your tone of voice, through the expressions on your face, through your posture—and most of all through your overall demeanor.

As the candidate, you set the tone for the campaign. No one likes to be around losers!

Visualize victory. Practice believing you can win. Think about what it will be like to win. You may end up being more disappointed if you lose in the end, but the odds of your actually winning will go up, because more people will make an emotional connection with you.

- *Always know to whom you're talking*

Every speech you make should be tailored to communicate to the audience that you are aware of whom you are talking to—that you understand the audience, their interests and needs. Generally, this requires good staff work and a quick briefing.

It may not require a major alteration in the basic stump speech. A few simple references to the group's accomplishments or major interests and to its leaders may suffice.

- *It helps to demonstrate that you are close to a group's leaders or that you have some other common bond with them*

Intimacy with a group grows enormously when you can demonstrate that you have something in common. Did a relative grow up in the country of their origin? Do you know someone who is his or her neighbor? Have you worked with the head of their senior center? Is there a story you know about one of their leaders? Did you have a common experience with one of their members—or with someone they know?

An easy technique is to mention the name of the spouse or children of one of the leaders of the group; that generates instant intimacy. Again this requires good staffing.

- *Acknowledge key leaders—and other political figures that are present*

Of course you can go overboard with this. But it is generally good to acknowledge several of the group's key leaders. They will love it, since it makes them look important. Just as importantly, it makes you look intimate with the group.

Before each speaking engagement, get a briefing from your staff or someone in the group on the key people who need to be recognized.

Acknowledging other political leaders who may be present, even your adversaries, makes you look generous and self-confident.

- *People love to be thanked*

You can't go overboard thanking people. When people help you, they love to be thanked, and they expect it.

Sending personal notes, or hand-written notes on computer-generated letters, makes a big impression on contributors or other supporters.

Calling people with the sole purpose of thanking them makes an enormous impact. Calls make people feel very important and tell them in no uncertain terms that you like them.

Systematic "thank you" programs in a large campaign require discipline, but they are absolutely worth it.

• *Write Notes*

In general personal notes are enormously useful and communicate that someone is special. You can use them to thank people, or to acknowledge some accomplishment (e.g., "I saw the letter to the editor you wrote today—it was terrific"). You can use them to acknowledge special events (e.g., "I understand you have a new grandson—congratulations"). You can use them to make people feel special about the job they did (e.g., "That was a terrific speech at today's meeting. Thanks for your clear sense of direction").

Writing notes like these doesn't take much time—especially if you have a staff assistant or secretary who takes dictation. Do them in the car on the way to work, or as you read the paper and see something you want to acknowledge.

People love to be acknowledged.

• *Don't try to be someone you can't be*

Every candidate is different. When it comes to making an emotional connection with the voters, everyone is not Bill Clinton. You don't have to be Richard Gere for someone to fall in love with you. You don't have to be Bill Clinton for a voter to like you.

Every candidate needs to play to her or his strengths. On the other hand, a number of the rules we just discussed involve learned skills or procedures that anyone can acquire and can be facilitated by good staffing.

As a candidate, there is no excuse for failing to do the best you can to make an emotional connection with the voters, and it may be the difference between victory and defeat.

QUALITY # 7—DOES THE CANDIDATE HAVE INTEGRITY?

All things being equal, voters want their leaders to be honest, both in their public and personal lives.

In particular, they don't want leaders to lie to them. They are especially offended by candidates who are hypocrites—who say one thing and do another. Ask Congressman Mark Foley of Florida, who chaired the Congressional Caucus on Abused and Neglected Children while he sent sexually explicit text messages to under aged Congressional pages.

Communicating integrity is particularly difficult in political campaigns because it is much easier to communicate that a candidate is dishonest than it is to establish that a candidate is honest. The reason for this is simple. A large number of voters are unfamiliar with candidates, even incumbents. If the news media or an opponent seizes on one symbolically dishonest act that receives considerable attention, this is likely to be the main thing a voter knows about the candidate.

As a result, even squeaky-clean candidates have to be very careful when it comes to the details of their campaigns and personal lives. Filing accurate reports on time, divesting a stock that might present an appearance of conflict of interest, taking or not taking certain campaign contributions—all of these are important.

Of course, the importance of integrity for determining voter support depends upon the interplay of all nine of the key candidate qualities. Governor George Ryan of Illinois was brought down by continuing allegations that he allowed corruption to thrive while he was Secretary of State. Though Bill Clinton's integrity was questioned constantly during his eight-year Presidency, he almost certainly could have been reelected had he been able to run against George W. Bush.

QUALITY # 8—DOES THE CANDIDATE HAVE VISION?

Voters want candidates with a vision of where they want to lead. Do they have a vision for the future of the city, state or nation? Do they have sense of where they want to take us?

Yogi Berra is supposed to have said, "If you don't know where you're going, any road will take you there." People want to know where their leaders are going.

George H.W. Bush's bid for reelection was significantly undermined by what he himself called, "The Vision Thing," the common perception that he had no clear vision for the future.

John F. Kennedy's 1960 campaign centered around his vision for the future. Kennedy's campaign themes: "A Time for Greatness" and "Leadership for the 60's," and "Getting America Moving Again" gave voters a sense that he had a clear vision for America's future.

In 1996 Clinton's attacks on Bob Dole for his lack of vision were devastating. In one commercial the Clinton campaign ran clips of Dole recounting how he had opposed Medicare, how he opposed the Department of Education and uttering his famous quote: "I'm not sure what everyone is looking for in a candidate for President. Maybe we shouldn't have one at all, leave it vacant. But there's going to be one, every country ought to have one, so we're out here campaigning."

The spot concluded: "No Vision: Wrong in the Past, Wrong in the Future."

Over the years, pundits and party activists have constantly beat up congressional Democrats for their failure to present clear pragmatic alternatives. In fact, hundreds of proposals, some of them with major scope, were presented by Democrats in each session for years.

The problem wasn't the lack of progressive programs or policies. The problem was a lack of defining vision for the future of America, for the world of our children and grandchildren.

It is particularly important for the national leadership of the Democratic Party and the progressive movement to provide a national vision framework for candidates. Providing a clear Democratic Party vision is the major component in any attempt to "nationalize" congressional races for instance. It's one of the reasons why history shows clearly that the party that is most successful at nationalizing congressional races is the most likely to win.

In 2002, the Democratic Congressional Campaign Committee took the opposite tack. It decided to focus local campaigns on local issues. That's one of the reasons the party lost seats that year.

The elaboration of that vision is especially important in a potential period of political realignment. Our ability to create an enduring Democratic majority electorate—and our ability to reframe the political dialogue in America—hinge largely on our ability to define and communicate a progressive vision for our future.

A vision paints a picture of the way we view of the future, and activates our basic moral frame.

A candidate's vision flows out of the values to which he is committed and applies those values to his understanding of the world and its future.

But a leader's vision also does something else that is critical. It gives the follower, or voter, a sense of the meaning and significance of our society and of each individual within it. It provides the framework that allows the leader to address the most pressing self-interest of all: the need for meaning in life. The ability of a leader to communicate his vision for the future enables the best of them to communicate Quality # 9—inspiration.

QUALITY # 9 — DOES THE CANDIDATE INSPIRE ME?

The final quality that voters look for any leader is inspiration. By inspiration, I mean something very specific. Being inspired is feeling called upon to be more than we are. It is a feeling of empowerment.

Great speakers inspire because of the way they make you feel. They inspire their listeners by making them feel *empowered* to go out and be more than they are today.

Human beings want to be inspired. They want leaders who call upon them to be everything they can be.

The sociologist David McClelland reports:

> We set out to find exactly, by experiment, what kinds of thoughts the members of an audience had when exposed to a charismatic leader.... They were apparently strengthened and uplifted by the experience; they felt more powerful, rather than less powerful or submissive. This suggests that the traditional way of explaining the influence of a leader on his followers has not been entirely correct. He does not force them to submit and follow him by the sheer overwhelming magic of his personality and persuasive powers.... In fact, he is influential by strengthening and inspiring his audience.... The leader arouses confidence in his followers. The followers feel better able to accomplish whatever goals he and they share. [7]

The most compelling symbols used to inspire are stories of heroism. Heroism is in essence nothing more than overcoming obstacles to accomplish some important task — usually for someone other than yourself.

Stories of the stranger who risks his life to rescue someone from a burning building are inspiring because they demonstrate the potential of human beings to be more than they are — to overcome great obstacles at peril to themselves in order to do accomplish something important.

Political scientist George MacGregor Burns describes two types of leadership.

Transactional Leadership involves exercising the normal everyday tasks of leading: enforcing standards, managing time, setting objectives, altering agendas, building a loyal team, listening, encouraging, reinforcing with believable actions.

The second is what he calls "transforming leadership."

Burns says that **Transforming Leadership** *is more rare. It is leadership that builds on people's need for meaning — that instills institutional purpose. All great organizations at one level or another have transforming leaders. Transforming leaders are not simply concerned with the minutiae of every day decision-making. They are concerned with a different kind of minutiae: the tricks of the pedagogue, the mentor, the linguist — the more successfully to become the value-shaper, the exemplar, the maker of meanings. His job is much tougher than that of a transactional leader. He or she is an artist. She is calling forth and exemplifying the urge for transcendence that unites us all. At the same time, she exhibits almost boorish consistency over long periods of time in support of her one or two transcending values.

Burns goes on to describe the characteristics of "transforming leaders:"

> Transforming leadership occurs when one or more persons engage with others in such a way that leaders and followers raise one another to higher levels of motivation and morality. Their purposes, which might have started out separate but related, in the case of transactional leadership, become fused. Power bases are linked not as counterweights but as mutual support for common purpose. Various names are used for such leadership: elevating, mobilizing, inspiring, exalting, uplifting, exhorting, and evangelizing. The relationship can be moralistic, of course. But transforming leadership ultimately becomes moral in that it raises the level of human conduct and ethical aspiration of both the leader and the led, and thus has a transforming effect on both.... Transforming leadership is dynamic leadership in the sense that the leaders throw themselves into a relationship with followers who will feel "elevated" by it and often become more active themselves, thereby creating new cadres of leaders." [8]

When we think about "great" leaders from history, we generally are talking about "transforming leaders." They are people who inspired their followers, and often still inspire us.

Of course, people can be inspired by leaders whom most of us believe are the embodiment of evil. Adolph Hitler and Osama bin Laden come to mind.

But for those of us who share progressive values, one of the greatest evidences that history is on our side is the unquestionable fact that the men and women whom we commonly view as the great "transformational" leaders of the past, are invariably bearers of progressive values. They are people like Jefferson, Lincoln, Roosevelt, Kennedy, King, Gandhi, and Nelson Mandela. They aren't Richard Nixon or Herbert Hoover—and they certainly aren't the Hitlers and the Mussolinis.

There is no question that leaders can inspire people with appeals to irrational, oppressive, or racist values. But these individuals are not the leaders who are ultimately revered by our common memory as people who called upon humanity to live up to its collective potential. They are not the "transforming leaders" who challenge society to provide the opportunity for all of its members to fulfill their potential as human beings.

THE NINE QUALITIES—POLITICAL MOVEMENTS AND PARTIES

Voters don't just look for these nine qualities in candidates. They look for the same qualities in political parties and movements.

Think about any of the qualities and apply them to the Democratic Party—or the progressive movement.

- Is the party on my side?

- Is the party committed to core values—or just winning elections?

- Does the party provide and advocate strong effective leadership—or is it ineffective and weak?

- Is the party self-confident—or does it appear to be directionless and unsure?

- Does the party respect me—or does it take me for granted or treat me like I'm stupid?

- Do I like the people in the party? Does it make me feel like I belong and connect emotionally to leadership?

- Does the party have integrity—or is it corrupt and self-dealing?

- Does the party have a vision for the future of our city, state, country our world—for the next generation?

- Does the party and my participation in it inspire me and empower me?

These are the qualities that determine both whether a voter chooses a candidate and whether he participates in, and has allegiance to, the Democratic Party, the progressive movement, or just about any other political organization or movement.

They are, in effect, the qualities we look for in the leaders and the movements that give meaning to our lives.

Communicating these nine qualities persuade swing voters. What messages motivate mobilizable voters?

CHAPTER TWENTY-TWO

Six Motivational Messages for GOTV

There are Six Major Messages That Motivate People to Vote.

We said earlier that while the subject of a persuasion message is the candidate, the subject of a mobilization message is the voter.

Why is it that some groups of people are generally more prone to vote than others?

Why did 82% of African-American voters turn out in the Chicago municipal elections that elected Harold Washington Chicago's first black mayor. Yet only 60% of African-American voters turned out in the last presidential election?

A lot of research has been done concerning why people vote and why they don't. We know that older people are more likely to vote than younger people; more educated people are more likely to vote that less educated people; higher-income people are more likely to vote than lower-income people.

In general, there are three major reasons why people stay home from the polls:

1) They think that their vote won't matter to the election's outcome.

2) They think that the election's outcome won't matter to their lives.

3) They think that very little of what they do in general affects their lives—so voting sure isn't going to affect them one way or the other.

Of these three, the third is the most important and most difficult to address.

The chart below tells the tale. Seventy-four percent of high-income people, who generally have a sense that their own actions can affect their lives, voted in 2000. Only 34.2% of very low-income people went to the polls, although arguably the results of the election had bigger consequences for them than their higher-income neighbors.

Voter Participation By Income

US Census Bureau Data on Voter Registration and Participation 2000

Annual Income	% Registered Voters	% Registered Voters Voting in 2000
Below $5,000	53.10%	34.20%
$5,000-9,999	57.10%	40.60%
$10,000-14,999	58.60%	44.30%
$15,000-24,999	65.00%	51.30%
$25,000-34,999	69.00%	57.30%
$35,000-49,999	72.30%	61.90%
$50,000-74,999	77.90%	68.70%
$75,000 and over	82.10%	74.90%

Studies at the Center for the Study of the American Electorate confirm that the sense that people have as to whether the actions they take affect their lives is the greatest single predictor of voter participation.

Messages about voter mobilization are not (as in the case of persuasion) about a candidate or party or political movement. They are about the feelings and attitudes of the voter himself and his or her relationship to the election and the society in general.

From my experience, there are six basic messages that will motivate people to vote:

GOTV MESSAGE # 1
YOUR VOTE MATTERS—IT'S CLOSER THAN YOU THINK

Is it worth my time to vote? Not if I think that the outcome is a foregone conclusion. In 2004, those in Presidential swing states were more likely to vote than those who did not. Minnesota, one of the most hotly contested states, had a turnout of 79%, but Hawaii, which Presidential candidates ignored, had only 50%. [1]

That's why you find campaigns communicating what might at first appear to be counterintuitive messages.

A candidate in the lead may decide to put out the message that his opponent is coming on—it's closer than everyone thinks. He needs to convince his hard-core voters that the outcome of the election is not a foregone conclusion. On the other hand, of course, it's easy to understand why a candidate that's being counted out would want show that his campaign is coming on—that he is within striking distance.

Remember that neither of these messages communicates about who *should* win. These are not persuasion messages about the wonders of a candidate. They are about the state of the contest and the likelihood that it's worth someone's time and energy to cast a ballot.

GOTV MESSAGE #2—INSPIRATION

Most important antidote to the sense that "nothing I actually do affects my life" is inspiration.

Inspiration is, after all, a feeling of empowerment. It is the feeling that the individual or group can rise to the challenge and overcome previously insurmountable obstacles. More than anything else, it was the inspiration—the feeling that African-Americans could actually win the mayoralty in Chicago—that gave the African-American community the sense of empowered that led to the 82% African-American turnout for Harold Washington.

The feeling that nothing you do will affect your life—the feeling of personal powerlessness—translates into a feeling of meaninglessness—of insignificance. Addressing this basic human need for meaning is the major component of the formula for voter mobilization—and social mobilization in general.

GOTV MESSAGE # 3—FEAR RESOLVED INTO ANGER

Simply stated, "Something bad could happen to me or my family as a result of the election—and I'm not going to let them do it."

Fear taken by itself is not mobilizing—it is immobilizing. We don't want people to be frozen in fear. We do want them to be afraid that the results of the election will injure them or someone they care about, and then be angry enough to do something about it—to vote.

"The Republicans want to privatize your Social Security."

"The Republicans want to cut Medicare to give tax breaks to millionaires."

"The Republicans want to cut student loans—Let's vote about it." The more concrete the potential assault, the better.

GOTV MESSAGE # 4—IT'S US VERSUS THEM

When the Chicago Bulls were on the verge of winning their sixth national title, everyone in Chicago was pumped, mobilized, excited following each game.

Very few of them stood to make any money or benefit personally in any way from the Bulls victory, but they were totally invested nonetheless.

They'd made an emotional investment in "their" team. They had "acted" themselves into belief in the team. In fact, they thought of themselves as part of the team. When the Bulls won, it was to be "their victory." Victory gave each person a sense of meaning and significance.

To motivate mobilizable voters, we have to make them feel like part of our "team." We want them to start rooting for our guy—not to persuade them (presumably they are already persuaded)—but to give them an emotional investment in victory. We want to make them think about our candidate's victory as "their victory." We want our candidate's victory to give them a sense of personal meaning and significance.

We want more and more mobilizable voters to be like the campaign workers who cheer, "We won!" on election night. They don't cheer, "*He* won.*" They cheer, "*We* won."

We generate that feeling by creating a sense of "us versus them," our team versus their team. Tough, brave, pugnacious candidates are more prone to provoke this reaction than bland, boring, cautious candidates. Candidates and campaigns that highlight the fact that they stand up for what they believe, candidates who project a vision and communicate inspiration, candidates that seem to do something heroic get "us versus them" responses from mobilize voters.

Candidates who understand that "the fight's the thing" provoke that reaction.

"Us versus them" is the second major reason why Harold Washington got out 82% of the African-American vote in 1983.

GOTV Message # 5—"Let's Get 'Em"

This message is about punishment. It's not about fear of what might happen in the future, but justice for what has happened in the past.

It's about showing them that we matter, that we're not going to allow them to push us around forever. They stole the election, or they took money that should have gone for our kid's education, or they ignored our communities, or they insulted us. This time we're going to throw the bastards out.

This message is important to mobilizing voters in much of the Democratic base. But it is used every day by Republicans as well. They use it every election to mobilize the people Frank talks about in *What's the Matter With Kansas?* They use it to mobilize against the "liberal elite" that they say is destroying family values, advocating gay marriage, and laughing at the "rubes" who believe in "intelligent design."

Progressives have to remember that while we need to stand up clearly and forcefully for science and religious freedom, it is a gigantic error to patronize, or mock those who hold opposing views. It plays into the hands of those who seek to mobilize the conservative base. If we communicate disrespect and contempt toward people, we help the Right get its vote to the polls. Clear, uncompromising disagreement with someone is *not* disrespectful—to the contrary. We should not give a moment's quarter to many of the positions taken by cultural conservatives. But if we fall into mocking or disrespecting them we do our own cause an enormous disservice.

GOTV MESSAGE # 6
"I WON'T GET OFF YOUR PORCH UNTIL YOU VOTE"

This is the "mechanical' message—and it works. The basic communication is simple: "I will knock on your door, call you, pass you leaflets, and continue to do it until you go to the polls."

Yale political scientists Alan Gerber and Donald Green have shown that the most powerful way to communicate this message is door-to-door. A living, breathing human being who comes around, multiple times, to remind you to vote has enormous impact on voter turnout. Door-to-door contact makes the act of voting concrete and personal; it translates an abstract concept into your life, into the here and now.

When SCG does GOTV programs we try to do two door-to-door canvass contacts before Election Day—and three door-to-door contacts on Election Day until that voter votes. These contacts are supplemented by reminder calls, "street action" (more on this in Section Six), radio, ethnic or cable TV and sometimes mail.

The point is to inundate the target with GOTV contacts that communicate the right mix of the six GOTV messages, and especially—"I won't get off your porch until you vote."

Below I've included some examples of effective graphic GOTV message.

This last image probably only has impact in Chicago. It is Chicago's first black Mayor, Harold Washington.

CHAPTER TWENTY-THREE

Symbols

POLITICAL COMMUNICATION IS ABOUT SYMBOLS

As we've seen, all communication involves symbols. But this is particularly true of political communication.

We've seen that people's understanding of the world is always mediated by symbols. Symbols allow us to make sense out of the thousands of inputs of information that we experience every day. They allow us to place facts into meaningful relationships that we can understand. That is especially true of the frames that call up our most basic moral concepts and metaphors that translate abstract concepts into concrete physical experience.

The most compelling symbols are the most concrete. If we can visualize, hear, smell, taste or remember a symbol it will be more persuasive and compelling than less emotive, more abstract symbols.

In *In Search of Excellence*, Peters and Waterman argue that people reason intuitively because they need ways of sorting through the infinite minutiae out there, and we start with heuristics—associations, analogues, metaphors and ways that have worked for us before.

We are more influenced and motivated by stories that make sense in themselves than by data—which are, by definition, abstract. This is particularly true of motivation. Motivation is achieved by communicating concrete symbols, not rhetorical abstraction.

So in convincing persuadable voters that a candidate has the nine qualities we have discussed above, we don't just say Candidate A is likable, or Candidate B is on your side. We present a symbol that makes the same point with emotional impact. We want our audience to viscerally experience the fact that Candidate A is likable or Candidate B is on your side.

TELL THEM A STORY

The best symbols are stories or narratives. They are the best symbols because they take abstract concepts and make them real. They communicate in terms of real life experience.

Former Senator Paul Simon was one of the best political stump speakers I've ever met. His speeches were generally nothing more than a series of interesting stories that communicated his message.

Abraham Lincoln was the consummate storyteller, and he was very intentional about his use of stories:

> *They say I tell a great many stories. I reckon I do; but I have learned from long experience that the plain people take them as they run, are more easily influenced through the medium of a broad or humorous illustration than in any other way...* [1]

Tom Peters and Nancy Austin highlight the importance of stories in A Passion for Excellence:

> *It turns out that human beings reason largely by means of stories, not by means of data. Stories are memorable... They teach... If we are serious about ideals, values, motivation, commitment, we will pay attention to the role of stories and myths....* [2]

As President Lincoln once said:

> *I believe I have the popular reputation of being a story-teller, but I do not deserve the name in its general sense, for it is not the story itself, but its purpose or effect that interests me. I often avoid a long and useless discussion by others or a laborious explanation on my own part by a short story that illustrates my point of view. So, too, the sharpness of a refusal or the edge of a rebuke may be blunted by an appropriate story, so as to save wounded feeling and yet serve the purpose. No, I am not simply a story-teller, but story-telling as an emollient saves me much friction and distress.* [3]

THE ELEMENTS OF GREAT STORIES — THE POLITICAL NARRATIVE

Great political messaging, in all cases, is very much like great storytelling. In fact, a powerful political message always involves creating a narrative. It involves many of the same elements as any great movie, novel or short story.

•**The Characters.** Like all great stories, political narratives must have a protagonist, the good guy; and an antagonist, the bad guy. In elections the protagonist is always our candidate. The antagonist may be our opponent. Or it may be someone else—outside special interests, the pharmaceutical companies, the toxic dumpers, or whatever. Like any great story, our characters must be developed in our communication. People need to get to know them.

• **Conflict.** All great stories involve conflict. Man vs. man; man vs. nature; man vs. society; man vs. himself; man vs. machine. Stories are about conflict and the resolution of conflict. If you see a movie or read a story with no conflict, your response is "nothing happened."

• **Setting.** Good stories set the stage. They create a sense of where they take place and the forces in play. Setting is necessary to allow the listener to understand the significance of the conflict that the story describes. Great political messages place the political conflict in historic context.

• **Foreshadowing.** Good stories generally give us a hint of the nature of the conflict even before it appears full blown in the plot. Foreshadowing creates drama and suspense. Drama and suspense create interest and curiosity in the listener.

• **Climax.** Every good story has a climax where the story's central conflicts are resolved. Political narratives might tell stories that involve resolutions of past conflict (say, the battle to defeat the privatization of Social Security or stop the Iraq War). But in every case the current conflict—the one embodied in the election or issue campaign itself—will be resolved in the polling place Election Day, or on the floor of Congress in an issue campaign. In electoral politics, the election is always the climax of the overarching narrative.

• **Point of View.** Every great story has a point of view, a perspective. It is told from the standpoint of a participant or an observer. In politics, our perspective in the overarching election narrative should always be the point of view of the voters. Of course, other stories that are told as symbols of candidate qualities during the campaign might be told from the point of view of distinct individual or of the candidate himself.

THE "CREATION MYTH"

Many successful candidates and campaigns have selected a "Creation Myth"—a story that describes how and why the candidate came to be running for public office. By using the term "myth" I don't mean to imply that they aren't true, only that the story takes on a "mythic" status for the campaign—a status that communicates a great deal about the candidate's values and motivation.

My wife Jan's "Creation Myth" was the story of how she and a group of six suburban housewives waged a successful national campaign to put "freshness dates" on food in the early 1970s.

At the time, there were no "freshness dates" on food products—only codes that allowed stock boys to rotate the stock at supermarkets. Jan, together with five of her friends, decided that they were tired of getting out-of-date food products, so together they formed an organization which they modestly called "National Consumers United."

They wanted to crack the codes that supermarkets used. Their data collection methods were simple. They would lean the stock boys up against the shelves and demand to know what codes meant. And as they discovered the meaning of various codes they would search the supermarkets for out-of-date food, load it into baskets and roll it ceremoniously to the manager so that it could be dumped.

In one of their more memorable actions, they bought stock in the National Tea Company (a Chicago area food chain) and confronted the management at their annual meeting—with NBC Nightly News in tow. The President of the company accused them of either being "Communists" or agents of Jewel (a competitor). It appeared on the national news that night.

Finally, they published a book that translated the codes into "freshness dates" and sold it through articles in women's magazines. They sold 25,000 copies.

In the end, they won. Now every supermarket in America has freshness dates on food, and in one survey conducted by Jan's first campaign for Congress, 80% of voters said they checked those dates before buying products like milk or meat.

When she talks about this story, she says that the freshness dates campaign may not have changed the world, but it certainly changed her life. It made her realize that by working with other people you can change the world, and that led her to a career as a consumer and senior-citizen advocate, a state representative, and finally a Member of Congress.

Stories like that connect with regular people. They also communicate the nine qualities we discussed above. They communicate about being on our side, commitment and values, effective leadership, respect for people, self-confidence and likeability. That story even contains elements of vision—of envisioning how things should change—and certainly of inspiration: six everyday housewives who took on an industry and won.

BOWTIES, ICE CREAM CONES AND AIRPLANES

Stories are very powerful symbols.

Of course they aren't the only symbols. Former Senator Simon always wore a bow tie. It became a symbol of his independence—that he was his own man and always stood up for what he believed.

Symbols can be caricatures. A powerful commercial in a New Orleans prosecutor's race portrayed the incumbent as a "Mister Softie"—an ice cream cone. The narrator explained how he was soft on criminals as a "Mister Softie" melted at the bottom of the screen.

A symbol can be a tag line that is always repeated as part of political communication. Jan's is: "Keep a fighter on your side." Bill Clinton's 1996 slogan was a "Bridge to the 21st Century"—a wonderful, visual image that made Clinton look visionary in contrast to Dole who was by implication a "Bridge to the 19th Century"—a person who was "wrong in the past, wrong in the future."

A symbol can be an issue. For many women a candidate who is anti-choice is simply not on their side.

A symbol can be a thematic—an organizing principle or frame. In 1996, Democrats successfully repeated the charge—over and over—that Republicans wanted to "cut Medicare to give tax breaks to the rich." For most Americans, and especially seniors, that meant that they weren't "on your side."

Symbols don't have to be related to politics. A memorable—and humorous—commercial in a Texas State Senate race observed that the opponent had landed his airplane with the wheels up "not once but twice at Tyler Pounds Field." It went on to say: "We can understand one mistake, but you have to begin to wonder, if he can't get his wheels down in Tyler, how is he going to keep his feet on the ground in Austin?"

Landing an airplane with the wheels up has nothing whatsoever to do with the job of a state senator, but it cast doubt on the candidate's competency—his ability to be a strong, effective leader.

CREATING "POLITICAL FACTS"

We've already discussed "political facts." In an electoral campaign, both sides project symbols that define their candidates. In issue campaigns you project "political facts." These are the images, stories, labels or factoids that come to be commonly accepted parameters for the debate. They come to be repeated over and over by the media, among opinion leaders or legislators and have a profound effect on the success of one side or the other.

Debates over reform of the civil justice system are often defined by the cases cited by the two sides to explain the issue. In the debate over medical malpractice "reform," defenders of the civil justice system try to make the issue real to the listener by citing a real case of a woman who died when a doctor removed the wrong kidney. Or there was the case of the lab that systematically analyzed only one of every three tissue samples to raise profits and caused the cancer of thousands of people to go undetected.

On the other side was the widely-touted story of the woman who successfully sued McDonald's for millions of dollars because she was scalded when her hot coffee spilled on her legs. That story was used effectively to argue that product liability law should be reformed—even though the award was drastically reduced in the end.

In an issue campaign, the symbols you choose—the "political facts" you create—have an enormous impact on how legislators and the public view the issue.

Symbols that Make You Feel and Visualize

When someone has a fantasy—be it a fantasy about a new job or a vacation, they don't recite the statistics about the warmth of the sun on the Caribbean beach. They visualize being on the Caribbean beach, or what it would be like to sit in the corner office.

When someone has a fantasy, they imagine how it feels and sounds and tastes to be something or somewhere they are not. That's why metaphors are so important at converting abstract concepts into physical experiences.

A great story or film does exactly the same thing. The storyteller tries to make the listener suspend disbelief, to actually experience 18th century England or to ride with Lawrence across the sands of the Arabian Desert.

Great political symbols allow people to visualize the story, to feel what it would be like to be out of work, to experience the sensation of success.

Great political symbols call upon the listener or viewer to visualize an experience, not just to think about it.

Good political communication is directed at people's emotions, not just their thoughts. And the simple fact is that emotions—feelings—are not thoughts. You actually feel emotions—*physically*. Emotions make you react. They make you feel sad, or excited, were inspired. They make you cry or laugh.

Emotional states occur when entirely different portions of the brain are engaged in the sectors involved in simple reasoning or thought.

It's fashionable for pundits to criticize candidates for appealing to raw emotion instead of reasoned thought. But we should remember that emotional states evolved in human beings, because emotional states are adaptive, and help us succeed and survive.

Just like messages aimed at reasoned thought, emotional messages can appeal to our basest feelings—or they can appeal to our most ennobling. Emotions control our levels of motivation. They can spur us to action—to heroic levels of performance and commitment. Or they can immobilize us with feelings of depression or sadness.

Our job as Progressives in politics is to engage emotions to motivate people to vote for our candidates, and involve themselves in the process in the struggle for a better world. That requires more than reason. It requires inspiration, passion, emotional commitment. It requires joy and sorrow, and hope and disappointment.

Great political communication engages emotions, not just logic.

CHAPTER TWENTY-FOUR

Addressing the Emotions and Unconscious

SOMETIMES PEOPLE HEAR THE WORDS, BUT LISTEN TO THE MUSIC—80% OF COMMUNICATION IS NON-VERBAL

As every parent knows, there's a big difference between hearing and listening. What you say may have little to do with the message you communicate.

Remember, 80% of communication is nonverbal and a lot of it is unconscious. People receive messages from your facial expressions, your posture, your dress, your tone of voice, your style, the way you walk, the sparkle in your eyes.

Think of Oliver North in the Iran-Contra scandal. Committee Democrats had the goods on an illegal, overt attempt to subvert the will of Congress and laws of the United States. But after days of hearings, North came out on top in the public's mind. His sincere attitude, crisp uniform, passionate delivery, chest full of medals—and the way he looked up at the Senators—carried the day.

Intellectual types and policy wonks are particularly prone to mistake the words they write for the messages people receive. Words can matter. But many times people may hear the words, yet they listen to the music that surrounds them.

A GREAT DEAL OF POLITICAL COMMUNICATION TAKES PLACE AT THE UNCONSCIOUS LEVEL

Daniel Goleman's book *Social Intelligence* describes the case of a man whose visual cortex has been destroyed by a stroke. His eyes could receive signals, but his conscious brain could not decipher them and turn them into conscious images.

When this patient was tested with various shapes like circles and squares, or faces, he didn't have a clue what he was seeing. But when he was shown pictures of angry or happy faces, he was able to guess at the emotions express at a rate far better than chance. How could this be?

Goleman explains:

Brain scans taken while patient X guessed the feelings revealed an alternative to the usual pathways for seeing that flow from the eyes to the thalamus, where all the senses first enter the brain, and then to the visual cortex. The second route sends information straight from the thalamus to the amygdala (the brain has a pair, right and left). The amygdala then extracts emotional meaning from the nonverbal message, whether it be a scowl, a sudden change of posture, or a shift in tone of voice—even microseconds before we yet know what we are looking at.

Though the amygdala has an exquisite sensitivity for such messages, its wiring provides no direct access to the centers for speech; in this sense the amygdala is, literally, speechless. When we register a feeling, signals from our brain circuits, instead of alerting the verbal areas, where words can express what we know, mimic that emotion in our own bodies. So patient X was not seeing the emotions on the faces so much as feeling them, a condition called "affective blind sight."

In intact brains, the amygdala uses the same pathway to read the emotional aspect of whatever we perceive—elation in someone's tone of voice, a hint of anger around the eyes, a posture of glum defeat—and then process that information subliminally, beneath the reach of conscious awareness. This reflexive, unconscious awareness signals that emotion by priming the same feeling (or reaction to it, such as fear on seeing anger) in us—a key mechanism for "catching" a feeling from someone else. [1]

In the last several years a new discipline has grown up in the marketing world called neuromarketing.

Neuromarketing evaluates the response produced by a product in a particular region of the brain to conclude whether or not the product makes a direct and immediate connection with the prospective customer. In an article in the *New York Times Magazine,* Clive Thompson explains the premise behind this new field, which has been developed by scientists at the Bright House Institute:

The Bright House Institute's techniques are based, in part, on an experiment that (Clint) Kilts conducted earlier this year. He gathered a group of test subjects and asked them to look at a series of commercial products, rating how strongly they liked and disliked them. Then, while scanning their brains in an M.R.I. machine, he showed them pictures of the products again. When Kilts looked at the images of their brains, he was struck by one particular result: whenever a subject saw a product he had identified as one he truly loved—something that might prompt him to say, "That's just so me!"—his brain would show increased activity in the medial prefrontal cortex.

Kilts was excited, for he knew that this region of the brain is commonly associated with our sense of self.... When the medial prefrontal cortex fires, your brain seems to be engaging, in some manner, with what sort of person you are. If it fires when you see a particular product, Kilts argues, it most likely to be because the product clicks with your self-image.

The result provided the Bright House Institute with an elegant tool for testing marketing campaigns and brands. An immediate, intuitive bond between consumer and product is one that every company dreams of making. "If you like Chevy trucks, it's because that has become the larger gestalt of who you self-attribute as," Kilts said, using psychology-speak. "You're a Chevy guy." With the help of neuromarketers, he claims, companies can now know with certainty whether their products are making that special connection.

Thompson continues....

Other neuromarketers have demonstrated that we react to products in ways about which we may not be entirely conscious. This year, for instance, scientists working with DaimlerChrysler scanned the brains of a number of men as they looked at pictures of cars and rated them for attractiveness. The scientists found that the most popular vehicles—the Porsche and Ferrari style sports cars—triggered activity in a section of the brain called the fusiform face area, which governs facial recognition. "They were reminded of faces when they looked at the cars," says Henrick Walter, a psychiatrist at the University of Ulm in Germany who ran the study, "The lights of the cars look like little eyes." [2]

Whether or not each of the findings of this newly developing discipline withstands the test of time, there can be little question that our brains respond to communication in ways that are not entirely mediated through our conscious thought processes.

Just as with commercial advertising, political communication must focus on the way it makes its audience feel about the candidate, the idea or the party—not the logical sequence of argument.

Is the voter a "George Bush kind of guy"? Does he make us feel a sense of connection—that he's on our side—that his leadership is consistent with our self-image—with our identity? How does he impact my own sense of who I am—my relationship to the world—to my sense of meaning?

We referred earlier to Malcolm Gladwell's book, *Blink*, that is entirely devoted to discussion of the "adaptive unconscious." He argues that "the only way human beings could ever have survived as a species for as long as we have is that we've developed another kind of decision-making apparatus that's capable of making very quick judgments based on very little information." [3]

Timothy D. Wilson writes in his book, *Strangers to Ourselves*: "The mind operates most efficiently by relegating a good deal of high-level, sophisticated thinking to the unconscious, just as the modern jetliner is able to fly on automatic pilot with little or no input from the human 'conscious' pilot. The adaptive unconscious does an excellent job of sizing up the world, warning people of danger, setting goals, and initiating action in a sophisticated and efficient manner." [4]

Wilson argues that we toggle back and forth between conscious and unconscious thought depending on the situation: "Whenever we meet someone for the first time, whenever we interview someone for a job, whenever we react to a new idea, whenever we're faced with making a decision quickly under stress, we used the second part of our brain." [5]

The same is true when you make an initial judgment about a candidate, party or political movement.

Gladwell makes these major points in *Blink*:

• Decisions made very quickly at the adaptive unconscious can be every bit as good as decisions made cautiously through deliberation.

He argues that the process of "thin slicing" data that is used when we make quick unconscious judgments may actually be more accurate at isolating the subtle pattern or gist in all the incoming data that allows us to make an accurate decision.

Gladwell uses the example of Allied interpreters who transcribed German Morse Code transmissions in World War II. Before long, the interpreters could recognize the distinctive "fist" of each German operator—the way he hit the key. That enabled them to track movements of German units by the "fist" of the key operators associated with each unit. [6]

Most other phenomena have distinctive "fists" or "gists" that are inscripted in voluminous amounts of data. But if your unconscious is good at "thin slicing" it can pick patterns out and add them to the "pattern of vocabulary" we described earlier.

Sometimes the very paucity of information makes the pattern easier to see. But regardless, we "thin slice" because we have to. Too many circumstances require rapid-fire decisions.

• Gladwell's second thesis is that while the unconscious is powerful, it is also fallible. It is fallible mostly because its decisions are based on a complex web of experiences, interests and emotions. Of particular relevance to politics is what he calls the "Warren Harding Error." People thought Harding would make a good president because he looked like a president. Their experience had led their unconscious at first impression to decide the people who were tall and distinguished had superior leadership skills. Turned out Warner Harding didn't.

Of course this error is the root of all irrational prejudice. The Implicit Association Test (IAT) is used by psychologists to measure unconscious assumptive associations. The test asks people to match categories very rapidly. The race IAT measures racial attitudes at the unconscious level—the immediate associations at *the moment*—before we have an opportunity to choose on a conscious level.

"The giant computer that is our unconscious, systematically crunches all the data it can from the experiences we've had, the people we've met, the lessons we've learned, the books we read, the movies we've seen and so on, and it forms our opinions. That's what's coming out in the IAT." [7]

It turned out that 80% of all those who had ever taken the race IAT ended up having pro-white associations, including Gladwell, who is half black.

But that gets to Gladwell's third point.

• Our snap judgments and first impressions can be educated and controlled in the same way we can train and educate our conscious decision-making.

Our first impressions are generated by our experiences and environment. We can alter the way we "thin slice" by changing the experiences that comprise those impressions. In other words, we can modify and supplement our "pattern vocabularies" the same way we can add to our conscious store of knowledge.

If, before you administer the racial IAT, you ask people to look over a series of pictures or articles about people like Martin Luther King, Nelson Mandela, and Colin Powell, the scores change. In other words, you can be primed by your experience to have a different unconscious reaction.

And this should come as no surprise. If you want to make someone into a great chess player, they need to practice chess—over and over—to build the "pattern vocabularies" of chess board situations that are recognized by the unconscious mind.

There are several key lessons for political communication implicit in Gladwell's three theses about the adaptive unconscious. They form the basis for our next principles of political communication.

Repetition, Repetition, Repetition Is Required to Eliminate Unconscious Prejudice in Favor of Conservative Values, and to Reinforce Progressive Values, Frames and Assumptions

To someone who doesn't know how to land an airplane, landings look difficult.

To someone who is an inexperienced chess player, it is impossible to understand how a grandmaster makes the right moves.

To someone who is not a great basketball player, it's almost magical how great players can sink the ball into the hoop over and over.

And it's very difficult to consciously explain to someone how a land the plane, choose the right chess moves, or sink the ball into the basket.

But we know that acquiring these abilities does not involve magic. They all involve practice—repetition, repetition, repetition. You practice landings. You practice chess. You practice shooting baskets over and over and over.

That practice allows our unconscious "computer" to store and recognize more and more patterns on the basis of which to make large and small decisions—decisions as large as the split-second call to abort a landing because you glimpse a plane approaching on a crossing runway, and as small as the unconscious, nuanced muscle movements that allow you to "grease" the landing.

To train the powerful computer in your unconscious mind requires repetition. This fact has two important implications for the communication of progressive values and assumptions.

As the late political consultant Matt Reese used to say, "Politics is repeated, persuasive contact." This is certainly true from the point of view of "breaking through"—getting people's attention (more on that later). But it's also true when it comes to communicating progressive values and assumptions. We think about values and assumptions mainly on an unconscious level. The deep frames that embody our moral systems are embedded in our neurons and, for the most part, function unconsciously.

Conservatives learned long ago that by unapologetically standing up for their values and assumptions, and referring to them every time they have a chance, they train voters to take those values and assumptions as unconscious "givens."

On the other hand, when Democrats soft-pedal their values, "finesse" them, apologize for them, or appear to accept the underlying assumptions of our conservative opponents, we train the unconscious of the voters to accept these frames as well. That's true even when we do it for what we think is short-term expediency.

Here's an example. How often have you heard conservatives say, "You have to let supply and demand set wage levels in the labor market place" or "the minimum wage interferes with the 'natural forces' of supply and demand to create wage levels that are artificially high"?

Now, how many times have you heard progressive proponents of raising the minimum wage say, "yes, but…" and then go on to make another perfectly sound argument for raising the minimum wage.

In fact, of course, there is nothing "natural" about allowing the process of supply and demand to determine how we distribute the goods and services in our economy—which is what wages are all about.

Supply and demand may provide an efficient means of allocating resources for some (certainly not all) social tasks. It might be an efficient way to send economic signals and focus the direction of investment and economic activity by pricing commodities and by influencing the rates of return to various investments. But supply and demand does not necessarily yield a fair distribution of our economic resources or assure that macro, or over-all, economy functions in the most efficient fashion.

In a recession or depression, supply and demand drive down wage rates. But lower wage rates give consumers less money to spend and cause the economy to slow further. You need more spending to stop a recession, not less.

Providing people a better life is, after all, the goal of the economy, not some side effect. People are not commodities like corn or beans or gold. There is nothing "artificial" about providing everyone who works with a living wage. That implies that our economic system is handed down by God or that it has some basis in natural law or science. In fact it is created by human beings to address our goals and priorities, not the other way around.

There is nothing "natural" about the fact that the average CEOs of the country's largest firms make more in wages (forget stock options and other extensive benefits) *before lunch on the first day of the year* than his minimum-wage employees make all year long.

CEOs of companies with more than $1 billion in annual revenue make an average of $10,982,000 per year. That is $42,238 per day or approximately $5,279 per hour. Even with a new higher minimum wage, it takes the average minimum-wage worker 52 forty-hour weeks (2,080 hours) to earn $13,500. It takes the average CEO two hours and 30 minutes to earn $13,500. The CEOs of large American companies have salaries 813 times higher than their minimum wage employees.

Now, the polling in a referendum or election may tell us that the most persuasive argument does not challenge these basic assumptions. As a political consultant I want to use those most persuasive arguments to win. But I also want to add the more fundamental challenge to conservative assumptions to our message package. Between elections, we have to repeatedly challenge and undercut conservative assumptions, to train the unconscious thinking of voters for the long haul. We have to end the prejudice in most voters' minds that allows them to unconsciously accept conservative frames and assumptions. By refusing to challenge their assumptions we help reinforce the voter's unconscious prejudice in favor of these assumptions as certainly as we would if we left unchallenged a racist assumption or attitude.

Training Progressive Leaders and Candidates Requires Repetition, Repetition & More Repetition— the Right Kind of Practice

Learning to be a great candidate or leader is just like learning how to fly an airplane; you have to accumulate hours; or in the case of political leaders, years of the right kind of experience.

Training leaders and candidates to exhibit the "nine qualities" and to communicate them—to make great speeches, give good interviews, raise money, connect with people, requires repeatedly doing it. As we've seen, it's not solely your issue positions or your resume that sell you to the voters. It's your ability to communicate qualities like strong and effective leadership, respect, integrity and likeability. Like so many things, this comes mainly from the unconscious. It is Bill Clinton's instinctive moves that make him a great politician.

The ability to communicate these qualities often comes from the millions of life experiences that prepare someone to be a progressive leader or candidate. That's what we mean when we say, "she's a natural." But as Gladwell makes clear, many can also be learned, intentionally. And they are learned, as my eighth-grade teacher said, through "the right kind of practice." Many candidates learn the wrong unconscious lessons and develop bad habits through the wrong kind of practice.

The job of great campaign managers and consultants, great trainers and mentors, is to give their trainees the right kind of practice. That's what will make them instinctive in making the moves that communicate the nine qualities that determine whether people follow them, and whether voters support them.

CHAPTER TWENTY-FIVE

Framing and Naming

FRAMING IS THE KEY

We've already seen that the way we frame any issue or fact matters enormously as to the way it is understood. The frame places it in the context, in a pattern of relationships to which we have an immediate and unconscious, positive or negative reaction. We've seen that deep frames communicate our fundamental moral system and surface frames are more limited.

When Republicans propose to cut taxes for the wealthiest Americans, they say:

"We must cut taxes to stimulate growth in the economy."

They framed their argument as a choice between taxes and economic growth. What goes unsaid is the unconscious assumption that tax cuts will, in fact, stimulate the economy. They know that if they say it often enough, and assumptively enough, people will be conditioned or primed unconsciously to believe it is true.

At the Emergency Campaign for America Priorities (ECAP), when we oppose these tax cuts, we say:

"We must stop the Republicans from taking food from the mouths of poor children to give tax breaks to millionaires."

This frame sets up the choice between food for poor kids and tax breaks for the rich. The effectiveness of this frame is rooted in the unconscious, unspoken assumption that it is unfair to deprive children of food in order to benefit the most economically prosperous people in America. It also assumes that the source of the funding for these tax breaks comes from child nutrition programs.

If we repeat our frame enough, people begin to unconsciously associate tax breaks for the wealthy with unfairness, with taking action that is morally wrong. Using this frame we seize the high moral ground in the battle over values. We don't discuss "tax policy" as something technical. We don't talk about "programs" or use the alphabet soup of policy wonk dialogue. We talk about right and wrong.

George Lakoff argues that Progressives and radical conservatives have two distinctly different deep frames that embody their contrasting moral systems.

Each of us has developed and will respond to both of these frames at some level. Some people use one frame in one aspect of life, perhaps at work, and another at home. For others, one frame or the other is active, and the other is passive, allowing us to understand situations involving the other frame.

Most importantly, he argues that many persuadable voters are "biconceptuals." They respond to both the progressive and conservative frames. The key is who activates the frame.

To win the battle with the right we have to consistently articulate, and consequently, activate the progressive frame. In other words, Lakoff believes that there is a tug-of-war in each swing voter between the progressive and conservative frames. To be in the competition, progressive frames must be called upon and reaffirmed regularly so that people will unconsciously react to new situations and issues using the progressive frame.

This goes for surface frames as well. Our unconscious mind has to be constantly trained—or primed—to rely upon progressive frames and values when it makes decisions and judgments. That is done through repeated, persuasive and confident reaffirmation of our frames and values.

To win the battle with the right, we have to constantly surround people with the progressive frames and values. We must provide the unconscious minds of American voters with the experience that allows them to make choices that actually reflect their own self-interests.

In Sections Eight and Nine, we will discuss these frames and values in much greater detail and explore further why a clear progressive vision of the future is so important to challenging the right's three-decade domination of political dialogue in America.

Naming Sets the Frame

The name we give an issue or situation itself provides a frame for the topic it symbolizes. A name automatically prejudices what we think or believe about a subject.

Some years ago, 18 of the wealthiest families in the United States decided to try to eliminate the estate—or inheritance—tax. The inheritance tax affects a tiny number of American families. It was first passed in the early 20th century—both to generate revenue and to help prevent the development of an American aristocracy.

Eliminating the estate tax today, as the Republicans wish to do, would cost the U.S. Treasury a trillion dollars over the next decade. That's tax money that will come from one or all of these places:

- Additional national debt left to all of our children;
- Services of government, like education, health care and nutritional programs;
- Taxes paid by someone else, not the inheritors of the fortunes.

By definition, every dime of that trillion dollars would go into the pockets of the sons and daughters of multimillionaires. They are the only taxpayers liable for the tax, which applies only to estates of several million dollars or more.

That kind of proposal—one that takes money from health care and education and gives it to the Paris Hiltons of the world—shouldn't be very popular with the public. But the proponents of this measure did something very ingenious—they named it the "death tax."

Everyone is against a "death tax." There is an unconscious repulsion to taxing someone when they die. And then they add that poor farm widows are forced sell the farm that has been in her family for generations, just to pay the "death tax."

Of course the advocates of abolishing the estate tax have never produced one real example of a farm sold to pay the tax.

But the main point is the name. Progressives have fought for years to fend off this horrible proposal which would have had no traction at all in the general population had it not so cleverly been named the "death tax."

Names really matter.

In the campaign to defeat the privatization of Social Security we won the name game. Polling and personal experience showed us that people were much less inclined to support the "privatization" of Social Security than "personal accounts."

Republicans fought mightily to give "personal accounts" traction, but "privatization" had already caught on with the press, and we did everything we could to brand that issue "Privatization." We won the battle over the name, and the issue itself. Our victory in the contest over naming rights was a big reason for our ultimate success.

At ECAP we referred to "tax breaks for millionaires" not "tax cuts for the rich."

You might think that these two phrases expressed the same idea, but people hear them differently. It turned out that they thought that "tax breaks" are for someone else and "tax cuts" were for them. It also turns out that most people knew they weren't millionaires, but a large number of middle-class people thought they were (or would one day) be rich.

Names matter.

PROGRESSIVE OR LIBERAL?

We are still fighting a daily battle in the press over what to call our own movement. Most people in the progressive movement refer to ourselves as "Progressives." The polling shows that when people hear the word "progressive," they think of forward-looking, visionary, action-oriented, modern, fair, efficient.

But when they hear the word "liberal," many people who think of themselves as progressive think of moral relativism and libertine attitudes with which they don't identify at all. The right has vilified the word so viciously that for many people it fails to communicate a true understanding of what we used to mean by a "liberal" philosophy.

As a result, many more people identify themselves as Progressives than identify themselves as Liberals. One poll asked people to classify themselves as Liberals, Moderates or Conservatives and then asked them to classify themselves as Progressives, Moderates or Conservatives. More people self-identify as Progressives than as Liberals. Moreover more people classified themselves as Moderates and fewer as Conservatives on the "progressive" scale than the "liberal" scale. In other words, more people felt they were a "Moderate"—when "Moderate" meant closer to being a "Progressive" than a "Moderate"—when it was closer to being a "Liberal."

Progressives need to mount a systematic effort to brand our movement as the "progressive" movement. Our organizations need to be referred to in the press as "progressive groups," not "liberal" groups.

CHAPTER TWENTY-SIX

Talking to Normal People

POLITICAL PEOPLE ARE NOT NORMAL PEOPLE

Whenever I do a seminar with political organizers or activists, there will come a time when I tell them that they are not normal people. They generally look at me as if I just insulted them.

But it's true. Political activists—people who volunteer in campaigns, manage campaigns or run for office—are not normal people. Normal people think about politics five minutes or 10 or 20 minutes a week. They aren't political junkies, they don't consume the *New York Times*, and they are not glued to C-SPAN.

Not that this wouldn't be a good thing. Unfortunately, Americans as a whole are far less interested in politics than the citizens of many other countries, a fact that is reflected in their lower-than-average voter turnout. One of our key jobs as Progressives is to connect the dots between politics and people's everyday lives.

But in general voters, especially persuadable and mobilizable voters, are not heavily engaged in or interested in politics. They are principally involved in the hundreds of concerns that make up everyday life.

The fact that political people are not normal people has two important implications:

• If political people make decisions about what is persuasive or motivational to normal people without asking them, *we will be wrong.* That's why we do research.

• The fact that normal people don't devote all of their time to politics means that there are four essential rules for successfully getting our message across to them.

THE 4 C's OF GOOD POLITICAL COMMUNICATION

There are four "C's" that describe key rules for successfully getting the message across to persuadable and mobilizable voters.

Clear. The message must be clear and understandable to everyone who receives it. In politics, we are not James Joyce and our message is not his novel *Ulysses* that English scholars have written tomes attempting to understand and interpret. We don't want people scratching their heads and wondering what we mean by a particular phrase or reference. When you go to an art gallery, it's fine to have to speculate as to the meaning of a painting. Great films can be open to many different interpretations. But in politics, we aren't looking for subtle. We want clear. We want to be able to take complex issues or questions and refine them to their clear essentials.

In a great commercial for a John Kerry Senate Race from the 1980s, he walks through a hardware store and picks up various items:

> *If you or I walked into a hardware store, we'd pay 22-cents for this plastic cap. The Air Force paid over $1,100 for it. And this 20-cent Allen wrench— the Navy spent over $9,000 for it. And the Pentagon paid $110 for this 10-cent diode. Anyone who thinks we have to spend like this in order to keep America strong, must have a screw loose.*

Using concrete items as symbols of military waste, Senator Kerry took a complicated subject and made it clear and understandable to everyone.

Concise. Since normal people think about politics five, or 10 or 20 minutes a week, we have to be concise and to the point. Hard-core partisan voters might want to spend hours listening to talking heads on CNN or Fox, but to reach persuadable and mobilizable voters, we have to get our message across in short, clear statements or images. The short sound bites used for radio and TV news place an even greater premium on being concise. The length of the average sound bite used on TV news has dropped in the last twenty years from somewhere around fifteen seconds down to eight seconds.

There are, of course, many who regard the tendency to be more and more concise as a race to make policy discussion more and more simple-minded. This may be true. However, being concise does have the benefit of making successful political communicators refine their message to its essence. Most writers and communicators, especially politicians, tend to think that it takes a lot more words to tell their story than are actually necessary. Good editors almost always improve a message by reducing its length.

If we want to communicate to persuadable and mobilizable voters in 21st century America, we need to be able to tell our story quickly and clearly.

Contrastive. In politics we are trying to convince the persuadable voter to make a choice between one candidate and another candidate. That means that the symbols we choose to describe our candidate's qualities should be contrastive. They should demonstrate the comparative advantage of our candidate compared with the other candidate. They must force the voter to make a choice.

In Jan's first race for Congress, one of her two opponents decided that a key symbol for his candidacy would be his tough stand on gun control.

Unfortunately, both Jan and her other opponent (there were three candidates in the primary race) *had equally tough stands on gun control.* The symbol he chose was not contrastive. It didn't demonstrate his comparative advantage.

Convincing. Of course, you can say whatever you want—pro or con—about a candidate. But to be effective, the symbols you choose have to be convincing—they have to ring true to the listener.

Again in Jan's first Congressional primary race, her record in the legislature was attacked because of her vote against an omnibus Republican crime bill that—among other things—cracked down on guns in schools. Jan had voted against the bill, since it included various draconian attacks on civil liberties as well as the gun provisions. But no matter, mailings were sent throughout the district claiming that Jan would allow guns in schools.

The problem was that no one believed it. Sure, they said, former teacher, mother of three is for allowing kids to take guns to school. It simply wasn't believable—it wasn't convincing.

PEOPLE ACT THEMSELVES INTO A BELIEF OR COMMITMENT MORE EASILY THAN THEY CAN BE "CONVINCED" BY ARGUMENT

In Section Three, we discussed this principle at some length—but it is germane here as well.

If you get someone to do something for your candidate, or your cause, they become much more likely to support the candidate or cause. Get them to come to a rally, or to make some phone calls, or to help with a fundraiser or house party and you're getting them to make an investment. Once someone makes an investment of his or her time, money or emotions, he or she is much more likely to believe. In this sense, politics is just like business. The more you have invested, the more you will invest.

People do not become invested in a candidate or cause by hearing about it. They become invested by committing time, money or emotional energy to it. Then they will invest more and believe more.

Want someone to buy into an organizational goal? Don't preach at them about it. Get them involved in the project. Just a little involvement will begin to cement the commitment.

THE FIGHT'S THE THING

A few years ago, I was asked to consult with the staff director for an incumbent Democratic member of Congress. He had a large bank account and had served in office for several terms, but the poll numbers didn't look good. The voters didn't have strong feelings about him one way or the other. He had no core constituency of passionate followers. Persuadable voters—if they knew him at all—thought he was just one of that undifferentiated mass of plain-vanilla officeholders. As far as they knew, he was there just to hold the position—because he was not passionate about any issue or cause.

The staff director was mystified why his boss had such low re-elect numbers, and also by the fact that he apparently had very little emotional connection with the voters.

I asked him to tell me about the last fight his boss had led. He replied that they tried to avoid fights or controversial issues. I said, "You can stop right there—the fight's the thing. If you want people to be passionate about your guy, they have to see him lead some fights."

The "fight's the thing" because people "act" themselves into beliefs and commitments. Rooting for "your team" is a form of acting. When you start "rooting" for a sports team, you make an emotional investment in the team and its players.

The more emotion you commit, the more you "believe" in the team— the more you care about the results of the game—the more you like the players—the more you buy the paraphernalia.

I have some friends in Louisiana who go to every Louisiana State University (LSU) home game. Their house is loaded with LSU pillows and trinkets. Their dog is named "Tiger" (after the LSU Tigers). They're not gamblers and they don't stand to make anything material from the success of LSU's football team. But they are completely invested in the team. They get part of their meaning and significance from LSU's success.

To feel that way about a political candidate, political leader, party or movement, there has to be a contest that forces you to choose sides—to root them on. Candidates who stand up for what they believe in—that "take 'em on"—develop a loyal core of supporters because the dynamic of the fight requires voters to choose sides and make an emotional commitment—to root for someone that they believe in.

In fact, politics can be viewed as the quintessential "reality" TV—real characters, real stakes, an outcome that is in fact settled by the audience.

Just as importantly, voters view candidates or officeholders who avoid conflict as people who have no values. That's because if you have strongly held beliefs, you fight for them. A party or candidate whose goal is to avoid being accused of anything will be viewed as a party or candidate who stands for nothing.

And by the way—the candidate who never led a fight, lost.

Fights run contrary to the inclinations of many politicians. Politicians as a class want everyone to like them. Their instinct is to try to please all the people all of the time. Quite apart from the fact that the idea of running for public office is to fight for your constituents, trying to please all the people, all the time, is just bad politics.

Once again, a political message is best as a storyline or narrative. Good stories always have conflict. Stories are interesting when they are about change, and change requires conflict.

THE LINE

If a new office holder wants to develop a strong base of passionate supporters, she should choose at least one good fight right away.

Immediately after Jan was first elected to Congress in 1998, some immigrant rights advocates came to her for help with a problem that demeaned and inconvenienced recent immigrants every day. The Immigration and Naturalization Service (INS) office in downtown Chicago had a huge line every morning. Hundreds, sometimes more than a thousand, people were forced to wait in the heat or cold outside of the office building every morning for service. People started lining up each day at 4 or 5 a.m.

The line was so long because the INS refused to do any serious business by phone. They didn't even have locations where you could pick up forms without waiting in line. If they lost your application (a frequent occurrence), you had to come back and wait in line to file a new one.

To make matters worse, the INS would only service 600 people each morning. But they didn't give out numbers and you couldn't make appointments, so you didn't really know if you were in the first six hundred until you had waited for hours for the office to open. If you missed the cut, you would have to come back another day—no matter that you had missed a day of work.

And even when you finally got into the office, you were treated with disrespect.

So one morning, Jan and her staff went to stand in the line incognito. They took a tape recorder to interview immigrants in the line—to find out why they were there—so they could understand the process from the point of view of INS's "customers." What they found was not pretty.

Jan happened to be in a spot in the line that didn't make the 600-person cut. But apparently she didn't move fast enough for the guard who yelled: "Move or go to jail."

Jan replied, "You have no right to speak to me like that." The guard said, "Well, who are you?" Jan said, "First, I'm a human being, and no one deserves to be treated like that. And second, I'm a Member of the United States Congress and this is going to change."

The guard protested that it was "unfair" that a Member of Congress should show up unannounced. She called the Regional Director who sent word asking her to come to his office. Jan sent word back that if he wanted to talk, he could come downstairs and discuss the matter with the rest of the people who had been in the line since 5 a.m.

The next week Jan returned to the line, this time with the press. She played the tapes of people's stories and demanded action to assure that recent immigrants were treated with respect.

The story played all over Chicago. And within several weeks, the line was gone. The INS national office intervened; reforms in procedures were made. New personnel were hired; the office began scheduling appointments.

That was years ago. Even today, Jan is often introduced at ethnic events by someone who retells the story of how she got rid of the hated line. That fight became legendary. For Hispanics, Asians, Russian Jews, Poles and many other ethnic groups that make up Chicago's melting pot, it was clear from that moment that Jan was on their side.

THE ACTION'S IN THE REACTION

Another reason why "the fight's the thing" is that very often, as Saul Alinsky used to say, "the action's in the reaction." Often, something becomes an issue, begins the word of mouth buzz, and shows up on the radar, not because of what you do or say, but because of the reaction it provokes in the other side.

The key event in Jan's visit to the immigration line was the guard's threat to "move or go to jail." The action was in the reaction.

In fact, sometimes you do or say things in politics, just to get the other side to "take the bait." You provoke them into a response. Sometimes when we run issue campaigns, we target members of Congress who are very unlikely to vote our way, but who will react loudly to being attacked. You'll remember we call them "squealers." The effect of their response is to frighten other members who may feel vulnerable if they vote against us.

Of course, if you've planned something without taking into account the reaction, the backlash can badly damage your cause and come to overshadow your original message. The Mexican flags that immigrants carried in the massive pro-immigrant marches in April and May of 2006 were meant as expressions of pride. But they provoked a backlash from the anti-immigrant fringe that damaged the immigrant cause.

INTENSITY MATTERS

In politics, intensity matters. Some opinions are deeply held and strongly felt. Others are very soft. Intensity obviously matters when it comes to altering opinions. If you start a campaign and the opponent has very high positives that are very intense, you have a much bigger problem than campaigning against an incumbent with high positives that are very soft.

The level of intensity with which a group reacts to an issue, or other symbol, may be very important as well.

Support for a preemptive, unilateral attack on Iraq is a case in point. During the run up to the 2002 elections, opinion polls generally indicated that a majority (though not a large majority) of voters supported war with Iraq. But throughout the country members of Congress from both parties received overwhelmingly more communication from those who were opposed to the war. Jan received 7,000 letters, emails and phone calls on the subject, and only 70 supported the President's position. The reason was a major imbalance in the level of *intensity* of war supporters and opponents.

Intensely-felt positions can become litmus tests for whether a candidate is on your side. They also have a much greater effect on motivating stay-at-home voters to go to the polls. In the 2002 elections, many Democrats stayed away from the polls because they had been "demobilized" by a feeling that Democrats weren't standing up for them. A sense that the Democratic leadership was failing to stand up to the President on the Iraq issue was a major contributing factor.

PEOPLE WANT TO MAKE A COMMITMENT — GIVE THEM THE OPPORTUNITY

We've talked a good deal about how from the most fundamental physical self-interests, meaning and significance often trump all other self-interests.

A lot of what people do can be understood as quests for this kind of meaning and validation, or in the escape from a feeling of worthlessness and irrelevancy.

Fundamentally, people fulfill their need for meaning through the commitments they make. It is through the commitment to a partner, family, children, job, ideology, art, sport, religion, nation, or leader that they gain the sense that their life matters. They will often trade security, money, sometimes their lives, to fulfill the commitments that give them meaning.

Great political leaders give people the opportunity to make a commitment: to their election, to the causes they espouse, to them—as people. That act of commitment fulfills one of their constituent's most basic needs in and of itself.

But that requires that the leader give constituents something to believe in. That's why the quality of commitment to your values is so high on the list of qualities people look for in their leaders. Leaders can't ask others to commit themselves to their cause if they are unwilling to make a commitment themselves.

Remember, the commitments we ask have two elements:

• We have to convince the voters that the cause to which we want them to commit is in itself significant.

• We have to convince each person that he or she can play a significant role, *personally*, in achieving the goal—whether by voting, volunteering, giving money, talking to neighbors, writing letters or participating in organizations.

BECAUSE PEOPLE ARE HERDING ANIMALS—SOCIAL CREATURES THEY LOOK TO THEIR NEIGHBORS TO VALIDATE THEIR VIEWS

Remember that one of people's major categories of self-interest is human interaction and approval. People live in groups, and what other members of the group thinks matters a lot. As I've said before, people are herding animals.

If the group gives someone "permission" to believe something or support someone, he is much more likely to do so. People look to their friends and neighbors to validate their views.

All you need to do is think about your own experiences in high school to realize that when a candidate becomes popular, her support begins to snowball, because the fact that popularity itself is persuasive to other voters. In other words, the well-known "bandwagon effect" is enormously important in politics.

If we communicate that our candidate is doing well in the polls, that fact *by itself* will persuade others to support her. If someone sees loads of yard signs in their neighborhood, that fact *by itself* will help persuade voters that the candidate is "on their side."

After the 2000 U.S. Census, Jan's district was redrawn to include the city of Park Ridge, Illinois. Park Ridge, where Senator Hillary Rodham Clinton grew, up had a reputation as a rock-ribbed Republican bastion. The goal of Jan's political organization was to turn Park Ridge blue.

When we first recruited door-to-door canvassers in Park Ridge and asked them to put up Democratic yard signs, the person on the other side of the door would inevitably say, "I'd love to, I'm a Democrat, but there aren't any other Democrats on this block." Then a couple of doors down, someone would say, "Gee, I'm a Democrat, but there aren't any other Democrats on the block."

By the time our canvasser was done with a precinct, it had blossomed in Democratic yard signs, and people would all say, "Gee, I had no idea how many Democrats there were in Park Ridge."

In 2006, Jan won Park Ridge by 56% of the vote. I'm betting that by 2008's Presidential election, Park Ridge will be blue.

CHAPTER TWENTY-SEVEN

Planning a Message Campaign

The remaining principles of political messaging pertain to the planning and execution of the political message campaign.

LEARN EVERYTHING YOU CAN ABOUT YOUR OWN CANDIDATE, AND THE OPPONENT, BEFORE YOU LAUNCH THE CAMPAIGN.

In elections, the subject of messaging to persuadable voters is the candidate, so the first task in planning the campaign is to find out everything you can about the subjects of the decision—the candidates contesting the race.

Our research has one major goal: to find symbols that will communicate one or more of the nine candidate qualities we've discussed above. In other words, the first thing we do in planning the campaign is to go on a symbol hunt.

We need to find symbols that will allow us to communicate the positive side of the nine qualities for our candidate, and the negative side of the qualities for our opponent. We also need to find symbols that will help us neutralize attacks that come from the other side.

Our goal is to raise the voter's positive valuation of our candidate and where necessary, raise the voter's negative valuation of the opponent or opponents.

That means we have to do opposition research and research on our own candidate as well. In both cases, we need to catalog and investigate symbols that are both positive and negative. If we don't do a thorough job on this research, two things can happen:

- We'll miss the most powerful symbols we can use to benefit our candidate or attack an opponent.
- We'll be unprepared when the opposition uses a symbolic vulnerability to attack our candidate once the campaign is underway.

There are a lot of sources to be checked:
- If either candidate is an officeholder, you need to review their history in public office—legislative voting history and news accounts of public remarks.

- You need to work with your candidate to review her life and background. You need to learn what she believes in. You need to get her to remember stories in her life. What meant a lot to her? You need to understand her family and family history.

- You need to review both candidate's business and professional history. What has been written in the public media about their work? Have they won awards? What does their professional life say about the nine qualities? Who's on the voter's side? What does the candidate believe in, etc.?

- You need to do a complete search of all other public documents and filings—lawsuits, criminal convictions, scrapes with authority, voting records.

- You need to interview selected friends and associates of the candidate. Look for mavens who know all the political scuttlebutt, who can inform your search.

Remember, you're looking for symbols that are powerful, visual—that communicate emotionally—symbols that surprise or make us laugh or cry or angry. The smallest detail could be the symbol you're looking for—like the pilot who was running for State Senator in Texas and "belly-landed his airplane at Tyler Pounds Field" or the candidate whose idea of fighting crime as a state legislator was to criminalize senior-citizen bingo players.

Of course, the best symbol could turn out to be something major and obvious like a candidate's position on the war in Iraq.

We also need to find our candidate's "creation myth"—what drove the candidate to run for office or to become involved in public life. And most important, we need to know what our candidate genuinely believes about people, about life, about issues. What values drive our candidate?

There are opposition research firms that specialize in this kind of research. In general, the most frequent mistake at this level is to ignore symbolic material that reflects negatively on *your* candidate. You have to know it's there in order to prepare for it.

Once you've done this research, a campaign can move to the next step.

Understand the potential interplay between your message and the likely message of your opposition—the message box

This is often done using a "message box."

A number of years ago, a friend and political consultant named Paul Tully created the message box. Tully was a consultant to many of the Democratic presidential candidates of the 1980s' and '90s'. His last client was Bill Clinton. Unfortunately, he died of a heart attack months before Clinton won the nomination and the presidency. But Tully's message box is still with us and is widely used by political campaigns.

We take all of the symbols we have discovered for our research and use the message box to understand their political interplay.

Essentially the message box describes the types of communication that will happen in the political campaign:

What Our Candidate Says About Himself	What Our Opponent Says About Himself
What Our Candidate Says About His Opponent	What Our Opponent Says About Our Candidate

There are four types of communication that happen in campaigns. Each of these interacts with the others in a dynamic fashion as the campaign unfolds.

There are two types of communication that we, the campaign, *can* control:

1) **What our candidate says about himself.**
    We have to determine exactly how the candidate is going to define himself. Which qualities will we highlight? What symbols will we use to do it?

2) **What our candidate says about his opponent.**
    Some campaigns don't require that we say anything at all about our opponent. Maybe the opponent is so poorly known that anything we say about him would actually improve his chances.
    But most campaigns, particularly in hotly contested races, absolutely require that we decide what negative qualities about our opponent we want to highlight, and the symbols we use to do it.

The second two forms of communication, we *cannot* control. But we have to plan.

1) **What our opponent says about himself.**
    We need to use our best information to determine how the other side will position their candidate. Which qualities will they highlight, what symbols will they use?
    The qualities and symbols we use to describe our candidate will be

impacted by our opponent's choice of message. The will also help us decide how we will discredit or minimize the importance of the opponent's positive message.

2) **What our opponent says about our candidate.**
How will our opponent seek to raise our candidate's negatives? What qualities will he attack? What symbols will he use? Of course a lot of this will be determined by how much he can find out about our candidate. What negative symbols can he dig up?
Our opponent will dig up symbolically powerful events, stories, votes, misdeeds, etc. through his own program of opposition research.

DETERMINE WHICH OF THE SYMBOLS IN EACH QUADRANT OF THE MESSAGE BOX ARE MOST PERSUASIVE

We need to know which symbols about our candidate are most persuasive in building his positives, and which symbols about our opponents are most persuasive at building his negatives.

We also need to know how effective the symbols are that are available as ammunition for the other side to attack our candidate because we need to plan how to neutralize these attacks.

Finally, we need to test the effectiveness of our opponent's positive symbols because we might need to neutralize them, too.

Of course, we could make these judgments based on our political experience. That might work fine, if the electorate were made up entirely of political junkies, but it's not. Political people are not normal people—that's why we have to do systematic public opinion research.

The purpose of this research is simple: to determine which symbols of candidate qualities are most persuasive to perusadable voters.

There are basically two general categories of this research. There is a quantitative research using public opinion polling techniques and qualitative research using focus groups and other methods for getting a more complex and subjective understanding of voter decision-making.

Of course, for a lot of voters, the public opinion poll embodies everything they don't like about politicians who will "say whatever it takes to win." Many voters hate politicians who put their finger in the air (through polling) in order to determine what position to take on a particular issue. Voters don't like politicians whose position depends on an issue's popularity in the polls—and well they shouldn't.

Polls should never be used to determine a candidate's position on an issue. Positions should be based on a leader's evaluation of what's right and wrong, not what is popular.

On the other hand, to run an effective election campaign, we need to find out which arguments—or symbols—are most convincing to persuadable voters. The only respectful way to do that is to ask them, to do polling. Candidates should not change their positions on issues based on poll results, but they can certainly learn which things to highlight in an election campaign and how to talk about them.

THE BASELINE POLL

Early in the campaign, you would do a "baseline" poll. Though it may be important for raising money and for lifting the mood of the candidate, a good baseline poll is mostly about identifying persuadable voters and refining the message communicated to them. A good baseline poll might have the following elements:

- Screen questions to qualify respondents as likely voters. (e.g., "Would you say you are likely to vote in the upcoming election?")

- Questions identifying issues that are important to the respondent.

- Questions indicating how favorably candidates are regarded by the electorate—and the name recognition of the candidates.

- Questions concerning the job performance of incumbent candidates.

- Questions having to do with the overall political atmosphere. For instance, we might ask about whether voters think things are on the "right direction or off on the wrong track."

- A "horse race" question: "If the election were held today and the candidates were Elmer Fudd and Bugs Bunny, would you support Elmer Fudd or Bugs Bunny?"

- Presentation of positive message about the candidates. This information is generally presented so as to resemble the positive message of each competing campaign. It is drawn from our research.

- A re-poll of the "horse race" question. "Having heard these descriptions of the candidates, if the election were held today and the candidates were Elmer Fudd and Bugs Bunny, would you support Elmer Fudd or Bugs Bunny?

- A test of various negative statements about the candidates: "Some people say that Bugs Bunny is a rabbit. Would you find this a very convincing, somewhat convincing, or not at all convincing reason to vote against Bugs Bunny?"

- Potentially a final re-poll of the "horse race."

- Demographic questions about the respondent: race, income, type of job, age, gender, etc.

Interviews are done with a random sample of voters. A universe of 400 interviews will give us an outcome that is accurate within a range of plus or minus 5%, 95 out of 100 times. For most campaigns, that yields good "top lines"—results that can be relied upon for the entire universe of people polled.

It also gives us a fair reliability, if we cut it into a limited number of subgroups—by gender, race, etc. But if we want to divide it more finely, we need to do a larger initial sample, since the reliability of the poll for any subgroup increases with sample size.

Once a campaign begins to connect with the voters, the baseline poll might be followed by several tracking polls. Trackers allow us to see how well our communication strategies are actually working, and allow us to test messages that we are inevitably forced to develop to respond to newly developed campaign situations.

Below I've reproduced a sample poll questionnaire that illustrates how the process works.

CITY COUNCIL POLL
JANUARY 2007

Phone Number_____
Interviewer_____
Sample Page Number_____
Date_____ Time Began_____
Time Ended_____

I'm calling from SCG Research, a public opinion firm. Your number was selected at random for a survey of important issues facing your community. We are not selling anything and I won't ask you for a contribution or donation. According to our research procedure, may I speak to _____(Ask for Name on List)?

Gender **(DO NOT ASK)** Record respondent's gender.
1.   Male
2.   Female
(When proper respondent is on the phone, begin the survey. Circle the number of the response.):

1. **First, are you registered to vote at this address?**
    1.   Yes (Continue)
    2.   No (Terminate)
    3.   Not sure (Terminate)

2. **As you may know, in March there will be an election to select the Mayor of Clark City and City Council members from each city ward. Is it very likely, somewhat likely or not at all likely that you will vote in those elections?**
    1.   Likely (Continue)
    2.   Somewhat likely (continue)
    3.   Not at all likely (terminate)

3. **Now, I'd like to ask you about some public figures. For each one, please tell me whether you have a VERY favorable, SOMEWHAT favorable, SOMEWHAT Unfavorable, or VERY Unfavorable impression of that person. If you haven't heard of someone, or if you don't know enough to have an impression, just say so and we'll move on.**

    First, do you have a VERY favorable, SOMEWHAT favorable, SOMEWHAT Unfavorable, or VERY Unfavorable impression of: (ROTATE READING ORDER)

    1. Lucy O'Connor
    1.   very favorable
    2.   somewhat favorable
    3.   somewhat unfavorable
    4.   very unfavorable
    5.   no opinion
    6.   never heard of

    2. Isabel Frederick
    1.   very favorable
    2.   somewhat favorable
    3.   somewhat unfavorable
    4.   very unfavorable

    5.   no opinion
    6.   never heard of

3. Karen Gold
    1.   very favorable
    2.   somewhat favorable
    3.   somewhat unfavorable
    4.   very unfavorable
    5.   no opinion
    6.   never heard of

4. Sidney Goldstein
    1.   very favorable
    2.   somewhat favorable
    3.   somewhat unfavorable
    4.   very unfavorable
    5.   no opinion
    6.   never heard of

5.   Looking ahead to the next election for City Council from this Ward, if the election were held today and the candidates were (rotate reading order of names) **Isabel Frederick or Lucy O'Connor, for whom would you vote? (IF "NOT SURE," ASK:) Well, which way do you lean at this time?**
    1.   Isabel Frederick
    2.   Isabel Frederick (lean)
    3.   Lucy O'Connor
    4.   Lucy O'Connor (lean)
    5.   Undecided
    6.   Refused

6.   Do you think that your community is safer than it was four years ago, less safe, or do you think there has been no change in the safety of your community?
    1.   More safe
    2.   Less safe
    3.   About the same
    4.   Don't know

7. Now I'd like to ask you about the current City Councilman, Isabel Frederick. How would you rate the way she has been doing her job as City Councilman for your ward? Has it been excellent, good, fair or poor?

1. Excellent
2. Good
3. Fair
4. Poor
5. Don't know

Now, let me read you descriptions of three candidates for City Council from our area. (ROTATE READING ORDER OF THE DESCRIPTIONS)

(a) When Isabel Frederick was first elected to the City Council 12 years ago, many people believed that the economic revitalization of our area was a pipe dream. Others warned that any attempt to revitalize the 51st Ward would jeopardize our neighborhood's racial and economic diversity. Isabel Frederick and the people of the 51st Ward have proven the skeptics wrong. Frederick has spearheaded the redevelopment of Maple Street, the Rosemont shopping district and the Hobart Park. She has brought two new schools, a library and over a thousand new units of affordable housing to the community. The crime rate in our community has dropped by 44%, test scores in our local elementary schools have steadily increased, and at the same time we have maintained our community's racial and economic diversity.

(b) Lucy O'Connor is a long-time community activist who has been a member of the Clark City Police District Strategic Plan Committee. Her priorities are fighting crime and involving the community in the decision-making process. She is an active member of the African-American Community. She is an experienced community development consultant and is committed to balanced development with equal attention to re-development and the creation of quality housing, as well as safe and attractive neighborhood shopping areas. She is a former board member of the Good Government Civic Committee, and has been an independent voice for residents and neighborhoods and she is not beholden to the boys downtown or the big money interests.

8.   **Having heard these descriptions, if the election for City Council were held today, for whom would you vote** (ROTATE ORDER), **Isabel Frederick, or Lucy O'Connor?** (IF "NOT SURE," ask:) **Well, which way do you lean at this time?**
1. Isabel Frederick
2. Isabel Frederick (lean)
3. Lucy O'Connor
4. Lucy O'Connor (lean)
5. Neither/other (IF VOLUNTEERED)

6.   Not Sure
7.   Refused

Now, let me read you some concerns people have mentioned about reelecting Isabel Frederick as City Councilman. For each one, please tell me if it is a very convincing reason, a somewhat convincing reason, or not a very convincing reason to vote against Isabel Frederick.

9.   Some people say that Isabel Frederick has been City Councilman too long. They say it is time for a change and that Frederick has lost touch with the community.
1.   Very convincing reason
2.   Somewhat convincing reason
3.   Not very convincing reason
4.   Not sure

10.   Some people say that Isabel Frederick has grown too close to developers. They say she helps force long-time, low- and middle-income residents from the community to make way for expensive new housing developments.
1.   Very convincing reason
2.   Somewhat convincing reason
3.   Not very convincing reason
4.   Not sure

11.   Some people say that Isabel Frederick's community service office is not effective at dealing with the problems of constituents.
1.   Very convincing reason
2.   Somewhat convincing reason
3.   Not very convincing reason
4.   Not sure

12.   Some people say that residents in the Vulcan Park neighborhood spend almost half of their retail dollars outside of the Ward because Isabel Frederick has not done enough to develop local businesses.
1.   Very convincing reason
2.   Somewhat convincing reason
3.   Not very convincing reason
4.   Not sure

13.   Some people say that Isabel Frederick is doing to little to fight crime in our community.

1. Very convincing reason
2. Somewhat convincing reason
3. Not very convincing reason
4. Not sure

Now, let me read you some concerns people have mentioned about electing Lucy O'Connor to the City Council. Please tell me if it is a very convincing reason, a somewhat convincing reason, or not a very convincing reason to vote against Lucy O'Connor.

14. A newspaper reported that when Lucy O'Connor was President of the Board of the Jones Community Center, she mismanaged the agency so badly that it went out of business and that all of its funds were never properly accounted for.

1. Very convincing reason
2. Somewhat convincing reason
3. Not very convincing reason
4. Not sure

15. Lucy O'Connor supports taking money from public schools and using them for vouchers to help parents who send their children to private schools.

1. Very convincing reason
2. Somewhat convincing reason
3. Not very convincing reason
4. Not sure

16. Now, if the election for City Council were held today, for whom would you vote, Isabel Frederick, or Lucy O'Connor? (IF "NOT SURE," ASK:) Well, which way do you lean at this time?

1. Lucy O'Connor
2. Lucy O'Connor (lean)
3. Isabel Frederick
4. Isabel Frederick (lean)
5. Neither/other (IF VOLUNTEERED)
6. Undecided
7. Refused

Finally, I'd like to ask you a few questions for classification purposes only.

17.   Generally speaking, do you consider yourself VERY progressive, SOMEWHAT progressive, moderate, SOMEWHAT conservative, or VERY conservative?
>1.   Very progressive
>2.   Somewhat progressive
>3.   Moderate
>4.   Somewhat conservative
>5.   Very conservative
>6.   Don't know/refused

18.   What is your age category? Are you? (Read Categories)
>1.   18-29
>2.   30-39
>3.   40-49
>4.   50-64
>5.   65 or older
>6.   Don't know/refused

19.   What is the highest level of education you have completed? (Read Categories)
>1.   Grade school
>2.   High school graduate
>3.   Some college or junior college
>4.   College graduate
>5.   Graduate school
>6.   Don't know/refused

20.   Are you married, single, separated, divorced, or widowed?
>1.   Married
>2.   Single
>3.   Separated/divorced
>4.   Widowed
>5.   Don't know/refused

21.   Are you a member of a teachers' union or labor union, or is anyone in your household a member of a teachers' union or labor union?
>1.   Yes—respondent
>2.   Yes—household
>3.   Yes—both respondent and household
>4.   No
>5.   Don't know/refused

22. How long have you lived in the Vulcan Park Community?
1.   Less than one year
2.   1 to 2 years
3.   2 to 5 years
4.   Over 5 years
5.   Don't know/Refused

23. Do you rent or own your place of residence?
1.   Rent
2.   Own
3.   Don't know/Refused

24. Are you a Protestant, Catholic, Jewish, Muslim, Hindu, or something else?
1.   Protestant
2.   Catholic
3.   Jewish
4.   Muslim
5.   Hindu
6.   Other _____
           (Do not leave blank, fill in a response)
7.   Don't know/Refused

25. And, what is your race? (Do Not Read)
1.   White
2.   Black/African American
3.   Hispanic (Puerto Rican, Mexican, etc.)
4.   Asian
5.   Other _____
           (Do not leave blank, fill in a response)
6.   Don't know/Refused

26. What is your zip code? _____

This completes the survey, thank you very much for your time. You have been most helpful. My supervisor may call you back to quickly verify the survey. Thank you again and goodbye.

27. Gender (DO NOT ASK.) Record respondent's gender.
1.   Male
2.   Female

The poll above is intended for use in a fictitious City Council race in the fictitious jurisdiction of Clark City.

A questionnaire like this is administered to a random sample of voters. The sample is usually drawn either from the voter file, or using what is known as random digit dialing. In either case, the first section of the poll is intended to screen for voters who actually intend to vote in the upcoming election.

It then goes on to ask for "favorable-unfavorable" opinions of various public figures, including the candidates in this race. It also tells us the degree of name recognition of the candidates. This is a key set of questions because it enables us to determine, for both our candidate and the opponent, where we begin the persuasion process.

If a candidate has a high ratio of favorable to unfavorable opinion and high name recognition, she is in good shape as the race begins. If she has a high ratio of favorable to unfavorable opinion but low name recognition, we have to introduce her to many of the voters and hopefully maintain the favorable to unfavorable ratio as we do it. In this case, she is also vulnerable to being "introduced" to many of the voters by our opponent.

If the candidate has a high ratio of unfavorable to favorable opinion and low name recognition, she is obviously in trouble—but not the kind of trouble she would be in if she had a high ratio of unfavorable to favorable opinion and high name recognition.

Low name recognition means we have to do a lot to get the candidate on the voter's radar, but even if she has low favorables, there are still many voters who can be introduced to her in a more favorable context.

Once we have completed the favorable to unfavorable battery, this poll moves to the "horse race." If the election were held today, for whom would you vote (or lean to)? This tells us where the race begins, but depending on the name recognition of the candidates, it may or may not mean a lot when it comes to the final outcome.

Next, this poll presents a paragraph of positive message—symbols— about each of the three major candidates, and then does a "re-poll"—that is, we ask the horserace question again. These paragraphs are intended to test the effect of what we believe will be the actual positive message of our opponents, and our best guess as to what would be a powerful formulation of our own positive message. In many polls we might do a "split sample" here—half of the respondents are asked to respond to one positive message for our candidate and half for another. This enables us to test the different effect of the two formulations.

The results of the re-poll are certainly interesting in the aggregate. But they are particularly interesting when we do the "cross tabs." The "cross tabs" are the cross tabulations of data from some questions (especially the demographic data) with the results of other questions. At the end of the poll, we ask demographic questions. We can then compare the demographic (and geographic) information with the results of the "re-poll" and see which respondents to the poll were most likely to be persuaded by the positive message about the candidates. Who moves to our candidate? Who moves to the other candidates?

The same kind of cross tabulation can be done on the results of the next set of questions that test the effect of various negative statements (or symbols) about the candidates. The questions are aimed at measuring the intensity of the negative response to various statements and, through the cross tabs, who exactly is persuaded by these negative statements.

Then, the poll does a final "re-poll" to judge the effect of the accumulated information, both positive and negative, on the voters.

The last section of the poll gathers the demographic information we use in the cross tabs.

Many polls have additional sections. For instance, they might test various positive symbols. They might test the impact of particular endorsements, or of particular phrases. A poll might ask whether respondents think that the community is on the right track, and which issues are of greatest concern. It might test anonymous profiles for candidates. But the main purpose of polls remains the same in all cases. Polls allow us to determine the messages that are most likely to persuade voters.

Along the way, they might help us to determine which segments of the electorate can be mobilized "blind" as a group (if any). For instance, if women over 55 break better than two-to-one for our candidate, we may choose to forego an ID program among these voters and simply attempt to mobilize as many of these voters as possible. After all, for every 10 new voters we would get 6.5 voters to the other candidate's 3.5 voters. For the 10 new voters we get out, we would come out ahead.

QUALITATIVE OPINION RESEARCH—FOCUS GROUPS

Polls can tell you a lot about the quantitative impact of messages. They have a limited use in allowing us to explore the nuances—the whys and wherefores—of opinions.

Focus groups allow us to spend an hour-and-a-half to two hours with a group of people and talk about how they *feel*.

Generally focus groups include from 15 to 25 people. Often the participants are somewhat homogeneous. That is so they will feel comfortable exploring their ideas and feelings with each other.

The groups are run by moderators who use a prepared questionnaire, or discussion guide. When we want to test the impact of specific slogans, radio or phone scripts, the questionnaires are followed quite literally. In other cases they are guides to more in-depth exploration of the group's feelings.

Focus groups are particularly useful at getting feedback on TV spots, written advertisements or other forms of messaging. We can use them to see what people remember from the messages they hear or see. We can get their gut reactions to candidates, and explore why people react in certain ways.

Since focus groups are so small, they can never be relied upon to provide statistically significant quantitative data. But they can be invaluable at determining what people really hear or see when we communicate with them.

Focus groups are the place where you really begin to understand the difference between "political people" and "normal people." A lot of times there is a great gulf between what "political people" think they have said and what "normal people" hear. What political people and particularly policy people often think is sophisticated conversation, sometimes sounds like "blah blah blah" to normal people. Often, of course, the "normal people" are absolutely right. But regardless of who is right, if we think we are saying one thing and "normal people" hear something else, we're not doing a very good job of communicating. After all, it is our job to get our message across. It isn't the message recipient's job to figure out what we mean.

When I was still in high school, quite a number of years back, I volunteered for a candidate in a race for Governor of Louisiana. The big debate among political insiders in Louisiana at the time was over whether the candidates were "controlled" by the remnants of the famous Louisiana Long organization (Governor Huey Long, Governor Earl Long, Senator Russell Long). The incumbent Governor, John McKeithen, ran for reelection using the slogan, "Vote for Me, I'm Uncontrolled." To political people this sounded just great. Of course "normal people" heard: Vote for me, I'm undisciplined—or Vote for Me, I'm out of control. A good focus group would have sorted the problem out at the get-go.

There are many variants on the focus group. ABC's "Nightline" sometimes selects a group of average people to do "dial testing." Each participant is given a dial to turn—one way if they like what someone is saying, or the images they are experiencing, and another way if they don't. These inputs are then aggregated by a computer and you get a graph of the average response to the words, appearance, images, or general impression, being given by a person or advertisement—word by word.

Polling is good at identifying which words and phrases work the best.

Focus groups are often essential to determine why one particular word or phrase works best. They allow us to get people to explain the thought process that goes into their understanding of what we have attempted to communicate.

Focus groups can also give us insights into the critical issue of intensity. Just finding the raw percentage of people who support a particular position may not be the most important thing you want to know about a position or an issue.

And remember the coalition rule: if you stand up for the most intensely felt bottom line of all of the potential coalition participants, they will give you a great deal of slack with respect to other interests that are less critical.

Politicians who look only at the quantitative polling data to see the lay of the land ignore the principal source of energy in the political process: intensity.

Select a limited number of key positive and negative messages for the campaign — and weave them together in a core message or narrative

Once the campaign has done its research, message box modeling and opinion research, it needs to select a limited number of key positive and negative messages that it will repeat throughout the campaign. The actual number should reflect the length of the campaign, the campaign's communication budget, the budget of the opposition and the quality of the symbols that you've identified. Generally no more than five or six are appropriate.

The symbols chosen should generally be aimed at focusing in on a cluster of the candidate's qualities that the polling has shown can be most persuasive. These should then be woven together into a core campaign message or narrative that communicates the qualities of the candidate that we intend to highlight. Each symbol should prove the message of the narrative. The narrative as a whole should be clear, concise, contrastive and convincing.

The narrative should have the qualities of any other story—it should contain the dramatic elements that are present in all great storytelling. It should develop the characters—our candidate, the protagonist and our opponent (or some other antagonist). It should describe a conflict and the setting of the conflict; and provide the other dramatic elements that make them compelling, interesting and engaging to the voter.

In the 2004 presidential race, the Bush campaign's positive message told a story about Bush as a strong effective leader who was firmly committed to solid core values and was standing up to the world-wide threat of radical Islamic terrorism.

The negative narrative set up a contrast with Kerry, whom it positioned as a flip-flopper with no core values. Rove used Kerry's vote for the Iraq War in 2002 and against Iraq War funding later as a powerful symbol of this character quality.

The ad, showing footage of Kerry surfing in flowered shorts, symbolized the same quality. To the millions of Americans who thought windsurfing was only for the "jet set" on the coasts, and had never thought of wearing a patterned swimsuit, it also symbolize that Kerry was not like them, not on their side.

Chapter Twenty-Eight

Breaking Through

Develop a plan to break through.

Once we've developd the core message—the narrative—we're ready to start communicating.

But the first problem is often the most profound. It is breaking through, getting the attention of the voters.

Before a voter can ascribe qualities to a candidate, they have to know that the candidate exists.

In dealing with this problem, we are not only competing with opposing candidates. We're competing with the thousands of other messages the voter receives and processes every day. We are competing with McDonald's, Pepsi, Hewlett-Packard, Ford, the weather report, the murder in the suburbs, the kid's teacher, the kids themselves, and the mother-in-law. We're competing with the bowling league, the church meeting, the boss's tantrum, the telemarketer at dinner, the bank statement, the babysitter, the dog needing to go out, Oprah, the movie review, the morning shock jock, Monday Night Football, Disney on Ice, reality TV, *Time* Magazine, the Cancer Society, thousands of billboards, street signs, and that's just a start.

In *The Tipping Point*, Gladwell reports that the New York-based firm Media Dynamics estimates that the average American is exposed to 254 different commercial messages a day, up nearly 25 percent since the mid-1970s.[1] And that's just "commercial" messages.

The first problem of political communication is to get our candidate on the "radar screen" of the voters.

There are two ways to achieve break-through:

- **Be Memorable**
- **Repeat, Repeat, Repeat**

MAKE THE MESSAGE MEMORABLE USING THE "STICKINESS FACTOR"

In *The Tipping Point*, Gladwell argues that we can think about memorability the way we think about the "stickiness" of a virus during an epidemic.

The worst flu epidemic of all time was the pandemic of 1918. It was first spotted in the spring of that year and was fairly tame. But over the summer something happened to change the virus. It became more deadly. Nothing changed in the way it was transmitted or spread, but once it infected a victim, the immune system had a much more difficult time purging it from the body—it became more "sticky." [2]

"Stickiness" is a critical element in social epidemics as well. We spend a lot of time thinking about how to make messages more contagious—to spread them to more and more people. But the first problem is to make sure that what we say doesn't go in one ear and out the other—that it "sticks" with us—that it has impact.

Think for a moment about Ice Hockey. There are a limited but intensely loyal number of loyal National Hockey League fans in the USA. Every night on the news during the hockey season there are sports items on hockey. For those who care about hockey, these sports items are followed avidly, and they register.

But if you don't follow hockey, I challenge you to tell me what it was that the sports announcer said about the NHL last night. The item goes in one ear and out the other. It isn't "sticky."

Most normal people think about politics that way. They may hear an item about politics on the news, but if it doesn't make an impact, it will simply go in one ear an out the other. That is why memorability is so critical. We have to make the symbols we use,—the stories we tell—"sticky."

There are a number of rules that we use for making messages memorable.

RULE NUMBER 1—THE MORE CONCRETE, THE MORE MEMORABLE

To be "sticky," a message has to relate directly to the listener's personal experience. It has to make the listener nod in acknowledgement or laugh in recognition. It needs to connect with the listener. The more a message relates to one's everyday experience, the more likely it is to be remembered.

In general, people don't experience concepts in their daily lives. They experience concrete events, specific people, social situations, emotional states, sounds, sights, tastes and smells.

That is why, in general, the more abstract a message, the less memorable it is. The more concrete the message, the more it is likely to stick with you.

Memorable messages don't just make you *think* about a subject—they make you feel, taste, smell or hear the content. They make you *experience* the content. A memorable message about pollution doesn't tell you about the concept of a polluted waterway—it describes a polluted waterway: its smell, its color, its toxicity.

It is one thing to hear that the ambient temperature of the earth has risen 1 degree Fahrenheit and may rise many more degrees over the next 50 years. It's another to hear that polar bears may soon be extinct, or that the Midwest "bread basket" may dry up, or that coastal areas could be flooded.

When the first President George Bush ran against Mike Dukakis in 1988, he didn't cite a bunch of statistics when he wanted to accuse Dukakis of having a bad environmental record as Governor of Massachusetts. Instead he did a TV spot about Dukakis' failure to clean up Boston Harbor, complete with pictures of waste and pollution.

Memorable messages are much more likely to paint a picture for the listener to make him experience the subject, not just hear about it.

That's another important thing about stories. It's no accident that throughout human history, cultural traditions have been passed from generation to generation in the form of myths and stories. Stories make concepts accessible from the standpoint of everyday experience, and they are much more likely to be remembered than a platitude or rule.

In *The Tipping Point*, Gladwell cites a study that tested the best approach to get college students to get tetanus shots. They gave one group a factual booklet and gave the other a "high fear" booklet that described victims in graphic terms. The "high fear" booklet was indeed more persuasive in convincing students of the dangers of tetanus and made them more likely to *say* they would be inoculated. But neither booklet resulted in a substantial number of students *actually* being inoculated.

Then they made one small change in the booklet that increased the vaccination rate from 3% to 28%. It was to include a map of the campus with the University Health Building circled and the times that shots were available clearly listed. Most students all already knew where the health center was, so they didn't *need* the information on the location of the health center.

Gladwell concludes: "...what it needed was a subtle but significant change in presentation. The students needed to know how to fit the tetanus stuff into their lives; the addition of the map and the times when the shots were available shifted the booklet from an abstract lesson in medical risk... and at once the advice became memorable." [3]

RULE NUMBER 2—A MESSAGE IS MORE MEMORABLE IF IT MAKES THE LISTENER REACT EMOTIONALLY

To be remembered, a message should not simply be concrete, it should force the subject to react emotionally. It is no accident that most people's earliest memories involve some (positive or negative) emotional event.

Not only are we are much more likely to remember something we feel than something we simply think; a memorable message makes you react.

It may make someone laugh, it may make them mad, it may make them cry; but one way or another it makes them react emotionally.

A classic Texas political spot sought to portray the opponent as out of touch with real problems. It started out with an image of a grandmother in a police mug shot. The announcer reported that:

> On March 26th, 1987, State Senator Doug Carl struck a blow against a dangerous class of criminals. Doug Carl voted to keep bingo games for seniors a crime. Bingo? That ought to make us all sleep better tonight. In times like these, our families need serious, hardworking leadership. We need a new State Senator. Richard Notte. Fighting for us.

The spot included the mug shot of a grandma who looks like she could have just come from a bingo hall. It never fails to get a laugh—and drills home the point with a concrete, memorable image. It's a sticky spot.

RULE NUMBER 3—SURPRISE IS MEMORABLE

Memorable messages often include an element of surprise. They include the unexpected.

The listener does not expect "making bingo games a crime." She also does not expect a respectable-looking grandma to be in a mug shot.

One of the best spots ever made in a Congressional race defeated former Congressman Fred Heinemann, a Republican from North Carolina. Heinemann had made the unbelievable comment that his reported income of $180,000 made him "lower middle class."

The spot that did him in, by media consultant Saul Shorr, looked out on stars with an announcer saying, "Earth To Fred…come in, Congressman…. Fred Heinemann thinks that middle class people make $300,000 to $750,000 per year….Earth to Fred, are you there?…And he thinks that his $180,000 annual salary makes him 'lower middle class'….Earth to Fred…over. Fred Heinemann….he's out of touch with average families here….Way Out… Earth to Fred Cooooome In…."

The spot was concrete. It stimulated a huge emotional response from its audience (a combination of anger, amazement and laughter), and it did so partially because it was so surprising that anyone could be so out of touch with the lives of everyday people in America.

The public had a similar reaction to the news stories about how the first President Bush was so fascinated that there were scanning machines used in grocery stores. The response was shock and amazement that any American could be so out of touch that he thought that scanning machines were a new technology in grocery stores, a decade after they first became common. That story did more than dozens of political tirades could have about how out of touch Bush was with average Americans. It was concrete, related directly to everyday experience, totally surprising, and of course resulted in countless jokes at the President's expense. It caused a memorable emotional response on the part of the listener.

Rule Number 4—Confusion Leads to Distraction

According to *Tipping Point* author Gladwell, as it prepared the first editions of "Sesame Street," the Children's Television Workshop did considerable research on the techniques for getting small children to remember the messages they wanted to communicate in their TV show.

Their chief finding was that confusion led to distraction. If the child did not understand the plot of a skit or a concept being discussed, she was much more likely to become distracted—to pay less attention to the show—and to remember less.

If we don't understand a subject, or the relevance of what is being described in a message, we begin to tune it out. It goes in one ear and out the other.

Back to the hockey news. If you don't follow hockey—if you don't care about hockey and don't know the teams or the players or the rules– it doesn't much matter to you if someone scored a "hat trick." What is a "hat trick" anyway?

If you've ever been abroad and tuned in CNN at your hotel, you probably caught the cricket news. But odds are good that 30 seconds after the announcer revealed who was "bowling" that morning, it didn't register. Without understanding the sport, the facts presented to you are not memorable. When the cricket news comes on, you begin to think about something else or go get a cold one from the fridge (actually, being in Europe, you probably get a warm one).

But if you are a cricket fan, you hang on every word. It is relevant to your life and experience and, just as importantly, you understand the context and importance of what you hear.

Like all pilots, I like to talk with other pilots about flying. I can re-member the most obscure detail in a conversation, article or TV show about flying. To most people it would sound like white noise and they wouldn't retain a thing.

Of course, the same goes for politics. If we talk in jargon that is unknown to most of the world, people don't try to understand the jargon, they simply tune out. They become distracted and don't remember what we say. Another case of "blah, blah, blah." It is for good reason that "clear" is one of our four C's of political communication. *Clear* not only makes things understood, it allows people to remember.

RULE NUMBER 5 — MEMORABILITY DEPENDS ON THE STRUCTURE OF THE MESSAGE

Our eyes register movement and shape over a very wide area. But the subject of what we actually see is displayed in what is known as the fovea of the eye only. The fovea focuses on what we "notice" and remember.

For that reason, Madison Avenue spends millions testing the structure of their TV spots, and print ads to understand where people's eyes actually focus. The beautiful model might make someone notice the ad, but if the eye doesn't move from the model to the car that is the object of the sale, then the ad does no good to the advertiser. The reader may remember the beautiful model, but does he remember the car?

The structure of a message has to do with the portion that you notice. Does the print ad, or direct mail piece, lead you to the candidate or just the clever tag line? Does the speech leave the audience remembering the message we hoped to communicate — or to some irrelevant story or fact that got in the way?

THE OTHER WAY TO BREAK THROUGH — REPEAT, REPEAT, REPEAT

The more you repeat something, the more it will be remembered.

Many people remember their primary education as endless repetition, and for good reason. Even if a message is not inherently memorable, repetition works; it makes people remember.

This is particularly true in politics. It doesn't matter how implausible, or illogical; repeating a message is key to being remembered and believed.

Just ask McDonald's how many thousands of times they repeat their messages. Or ask President W. Bush. No matter that there was no evidence that Osama bin Laden was connected to Saddam Hussein, Bush knew that if he said it enough people would remember it — and believe it.

The rule in political communication is that it takes at least five impressions of a TV commercial to "burn through" — to be noticed by a viewer. The same goes with direct mail. You do not boost your name recognition as a candidate with one piece of mail. It takes six or 10 pieces of mail before the voters begin to notice.

It may take fewer impressions of a message to break through if the message is inherently memorable. But any message takes multiple repetitions, no matter how inherently memorable it may be.

The necessity of repeating the message is the major requirement of politics that makes campaigns so expensive. You buy TV time by the point. One point represents one percent of TV households in a market. To buy the number of TV impressions equal to the total viewing audience in a market, you have to buy 100 points of TV. To get five impressions, you need to purchase 500 points.

Most people in politics would tell you that it makes little sense to put less than 500 points behind a particular TV spot because it won't "burn through;" it won't be noticed and remembered.

In some markets, TV costs $40 or $60 a point, so the total cost of 500 points would be only $20,000 to $30,000. But in other markets a point may cost $400 — and the cost of 500 points would be $200,000.

One of the key things to measure in a campaign plan is how much it will cost per impression to communicate with the voters.

Through whatever means — TV, radio, earned media, outdoor advertising — successful political messages must be repeated and repeated and repeated. Political communication is "repeated, persuasive contact."

CHAPTER TWENTY-NINE

Message Context

CONTEXT CAN HEAVILY IMPACT HOW PEOPLE INTERPRET A MESSAGE

It's obvious that the historic context in which you deliver a message can radically alter the way it's understood. Americans heard messages about terrorism very differently after 9/11.

But the power of context goes well beyond the way major events shaped the prism through which people hear what we say.

The most subtle changes in context can fundamentally transform the meaning of what we hear and can themselves fundamentally alter human behavior.

In *The Tipping Point*, Gladwell cites a number of psychological studies to reinforce this point. The most famous of course, is the "broken window" study that shows that if a car or house has broken windows, it is more likely to be vandalized.

He also cites the immediate—and precipitous—decline in serious crime (assault and robbery) that occurred in the New York City subway after the transit authority conducted a successful campaign to eliminate graffiti from the once-covered subway cars. The head of the Transit Police at the time believed (correctly) that "the graffiti was symbolic of the collapse of the system." [1]

Gladwell argues that these minor, seemingly insignificant, quality-of-life crimes were tipping points for violent crime. They created an environment of chaos and seeming anarchy that triggered an epidemic of violent behavior--that the chaos seemed to make it acceptable.

The Tipping Point contends that it is generally true "that in ways that we don't necessarily appreciate, our inner states are the result of our outer circumstances."

For instance, he cites a well-known study by a social psychologist named Phillip Zimbardo at Stanford. Zimbardo took a randomly chosen group of volunteers and divided them into "guards" and "prisoners" in what was supposed to be a two-week-long experiment on the impact of a prison environment on the two groups. The prison environment and role of the subjects substantially changed their behaviors. The guards, some of whom had previously identified themselves as pacifists, fell quickly into the role of hard-bitten disciplinarians. Some became positively sadistic. The prisoners (even though they knew they were really part of an experiment) became depressed and passive. After 36 hours, one prisoner became hysterical and had to be released. Four more then had to be released because of "extreme emotional depression, crying, rage and acute anxiety." The experiment was called off after six days. [2]

Zimbardo's conclusion was that there are specific situations so powerful that they can overwhelm our inherent predispositions.

Gladwell cites another study conducted on divinity students at Princeton Theological Seminary. Each student was asked to give a presentation in another building on the story of the Good Samaritan. After being given the assignment, half were told that they were late and had to hurry to make the presentation. Half were told they had plenty of time. Some were given the text of the story of the Good Samaritan to study. Some were not. They were also interviewed before the experiment on what had motivated them to come to Divinity School.

On the route to the location of the presentation, the experimenters placed a man who was obviously in distress—slumped over, head down, eyes closed, coughing and groaning.

The question was, what factors affected who would stop to do what the Good Samaritan did, while on the way to make a presentation about the Good Samaritan?

Turns out that it didn't matter whether the student was given the text to study. It didn't matter what his motivation was in going to Divinity School. What did matter was whether he was told that he was late to the presentation, or that he had some time.

Sixty-three percent of the group that thought they had time stopped. Only 10% of the group that was told they were late stopped.

Gladwell concludes that "what the study is suggesting, in other words, is that the convictions of your heart and the actual contents of your thoughts are less important, in the end, in guiding your actions than the immediate context of your behavior. The words 'oh, you're late' had the effect of making someone who was ordinarily compassionate into someone who was indifferent to suffering…" [3]

CONTEXT AND MOTIVATION

In my experience, five key elements of context are especially important in generating motivation:

1) *Light.* Bright lights tend to be motivational. At a campaign rally I never lower the lights in the audience. Spotlights on the speaker with a

darkened audience may be dramatic as someone enters, but darkened lights take people out of the action if they persist.

And a common mistake at rallies and other events is the failure to make certain that the speaker is well lit. To the extent possible, you want his face lit brightly (not in the shadow), so that people can understand the communication from his facial expressions, not just his words. Large TV monitors help when you have a large audience.

2) *Music.* Nothing communicates emotion more effectively—or more quickly—than music. Music creates emotional states. Upbeat music generates motivation. Downbeat, slow or "relaxing" music cools a crowd. Stadium anthems, fight songs, Bruce Springsteen, Aretha Franklin—these are the ticket for rallies or motivational events.

3) *Crowd.* It is motivating to feel that more people arrived, at any event, than were expected. If you want to motivate, never have empty chairs. To the extent possible, you want a standing-room only crowd.

Set the room for fewer than expected and bring out more chairs at the last minute. Spread the room and used tables or dividers to make the room look full. Choose rooms with high ceilings, since the same size crowd looks bigger there.

4) *Signs and Other "Chum."* Signs and "chum" build momentum (political people often refer to the regalia of politics as chum). Fans, noisemakers, stuff for people to hold or waive or blow build excitement.

5) *Sound.* In most meetings and public events, people experience the event through the sound. If the sound is clear and understandable, people will pay attention, stay focused and be motivated. If the sound is garbled or too soft, they will become distracted and disengaged.

We have a rule for events: "At events and rallies, if anything can go wrong it will be the sound."

The surest way to snatch defeat from the jaws of victory at an event aimed at motivating is bad sound. That means the sound must be checked, maintained and, if possible, managed by professional sound people.

Sometimes the Context Is the Message

Not only does context frame and often determine what and how we hear a political message, sometimes the context itself might *be* the message. That's particularly true of GOTV messaging, where the goal is not to convince but to motivate.

At a rally where an inspiring speech is delivered in a bright, exciting, packed room, where the audience has been pumped up by upbeat music and treated to a dramatic entrance by the candidate the message is the excitement generated by all of the elements that create *emotional context.*

Think about the "message" the next time you want to get romantic. It's not so much the words you say, it's the context that communicates "romantic." You turn down the lights, put on some smooth jazz and pour some champagne. That's romantic.

If you turn up the lights, flip on the football game and put on Big 10 fight songs, that's not romantic, at least for most of us.

CHAPTER THIRTY

Controlling the Dialogue

CONTROL THE DIALOGUE — STAY ON THE OFFENSIVE — IF YOU'RE ON THE DEFENSE, YOU'RE LOSING

I already mentioned that President Clinton's 1992 Campaign Manager, David Wilhelm, says that his first rule of political communication is: stay on the offensive. If you're on the defense, you're losing. That means we have to control the political dialogue.

The plain fact is that people can't focus simultaneously on scores of subjects. Individuals and groups shift their focus of attention constantly. And one of the most important elements of leadership is the ability to define that attention agenda.

That is one of the reasons why control of the White House — or a Governor's mansion or a house of Congress — is so critical in politics. Control of the levers of power helps you to control the subjects that are front-and-center for the voters. One of the major reasons why President Bush's positive ratings continued to dive after the 2006 Midterms is that the Democratic control of Congress gave us back the ability to set the Congressional agenda — and investigate his administration.

In the lead-up to the 2002 Mid-term Election, President Bush's political strategy was spelled out in a PowerPoint presentation that an aide inadvertently lost in Lafayette Park across from the White House.

The strategy: First, confuse the voters when it came to the costs of pharmaceuticals and the Republicans' proposal to privatize Social Security; second, change the subject to War. It was simple, and it worked. But it only worked because Democrats had made their own decision not to communicate a national message. A decision was made to intentionally avoid communicating a national message and instead focus on "local issues" in the 2002 Congressional races.

That decision was clearly wrong. It was wrong because by allowing the Republicans sole control of the agenda for national discussion, they focused the attention of swing voters on the national security issues that were their strength, and neutralized the issues on which we had comparative advantages. They neutralized issues like pharmaceutical costs and Social Security through obfuscation and, to some extent, with outright lies (repeated over and over). They claimed they had pushed for coverage of pharmaceuticals through Medicare (simply not true), and that they opposed the "privatization" of Social Security (also not true). But they confused the voters adequately to allow the focus on War to carry the day.

In 2006, Democrats took a completely different tack. Democrats nationalized the campaign. And just as importantly, we controlled the dialogue as we went into Election Day. As a result, we won by a 15 percentage-point spread among the 19% of the electorate who made their voting decision in the last four days leading to the election. It was critical that our message was on the minds of the massive number of decisive voters who made their minds up near the end of the campaign. If we had lost control of the dialogue at the end, many of these voters might have voted differently.

In politics, our job is to keep the political dialogue on our side of the message box, particularly as people go to vote.

Every candidate, every party and every political movement has its own comparative advantages and disadvantages. The candidate, party or movement that can focus the voter's attention on their advantages—and prevent the voters from focusing on our disadvantages—generally wins.

Wilhelm is right; it is rare to see a winning political campaign that is more often on the defensive than on the offensive.

Remember the Clinton campaign's 1992 "War Room"? The Clinton team was determined never to allow a political attack by their opponents to go unchallenged in the same media cycle. It took the offensive. It was always on the attack, always defining the issue, never thrown off their own message by their needs to respond to the other side.

The famous slogan: "It's the economy, stupid," reminded them constantly to keep the voters' attention on our comparative advantages— Bush's economic policies and the economic stagnation they had caused.

About mid-August 2005 when the tide turned against the Bush administration in the American media, I remember Congressman George Miller remarking on why it was especially important for Democrats to force them to play defense. "These guys in the Bush administration are CEOs," he said. "They're used to people doing what they say, or they'll be fired. This equips them to move right ahead on the offense; they never second-guess. But CEOs are not experienced in being on the defensive. They won't know how to handle the attacks." They didn't. That brings us to the use of negatives.

Smart Use of Negatives

Every candidate has negatives—qualities that bring down the candidate's level of support. In most closely contested campaigns, we have to focus the voter's attention on those negatives. If we don't focus the attention of the voters on an opponent's negatives, we often will lose.

The problem with negatives is that they often create a backlash of "unlikability" for our own candidate. When we deliver an attack on the other candidate that tends to make the candidate making the charge less "likable" or "mean" in the eyes of many voters.

How then to deliver negative messages that do as little damage as possible to the "positives" of our own candidate?

There are several key rules:

Rule # 1—Build Our Positives First

If the first thing that the voters learn about our candidate is that he is attacking the other candidate, we risk the first impression of the voters (particularly persuadable voters) being negative for both our opponent *and* ourselves. This is particularly dangerous if our candidate begins the race without much name recognition.

So if it is at all possible, we need to boost our name recognition with a positive message about our candidate before going on the attack.

There are of course exceptions to this rule. Let's say our opponent is not well-liked at the beginning of the campaign. A champion who is willing to take him on might be just the ticket, even as a first impression.

If our candidate is competing first in a lengthy primary, then the "persuadable" primary voters may want very much to hear from a candidate who will take on the Republican. Of course, as our name recognition improves, we have to be careful to present enough positives to the general-election "persuadables" to assure that their first impressions of our candidate is not someone who is simply "negative."

Rule # 2—Use Humor

Humor is one of the best ways for campaigns to deliver negatives that deliver the message without making our candidate look "mean." This kind of humor cannot appear shrill; it has to sound lighthearted and clever. But it can deliver a terrific wallop.

A classic humorous negative TV spot was used to attack GOP candidate and former Klansman David Duke when he ran for Governor of Louisiana a few years ago. The spot was a parody of the "Jeopardy" TV quiz show. Panelists were given "answers" for which the appropriate question was always: "Who is David Duke?" Here's the script:

Host: Welcome to "Jabberwocky," the game show that all America loves to watch. Bill, Allen and Debbie, are you ready?

Bill, Allen and Debbie: Ready!

Host: Debbie, you first.

Debbie: I'll try False Patriots for $300, Paul.

Host: He was kicked out of ROTC, lied about serving his country and never served a day in the military.

Buzz.

Debbie: Who is David Duke?

Host: Right!

Debbie: Good Buddies for $300.

Host: He hired Ex-Nazis to work on his political campaign.

Buzz.

Host: Bill.

Bill: Who is David Duke? Paul, I'll try Tax Cheats for $200.

Host: He failed to file state income taxes from 1984 to 1987. Allen.

Allen: Who is David Duke? Crazy Ideas for $400, Paul.

Host: He has advocated that America be divided into separate –race-nations.

Buzz.

Host: Debbie, again.

Debbie: Who is David Duke? Basement Booksellers for $300.

Host: He says he changed his ways, but just this year he was caught selling Nazi books and tapes from the basement of his office.

Buzz.

Host: Allen.

Allen: Who is David Duke?

Host: And that's the end of round two. Stay tuned, folks, we'll be right back.

Here is another script from a humorous negative campaign spot:

Last August, Lacey Smith moved from Palm Beach, Florida to Madisonville. Smith had hardly been in Kentucky long enough to unpack his boxes when Lacey decided to move again…. this time to Washington. The only hitch was that Lacey Smith needed our help to go to Congress. Now, we're not opposed to visitors in Kentucky, and we like a man with ambition. But when the tourists start running for Congress, it's time to draw the line. Let's tell Lacey Smith that there's more to being a Congressman than having the urge to travel.

The visuals included a stand-in for Lacey Smith carrying a suitcase and unpacking boxes and a Rolls Royce towing a U-Haul with a "Lacey Smith for Congress" banner.

The tone was light and whimsical—not sarcastic or strident. All in all, a very effective use of humor in a negative spot.

RULE # 3—USE OF THIRD PARTIES

It is pretty obvious that one of the best ways to prevent a negative backlash onto our candidate from the delivery of a negative is to have someone else deliver the negative. That's one of the reasons why third party "issue ads" are so useful. A negative attack delivered by the NRA or AFL-CIO simply delivers the negative—it does not make the candidate on whose behalf it is shown look "mean."

When Dick Durbin first ran for the Senate, his opponent was a right-wing Republican State Senator named Al Salvi. Jim and Sarah Brady did a spot for Durbin that was extraordinary powerful. They had enormous credibility on the gun issue and by delivering the message, they prevented Durbin from being viewed as a "negative campaigner."

The Brady's spoke directly into the camera:

Jim Brady: I'm an Illinois native and I was proud to serve as President Reagan's Press Secretary. When President Reagan was shot, I was wounded too. You should know about Al Salvi's extreme view of guns.

Sarah Brady: All Salvi wants to make assault weapons legal again. And Salvi wants to let people carry concealed guns in public places.

Jim Brady: Al Salvi's view on guns are too extreme for Illinois.

RULE # 4—USE THEIR ATTACK ON US AS AN OPPORTUNITY TO DELIVER AN ATTACK ON THEM

In a tightly contested race, it is almost certain that our opponent will "go negative" and attack our candidate for something. That is why we test the impact of our own negatives and develop ways to neutralize their attacks before the fact.

Good campaigns go a step further. They develop the ability to change the subject when the attack comes. And often the new subject is an attack on our opponent.

Their attack on us is usually a great opportunity for us to deliver negatives against them. Voters view counterattacks as "self defense."

For example, a piece of mail might start off:

Why is "Candidate A" slinging Mud at "Candidate B" (picture of our candidate with mud on her face). (inside) Because he can't match "Candidate B's" Record or her lead in the polls.

Then follows our attack on "Candidate A's" record—which now appears entirely in self-defense.

RULE # 5 — USE POLITICAL JUJITSU; TURN THE ENERGY OF THEIR ATTACK BACK ONTO THE OPPONENT

Sometimes an opponent's attack on our candidate can be a godsend. It can be sent sailing right back at our opponent as a devastating negative.

When Jan was first running for State Representative, her Republican opponent was Joan Barr, the Mayor of Evanston, Illinois. Barr had made her reputation as a "moderate" Republican and a decent person.

Unfortunately for Joan, her campaign had been hijacked by the State Republican Committee who had employed the services of a notorious national Republican "hatchet" man named Roger Stone.

Stone sent a letter to all of the district's seniors over the last weekend of the campaign designed to look like it came from "Medicare." On the outside of the envelope was printed: **"Medicare Cancellation Notice Enclosed."** Inside was a letter charging that because Jan supported universal health care, she was in favor of abolishing Medicare.

The letter was sent the last weekend, so our campaign wouldn't have the ability to respond with paid media. Unfortunately for Barr, Stone forgot about the press.

Apart from the fact that at the time Jan was the Executive Director of the State Council of Senior Citizens, and a huge backer of Medicare, the mailing also terrified a large number of the district's senior citizens. Some of them were afraid to open it. Others called their children in fear that their Medicare coverage was, in fact, somehow being canceled.

So a number of seniors held a press conference denouncing the mailing as an unconscionable scare tactic and, by the way, totally untrue. The last frame of one of the TV stories that ran the Sunday before the election was a "freeze frame" of Joan Barr going into her home—looking more like a fugitive than a candidate for state representative. The tactic completely backfired on the Barr campaign and made her look like a woman who would unscrupulously frighten senior citizens in order to win an election.

A similar fate awaited one of Jan's opponents in her first primary for Congress, State Senator Howard Carroll.

The week before the election, Carroll began airing an ad with vivid pictures of the terrorist attacks in Oklahoma City and New York. The spot asked:

Remember the Hamas terrorist attacks in New York, the bombings in Oklahoma City…165 killed, 20 were children in a day care.

Would you support the death penalty for terrorist acts?

Jan Schakowsky opposes the death penalty, even for murderous acts like the bombings in Oklahoma and New York.

Howard Carroll sponsored the law imposing the death penalty for terrorists like McVeigh and Hamas.

Howard Carroll for Congress.

Jan's terrific research consultant, Don Weiner, found a wonderful man named Bud Welch whose daughter had been killed in the Oklahoma City bombing. But Welch was opposed to the death penalty, and in fact he had become involved in national efforts to repeal the death penalty. We got Welch to come to Chicago and conduct a widely-attended press conference where he accused Carroll of "using my daughter's body to try to win an election."

Just as bad, said Welch, Senator Carroll was a hypocrite because Carroll himself had opposed the death penalty for the entire 27 years he had been in the State Legislature and changed his position in order to run for Congress. Welch's counterattack had enormous credibility. It was also used as a basis for a piece of mail that was delivered to district voters immediately before the election.

The counterattack put the nails in Carroll's political coffin. We had succeeded at turning his attack around. Instead of raising the question of whether Jan was "on your side" it raised the question of Carroll's commitments to his positions, his values and his integrity. It made people think that Carroll was a flip-flopper for political gain. It was political jujitsu.

STAY ON MESSAGE — REPEATED, PERSUASIVE CONTACT

Bill Clinton was a genius at political communication. But even Clinton had a flaw that drove his political staffers wild. When the press would yell out questions after a planned communication event, Clinton would often be tempted to engage the reporter, and provide the answer. In normal life that might be a good instinct, but in politics it was not helpful since it sometimes meant that Clinton would "step on" his own message. His impromptu comments would prove more newsworthy than the message that the campaign intended to deliver.

The problem is that in a given day or a given news cycle, only one message is going to be delivered to the voters through the earned media.

To control the dialogue, the campaign needs to decide what that message will be, and stick to it.

Even more importantly, the campaign as a whole has to stick to its message plan: which qualities are we going to communicate about our candidate and our opponent? What symbols are we going to use to communicate those qualities?

In most campaigns, there is not time or money to communicate more than a limited number of symbols. Those symbols must be carefully chosen, since they are the vehicle—the vector—that we will use to communicate the candidate's qualities to persuadable voters.

The candidate—and campaign insiders—might get absolutely sick of delivering the same basic message day after day. They may wretch as the very thought of talking about the "Bridge to the 21st Century" (Clinton's 1996 campaign slogan) or of the telling of a particular story. But if those symbols are not repeated, they will not "burn through" to normal voters. Winning campaigns stay on *message,* day in and day out, for the entire length of the campaign.

At the beginning of this Section we described how George Bush the First eviscerated Michael Dukakis with his relentless attack line—"He wants to do for America what he's done for Massachusetts: Americans can't afford that risk." He did it over and over and over again, using different symbols to prove the same message. He framed the campaign dialogue, he framed Dukakis and convinced Americans that Dukakis just wasn't on their side.

The key was choosing a limited number of powerful symbols that were repeated over and over and all proved the *same* message.

CHAPTER THIRTY-ONE

The "Inherent" Conflict Between Persuasion and Mobilization is a Myth.

These message principles—or their rough equivalent—are appropriate to candidate and issue campaigns, as well as to the overall campaign to move the center of American politics and create a long-lasting progressive majority.

We have seen that the messages that mobilize and persuade voters are different, but they do not need to be incompatible or contradictory.

The most important single conclusion of this analysis is that, in most cases, the messages that can persuade swing voters on the one hand and motivate mobilizable voters on the other are often different, but they are rarely in conflict. In fact they share many elements.

A small industry has developed debating the relative importance of appealing to the "base," and "moving to the center" to attract swing voters. Generally, this debate ignores the basic principles of political communication or the factors that people really use to make political decisions. It assumes that the messages are about "issues" and not the qualities of the candidates.

In fact, with both base and swing voters, the progressive candidates who are most effective self-confidently communicate a progressive vision; they constantly appeal to voters' progressive values and inspire them with their own passion and commitment. Candidates are more effective with both persuadables and mobilizables if they show that they will stand tall for the baseline concerns that people identify as "their side," and treat people with respect and empathy.

The issue and policy positions taken by candidates and parties are certainly important symbols of a candidate's qualities. But they are rarely as important as the ability of the candidate to appeal to the full range of physical and nonphysical self-interests, and especially to give the voters a sense of their own meaning and significance.

This means that if we proceed properly, the old conflict between appealing to swing voters and to base voters *simply does not exist.*

Battles over resource allocation between persuasion and mobilization — or scheduling candidate time between swing and base areas — will always be part of progressive campaigns. But if we follow these principles of communication and attempt to address the full battery of voter self-interests, there is no fundamental conflict between the two.

Those who argue that in order to win, progressive candidates must play down their values, moderate their positions, or avoid progressive battles — are generally wrong.

Nobody ever followed a leader who was in a defensive crouch. Defeating the right demands instead that Progressives listen to their mothers, and *stand up straight*.

SECTION 5

Planning Campaigns

CHAPTER THIRTY-TWO

Winning Elections:
Persuading "Persuadables,"
Mobilizing "Mobilizables"

Let's turn now to the concrete task of winning elections. First, a review of some of the basic principles that we've discussed so far.

THE THEORY OF CAMPAIGNS

For a number of years, I was privileged to have, two of America's best strategists and organizers, Jerry Morrison and John Hennelly, as my partners at SCG (now both are in senior positions at the Service Employees International Union). Over time, we developed an approach to election campaigns – a theory of campaigns –that is described below. It starts with this premise: when it comes to winning election campaigns all voters are not created equal.

The reason is simple. The purpose of a political campaign is not public education. It is not to raise issues. It is not to raise the flag. The purpose of a political campaign is to elect a candidate.

To achieve that end, campaigns are not organized to get people to do what they would do anyway, whether or not the campaign had been organized.

Political campaigns are intended to **change the behavior of the voters.** If a campaign does not change the behavior of the voters—if it does not get them to do something other than they otherwise would do—why waste all the money and time? You might as well just let voters do what they would do naturally.

So the people who are the focus, or target, of campaign activity must be people whose behavior we can change. These are people who would not have voted for our candidate if the campaign did not exist.

First, to matter to a campaign, a person must be registered to vote. That means that the campaign has to do whatever is necessary to get *all* of our potential voters registered.

The fact is that if everyone voted, Democrats would win most of the time. So as Democrats, we want to get as many people on to the voter rolls as possible—both because it's right and because it serves our interest. More on the importance and structure of voter registration drives later.

Once someone makes the cut of being registered to vote, all voters are still not equal from the point of view of the resources of a successful campaign. As we've seen, winning campaigns focus on a very narrow subset of all registered voters:

- Persuadables
- Mobilizables

Remember, they are the only two groups who are the targets of message in a good electoral campaign because they are the only two groups whose behavior can be changed.

Persuadable voters have two characteristics:

- They generally vote
- They are undecided

Mobilizable voters also have two characteristics:

- They would support our candidate
- They are unlikely to vote unless they are mobililzed to do so

FINDING PERSUADABLES AND MOBILIZABLES

So the first task of a political campaign is to find out who the persuadables and mobilizables *are*.

The late veteran political consultant Matt Reese used to say that if persuadables had purple noses, and mobilizables had green ears, it would be easy to find them. But they don't and that's why campaigns do *targeting*.

To find these voters we have to get two pieces of information:

- How is the voter likely to vote—is she likely to vote Democratic or Republican, or is she undecided?
- How likely is the voter to go to the polls?

These are the two pieces of information that define persuadable and mobilizable voters.

FOUR SOURCES OF INFORMATION

There are four sources of information that allow us to find the persuadables and mobilizables so we can communicate the campaign's message to them.

SOURCE # 1 — GEOGRAPHY — WHERE DO THEY LIVE?

One reason that geography is important to finding persuadable and mobilizable voters is because people tend to behave like their neighbor, whether it's buying habits, religious affiliations, cultural practices or political views; people in geographic communities tend to act alike. That's why marketing firms have spent millions creating and refining census block clusters that allow them to target people who have particular tastes — and the propensity to act in certain ways.

But there's another reason why geography is so important to politics. We have secret ballots in America, so we don't know exactly how each voter casts his ballot in each election. But we do know how a given precinct, or township, or legislative district votes in each and every election. As a result, we can predict what percentage of a particular geographic area is likely to be comprised of Democrats or Republicans, how likely it is that a voter in a precinct will come out to vote, and how many persuadables and mobilizables reside there.

If someone lives in a precinct that votes 65% Democratic, we know — without knowing anything about him — that there are two-to-one odds he's a Democrat.

The National Committee for an Effective Congress (NCEC) specializes in geographic targeting. Every election cycle, NCEC does targeting information for every precinct in the United States.

The chart below is a typical NCEC spreadsheet. It is helpful both at demonstrating the power of geographic information to target, and the concepts of persuadable and mobilizable voters.

STATENAME	CD2002	REG	TRNOUT PCT	EX VOTE	PERS PCT	PERS IDX	DEM PERF	GOTV IDX	GOTV PCT
Florida	21	253937	51	129395	16.7	21667	43.5	47806	18.8
Florida	17	267471	45.8	122498	11.7	14374	80.5	77536	29
Rhode Island	2	329265	58.7	193295	20.5	39558	55.7	56810	17.3
Maine	2	450968	47.6	214438	25.6	54817	54.9	80640	17.9
S Carolina	5	374451	51.8	194021	18.2	35384	50.8	22967	6.1
Illinois	17	435616	51.2	222864	23	51227	51	45196	10.4
Colorado	7	369482	52.4	193723	17.4	33697	48.9	23793	6.4
Louisiana	5	413015	48.8	201327	20.9	41993	47.4	50251	12.2
Arizona	1	337960	53.5	180870	14.2	25719	51.6	40672	12
New York	16	262371	29.1	76310	3.9	2943	94.6	58518	22.3

The first two columns represent the geographic area being analyzed. It could be a precinct, a legislative district, a state, a TV market or a Congressional District. The data on the chart above is for Congressional Districts.

The third column represents NCEC's projection of the number of registered voters that will reside in the District for the 2002 election. The projection in this chart happens to have been made before the 2002 election and was based, like all of the other data here, on the past performance of the District.

Column four is NCEC's projection of turnout percentage in the district. Again, this is based on similar previous elections. Since 2002 was a non-Presidential election, NCEC looked at past turnout in non-Presidential elections to predict future turnout in the area. Generally, these projections assume that whatever Get Out The Vote (GOTV) operations have happened before in the district will happen in the upcoming election.

Column five is NCEC's projection of the actual number of voters who are expected to cast ballots in the upcoming election. It is simply the number of Registered voters times the percentage who are expected to vote.

Column six represents what NCEC calls the persuasion percent. This is the percentage of those who are likely to vote who are switch hitters in any given election. These are the people who are persuadables. They generally vote, but they vote for a Republican in one election and a Democrat in the next. Or they vote for a Republican and Democrat for different offices in the same election.

Two things are very important here. First, there is a considerable variation in the percentage of persuadables from one Congressional District to the next (or one precinct to the next). In the second District in Maine, 25% of the voters are persuadables. But in the 16th District of New York, only 3.9% are persuadable.

Second, the percentage of persuadable voters never gets above about a quarter of the electorate. Yet this relatively small cross-section of the electorate is the subject of most of the political messages communicated in American politics. Virtually all of the TV ads and most of the Radio, mail and "earned media" are aimed at this group.

Nationwide, for the last decade, each party had a base of about 45% of the electorate. Since 2004, the number of self-identified Democrats has grown relative to self-identified Republicans. However, nationally, we are still battling for the allegiance of only 10% to 15% of the voters.

The next column is called **Persuasion Index.** This is the number of living, breathing people who are expected to be persuadables in the Congressional District. It is simply the number of people expected to vote times the persuasion percent.

The eighth column is called **Democratic Performance** — or the Democratic Performance Index (DPI) for the District. This is the average percentage of Democratic votes cast in the District. It is derived by taking a weighted average of various races in the recent past. The chart above includes the Democratic Performance for all kinds of races. NCEC often also generates a Federal, State, Congressional, Senate or Presidential Democratic performance because in many areas these numbers systematically differ from one another. For instance, an area may have a popular incumbent member of Congress that gets a sizeable vote every two years, but the district may still vote for the other party most of the rest of the time.

Next is the Get Out the Vote (GOTV) Index. This is the number of registered voters who are not expected to vote in the upcoming election, but would vote Democratic if they did, and have some history of voting. These are the mobilizable voters.

It is derived multiplying the Democratic Performance times the number of voters who are registered, not expected to vote, and have some history of voting. These are the voters whose behavior we are likely to change through a get out the vote (GOTV) campaign.

The reason a voter generally has to have some voter history in order to be included in the GOTV Index is that we are substantially more likely to mobilize someone who has voted—even once—than someone who has never voted before. In the case of newly registered voters, they are generally about as likely to vote as the average low-propensity voter who has cast a ballot in the past.

The final column is the GOTV percent. This is the percent of all Registered voters represented by the GOTV Index.

Several important points:

- **The GOTV Index varies widely between Congressional Districts (or precincts).** A higher Democratic performance drives up the index. A higher expected turnout drives down the index. In the table above, the GOTV Index varies from 18,845 in California's 22 District to 80,640 in Maine's 2nd District.

- **The GOTV Index is often at least as large as the Persuasion Index.** In other words there are often many more voters whose behavior can be changed by the campaign and who are Get Out The Vote targets than there are who are persuasion targets. Yet very often, campaigns spend disproportionate amounts of resources on persuasion and not enough on mobilizing voters who would vote Democratic if they would only go to the polls.

Note that the GOTV percent number is not really comparable to the Persuasion percentage. The GOTV percent is a percentage of Registered voters, whereas the Persuasion percent is a percentage of the smaller number of expected voters.

For the purpose of planning campaigns, we normally refer to precincts with 65% or better Democratic Performance Index (DPI) as Democratic precincts. Those with 35% to 65% DPI are Swing Precincts. And those with 35% or below as Republican Precincts.

SOURCE #2—DEMOGRAPHY—WHAT KIND OF PERSON ARE THEY?

The second source of information that allows us to find persuadable and mobilizable voters is demography—what kind of person they are.

As we've seen, even if we don't know anything about someone's actual opinions or voting habits, we can imply a lot simply from their demographic characteristics.

For instance, if you are a white male, who is not Jewish, not gay and not a labor union member, the odds are almost 80% that you will vote Republican.

If you are an African-American, the odds are over 90% you will vote Democratic *(African-American voters are the smartest voters in America.)*

If you are a non-Cuban Hispanic, the odds are about 65% you will vote Democratic. The same is true if you are an Asian-American.

Where can campaigns get demographic information? Of course there's the U.S. Census. Sometimes the information comes from voter registration roles. In "Voting Rights Act" states of the South, race is on the voter registration list. That, of course, is terrific news for Democrats, since it affords us a fairly precise way to find African-American voters.

There are also computer programs that provide "surname directories" for various ethnic groups. These directories can locate many if not virtually all members of a particular ethnic group.

And it is often the case that more precise demographic information can be derived from a campaign's polling that will help us identify persuadable voters with great precision—say, Catholic women over 55 years old.

SOURCE # 3—THE VOTER FILE—WHAT DO WE KNOW ABOUT THEIR PAST VOTER HISTORY?

Because we have secret ballots, there is no record of how each individual votes. But there is a clear, highly accessible record of whether or not they go to the polls.

In most areas this information is maintained on computerized voter files that are available from public election authorities—and often from private firms that enhance voter files with other data.

Whether someone votes or not can obviously shed a great deal of light on one of the major criteria for finding persuadable and mobilizable voters—the likelihood that someone is going to vote in the future.

If someone has voted in three of the last six General Elections, we can determine—with reasonable confidence—that the person is 50% likely to vote in the future.

That's because the best predictor of future behavior is past behavior. This, by the way, is one of the fundamental principals of organizing good political campaigns. Left to their own devices, the way people have behaved in the past is the best predictor of what they can be expected to do in the future. If they have voted with us in the past, that's just fine. If not, the job of the campaign is to change that behavior.

If we know that someone lives in a predominantly African-American area and we know from the voter file that he has voted only once in the last four General Elections, we can say with great certainty that he is a mobilizable voter. Because he is an African-American, we know that the odds are he will vote Democratic. Because he has voted only 25% of the time in past General Elections, we can predict that he has only 25% odds of voting this time—unless we mobilize him to increase the odds that he will actually go to the polls.

But the voter file not only tells us about someone's likelihood to vote. Some states provide information on voter history in primaries. If an individual generally votes in the **Democratic Primary,** we also know that the odds are very high that she will vote Democratic in a General Election—if we can get her to the polls.

In some states, voters register either as a Democrat, Republican, Independent or some other party. Though it is not as predictive as voting in a party primary, **party registration** can also predict how someone will vote in a General Election.

Of course, the degree of certainty that a registered Democrat (or a particular type of registered Democrat, e.g., a female registered Democrat) will vote Democratic can be greatly increased by doing a random sample of registered Democrats.

This is of course true of any demographic or political group. If we can draw a line around a group with similar geographic, demographic or political characteristics, we can do a random sample of that group and determine the likelihood how the group as a whole, and anyone within the group, is likely to break in the election. This might enable us to target an entire group as a mobilizable or persuadable group.

SOURCE #4—THE CANVASS—ASK THEM

None of the sources of information we've used so far require that we pick up a phone or knock on a door. All of them come from sources of pre-existing information. The only work a campaign has to do to use these forms of targeting information is research and analysis.

In most campaigns, these pre-existing sources of targeting information aren't enough. To finish the job we have to turn to the final source—we have to ask them. Asking them usually involves either a **door-to-door or telephone canvass: "can we count on your support for our candidate?"— yes, no, or undecided.**

These four sources of information: geographic data, demographic data, the voter file and canvass information allow campaigns to target persuadable and mobilizable voters with some precision.

Whatever the source of information, once we find someone who supports our candidate, but is unlikely to vote, we have a mobilizable voter. Once we find a voter who is undecided, but likely to vote, we have found a persuadable voter.

ONCE WE FIND THEM, WHAT DO WE TELL THEM?

Identifying the persuadable and mobilizable voters tells us which voters' behavior can be changed. We then set about changing that behavior by communicating the **Campaign Message.**

As we've seen, the Campaign Message is the core narrative communicated by the campaign to accomplish its two central functions.

Remember that there are actually two—very distinct—components of the campaign message.

The component directed at persuadables is intended to convince them to support our candidate.

The component directed at mobilizables is intended to motivate voters who already support our candidate but who are unlikely to vote, to go to the polls.

We apply the lessons of Section Four to develop these messages.

Let's turn now to a more detailed look at how to use targeting information to find mobilizable voters.

TARGETING MOBILIZABLE VOTERS—THE FIRST STEP IS TO FIND OUR CANDIDATE'S SUPPORTERS

The first criterion for a mobilizable voter is that she must support our candidate. So to find all of the mobilizable voters, the campaign's first problem is to find all of its supporters.

In the best campaigns, the goal is to assemble a **"Run Universe"** for Election Day **large enough to win the election**. In other words we want to go into Election Day knowing the names of enough voters who support our candidate, that we can win the election if we just "run" them to the polls.

THE WINNING NUMBER

Our first problem in constructing this "Run Universe" is to determine a **"Winning Number."** How many votes will be needed to win the election?

Of course, to find the "Winning Number" we first have to determine how many voters are expected to go to the polls. Past history is the guide for expected turnout—and in many races the NCEC projections are often used as a baseline. Of course, past history has to be adjusted for Get Out The Vote (GOTV) efforts that exceed historical precedent.

Once we've settled on a projected turnout, we have to determine what percent of the vote will result in victory.

In a two-way General Election, that calculation is pretty simple: 50%, plus one, wins. It is a **minimum winning number**. Most campaigns use 52% as a **safe winning number.**

But in multi-candidate fields where a majority of the vote is not required, things get a little trickier. In a three-way race, for instance, what is a **minimum winning number?**

If you said 33%, plus one, you're right. But what about a safe winning number in a three-way race? Is it 35%?

Wrong. It is still 52%, since one of the candidates could conceivably get zero votes. The calculation of a safe winning number in a multi-candidate field depends upon how the candidates bunch, so to make the call a Campaign Manager has to use some art, not just science.

In a 10-person race, the minimum winning number is 10%, plus one. But the safe win number is still technically 52%. Of course, no one will actually get 52% in most 10-person races, so finding a "Run Universe" of 52% will be impossible, too. What is a reasonable number to target, upon which to base a campaign strategy? We have to decide how many candidates are strong and how many are "also-rans." Then we have to make an educated guess. If several of the candidates in the field are fairly strong, maybe a true safe win number is 25%, if fewer are strong it may be 40% or 45%.

CONSTRUCTING THE "RUN UNIVERSE"

Now we go about finding enough voters to meet our winning number. To do this we turn to the four sources we described above: geography, demography, the voter file and the canvass.

Let's say our winning number is 100,000 votes in a General Election campaign. We start off by trying to find as many voters from the first three sources that are immediately identifiable without having to canvass anyone.

First we take voters from the voter file who have voted in Democratic Primaries. We know that if they vote, they will almost certainly vote Democratic. Let 's say there are 50,000 of these voters.

	Run Universe	Plus Voters
Democratic Primary Voters	50,000	50,000

We add 50,000 voters to our list to our "Run Universe" for Election Day, and expect that they will yield about 50,000 plus Democratic votes, were they to actually vote. We may or may not actually communicate a mobilization message to all of these voters in the period leading up to the election; it depends upon available resources.

Next we add voters who only vote in General Elections (no primary voter history), but who live in precincts that have a history of voting 65% or better Democratic. All of these voters will not necessarily vote Democratic were they to vote. However, if we were to mobilize 100 of them who would not ordinarily vote, we know from the past voter history of the area that 65 of them would vote Democratic and only 35 would vote Republican. In other words we would come out ahead by a two-to-one margin.

Let's say there are 10,000 of these voters. We can add them all to the "Run Universe" column, but we can expect only 65% of these (or 6,500) to the number of "plus" voters if they all go vote. In other words, we would have to "run" 10,000 voters to get 6,500 Democratic votes.

	Run Universe	Plus Voters
Democratic Primary Voters	50,000	50,000
General Election only Voters in 65% or more Democratic Pcts.	10,000	6,500

Now we add demographic or political groups (like Registered Democrats) who would break 65% or better Democratic if they voted. Let's say in our example there are 2,000 voters who have not already been listed as part of our "Run Universe" but are Registered Democrats or African-Americans. Again, we can could all of these voters as part of our "Run Universe" for the pre-election period, but can only expect some percentage of them to vote Democratic.

	Run Universe	Plus Voters
Democratic Primary Voters	50,000	50,000
General Election only Voters in 65% or more Democratic Pcts.	10,000	6,500
Demographic or Political Groups that break 65% or better	2,000	1,300

Next we can add supporters or donors to the campaign that are not in the other categories. This time, we can safely assume that almost all will vote for our candidate, if they vote.

	Run Universe	Plus Voters
Democratic Primary Voters	50,000	50,000
General Election only Voters in 65% or more Democratic Pcts.	10,000	6,500
Demographic or Political Groups that break 65% or better	2,000	1,300
Supporters and Donors	500	500
Total Identified Before Canvass	62,500	58,300

So far, we have identified 62,500 people for our "Run Universe." If the entire "Run Universe" voted, we would yield approximately 58,300 plus Democratic Votes. That means we have to find 41,700 plus voters through the canvass to reach our winning number.

Safe Winning Number	100,000
"Run Universe" Before Canvass	58,300
Plus Voters to be found through Canvass	41,700

In this example, if the canvass is executed properly, on Election Day we would end up with 104,200 voters in our "Run Universe." And that would yield 100,000 votes if they came out.

Whom to Canvass — Targeting

So where do we canvass to find these voters? Obviously, we don't canvass the voters who we have already put in our "Run Universe." We already know, or can project, how they will vote.

In addition, there is no reason for us to canvass Republican Primary voters. We know that they will vote Republican almost all of the time.

So we go hunting for Democratic votes among voters who only vote in General Elections (Democratic Primary voters are already counted, and Republican Primary Voters have been excluded), who live outside of Democratic (65% or better) precincts. (Remember, those who live in 65% or better Democratic precincts are already in the "Run Universe," too.)

If we start out with a voter file of 325,000 and 62,500 are in the initial "Run Universe" and, let's say, there are 75,000 Republican primary voters, then we have only 187,500 voters among whom to "hunt" for "plus" voters.

All Voters in Voter File	325,000
Initial Run Universe (before canvass)	-62,500
Republican Primary Voters	-75,000
Remaining Contact Universe	187,500

But no matter how hard you try, only a percentage of any given Contact Universe can actually be contacted either by phone or door to door. Some people will never be home, never pick up the phone, or whatever. We normally assume this percentage — or **maximum penetration rate — is about 75%.**

Contact Universe	187,500
Penetration Rate	75%
Actual Potential Contacts	140,625

So in our example, if we execute the canvass flawlessly, we can expect to contact about 140,625 voters. Since we need to find 41,700 plus votes, that means we're going to have to find a plus voter in 29.65% of the contacts we make.

Number of Pluses Needed	41,700
Potential Actual Contacts	<u>140,625</u>
Percentage Plus Rate Needed	29.65%

It also means that if there are 100 days left to conduct a volunteer canvass, we need to contact an average of 1,406 people in our contact universe every day.

How Do We Prioritize the Canvass?

Since the goal of the canvass is to find plus voters, the first place we will "mine" for these voters is where we have the richest veins of ore. So we go first to the highest Democratic Performance Precincts that are not already in the "Run Universe"—precincts that have a 64.9% Democratic Performance—and we work down. These are the precincts where we'll find the largest number of plus voters per hour of canvass contact.

If we have enough resources to canvass all precincts—all the way through the most Republican precincts—that is terrific. If resources are short, we go first where we get the biggest bang for the canvass buck. It's like mining for gold. You go to the richest veins first.

How Do We Prioritize our "Run Universe" for Get Out the Vote?

By creating the "Run Universe" of potentially plus voters, we have only done half of the job of finding the "mobilizable" voters that are one of the two targets of the campaign. The "Run Universe" tells us who is likely to vote Democratic. To be a "mobilizable" voter, the individual must indeed be likely to vote Democratic. But to be a target for mobilization, he or she must also be unlikely to vote. After all, a Democratic supporter who always votes, will vote for us, no matter what action is taken by the campaign. The campaign is about changing behavior.

The truly mobilizable voters are those portions of the "Run Universe" (our supporters) who have been shown by their past voter history (in the voter file) to be low propensity voters. In general then, the less likely someone is to vote if left to his own devices, the higher priority he is for Get Out The Vote. Voters who have no voter history are very unlikely to vote no matter what we do, so they are lower priority targets for mobilization.

But a voter with a 25% or 50% history of voting is a very high priority for mobilization. We also treat new registrants as low propensity voters.

In the period leading up to the election—and Election Day—if we have enough resources we would like to mobilize *the entire* "Run Universe," if that is possible, since some of those who have voted before might indeed fail to go to the polls this time if they are not mobilized. But the rule for prioritizing the "Run Universe" for GOTV is very simple:

We prioritize voters who have some voter history, but are least likely to vote.

To some people who are involved in campaigns for the first time, this may sound counter-intuitive. But when you think about it, these mobilizable voters are precisely the people whose behavior can be modified by the campaign.

Targeting Persuadable Voters— Creating the Persuasion Universe

Recall that persuadable voters also have two characteristics: they are likely to vote, and they are undecided. Our sources of information are exactly the same as we used to find mobilizable voters: geography, demography, the voter file and the canvass.

The Canvass

One source of data is obvious. If, during the **canvass**, a voter self-identifies as undecided, we take them at their word and consider them undecided. Of course, respondents to phone or door to door canvassing who say they are undecided are sometimes minuses—they actually support our opponent and just don't want to tell us. But a large percentage of undecided canvass contacts are telling us the truth—they are actually undecided.

Demographics—Polling

The second major source of information on undecided voters—and the one that is most widely used—is polling. **As we described in the last Section, polling combines a series of questions about the voter's views with questions about their demographic characteristics to target undecided voters.** Of course, the purpose of the poll is also to identify and refine the campaign's persuasion message—to determine which message is most convincing to voters who are persuadable.

Our door-to-door or phone canvass can identify which individual voters say they are undecided. Polls can find voters who are actually undecided, but may not say so to a partisan canvasser—voters who can be persuaded to abandon one candidate and support another. Polls can also find undecided voters much earlier than a canvass that may not be completed until the last week of the election campaign.

The demographic information in the poll is cross-referenced to find out whose opinion was altered by the information presented in the poll. Which demographic groups changed their opinion after the presentation of positive and negative messages about the candidates? These demographic groups then become the targets of persuasion. For instance, our polling could show that the most persuadable demographic group is Catholic women over 55 years of age.

Let's say it again: Polls don't tell us what to believe. They tell us the things we should communicate in order to convince persuadable voters.

The goal of an election campaign is to win and to do that; we need to convince persuadable voters. That means we should talk about the things they care about—the things that will move *them*, not the things that we *think* should persuade them.

Going into an election campaign without a poll is like flying an airplane in the clouds without instruments. If we try, we might luck out, but nine times out of 10 we will be wrong. And the reason is simple:

Political people are not normal people. Normal people think about politics 5 or 10 minutes a week. If people involved in politics try to decide what is important to normal people without asking, *they will be wrong.*

Taking a poll is asking normal people what is important to them.

GEOGRAPHY

The NCEC data will tell us which precinct has the highest percentage of persuadable voters based upon the past voting history of the precinct. That means we can target persuasion communication to the geographic areas that have the highest likelihood of having persuadable voters.

Depending upon our resources, this means we can increasingly narrow our focus. Let's say we are short of resources for our direct mail persuasion program. Instead of mailing to all Catholic women over 55 years of age, we might decide to mail instead to Catholic women over 55 who live in the 100 precincts with the top persuasion percents.

VOTER FILE

The voter file can help us refine our targeting further. Obviously we don't try to persuade partisan Republicans or partisan Democrats. Anyone whom we have already put in the "Run Universe" is by definition not a persuadable voter. To be in the "Run Universe," you have to be a supporter of our candidate. To be persuadable, you have to be "undecided."

So we would not just target women over 55 who live in the top persuasion precincts. We would exclude all women over 55 who are in the "Run Universe." We would also exclude Republican primary voters. So the only voters we ever target as persuadables in a General Election are General Election-only voters—voters with no history of voting in partisan primaries.

PRIORITIZING THE PERSUASION UNIVERSE

Of course, being undecided does not by itself make a voter a persuasion target for a campaign. Persuadables are both undecided and likely to vote.

As a result, the more likely the voter is to go to the polls, the more intensely we contact them with persuasion message.

If we spend a dollar sending mail to an undecided voter who is 50% likely to vote, we have wasted $.50. If we spend the same dollar on a voter who is 100% likely to vote, we get the maximum bang for the persuasion buck.

In other words, the priority for persuadables is just the reverse of the priority for mobilizables. With mobilizables, among voters with any voting history, we prioritize those who are *least* likely to vote. With persuadables, we prioritize those who are the *most* likely to vote.

As a practical matter, then, a campaign creates two lists of voters. One is a list of supporters—our "Run Universe." The other is a list of voters who are undecided. Each list is sorted by the likelihood of the voter to go to the polls. At the top of the list of persuadables are those who are most likely to vote. On the top of the list for mobilizables are those with some voter history but who are least likely to vote.

The more money or volunteer time to which a campaign has access, the lower down each list it can afford to go as it communicates its persuasion message to persuadables, and its mobilization message to mobilizables.

Of course, if we're using TV or radio as persuasion media, targeting cannot be done on a name-by-name basis, but the principle remains the same for prioritizing all campaign communications, and we attempt to approximate the model as closely as possible.

Prioritizing Money and Time in a Campaign

In a business enterprise the goal is to maximize profit. Every investment decision or commitment of time is measured according to those criteria.

In a not-for-profit organization, the goal is to maximize the achievement of the nonprofit's goal.

In an election campaign there is only one criterion for prioritizing the expenditure of money, volunteer or candidate time:

The goal is to maximize the campaign's ability to increase marginal votes for our candidate per dollar or per hour of volunteer time.

Every decision of a campaign should be made with reference to this criterion.

The manager of a business would get a bonus if she had a huge surplus of funds available at the end of a fiscal year.

The manager of a competitive political campaign would be shot (figuratively, of course) if he had a big balance in his account on Election Day. That money would represent votes that could have been persuaded or mobilized and weren't. His goal is to maximize votes for his candidate, not money in the bank.

How much should a campaign spend on mobilization and persuasion?

For every campaign there is a different answer to this question. The answer depends entirely on how many persuadables and mobilizables there are in the district and the resources the particular campaign has to communicate.

The answer also depends heavily on the nature of the candidates in the race. How powerful are the available persuasion messages? How hard will it be to organize a mobilization effort? How much will the other candidate spend on either persuasion or mobilization?

For every campaign there is a point of maximum efficiency in spending for both the persuasion and mobilization efforts. For example, a TV commercial generally does not begin to have maximum impact until the viewer has seen it five times. Then it begins to sink in, to break through. So spending the dollar that buys the 500th point of TV (one point represents one percent of the viewing audience) is much more efficient (votes per dollar) than the dollars that bought only 100 points of TV. Every dollar you spend for the 500 points will yield more votes than every dollar you spend for only 100 points because without making multiple impression you don't break through.

On the other hand, the dollar spent on putting up the 10,000th point of the same commercial will be much less efficient. It will generate far fewer marginal votes per dollar than the dollar that put up the 500th point.

The same is true of mobilization programs. Let's say a Congressional race spends money on one field director who attempts to organize volunteers. The number of votes affected per dollar here is much lower than if the campaign put 15 full-time staff in the field over a four-month period. This is true because the 15 people can organize a serious, high-intensity effort—a crusade that takes on a life of its own and massively boosts turnout among Democratic voters. On the other hand, the dollar the campaign might spend to put the 100th full-time organizer in the field will produce many fewer votes than the dollar you spend on the 15th person.

In general the efficiency of spending in both the persuasion and mobilization campaigns is determined by where the spending falls on a bell curve. Its efficiency goes up for a time; it peaks and then begins to drop.

The trick to running a great political campaign is to locate the point of maximum efficiency in both the persuasion and mobilization areas, and to make sure you are spending at the maximum efficiency point on both elements of the campaign, before you begin to spend more inefficient dollars in either side of the campaign.

In other words, it's not smart to spend so much on TV or mail that each new dollar of spending is less efficient at producing votes than a similar dollar spent on field operations. This is a mistake that has been made by many Democratic campaigns over the last 20 years. You simply can't afford not to spend money on field operations in most Congressional races. And a high-intensity field operation is much more efficient at producing new votes per dollar than a low-intensity, small-scale, poorly organized effort.

It is also important to remember that mobilizable votes are less "fragile" than persuadable votes. If a campaign put up a million dollars on TV to do persuasion and their opponent did the same, there is no guarantee that the million dollars will yield any more votes at all. It's entirely possible that the other side's TV ads are more persuasive than ours.

But the new votes added by mobilization programs are not subject to being "stolen" by the other side at all. Mobilizable votes—by definition—already intend to support our candidate. They won't be swayed by persuasion TV from the other side. If we can get them to the polls, they are money in the bank. They add to the new votes we will get with an effective persuasion campaign. But if we don't go after them with a mobilization effort, no amount of persuasion advertising will add them to our vote totals.

Moving the Center: Persuading the Persuadables, Mobilizing the Mobilizables

So what does all of this have to do with beating the right—with realigning American politics?

What's true in a campaign is also true in the larger campaign to move the center of American political dialogue, the control of Congress, the White House and the Courts.

There is a potential emerging Democratic majority in America. But to make that potential majority into a real majority it has to include both persuadables and mobilizables and we have to conduct two simultaneous campaigns to change the electoral behavior of both groups.

Our ability to do that depends on recognizing that both tasks are critical; it depends on crafting creative strategies to target and communicate with both groups; and it depends heavily on our ability to craft messages that will mobilize and persuade.

CHAPTER THIRTY-THREE

Battling for the Progressive Agenda — Issue Campaigns

I regularly run into people in D.C. who work for wonderful, progressive, issue-advocacy organizations. We begin to discuss their work, and they say, "I don't get involved in elections; our organization is non-partisan."

Now I completely understand the imperatives of organizational tax status, but whether or not your organization gets involved in elections, someone who cares about an issue should care about elections, because the most important lobby day is Election Day.

One of the least appreciated things about the American political system is the extent to which the party in power in Congress completely controls the issue agenda. People picture Congress as a larger version of their student council: anyone who has a motion is recognized to speak. Amendments are offered under Robert's Rules of Order.

Congress does *not* run according to Robert's Rules of Order. As a practical matter, nothing is considered on the floor of the House without the approval of the majority party leadership. In the Senate, the minority has somewhat more power, but still the agenda is set by the majority party.

The basic parameters for potential changes in public policy are always determined by what happens Election Day. So if you want to make progressive change in public policy, you'd better make sure that progressive Democratic leaders are in charge of the Congressional agenda. It's like football—if you're going to have a successful season, you would be wise to recruit good players.

Notwithstanding the enormous importance of Election Day, it is critical that Progressives wage effective issue campaigns between elections.

When the Republicans were in the majority, progressive issue campaigns played three critical roles:

- They prevented passage of horrible policy initiatives like the Bush plan to privatize Social Security.

- They set the stage for the next election by demonstrating to voters that Progressives have the nine qualities that are persuasive, and empowering and motivating mobilizable voters.

- Within limited confines, we actually scored some victories that benefited everyday Americans.

With the Democrats back in the majority, issue campaigns are more important than ever. The reason why twice as many Americans know what conservatives stand for than what Progressives stand for is that for the last 12 years we have primarily been fighting conservative initiatives. Now we have to offer up clear progressive initiatives, both in order to pass them and benefit ordinary Americans, and to brand the progressive program and progressive values.

We need to deliver a down payment on the progressive agenda and set the stage for more serious initiatives to fundamentally restructure the political economy to benefit ordinary Americans. As a practical political matter, most of those major initiatives will not be passed and signed into law so long as there is a Republican president. But until then we can indeed make a down payment on change and set the terms of political debate.

By generating a groundswell of support for progressive policy initiatives, we help give Democrats in Congress the ability to demonstrate that they can deliver the goods, so that they can govern effectively.

And, of course, we need to do everything in our power to end right-wing policies like the disastrous war in Iraq.

How do we run these kinds of issue campaigns?

LEARNING RULES FOR RADICALS

I've been running issue campaigns for almost four decades. My first serious issue campaign involved pollution and the legendary community organizer Saul Alinsky.

The story is told that in late 1969, Alinsky had lunch one day with *Chicago Daily News* columnist Mike Royko in the Billy Goat Tavern — made famous by Saturday Night Live and John Belushi — "cheezborger, cheeszborger, cheeszborger."

They had a discussion bemoaning the state of Chicago's air — and the polarization of working white and black Chicagoans. Finally, Alinsky told Royko that he would start an organization that involved both whites and blacks to fight the common problem of Chicago's worsening air pollution — if Royko would write a column to solicit recruits.

Soon Alinsky's Industrial Areas Foundation had deployed a half-dozen organizer trainees to begin the organization.

Alinsky, and his book *Rules for Radicals*, had a big impact on a generation of progressive organizers.[1] He had a laser-like understanding of people's self-interests and their importance as the core of successful political organizing.

After I graduated from Duke, I began a graduate program at the University of Chicago in a field called "ethics and society." I did work in the Divinity School and the Department of Economics. Not long after I arrived in Chicago, I hooked up with the Industrial Areas Foundation's organizing project on a part-time basis and became the new organization's chief bureaucrat.

The Campaign Against Pollution (CAP) was born in late 1969 and organized a frontal assault on Commonwealth Edison, the electric power utility in Chicago. CAP demanded that ComEd either put scrubbers on its power generators or stop using high-sulfur coal that was emitting massive amounts of sulfur dioxide, the chief ingredient of smog, into Chicago's air.

The plan was to pack the company's shareholder meeting in the spring. Organizers were deployed to recruit churches and community groups to buy small blocks of stock. In addition, CAP organized a campaign to collect pledges from customers to withhold their electric bills if the company didn't comply. Finally, CAP began targeting Ward Committeemen and Aldermen from Mayor Richard J. Daley's Democratic machine.

Just before the company's shareholder meeting, and around the time of America's first Earth Day in 1970, ComEd agreed to stop buying high sulfur coal. CAP's first victory ultimately cut sulfur dioxide in Chicago's air by two-thirds.

The organization went on to broaden its agenda and become the Citizen's Action Program. It ran a campaign to end the unfair real estate assessment practices that cost homeowners millions by under-assessing large industrial and commercial property. And for the first time anywhere in America, it developed the mortgage redlining issue and ran campaigns against lending institutions that "redlined" whole neighborhoods and refused to loan funds or sell insurance in those communities.

In 1974, I co-founded Illinois Public Action, which became Illinois' largest public interest organization and progressive coalition. Public Action built a membership of 250,000 and had 130 affiliated unions, community and senior citizen groups.

Originally, the organization ran issue campaigns aimed at changing state policy. Several years later, we teamed up with similar organizations to found a national organization—Citizen Action—to conduct national issue campaigns. Public Action's political committee also backed progressive candidates and helped organize campaigns for progressive Democrats. It was especially instrumental in electing U.S. Senator Paul Simon in 1984.

Many of the people who were involved in Public Action have gone on to play significant roles in progressive politics. They included people like Congressman Rahm Emanuel—who served as senior adviser to President Bill Clinton, was chairman of the Democratic Congressional Campaign Committee in the successful 2006 midterm elections, and is now Chairman of the House Democratic Caucus. Emanuel started working for Public Action when he was 22 years old.

The people around Public Action included guys who would become prominent consultants like Pete Giangreco and David Wilhelm. It included progressive activists like Heather Booth and Midwest Academy Director Jackie Kendall, as well as former Congressman Lane Evans and Congresswoman Jan Schakowsky. To me, of course, Jan was particularly important since she became my wife in 1980.

CHANGING THE BEHAVIOR OF DECISION-MAKERS

To win an election campaign, we have to change the behavior of persuadable and mobilizable voters. They are the key decision-makers. In issue campaigns, our goal is to change the behavior of key decision-makers as well.

These decision-makers can be members of Congress or other legislators, public executives (the President, a governor, a bureaucrat), or a private sector decision-makers like a corporate executive.

In this book, the major attention will be focused on campaigns aimed at Congress, but the same general principles apply to state legislatures and other key decision-makers as well.

THE FIRST STEP—A SELF-INTEREST INVENTORY OF THOSE WHOSE BEHAVIOR WE SEEK TO CHANGE

Using the self-interest spectrum we discussed in Section Three, our first step is to inventory the self-interests of the actors who are affected by the issue on the table. Of course, the most important actors are the decision-makers themselves, Members of Congress.

By virtue of their roles, legislators generally share a number of categories of self-interest—some obvious, some not so obvious.

General Self-Interests of Legislators and Members of Congress

1) Desire to Get Re-elected.
    The legislator's electoral status defines a key self-interest.

If a legislator is worried about winning his next general election, he will generally find the views of swing, persuadable voters very important.

If he has a Party primary challenge, his base party voters will move to center stage.

A legislator who feels completely invulnerable to electoral attack may not be as concerned about the direct electoral consequences of his actions, but it doesn't mean he doesn't care about a lot of other things that make him vulnerable.

2) *Need to Raise Campaign Funds.*

A specialized aspect of the legislative imperative to seek reelection is the need to raise campaign funds. This may also operate in the case of legislators, who are as safe electorally, but need to raise money to help their party contest for control of the body—or to garner support for a leadership position. There's a saying about Congress that goes something like, "if you can't take their money, drink their booze, go to their on their trips, and eat their dinners, and look them in the eye and vote against them, you shouldn't be here." [2]

Honestly, if that were the test, the Capitol would be pretty empty. People are always influenced by other people who provide the things they need.

Some members get on "exclusive committees" mainly because it gives them a rationale to raise funds from the groups with interests before that committee.

The bottom line is that in order to have a government that is truly Democratic, we have to have public financing of elections. But until then, luckily, funding is not the only self-interest of Members of Congress.

3) *Desire to position himself to run for higher office.*

This interest may mean that the perception of voters far distant from a Congressman's home district may enter his decision-making calculus. When former House Budget Committee Chairman Jim Nussle decided to run for Governor of Iowa, it made him vulnerable to pressure from voters all over Iowa—not just in his own home district.

Some legislators may be seeking an appointment to a judgeship or executive office, so the people who make those appointments and the legislators who confirm appointments may be important to them.

4) Desire to stand up for strongly held beliefs and convictions.

Notwithstanding the general reputation of politicians as a group of self-promoters who don't care about principles, strongly held beliefs and convictions play a very important role in congressional decision-making. In fact, in my experience there are actually more "true believers" in Congress than most legislative bodies.

In the final analysis, after all, a sense of meaning and importance in life is, for most people, an over-arching self-interest often is manifested in a strongly held belief system. People really care about their own self-image.

5) Desire to please legislative peers and move up the leadership ladder in the legislative body.

Legislative bodies are institutions with their own rules and social structures that become very important to their participants. If you cross someone today, will he retaliate on some completely unrelated matter tomorrow?

Legislative leaders are especially concerned about the feelings of their peers. After all, the members of the body are their constituents every bit as much as the voters in their districts.

Ambition for legislative leadership or committee positions is also very important, as is the goodwill of a powerful committee chair.

6) Need to deliver benefits to the district.

Legislators factor in the degree to which particular positions affect those who are capable of impacting these district benefits. These often include legislative leaders, heads of appropriations committees, Presidents, governors and other officials in an executive branch.

7) Party considerations.

Legislators, and particularly legislative leaders, have broad party considerations that transcend the impact of a vote on their particular district's voters. How will a vote affect voters in swing districts, upon whom leadership depends? How will an issue affect the election of candidates for governor or the presidency?

Many Members of Congress—particularly those who are most active at crafting the legislative agendas of their caucus—often tend to be party stalwarts who always factor in the impact of legislative action on the fate of party interests.

8) *Desire to please major secondary players upon whom a legislator depends — or with whom they have a relationship.*

It may be that the legislator knows he will need a favor down the road.

It may be that the political player is the legislator's political sponsor — the person upon whom the legislator depends for his political life.

Or a legislator simply may not want to have a powerful political enemy lurking out there.

9) *Desire to please friends with whom a legislator has a personal relationship (political, ethnic, personal or business).*

Legislators are like everyone else, they don't like taking actions that alienate political, personal or business friends. (After all, friends are not so easy to come by.)

Lobbyists spend years developing friendships with members of legislatures, both so they can have access, and also to force the legislator to make an emotional investment in their friendship. Let's face it: if a friend asks you to do something, you're much more prone to do it.

10) *Desire not to alienate people who work for a legislator's reelection — or people with whom they identified politically.*

Hard-core supporters often have an extremely powerful influence. Legislators don't want to make their closest political allies mad. That also goes for the political "family" with whom the legislator identifies.

11) *Desire to be part of the "mainstream."*

Remember, human beings are pack animals. If the group gives someone "permission" to believe something or support someone, he is much more likely to do so.

If a particular position seems increasingly popular - both among voters and with other legislators - that fact by itself will persuade others to support it. On the other hand, as my friend Wiley Pearson says, *politicians don't want to be the nail sticking out of the board, because they're likely to get hammered.*

12) *Desire to avoid diverting time and energy to deal with a persistent set of constituents.*

Time and energy are important assets to legislators.

Legislators often have a self-interest in settling a dispute with a group of constituents simply to avoid the expenditure of time and energy, regardless of the content. Even small constituencies can divert enormous amounts of time and emotional energy.

13) Desire to get a job with a special interest after his term of office is completed.

Legislators at all levels are subject to the temptation to think about jobs or positions they might have when and if they leave office.

These opportunities - whether concrete or abstract - sometimes materially affect the behavior of Members of Congress. Over the years, legislators have taken me aside many times as I advocated for progressive legislation, and said: "Gee, Bob, I'd love to vote for this legislation, but you know, this is my last term, and the people in the widget industry are talking with me about a job."

Probably the best-known recent example of this phenomenon is the case of Congressman Billy Tauzin. Tauzin was chairman of the House Energy and Commerce Committee when he crafted the Bush administration's notorious "Part D" of Medicare—the prescription drug program that benefited the pharmaceutical companies more than seniors. "Part D" actually prevented Medicare from negotiating with private drug companies for the lowest price. Similar negotiations by the Veterans Administration lowered prices by 40%. As he was negotiating these provisions with the drug companies, it was rumored that Tauzin was also discussing an informal offer to become the CEO of Pharma, the drug company lobby organization. He now holds that job and receives a multimillion-dollar annual salary. In recognition of his role, Americans United made Tauzin the poster child for the corruptness of Medicare "Part D."

14) Need to be liked by constituents, colleagues, friends, lobbyists, and other associates, etc—the fear of anger.

It is hard to overstate the importance of "need to be liked"— especially for politicians.

That is one of the major reasons so many politicians try to craft deals and make everyone happy. They don't like people being angry with them.

Unleashing the passion of anger also has unpredictable consequences, and most politicians don't like "unpredictable." Anger can spin out of control.

15) Turf.

Legislators are very territorial. In Congress, a major source of power is committee jurisdiction. It is of considerable concern to committee members, and especially to committee chairs and ranking members. The same goes for an individual member's sponsorship or primary responsibility for trademark issues. Members often develop an issue niche that becomes their specialty. Encroachment by another member is often a big concern.

The threat of encroachment may propel members to oppose bills for reasons that have nothing to do with the substance.

CHAPTER THIRTY-FOUR

Conducting a Legislative Issue Campaign

FILLING A LOW-PRESSURE ZONE

Issue campaigns, and I suppose political movements in general, can be thought about the way we think about storms. Everyone has seen the TV weatherman say: "This storm is beginning to get organized," or "this storm is beginning to fall apart," or "this storm is very well organized and packs quite a wallop."

Issue campaigns are the same way—and to some extent for the same reason.

Every low-pressure wave in the atmosphere doesn't develop into a powerful storm. Atmospheric forces have to conspire to create circulation around the wave that concentrates its power into a storm and causes it to intensify.

Most of the time when there is a highly successful movement or issue campaign, history has created a demand for action that isn't being filled—an historic low-pressure zone. Then someone, or some group, organizes the circulation around that zone. Someone steps up and provides leadership and organization and attracts a storm of action surrounding them.

It was true with the civil rights movement, the women's movement, campaign to defeat the privatization of Social Security, and the campaign to end the war in Iraq.

The first step in any issue campaign is to assemble a critical mass of forces that will begin that kind of "circulation."

You look for the actors on the self-interest spectrum who share your self-interest or those who can be recruited as allies. Then you bring those actors together into a powerful vortex that magnifies the energy of the participants. As a result, you intensify the low-pressure "wave" into a storm of action that attracts the other actors interested in the issue as surely as a "low pressure zone" sucks in the surrounding atmosphere.

Successful issue campaigns require careful execution. But first and foremost they require leaders who are ready to step up and take action.

By 2007, the public opinion battle to end the war in Iraq was won. Most Americans opposed the war. But a vacuum existed. For all their wonderful work, none of the major anti-war groups was organized to mount a strategically focused campaign to eliminate support for the Bush Administration's war policy among Members of Congress.

The President's announcement of his "surge," or escalation, of the war provided the precipitating event that caused MoveOn.org and USAction to create Americans Against Escalation in Iraq (AAEI), with the explicit purpose of filling that vacuum and pressing Congress to end the war.

MoveOn.org's Washington Director, Tom Matzzie, became the Campaign Manager for AAEI. I became General Consultant to the campaign.

AAEI rapidly attracted major organizations that wanted to join the battle. MoveOn.org and USAction were joined by the Service Employees International Union (SEIU), Americans United for Change, Win Without War, the Center for American Progress (CAP), the Campaign for America's Future (CAF), Vote Vets, the United States Student Association, Campus Progress Action, Working Assets and the National Security Network.

AAEI's strategy to ultimately end the Iraq War was to unite Democrats, divide Republicans and isolate the President. We believed that if there was any chance of getting President Bush to change course in Iraq, before a new President took office, a significant portion of his Republican support had to collapse. The forces assembled by AAEI grew by the day.

Anti-war members of Congress and their staffs began to coordinate with AAEI's communication and lobby team.

Generals and former national security officials were engaged by Vote Vets and the National Security Network. They became the face of the movement to end the war in Iraq.

Progressive bloggers worked closely with the coalition.

Progressive donors stepped up to fund millions of dollars of advertisements targeted at specific members of Congress, a talented press staff, fly-arounds of generals and Iraq Vets, and an expanding field structure that included an "Iraq Summer" project that deployed 90 organizers into target districts to dog Republican targets for months at a time.

The 3.5 million MoveOn.org membership generated calls to Congress and millions in contributions. Their calls were supplemented by hundreds of thousands of patch through calls to Congressional targets.

AAEI had filled a low-pressure zone and created a storm of action.

WHAT WILL IT TAKE TO WIN?

In a legislative campaign, the next step involves a targeting analysis and research on the self-interests of potential targeted legislators. The threshold problem is simple: how do we piece together the number of votes we need to get the results we want?

Do we need a simple majority? Do we need to invoke cloture in the Senate, with 60 votes? Do we need only 41 votes to stop the other side from getting cloture and cutting off debate?

The Senate has rules that give minorities a great deal more power than in the House. The most important is the requirement that debate on a measure can only be stopped on most bills with the cloture motion. That requires 60 votes to succeed, and as a result, 41 senators can stop most normal legislation, unless it is moving under the cover of special rules.

Will we hang on to all the Democrats? Where will the leadership be? How many Republican members do we need in order to win?

Targeting — Changers, Squealers, Exemplars

In campaigns aimed at Congress we generally target three types of members:

- Members whose decisions we seek to change directly. These are the members whose votes we can move—changers.

- "Squealers"—whose behavior affects the decisions of others. As you recall, "squealers" react loudly to pressure. They raise the "subjugation costs" that their leadership has to pay to keep them in line. They also demoralize fellow adherents to the conservative position.

- Exemplars—Targets who become examples for others (remember you don't have to hang them all—just one, in the public square).

As we do our targeting, we need to be analyzing the self-interests of potential target members on all of the parameters we discussed earlier. Our sources of intelligence include:

- Voting records in Congress and the political history of the legislator. For Congress, the *Political Almanac, Congressional Quarterly,* or *National Journal* give us a lot of what we need.

- Public statements and news accounts about the legislator, and his views on the issue in question.

- The legislator's campaign-contribution history.

- Voting history of the legislator's district.

- The legislator's work, employment and business history.

- An analysis of the legislator's personal financial disclosures.

- Intelligence gathered through personal conversations with those who know the legislator—particularly those with whom he or she works at the Capitol.

- First-hand personal knowledge of the legislator.

MESSAGING TO LEGISLATORS

Simply put, the messages directed to target legislators in issue-based legislative campaigns need to address whichever set of his self-interests matter most to a legislator, or group of legislators.

Messages have to be designed to address those self-interests directly. Sometimes they need to address the content of the issue. Other times they don't.

The real message may be that close political associates want him to support our position, or that everyone else with whom he identifies is supporting our position, or that he will face primary opposition if he opposes us. Or it may be a direct appeal to his or her concern over low quality and failing schools, or poor health care. The right message depends on which self-interest really matters to the target.

METHODS OF COMMUNICATING WITH LEGISLATORS

As with most media decisions, the first critical element in communicating with legislators is our ability to break through—to get on their radar.

Different media have different effects.

VERY FORCEFUL

• **Personal meetings with the legislator.** This would be a one-on-one meeting or a meeting with a small group. An actual, physical meeting focuses all of the legislator's attention during the meeting. If you have a choice between a phone call or a meeting, take the meeting.

• **Large "town hall" style meetings with constituents.** These include meetings that are completely under your control, and meetings that may be put on by the legislator where you have a major presence. The emotional impact of a large group of constituents passionately advocating their position can't be topped for real impact.

• **"Actions" at the legislator's office.** Legislators and their staffs really pay attention to groups that show up in the office—especially with the press in tow.

• **Other protests events.** Constituents on TV, demanding action from a member of Congress gets their attention.

• **Conversations with other legislators, and secondary players (Mayors, Governors, the Speaker).** Legislators pay close attention to what their colleagues and other political actors think about an issue. A call from a Governor of the same party, for instance, gets noticed.

• **Calls from constituents who are leaders in the community.** These are often referred to as "grass tops" contacts. Good friends, business associates, the Bishop, and people the legislator knows or respects are especially important.

• **Contacts from groups that are close to the legislator, or that can impact the outcome of a close election.**

• **Contacts to a legislator by members of the media—often responding to an issue campaign's statements or charges.** Sometimes a reporter can be your best lobbyist—unintentionally. If your press operation can get a press person to call about a position or issue, it breaks forcefully into the members' consciousness.

• **Meetings with staff.** In Congress, staff play pivotal roles in the legislative process. Less so in most state legislatures.

• **TV, radio or print ads viewed by the legislator—especially in his home district.** The idea that there is a spot about him on TV really focuses a legislator's mind. Often a small TV buy can be used as a news hook for an earned-media story that has a lot of impact beyond this spot's viewership. In addition to spots in the district, spots run on CNN, Fox News and other cable channels in the D.C. area are helpful because they are frequently watched by members or their staffs. Print ads in the home district or the "trade press" read on Capitol Hill also have impact.

• **Other earned media stories that are seen or read by the legislator—especially when they communicate positions of key constituencies or polling data.** In long-term efforts, regular stories in the press are extremely important to keep the issue on the agenda week after week.

These methods of member contact are especially forceful because they grab the attention of the members and their staff. In general the more emotionally engaging the medium, the more forceful it is at breaking through.

Less forceful methods don't get as powerful a grip on members and their staffs, but they still are important. Generally, the greater the "physical presence" of the medium, the better. For instance, physical letters make more impact than e-mails per piece of mail.

MEDIUM FORCEFUL

• **Grassroots phone calls to legislators or their offices.** Remember the cockroach theory of lobbying. If the legislator hears from a hundred people a day about an issue, most think that there are thousands out there who shared this view. In Congress, you constantly hear the question, "Are we getting any calls on this issue?"

Automated "patch-through" calls and e-mails to activists and groups are especially well-suited to generating oceans of calls. Remember that to generate "patch-through" calls to Congress, you do high volumes of auto calls to voters, so they give the campaign a "twofer." You generate voter contact on an issue and at the same time you generate massive numbers of constituent calls to flood a legislator's office over a period of days, weeks, or months.

One of the little highlights of the campaign to limit the Bush tax cuts was when I received a call from a staff director of a "moderate" Democrat, who had refused to commit his vote. She called me at the office after 1,700 calls had inundated her office in two days, and "grass tops" leaders had been tracking the senator down all over the country. She simply said, "Okay, okay....We give up.... Call them off."

• **Individually written "grass tops" letters that are mailed to a legislator's office.**

• **Hand-delivered position papers.** Members' staffs are very interested in position papers that outline an organization's stance or any research the organization might have on a subject. Generally it is the staff's job to write a summary of an issue for the member. When we give them a position paper it helps them solve this problem. It should summarize the facts and arguments in our case, which the staffer is likely to have to do anyway. Our position paper should frame the issue our way.

• **Faxes to legislative offices.** In my experience, fax communication to legislative offices has more impact than e-mail, because they have greater physical presence (unless the office computer processes faxes electronically, in which case there is no difference in impact).

LESS FORCEFUL

- **E-mails to legislative offices**
- **Form letters**
- **Post Cards**
- **Petitions**

SYSTEMATIZING "GRASSROOTS" AND "GRASS TOPS" CONTACT

As part of a serious campaign, it's important to systematize grassroots and grass tops contact. In this respect, good issue campaigns are run like electoral campaigns—they have the same sense of urgency; they chunk down the activity into "doable" parts; and they deliver the message in a disciplined, measurable way.

In electoral campaigns, everyone generally understands that the top priority is delivering messages to voters. The same is true in an issue campaign. The most important single activity is directly communicating with "the deciders"—the members of the legislative body, or the executive making the key decisions.

A lot of advocacy organizations make the mistake of thinking that they are involved in an issue campaign if they hold meetings of advocates, track legislation, send over some position papers and have a few press events. These are not unimportant activities, but in issue campaigns, where the rubber hits the road is at the point where we communicate directly with the people who make the decisions—the members of Congress, heads of the agencies, or whomever. And there is no better group of communicators than the voters upon whom they depend for votes at election time.

That's why call-in days, patch-through calls, and systematic "grass tops" programs are essential elements of great issue campaigns.

Here are some key tricks of the trade:

- Set weekly targets for grass tops phone calls to members of Congress.
- Systematically work leadership networks for crucial constituencies.
- Recruit and train leaders who can lead confrontations with members of Congress at public appearances, town hall meetings, or their office.
- Demand meetings with members of Congress for leaders and large groups. If the member won't meet, run a campaign to drum up pressure for the meeting.
- Run campaigns to pass resolutions by local and state legislative bodies, organizations, etc.
- Set quotas for individually written letters to members of Congress each week.
- Set quotas for letters to the editor from key leaders each week.
- Use the press operation to book leaders on local talk shows.
- Assure that leaders from key constituencies are highlighted in earned media that is seen by the target member of Congress.
- Involve local leaders in nationwide events; it gives them a clear understanding that they're involved in something important.
- Recognize that the same tactics are not appropriate for all targets. A generally friendly Democrat should never be treated the same way as a generally unfriendly Republican.
- Consider using "Webinars"—seminars held over the web to get your grassroots network up to speed.
- Use "virtual marches" that organize phone callers through email to call the Capitol at specified times during a day when the goal is to completely clog the phone at a Congressman's office.
- Remember each member has his own distinct set of self-interests.

DELIVERING ISSUE MESSAGES TO THE VOTERS

Of course, in order to win an issue campaign we may need to change the underlying political dynamics of an issue. In the Social Security battle, we used earned media to move public opinion and make it politically radioactive to support privatization.

A good issue campaign often involves changing public opinion. It involves moving poll numbers just as surely as an election campaign.

And there is another reason to use issue campaigns to move public opinion. Issue campaigns are important methods of changing the overall political dialogue, moving the political center and modifying the underlying value frame of political discussion.

How do we use issue campaigns to affect the attitudes and value frames of the voters?

The key to effective issue campaigns, such as the campaign that defeated the privatization of Social Security, are field and press operations aimed at voters—both nationwide and especially in targeted districts.

In communicating with voters in issue campaigns, we use all of the rules of political messaging we discussed in Section Four.

First, we analyze the self-interest of the voters. With voters—and with legislators, too—the question is, of course, not *actual* self-interest but *perceived* self-interest.

Then we develop alternative formulations of our message to the voters. Once again, we're looking for a narrative. But this time we're looking to persuade voters about an issue position, not a candidate. And we're seeking to mobilize voters to take action vis-à-vis a legislator or other public official.

In evaluating self-interest, testing message and symbols, we use the same tools we do in elections: research, polling, and focus groups. Then we settle on our message, and consistently communicate using a variety of media.

MEDIA FOR COMMUNICATING ISSUE MESSAGES TO VOTERS:
- Direct Mail
- Robo-Calls
- Radio
- Earned Media
- Print Advertising
- Blogs
- Door to Door Canvassing
- Mass meetings
- Volunteer Phone Banks
- E-mail and Web Sites
- Passing leaflets and other material at mass locations
- Outdoor Advertising
- Paid TV
- TV coupled with earned media
- Organizational networks, meetings and newsletters (churches, union locals, etc.)

In order to determine the targeting for issue campaign messages to the general public, we first have to develop a plan with respect to each target member of the legislative body. Then we test the message using polling and focus groups. Then we choose the media with which to communicate.

Framing and naming the debate are especially important in issue campaigns.

Are we talking about a "death tax" that unfairly taxes families when someone dies and evicts farmers from their land? Or are we talking about a tax break for the heirs of multimillionaires like Paris Hilton that will be paid for by cutting funds for health care and education?

STARTING SOMETHING IS HARDER THAN STOPPING SOMETHING

In life and politics, it is generally harder to start something than to stop something. Once something becomes a fact on the ground, a wide array of people develop self-interests in its continued existence. And it's easier to get people fired up to protect something concrete that they have, than it is to crusade for something they hope to have in the future.

This general law of human nature is magnified when it comes to Congress. In the federal system, it is much more difficult to change policy than in many parliamentary systems. The 60-vote Senate rule on stopping debate and the bicameral structure of the Congress themselves place big impediments to change (from either the left or the right).

From 1994 to 2007, Progressives have used all of these levers to slow right-wing initiatives. Now we have to overcome them.

But the general principle that it is harder to start something than to stop it from happening presents itself in most legislative battles at every level of government—and for the least significant issues as well as the most momentous.

There are many stakeholders in the status quo; there are only "potential stakeholders" in change.

In Section Nine, we will look at just how critical it is for progressive victory that we make structural change our top priority. We have to create new facts on the ground in order to take advantage of the natural forces of self-interest, instead of pulling against them.

It's a lot easier to defend Social Security or to protect Medicare than to create a new national health system. Real, current stakeholders have tangible self-interests in these programs and can be mobilized to resist attacks.

It's a lot harder to get Congress to provide universal access to higher education than it would be to defend the current system of universal post-secondary education. Taking away post-secondary public education would cause a firestorm. It is inconceivable.

It would be just as inconceivable to eliminate universal access to higher education if such a program were put in place. But putting it in place is a different matter. That's a lot harder.

People fight harder to protect what they have than to get something they don't yet have.

In general, then, it's easier to stop something than to start it. Repealing something that has recently been passed is even more difficult, since the Members of Congress have already taken whatever heat for passing the initiative in the first place. Getting them to reverse themselves? That's tough. That's why the repeal of the "catastrophic health care plan" after the Rostenkowski chase by senior citizens was such a remarkable and unusual event.

CHAPTER THIRTY-FIVE

Campaigns Aimed At Government Agencies

BUREAUCRATIC SELF-INTERESTS: DON'T MAKE WAVES

Bureaucrats and executive officials of the government have many of the same general self-interest as legislators. Of course, they don't have to get reelected, but many of the other categories of interest definitely apply.

As a group, public employees are one of the most dedicated and hardworking groups of Americans I know. Many care deeply about their jobs and the goals of the organizations they staff.

But managers in public bureaucracies often share an important self-interest. Bureaucrats don't want to make waves—they don't want to be accused of screwing up. They want to stay out of trouble, to keep their heads down.

As a consequence, if you're running an issue campaign aimed at a decision-maker who is a bureaucrat, the major goal is to convince the target that you will cause him more trouble if he *doesn't* do what you want, than the trouble he will face if he *does* do what you want.

Of course, the same calculus is involved in any target, but bureaucrats are particularly vulnerable because their success and failure are often defined by whether they stay out of trouble. This mentality functions equally in both public and private bureaucracies.

Bureaucrats are particularly vulnerable to publicity and the threat of publicity. And the last thing they want is to become a problem for someone up the line, particularly top management. If you can stir up so much trouble that a guy up the line has to get involved, that is often a huge problem for your target.

When Jan went after the local Immigration and Naturalization Service, her major goal was to cause such a media problem for the local INS director that the national office would require action. By the way, bureaucrats hate to become involved with elected public officials like Members of Congress. That's why a major hassle for bureaucrats is to get elected officials involved with an issue, even if they don't directly oversee the bureaucrat or his agency.

Jan spends hours on the phone with U.S. embassies abroad, calling personally to get them to take action on visa applications for constituents. Her major power in these matters is simply forcing the official to spend so much time on her request that it's easier to just get it done.

PROTECTING THE BUDGET

A second generic bureaucratic self-interest is to protect their budget. Budgets are the source of power and prestige in a bureaucracy. To the extent you can engage this interest, you're way ahead of the game.

TURF

Bureaucrats in any institution (public or private) tend to be extremely jealous of their territory. Encroachment from another competing bureaucracy or bureaucrat is a constant concern. In fact, any encroachment on one's bureaucratic prerogatives is a concern.

The classic battle between the FBI, CIA and Department of Defense is a good example.

Bureaucratic competition becomes more important as jurisdictions overlap. Territorial, jurisdictional disputes, or fear of encroachment, can work for you or against you in an issue campaign. If possible, you need to design a campaign so that you engage the bureaucrat's jurisdictional self-interest, rather than running into the bureaucratic buzz saw.

CHAPTER THIRTY-SIX

Campaigns Aimed At Corporations

THE SELF-INTERESTS OF CORPORATE DECISION-MAKERS

Labor unions, community and consumer organizations and civil rights groups often run campaigns aimed directly at businesses. The goal is often to bring the business to the bargaining table, change its environmental policies or its corporate priorities.

Whole books have been written on corporate campaigns. Just a few words here.

Each corporation has its own constellation of interests. But for most, there are several that predominate.

Clayton Christensen of Harvard Business School argues that the most important self-interest of most businesses is, of course, its bottom line.[1] And the major forces that impact on the bottom line are the two stakeholders who control the flow of resources to the firm:

- Customers
- Investors

If you want to exert pressure on a business, focus on one of these two groups.

There are lots of ways to do it—some direct and some indirect. If the firm is a retail establishment, its customers are directly vulnerable to mass communication. If its customers are businesses, you can drag them into the fray.

Anything that causes Wall Street to worry about a firm's prospects has big implications for top management. Often this pressure is indirect, like the threat of some form of government regulation or simply a run of bad publicity. Remember, it was a series of articles in the *Wall Street Journal* that precipitated the collapse of Enron's house of cards.

Of course, the bureaucrats in business have the same sets of self-interest as those in the public sector. They want to keep their heads down; they don't want to be associated with a screw-up; they care about their jurisdiction.

Mid-level managers also want to advance their careers by sponsoring successful new product initiatives and profitable innovative programs.

They don't want to be associated with problems or failures. If you can threaten to pin a failure on someone in the corporate hierarchy, you have a handle on them.

Finally, business fears regulation by government at any level, and often regulation is the only thing that *will* make a corporation respond.

When designing campaigns aimed at corporations we use the same research and self-interest analysis we described in the congressional context. As in all campaigns, we want to engage people's self-interests and make their self-interests work for us, not against us.

Here are five quick examples of corporate campaigns involving widely varying tactics. All involved a careful analysis of the self-interest of corporate or government targets.

Pesticides and Lysol

In the 1990s, the organization of which I was director, Illinois Public Action, together with the national organization Citizen Action, was waging a campaign to eliminate many dangerous pesticides that were used on food products. Scientific studies had shown that pesticides widely in use caused cancer, birth defects, and other serious health problems. They continued to be used because of pressure from the large chemical companies.

We were targeting a class of chemicals that were widely used in pesticides sprayed on fresh fruits and vegetables, and had been shown to cause cancer.

To dramatize the issue, I held a press conference, where I demonstrated to reporters that allowing the chemical to be used as a pesticide was like using Lysol disinfectant as a salad dressing, since Lysol contained the same chemical. I poured Lysol on a salad for the TV cameras to demonstrate.

The press conference played prominently on television, and Citizen Action repeated the same event in other cities over the next few days.

Our target was the pesticide industry, EPA and Congress. But we had apparently hit another nerve. The day after the press conference I got a call from a good friend at a major PR firm. He had just been retained by the makers of Lysol. They wanted to meet. They were very worried about the image of their product as a carcinogen.

We said we'd be happy to meet and began some quick research on the properties of their product. It turned out that the scientific community was in fact very concerned that their product contained the chemical.

These meetings led to a commitment by the makers of Lysol to reformulate their product and eliminate the *cancer-causing chemical* within the next several months. In exchange, we made the commitment not to repeat our press conferences with the Lysol as salad dressing in other cities. There were, after all, lots of other cleaning products on the market. The last thing the Lysol people wanted was to be known by potential customers as the cleaning alternative that could give them cancer.

SANDWICHES AT O'HARE FIELD

About the same time, a guy came to see me, who represented a union local that was involved in a contract dispute between a food service vendor at O'Hare Field and its workers. The vendor, Carson's International, had been recalcitrant about negotiating a contract. The union had something that they hoped would be their silver bullet—sandwiches.

One of the food service workers laid them out on my desk. "Thing is," he said, "they're *way* out of date. Made weeks ago."

"How do we prove it?" I asked. "These codes," came the reply. "They're color-coded. Here's the list of the codes." I felt like I was back in the 1960s in Jan's campaign for freshness dates in supermarkets.

The press and many politicians don't care so much about a contract dispute with workers. They care a lot about being sold out-of-date food at the airport.

The next day, together with representatives of the union, I held a press conference to display the sandwiches and the code list. There was a lot of coverage.

As the press left, I turned to the guys from the union and one of my associates and said, "Two bits says I get a call from Jasculca-Terman or Burston-Marsteller by the close of business." They were two of the most prominent PR and government affairs firms in Chicago. Carson's International would almost certainly hire one of them to try to cauterize this problem.

Sure enough—it must not have been a half an hour—I got a call from Rick Jasculca. He'd just been retained by Carson's International to try to work this out.

This time, the answer was simple. "Tell them to give the workers a fair contract and stop selling out-of-date sandwiches and we'll shut up," I told him.

It only took a few days before the strike was settled and Jasculca sent us the firm's new food rotation policy.

Of course, he knew that our next step would have been to call on the city to re-examine the firm's franchise as a vendor at O'Hare. They didn't want to go there.

WAL-MART AND THE LIVING WAGE

The best-known corporate campaign today is aimed at Wal-Mart. Several organizations, including Wal-Mart Watch, have dedicated themselves to preventing Wal-Mart, the largest private employer on the planet, from continuing to lead the race to low wages and benefits—not only in the U.S., but worldwide.

In the fall of 2006, my good friend Joe Moore, Alderman of Chicago's 49th Ward, proposed a city ordinance that would require a "living wage" and benefits for employees of all retailers with more than 90,000 square feet of floor space, including Wal-Mart.

The notoriety of Wal-Mart's bad employment practices gave the proposal considerable traction. SEIU, The Jobs With Justice Coalition, ACORN, and the Living Wage Coalition organized throughout Chicago to support the ordinance. The large retail sector went crazy. The Chamber of Commerce called on Chicago's Mayor Daley to oppose the ordinance, saying it would be bad for new development. But the political and economic climates, where median wages for average workers had not increased for years, coupled with local organizing efforts, prevailed. The ordinance passed the Chicago City Council, 34 to 14.

It took two months for the business community and the Mayor to successfully pressure several members of the City Council to change their positions and vote to sustain a veto, which the Mayor issued in the early fall.

Moore and the advocates of the "living wage" in Chicago plan to go back to the Council with a living wage proposals that will cover all larger businesses—not just retailers. The controversy helped spur the Illinois Legislature to raise the state's minimum wage in November of 2006.

The Chicago campaign was also part of a broader effort to tackle the shrinking wages available to average workers in America. A flurry of referenda calling for increases in the minimum wage were passed in the 2006 Midterm elections. And the new Democratic majority in Congress passed a nationwide increase early in 2007.

Of course, the notion that the "minimum wage" should be a "living wage"—that anyone who works 40 hours a week, at any job, should be able to earn enough to support themselves—is a critical element in the overall progressive value frame.

Campaigns aimed at specific businesses—like Wal-Mart—and specific sectors—like the "Big Box Stores"—can help promote broader policy changes.

SEARS AND U.S. STEEL

Earlier I mentioned the campaign of Citizens Action Program (CAP) in the 1970s to reduce pollution at U.S. Steel's South Chicago plant.

That was a tough one. U.S. Steel sold product to big wholesale customers. We didn't have a lot of handles. So we had to go for a number of "bank shots." We had to put pressure on *secondary* players who would, in turn, put pressure on U.S. Steel.

Several were particularly notable.

First, it turned out that a member of the U.S. Steel Board was also the Chairman and CEO of Sears. Now Sears is a retail company. We could get to their customers and generally cause them trouble. So we decided to very publicly demand a meeting with the Sears Chairman.

To support that demand, we began sending delegations to the stores on weekends all across the Chicago area. Each delegation was equipped with a person in a clown suit, a large supply of helium and balloons. Printed on the balloons were the words: "Sears + U.S. Steel = Pollution. Call xxx-xxxx." That was the phone number of the local store manager. We also passed out leaflets explaining the issue and asking customers to call the store manager and ask him to call the chairman of Sears who, we explained, was on the U.S. Steel Board. "Tell him your customers want him to stop the pollution and meet with CAP," it said.

Kids would take the balloons—and pretty soon scores of them were bobbing through the Sears store. We did our best to have metro or local press along for a picture. It took about two weekends of these events to get a meeting with the Chairman of Sears.

The vice president-midwest of U.S. Steel, Edward C. Logelin Jr., was not pleased that his board had been dragged into the fray. He was even less pleased when our delegation showed up at a national meeting of the General Assembly of the Presbyterian Church, which was being held in Buffalo, New York. Logelin was running for Moderator (or, chairman) of the General Assembly of the Church. We put up a picket line in front of the meeting and passed out leaflets asking how a church can elect someone who was such an irresponsible steward of the environment. Logelin was not elected.

Back in Chicago, we put a good deal of pressure on the city Department of Environmental Control. We asked them to put monitoring stations near the plant, and to participate in three-way discussions between CAP, U.S. Steel and the city to develop a pollution abatement plan.

After considerable pressure, U.S. Steel agreed to participate. But the day of the first meeting, we had a surprise for them.

For some time CAP had been involved in a campaign to end the under-assessment of large downtown commercial properties, since it led to higher property tax bills for everyone else. The County Assessor at the time, a guy named P. J. (Parky) Cullerton, was an old-school political boss, who had all sorts of deals with big developers and real estate bosses for huge tax breaks. CAP had done a number of studies of many of these properties in conjunction with reporters at the *Chicago Daily News*, then one of Chicago's afternoon newspapers. It was the sister paper of the *Chicago Sun-Times*.

As we began to work on the U.S. Steel campaign, we decided to look at their assessment as well. We calculated that based on the industry standard of the capital cost-per-ton of steel produced, it would be impossible for the U.S. Steel South Works to produce the amount of steel it churned out if the plant were only worth the market value that was indicated in its real estate tax assessment. Company press releases about the cost of their new Basic Oxygen Process Shop Furnace confirmed our results. It turned out that the U.S. Steel South Works was under-assessed by tens of millions of dollars.

The Chicago Daily News hit the stands at 10 a.m. each day. As we walked into the meeting with representatives of US steel to talk about their pollution—at exactly 10 a.m.—we flopped down the afternoon paper on the table. The banner headline read: "U.S. Steel Under-Assessed." That got their attention.

Fairly soon, U.S. Steel and the city came to terms on a pollution control and monitoring plan. And their real estate tax assessment was increased. U.S. Steel wanted out of the spotlight, so they did business.

As a postscript, U.S. Steel South Chicago Works was closed 20 years later. It was a victim of the American steel industry's failure to come to terms with the invasion of mini-mills as a new technology moved from the production of cheaper, lesser-quality sensitive steel up-market to structural steel. The fact that it closed had little or nothing to do with pollution abatement costs. In fact, when the U.S. Steel (by then USX) South Chicago plant closed in 1992, that left only one integrated North American structural steel maker—Bethlehem. Bethlehem closed its last structural steel beam plant in 1995, leaving the US market entirely to firms utilizing mini-mill technology. [2]

CAMPAIGNS AIMED AT BUSINESSES

In all these cases, the issue campaigns targeted the firms' bottom lines, either directly or indirectly, through media and government. They supplemented these attacks with mini-campaigns aimed personally at primary decision-makers.

A Combination Campaign aimed at Business and Government — "Save the Swordfish... Try the Pasta!"

In the late 1990s, our firm worked with a wonderful organization called SeaWeb. Its goal was to end the over-fishing of Atlantic swordfish that was endangering the existence of the species—and the viability of the fishery. Questions of fishing rights have been controversial since humans were hunter-gatherers hundreds of thousands of years ago.

The problem in the modern world is a combination of increasingly efficient fishing technologies and a lack of strictly enforced regulation of fish stocks.

It doesn't take a genius to understand that if you fish a species to the point where it reproduces at a rate lower than the annual catch, it will ultimately disappear. That's particularly true if you fish nursery areas and catch juvenile fish before they can reproduce.

This problem has become increasingly acute for larger, slower-maturing fish since replacement times are a matter of many years. And modern mass-marketing hasn't helped. The Patagonian Toothfish was not a big seller to restaurants or grocery fish departments. But it flew out of kitchens when marketers renamed it Chilean Sea Bass. Its massive popularity, and mostly illegal, foreign catches have caused the species to be fished almost to extinction.

The SeaWeb campaign to replenish Atlantic Swordfish was conducted together with a coalition of environmental groups. Its tactics were very innovative. The plan was to work with a progressive organization called the Chef's Collaborative to get restaurant chefs to sign a pledge not to serve swordfish until the U.S. Department of Commerce and the International Tuna Conference put new rules in place that protected the long-term viability of the species and the fishery.

Of course, everyone in the fishing industry recognized that you can't overfish common stock and continue a viable fishery. But no one wants to cut their own catch, either. That's why the forces of the "market" are inadequate to effectively allocate fish resources. Everyone acting together has to set rules to protect the common store of fish. Left to the market, that common resource would disappear.

Our campaign involved directly recruiting chefs to join the moratorium, and to place cards on tables explaining why there was no Atlantic Swordfish on the menu. This activity was accompanied by an active press campaign and direct lobbying of the U.S. Department of Commerce, which is in charge of both fisheries regulation and the U.S. position at talks of the International Tuna Commission that hammered out common rules and quotas for world fisheries.

In the course of the effort, the Coalition met with the Secretary of Commerce William Daley. Daley, whom both Jan and I have known for some years, said that he had been warned that the most controversial issue he would deal with as Secretary of Commerce would be fishing issues.

During our campaign, we recruited thousands of chefs to participate in the boycott and generated substantial media attention for this novel tactic. But our real targets were the Department of Commerce and the International Tuna Commission. In the end, the Clinton Administration issued regulations that set new standards substantially improving the regulation of the Atlantic Swordfish fishery in American waters. It included a program to buy out fishermen who wanted to move into other industries or fisheries. With U.S. support, the International Tuna Commission also improved international standards.

The Swordfish population has begun to bounce back—but the need for protection of our marine resources remains a major and urgent concern that will impact the future of life on the planet.

SECTION SIX

ORGANIZING FOR VICTORY

CHAPTER THIRTY-SEVEN

Organizations and Their Capabilities

As important as they are, progressive victory does not simply require great messaging and strategy. It also involves great organizing.

It involves creating progressive campaigns and organizations to engage the energy of millions of ordinary Americans in a serious progressive movement.

It's easy to pay homage to great organizing. It's something else again to do it—to execute.

This chapter will deal with the elements of great organizing, and the characteristics that progressive political organizations need to succeed.

Organizations are not simply the sum of the individuals who participate in them. All organizations, including political organizations, develop characteristics in and of themselves that heavily impact their capabilities to achieve goals.

In his book *The Innovator's Dilemma*, Harvard Business School's Clayton Christensen argues that there are three essential factors that affect what an organization can and cannot do: it's resources, its processes, and its values.[1]

RESOURCES

In a business context, resources include people, equipment, technology, money, relationships with suppliers, distributors and customers, brands, information, and product designs. In a political context, an organization's most important resources are its people (employees, leadership and members), money, name, technology, equipment, information, vendors and relationships with other political actors.

Resources are people, things and assets. They can be recruited, hired, fired, sold, depreciated or enhanced. They can generally be transferred across the boundaries of organizations more easily than processes or values.

PROCESSES

In a business context, processes are patterns of interaction, coordination, communication and decision-making through which companies transform inputs of resources into products and services of greater worth. In a political context, they are the patterns of interaction, coordination, communication and decision-making through which the organization alters the behavior of those who it seeks to influence.

Some processes are formal. They are explicitly defined, documented and consciously followed. Others are informal. They are habitual routines for ways of doing business that evolve over time. At some point, these processes become so highly inculcated in the organization that they become part of the organization's culture.

In all organizations, processes develop as a means to tackle specific problems that the organization normally confronts. Christensen argues that when an organization attempts to use processes that were developed to solve one set of problems to solve a very different set of problems, it may well fail. Processes that define the *capabilities* of an organization with one goal, also define a *disability* when it comes to confronting another goal.

By their very nature, processes and organizations are developed to perform routine tasks efficiently. They are not meant to *change*. When the task changes, it is often difficult for organizations to change their processes.

In political organizations, some of the most critical processes are those that affect decisions regarding the allocation of resources.

VALUES

The values of any organization are the criteria by which decisions about priorities are made. In political organizations, these include the values used to determine the types of goals the organization seeks to achieve, those whose behavior it attempts to influence, the processes it emphasizes (including the day-to-day focus of its people, its organizers and its members), where it spends its money and the tactics it considers most effective.

The more broadly an organization's values are shared throughout the organization at every level, the more likely it is that everyone in the organization will make independent decisions about priorities that are consistent with the organization's strategic direction and priorities. A key characteristic of great organizations is that consistent values permeate the organization's structure.

Like processes, an organization's values can also become embedded in its culture, and that makes them very hard to change, especially if the organization is confronted with tasks for which its values are inappropriate.

Strong organizational values, then, heavily influence the organization's *capabilities* and its *disabilities*.

Together, the processes and values of an organization come to define an organizational culture. Peters and Waterman, in their book on great companies, *In Search of Excellence,* come to one overriding conclusion:

Without exception, the dominance and coherence of culture proved to be an essential quality of excellent companies. [2]

Generally, an organization's culture is defined by stories, heroes, role models, mentors, and above all, the kind of "transforming leaders" we discussed in Section Four. These are leaders that view themselves as teachers, as the shapers of values. They lead others into motion, and then label or name the values the actions exemplify. If these actions and the processes they compose are repeated often enough, the processes and values they define are learned by the unconscious of the organizational participants and become the culture. When that happens, the participants act according to the processes and seek to maximize the values *automatically.* The culture becomes "common sense."

In the early stages of an organization's history, much of the organization's capabilities reside in its resources, especially its people. The people who found organizations bring their own values and define the processes that will characterize the organization in the future.

But Christensen argues that, as the organization grows and gains experience, the locus of its capabilities shifts toward its processes and values. As people work together successfully to address recurrent tasks, processes are defined. It also becomes clear which types of priorities are most likely to achieve the organization's goals, and values coalesce.

You could put the same highly capable people in organizations with one strong culture, and they will be successful. If you put them in a different organization with another strong culture, and they may not be successful.

In other words, an organization's processes and values—its culture— exist independently of the people within it. The culture becomes a characteristic of the organization that can only be changed with great difficulty and the intense focus of the organization's top leadership.

On the other hand, it is critical to create a strong culture in order to succeed over the long run. For an organization to become large, powerful and effective, you can't rely on the wisdom of a few organizational founders. You have to have a broadly shared culture that defines the organization itself. One of the reasons why many progressive organizations and startup businesses are successful at first and then "flame out" after a short while is their failure to create a strong culture of processes and values that moves the locus of the organization's capabilities from a small group of people to the culture of the organization itself.

CHAPTER THIRTY-EIGHT

The Qualities of Great Organizers

What entrepreneurs are to business, political organizers are to political organizations.

While there are many roles that are critical in effective political organizations, none is more important than that of political organizers. In politics, and especially election campaigns, we constantly create new organizational structures. In fact, one of our great needs is increased institutionalization of these structures. But regardless, the political organizer and the organization's initial leaders are critical to creating the organizational building blocks of the progressive movement and fashioning the culture, the processes and values of those organizations. This is especially true of startup campaigns. But it is true at almost every level, from attempts to create new organizing committees around issues; to coalitions like USAction, Americans United for Change, and the Emergency Campaign for America's Priorities; to major institutions like labor unions and the Democratic National Committee. Just as in business, different values and processes are often necessary in organizations to complete different tasks. But there are two categories of organizational values that are almost always critical to create effective political organizations. I call them:

1) Thinking like an organizer
2) Excellence in Execution

These two constellations, or sets of values, define appropriate processes that are critical to the success of almost any progressive political organization.

THINKING LIKE AN ORGANIZER

As we build progressive organizations, we should make "thinking like an organizer" a value set that is emulated throughout the organization— by everyone. Like other key elements of the organizational culture it should not be restricted to leaders or staff people who refer to themselves professionally as "organizers."

Some of them we've discussed before in other contexts. Here's the list:

UNDERSTANDING SELF-INTEREST

The first and foremost value in this set is—"understanding self-interest".

Great organizers are masters at decoding people's self interests, and at picking up the signals that allow them to understand what motivates other people. Everyone has a constellation of self-interests, including their physical needs, needs for control, needs for structure, needs for social interaction, needs for intellectual stimulation and above all, the need for meaning—for significance. Great organizers unpack someone's self interests the way a private eye solves the case. They look for all the clues, the facial expressions, the words, the posture, the things people wear, the activities they value, the people with whom they associate.

ASSESSING THE CAPABILITY OF THE INDIVIDUAL TO BECOME INVOLVED

To move people into action, you have to understand the self-interest that motivates them. But you also have to understand the capability or capacity they have to become involved, donate money, execute a project— the skills, the capacity, the time—the wherewithal.

When you want someone to give you money, you have to give them the will, based on your understanding of their self-interest. But they also must have the wherewithal to give—the money in the bank. The same goes for everyone else who you want to motivate to participate in an organization on whatever basis.

Great organizers are good at understanding self-interest. They are also good at assessing the capability of the individual to make a contribution to the effort and to put the right-sized peg in the right-sized hole.

MEANING IS THE GREATEST MOTIVATOR

Great organizers understand that meaning is the greatest motivator. They're constantly refocusing members, staff and leadership on why what they're doing is so important—and why each person is so important to the effort.

Remember that there are *two needs* represented by this desire for meaning. On the one hand, people want to feel they are involved in something bigger than themselves, something important. On the other hand, they want to stand out, to play an important personal role. Our organizers need to satisfy both sides of that equation.

BEING AN AGITATOR

In Section Three, we discussed the importance of agitation — particularly with allied activists and leaders and those who share our self-interest but don't yet realize it.

Thinking like an organizer involves *being an agitator*, rubbing raw the sores of discontent, bringing into consciousness the injustices that people have learned to take for granted, ignore or look past.

Progressive organizing is about change. Change requires that people reawaken to the elements of injustice that we have come to accept as "normal." In the South, it used to be "normal" that whites and blacks had different drinking fountains, sat in different bleachers at the ballpark and attended different schools. It was "normal" that blacks never had powerful jobs and were never elected to office.

Just 160 years ago, it was "normal" that Americans "owned" slaves.

Today it is "normal" that schools attended by children of wealthy parents are better equipped and funded and hire better teachers than schools attended by children of poor parents.

Agitators reawaken us to the injustices that we have come to accept as commonplace. They make us see them in a new light. Once they are brought to consciousness. They force us to focus on the uncomfortable — "Hey, I see you have a spot on your pants."

Agitators keep us slightly on edge — in motion. They dispel complacency. To think like an organizer some part of you has to be an agitator.

ONE STEP AT A TIME — TAKE THEM TO 95TH STREET

In Section three, I wrote about my first supervisor, Pete Martinez, and how he repeatedly lured me to take him all the way to his home on 95th Street from our office on the North side of Chicago. He asked me first just to take him down town, then a little further south but not out of the way — and finally, once I was closer, all the way to 95th Street.

Thinking like an organizer is about taking them to 95th Street — one step at a time. We get people into action, and then get them more and more committed to the project, organization or campaign; doing more and more, committing more and more every step of the way.

REPEATED, PERSUASIVE CONTACT

Thinking like an organizer is remembering this key principle of political communication *all the time*. Want someone to come to the meeting? Remind them several times. Want the press to cover the event? Talk to the assignment desk– several times. Want to make a point? Come back to it, over and over.

The Art of the Ask

Everything about effective political work, about thinking like an organizer, is about asking. You ask people to canvass their block. You ask people to make phone calls. You ask people to give money. You ask people to vote. You ask what people are thinking.

Believe it or not, people love to be asked. It makes them feel important, needed, meaningful.

Tip O'Neill, the former Democratic speaker of the House, told a story about his first attempted run for public office, which he lost.

The morning after the election, he strode slowly down the walk to his mailbox. There in the yard next to him was Mrs. O'Brien, his neighbor of many decades. "How are you this morning, Tip O'Neill?" she said.

"Oh, not too well," O'Neill is said to have replied. "I just lost the election. But thanks for so much for your vote, Mrs. O'Brien."

"Oh, I didn't vote for you, Tip O'Neill," she said.

"Why, Mrs. O'Brien," he replied, "I've been your next door neighbor for years. Why didn't you vote for me?"

"Because you never asked," she said.

People love to be asked. They hate to be ignored. They hate to be taken for granted.

When Jan first started out in politics, she would go to the fairs and summer festivals, but she was reluctant to interrupt the people having a cold one and a brat in the beer tent. She quickly learned that they were happy to be interrupted by someone running for public office. By and large, they love to be asked for support. They love to be asked their opinion.

The outcome of a good campaign field operation is entirely a function of the *quality* and *quantity* of asks. The art of the ask is the art of great organizing.

Listening

The corollary of the art of the ask is the art of listening. Thinking like an organizer is about listening, and not talking.

When I was in high school in Shreveport, Louisiana, on the weekends, one of our favorite summer activities was water skiing. The father of a particular high school girlfriend didn't like me very much. Regardless, one Sunday she and I were going water skiing with her dad.

My plan was to try to get myself into the father's good graces. Many major issues, like how late I could keep his daughter out on dates, hung in the balance.

I decided to spend the afternoon on the boat asking him all about what he did for a living. Unfortunately, he sold insurance—not your most interesting subject. But by the end of the afternoon, I had heard all about selling life insurance.

When I got home the phone rang. The girlfriend was on the line. "Daddy loves you," she said. "He thinks you're so smart."

Now, remember, I hadn't said much of anything all afternoon. I had just asked him about his business and listened. Then again, people think that if you're interested in them, and the things that they are interested in, you must be pretty smart.

Listening is critical to great organizing because it is critical to our ability to analyze someone's self-interest. And it is equally critical to our understanding what capabilities and abilities someone has to contribute to the campaign organization.

As a consequence, I have a somewhat facetious 70-30 rule. Seventy percent of the time a good organizer listens. Thirty percent of the time you ask questions. This doesn't leave a lot of time to talk. Clearly my rule is an exaggeration, but you get the idea.

CLOSING THE DEAL IS ABOUT QUID PRO QUO

Thinking like an organizer is understanding that when we ask people to do something, we never beg. We never go to people hat in hand and plead with them to do whatever it is we want.

Closing the deal—getting them to commit to any action—is always about a quid pro quo. We always "pay" them in some currency drawn from the menu of their self-interests.

When we ask a senior citizen to volunteer to help on a campaign, we "pay" them by fulfilling their desire to "get out" and have much-needed social interaction. They get to feel needed, like they're important, part of something meaningful. Maybe they also get some pastries or sandwiches; free food is always a good thing with seniors. Humorist Garrison Keillor quips that "the crucial questions when you turn 64 are: Will I be needed and will I be fed?" [1]

Closing the deal is always about some quid pro quo.

BUILDING RELATIONSHIPS

Thinking like an organizer is about building relationships. It's not about managing lists or treating people like pawns on a chessboard. Great organizers spend time meeting with people face-to-face—asking them about their lives, meeting the kids—getting to know who they are and letting them get to know who *they* are.

Great organizers address people's critical self-interest need for human interaction that is about *relationships*. They address the need for people to feel important and meaningful. Relationships provide that, too.

When the chips are down, a volunteer or employee is always more likely to deliver if they're asked to go to the extra mile by a friend rather than a stranger.

Great organizers, and especially great campaigns, forge strong relationships. Ask anyone who's been in a real battle—in real warfare—how he feels about his buddies. For many of the now-aging vets of World War II, the relationships they forged 60-plus years ago were the strongest of their lives. The same goes for other battles, for great campaigns. It's the sense of camaraderie—of close relationship—that attracts many people to campaigns in the first place.

THERE IS NO SUCH THING AS APATHY

The story is told that organizers would meet with the late, organizing guru Saul Alinsky and complain about how apathetic the people were in the community they were assigned to organize. He looked up and said, "There is no such thing as apathy—only bad organizers."

Thinking like an organizer is about realizing that it is *our* responsibility to organize others, it's not their responsibility to fall into our arms. We have the responsibility to persuade them, and mobilize them.

If someone has a set of self-interests that should lead them to be progressive, yet they aren't, it doesn't help for us to disparage them, or view them as stupid. It helps to take responsibility to engage their self-interests—to actually recruit them.

History will not simply hand victory to Progressives in our battle with the right. It is up to us to organize and persuade. If someone appears apathetic, it's only because *we* have not yet figured out how to ring their bell.

EXCELLENCE IN EXECUTION

The second overall constellation of values that are critical to an effective political organization has to do with excellence in execution. In general, I find that issue and electoral campaigns are much more prone to fail because of poor execution than they are because of poor strategic or message decisions.

Being a great political organizer is not about being great at political repartee, or being a clever pundit, or hanging around the water cooler, spinning out political analysis.

Being a great political organizer is all about execution.

PRIDE AND TEAMWORK

The first value to be maximized in this category is pride and teamwork. In electoral campaigns, there is a tendency to jockey for position, to cover your own rear in case things go south. But in reality, most of the time, it is my experience that if you win, everyone gets the credit, and if you lose, everyone gets the blame.

The same goes for the entire progressive movement. There is always a temptation for organizations to vie for credit, to backstab other organizations. But to be effective—to be victorious—we need a sense of teamwork and common vision, and a common pride in each other's success.

Effective organizations, and an effective progressive movement, must have an ecumenical spirit where the success of all is more important than self-promotion.

It is simply wasteful to expend our scarce energy and time backstabbing and ass-covering. We need to create a culture where that's not encouraged, not tolerated and not necessary.

And that sense of teamwork needs to include a sense of pride—of *esprit*—a sense of pride not only in each other, but in the quality of our work.

There has to be a sense that we owe it to each other to execute everything we do with precision and commitment, with an understanding that going through the motions is never good enough. In a great organization, each of us expects the other to put out every ounce of energy necessary to succeed, and feels an obligation to everyone else to do so as well.

Great organizing is about spit and polish. It's about not being sloppy. It's about precision. It's about believing that no task is too small to be done well—or as my dad used to say, "If it's worth doing at all, it's worth doing right."

Focus

Excellence in execution is about focus. In issue and electoral campaigns, there are millions of distractions—people and circumstances that can lead the organization or campaign astray.

Great organizers are like great wide receivers in football. A great wide receiver may have five 300-pound tacklers bearing down on him. But he blocks them out of his consciousness and "looks" the ball into his hands. Great wide receivers have a laser-like focus that can filter out the clutter and concentrate on what matters—catching the ball.

At times of maximum danger, our brains and bodies are programmed by evolution to narrow our focus to the danger at hand. Our field of conscious vision actually begins to shrink, and we block out extraneous noise. At your peak level of awareness—where your heart rate goes to about 125 beats per minute—time seems to move more slowly. So we can more carefully process sensory inputs.

In *Blink,* Gladwell cites studies that showed that if you become overstimulated (heart rate of 175 beats per minute or more) because of a dangerous situation, your ability to process sensory inputs begins to sharply decline. In particular, you enter what he calls a temporary state of "autism"—unable to "mind read"—to understand or process facial expressions and other cues to human emotions and intention. It turns out that the major way to protect against this kind of over-stimulation is practice. When police, for instance, practice dangerous encounters on firing ranges, their heart rates drop and they can take control and focus at peak performance on the danger at hand.

Even when circumstances do not cause people to react physiologically to focus their senses, great organizers practice and teach the art of sharp focus—*looking the ball into their hands*—or the task to completion. They practice their craft over and over so that in the heat of battle, they can continue to focus with precision.

You Are the Message

A key element of the culture that values excellence in execution in politics is the understanding that each person is the message, personally.

In election campaigns, one of the most powerful symbols of the candidate is the campaign itself. If the campaign is exciting, on time, welcoming, inspiring, fun to be part of and effective, people think that the candidate is exciting, on time, welcoming, inspiring, fun to be with, and effective.

If the campaign is boring, unwelcoming, flat, no fun to be part of, and disorganized, people think that the candidate is boring, unwelcoming, flat, no fun to be with and ineffective.

The same goes for organizations and the progressive movement in general. The most prominent symbol of who we are and what we believe is the people who are part of our organizations. People vote for people, even when there's no election. They vote with their feet, with their heads, with their contributions, with their participation. What they vote for, or against, is the *people.*

The culture of the great organization, movement, or campaign, highlights the responsibility of each individual to represent the organization, campaign or movement, every day.

A WINNING ATTITUDE

We already talked in Section Three about people's conviction that they are winners. People want to be part of winning—not losing—organizations and campaigns. They look to their peers for validation and credibility. The bandwagon matters; winners are on the bandwagon.

So it is absolutely critical that the organization have a culture that always encourages a winning attitude and never allows a losing attitude to spread. Defeatism and negativity are like cancers in an organization or a movement.

Political organizations in many respects resemble sales organizations. Just like salesmen, our job is to persuade and motivate. As we have seen, being a great salesman is about subconscious behaviors. Above all it is about having a positive, winning attitude. In great sales organizations, people feed off each other's energy and emotion, and as we have seen, emotions are contagious. A telemarketer is never as good at calling from his own home as he is from a phone room because he doesn't feed off the positive energy. A winning attitude is like the gasoline for great sales organizations, and it's exactly the same for political organizations.

I don't care how bleak it looks, great organizations never admit defeat before the end of the game anymore than great sports teams do. They keep looking for a way to win, they believe they can win, and sometimes—they do.

One thing is for sure, if you don't believe you can win, you never will.

Excellence in Execution Requires a Culture Designed to Produce Winners

Since most people think of themselves as winners, a primary task of great organizations is to create an environment that continually reinforces this notion. If you label a person a loser, he'll act like one.

However overrated our view of ourselves, it doesn't help to make people feel more average or less successful. People want to be successful. They want to be part of organizations, and to follow leaders, who can make them succeed and make them feel successful.

Great leaders and organizers create systems designed to produce winners. They are trained to celebrate winning when it occurs and *set goals so that most people can be successful.*

FLEXIBILITY

As much as we aspire to spit and polish—to execute with precision—most political campaigns and political movements have to live with the reality that they must be extremely flexible. Resources are generally scarce; they're more like a guerrilla force than a standing army. That means they must learn to live off the land, and be ready to turn on a dime.

This does not mean the political organizers are free to be disorganized. Just the contrary, our operations have to be lean and flexible, and that means super-well organized, self-sufficient and self-confident. Great political organizers are great scroungers. They are people who can make do, jury rig and improvise. In order for people to have these qualities they require the highest skills and best training. They are the special forces of political life.

Excellence in execution in politics means that you carefully develop a plan and build into the plan the likelihood that the plan itself will have to be changed. That's because the first casualty of war is always the plan.

Flexibility does not mean you do without a plan or fly by the seat of your pants. It means that you carefully analyze the self-interests involved in the campaign, develop a plan to persuade and mobilize. But the plan must include the recognition that you and your colleagues must be flexible enough to make key calls based on "thin slices" of information once you're in the heat of battle. You build in that flexibility not simply because you have no other choice. Often the gut calls made by practiced organizers using "thin slices" of information, combined with our adaptive unconscious, make better decisions than those made through a highly deliberative bureaucracy that takes forever to decide and move.

Excellence in execution requires flexible fast paced decision-making. It requires that people be taught to do it well.

No Whining

Excellence in execution requires an organizational culture that does not tolerate whining.

Let me be clear. No whining is very different than a culture of "yes men" who blindly execute. We highly value independent initiative in identifying problems and solving them. Whining is constant complaining without solution. Whining is negative energy that spreads and infects a campaign or organization and, in addition, is downright unpleasant.

Great organizers don't expect everything to be perfect. They expect to confront and solve problems, not whine about them. Great electoral campaigns tolerate no whining; zero tolerance. They serve notice on the first day: if you want to whine, go somewhere else. Whiners don't attract followers. Organizations that tolerate whining don't, either.

Nuts and Bolts

In the end, excellence in execution in politics is more about nuts and bolts than grand strategies or plans. It is about carefully and correctly executing the voter I.D. and GOTV plans. It's about high-quality research and thoroughness in preparing the message plan.

Execution is definitely about clever messaging and excellent strategy. But if I had to choose, I'd take great execution of nuts and bolts every time.

In my view, the world can be divided into people who tell you why they can't achieve a goal and those who achieve them. We can hire or recruit any Tom, Dick or Harry to tell us why things *can't* be done. They are worthless to accomplish our goals. In politics we're looking for people who can find a way to succeed—*to execute.*

DISCIPLINE

In effective political organizations, a high premium is placed on discipline. It's hard to do a hundred thousand voter I.D.s. It's not so hard to do a thousand voter I.D.s per day over a hundred days.

The key to the successful execution of issue and political campaigns is to chunk the project down into doable parts and execute each discreet part with rigor and discipline.

As the military knows, a disciplined approach to the task is not simply a function of the type of individuals who populate organizations. It's very much a question of the organizational culture, of the values and procedures that are put in place about leadership.

When we do organizer training we make it clear from the first day that every session will start *exactly* on time. It only takes one or two embarrassing late entries by a lone straggler to get everyone into the rhythm. Punctuality is extremely important to all other forms of discipline in an organization. If the culture of the organization does not put a premium on punctuality, it is impossible to create a disciplined culture that values precision.

In general, discipline is much easier within an organizational context than outside of it. It is easier for a phone banker to be disciplined about making calls in a phone room than it is at home where his refrigerator, e-mail and television await. It is easier for a candidate to raise funds in a call-time routine, working with the call-time coordinator. In general, institutionalizing settings, routines and procedures massively increase the ability of human beings to be disciplined.

Let me give you an example of the importance of discipline, chunking things down into doable parts.

YEAR ROUND DOOR TO DOOR

In 1973, I met a fellow named Marc Anderson. He called one day to ask if the Citizens Action Program (CAP), where I was Associate Director at the time, wanted some money. The answer to that was easy. Anderson had been a successful door-to-door guy—selling encyclopedias. He believed he could use the same techniques to raise funds and recruit members for public interest organizations. Anderson had founded an organization to prove this premise. He wanted to team up with CAP so his people could have an ongoing action program to talk about at the door.

Anderson recruited motivated young people to go door-to-door. Their job was to present the organization's program, ask for a signature of support for the organization's goals, and recruit a membership contribution. Each canvasser had a quota of contributions that they had to raise each night and would canvass for four to five hours.

Many people could not believe that someone could go door-to-door in a neighborhood of perfect strangers and return at the end of the night with today's equivalent of $130 or $150 that had been given willingly by a dozen supporters. But Anderson's door-to-door operation worked brilliantly and became the basis for the pre-Internet public interest movement. For over 30 years, canvassing programs spread across the country for Citizen Action, the Public Interest Research Groups (PIRGs), Clean Water Action, Greenpeace, the Sierra Club and dozens of other progressive organizations.

The canvass operations used all of the principles that yielded "excellence in execution."

That Which Is Not Measured Is Not Done

The ultimate key to discipline—and to excellence in execution in general—is the regular measurement of results. Projects must be chunked into goals and timetables and progress must be measured constantly.

In an organizational context, there are many distractions—many claims on time and resources. The goals that are actually accomplished are always the goals that are measured for everyone in the organization to see.

Both the research on management outcomes and personal experience leads me to believe, without exception, the actual focus of an organization is a direct result of which outcomes are measured. *That which is not measured is not done.*

Rules About Measurement

• **Measurement Rule # 1.** You should not measure performance solely with respect to fixed goals that are set by the organization or its leadership. People are particularly responsive to measuring their performance relative to their peers. For the many years that I directed Illinois Public Action (IPA), the organization had a paid door-to-door canvass operation. We would always display a chart on the wall that measured each canvasser's nightly performance—for everyone to see. People need to compare themselves with each other. They don't want to fall behind the pack. Measurement systems need to engage that key self-interest.

• **Measurement Rule #2.** Set short-term, daily goals. Proximate, short-term goals are critical to maintaining disciplined performance. You can't expect the people in your organization to know how they're doing—or to focus their energy a disciplined way—if the only benchmark they have is six months in the future. There are too many distractions in life, and at work. Each of our canvassers at IPA had a daily quota and a weekly quota. Quotas—or short-term goals—are essential to long-term success in any endeavor that requires routine execution. Without them an organization cannot achieve long-term goals. Without short-term quotas, an organization cannot seriously accomplish its intended goals.

• **Measurement Rule #3.** Quotas and goals should never be set so high that most people in the group cannot achieve them with regularity. Quotas are certainly intended to stretch individual performance. They are intended to remind a canvasser that if he just gets one more voter registration, he'll meet his quota—even though he started thinking about going home 15 minutes before quitting time. But quotas should not stretch people so far that only the very best meet them. People think of themselves as winners. We need to give them the opportunity to be successful most of the time. Success motivates people to do more, to stay at the task, to endure hardship. Success makes people feel meaningful and significant and empowered.

Failure demobilizes people. It makes them feel insignificant, unempowered, bad about themselves and insignificant. People have plenty of opportunity to encounter these negative feelings for themselves. They don't need to be part of a political organization or campaign that makes them feel that way.

• **Measurement Rule #4.** Expect each member of the team to reach the goal. Expect victory. People need to assume that the goal is achievable. When they believe it, they can do it. If they don't believe it can be done, they won't do it. Many years ago, Illinois Pubic Action's telephone fund-raising operation began a new program. It was called the Public Action Leadership Club—or the PAL Club. To be a member, you had to agree to give the organization $10 per month—either by authorizing us to charge your credit card each month for 10 bucks, or making a lump sum payment of $120.

Twenty years ago that sounded like more money than it does today, and the first night, none of the fundraisers could get anyone to join the program. I was working late, and the manager on duty came to see me to tell me of the difficulty.

About that time, Kim, our premier fundraiser, joined the group. She had had a doctor's appointment and got in an hour later than usual. She sat down and knocked down three PAL members in a row. Then the telemarketers had a brief meeting, and she told everyone how easy it was to recruit PALs. Everyone returned to their workstations and proceeded to systematically recruit PAL memberships. It wasn't because Kim showed them how to do it. It was because she had shown them it was possible.

If people believe they can achieve a goal, they generally will. If you want them to stretch, they have to believe they can.

•   **Measurement Rule #5.** Goals must be concrete, specific and quantitative. *Some is not a number. Soon is not a time.*

Some people don't like numbers. These people don't belong in politics. Like it or not, politics is about numbers. It's about the number of votes you get. It's about the number of voters who come to the polls. It's about the number of "asks" you make. It's about how many phone calls you generate to a Senator's office. Everything in politics has something to do with numbers. Numbers involve precision, and excellence in execution demands precision.

You don't have to love math. You just have to understand that some is not a number, and soon is not a time. The answer to the question, "How many people are coming to the meeting?" is not "a lot" or even "about 50." The right answer is—"we currently have 33 hard commitments and another 200 calls out."

Numbers are about precision; that's why they're so important.

In my experience, people who chafe at being held accountable to perform at a quantitative level—with respect to a number—aren't really objecting to the use of numbers at all. They just don't want to be held accountable—which brings us to the next critical aspect of organizational culture that produces excellence and execution.

ACCOUNTABILITY

Great political organizations establish procedures that assure accountability. And they have values that emphasize its importance. These aspects of organizational culture are institutionalized from the first day.

The expectation of accountability should run in all directions. There must be accountability to the decision-making structures and leadership of the organization. But there must also be accountability to each other—

to one's peers—to the team. Each person needs to feel that when he's at bat, he can't let his teammates down.

In fact, peer-to-peer accountability is often more critical than account-ability to the organizational hierarchy. We've all been in organizational contexts where rank-and-file members are cynical about the decisions and goals of the leadership. In that situation, the rank-and-file often conspire to do what is necessary just to get by.

Excellence in execution demands a sense of mutual accountability. That means that the organization's goals have to be embraced by the team itself; if you don't pull your weight, you're betraying your mates, not just top management. That's another reason why positive energy and attitude is as critical to a political campaign as it is to a sales force.

The Values and Procedures of Effective Organizations Encourage the Use of Positive Reinforcement and Intrinsic Motivation.

The literature on management is nearly unanimous. In looking at excellent companies, Peters and Waterman found that the key to effectively using rewards and punishments to influence behavior is the use of positive reinforcement. The key to lasting commitment to the task is intrinsic motivation.

There is an asymmetry between positive and negative reinforcements (e.g., threats and sanctions). Negative reinforcement will produce behavioral change, but often in strange, unpredictable, and undesirable ways. Positive reinforcement causes behavioral change, too, but usually in the intended direction. [2]

Studies show that negative sanctions simply don't work very well. They usually result in frantic, unguided activity. And they don't suppress the desire to "to be bad."

The psychologist B.F. Skinner wrote, "The person who has been punished is not thereby simply less inclined to behave in a given way; at best, he learns how to avoid punishment." [3]

On the other hand, positive reinforcement not only shapes behavior but also teaches and in the process enhances an individual's "self-image." Positive reinforcement nudges good things onto a person's agenda—negative reinforcement rips things off the agenda.

Positive reinforcement makes someone want to spend more time engaging in the rewarded activity. Negative reinforcement prevents spending time on the sanctioned behavior.

Positive reinforcement enhances the self-image of the "winner" and motivates the individual. Positive reinforcement enhances one's sense of control of an activity.

Negative reinforcement diminishes one's sense of being a winner and results in feeling less in control.

Positive reinforcement, in other words, works with people's basic self-interests. Negative reinforcement works against them.

To the extent the leader or manager must use negative psychological sanctions; they should involve "disappointment"—not "criticism." Disappointment implies the belief on the manager's part that the individual has the potential to be successful. Criticism implies that he or she is a failure.

There are number of rules for providing an effective positive reinforcement:

- Positive Reinforcement Rule #1: It should be specific—it should reward concrete action. Rewarding achievement of a concrete goal is more effective than rewarding overall performance.

- Positive Reinforcement Rule #2: It should be immediate. The closer the reward is in time to the action rewarded, the better.

- Positive Reinforcement Rule #3: Reward small wins as well as large ones. One of the biggest problems in maintaining momentum in a long political struggle is constantly reminding the participants that it's all worth it, that they can win. It is extremely important to reward small interim wins and successes.

- Positive Reinforcement Rule #4: Intangibles like leadership attention are important forms of positive feedback. Use all the self-interest arrows in the quiver. Making people feel special through praise from management or leadership may be more important than financial rewards or bonuses. Making people feel important is an especially significant form of positive reinforcement. Making people feel small or insignificant is probably the most onerous form of negative sanction.

- Positive Reinforcement Rule #5: Unpredictable and intermittent reinforcements work best. A volunteer of the week is good. A special recognition for yesterday's spectacular work is better yet. It seems more special and it's more proximate to the success of being celebrated.

- Positive Reinforcement Rule #6: Small rewards are sometimes more effective than large ones. Given the choice, small special rewards that are spread around are generally better than one large reward that goes to one person.

INSPIRATION LEADS TO SELF-MOTIVATION

Accountability by itself will not result in truly excellent execution. If we want each team member to be intrinsically motivated, each must be inspired to do so. The key to lasting commitment to a task is intrinsic motivation.

Inspiration is key, because it appeals to the most basic self-interest, the need for meaning and significance.

Recall that all inspiration has two elements. First, one must be convinced of the essential significance, the intrinsic value, of the task they are given. Second, they must be given a sense of empowerment themselves. They need to believe that they can make a special contribution to help achieve the goal.

Once again, to feel a sense of meaning, one must feel one is committed to something bigger than oneself, but also that one can "stand out," that one can make a major contribution to accomplishing the meaningful goal.

Take for example, a potential volunteer who comes into the campaign office of Candidate A and is initially ignored by the campaign's organizers. Finally, he is given a list to call, is set off in the corner, and ignored for the rest of the night.

As he's about to leave, he struggles to find someone to give his list to. He's only made 30 contacts in three hours of attempts and identified just 10 new voters for the candidate. As he hands over his list, the distracted organizer says, "Thanks, just put the list over there."

The odds of this volunteer returning are about *zero*.

On the other hand, here comes a potential volunteer to the campaign of Candidate B. As he walks in the door he is met by a volunteer coordinator who says, "Oh, Mr. Smith, we've been expecting you. First come to this area for a quick briefing." There he finds 10 other potential volunteers.

The group is then briefed on the state of the campaign and the critical role of the field program. They're told to expect to reach about 90 people each during their three-hour shift on their predictive dialer. The briefer then explains that three other offices are doing the same program tonight and every night. The between these 30 people, the campaign will reach 2,700 households tonight and every night for the in next 60 days.

"We've already contacted 20,000 households in the last 10 days. By the time were done, we'll have reached over 180,000 households of swing voters. After we're done tonight at nine, we'd like you to stick around if you can for some popcorn and a quick debrief on what you've heard. I'll be here all night so let me know if you have any questions. Here's your canvass packet, including your voter phone list, a sample phone rap and a set of questions and answers."

Our briefer continues with a short discussion of the dos and don'ts of phone canvassing.

"And above all," she says, "*smile* on the phone. The smile changes your tone of voice. Now let's go to work. I'll be checking in with you. Refreshments are on the counter."

Crisp, knowledgeable, organized. Above all, the volunteer thinks he's part of something important and that his personal effort will make a difference.

Every night, the volunteers are briefed on new potential developments by someone who consistently returns to the themes of why this election is so important. The difference between Campaign A and Campaign B is like night and day. Campaign B's volunteers will come back, and maybe they'll bring a friend. They're pumped. They're inspired.

GREAT POLITICAL ORGANIZATIONS MOVE PEOPLE INTO ACTION

We've already seen how people "act" themselves into beliefs and commitments. But many organizations act as if the proclamation of policy and its execution were synonymous.

Only if you get people acting the way you want them to, even in small ways, will they come to believe in what they're doing. We succeed by the explicit management of the after-the-fact labeling process: publicly and ceaselessly lauding the small win.

Excellence in execution requires a culture that prioritizes putting people into motion.

THE CULTURE OF GREAT POLITICAL ORGANIZATIONS IS FUN

I suppose this goes for most organizations, but it seems especially true in politics. The best organizations are fun places to work, volunteer, hang out.

Democrats need to be the fun party—the cool party. That means that while we always have to be serious about our goals, we can't always take ourselves too seriously.

Fun is especially important in politics, because politics is so dependent upon volunteers. But it's also important because fun is attractive, and, especially in the electoral realm, the campaign itself is a major symbol for the qualities of the candidate.

And don't think that fun and disciplined hard work can't go hand-in-hand. Anyone who has really committed to a cause knows that the people who work the hardest can also play the hardest. Relationships between members of the team are forged when people relax and socialize together in the heat of battle, when they kid and joke together.

Many people volunteer in politics mainly because of the camaraderie and social time that are part of the best political organizations and campaigns.

About two weeks after I first started supervising other organizers at CAP 37 years ago, Pete Martinez asked, "Have you planned a party for your organizers yet?" He was right.

Great organizations are about relationships and team building. Both are forged in informal get-togethers and social time. The bonds of relationship and sense of team may be nurtured in the soil of hard work, but the fertilizer you want to add to the mix is *fun*.

Turning Negatives into Positives

One of the major lessons I learned from the culture that Saul Alinsky created around his community organizations was the importance of turning negatives into positives.

Political organizations, particularly those that start out with less power than their adversaries, must put a higher priority on looking for opportunities to do political jujitsu: turning the energy of someone's attack back onto the adversary himself.

In Section Four, I described political jujitsu when it comes to political messaging. But the principle has broad applications. As Clayton Christensen says, an organization's capabilities also define it incapacities—and vice versa.

A small organization may have fewer resources, but that makes it more nimble. A candidate without much political experience may seem "green," but he is also "a fresh face"—a huge asset if voters are looking for change. The fact that the target of an issue campaign is very well known could be a problem, but we can also make it our asset if we use his own notoriety to attract press coverage for our attacks.

Politics involves contests. In a contest, you always have a set of strengths and weaknesses. But the traits that are strengths in one context might be weaknesses in another. Every positive candidate trait can morph into its own negative evil twin, and vice versa. It depends upon how the trait is framed and positioned.

For example, commitment can become stubbornness. Self-confidence can become arrogance. Showing respect can become "pandering." Integrity can become priggishness. Being visionary can become "impractical" or "having your head in the clouds." Inspiring can become "demagogic."

Great organizers put a premium on constantly searching for opportunities to turn negatives into positives.

HIRE FOR ATTITUDE—TRAIN FOR SKILL

Excellence in execution is mainly about attitude. Great political organizations hire people with attitudes compatible with the values and procedures—the culture—I have just described. If a candidate for a job, or volunteer position of responsibility, has political experience or skill at particular tasks, that's great, but it's not as important as attitude.

Successful political organizations value first and foremost the attitudes that are compatible with a successful organizational culture. It's much easier to train for skill than to change ingrained attitudes or habits.

THE CULTURAL FOUNDATION FOR PROGRESSIVE SUCCESS

The elements we have just described:
- Thinking Like an Organizer
- Excellence in Execution

They are the building blocks of culture for successful progressive organizations, and for a progressive movement. It's up to progressive leaders to create this kind of organizational culture and to infuse the progressive movement with these values.

THE ROLE OF PROGRESSIVE LEADERS

When I discussed the importance of a candidate's ability to inspire in Section Four, I referred to MacGregor Burns' concept of transformational leadership. But it's not just candidates and public officials who must be transforming leaders.

To create the culture I've just described, transforming leaders are needed throughout the progressive movement: the campaigns, advocacy organizations, publications and party structures.

Organizational culture is forged by leaders. The role of the transforming leader is one of the orchestrator and labeler, taking what can be gotten in the way of action and shaping it (generally after-the-fact) into lasting commitments to a strategic direction. Transforming leaders create commitments to procedures and values that become the organizational culture. In short, he or she makes meanings.

To be an effective transforming leader requires two attributes:
- Believability
- Excitement

BELIEVABILITY

Believability is established by being able to do yourself whatever it is you ask your followers to do. That's why great political organizations have cultures that value leading from the front, cultures where leaders at all levels know that execution is paramount and are willing to get their hands dirty to make it happen. People who talk a good game but cannot execute need not apply.

Military historian John Keegan's book *The Mask of Command* looks at the leadership styles of several of history's greatest generals.[4] Alexander the Great was the quintessential example of leading from the front. Alexander actually led his troops into battle on the front line. That may have some limitations for modern generals that need greater perspective on the battlefield, but it inspired Alexander's army to create a massive empire. Alexander's willingness to do himself whatever he asked of his troops is a good role model for someone who leads great political organizations.

Alexander was believable. Alexander would have made a great canvass director.

One night, our telemarketing manager at Illinois Public Action was confronted by a chorus of whining. "Oh, the people on this list are so reluctant to give." I watched him as he called everyone into his office and said, "Hand me a call sheet, any call sheet. Now, watch." As everyone watched he called three randomly chosen leads and received contributions from each. When he was through, all he said was, "Now, let's go raise some money." They did.

EXCITEMENT

Excitement is provided by purpose. Purpose is provided by leaders who communicate the intrinsic meaning of the required tasks and appeal to their followers' own need for meaning and purpose.

Purpose is communicated by teachers. *A great leader is a great teacher.*

BUILDING PROGRESSIVE INSTITUTIONS

When we talk about institutionalizing some pattern of behavior, we're really talking about creating an organizational culture. The art of the creative leader is really the art of institution building

- *To institutionalize is to infuse with value beyond the technical requirements of the task at hand.*
- *The institutional leader, then, is primarily an expert in the promotion and protection of values.* [5]

CHAPTER THIRTY-NINE

An Example of The Critical Importance of Organization—Campaign Field Operations

The first use of television in a political campaign came in the campaign of Senator William Benton of Connecticut in 1950. It was quickly followed by one from Dwight Eisenhower's campaign in the presidential contest of 1952.

Since that time, "sophisticated" political consultants have tended to de-emphasize the importance of field operations in major campaigns in favor of the "modern" precinct captain—*television.*

This was a huge strategic mistake, particularly for progressive candidates.

This tendency was furthered by the emerging structure of the political consulting business. Bigger money was available from the production and placement of TV commercials than the tedious construction of field structures.

The demise of big-city patronage-based organizations during the 1970s and '80s also reduced reliance on field operations.

The failure of the Democratic Party to cultivate and maintain serious field structures was one of the major factors that led to the Republican domination of American politics during the last part of the 20th and early 21st centuries.

A swing of 94,000 votes in the right places out of the 75,723,756 votes cast would have changed the control of the House and Senate in 2002. Clearly, a serious investment in field operations would have made a big difference.

Though this trend has begun to reverse itself, there are still many entrenched self-interests that tend to prevent the allocation of resources that are necessary to right the imbalance. Both the procedures and values—the entire culture—of the Democratic Party and of the progressive movement generally have to undergo fundamental change to solve this problem. But, of course, changing the culture of movements and organizations is much more difficult than changing personnel.

WHY ARE FIELD OPERATIONS CRITICAL?

1) Fully half of the target voters whose behavior can be changed in most campaigns are low-propensity voters who would support our candidate if they were motivated to go to vote. A look at the NCEC data for virtually any district will show that there are almost always as many "GOTV" or mobilizable voters in a given swing district as there are "persuadable" voters. You run only half a campaign if you focus solely on persuadables. Campaign professionals who focus only on persuadable voters in major races are guilty of malpractice. But to do serious mobilization, you have to have a field operation.

Virtually all of the research on voter turnout shows that door-to-door contact is by far the most effective medium for communicating a GOTV message, especially the all-purpose message: I won't get off your porch until you vote." The work of Gerber and Green at Yale is particularly clear.[1] It is confirmed by many practitioners of serious high-intensity GOTV operations.

Other media like phone calls, radio, mail, sound trucks and "street action" are important supplements, but door-to-door contact is by far the most effective medium for Get Out The Vote.

Our firm participated in an experiment aimed at determining just how effective door-to-door operations are in increasing voter turnout in the fall of 2005. Our client was New Jersey Citizen Action. A group of funders, who put money into nonpartisan Get Out the Vote operations, was interested in scientifically measuring the effect of various approaches.

The contact universe included 85,000 low-propensity African-American voters in the New Jersey 2005 statewide election. Discrete segments of these voters were contacted using different methods at different frequencies. The actual voting performance of these voters was then measured against control groups who received no contact from the program. Several of the results were striking:

- The first and second attempts to contact voters improved voter turnout by 11% to 12% each
- Additional contact by live phone calls increased actual turnout by 3.6%
- The most effective times to contact voters, as one might expect, turned out to be the day before the election and Election Day.

Note that the study simply measured the mechanical effect of strong GOTV—the "I won't get off your porch until you vote"—effect. It did not measure the relative effect of different GOTV messages, nor did it measure the effect of early vote or mail ballot operations. It also measured these effects only for very low-propensity voters.

But just the effects that were measured have an enormous impact on the outcome of elections. In a close general election, a typical congressional vote turnout may be 200,000. Let's say the campaign has a field operation that can reach 35,000 low-propensity, mobilizable voters (voters who would vote for our candidate, but won't vote unless they are mobilized) on Election Day and the day and night before. Just the mechanical effect of the door-to-door contacts would yield an increase of 4,025 voters. That's a 2% improvement in our candidate's final result—much more than the difference in most competitive House races.

A high-intensity field operation for a congressional district general election can be organized for roughly $250,000. Of course, a good field operation would provide many other direct benefits to a campaign: both persuasion and the mobilization of other voters who might not vote unless they are motivated to do so. But assuming that the field operation provided no other benefit than getting an additional 4,025 votes, the cost per marginal vote would be $62.

To achieve a comparably efficient cost per marginal vote using persuasion TV, a congressional campaign that spent $1 million on TV (small sum for a competitive race) would have to move 16,000 persuadable voters—representing an 8% swing in the vote—a very impressive performance in a marginal congressional district.

Just as important, a campaign could spend its million dollars on TV and actually lose marginal votes, because the opponent's TV or some other aspect of his campaign could be more persuasive. The 4,025 votes generated by the door-to-door contact among the most marginal voters, on the other hand, do not depend on the persuasion campaign, because these mobilizable voters are not subject to persuasion by the other side. If the campaign simply executes the program, these voters are very likely money in the bank—a foundation upon which the persuasion campaign can build.

Field operations are much more reliable at generating new votes for a campaign than any element of a persuasion campaign. They're not competing with the other side for the decision of the target voters since the target voters for mobilization already support our candidate. The only question, in their case, is whether they are likely to vote. If the field operations are properly executed, the number of votes for our candidate will go up, regardless of what is done by the opposition.

Finally, GOTV operations generate votes that no amount of persuasion can deliver. They add votes to the total generated by persuasion. That's why the campaign that uses only persuasion is only doing half a campaign.

Television—"the modern precinct captain"– is virtually useless for GOTV. The reason is that it is a broadcast medium. TV goes to all the voters. It's fine that we should spill over beyond our persuasion universe with TV-based persuasion messaging. It may waste money, but it won't cost us voters. It is not fine to mobilize the other side's low-propensity voters. We want to lull them into a deep sleep, not turn them out to vote. That's why TV is rarely used for GOTV unless its audience is appropriately segmented. Ads on Black Entertainment Television (BET) or Spanish-language TV can be used to supplement field-based GOTV. Not so for broadcast TV or cable TV targeting the mainstream market.

2) **Door-to-door and volunteer-based phone operations are enormously powerful "persuasion" media**. When it comes to persuasion, paid TV, radio and mail are very important media, as is earned media. These are generally necessary to win swing races, but none of these media have the credibility of personal contact.

Just as important, as we saw in Section Three, word-of-mouth remains a major critical communications media, particularly for "normal people" who think about politics five minutes a week. The fact that human beings are "pack animals" also plays a role. It is very influential to an undecided voter to hear a neighbor legitimating support for a candidate, particularly in a low-visibility race.

This persuasion aspect of field is especially important in early Presidential primaries. We've already discussed the critical impact of the different approaches that were taken to field operations by Dean and Kerry in Iowa in 2004. Personal communication always has a big impact on the voters in early primary states.

One final advantage of field operations as persuasion media is their surgical ability to reach actual voters just as they are about to make their decision.

Our consulting firm sometimes has clients who are candidates for judge and running countywide in the Chicago area's Cook County. No one knows the candidates in a countywide race for judge. But voters cast ballots based on what they do know; so when the voters don't know much about any candidate, the name of the game is to define them right as they walk into the polling place. We advise clients of this sort that their major strategic goal should be to assure that someone passes a "palm card" with their name and "punch number" as they enter the polling place Election Day. This might be the local Democratic precinct organization, a campaign volunteer, or a paid passer—but regardless of who passes the card, it will have more influence than any other single campaign expenditure in that kind of race. Of course, if someone you know and respect gives you the "palm card," so much the better.

In high-visibility races, many voters come to the polls already knowing whom they will support. Although even in this case, voter contact at the precinct immediately before voting can affect the outcome in marginal races.

In low visibility races, voters often don't decide until they get to the candidate's name on the ballot. Sometimes they don't even know about the race until they get to the name on the ballot. Here, they make their voting decision based on whatever they know.

If all that the voter knows is that the candidate has a Polish name or an Irish name, he'll vote based on that fact. The best way to get elected judge countywide in Cook County is to be endorsed by the regular Democratic Party, which has precinct captains in many precincts. The second best way is to be an Irish woman. Irish women seem to have particular appeal in a town like Chicago first because none of the many ethnic groups that make up the city (Poles, Germans, Lithuanians, Jews, Russians, Italians, African Americans, Mexicans, Puerto Ricans) appear to have brought strong hostilities against the Irish their home countries. Second because all things being equal, more voters appear to be willing to trust women to be judges than men.

Even if a voter simply recognizes a name, he is more or less likely to vote for the candidate depending on his predisposition toward the name. After the Oklahoma City bombing, a candidate named Timothy McVeigh would have had a tough time running for judge. A candidate named George Clooney would do pretty well. Voters vote based on whatever they know.

In a low-visibility race, the passing operation on Election Day would be supplemented with whatever else we can do within the confines of the budget to raise the candidate's name recognition and connect the name to a positive connotation.

We often use outdoor advertising, earned media, phone calls, and direct mail for this purpose. The most cost-effective of these media is outdoor advertising on billboards, buses, bus shelters, commuter trains, etc. Outdoor media give us the most repeated "impressions" of the name voters will see on the ballot per dollar spent.

Of course, as I said in Section Four, a major addition in any campaign is the yard sign. The extent to which yard signs bloom in communities is directly related to the strength of the field operation. They have the same advantages as paid outdoor advertising in efficiently putting a candidate's name before the voters. They have the additional value of legitimating the candidate and communicating that he's "on our side." A sea of yard sign says: "Your neighbors support this candidate and its okay for you to support her, too; she must be an on our side because other people in the 'pack' support her."

Persuasion phone contacts are also extremely helpful, particularly from volunteers, and particularly from neighbors. The ability of the phoner to sound as though they share the same "home turf", or at least share some characteristic with that voter, is obviously a plus when it comes to persuasion.

Regardless, a door-to-door contact or phone call is often much more effective at grabbing the voters' full attention to a race—at breaking through—than the best TV or radio commercial. We know that TV commercials need to run at least five times to "burn through." TV and radio spots can run in the "background" of your consciousness. Phone calls get your *full* attention the first time. You have to drop what you're doing and pick up the receiver. Door-to-door contacts have even more impact. They demand your full attention; you have to get up and answer the door. It's harder to "hang up" on the guy on your doorstep. That's why door-to-door and phone contacts can be annoying at dinner time. It's also why they are so effective. Of course, this ability of canvassing and phone calls to "break through" is also one of the things that make them so important to GOTV.

3) Field operations put people in motion. As we've seen, the key first step of developing passionate support for a candidate or cause is to get people to "act themselves" into commitment. Field operations do just that.

Good field operations in a congressional district have 1,500 to 2,000 volunteer participants by Election Day. By volunteering in the campaign, the volunteers' levels of commitment and passion for the candidate increase tremendously. The same goes for the likelihood that they will influence *their* family and friends, who will in turn influence their family and friends in the political equivalent of the same type of word-of-mouth "epidemic" that generates attendance for a great movie or sends customers to the latest hot restaurant or makes the newest brand of sneakers popular.

Volunteer-based, Democratic field operations not only "act people" into supporting candidates, they "act people" into commitment to the Democratic Party and the progressive cause.

Jan hasn't had a seriously contested congressional race since her first primary in 1998, yet she has a full-time, year-round political director as well as a full-time fundraising director and half-time assistant fundraising director. They involve her constituents in regular meetings, fundraisers, rallies and field operations, both in and out of the district. That's why she was able to send thousands of people by bus to work for Kerry in Wisconsin in 2004, and to support other congressional candidates in swing Illinois districts in 2004 and 2006. It's why she can send hundreds of thousands of dollars to support the Democratic Congressional Campaign Committee and Democratic campaigns across the country, and why she can play a major role in turning out voters for statewide candidates in Illinois. It's why she has such a large, passionate core of supporters, and one of the reasons why she has maintained such high positive ratings among rank-and-file voters. People know people who are committed to her and the political movement around her. Of course, these are the same very important reasons why she consistently wins more than 70% of the vote. Every Democratic Member of Congress could benefit from a similar operation.

HIGH-INTENSITY FIELD OPERATIONS IN ELECTORAL CAMPAIGNS

There are a variety of different approaches to developing a high-intensity field organization for a campaign. You can rely more heavily on paid canvassers, or more heavily on volunteers. How you develop your plan also depends upon the mission of the organization.

Sometimes the organization's mission is simply to Get Out the Vote. In 2004, our firm helped construct many operations to mobilize low-propensity voters, primarily African-Americans, who would break heavily for progressive candidates if we could just get them to the polls.

In most campaigns, however, the field operation has five key missions:

1) **I.D.** To conduct a door-to-door and phone canvass of whatever size necessary to create a "run universe" that banks enough votes to win the election.

2) **Persuasion.** To persuade undecided voters through person-to-person contact during the canvass, and at the polls on Election Day. This persuasion function is supplemented through the effects of signs and other means of visibility distributed by the field operation.

3) **Get Out the Vote (GOTV).** To motivate our mobilizable voters to go to the polls—voters who would support our candidate, but have a low propensity to vote. In other words, to run a high-intensity GOTV program.

4) **Candidate Advance.** To find and staff events for candidate appearances that provide opportunities to recruit volunteers, and persuade or mobilize voters. This function is always done in conjunction with the scheduling operation, and sometimes with the advance staff.

5) **Voter Registration.** Where there are adequate resources, campaigns or organizations register new voters who are likely to break for our candidates.

334 · SECTION SIX   ROBERT CREAMER

Organizing a High-Intensity Field Operation

As an example of what I mean by a high-intensity field operation, we'll walk through the typical steps that our firm might use to set up a field structure for a congressional race.

Normally, we begin the process six months before Election Day, though the work of advancing candidate appearances is usually begun much earlier.

Good field operations are typically managed by an experienced Field Director—someone who has done it before, or has been an outstanding organizer in another field project. In my view, it is extremely difficult for someone to be a good field director if they have not participated as an organizer in a serious field operation. A strong field director is the key to a good field operation.

The Field Director reports to the Campaign Manager. In field programs conducted by our firm we support the Field Director with an experienced senior consultant. In most races, we prefer to build an army of volunteers around a skeleton of 10 to 15 full-time paid organizers. We typically recruit these organizers from the ranks of people who are potentially interested in careers in political organizing and want to develop organizing experience. In fact, our firm runs a Campaign Management Program aimed at recruiting and training entry-level organizers who are seriously considering political and/or organizing careers.

We hire for attitude and train for skill. We also demand that our organizers be prepared to work 14 hours a day, seven days per week, for at least 17 weeks prior to the election. In other words, we want organizers who are prepared to devote themselves to the cause. With some exceptions, we generally prefer that the paid organizers come from out of town so they don't have a life beyond the campaign. That frees organizers from the distractions of home life and the gives them the ability to bond with the rest of the team on a level playing field. This also lets them see that it's not who you already know, but it's *how to meet* the people that you *should* know, wherever you are.

When they report to duty, the organizers have a five-day training program that covers the theory of campaigns, message, field, GOTV, advance, mail, press, polling, and the basics of organizing. Our view is that the more they know about the theory of what they are called upon to do, the better job they will do.

They are also oriented to the campaign and receive briefings from the candidate and campaign management. They receive briefings in the district, a tour of the district and spend social time bonding as a team.

Finally, they receive turf assignments and specific quantitative goals for volunteer recruitment, voter registration, voter I.D.s, sign placement and other elements of the early field operation.

Systems are set up to measure every aspect of the operation, every day. Nightly reports on performance go to the campaign management and to our firm's Chicago support staff.

It is made clear from the first day that everyone is expected to meet our standards of performance every day. Those who don't are released. In this and other similar operations, it is critical to maintain standards. Meeting quotas has to become second nature—a part of the organization's culture.

THE FIELD PLAN

Every operation needs a carefully articulated field plan that is part of the overall campaign plan. The field plan includes:

- *Components of the "Run Universe."* How many voters do we need to win? Using the formulas described in Section Five, we decided how many "plus" voters we can identify without using a door-to-door or phone canvass. These generally include Democratic primary voters, General election-only voters, people who live in 65% or better Democratic precincts, and political and demographic groups that will break 65% or better for Democratic candidates (this will include Democratic registrations if available). The plan then calculates how many "plus" voters need to be identified through the canvass to exceed our "winning number."

- *Voter I.D. Goals for Phone and Door-to-Door Canvasses.* The field plan sets targets for I.D.s, "plus" voters that need to be identified through the phone and door-to-door canvass operations. In general the phone canvass is the most efficient means of doing voter I.D., so the goal is to maximize phone I.D.s and use door-to-door canvass to make up the difference of what is needed.

The field plan also includes:
- A GOTV plan. Much more on that later.
- A volunteer recruitment plan.
- A visibility plan.
- A plan for managing candidate appearances.
- A statement of the basic persuasion message that should be used by phone and door to door canvassers.
- A field program budget.

BUILDING THE VOLUNTEER OPERATION

Volunteers don't generally organize themselves. Full-time organizers are usually necessary to create a highly-structured volunteer operation.

The organizer's first assignments begin the process of enlisting the volunteers into the field organization that they need to build in their sector. They're given lists of potential leads in the area and taught how to find additional leads in the community. Early leads include previously-identified activists, the candidate's family, party officials, and constituency group leaders.

Organizers should, of course, look especially for the four major groups of communicators: connectors, mavens, salesmen and leaders.

Remember, connectors have many different contact groups and move between groups. Mavens know everything about some aspect of the area and where to find out what they don't know. They are also interested in sharing these things with others. Salesmen are people who have the gift of persuasion. Leaders have followers.

In general, the steps necessary to build a volunteer organization include:

- Identifying connectors, mavens, salesmen and leaders.
- Conducting one-on-one or small group meetings.
- Gathering lists and referrals.
- Recruiting volunteers.
- Activating volunteers.
- Delegating responsibility—assigning roles and creating an accountability structure.

The purpose of the one-on-one meetings is to analyze the individual's self-interest, assess his capacity to become involved in the effort, and obtain a commitment from him to take a first step toward involvement in the campaign. It is also intended to get further referrals for additional leads. No organizer should ever leave a meeting without a list of potential new recruits.

RECRUITING VOLUNTEERS —
WHY DO PEOPLE VOLUNTEER FOR CAMPAIGNS?

Organizers can tap into scores of different self-interests to recruit volunteers to work in campaigns. A few include:

- True believers. People who are fundamentally committed to the progressive cause.

- People who personally support or have a strong attachment to the candidate.

- A new person in town may want to meet like-minded people.

- Build a resume. Campaigns are a great way to build a resume for future employment or educational opportunity.

- Looking for a job. Potential volunteers may want to work for the candidate if she is elected, or for one of her supporters.

- Social contacts. A senior may want an opportunity to spend time with people. The stay-at-home spouse may want adult company. A young person may love the camaraderie and responsibility.

- Motivated by a single issue. Potential volunteers may see the campaign or the election as a way to advance an issue agenda.

- Want to get out of house. The campaign may provide a structured way to get out, to do something different or exciting.

- Provide meaning or purpose. The campaign provides meaning and purpose for its participants, the opportunity to be part of something important.

- Likes to be around politicians. Some people find politicians exciting.

- Looking for connections in the community. Campaigns are a great way to meet useful contacts.

- Looking for a date. Campaigns are pretty good way to troll for personal relationships, too.

There are, of course, many more.

From the organizer's point of view, which of these is the "best" reason to get involved in a campaign?

All of them.

The organizer's job is to identify a self-interest that the campaign might address and make an implicit—or explicit—arrangement with the prospective volunteer to address it in exchange for some level of participation. Remember that to identify self-interest, you *listen*. You ask questions, then follow up with more questions. People love to talk about themselves.

And remember that a good organizer doesn't "beg" someone to become involved. They don't ask them to become involved in order to solve the organizer's problem. They make a *quid pro quo* arrangement with the prospect for their participation.

If someone agrees to work his precinct in exchange for $300, the arrangement is very explicit. If the prospective volunteer is likely to get involved because he's looking for meaning in life, the arrangement may be more implicit—but from the organizer's point of view it is always a quid pro quo.

WHAT DO YOU ASK POTENTIAL VOLUNTEERS TO DO?

Every campaign has a hierarchy of needs for volunteers. Generally, it involves things like:

- Coordinate an area, recruit and supervise precinct coordinators
- Precinct coordinator, to canvass his precinct several times before Election Day and create a local GOTV operation (including early voting and mail ballot operations)
- Host a house party for other prospective volunteers
- Precinct volunteer—work with a precinct coordinator to accomplish his goals
- Volunteer to work Election Day in a precinct
- Phone canvasser—make voter I.D. or GOTV calls
- Put up a yard sign
- Attend a candidate house party

There are many other volunteer roles in a field organization, but these are some of the most important. You start by asking them to do the highest item on this kind of hierarchy of volunteerism for which you think they're qualified. You won't ask someone to coordinate an area, for instance, until you know they can deliver and have an attitude that reflects the organizational culture.

But you probably would start with asking someone to be a precinct coordinator. If he won't do that, you move down a list until they agree. Once you get him into motion doing something, you try to take him back up the list, to gradually get him more involved in the operation. You take him to 95th Street.

People often first get involved in a campaign by agreeing to put up a yard sign or attend a house party where the candidate makes a brief appearance or someone plays a campaign video and explains how important the campaign is, and how it is set up—and then asks his neighbors to become involved. They end up making major commitments to the effort.

In general, the people who are the busiest and the most involved in community or political activity are the most likely to devote even more time to the campaign effort. Remember that people's past behavior is the best predictor of future behavior.

CLOSING THE DEAL

Closing the deal—getting someone to participate in the campaign—involves exactly the same elements as closing any sale. The keys are:

1) **Always be asking.** Volunteer recruitment success is entirely related to the quality and quantity of asks. If you're an organizer, never end any conversation without making an ask. Ask everywhere. We often find that when an organizer accompanies a candidate to a mass location, that one in 20 people will actually agree to volunteer after they've met the candidate, even for a matter of seconds, if they are asked to become involved.

2) Always **engage their self-interest** when you ask.

3) **Know before any meeting with a prospective volunteer what you want to ask them to do.**

4) **Follow the hierarchy of volunteerism.**

5) **Use silence. It's your friend.** A lot of organizers talk their way out of commitments. They ask and then qualify. Or before the respondent answers, they feel compelled to back off: "But, if you can't do that, how about...." They hate the dead air. Ask, and then shut up. Let it hang there; wait for an answer. You're much more likely to get a yes if you use silence as your friend.

6) Always get a **"real commitment."** A lot of organizers ask things like: "Can I count on you to make some voter I.D. calls?" And when the prospective volunteer says yes, they leave it at that. That is not a "real commitment." A real commitment has three elements.

   - A commitment to take a particular action;
   - At particular time and place;
   - For a specific duration of time.

   A real commitment is a yes to the question: "How about doing voter I.D. calls at the campaign office, this Wednesday night from six to nine?"

7) Before the meeting ends, **review the commitment** so there is no misunderstanding.

8) **Re-contact the perspective volunteer to remind her of the commitment before the agreed date.** Remember, this is not a test of the perspective volunteer's commitment, integrity or memory.

You want her to show up, both because you want the work to be done, and because you want to get her in motion so she'll "act" herself into greater commitment.

9) **Routinize Activity.** People are more likely to routinely participate in activity if they are put on a regular schedule. They're more likely to show up every Wednesday at 6 p.m. than at irregular times.

10) If someone has indicated they are willing to volunteer, say by turning in a volunteer card, **contact him within 24 hours** of his indication of intent. Strike while the iron is hot. The likelihood someone will actually be activated drops with every moment that passes after something has spurred someone to take the first step to become involved.

11) Make contact with every volunteer in the organization **at least once per week** during the election campaign. People need to be kept in the loop and made to feel important.

12) **Always treat every volunteer with respect,** and remember that meaning is the greatest motivator. Volunteers must constantly be reminded of how important the effort is, and how they are crucial to success.

13) **Celebrate short-term victories**, and the achievement of immediate short-term goals.

14) Never hesitate to **hold a volunteer accountable**. If they don't show up, call them. Tell them you were depending on them, that a phone was set aside or that the campaign is now behind in its work because of their absence. If you don't hold volunteers accountable, they will not believe that their work is important. If you act like a campaign is as important as it is, volunteers will respond and act that way to. If you act like you couldn't care less if someone fulfills their commitment to volunteer, they will receive the message that their work, and the campaign, don't matter.

15) **Don't ever say no for anyone.** Make them say no. Many organizers are prone to say, "Oh, let's not ask Nancy, she's so busy she'll probably say no." In effect, you're saying no for Nancy. Give her the respect of allowing her to give you an answer. You'll be surprised at how often she says yes, or at the very least offers you another hot lead instead.

16) **Never stop looking for leaders.** The best way to recruit volunteers is in groups. Leaders have groups of followers, and often their desire to please, impress or be accountable to that leader is more than you could have gotten from them directly. Leaders who can deliver groups of volunteers are much more valuable than volunteers who were recruited one at a time.

17) **Investment in training is never a waste of time.** Providing volunteers with skills and a "big picture" sense of the campaign will massively increase commitment and output.

18) **Keeping people motivated requires regular contact** with other activists in the campaign. Hold regular meetings of volunteers. The motivation of volunteers must routinely be reinforced--it's contagious, and it comes from contact with other people.

Structuring the Field Operation

There are a number of different field structures that are appropriate for different campaigns depending upon the mix of volunteers and paid canvassers, lead time and the nature of the community. Some rely on a more centralized command and control structure. Others are more decentralized. *All must be highly accountable.*

In some contexts, it is better to deploy volunteers or paid canvassers from headquarters on a regular basis. In more mature organizations, it is better for precinct coordinators to manage canvass operations on a precinct-by-precinct basis.

In the precinct model, several precinct workers report to the precinct coordinator, who reports to area coordinators with responsibility for five or six precincts. Area coordinators all report to the Field Director. During the height of the canvass operation, reports are generated daily on voter contact progress. Ideally at each level, the supervisors understand that it is not just their responsibility to receive reports. *It is their responsibility to recruit volunteers, motivate them and ultimately to get the job done in their areas one way or the other.*

The culture must always be about accountability and excellence in execution, getting the job done.

Executing the Plan

Voter Registration

Some states (like Wisconsin) have same-day registration. That makes registration drives somewhat less important, although a case can be made that a person who is registered before the election is more likely to vote than one who is not, even in those states.

If voter registration is part of the plan, it generally takes place in two phases.

Long-term registration programs can begin many months before elections. These long-range programs generally involve using personnel who are paid per registration and must meet daily quotas. Some states (like Florida) have banned payment per registration. In these states, salaried personnel may still be required to meet production quotas for quality control.

There has been a long debate about the relative benefit of recruiting voter registrations at mass locations (shopping centers, street corners, summerfests, driver's license facilities, etc.) compared to door-to-door registration.

While there is little question that it costs less to recruit registrations at mass locations, door-to-door registration can be preferable in two circumstances:

- Door-to-door allows you to more effectively target a demographic or political group. After all, progressive organizations are interested in registering progressives only. The other side will do a fine job with conservatives without our help.

- If the same people who canvass for registration, such as a precinct captain who will work the precinct throughout the campaign, he or she may be able to develop a relationship with those voters during the registration process.

Long-term voter registration programs are most effective if they are organized using all of the principles we described above, with daily accountability and measurement of results.

The second phase of voter registration should be part of the first GOTV canvass conducted two months prior to Election Day (generally registrations end one month before elections). Those details will follow.

THE VOTER I.D. CANVASS

In a Congressional race, both the phone and the door-to-door voter I.D. canvass generally should begin no later than 16 weeks before Election Day. The contact goal should be chunked down into the daily pieces, as discussed earlier. A large portion of the canvass can be accomplished on the phone, with door-to-door contact to all voters that can't be reached by the phone operation. Both phone and door-to-door operations must generally be conducted simultaneously. Timing of the I.D. must be massively compressed in areas with late primaries. In our experience, volunteer-generated I.D. calls are more accurate and persuasive than paid calls, though paid calls can help get the I.D. job done. Volunteers using web-based predictive dialing technology have all of the speed of paid I.D. calls at less than half the cost per I.D.

Remember that the targets of this canvass are general election-only voters and new registrants who do not reside in 65% plus Democratic precincts and have not somehow already qualified as a supporter of our candidate (see Section Five).

Congressional general election races often involve the necessity of finding 30,000 to 50,000-plus voters using the canvass. This will usually require 120,000 to 150,000 or more voter contacts, which will yield about 100,000 I.D.s.

Each I.D. canvasser should be comfortable with their "rap". A good voter I.D. "rap" includes:

- Introduction
- I.D. question
- Volunteer ask
- Persuasion message (if needed)
- Possible Issue I.D
- Farewell

Pre-Election GOTV Canvasses

Canvass #1 — Two Months Out

In the best GOTV operations, there are at least two door-to-door GOTV canvasses before Election Day. One is conducted two months before the election. All elements of the "run universe" known at that time are contacted. In addition, in 65%-plus Democratic precincts we should knock on every door during this canvass — even where there is no registered voter, since we want to register remaining voters who might break Democratic.

Canvass #2 — 72 Hours Out

We should also canvass all voters in the "run universe" in the three days prior to the election. This canvass should include a reminder to vote and a request for a commitment from the voter to go to the polls. Get Out the Vote material with polling place location and voting times should be handed out or left as a door hanger or "Post-it Note" on the door. The door hanger should be large, colorful and impossible to miss.

If the campaign has scarce resources, the canvass should be directed entirely at the portion of the run universe with a low propensity to vote. Low propensity voters who support our candidate are the mobilizable voters. They are the voters whose behavior we can change. But where resources allow, we should contact everyone in the "run universe" so no one slips through.

Just as with I.D. canvassers, a script or rap sheet should be provided to all GOTV canvassers as a model for their work. A typical "rap" sheets includes the following elements:

- Introduction
- Voter registration question
- GOTV ask
- Reiterate GOTV message
- Second GOTV ask (if necessary)
- Reiterate GOTV message
- Third GOTV ask (if necessary)
- Volunteer ask
- Farewell

You'll notice that the script for the GOTV canvasser is very persistent. Remember, we don't have to worry about persuasion among mobilizable voters. We're not going to loose their support because we're too persistent about asking them to vote. Our goal is to agitate them to take action—to go to the polls. The worst-case option with mobilizable voters is that they won't vote—which is precisely what they would have done if we hadn't contacted them in the first place. So GOTV canvassers should be encouraged to be as persistent as possible to get people to act.

OTHER METHODS OF DELIVERING THE GOTV MESSAGE

Door-to-door contact is the most effective method of delivering GOTV message. It's got to be our highest priority, both in the period leading up to the election and on Election Day itself. If you can't do anything else for voter mobilization besides door-to-door GOTV, that's the thing to do.

There are however, other supplemental methods of delivering our six GOTV messages in a symbolically powerful way.

PHONE CALLS

We've seen from the data that live phone calls are an important supplement to door-to-door. In the New Jersey study, live GOTV calls increased voter turnout by 3.6% when they were used in conjunction with door-to-door contact.

Auto calls are only effective as supplemental "reminder" contacts. We generally deliver one auto call the evening before the election and one early in the morning of Election Day. They'll serve the function of reminding voters who already intend to vote to go to the polls. They are more effective if they can be programmed to include the address of the voter's polling place.

Live phone calls have the advantage of being able to ask a commitment of the voter—"Will you go to vote?" If a voter makes a commitment to a live person, they are more likely to act on it. In our experience, GOTV calls are best when delivered by volunteers on the weekend before the election and on Election Day. Paid live calls for Get Out the Vote are extremely expensive relative to other media, but they can be important if volunteer phone calling and door-to-door are not available.

Outdoor and Yard Signs

Plaster Democratic-leaning areas with messaging. Yard signs and signs put up in construction sites and telephone poles (if legal) are excellent, inexpensive ways to deliver many repetitions of a simple, but symbolically powerful GOTV message. The key here is *weight*. Communicating motivation in any medium requires symbolic power and massive repetition. Our goal is to create a bandwagon effect for the importance of voting.

Paid outdoor GOTV signs are a more expensive way to supplement yard signs. But they are much less expensive than many other media. We use paid outdoor for GOTV frequently on buses, billboards, elevated trains and buildings.

Targeted GOTV Radio and TV

We don't use radio and TV to general audiences for Get Out The Vote, because we don't want to increase voter turnout everywhere, only among our supporters. But TV and radio are powerful media for GOTV where the audience for the stations we use mainly includes voters who support our candidate.

African-American and Spanish-language radio and TV generally reach predominantly Democratic voters. African-American and Spanish language radio are particularly powerful and spots on radio are inexpensive to produce. Black Entertainment Television (BET), Univision and Telemundo TV networks and local affiliates are also excellent media.

Once again, symbolic power and weight are important. Lots of repetition within a short time frame is required. Generally, GOTV radio and TV should be delivered in high concentration in the last two weeks prior to the election.

STREET ACTION

In the 72 hours before the election, "street action" is an important medium—particularly in highly concentrated target communities. As with TV and radio, you don't want to concentrate "street action" in communities that won't break Democratic. But where they will, people passing leaflets at mass locations, loudspeakers, announcements at gatherings—generally making noise about voting is very important.

In big cities, personnel should be deployed at mass locations throughout target areas—elevated train stops, high-volume bus stops, ballgames, large church services, shopping centers, high-traffic street corners; all are useful locations. Massive repetition—lots of weight is the key. Street action includes Election Day passing at mass locations—especially as people leave work. Again, we're looking for that bandwagon effect. We want to make voting something everyone in the target community seems to be doing.

SOUND TRUCKS

The two weekends before the election we often supplement our other GOTV activities with sound trucks that ride through target communities calling on people to go vote. Like Street Action and outdoor media, this medium is only appropriate in 65%-plus Democratic areas. It gets people's attention.

GOTV MAIL

GOTV mail can help supplement the array of GOTV messages in campaigns with plenty of resources. It's the most costly medium per contact. It does have the advantage of engaging the voter visually and giving her something that will lie around the house waiting for Election Day. The ability to target a voter with precision is another enormous advantage.

It's also a good medium to deliver polling-place address information. A caveat is in order about polling-place information, however. We have to be careful to get it right. The wrong information about polling place location can cost us votes. In fact, systematic mistakes in the distribution of polling place information can cost us an election. In fact it is so critical that it is not unheard of for operatives of opposition campaigns to distribute incorrect information about a voter's polling location.

In this and other mission-critical aspects of the campaign, we have to use tight systems of quality control to assure accuracy.

Institutional GOTV

African American churches in highly Democratic areas should be enlisted to have "Empowerment Sundays" and to systematically promote voter registration and Get Out the Vote among their members.

The same goes for other large institutions, nonpartisan social service agencies and community organizations. Get Out the Vote does not require a partisan or persuasion pitch for a candidate, only an appeal to go vote.

Election Fairness Operations

In the last two presidential elections, there is very a good case to be made that the elections were stolen. In the highly publicized Florida case in 2000, and the lesser-known Ohio case in 2004, enough votes were changed by manipulation of the voting apparatus to change the outcome of the election—and history.

Robert Kennedy Jr. summarized the facts of the Ohio case in a compelling article in *Rolling Stone* magazine. [2]

In both these cases, the theft hinged on elements of the electoral process we can do something about. Before Election Day, the campaign should:

- Assure that an adequate number of voting machines will be available in all Democratic precincts. The time to fight about the number is well before Election Day. Use the press, courts, demonstrations, whatever is necessary to assure adequate equipment. With most voting equipment, a precinct should have a minimum of one machine for 200 expected voters. Many Ohio voters had to wait in line for hours in 2004. There is no doubt that thousands left before voting, or were discouraged from going to vote at all.

- Check ballot configuration and do whatever is necessary to avoid confusion.

- Identify precincts where judges of elections have caused problems in the past. These are usually precincts with mixed partisan registration in jurisdictions where the election apparatus is in unfriendly hands

- Verify the procedures to assure all registered voters are on the rolls. In Ohio in 2004, many thousands of voter registrations were not accepted by the voting authorities.

- Verify the provisional voting procedure.

- Set up a legal team for rapid response.

- Assure that problem precincts have poll watchers in the polling place even if none is necessary to monitor who has voted.

In the event of problems on any of these fronts, high visibility press, demonstrations, or legal action should be taken *before* Election Day. Of course, the message to low-propensity voters should be that these problems *are fixed,* that they *will* be able to vote. You don't want to frighten people into not voting.

EARLY VOTING AND MAIL BALLOTS

It used to be that we thought of elections as a one-day sale. But many jurisdictions now have early vote and mail ballot procedures that have become a major focus for our efforts in serious field operations.

Oregon has gone exclusively to mail ballots, and in many states in the West over half of all votes are cast by mail.

Both of these mechanisms provide important means to bank large chunks of low-propensity voters before Election Day. In fact, heavy use of mail ballots makes Election Day almost a month long in some jurisdictions. That means that many campaigns need to adjust their calendars to begin Election Day style GOTV a month earlier than would otherwise be the case.

During these periods we call low propensity voters or visit them at the door to encourage them to cast their vote early.

Many of the jurisdictions which rely heavily on mail ballots make lists of "match backs" publicly available. Match backs are lists of voters who have already cast their ballots, which allows us to narrow our "run universe" throughout the mail ballot or early vote period. They also provide us with a much-narrowed "run universe" on which to concentrate on Election Day.

PREPARING FOR ELECTION DAY

In a typical Congressional district where mail ballots are restricted to limited classes of voters (sick, out-of-town, older, etc.), you need about 1,500 to 1,700 volunteers to run a serious Election Day operation.

This will allow the campaign to knock on the door of everyone in the run universe three times during Election Day. It will also allow us to monitor who has voted so we can continue to narrow the remaining universe of voters as the day goes on. It will also allow us to pass persuasion "palm cards" to all voters during major rush periods, and also to do two volunteer phone contacts.

Overall, then, our GOTV goal for Election Day is to contact each voter up to five times, until he votes—three times door-to-door and twice on the phone.

TRAININGS

We try to assure that at least 80% of Election Day volunteers attend a pre-election training. The trainings achieve three things:

- They allow us to see who will show up, and who will not, before the critical day itself.

- They allow us to completely train and orient volunteers on Election Day procedures, schedules and skills.

- They inspire volunteers. When volunteers Bonnie and Cheri show up at one of many packed-house campaign trainings, you might hear Bonnie say, "Wow, Cheri, there are so many people here, this is great; maybe Sue wants to do this, too!" People pump each other up, they communicate motivation to each other, and they react to a dynamic team environment.

The keys to a great Election Day are well-organized, well-trained, motivated volunteers. We want volunteers who will break down walls to turn out the last vote. We want volunteers who understand that even though they have worked for 12 hours, during the 10 minutes before the polls close they still have time to drag out the last vote—because that's the vote that could make the difference in winning and losing. Remember that in 2000 in Florida, 500 votes made the difference between one historic direction for America and another.

THE 72-HOUR DRILL

In the 72 hours before the election our organization needs to complete six additional tasks:

- Knock on the door of all households in the "run universe." If a face-to-face contact is not possible, a door hanger should be left motivating the occupant to go to the polls and containing the address of the polling place.

- Finish preparation of all Election Day materials.

- Complete volunteer phone contact with all "run universe" households.

- Deliver an early evening auto call to all "run universe" households.

- Deploy street action and sound truck operations—including Election Day passers at mass locations.

- Assure that legal and "election fairness" operations are executing their plan.

Preparation for Election Day is equally about two things: *intensity* and *precision*. To have a great Election Day operation, you need both.

How Many Volunteers Do We Need?

I said earlier that to complete a high-intensity GOTV operationally generally estimate that you will need 1,500 to 1,700 volunteers in a congressional district. Here's how to calculate what you *actually* need to do the canvass portion of the program:

- Determine Number of Low Propensity Voter *Households* (household may contain more that one voter) in the voter file.

- You can either get that number directly from the voter file, or it can be estimated by multiplying the number of low propensity target voters by .7 (this percentage accounts for "householding").

- Multiply by the maximum penetration rate possible at the door (approximately 65%).

- Divide the number of low propensity households by the contacts per hour at the door (maximum 10 to 12). This will give you the number of canvasser hours.

Example:
- 100,000 low propensity voters x .7 = 70,000 (householded percent)

- Max Penetration Rate door-to-door = 70,000 x .65 = 45,400

- 45,400/12 = 3,791 canvasser hours per canvass pass

- If you want to complete one canvass pass in 10 days, you must average 379 canvass hours/day

- If each canvasser knocks on doors for 3 hours per day, the campaign will need 126 canvassers each day

Example Within a Precinct Structure:

- Precinct has 800 low-propensity voters

- 800 x .7 = 560 households

- 560 x .65 = 364 maximum penetration

- 364/12 = 30.33 canvass hours required by precinct captain and assistants

- If you want 2 canvass passes before the election, it will require 60.66 canvass hours.

- This would only be 20 hours each for 3 people.

How many volunteer hours do you need to contact the run universe by phone?

- If the number of low propensity voter households is 70,000, the number with good phone match is approximately 70,000 x .7 = 49,000. (If you have the number of actual households with phone numbers you can use that. If not, for planning purposes you can multiply the number of households by .7)

- Maximum penetration rate by phone = 49,000 x .65 = 31,850

- Number of Phone Hours needed with Web-Based Dialer = 31,850/35 contacts per hour = 910 hours.

- This could be completed by 15 phoners working 21 three-hour shifts.

- Number of Phone Hours needed without a Web-Based Dialer = 31,850/17 contacts per hour = 1,873 hours.

- This could be completed by 31 phoners working 21 three-hour shifts.

On Election Day itself there are basically three structural options:

- Precinct-Based Structure—Area Coordinators, Precinct Coordinator, Runners, (potentially) watchers

- Swat Team Configuration—Run/Canvass Teams of four to six— broken into sub-teams of two

- Mix

If volunteers are plentiful, the preferred option is to rely mainly on precinct-based structures for Election Day, and the I.D. and GOTV canvass preceding it. In the best operations, a local precinct captain can be recruited to take complete responsibility for all of these functions, including recruitment of local precinct volunteers.

In practice, you generally rely on a mix of these two structures to allow you to have personnel that can be deployed quickly from the central headquarters to weak spots.

How many volunteers do you need for Election Day?

- Approximately 1 all-day runner per 100 households in run universe
- 1 to 2 checkers per polling place
- 1 or 2 passers (peak times)
- One area coordinator per 6 precincts
- 2 lawyers for 100 normal precincts (more in problem areas)
- Phone Bankers (*only* personnel who cannot run)

Here an example of how to calculate the number of volunteers you actually need for Election Day in a race with a run universe of 10,000:

Run universe = 10,000
10,000/100 = 100 all-day runners
If half of runners work all day and half work ½ day = 150 runners
30 polling places = 30 half-day checkers and 30 passer/runners
30 polling places/5 = 6 area chairs
10 phones lines, requiring 40 phone bankers
2 lawyers
3 headquarter volunteers

Runners	150
Passers	30
Checkers	30
Area chairs	6
Phone bankers	40
Lawyers & HQ	5
Total Volunteers:	261

WHAT DO ELECTION DAY VOLUNTEERS DO?

- Area Chair: Responsible for conducting of the Election Day operation in five to seven precincts
- Runners: Go door-to-door turning voters out
- Passers: Greet voters at the polls and give them a palm card
- Checkers: Serve as poll watchers in the polling place, and check off "plus" voters as they vote
- Phone bankers

Below is a typical Election Day "coverage sheet" that allows you assign personnel and fill holes in the structure.

Name	Open	6 to 7	7 to 8	8 to 9	9 to 10	10 to 11	11 to Noon	Noon to 1	1 to 2	2 to 3	3 to 4	4 to 5	5 To 6	6 to 7	Close
1. George Jones															
2. Ron Rundus															
3. Roger Fisk															
5. Holly Hunter															
6. Joyce Zwick															
7. Lauren Hall															
8.															
9.															
10.															

Election Day materials instructions include:

- Packet (envelope) marked with precinct number, contact information, coordinator name and phone number(s)
- Precinct Map
- Map of how to get to precinct
- Script
- Pen or pencil
- Credentials if needed
- E-Day Instruction Sheet

Election Day instructions include:
- Hints for Runners
- Number to call for coordinator
- Number to call for legal help
- Summary of election rules
- Location of victory party
- Reasons why E-Day is so important
- E-Day Schedule
- Address of the Victory Party

A typical Election Day schedule looks like this:
- Openers—opening polling locations
- Potential Passing for morning rush hour
- First Turnout Report (10:00 a.m.)
- First Running of the Voters
- Noon Report
- Lunch
- Second Run
- Afternoon Report (2:00 p.m.)
- Continue to Run
- Final Report (4:00 p.m.)
- Final Run
- Closers—get final numbers from each poll

A Schedule for Election Day Phone operations includes:
- One round auto-calls night before election
- One round auto-calls a.m. Election Day
- Two Rounds of live calls Election Day

A model Election Day Field Operation has:
- **At least 3-deep in each precinct all day**
- **1,500 to 1,700 people per C.D.**
- **Contact each plus voter 5 times E-Day (3 times door-to-door and 2 times on the phone)**
- **Match Banks throughout the day**
- **Mass Location Passing on Election Day**

A high-intensity voter I.D./GOTV effort of this sort materially increases turnout among mobilizable voters. A program of this sort can be conducted in a congressional race for $250,000 to $350,000.

All serious congressional races spend well over $1 million on persuasion TV and mail. In virtually every one of those, an investment of this type of field program will generate more additional or marginal votes to the candidate than the expenditure of an additional $250,000 to $350,000 on efforts to move persuadables using TV, radio or mail.

Of course, in most circumstances, GOTV cannot win elections in the absence of serious persuasion programs either. The rare campaign that has a field program and no serious media persuasion program will almost certainly lose.

In most serious swing campaigns, you must have both systematic persuasion and high-intensity mobilization to maximize the odds of progressive victory.

Remember one more thing about field programs—they put people in motion. They move thousands of people to make a passionate commitment to the progressive cause.

Election Day, in particular, will change your life. People see everything come together on Election Day. Organizers who have sworn for months that they would never be willing to do "all this hard work" again, miraculously change after Election Day. Win or lose, they are likely to come in the next morning and ask where to sign up to do it again.

Election Day is a transformative experience for organizers and volunteers. For many, it's almost an epiphany—you suddenly see clearly why this is all so important. It is also intoxicating, addicting. It's as if a virus is gradually infecting you during the campaign and grabs you completely on Election Day. I've seen it happen hundreds of times.

The progressive movement is not a bunch of ad agencies or consulting firms, as important as we all are. It is millions of people set in motion by their commitment to progressive values and a better world.

Campaign field operations not only win elections, they create and inspire thousands of progressive activists. They make a true progressive movement possible.

SECTION SEVEN

THE BATTLE OVER VALUES —
THE RIGHT IS WRONG

CHAPTER FORTY

Two Contrasting Sets of Values

To beat the right, we have to understand the battle that is underway in American society between traditional progressive American values and the values of radical conservatives.

Traditional progressive values have served as the foundation for the expansion of human freedom that has been the central theme of American history. Those values define what most people mean when they discuss civilization and human progress. They underlie the great documents of American freedom and the international affirmation of human rights contained in the United Nation's Universal Declaration of Human Rights.

Yet these values have been under constant, effective assault—in the United States and elsewhere—by radical conservatives that embrace a very different set of values.

In this Section we will analyze the contours of this battle of values. In Section Eight, we'll see why progressive values are the farthest thing from being "soft" or "weak," as they are characterized the right. In fact, they are critical to our long-term security—to the survival and success of American society and to human society as a whole.

We'll also discuss why, in order to affirm these values—and win politically—we need to communicate a clear progressive vision for a future that embodies them.

We'll begin our look at the battle over values by returning to cognitive linguist George Lakoff. The family is such a powerful metaphor for values, because it is the formative social unit—for each individual and every human society. Most human beings grow up and learn about human relationships first in a family context, so family structures provide a clear experience-based metaphor for all human relationships.

The kinds of values you experience growing up typically have a big impact on your broader view of right and wrong and how human society should be organized. Lakoff argues that "strict father" and "nurturant parent" family are important metaphors for radical conservative and progressive values. In American society, virtually everyone has some experience with, and understanding of, both the "strict father" and "nurturant parent" family models. That allows them to serve their role as powerful metaphors for our views of the broader society—which we often think about as an extended family—or national family.

Here's how Lakoff describes the strict parent model:

There are two parents, father and a mother. Morally, there is absolute right and absolute wrong. The strict father is the moral authority in the family; he knows right from wrong, is inherently moral, and has the authority to be head of the household. A family needs a strict father because:

- *The family should be run on a moral basis and the authority should be a moral authority. The authority of the father must not be seriously challenged.*

- *There is evil in the world, and the family needs a father strong enough to protect it from evil.*

- *There is competition in the world. There will always be winners and losers. To support the family, a father has to be able to win in a competitive world.*

- *Children are born bad, in the sense that they want to do whatever feels good, not what is right. They need a strict father to teach them right from wrong. Moral action is obedience to the moral authority, the father. Children learn right from wrong and become moral beings in only one way: punishment when they do wrong—punishment painful enough, either physically or physiologically, to give them an incentive to do right. Only in that way will they develop the internal discipline needed to function as moral beings. Such punishment is seen as an expression of love, and is called tough love.*

- *The authority should be the father, since "mommy" is not strong enough to protect the family, not able to win competitions and support the family, and not strict enough to discipline their children sufficiently.*

- *The mother's role is to uphold the authority of the father, take care of the household, and comfort the children when they need it.*

- *Affection is important, either as a reward for obedience or to prevent alienation through a show of love despite painful punishment.*

- *Discipline has an important secondary effect. If you're disciplined, you can pursue your self-interest to become prosperous.*

- *The mechanism for this is a version of free-market capitalism: if everybody pursues his or her own self-interest, then the self-interests of all will be maximized, as a law of nature (as Adam Smith said, by the invisible hand). It is therefore moral to pursue your self-interest, since by doing so, you're helping everyone.*

- *Correspondingly, it is wrong to give people things they haven't earned, since it will take away their incentive to be disciplined, which will make them dependent and less capable of acting morally. It is also wrong to take away the rewards of discipline, since it removes the incentive to be disciplined.*

- *Since both morality and prosperity come from self-discipline, morality correlates with prosperity. If you're not disciplined enough to be prosperous, you're not disciplined enough to be moral, so you deserve your poverty. This creates a natural hierarchy of morality, paired with wealth and power. In a well-ordered world, those in authority should be the moral people, since they deserve to be in authority.*
- *Mature children should ideally have become sufficiently disciplined to function on their own, support themselves, and be their own moral authorities. At that point, they are their own moral authorities, free from obedience to the strict father, and from then on he should not "meddle" in their lives.*
- *A mature child who is not sufficiently disciplined is never coddled but needs more tough love, and so is sent out to face the discipline of the world.*

Ideally, the father will protect and support the family, exercise his authority well, and raise disciplined, moral, well-behaved, obedient children who can prosper in the world and form their own strict father families. He will never coddle or spoil his children, never show weakness or indecision, never yield his authority, never allow himself to be manipulated. This is tough love, but it is what love is in this model.

Lakoff continues:

The strict father model of the family unites many themes into an intuitive seamless whole and, via the nation as family metaphor, structures right wing politics in terms of the political version of those themes.

Lakoff goes on to describe the nurturant parent model:

In this model, both parents (if there are two) are equally responsible. There is no gender hierarchy. The job of the parent is to nurture his or her children, and to raise the children to be nurturers of others. Nurturance involves empathy and responsibility (for both oneself and others), as well as everything that responsibility requires: strength, confidence, endurance, and so on.

Nurturant parenting is the opposite of permissive parenting, since it stresses caring about others, responsibility for oneself, and responsibility for others.

Nurturant parents are authoritative without being authoritarian. That is, because they are responsible for and to their children, they become competent parents, learning what they need to learn, and earn the respect of their children—in part by respecting the children. They set fair and reasonable limits and rules, and take the trouble to explain and discuss those limits and rules with their children. [1]

The traditional progressive value package rests on the twin values of empathy and responsibility for self and others. The radical conservative alternative rests on the values of moral authority, discipline and self-reliance through the individual pursuit of self-interest and responsibility for the self.

These are two sharply contrasting moral systems. But as we've seen, this does not mean that the elements of each of these frames cannot exist in the same person's brain. A person can apply the "strict father" moral system at home and a "nurturant family" system at work—or in political life.

And let's remember that we must activate our moral system as we frame debates and present symbols to represent candidate qualities. We need to use language that refers to our moral system, a system which is shared to some degree at least by most persuadable voters, in order to persuade them. If we allow the debate to reference only the right-wing value system, we will lose.

These two competing moral systems involve sharply contrasting philosophical assumptions.

CONTRASTING VIEWS OF THE NATURE OF RIGHT AND WRONG

First and foremost, the radical conservative morality assumes the existence of an immutable moral law. Actions are defined as right or wrong. Moral behavior is imbedded in a set of rules that are generally understood to be divinely inspired. Being moral is being obedient to the moral law.

In contrast, Lakoff refers to the traditional progressive view of morality as "virtue ethics." In various forms its roots go back to Aristotle as well as to early Christianity. For Aristotle, a good society is one that helps people fulfill their "potential to flourish." The goal of ethical behavior is not strict adherence to immutable moral rules, but the outcome of human fulfillment—which he conceived as the development of personal and civic virtues.

Early Christianity was equally clear in its rejection of what St. Paul viewed as a hidebound traditional law that had lost touch with the fundamental value of a loving one's neighbor as oneself—the golden rule. This was a central precept of early Christian moral teaching.

Throughout the Jewish Torah, and the entire Old Testament, we also read of a constant conflict between those who promoted the immutable moral law of the scribes on the one hand, and the view of the prophets on the other, who promoted a morality that focused on the consequences of human behavior and the ability of *others* to lead fulfilling lives. For the prophets, morality was about justice—about "Tikkun Olam"—repairing the world.

A system based on immutable moral law requires discipline to the law and sacrifice. What is best to assure that humans survive and flourish may, however, violate the law and as a consequence is seen as immoral.

A virtue-based system requires discipline to an ethic of responsibility for yourself and others—to assure first and foremost that everyone flourishes.

In a moral law-based system, character and strength are defined as the ability of individuals to say "no"—to discipline themselves strictly to the moral code and resist temptation to stray from a prescribed code of behavior.

In a virtue-based system, character consists of having a clear commitment to the primary virtues of empathy and responsibility for the self and others. A virtuous person does whatever is necessary to realize these values in the real world.

Neither of these systems is "relativistic"—where anything goes. Both requires disciplined commitment—to a strict moral code on the one hand, or a *fundamental* moral principle on the other.

CONTRASTING VIEWS OF HUMAN NATURE

The radical conservative system of morality is inherently pessimistic. It assumes that humans are innately bad and require discipline to behave as moral actors. Radical conservative ethics are heavily concerned with preventing human beings from succumbing to inborn instincts and to outward temptations that lead them from the moral path. Children must be disciplined to force them to ignore their innately bad instincts in order to follow the dictates of morality. Moral commands mainly involve proscribed behavior—things you are commanded *not to do.*

Traditional progressive morality is inherently optimistic. It assumes that human beings are innately good—to be nurtured so their innate goodness can flourish. It recognizes acutely that people are capable of horrible acts of cruelty, but it does not assume that humans are doomed to immoral behavior unless they are constrained by the absolute moral law. It assumes that human beings are innately capable of goodness. It focuses heavily on one's responsibility to take action to improve the lives of others, and assure that they flourish. That is why progressive values are about *hope* not *fear.*

CONTRASTING VIEWS OF REALITY AND HISTORY

Underlying a radical conservative system of morality is a bifurcated view of reality. It implies that an ideal reality—an essential state—exists independent of material reality. That ideal reality defines good, evil, beauty and truth and is only indirectly reflected in the material world. In this view, the spirit—or souls—of human beings exist independent of material reality. Human beings are understood to have an immutable essence that exists independent of history and social forces.

The progressive system of morality assumes that human beings, their thoughts and spirits, are part of one unified material reality. They are products of history, and also nodes of creativity in history. Humans are viewed simultaneously as products of this history and as creators of their own futures. They're not just corks bobbing in the stream of history; they can re-create the future. At the same time, their nature is not independent or apart from history either. They are not simply embodiments of some essential ideal of the human being that exist independent of the material world. They are simultaneously products and creators of historic and biological evolution.

In a world that changes before our eyes, it is very difficult for anyone to ascribe to a view of reality that does not recognize the reality of change. For much of human history it was easy to reject the notion of change. Changes in technology and social relations were glacial. They weren't noticeable in a lifetime. Today, change is the essential constant of human existence.

While the conservative view recognizes these changes, it implies that the essential nature of human beings and moral behavior do not change, since they are rooted in ideal essences unrelated to the flow of historic evolution. Human society may change, but the essence of human beings stays the same.

The progressive view implies that human society, social institutions and reality in general are not a static essence. They are a process. They're always becoming something new. The moral question this presents is whether they become something that enhances the ability of human beings to flourish—or something that endangers human survival and success.

Progressives believe in the expansion of human possibility—we do not believe that the "poor will always be with us" any more than we believe that polio or smallpox must always be with us. We believe in the expansion of the realm of human freedom and our ability to create a truly democratic society that allows everyone to fulfill his or her needs and dreams.

CONTRASTING VIEWS OF CAUSATION

Lakoff argues that the radical conservative moral system assumes that all events with moral consequence involve *direct* causation: when a single agent purposefully acts to influence another. One agent; one entity affected.

The conservative moral system rejects, or at least ignores, the notion that systematic causation that involves the interactions of complex systems can have moral consequences.

In the conservative moral system, only actions involving direct causality take on a directly moral connotation. Directly stealing, or taking someone's life, or sexual abuse: all involve direct causality and the action of one person directly on another. These kinds of direct action are much more easily subject to immutable moral commands.

Complex systems function over a period of time. Though they are subject to human intervention, they are much more difficult to pin down than the single events involved in direct causation.

The conservative moral system tends to ignore the harm caused by systematic causality—global warming, the depletion of environmental resources, the effects of a culture of poverty on a child's likelihood of educational success.

The response to a child born in poverty is to expect him to "pull himself up by his bootstraps" to achieve personal success. In fact, conservative morality considers any help the society might provide is likely to cause dependency, which in the conservative moral code is an immoral result. Self-reliance is the central value. The effect of poverty on the child's potential is not considered to have a moral dimension. Instead, it is considered to be part of the amoral process of economic competition. To the radical conservative moral system, the only "moral" implication of poverty involves one's individual attempt to escape it—not the systematic violence it inflicts on millions of people.

It just doesn't compute to a radical conservative when we talk about the moral challenge of global warming. In their view, subjects involving moral challenge involve personal actions that are subject to specific moral commands and have a direct and immediate result.

The fact that action having indirect long-term effects appears to conservatives to be amoral is partially a result of their view that the soul, spirit or moral center of human beings is a reflection of an essence that has its roots in an ideal realm rather than the processes of history and the material world.

Progressives view humans as products of complex historic processes, and the future is something humans can affect by their behavior today. For Progressives, actions to affect complex patterns of events in the future have an essentially moral content since they will directly impact whether or not other human beings survive and flourish.

CONTRASTING VIEWS OF INTERDEPENDENCE

Underlying the conservative moral system is a radical commitment to self-reliance. Because a person's moral core—or soul—is an expression of an ideal essence that is not impacted by their histories, they are morally responsible *individually*. They are seen as having free will that is independent of social context.

In a fundamentalist Christian religious context, this moral individualism is played out insofar as it is only possible for each separate individual to be "born again" and achieve salvation. Individuals are held responsible to proselytize other individuals with the Gospel—but salvation has little to do with group or collective action.

This view is reflected in economic life as well. In the conservative moral universe, moral success is achieved by individual self-discipline. That individual discipline is also seen as the key to individual economic success. As a result, those who succeed economically are viewed as virtuous since their individual discipline has been responsible for their success.

Individual success is not attributed to social context, cultural advantage, the inventions and innovations of prior generations—or the advantage provided by American society. Individuals are understood to be successful because they *earned* it, through individual discipline and effort.

Traditional progressive morality assumes that individuals are part of the complex web of history and social relationships. People are what they are because of generations that have come before; because others that came before them invented agriculture and writing and science and all the other forms of human knowledge. They are seen as responsible to pass on to the next generation yet a greater store of knowledge and understanding—to pass along the world a better place than they found it.

And they are bound by the principles of empathy and responsibility to recognize that they are responsible not only for their own success, but for the success of all other people.

Progressives understand that no one is independent. The only question is the form of their interdependence.

In the wonderful film, *"A Day Without a Mexican,"* all of the Latinos in Southern California magically disappear for a day. Of course, nothing could function. Upper-middle-class Anglos could not go to work because the nanny didn't arrive. The restaurants didn't serve because there were no workers. The hotels shut down, the factories closed, the food was not harvested.

Progressive morality presupposes that we are all interdependent, even with those whose work is often invisible in society.

Finally, the progressive view of interdependence implies that ultimately each individual and group will be better off, if everyone is better off. One person doesn't have to diminish another to advantage himself, his family, or his country. *You* don't have to be poorer for *me* to be richer. For me to have freedom, you don't have to be my slave. If all of the Third World children could learn and achieve their greatest potential, the whole of human society would benefit from their success.

The progressive moral view is optimistic that human societies are not doomed to fight with each other to divide up scarcer and scarcer resources. It assumes that if we all move into the future together, we will all be better off.

This assumption is extremely important to the progressive worldview. It is especially important in light of the massive challenges facing the world during the next century.

Perhaps this assumption should be restated: it is possible to make the decisions that prevent the struggle for our survival from being a zero-sum game. If we fail to do so, it is also possible that the sum of history's game could be zero. But one thing is certain: values that legitimate conflict over scarce resources in an age of exponentially expanding human technological power will all but guarantee a game with a tragic end.

CONTRASTING CONCEPTS OF COMPETITION

The conservative moral system presupposes that everyone is responsible to pursue his own self-interest. Logically, it concludes that if everyone does so, the self-interest of all will be maximized.

This moral assumption is the ethical embodiment of Adam Smith's "invisible hand" of competition. There is a moral imperative to pursue one's own self-interest, because if everyone does so, we will all be better off.

The efficacy of this view is reinforced by the conservative moral systems and the assumption that actions involving complex systematic causation have no moral consequence.

If trade policies are set to maximize one group's self-interest, but indirectly harm others, not to worry. There is no moral culpability for the harm caused to others by trade policies. These economic actions do not involve direct causation. A beneficiary of these policies might say: "I didn't steal food from that Mexican child or prevent a laid-off worker from earning a living. These are just the natural consequences of the way the competitive market functions. In the end, we'll all be better off."

As far as conservative morality is concerned, harm inflicted through economic competition—or competition for scarce resources, or externalities (like pollution or deforestation), are simply *not* moral issues. They may be economic, or environmental, or political issues, but not moral issues. For the progressive moral system, these are critical moral questions that involve right and wrong, because they are questions that involve the success and survival of others. They involve our moral responsibility that flows directly from our responsibility to others and a commitment to the view that we are all in this together.

CONTRASTING VIEWS OF THE COMMON GOOD

In a radical conservative moral universe, the common good is served as each individual pursues his own interest. That done, the "invisible hand" will do the rest.

In the traditional progressive moral system, the common good is served if everyone is responsible for himself and each other.

This contrasting view of the common good is probably the sharpest divide between the traditional progressive values and the radical conservative values that are attempting to displace them.

Of course, the fallacy of the radical conservative moral system is directly related to the fact that as often as not when individuals all act simply to maximize their own self-interest, the common good does not result.

Several examples should suffice to drive this fact home.

The first is referred to as the "tragedy of the commons." Suppose an island nation depends for its livelihood on the fishing harvests from the surrounding sea. It would obviously be in the interest of the community never to take more fish from the sea than can be replenished through the reproduction of fish. That way, everyone on the island will continue to have fish for the long haul.

But it is in the interest of each individual fisherman to catch as many fish as he can. This is especially true if the fish grow scarcer. To continue to have enough fish for himself and his family, each fisherman competes more and more vigorously for the remaining fish. In the end, this behavior will *assure* that the fish supply is depleted, and that no one has any fish.

In this situation, if everyone pursues his own individual interest, the common good is not served. But if everyone looks out for each other, and recognizes that all have a common group interest, they will manage the fish resource to assure a self-sustaining fish supply that can feed everyone for years to come.

The other example is the classic case of economic recession comes from Keynesian economics. In a recession, it is in each economic actor's self-interest to increase his savings and cut spending since the recession threatens his income. But by each pursuing his own individual interest, all of the actors together reduce the economy's overall spending. And that deepens the recession. If, on the other hand, the entire group of economic actors works through its government to increase national spending and reduce overall savings, it will stimulate the economy and the recession will end—benefiting everyone.

CONTRASTING VIEWS OF THE ROLE OF GOVERNMENT

These two competing value systems produced ultimately different views of the role of government—and the relationship of government to individual action.

The traditional American progressive view, as summarized by Lakoff:

A nurturant family uses its resources for the good of the family as a whole— for the common good—so that each member can have the freedom to pursue his or her individual goals. The parents put aside money for education of the children, or to get a new house, or a new family car, or for a down payment on a home for a grandchild, or to enable one of the partners to make a career change, or for disabled child's medical expenses. So that family members can be free to fulfill their needs and their dreams, the family's common wealth is often necessary. [2]

The central role of government, in other words, is to use the commonwealth for the common good—to make individual freedom possible—to allow each individual to realize the six categories of self-interest we discussed in Section Two. "The Commonwealth builds the infrastructure for freedom," says Lakoff. [3]

Radical conservatives would challenge the progressive view as "collectivist"—wishing individual citizens to "march in lockstep"—making individuals dependent on government. Nothing could be more fundamentally off the mark. The traditional progressive moral system views the actions we take together, through our government, as the critical foundations upon which each individual can have the greatest ability to achieve his or her individual goals and dreams.

It would not be possible to operate a business without a state rule of law—the ability to settle disputes through legitimate courts and without resort to violence—without personal security and safety.

Government action assures the public health, provides public education, maintains the public infrastructure for our common life—from streets, to parks, to airports, to mass transportation. Government is the expression of our common life—our life as a community; in democratic societies, it is more accountable to average citizens than any other major decision-making structure, including large corporations.

The radical conservative view of the role of government is summarized by Grover Norquist, the leader of the Republican efforts to slash taxes for the wealthy. He believes that government needs to be "shrunk to the size that it can be drowned in the bathtub." In his view, government is the enemy of moral purpose, which resides in the ability of individuals to pursue their own individual self-interest.

CONTRASTING VIEWS OF FREEDOM

In Lakoff's book *Whose Freedom?*, he analyzes in detail the implications of these two contrasting moral systems for the concept of freedom.

Traditional progressive and radical conservative moral systems are both concerned with freedom *from* and freedom *to.*

In the traditional progressive view, freedom is necessary for fulfillment in life. Freedom fulfills one of the six major groups of self-interest that motivates human beings–it affords us control over our lives.

In the progressive view, freedom requires opportunity. One's freedom is a direct result of his history and culture. You can't be free and live in abject poverty. It also requires security. Fear of coercion and physical attack negate freedom.

Progressives believe that individuals should be free to pursue their own interests and dreams. Free to speak and think and explore the world; free to hold the beliefs and religious convictions of their choice; free to make their own commitments and find meaning in their lives. We believe that to allow this freedom, people must also be free from want, and free from fear.

This is the traditional American formulation of the concept of freedom. It is essentially a restatement of Franklin D. Roosevelt's Four Freedoms: freedom of speech and expression, freedom of religion, freedom from want, freedom from fear.

In stark contrast, the radical conservative concept of freedom involves a radical commitment to pursue individual self-interest without any recognition that the exercise of freedom requires opportunity. Freedom here is viewed as freedom to become disciplined, freedom from government interference, freedom to enter the free market and become personally prosperous.

Both moral systems profess a commitment to expand the realm of freedom. The progressive view understands that to expand the realm of human freedom, one must expand opportunity and democratize political power. The radical conservatives want to expand the realm of free markets in which individuals can pursue self-interests without interference from government.

Throughout human history, the tradition of progressive freedom has driven America to expand the realm of freedom. The progressive concept of freedom, and the progressive moral system upon which it is based, have been ethical engines that have systematically broken down the barriers to freedom throughout our history. There was a time when only white landowners had the right to vote in America. The progressive concept of freedom drove the expansion of the franchise first to non-landowners, to African American men, and then finally to women. It has provided the ethical basis for unionization, and laws to regulate the exploitation of labor, our environment and our children. It has led to a historic commitment to universal public education and public health. Progressive values provide the foundation for Social Security and Medicare. They have driven the expansion of rights to ethnic minorities, gays, bisexuals and lesbians. Progressive values are the underlying theme of the story of American progress. Progressive freedom is American freedom. We cannot allow the radical conservatives to redefine freedom and transform freedom into its opposite.

THE RIGHT-WING COUNTER-REVOLUTION

When Barry Goldwater was defeated in 1964, the right in America organized itself. What emerged was a self-conscious, ambitious plan to change the dominant frame of American politics — to change the definition of "common sense."

The right developed leaders through their "farm team" in local and state government. They developed think tanks and publications. They seized beachheads of power.

The Reagan Revolution put them in a dominant position to control the political dialogue. With the 1994 Gingrich-inspired congressional takeover, they bounced back from Clinton's 1992 victory and aggressively moved once again to restructure the debate.

George W. Bush's victory, and the right's control of both the House and Senate, gave them the best chance in a generation to realign American politics for the foreseeable future.

Their goal was to roll back most major elements of the New Deal, free corporations from regulation, transfer wealth to the wealthy, and transform American foreign policy to conform with neoconservative principles.

In short, Karl Rove's vision of society looked very much like the late 19th century Gilded Age.

The right intended very explicitly to take actions that would reverse the spread of the traditional progressive realm of freedom. The Midterm elections in 2006 have begun to reverse this tide. It's now up to Progressives to retake the offensive in this historic battle.

THE RELIGIOUS MANIFESTATIONS OF RADICAL-CONSERVATIVE AND PROGRESSIVE VALUES

American fundamentalists, and especially American fundamentalist Christians, represent the religious embodiment of the radical conservative, "strict father" moral system.

Ultra-fundamentalists represent a distinct minority among American Christians, but they have come to have a disproportionate voice. They believe that the Bible must be understood literally, and they must obey the moral commands of God and promote the truth of the Gospels in order to be saved.

Ethically, they adhere strictly to moral law. They believe that morality consists of following commandments from God, and focus ethical concern entirely on actions that involve direct causation—one person directly affecting another.

They conceive of God as a "strict father" who demands disciplined adherence to his commandments and punishes those who disobey. Humans are viewed as innately sinful, and in need of redemption that only a commitment to God as manifested in Jesus and their view of Christian faith can provide. Fundamentalist faith calls for the execution of the "strict father" family model at home as well as in the broader society.

Progressive Christianity sees God as a nurturant parent, offering unconditional love and grace. Jesus in the progressive tradition is a model for living. His life was the embodiment of progressive values, of empathy and responsibility. The model for a Christian life in the progressive tradition is simple: *love your neighbor as yourself.*

Ethically progressive Christians seek to live life in Christ's footsteps— to live a Christian life not founded on rules and commandments, but on one's responsibility to help lift all of humankind to flourish and succeed.

Jesus' life was hardly a life spent maximizing his own self-interest and assuring that the invisible hand would maximize benefit for all. Jesus was committed to a life of nonviolence, of responsibility for others—of healing the sick and helping the poor. Jesus challenged entrenched authority and the values of selfishness and greed. Jesus threw the money changers from the temple.

Adherence to the "strict father" morality is not unique to Christian fundamentalism. It characterizes all forms of religious fundamentalism, including ultra-Orthodox Judaism and fundamentalist Islam.

All of them rely on male-dominated father figures, a concept of moral law that requires strict adherence to prescribe rules and rituals. All of them assume that human beings are innately sinful and must be prescribed from violating the moral law. They all rely heavily on discipline. Fundamentalist Islam deviates from its Christian and Jewish counterparts in its attitudes concerning the economy. But still it carries the fundamentalist unwillingness to separate church and state to its logical conclusion—theocratic states.

CHAPTER FORTY-ONE

What Are Progressive Values?

Values are the criteria we use to set priorities and make decisions. Moral values of the sort we have been discussing are the criteria that form the most fundamental precepts for human behavior and the structures and priorities of human society.

What then are the progressive values that define our understanding of the fundamental priorities for people and societies? I frequently hear that question from our right-wing opponents. So it is useful to lay them out systematically.

Progressive values definitely involve the twin precepts of empathy and responsibility. But these precepts presuppose an even more fundamental value.

1) The fundamental goal of action is to promote human survival and success—to allow all human beings to flourish.

This precept is at the root of both progressive religious teaching and secular progressive moral thinking. It is the underlying goal of "virtue ethics" of all types.

There may be variation among progressive moral systems with respect to what it means for human beings to flourish and succeed, but the fundamental goal remains the same—human fulfillment and survival.

This fundamental principle for action does not conflict with a religious, God-centered morality. Many progressive religious traditions make oneness with and obedience to God the central precept of morality. However, they affirmed the sanctity and fulfillment of human life as the material manifestation of God in the world.

The Christian New Testament relates the quintessential Christian understanding of ethics in the 10th chapter of the book of Luke in the parable of the Good Samaritan:

> On one occasion, an expert in the law stood up to test Jesus. "Teacher," he asked, "what must I do to inherit eternal life?"
>
> "What is written in the law?" He replied. "How do you read it?"
>
> He answered: "Love the Lord your God with all your heart and with all

your soul and with all your strength and with all your mind, and, love your neighbor as yourself."

But he wanted to justify himself, so he asked Jesus, "and who is my neighbor?"

In reply, Jesus said: "A man was going down from Jerusalem to Jericho, when he fell into the hands of robbers. They stripped him of his clothes, beat him and went away, leaving him half dead. A priest happened to be going down the same road, and when he saw the man, he passed by on the other side. So too, a Levite, when he came to the place and saw him, passed by on the other side. But a Samaritan, as he traveled, came where the man was; and when he saw him, he took pity on them. He went to him and bandaged his wounds, pouring on oil and wine. Then he put the man on his own donkey, took him to an inn and took care of him. The next day he took out two silver coins and gave them to the innkeeper. "Look after him," he said, "and when I return, I will reimburse you for any extra expense you may have."

"Which of these three do you think was a neighbor to the man who fell into the hands of robbers?"

The expert in the law replied, "The one who had mercy on him."

Jesus told them, "Go and do likewise."

In the material, social world, the cornerstone of Christian ethics is "love thy neighbor as thyself." That simple statement, and the story of the Good Samaritan that followed, makes it clear that the central goal of ethical behavior should be assuring that all human beings flourish. In the Christian tradition, one should seek to satisfy the same basic self-interests and needs for *all* human beings that we would wish to see fulfilled for ourselves.

The universality implied by the parable of the Good Samaritan is central to the progressive ethical system. Samaritans and Jews were not close at the time. Yet the disliked Samaritan was the true neighbor. The story was intended to drive home the universality of the fundamental ethical premise—"love thy neighbor as thyself."

"And who is my neighbor?" asked the expert on the law. "Everyone," Jesus replied.

The importance of the principle of universality must be understood in the context of human development. For millions of years, "everyone" was not the answer that most humans would have given to this question. For bands of hunter-gatherers, or tribes of later human societies, the answer was "another member of our kinship group or band—or another member of our tribe."

Jared Diamond' study of human development, *Guns, Germs, and Steel: The Fates of Human Societies*, points out that the first question for a typical member of one band of hunter-gatherers, when he encountered a member of another band, was why he should not kill them on the spot. [1]

The universality of the ethical demand to "love thy neighbor as thyself" is a very recent development in human evolution. It has emerged only over the last several thousand years of our approximately seven million years of evolutionary history. Previously, most behavior involving moral content pertained only to members of our own band, tribe or ethnic group.

Today, of course, there are many occasions when the principle of universality is wantonly violated. When countries go to war, they go to great lengths to "objectify" or dehumanize the enemy. Enemies are not viewed as people, but "gooks," "Krauts" or "Japs."

Ethnic and communal conflict underlies many of the world's most intractable problems. The rationales given for murdering, imprisoning, and oppressing the rival group often completely ignore the principle of universality. The oppressor group argues that the right of the rival group to be treated according to the moral imperative to "love thy neighbor as thyself" does not "in this case" have "moral equivalency" to his own group's claims.

The fundamental progressive value is to prioritize the survival and success of human beings—*all human beings.*

By survival we mean both the lives of individual people and the continuation of the human species.

By success, we mean the ability of each individual and each society to maximize the six categories of self-interest with which we began this book: physical needs (food, security, health, warmth, etc.), control of your life, providing a structure for your life, social interaction, intellectual stimulation, meaning and purpose.

Before going further I should acknowledge that there are those who share a progressive value system for whom the first principle of morality is not the success and survival of human beings (whether or not this principle results from God's will or a secular imperative). In their view, the first principle of morality is the protection and survival of the earth and all of its creatures—of the entire ecological system.

While this difference in first ethical principles may have implications in some circumstances, we will see in the next Section that those implications are rare—since human survival and success is heavily dependent on the protection and survival of the earth's ecology.

2) *Empathy.*

The second key progressive value follows from the first. To accomplish the ultimate goal, Progressives must put great emphasis on the priority of empathy with others. To understand others, we have to put ourselves in their place—to understand the way they see the world, their commitments, their sense of meaning, their identity, their self-interests, needs and history. To feel what someone else feels is necessary in order to motivate us to act to maximize their self-interests as well as our own.

Empathy is not only critical ethically; it is the central task of political organizing. Empathy is the way we come to understand someone else's perception of their own self–interests, and how we might engage it. Empathy is critical if we want to succeed at the political task of changing people's behavior.

As we've seen, evolution has hardwired human beings for the task of empathy. Our ability to communicate and to "mind read" from facial expressions are parts of the apparatus. Facial muscles affect emotional states and are "read" by others.

In *Social Intelligence: The New Science of Human Relationships,* Daniel Goleman reports that Swedish researchers have found that, "Merely seeing a picture of a happy face elicits fleeting activity in the muscles that pulled the mouth into a smile. Indeed, whenever we gaze at a photograph of someone whose face displays a strong emotion, like sadness, disgust, or joy, our facial muscles automatically start to mirror the other's facial expression." [2]

Earlier, we saw how inputs to the amygdala section of the brain do not register at the level of conscious thought, but cause the individual to *"feel"* the emotion of another person.

Our brains are wired for empathy.

In addition to the amygdala that mimics feelings and moods, Lakoff describes the mirror neuron system linking the premotor cortex (which controls complex movements) and the parietal cortex (which integrates sensory information). Through experience, the system develops the ability to link control of behavior with perceptions of the behavior of others. The mirror system fires when you take action or perceive someone else, too.

Several studies published in *Current Biology* shed light on how neural mirroring works and its consequences. By measuring brain activity using magnetic resonance imaging, you can observe that when you see someone else scratching his head or furrowing his brow, many of the same neural pathways are activated in your brain as would be activated if you yourself took the same actions. Your brain allows you to *experience* the act of another person as if it is your own. This is the physical basis for empathy.

Cognitive psychologist Arthur Glenberg says that "we empathize with other human beings because of mirror neurons rather than rules. I know what it is for you to be sad because I know what it is to be sad myself. When I see you hurt, my mirror neuron system is responding, is giving me a sense of pain." [3]

The study points to another interesting conclusion. The mirror systems also seem to be included in the human capacity for language. The word "give" may activate the plan for stretching out the hand with the thumb touching the index finger and opening the fingers. This way the human brain connects an abstract concept to a concrete act. When we hear words, we act them out in our brains. [4]

Lakoff notes that:

> Though we come wired for it, that neural wiring still has to be developed and used or it can decay or fail to develop further. Feeling someone else's pain and joy—viewing what another feels—is the mark of empathy. Empathy is at the center of progressive values. Caring about others as well as yourself is at the heart of the value system. [5]

Complete inability to empathize is generally considered a serious pathology. In social psychology, the definition of a sociopath is someone who is incapable of feeling empathy. The child who tortures pets has classic symptoms of inability to develop empathy and is a serious candidate to be a sociopath later in life.

3) Responsibility. Progressive values require that each person be responsible for himself and for all people.

Carrying out the principal progressive ethical demand of promoting the survival and success of all human beings requires more than empathy. It requires action. In the progressive ethical system, people must take responsibility for their own well-being and act affirmatively to work for the well-being of others.

And it turns out that evolution has also hardwired our brains to incentivize altruistic behavior—behavior that involves being responsible to others. Well it should, since responsibility is an adaptive trait.

An October 2006 study published in the *Proceedings of the National Academy of Sciences* shows that when people donate to others, the brain's reward center—the mesolimbic pathway—fires. This is the pathway in the brain responsible for dopamine-mediated euphoria. In other words, the warm glow associated with charitable giving has a physiological basis. [6]

Remember that in the progressive value system, people are understood to be actors—nodes of creativity. They are not simply formed by history— they reshape history—they make choices that affect the future, they take action.

Dependence has no place in a progressive values system. But the progressive worldview understands that no one is independent, either. Everyone is to one degree or another interdependent and should strive to be mutually interdependent. Many people are, of course, disproportionately dependent on others. Someone who is terribly ill in a nursing home is going to be disproportionately dependent on others. But Progressives view that disproportionate dependency as a tragedy, not a positive value.

Progressives favor empowering everyone—allowing them to enter into relationships of mutual interdependence—not dependence.

That's why Progressives support the independent living movement in the disability rights community that seeks to "mainstream" as many people with disabilities as possible. The independent living movement wants to do everything possible to empower disabled people to be contributing—mutually interdependent—actors in the community, not dependent wards of the state.

The moral imperative for responsibility underlies the importance Progressives placed on empowerment and democracy. We seek to empower everyone so we can be mutually interdependent, and as a consequence take responsibility to assure that they can maximize their own interests, and simultaneously help each other in achieving the common goals of society.

4) Competency. Progressive values require a heavy emphasis on developing the capability of everyone to exercise his responsibility for himself, and for each other.

This includes the development of skills, knowledge, technologies, work habits, and procedures that allow people to meet their responsibilities—and confidently select and achieve goals.

Empathy and responsibility provide the motivation—the will—for moral action. Competency gives the ability—the wherewithal—to act in a moral way.

The package of skills, knowledge, technologies, work habits and procedures that is necessary for individual success varies depending upon your role and occupation in this complex society. But progressive values require that everyone has the ability to develop his skills and abilities to contribute to society to the maximum degree. They also require that society as a whole strives to increase the overall competency of the community with each generation. A critical progressive value is to increase the community's store of skills, knowledge, technologies, work habits and procedures over time—so we can leave a better world to our children.

As a consequence, Progressives value scientific inquiry, education, discipline, endurance, creativity, critical thought, innovation and curiosity.

For Progressives, the diffusion of scientific inquiry and knowledge is a moral question, since it directly affects people's ability to act as responsible moral actors with the competency to successfully benefit human society.

That's why universal access to broadband, for example, has a moral dimension.

5) Equality. Progressive values require that every human being's success and survival are just as important as everyone else's—both individually and as groups.

Progressive values require us to end inequality and create societies where everyone can fulfill the six categories of self-interest we discussed in Section Two.

The principle of equality has many concrete consequences. It also runs into many complications that have resulted as human social structures have evolved and become more complex over the last 13,000 years. All complex societies have evolved decision-making elites of one sort or the other that have aggregated massively disproportionate levels of power and resources. In the next section, we'll begin to discuss in detail the challenges these complications present, both to progressive morality, and to long-term human success and survival. We'll also look at the implications of our next principle.

6) Democratic Society: Progressives believe that in order to maximize the success and survival of all people, power must be diffused to everyone.

This is true for two reasons:

- We must do so to assure that the interest of each individual and group are represented in social decisions. To achieve the value of equality—to maximize everyone's interest—each person has to have the power to hold decision-makers accountable.

- Democratic societies are necessary to assure that the society does not make decisions that benefit elites, but are destructive of the entire society. Historically this problem has been one of the major factors when societies fail or collapse.

In short, we believe that the self-interests inherent within the structures of society itself should promote moral behavior, behavior that benefits everyone and not just a portion of the population.

7) Hope.

Progressives have an optimistic view of human beings. We realize human beings are capable of unbelievable horrors. But we believe that they can aspire to great possibility—to act out the progressive values including empathy, responsibility and competence.

We believe that hope trumps fear. We know that when people are called upon to be more than they are, they can excel. In Senator Barack Obama's words, Progressives believe in the "audacity of hope."

8) Unity—We're all in this together.

Progressives believe that our goal as a society must be to empower every person everywhere in the world to live up to his or her potential as a human being. This assures each person has the power to seek his own meaning in life, to make commitments of his own choosing, to live out his own dreams and to develop his intellectual, physical and spiritual capabilities to the maximum extent he desires.

Progressives believe that we're best able to achieve this goal together—not separately. We believe that our combined talent and spirit allow all of us to be more successful than any of us could be by ourselves. We do not believe—as do the proponents of the so-called "ownership society"—that we're all in this alone. We believe that we are most successful as a community when we stand up for each other, educate each other, take care of each other, and help each other succeed—not when we focus solely on looking out for ourselves.

Finally, Progressives believe that this goal, and our commitment to achieving it together, function not only to benefit all of us as a community. It is also the best way to benefit each of us as individuals. In other words, we believe that society is *not* a zero-sum game.

Progressives don't believe that it is necessary for people in the Third World to live in poverty in order for those in the developed world to have prosperity. We don't believe that gays and lesbians must be denied the ability to participate in fulfilling marriages in order for straight couples to have fulfilling marriages. We don't believe that one race of people need to be made to feel inferior in order for another race to have a sense of meaning and status. We believe that by giving every child a good education, the growing store of human knowledge will make each of us smarter. We believe that by allowing people everywhere to be more productive, each of us will ultimately be richer. We believe that by ending sickness and disease everywhere, each of us will ultimately be healthier. And we believe that the elimination of misery, hunger and hopelessness everywhere will make each of us safer and more secure.

9) Nonviolent Resolution of Disputes. Progressive values call for the creation and protection of nonviolent methods of dispute resolution.

The evolution of human society has heavily relied on the creation and protection of methods through which strangers can resolve disputes without violence. Regardless of the degree of democratic diffusion of power in society, disputes arise. In small kinship bands or tribes where everyone knew each other, these disputes were resolved through kinship structures.

Jared Diamond says, "A fact further defusing potential problems of conflict resolution in tribes is that almost everyone is related to everyone else, by blood or marriage or both. Those ties of relationship, binding all tribal members, make police, laws and other conflict-resolving institutions of larger societies unnecessary, since any two villages getting into an argument will share many kin, who apply pressure on them to keep it from being violent." [7]

These forces are no longer in play in larger societies. The maximum size of about 200 is necessary for everyone in the group to know each other.

Dispute resolution structures have evolved at increasingly large levels of social interaction over the last 13,000 years. Today effective and legitimate structures to avoid violent conflict are just forming at the world-wide level.

The danger posed by the use of war or other means of violence such as terrorism to resolve conflicts has greatly increased because of the growth of our technological capability, global communications and interdependence.

10) Fairness and the Rule of Law.

Not only does the progressive value system prioritize the creation of nonviolent methods of dispute resolution, it also mandates fairness and its necessary corollary: the rule of law.

If each individual is equal, then the standards used to resolve disputes arising from his or her behavior must be the same—standards that are embodied in widely accepted laws that are approved through democratic procedures.

We distinguished earlier between the progressive system of "virtue ethics" and the conservative system of "moral law." By rejecting the "moral law" approach to ethics, Progressives are not rejecting the rule of law. "Moral law" assumes immutable, divinely inspired standards for human conduct. The rule of law requires that to meet the mandate of equality and fairness, common humanly crafted standards should be used to structure society, set its priorities and resolve its disputes.

Progressive morality rejects "moral law" but requires the "rule of law."

The rule of law protects people from the arbitrary, capricious, and oppressive use of power; in other words, it protects us from unfairness and tyranny.

11) *Individual Privacy and Minority Rights.*

Progressive morality requires that society respect the rights of individuals to select and achieve the goals that they wish, so long as their actions do not interfere with the ability of the entire society, and other individuals within it, to survive and succeed. Where they do conflict, it requires that disputes be resolved through fair, nonviolent dispute resolution procedures. Where they do not conflict, progressive values validate the individual's right to set his own priorities for action within a zone of privacy that is not subject to public decision.

In other words, in the progressive view, each individual has a right to privacy. What's more, groups in the society can't be singled out for unequal or unfair treatment, even if it is the will of the majority, since that would violate the fundamental principles of equality and fairness.

12) *Tolerance for Diversity, Innovation and Critical Thought.*

Progressive morality puts a premium on tolerance and diversity. These values are mandated by the basic value of empathy as well as equality and fairness. But they also result from the progressive commitment to competency and the consequential necessity of creative critical thought, innovation, and curiosity. Conformist values and homogeneous cultures help avoid social conflict. But they also fail to produce creative critical thought and innovation.

The voices of Copernicus, Galileo and Darwin were all controversial minority opinions at one time. A world society that seeks the scientific, technological and social solutions to our many problems needs to foster and encourage tolerance and diversity.

13) *Self Respect, Mutual Respect.*

It's pretty obvious that, for people to act in ways that promote everyone's success and survival, we need mutual respect. Just as important, for an individual or group to fulfill its own potential—to act responsibly with competence—each person needs self-respect, and belief in their own importance, significance and goodness.

In my view, the most debilitating disease limiting the development of human potential—particularly among children—is lack of self-respect— lack of self-confidence in your own competency and self-worth.

Progressive values require us to create a society that teaches everyone, especially children, both self-respect and respect for others—the innate significance of everyone including one's self.

14) *Responsibility to Future Generations—the Long Term View (the Cathedral Builder Mentality).*

The progressive value system requires responsibility not only to our contemporaries, but to the generations that follow—to the future of human society. That means we must create a culture steeped in the importance of the long view.

During the Middle Ages, whole generations worked to build the great cathedrals of Europe without ever seeing their completion. They did their part in a great multigenerational project.

Progressive values require that we create a society with a cathedral-builder mentality—not a society focused only on immediate short-term reward.

Someone wise once said, "A civilization flourishes when people plant trees under which they will never sit."

This value is becoming more important to our survival each day but it is far from new.

You can see it in the immigrant mother struggling at multiple menial jobs so her child can be the first in the family to go to college.

You can see it in parents of all sorts who dream that their children have more opportunity, and a better standard of living than they do.

Progressives need to call on people to commit themselves to be part of a great multi-generational quest to build a society where all men and women can be free—free of oppression, free of want, free to explore every possibility of life, free to create their own future.

15) *Economic Efficiency and Democracy. The goal of human economic systems is to maximize the primary values of human success and survival and all of the progressive values that flow from it.*

Economic systems are human creations. They do not, as conservatives sometimes argue, involve "laws of nature." And, contrary to the conservative moral view, progressive believe that economic systems have moral consequences.

In the progressive moral system, our society's economy must serve the values of empathy, responsibility and competency. It must promote equality, democracy, unity, hope and responsibility to future generations. It must include and nurture systems for the nonviolent resolution of disputes, fairness and the rule of law, and respect the privacy of the individual. It should embody the spirit of innovation, critical thinking and creativity and function in a way that promotes mutual respect between members of society. And perhaps most important, it should advance the goal of a more democratic society. That doesn't sound much like the model of laissez-faire free-market capitalism that is at the core of the radical conservative economic theory and practice, does it?

The reason is that the premise of laissez-faire free-market capitalism is wrong. If each person pursues only his narrow, short-term self-interest, the "invisible hand" does not create a result that is always in the best interests of society as a whole.

We've already discussed two examples in which the individual pursuit of self-interest doesn't benefit the society as a whole—the tragedy of the commons (our example of the island fishery) and the classic problem of savings in a recession.

Several other examples make the point even clearer:

The Conditions for Market Competition

The pure "Adam Smithian"[8] theory of competition requires that to function as a competitive market several conditions must pertain. Among them are the requirements that:

- The product being bought and sold must be a commodity. The products offered by various competitors must, in other words, be interchangeable—indistinguishable. Corn, beans, oil, gold, shares of stock, are all commodities. Automobiles, furniture, homes, new innovations often are not.

- Firms must be able to enter and exit a market easily.

- No seller may control a large enough segment of the market to be able to affect the price. This is typically the case in true commodity markets. In these markets, the seller must take the market price. It is not true in most administered-price industries like automobiles, computers, furniture and medical care, where the seller sets his own price.

- Consumers must have perfect information about prices and quality. Where this is the case, a truly competitive market will have only one price at a given moment for products of comparable quality. After all, no buyer would pay a price higher than the lowest price available. For instance, the price of gold is one fixed-dollar number at the close of trading.

According to market economic theory, these conditions provide accountability and discipline that forces the most efficient deployment of resources.

Though these conditions do not pertain for many sectors of our economy, it is true that even imperfectly competitive markets do efficiently allocate resources for a range of product and services. As such, they often do serve progressive values.

Even where this is true, however, it is always necessary to create regulatory structures that enforce the "rules of the game." Market competition cannot function without courts to resolve disputes, regulatory bodies to ensure transparency and honesty. Efficient markets without rules and regulations are no more possible than a basketball game without rules and a referee.

But in many sectors, the conditions for competitive markets simply do not exist—and in others it is more efficient, and more likely to serve the interests of society, to organize economic activity differently.

SECTORS WHERE THE USE OF COMPETITIVE MARKETS IS INAPPROPRIATE

The most obvious are sectors for what are known economically as "public goods."

By their nature "public goods" cannot be bought and sold because they are available to everyone in society, whether one pays for them or not.

The most often cited examples are national security and community safety. Everyone theoretically benefits from national security activity. It is not a commodity, whose consumption can easily be privatized.

But there are also many other sectors of economic activity were the conditions necessary for a truly competitive market don't apply, or where all of us together can more efficiently produce and distribute goods and services through government or some other community structure.

Products and services that have traditionally been provided by the public sector in the United States include police and fire protection, public education, the vast majority of healthcare services, a portion of the retirement system (Social Security), management and protection of public lands and natural resources, and our criminal and civil justice systems.

Fire protection is a good example. It is simultaneously more efficient and more humane to provide fire protection, jointly, through our government. If each individual had to buy his own, and the person next door failed to do so, you could not protect yourself from the fire that starts next door and spreads to your home.

And it would be morally unacceptable to refuse to rescue a child in a burning house just because the parent had failed to hire a fire protection company.

The radical conservatives have tried to "privatize" Medicare—and seek to introduce more "market" incentives into the still semi-market-based healthcare system.

In fact, healthcare is just like fire protection. It is both more efficient and humane to have one national health insurance system that covers the cost of health care for everyone—Medicare for all.

Competitive market healthcare is obviously not more efficient. We've tried it. Every other industrial country has a universal healthcare system. In the US we pay 40% more per capita for health care than any other country and have only mediocre healthcare outcomes when compared with other developed countries. Each year we waste billions of dollars on an inefficient healthcare system—yet the number of people with no health care coverage at all continues to rise; it's now at 46.9 million people. And we're not just talking about the working poor. Seventeen million of them have family incomes in excess of $40,000.

The Washington Post reported on one typical example. Vicki Readling is a 50-year-old real estate agent who makes $60,000 a year. But like most real estate agents she is an independent contractor and receives no health insurance from her employer. She tried to buy health insurance on the private market, but as a cancer survivor, she was quoted a price tag of $27,000 a year, which was more than she could pay. [9]

Independent presidential candidate Ross Perot used to say that when it came to healthcare we were paying first-class tickets and getting bleacher seats. The reason is simple. Trying to squeeze healthcare into the competitive market model is like trying to squeeze Cinderella's slipper onto the wicked stepsister's gnarly foot.

With health care, none of the conditions for competitive markets is ever present. Healthcare is the farthest thing from a commodity. Consumers have virtually no knowledge of which therapy or treatment is most appropriate or most "cost effective." In fact, most medical decisions are made by medical professionals and not by the customer at all. And major segments of the healthcare economy set their own prices. (Except where government is the consumer—and often, even then). This is a particularly true of the pharmaceutical industry.

You don't come in one day and say, "Gee, honey. I got a raise. Now I can have cancer," or, "Wow, we've saved enough to have a heart attack."

Healthcare expenditures are prompted by conditions that are often beyond the individual's control. And there is no relationship between the price of the service and its relative benefit. A $10 vaccination can save a child's life, yet a $100,000 operation could buy someone two more months of life in a hospital.

Most Progressives believe that the best approach is to maintain a public health insurance plan for everyone and give individuals a complete choice of an array of private doctors and hospitals. Government is especially efficient at providing insurance. The overhead costs of Medicare per dollar paid out is tiny compared with private health insurance plans. At the same time, public investment in the efficient and high-quality VA health system and in public hospitals and clinics is critically necessary as well.

Social Security is another sector where government is more efficient. Social Security provides a guaranteed benefit to most Americans, financed by Social Security taxes they have paid in during their working years. Administrative costs are tiny compared to private pension plans. The right-wing proposal to privatize Social Security would have cut guaranteed benefits so that people could speculate in the stock market, with part of their Social Security dollars. In this case, the so-called "ownership society" really becomes, "You're on your own, buddy" if your stock picks don't work out. The right wanted to convert Social Security to a risky investments scheme that would benefit Wall Street and destroy this critical sector that is based upon progressive values. Their proposal was defeated, because Americans don't want it.

Progressives support the use of competitive markets when they can efficiently and equitably meet the goals of our society. We support using the public sector in the many instances where it can more efficiently and equitably meet society's goals.

Unlike conservatives, Progressives are not wedded to the idealized "competitive market" to solve all of society's problems.

And contrary to the assertion of many "free market" ideologues, the unrestricted reliance on market mechanisms does not necessarily improve the country's competitiveness. The 2006 ratings of competitiveness, issued by the World Economic Forum, showed that the Scandinavian economies—which have large public sectors and generous welfare safety nets—are among the most competitive. Finland and Sweden are ranked second and third in the survey (Switzerland ranked first). The U.S. dropped to sixth in 2006. [10]

We need to stop being cowed by the conservative obsession with private markets. Private markets are not goals; human success and survival are the goals. We must unapologetically, forcefully support the public sector and its appropriate use to allocate resources through the democratic process.

CHAPTER FORTY-TWO

The Progressive View of Labor, Wages, Income and the Control of Wealth

HUMAN BEINGS AREN'T COMMODITIES

Progressives categorically reject the right's claim that wages should be set by "private" markets and anything else is "artificial" or "unnatural." Human beings are not "commodities" to be bought and sold. They're the purpose of the economy, not objects to be chewed up and spit out when they're no longer needed. There is a huge population of unemployed workers in the developing world. In rural China alone there are 600 million people that not necessary to produce food and must be integrated into the non-agricultural economy. If we allow the right wing to make supply and demand the sole basis for wage rates and payment for labor, we will see a continued race to the bottom, lower and lower wages and salaries, and in the short-term, higher and higher corporate profits.

In August 2006, the *New York Times* reported that:

- Federal Reserve study showed that, "Wages and salaries now make up the lowest share of the nation's gross national product since the government began recording data in 1947; while corporate profits have climbed to their highest shares since the 1960s."

- In the third quarter of 2006, wages and salaries represented 45% of gross domestic product, down from about 50% in the first quarter of 2001 and 53.9% in 1970 according to the Commerce Department.

- A separate report from Goldman Sachs said: "The most important contributor to high profit margins over the past few years has been the decline in labor's share of national income."

- The cause of this decline is not decreased productivity of labor — far from it. From 2000 to 2006, worker productivity rose 166%, but total median compensation rose only 7.2%, according to a report for the Economic Policy Institute.

- According to the U.S. Census Bureau, median household income in the US dropped 5.9% from the 2000 census through 2005 — from $49,133 to $46,662. [1]

For many months in early 2006, the Republicans lectured the media, complaining that they had not been given credit for the country's high level of overall economic growth.

Of course, to start with, economic growth under Bush hasn't blown anyone's socks off. Bush claimed in his 2007 State of the Union message that "the recovery" has added more than 7.2 million jobs since August 2003. But the net number of jobs added since Bill Clinton left office in January 2001 was only 3.6 million because so many jobs were lost in the first years of Bush's Presidency. And 3.6 million pales in comparison to the 18 million jobs that the Bureau of Labor Statistics says were added by the sixth year of the Clinton Presidency. [2] Economist and columnist Paul Krugman responded to the Bush Administration's economic cheerleading in his column in The New York Times:

> Here's what happened in 2004. The US economy grew 4.2%, a very good number. Yet last August, the Census Bureau reported that real median family income—the purchasing power of the typical family—actually fell. Meanwhile, poverty increased, as did the number of Americans without health insurance. So where did it go?
>
> The answer comes from the economists Thomas Piketty and Emmanuel Saez, whose long-term estimates of income equality have become the gold standard for research on this topic, and who recently updated their estimates to include 2004. They show that even if you exclude capital gains from the rising stock market, in 2004 the real income of the richest 1% of Americans surged by almost 12.5%. Meanwhile, the average real income of the bottom 99% of the population rose only 1.5%. In other words, a relative handful of people received most of the benefits of growth.
>
> There are a couple of additional revelations in the 2004 data. One is the growth didn't just bypass the poor and lower middle class, it bypassed the upper middle class, too. Even people at the 95th percentile of the income distribution—that is people richer than 19 out of 20 Americans—gained only modestly. The big increases went only to people who were already in the economic stratosphere....
>
> In short, it's a great economy if you're a high-level corporate executive or someone who owns a lot of stock. For most other Americans, economic growth is a spectator sport. [3]

These changes in income distribution are not the result of "natural laws." They are the result of systems set up by human beings that differentially benefit different groups in the society.

At the beginning of the Great Depression, income inequality, and inequality in the control of wealth, was very high. Then came the great compression between 1929 and 1947. Real wages for workers in manufacturing rose 67% while real income for the richest 1% of Americans fell 17%. This period marked the birth of the American middle class. Two major forces drove these trends—unionization of major manufacturing sectors, and the public policies of the New Deal.

Then came the postwar boom 1947 to 1973. Real wages rose 81% and the income of the richest 1% rose 38%. Growth was widely shared, but income inequality continued to drop.

From 1973 to 1980, everyone lost ground. Real wages fell 3% and income for the richest 1% fell 4%. The oil shocks, and the dramatic slowdown in economic growth in developing nations, took their toll on America and the world economy.

Then came what Krugman calls "the New Gilded Age." Beginning in 1980, there were big gains at the very top. The tax policies of the Reagan administration magnified income redistribution. Between 1980 and 2004, real wages in manufacturing fell 1%, while real income of the richest one percent rose 135%.

Much as they like to tout the magic "natural" effects of the market on levels of wages, conservatives have not been shy about using the power of government to effect the distribution of the fruits of the US economy. They have slashed taxes for the rich and for corporations, and increased the relative tax burden on working people. And by cutting taxes for the rich, they have transferred wealth to the most affluent people in America from all of our children by increasing the federal debt.

Increased income inequality is completely unrelated to the relative contribution of various classes of the population to the nation's economic prosperity. It is also innately unfair and violates the progressive principal of equality. Finally, as McCarty, Poole and Rosenthal show, it causes political polarization. Their study found that there is a direct relationship between economic inequality and polarization in American politics. [4]

They measured political polarization in congressional votes over the last century, and found a direct correlation with the percentage of income received by the top 1% of the electorate.

They also compared the Gini Index of Income Inequality with congressional vote polarization of the last half-century and found a comparable relationship.

Of course, the increasing inequality of income leads inexorably to increasing inequality in the distribution of wealth. The net consequence is completely undemocratic. Power in the society is more and more concentrated in the hands of a few.

A May 2006 report from Citizens for Tax Justice summarizes the continuing trend toward wealth concentration:

> The new Federal Reserve report, Currents and Undercurrents: Changes in the Distribution of Wealth, 1989-2004, is based on the latest data from the

survey of consumer finances, which is generally recognized as the best data source for measuring wealth inequality in the US.

- *The wealthiest 1% of Americans owned 33.4% of the wealth in 2004, up from 30.1% in 1989.*
- *The wealthiest 5% of Americans held 55.5% of the wealth in 2004.*
- *The poorest 50% of the American population collectively owned 2.5% of the wealth in 2004, down from 3% in 1989.*
- *The very wealthiest 1% of Americans now own a bigger piece of the pie (33.4%) than the poorest 90% put together (30.4%).*

For some specific types of wealth, this inequality is even greater:

- The wealthiest 1% of Americans owned 62.3% of business assets in 2004.
- The wealthiest 5% collectively owned 88.7% of business assets.
- The wealthiest 5%, also own 93.7% of the value of bonds, 71.7% of non-residential real estate, and 79.1% of the value of stocks.[5]

For Progressives, there are four major means of affecting the distribution of income in America's mixed economy:

> • **Unionization.** Unions are premised on the notion that supply and demand is not the be-all and end-all for determining who gets what share of the national income. The right to collectively bargain wages and benefits fundamentally negates the ultimate status of the marketplace in determining who gets what.

> • **Minimum wage and living-wage laws and other laws governing labor rights.** Minimum wage laws are set to provide a floor on wages. They should assure that everyone who works receives enough income to allow him to have a reasonable standard of living. Minimum wages should be living wages. Before the new Democratic Congress raised the minimum wage in early 2007, it had fallen to a 50-year low (adjusted for inflation). At the same time CEOs salaries had skyrocketed. We have seen that before Americans broke for lunch on January 2, 2007, the CEOs of the nation's top companies—those with $1 billion or more in annual revenue—*made more in the first two hours and two minutes of the first work day of the year than a full time minimum wage worker will make the entire year.* No economic theory can justify that.
> The slide in the minimum wage helped keep massive numbers of Americans in poverty—37 million. In 2005, half of those were below the "half poverty" line—in "deep poverty"—$7,500 for a family of three ($150 per week). [6]

By increasing the minimum wage in 2007, the Democratic Congress made a down payment on a "living wage" that must remain a fundamental progressive goal.

Left to itself, the "market" will do nothing to stop child labor, to prevent workers from being endangered by on-the-job hazards and shortened work weeks, or to end sweatshops. Unions and government are necessary to provide these protections.

• **Policies that determine who pays for and gets benefits from government.** The combined effects of the tax and service cuts of the Reagan and Bush eras have shifted trillions of dollars from average Americans to the wealthiest 1% of the population. If they had their way, the repeal of the estate tax by itself would shift another trillion dollars to the sons and daughters of multimillionaires and take it from education, healthcare, nutrition programs and other programs of our government.

On the other hand, as Franklin D. Roosevelt demonstrated, the actions of government can massively affect who gets how big a piece of the common economic pie.

• **Trade Policies.** Trade policies have a big impact on the distribution of income. Manufacturing wages have dropped in substantial measure, because there is a gigantic Third World workforce willing to work for much less than what is necessary to provide good wages for Americans. Government policy throughout the last 25 years has allowed the race to the bottom to continue unimpeded.

The United States trade negotiators have turned somersaults in order to protect property rights and have done virtually nothing to protect the rights of labor to unionize or to have protection from exploitation.

Worldwide economic integration is inevitable and desirable. The question is whether it is to be done the way that the European Union integrated Europe—by bringing low-income nations like Ireland, Portugal, Greece and East Germany up—or by bringing the standard of living in America down (at least for most Americans) to the level of the developing world.

There is no reason why our trade policy cannot protect the rights of labor and worldwide environmental standards in the same way it protects the rights of capital and intellectual property.

Big international business wants unfettered access to cheap labor with no restrictions worldwide. If it is allowed to prevail, that policy will yield a low-wage economy in the United States that is completely inconsistent with progressive values.

A HIGH WAGE ECONOMY—BOTTOM-UP NOT TOP-DOWN GROWTH—FORGET ABOUT TRICKLE-DOWN ECONOMICS

When I was in the federal prison camp at Terre Haute, my job as an inmate was working in the library. For this I received $5.25 *per month*—that's right, per month. It was the extreme case of a low-wage economy.

In the library, we managed the interlibrary loan program for the entire Terre Haute federal prison complex, which included our prison camp, and the medium and high security prisons. The only thing was, we did this without the benefit of computers or a database. We did it manually. What would take seconds on computers would take hours manually.

Allegedly we had no computers to track hundreds of books, borrowers and source libraries, because the Bureau of Prisons was afraid that if inmates had excess to computers (not to the Internet, just computers), they could be dangerous. I have yet to figure out exactly how. But you can bet that they would have found a way to allow us to have computers if they had to pay me $20 an hour, rather than $5.25 a month to manage the data. And that's a very import an economic fact.

Innovation in labor-saving technology—the development of processes and technologies that increase productivity—do not occur when labor prices are cheap. They occur when wages are high.

A high-wage economy leads to major long-term economic dividends:

* It incentivizes companies to invest in higher productivity technologies that increase overall productivity and provide real economic growth.

* It creates customers with spending power to drive economic growth. There is a natural tendency of market economies to use low-cost labor and increase profits. That's good for each company's bottom line, but it kills off the goose that lays the golden egg by reducing the buying power of its ultimate customers—the people who work for all the companies in the economy combined.

Government policies that encourage unionization and a living minimum wage offset that tendency and help the economy grow over the long haul. They provide a break on the natural tendency of market economies to concentrate income and wealth among the owners of corporations.

While low-wage economies may be good for specific companies, high-wage economies are good for everyone—by incentivizing innovation that increases productivity and by turbocharging economic demand.

That is why the progressive vision of the economy is one that begins with the premise that the economy is driven from the bottom up, not the top down. We do not believe that the engine of economic growth is supply. It is demand. Productive investment in innovation responds to the presence of demand, not the other way around. This is perhaps the clearest contrast between radical conservative economic and progressive economics. "Trickle-down" economics has never worked to stimulate long-term economic growth, and it never will. It only works to legitimate the insatiable appetite of the very rich.

And it is just one more example where the radical conservative moral system and its commitment only to the pursuit of individual interest fails to deliver. The private self-interest of a few undermines the interest of the society at large.

In *Wealth and Democracy: A Political History of the American Rich*, Kevin Phillips summarizes his case against "trickle-down economics."

He argues that the economic history of the 20th century demonstrates that economic growth happens from the bottom up, not the top down. He points out that:

- From 1933 to the early 1970s, real disposable income increased by over 130% for average Americans. Gross domestic product grew virtually continuously. That growth occurred on the strength of a broader and broader distribution of wealth and income—more consumers who could buy products. This was the same time when hundreds of new protections for average Americans were passed by our Congress—Social Security, Medicare, the Wagner Act that allowed serious labor organizing, and the minimum wage. 1968 marked the century's peak of purchasing power for the federal minimum wage.

- During the same period, the percentage of wealth on the top 1% of the population shrunk from a high in 1929—the year of the stock market crash—to a low in 1976.

- Since the early 1970s, the percentage of wealth on the top 1% has once again skyrocketed to 1929 levels—all as part of the new "supply side" philosophy that claimed that the increased wealth of a few would "trickle down" to everyone else.

- But today, the median income of the typical American family is right now almost the same as it was in 1969. [7]

The myth that tax cuts for the rich somehow benefit the economy as a whole, as well as average workers, has proven to be baloney. Phillips points out that during the greatest war of the 20th century, it was wealthy

Americans who were called upon to pay more for the war effort—not given tax breaks as they have been during the war on terrorism and the war in Iraq.

- During World War II, the tax bite on wealthy Americans was close to punitive (the highest bracket was 91%). But that didn't hurt the economy; far from it. By war's end, Americans were rolling in cash. The average weekly pay had been boosted from $24.20 in 1940 to $44.39 in 1945. Many families had their first discretionary income.

- Between mid-1943 and mid-1945, Americans stashed away about a quarter of their take-home pay. By 1945, they had $140 billion in liquid assets (mostly small savings accounts and war bonds)—twice the entire national income for 1939.

By the most conservative measures, the inflation-adjusted average wage of American workers has stagnated, while those of other industrialized countries has increased. Wages in those places rose during the 1980's and 90's, while their working hours shortened. U.S. wages stagnated while our hours increased.

- Phillips writes: ".... the evidence indicates the transformation of the United States from its high wage and best working condition status during the quarter century after 1945 to a society that, for the bulk of its workforce, was increasingly middling in wages, harsh in hours worked, and more stinting in its benefits."

- "The probable slippage of US wages below those of Holland, Denmark, Switzerland, Sweden, and Norway by the end of the 1990s was only part of the story. The yearly hours worked in those five nations, for example, were so much less than the 1,966 put in by Americans in 1997—just 1,300 in Norway, 1,552 in Sweden, 1,643 in Switzerland, 1,689 in Denmark and 1,679 in Netherlands—that data showing the five's superior health coverage, lower stress and hypertension, vastly longer paid vacations, serious job retraining programs, and lengthier dismissal notice requirements, burnishing already strong comparison. The bottom economic two-thirds of the population in these countries had overtaken their American counterparts." [8]

The myth of laissez-faire capitalism that makes fortunes is just that. The fact is that political and governmental power underlies most great fortunes—and economic success in general.

- Whether it is through the management of governmental debt, expanding or contracting credit in the money supply, the use of tax policy, governmental purchasing power, or investments in new cutting-edge technologies—governmental action has been involved in the creation of wealth throughout modern history.

- The question is not whether the power of government will be used to shape the economy—the question is whether it will be used to benefit the wealthiest in America or everyone else.

- The financial community loves to talk about leaving the market free to work its will—but consider what has happened when the interests of the financial community itself are put at risk: bailouts—to the tune of hundreds of billions of dollars. For example: the bailout of major banks (like Continental Illinois), rescue from a threatened Latin American default on bond payments (1983), a stock market flooded with liquidity on the day after its October 19, 1987 crash, the Savings & Loan bailout, the rescue of the collapsing Mexican peso—with its threat to US bondholders—the rescue of Asian currencies in banks (1997), and the arrangements by (former Federal Reserve Chairman) Alan Greenspan for Wall Street to bail out Long Term Capital Management (1998). [9]

THE ECONOMY AND THE LONG RUN

Over the last 50 years, the U.S. economy has become more and more focused on short-term results at the expense of the long run. That's because of the increasing securitization of assets.

Where at one point in history, a corporation or individual might own plants, equipment or companies, today they own securities that can be sold in highly liquid markets. Mortgages are packaged and resold as securities on secondary mortgage markets. Risk is repackaged, sliced and diced as derivatives. All of this makes capital markets more efficient—and transparent. But it also makes the owners of capital very impatient.

If returns drop, you can make a trade in seconds to a more profitable stock, bond, derivative or share.

As a result, managers are forced to concentrate ever more heavily on short-term return in order to support its company's stock price. Next quarter looms larger and larger at the expense of the long run.

Government representing the community's interest, and unions representing employees, must set rules of the economic game that require focus on the long run. Stockholders and highly liquid capital markets simply will not do so. This is particularly true when it comes to social costs that can be externalized by companies, like the disposal of effluent or the effects of greenhouse gases.

The success and survival of society requires a focus on the long run. But management is required by the discipline of the impatient market to focus on the short run instead.

Now let's summarize several key progressive values when it comes to the economy:

- Progressives believe that the market "supply and demand" by itself is not the "natural" or appropriate means of distributing the fruits of our economic activity. We believe that everyone deserves enough income to provide the basic conditions of human existence in American society—a living wage. That should be a baseline requirement for the economic game.

- Progressives believe that employees deserve to have the kind of power over their conditions of employment that can only be provided by free, independent unions and that unionization should be encouraged, not shackled by government policy.

- Progressives believe that private markets should be used to allocate resources where they are appropriate, but that democratic governmental structures should be used when *they* are most appropriate—including health insurance, Social Security and many other key economic activities.

- Progressives believe that trade agreements must place just as much priority on the rights of labor and the environment as they do on property rights. Trade deals should be structured to bring developing countries up to our standards of living, not drag our economies toward developing world standards of income.

- Progressives believe in a high wage economy, not "trickle-down" economics. We believe that a high wage economy helps spur innovation and productivity growth and produces high levels of economic demand for products and services. We believe that economic growth is driven from the bottom up, not the top down.

- Progressives oppose great inequality in the distribution of income and wealth. These differences do not reflect the relative contribution of various groups to economic productivity; they cause social and political polarization, and violate the progressive principle in equality and fairness. And most importantly, they serve to concentrate economic power and create an undemocratic society.

WE'RE ALL IN THIS TOGETHER

Our battle with the right in America is far from a simple dispute over which policies are best for the country. It centers on two very distinctly different worldviews, moral systems and visions of the future. And the stakes could not be higher.

In order to win we must ground our argument, our messaging, and our imagination in these values. Our values and our assumptions about the world form the basis for the most critical metaphor we use to describe what we believe—our vision of the future. When people are asked to follow, they want to know where you want to take them. It is to a progressive vision of the future that we now turn.

SECTION EIGHT

THE PROGRESSIVE VISION FOR THE FUTURE

CHAPTER FORTY-THREE

It's a High Stakes Game

SYLVIA LAZAR

For the first few years after my wife, Jan, and I were married in 1980, her Great Aunt lived with us during the week. Jan and I both worked, so Aunt Sylv looked after the house and was very involved in raising Jan's two kids and my daughter.

Sylvia Lazar was a warm, wonderful woman who by that time was in her 70s. She'd come to the United States as a teenager from the Ukraine, and still spoke with a thick accent.

Sylvia had grown up in a Ukrainian *schtetle* — a small peasant town where the family purchased water each day from a salesman who carried two buckets from the river on a yoke over his neck. Oxen and horses were the principal means used to transport goods and people. Life in her *schtetle* was very much as it had been for hundreds of years.

Her family moved to the United States by way of Canada in the early part of the last century to escape anti-Semitism and find a better life.

By the time she died in the mid-1980's, the world around her had been transformed. In the place of oxen, she had flown on jet planes, lived in air-conditioned homes with running water and indoor plumbing. She lived to see the development of antibiotics that changed forever the treatment of infectious disease. She watched a television as men landed on the moon.

Worldwide, life expectancy had skyrocketed. The standard of living in the developed world had exploded.

But Sylv had also lived through two great world wars that had killed tens of millions. She had seen six million of her fellow European Jews systematically slaughtered in the Holocaust. She'd seen pictures of the explosion of the atomic bomb and lived through an accelerating arms race and cold war between America and the USSR that included her old homeland.

She watched with all Americans as the world approached the edge of the nuclear precipice during the Cuban missile crisis. And she had cheered on her niece Jan, who become active in fighting the growing environmental crisis brought on by exploding human economic activity.

Over the tiny span of one lifetime, Sylvia Lazar had been witness to the qualitative transformation of society its culture and technology. She had seen both the breathtaking possibilities and the horrific dangers unleashed by the accelerating march of human history.

Whenever I think how hard it is to make social change, I think about Aunt Sylv.

In the thick of political battle, it's often difficult to see the qualitative change. But all you need to do is back up a little distance from the everyday struggle to see how quickly our world has been, and is being, transformed before our eyes.

Only 152 years ago, America was ending its great Civil War. Human slavery was abolished in America a mere seven generations ago.

That century-and-a-half represents .002% of the 7 million years of human evolutionary development. It represents only 1% of the 13,000 years since humans made the critical evolutionary advance — agriculture.

Politics is fundamentally the means through which human societies make choices about their futures. In this section we will explore the progressive vision of what our future should be.

Radical conservatives like to argue that the world is a dangerous place—that the tough, hard-nosed values of the "strict father" metaphor are necessary to protect our survival. They claim that only by standing up fiercely for our own self-interest will we be successful at defending America and the values of "Western civilization." They claim that radical conservative values are tough, and that progressive values are soft.

THE WORLD IS A DANGEROUS PLACE

But progressive values are the farthest thing from "pie-in-the-sky," "soft," "unrealistic," "head-in-the-clouds" precepts for action. In fact, progressive values allow us the best opportunity to survive and succeed in the future world that is simultaneously bristling with unprecedented danger, and beckoning with undreamt-of opportunity for our children and future generations.

If radical conservatives are allowed to continue using their values to chart our future course, human society as a whole could face calamity, much as isolated segments of human society have in the past.

A great deal is at stake in the political decisions we make over the next several decades.

Our progressive vision for the future is defined by how we apply our values to our historic situation, to the challenges and possibilities presented us by history. So to discuss the progressive vision, we have to start by looking at the major challenges and possibilities facing human society in the 21st century. First we'll put things in context by quickly summarizing the major developments on the path of social evolution that got us here to this critical crossroads.

CHAPTER FORTY-FOUR

Seven Million Years of Social Evolution—Diamond's Analysis

In his Pulitzer prize-winning book *Guns, Germs, and Steel*, physiologist and ethno-geographer Jared Diamond analyzes the forces of human social evolution since the end of the last ice age. His study identifies major characteristics of social evolution that I believe are central to understanding the challenges we face as we discuss the progressive vision of the future.

This chapter summarizes a portion of Diamond's analysis.

Human history—as something distinct from animals—began about seven million years ago when a population of African apes broke into several groups. One evolved into the modern gorillas, the second into modern chimps, and the third into humans. [1]

For the first five to six million years, human ancestors remained in Africa. Somewhere between one and two million years ago, there is evidence that the human ancestor Homo Erectus had migrated to Asia. The first unquestionable evidence for humans in Europe occurred about 500,000 years ago. That is also about the same time that Homo Sapiens evolved out of Homo Erectus. About that time we also have the first documented evidence of human use of fire.

From that point forward, human populations in Africa and Western Eurasia seem to have diverged. Neanderthals, sometimes classified as a separate species Homo Neanderthalensis, came to dominate Europe for about 200,000 years.

Human history really took off around 50,000 years ago with a great leap forward and the emergence of Cro-Magnon humans that were biologically and behaviorally modern humans.

Diamond argues that this great leap was caused in considerable part by the development of the human voice box that provided the anatomical basis for modern language upon which the exercise of human creativity is dependent. Others focus on a change in brain organization.

About 40,000 years ago, Cro-Magnons moved into Europe. Within 5,000 to 10,000 years, they had completely displaced Neanderthals. The Neanderthals appear to have been an evolutionary dead end.

The great leap coincided with the first proven major extension of human geographic range since the human expansion from Africa to Eurasia. Humans occupied Australia/New Guinea (then a single continent). During the Ice Age, so much of the ocean's water was locked up in ice caps that worldwide sea levels dropped hundreds of feet lower than today—leaving much of the shallow sea separating archipelagoes of Southeast Asia completely dry. But Australia was always divided from Southeast Asia by a deepwater channel. So the expansion of humans to there constituted the first known use of watercraft and navigation skills.

The Americas were first colonized between 35,000 and 14,000 years ago. The first unquestioned sites of human habitation are dated about 12,000 B.C. in Alaska. Humans had migrated over the Bering Strait land bridge from Siberia (which itself was unoccupied until about 20,000 years ago). The entire North and South American continents were occupied within about a thousand years. That completed the occupation of most habitable areas on continents and continental islands.

The settlement of the world's remaining islands was not completed until modern times—the Mediterranean islands between 8500 and 4000 BC; the Caribbean islands around 4000 B.C; Polynesia and Micronesian were occupied between 1200 B.C. and A.D. 1000; Madagascar between A.D. 300 and 800; Iceland in the ninth century A.D.; and the high Arctic around 2000 B.C. Only the most remote islands in the Atlantic and Pacific (Azores and Seychelles) and Antarctica remained for European exploration over the last 700 years. [2]

The second great qualitative event in human history occurred after the last ice age—about 13,000 years ago. It was the discovery of food production and agriculture.

For most of their seven-million-year history, humans were hunter-gatherers. They hunted wild animals and gathered wild plants. Food production involved domesticating wild animals and plants and eating the resulting livestock and crops. Today most people eat food that they produce themselves or what someone else has produced for them. Diamond predicts that at the current rate, the few remaining bands of hunter-gatherers will abandon their ways, die out, or disintegrate within the next decade, ending our millions of years of commitment to the hunter-gathering lifestyle. [3]

Diamond argues that the geographic advantages that allowed some groups to develop food production before others were heavily responsible for the accelerated capacity and power of human societies in Eurasia, compared with the rest of the world:

> In short, plant and animal domestication meant much more food, and hence much denser human populations. The resulting food surpluses, and (in

some areas) the animal - based means of transporting these surpluses, were
a prerequisite for the development of settled, politically centralized, socially
stratified, economically complex, technologically innovative societies. Hence,
the availability of domestic plants and animals ultimately explains why
empires, literacy, and steel weapons developed earliest in Eurasia, and later
or not at all on other continents. The military uses of horses and camels, and
the killing power of animal - derived germs, complete the list of the major
links between food production and conquest... [4]

FROM HUNTER-GATHERERS TO MODERN SOCIETY

Diamond has done substantial work among the societies in New
Guinea. In *Guns, Germs, and Steel,* he introduces his readers to the Fayu
people. The Fayu lived in single families scattered through the swamp that
came together once or twice a year to negotiate exchanges and brides.

They consist of 400 people, divided into four clans, wandering over 500
square miles. According to their own account, they formally numbered
about 2,000, but the population had been depleted by Fayu killing Fayu.
They lack any political or social mechanisms to achieve the peaceful
resolution of serious disputes.

As recently as 1500, less than 20% of the world's land area was marked
off by boundaries into states run by bureaucrats and governed by laws.
Today all of the land except Antarctica is divided into states.

"Descendents of those societies that achieved centralized government
and organized religion earliest ended up dominating the modern world.
The combination of government and religion has thus functioned,
together with germs, writing and technology, as one of the four main
sets of proximate agents leading to history's broadest pattern," [5] writes
Diamond.

Diamond divides human societies into four general categories: bands,
tribes, chieftains, and states. Fayu bands and modern state-based societies
represent the opposite extremes along the spectrum of human societies.

BANDS

Bands typically consist of five to 80 people, most close relatives by
birth or marriage. Today all modern bands are or were nomadic hunter-
gatherers, not settled food producers. Most today live in resource-poor
areas. Most that live autonomously do so today in Amazonian and New
Guinea.

Most likely all humans lived in bands until 40,000 years ago. Most still
did as recently as 11,000 years ago.

Bands have no permanent single base of residence. Land is used jointly by members of the entire group. There is no regular economic specialization except by age and sex. All able-bodied individuals forage for food.

There are no formal institutions to resolve conflicts—within or between bands. Social structure is egalitarian in the sense that there is no formal social stratification, no hereditary leadership, no formal monopoly on information used to make group decisions. Leadership is informal, but is acquired through many of the same qualities voters use to choose candidates—personality, strength, intelligence and fighting skills.

Populations are not dense, because the hunter-gatherer lifestyle can support only a limited number of individuals on an area which they occupy.

The band is a form of social organization that we inherited from millions of years of evolutionary history. Our closest animal relatives, guerrillas, chimpanzees and the baboons of Africa still live in bands.

As humans began to develop more complex social structures during the last tens of thousands of years, the first step was the tribe.

TRIBES

Tribes typically included hundreds, rather than dozens, of people and generally have fixed settlements—though some tribes and chiefdoms are herders that move annually.

Tribes are all now variously subordinated to nation-states. They still occupy much of New Guinea, Melanesia, and Amazonia.

Tribes began to emerge around 13,000 years ago in the fertile crescent located between the eastern Mediterranean Sea and the Persian Gulf, extending into portions of present-day Turkey.

The prerequisite for living in settlements is either food production or else a productive environment of extremely concentrated resources such as some groups of Native Americans found in northwest North America. Settlements and tribes began to proliferate in the Fertile Crescent about 13,000 years ago when climate changes that came at the end of the last major Ice Age combined with improved technology to permit abundant harvests of wild cereals.

Tribes differed from bands not only in size, but because they consisted of more than one recognized kinship group—called clans. These clans exchanged marriage partners and often owned land rather than it belonging to the entire tribe.

Tribes were still small enough so that everyone knew each other by name or relationship. The maximum number where this is possible is a group of several hundred. As we've seen, groups of larger size require structures—missing in tribes—to resolve disputes between strangers.

Tribes still had informal systems of government. Information control and decision-making were communal. Leadership was taken by "big men" who had no independent decision-making authority and achieved their status by their own personal attributes. The position was not inherited.

There were no ranked lineages or classes. Like bands, tribes lacked bureaucracy, taxes and police forces. There was little economic specialization. Every able-bodied adult—including the big men—participated in growing, gathering or hunting food.

The economies of tribes were based on reciprocal exchanges between individuals and families. There was no redistribution of tribute paid to a central authority or need for a market economy.

CHIEFDOMS

In A.D. 1492 when Columbus landed in the New World, chiefdoms were still widespread over much of eastern North America, South and Central America, sub-Saharan Africa and Polynesia.

They rose for the first time around 5500 B.C. in the Fertile Crescent and by 1000 B.C. in Mesoamerica and the Andes.

Chiefdoms were considerably larger than tribes, ranging from several thousand to tens of thousands of people. Because the vast majority of people in the chiefdom did not know each other or have a kinship relationship, chiefdoms required that people develop mechanisms for resolving conflicts between strangers—how to encounter strangers regularly without attempting to kill them.

Part of the problem was solved by designating one person—the chief—to exercise a monopoly on the right to use force.

Chiefs held recognized positions of leadership and inherited the office. They established a permanent centralized authority, made all significant decisions and had a monopoly on critical information. In general, the large populations of chiefdoms required food generated by food production—though in a few isolated chiefdoms, dependence on hunter-gathering existed in very rich areas.

Chiefdoms were characterized by public architecture and luxury goods that were not available to commoners. They included multiple lineages. But whereas the lineages of tribes are equally ranked, those of chiefdoms have hereditary perquisites.

Chiefdoms required greater economic specialization—and required craftspeople and menial servants. These jobs could be fulfilled by slaves captured in raids on other groups.

While continuing to rely heavily on reciprocal exchanges, and without markets or money, chiefdoms developed the addition of a redistributive economy. The chief would receive a portion of the harvest and redistribute a portion of that to commoners, with a portion returned to support craftsmen and retainers of the chief.

From the commoners, the chief claimed both goods and labor to construct public works, which might benefit the entire tribe or merely benefit the chief. Chiefdoms varied considerably by size and complexity.

Chiefdoms introduced the problem which characterize all complex, centrally governed societies. On the one hand, they developed a class that did not engage directly in food production and enabled activity that made possible large projects that benefit everyone, but were not possible for small groups of individuals to undertake on their own. At the same time, they functioned as kleptocracies transferring wealth from commoners to the upper classes.

Diamond points out:

> The differences between a kleptocrat and a wise statesman, between a robber baron and a public benefactor, is merely one of degree: a matter of just how large a percentage of the tribute extracted from producers is retained by the elite, and how much the commoners like the public uses to which the redistributed tribute is put. [6]

Elites throughout the ages have used a mixture of four solutions to solve this problem:

1) Disarm the populace and arm the elite—create a monopoly on physical force.
2) Make the masses happy by redistributing much of the tribute in popular ways.
3) Use the monopoly of force to promote happiness, by maintaining public order and curbing violence. The archaeological evidence shows that murder was the leading cause of death in bands and tribes. Resolving conflict without violence was a critical competitive advantage of more centralized societies.
4) Construct an ideology or religion justifying the elite's power. Supernatural beliefs were held by tribes and bands, but they were not used to justify central authority or the transfer of wealth, or to maintain peace between unrelated individuals. When supernatural beliefs and other ideological systems became institutionalized and gained this function, they were transformed into religions.

Chiefdoms typically have an ideology or system of religious beliefs to buttress the chief's authority. Chiefs often combine their positions of political leadership and priest—or supported a separate group of priests.

Religion and ideology not only justified the chief's power, they also provided a bond not based on kinship and a motive for sacrificing their lives on behalf of others. This was an enormous competitive advantage since, at the cost of a few individuals who died in battle, the whole society becomes more effective at conquering other societies and resisting attack.

STATES

States arose for the first time around 3700 B.C. in Mesopotamia and around 300 A.D. in Mesoamerica, over 2000 years ago in the Andes, China and Southeast Asia, and a thousand years ago in West Africa. They have continuously evolved out of chiefdoms.

Today, states rule all the world's land area except Antarctica. Whereas chiefdoms have populations of thousands, or tens of thousands, states range in size upwards to China's 1.3 billion.

The paramount chief's location becomes a capital city. Other population centers become cities as well, which are lacking in chiefdoms.

Cities differ from villages in their large public works, accumulation of capital from taxes, tribute or other means of capital accumulation, and in the concentration of many people other than food producers. Early states had hierarchical leaders, with titles equivalent to King. They exercised even greater monopolies of information, decision-making and power.

Central control became more extensive, and economic redistribution through taxes more far-reaching. Economic specialization grew substantially, to a point where today even farmers are not self-sufficient.

Many early states adopted slavery on a much larger scale since economic specialization, with more mass production and public works, provided more uses for slave labor.

There was a proliferation of vertical levels of bureaucrats and horizontal specialization. Internal conflict resolution became formalized in laws, a judiciary and police.

Most states developed a literate class. (The Incas did not). Writing developed around the same time as states in both Mesopotamia and Mesoamerica. Initially writing was used to keep track of goods, especially food. Later it was also used extensively to record bureaucratic or kingly actions, histories and laws.

Early states had state religions and standardized temples.

States developed and extended many of the characteristics of chiefdoms, but also added new qualitative changes. States were organized around geographic areas instead of kinship groups. Chieftains, tribes and bands usually consisted of one ethnic or linguistic group. States, especially empires founded by amalgamating states, were often multiethnic and multilingual.

State bureaucracies were no longer selected mainly based on kinship, but as professions on the basis of training and ability.

In latter-day states, leadership has become non-hereditary and many states have abandoned the entire system of formal hereditary classes handed down from chiefdoms.

THE TREND TOWARD COMPLEXITY

Diamond argues that "over the last 13,000 years, the predominant trend in human society has been the replacement of smaller, less complex units, with larger, more complex ones." [7]

This is because larger structures have a comparative advantage when two societies collide. Larger, more complex societies start with a numeric advantage. Their complexity gives them the ability to develop technological superiority. They have centralized decision-makers that can concentrate troops and resources, and they have official religions and patriotic fervor that can make their troops fight suicidally to defeat an enemy.

This last feature is a major break with previous human history. The idea that someone would willingly die for his state or religion would never occur to a member of a band or a tribe.

Diamond points out that in his experience in New Guinea there has never been a single hint of tribal patriotism, of a suicidal charge or any other military conduct carrying the accepted risk of death. Instead, raids are initiated by ambush or by superior force to minimize at all costs the risk of death. But this attitude puts severe limits on the military operations of tribes and bands.

What makes patriotic and religious fanatics so dangerous is their willingness to accept the deaths of many of their numbers, including themselves, to destroy the enemy.

"Fanaticism in war, of the type that drove Christian and Islamic conquest, was probably unknown on earth until chiefdoms and especially states emerged within the last 6000 years." [8]

Diamond argues that the major factor contributing to complexity is population size, and a major factor enabling the growth of population per area was the development of food production. Social complexity, in turn, led to even more intensified food production.

Food production also contributed to social complexity in other ways:

- Food production allows the production of stored food surpluses, which permit economic specialization and stratification. The surpluses enable the development of nonfood-producing classes — chiefs, bureaucrats, scribes, craftspeople, soldiers and farmers who during some of the year can do public works. This enables the deployment of time and labor for the creation of technological innovation, accumulation of knowledge and investment in improved agricultural production. If all members of the society are engaged in feeding themselves, society never has the resources to invest in increasing future productivity. In economic terms, it only consumes; it never invests.

- It allows seasonally pulsed inputs of labor. When surpluses are stored, farmers can be called upon to build monuments, fight wars, or undertake investment activities that increase production (e.g., irrigation projects).

- Food production requires people to adopt sedentary living, which is a prerequisite to accumulating possessions, economic investment, the development of elaborate technologies and crafts, and building public works.

The larger population densities, made possible by food production, made more complex societies inevitable.

Growth of population requires the development of institutions to resolve conflicts between unrelated strangers. Size makes it impossible to continue with completely communal decision-making. Many more decisions must be made and their responsibilities must be delegated to specialize decision-makers. Society-wide decisions must be centralized.

Economic necessity also requires that larger societies can no longer function with reciprocal or barter types of economy. There are too many pairs of people, and increasingly too many specialists. Means must be found to capture surplus production and redistribute it to nonfood producers. Characteristically, this happens through governments, or through markets and money.

Finally, as population increases, population density also increases. This forces people to deal with each other continuously, where with less population density they did not have to do so. Holland, for example, could not divide its 16,000 square miles and 16 million people into 800,000 individual territories each encompassing 13 acres and serving as home for a band of 20 self-sufficient people.

How does the process of amalgamation of small societies happen? Diamond says:

Societies with effective conflict resolution, sound decision-making, and harmonious economic redistribution can develop better technology, concentrate their military power, seize larger and more productive territories, and crush autonomous smaller states one by one.... More generally, large units potentially enjoy an advantage over individual small units, if—and that's a big "if"—the large units can solve the problems that come with their larger size, such as perennial threats from upstart claimants to leadership, resentment of kleptocracy, and increased problems associated with economic integration. [9]

Historically, societies have merged only in one of two circumstances:
- Merger under common threat
- Actual conquest

Various examples abound. The United States was born out of a common conflict with Britain. The European Union was organized to prevent any of its members from once again launching a debilitating war against the others and as part of a strategy to bolster Western Europe against the Soviet bloc in the Cold War. The Aztec, Inca and Roman empires were all formed by military conquest.

Wars or threats of wars have historically played a key role in most amalgamations in society.

Though wars have been a factor throughout human history, their effect in causing amalgamations has accelerated as population density has increased. This is because of the impact of population density on the fate of the vanquished.

If population density is low, losers simply move their hunter-gathering to greener pastures. If density is moderate, survivors have nowhere to go. The tribal societies have no economic specialization and no use for slaves—except perhaps to take women in marriage. Men are killed and the victor occupies the territory of the losers.

If population density is high and the conflict is between states, the losers still have nowhere to go, but the victor has two options. Because of economic specialization, the victor can make slaves of the losers. Or, if the losers produce substantial food surpluses, they can be left on the land, deprived of political autonomy, and made to pay taxes or tribute. This is the usual result of battles leading to the formation of states or empires.

TECHNOLOGICAL DEVELOPMENT

Diamond's discussion of the process of technological development is particularly important for understanding the challenges that face us today.

For millions of years, human technological development was barely discernible. Today it has accelerated to a dizzying pace.

Major qualitative increases in the spread of technological development occurred at the two key milestones in human development:
1) The period of the "great leap forward" 100,000 to 50,000 years ago. This was associated with changes in human brain structure and anatomy and led immediately to great innovation in tool making.

2) The development of a sedentary lifestyle, made possible by food production 13,000 years ago. Sedentary life was decisive, because it made possible non-portable possessions. It also allowed for the development of economic specialization by nonfood producers, fed by food-producing peasants.

Technology tends to develop most rapidly in a context with the fewest barriers to diffusion. The more societies and people are available to serve as opportunities for innovation, the more likely innovations will occur and survive. As a result, technology develops fastest in large productive regions with large populations, many potential inventors and many competing societies.

The continent with the earliest development of food production and sedentary communities, the largest population, and fewest barriers to diffusion was Eurasia.

The importance of diffusion can't be overstated. The spread of the technology of food production itself occurred most easily in Eurasia because it lay on an east-west axis with common climate and no insurmountable physical barriers. This allowed the food package (wheat, barley, etc.) that first developed in the Mediterranean climate of the Fertile Crescent to spread speedily to Europe, Egypt and the Indus Valley.

The food package that developed indigenously in Mesoamerica did not spread easily north and south because of the ecological and physical barriers posed by the climatic changes that occur over different latitudes of the north-south axis. It was further complicated by the barrier of the Isthmus of Panama.

The same was true of other technological innovation. For instance, wheels were invented in Mesoamerica. Llamas were domesticated in the central Andes. But over a period of 5000 years, America's sole beast of burden and wheels did not come into contact.

The values of various societies also played major roles. The Japanese were very impressed by the guns they encountered when first visited by the Portuguese. By 1600 A.D., they owned more and better guns than any other society. But for the samurai warrior class, swords were symbols of social status and a means of subjugating the lower classes. They moved to restrict gun production and ultimately virtually eliminated guns from Japan. As an isolated island society, Japan could take this step until its situation changed with the arrival of Admiral Perry.

After successful development of navigation technology, China abandoned oceangoing ships, mechanical clocks and water-driven spring mechanisms for cultural reasons for generations.

One of the reasons that the Norse Greenland society of the Middle Ages ultimately collapsed was its cultural unwillingness to adopt technologies from the neighboring Inuits. These include boat designs and hunting techniques that were adapted to Greenland and could have massively increased their food base. But these innovations would have challenged the values—and the power, prestige and narrow interests of their chiefs–so they were not adopted. Instead, they stubbornly stuck with the European values and technology they brought with them—and ultimately starved.

Most new technologies are not invented by societies. They are borrowed. That is one of the reasons why diffusion and openness to change are such important factors in spurring technological innovation. Writing, for instance, had only a few independent origins. Others, like the water wheel, the magnetic compass, the window, the camera obscura, were only invented once. That's because a new innovation can spread more rapidly than it can be independently invented.

Technology spreads in a one of two ways:

1) Other societies see or learn of the innovation and adopt it.
2) Societies lacking innovation find themselves at a competitive disadvantage vis-à-vis the inventing society and are overwhelmed or replaced if the disadvantage is great enough. The gun is an obvious example.

Contrary to myth, technological innovation does not normally occur to solve an unmet need. Instead, it results from people driven by curiosity or love of tinkering who look for an application once a device is invented.

Christensen, in *The Innovator's Dilemma*, makes this point in the context of modern business. He argues that one of the reasons why disruptive technologies are not often developed by large companies is that there is no way to measure a potential market for these new innovations. The small companies that develop these technologies "develop" new markets—i.e. new applications and needs. [10]

Finally and perhaps most important as we look to the future, Diamond argues that:

> *Technology's history exemplifies what is termed an autocatalytic process: that is, one that speeds up at a rate that increases with time, because the process catalyzes itself. The explosion of technology since the Industrial Revolution impresses us today, but the medieval explosion is equally impressive compared with that of the Bronze Age, which in turn dwarfed that of the Upper Paleolithic.* [11]

There are two especially important reasons this is so. First is that technological advances depend on previous mastery of simpler problems. Stone Age farmers did not advance directly to extracting and working iron, which requires high temperature furnaces. Iron ore metallurgy grew out of thousands of years of humans working with natural outcrops of pure metals that could be hammered without heat. It grew out of thousands of years of developing furnaces to make pottery, and then extruding copper ore and making copper alloys (bronze). Iron metallurgy, and ultimately steel technology, was built on the experience of years of bronze metallurgy.

The second reason for an autocatalyst is that new technologies and materials make it possible to make still newer technologies through recombination.

In 1700 B.C., an unknown printer in Crete printed writing on what is known as the Phaistos disk. It was the earliest known printed object. The disk's signs were punched into the clay with stamps that bore a sign as raised type. Why didn't this result in the spread of printing 3000 years before Gutenberg? Because many additional technologies had been invented by Gutenberg's time to give printing useful application—paper, movable type, metallurgy, presses, ink and scripts.

Paper and movable type came from China. Gutenberg's typecasting came from metal dies to solve the problem of non-uniform type sizes. His screw press had been developed for presses used for winemaking.

Finally, there was little demand for printing in 1700 B.C. because the knowledge of writing was confined to a small elite. The potential of a mass-market in medieval Europe induced many investors to lend money to Gutenberg.

Technological development accelerates for these reasons—and it is accelerating to warp speed in the modern world.

COLLISIONS OF SOCIETIES—THE MECHANISMS OF SURVIVAL AND DOMINANCE

In many ways the most telling event in recent history was the collision of European society and the peoples of North and South America. It began in earnest with Columbus's expedition in 1492. Many American societies were highly advanced—the Inca and Aztec empires in particular. In 1492, North America's population was a large fraction of Eurasia's, though it was divided into islands of population with only tenuous communication between them.

Within several hundred years, most of the Native American population had disappeared. European-based societies invaded, conquered and colonized all of the Americas. The Native Americans that remained were either integrated into the new societies, marginalized in small vestigial communities, or exterminated.

How did this happen?

Diamond posits four proximate factors that were determinative:

- European Germs
- Superior Technology
- Superior Political Organization
- Writing

For centuries, infectious diseases had been visited on crowded European societies. These diseases had evolved from the domesticated animals with which Europeans had close regular contact. As a consequence, much of European society that survived these diseases had evolved immunities.

Native Americans had no large domesticated animals. When humans first arrived in the Americas, they apparently exterminated all of the large domesticatable mammals except South American llamas. These large domesticatable mammals had evolved without humans, and apparently without fear of humans. So that while Eurasians were able to domesticate pigs, cattle, horses, sheep and goats, that possibility did not present itself to Native Americans.

This had important consequences. Native Americans did not have use of large mammals for energy, transport, plowing or warfare. That in turn led to slower development and less complex, densely populated societies.

Second, the lack of domesticated animals reduced their exposure to infections jumping from other creatures.

Infectious diseases require dense population centers and regular interaction between them. To survive, the disease must infect a large group. After the epidemic, everyone in the group will either die or become immune. The disease must then find its way to another group, to repeat the process with another generation of non-immune victims. Densely populated societies that have frequent interaction with other groups make this possible. The much less densely populated American continents were never connected by fast, high-volume trade routes. They also lacked domesticated animals to carry new pathogens into human populations. As a result, they did not support large crowd-infectious diseases. Diseases like smallpox, measles, influenza, plague, tuberculosis, typhus, cholera, or malaria never developed in America. The sole crowd-infectious disease that can be attributed with certainty to pre-Columbian North America was syphilis.

Ninety-five percent of Native Americans were wiped out by European infectious diseases to which they had no immunity.

The second proximate factor of the European conquest of America was superior technology, particularly the technology of war.

Europeans had developed steel. Native Americans used only naturally occurring metals like copper, silver and gold for ornamentation. Stone, bone, and some copper were used to make tools even in advanced American societies. Europeans had steel swords, lances, daggers, body armor, and helmets made of steel; and of course they had guns and artillery. Americans had clubs, axes of wood or stone, slings, bows and arrows, quilted armor and no animals on which to oppose cavalry mounted on horseback.

Later Native Americans became wonderful marksmen and horsemen, but by then their societies had been decimated.

Europeans also had a huge advantage in developing sources of power to operate machines. They began with large mammals and extended to wind and water power, which had been harnessed in Europe, but not in America. Europeans had harnessed non-human energy. Native Americans relied only on their own muscle power.

This translated into a massive advantage in transportation, which was supplemented by European sea transport technology, from ship designs to the compass that allowed them to conduct trans-oceanic voyages and come to America in the first place.

Third, Europeans had greatly superior levels of political organization. They had many states (Spain, Portugal, England, France, Holland, Sweden and Denmark) with centralized decision-making that could mobilize substantial resources, people and state religions to contribute to state cohesion, sanction leadership and legitimate wars against other people.

Native Americans had only two empires—the Aztec and the Incas—that could compete with European state at mobilizing resources. The rest of the population was organized into chiefdoms, tribes and bands.

The final European advantage was writing. Most European states had literate bureaucracies and large numbers and literate citizens. This facilitated public administration, economic activity, technological innovation, and the planning and mobilization of exploration and conquest.

Writing in America was confined to a small elite in Mesoamerica. The Incas had some ability to account, but no system for writing to transmit detailed information.

Diamond argues that these proximate factors all sprang from geographic advantages that led to early food production, social and technological development in Eurasia and provided huge competitive advantages to Europeans in the collision of these two cultures.

Five Lessons for the Future

Five critical lessons emerge from Diamond's analysis of human development that I believe have fundamental implications for the progressive vision of the future.

First, human history is indeed a story of both our biological and social evolution. *History is about what we are becoming.* It is not a series of endless cycles. It is not a pendulum intermittently swinging one way or another. It is not true that there is "nothing new under the sun." History is about change. It's about accelerating change. Larger populations, greater complexity and the autocatalytic increase of technological innovation push the throttle faster and faster.

Second, human history is about *qualitative change.* **Hegel and the other proponents of dialectical thought were right.** Quantitative change builds to a tipping point and is then transformed into qualitative change in the nature of the object or process. Evolution qualitatively transformed apes into humans. Bands were qualitatively transformed into tribes, chiefdoms and states. Food production qualitatively transformed the nature of human society and technology.

Third, the values—or priorities—that are appropriate to evolutionary success at one point in history may be different than those that are appropriate at other points. Evolution is indeed about the survival of the fittest. But we must remember that nature and history define fitness in only one way—that which survives, survives. The choices that lead to survival at one point may lead to collapse of the society at another.

Historically, many of the elements that we have described as progressive values have in fact been associated with survival, with evolutionary success.

- As world population has increased, there has been an increasing need to develop systems of nonviolent dispute resolution, encompassing more and more relationships.

- This, coupled with increasing social complexity and economic interdependence, has required people to become empathetic with a wider and wider range of other people. Where at earlier stages of human social development it only made sense to empathize only with your kinship group or clan, it became necessary to empathize with broader groups in chiefdoms and states—and, increasingly, with all of humankind.

- Values that prioritize creativity, openness and innovation—and tolerance for new and different people and points of view—have given societies enormous technological advantages. They are critical to the diffusion of innovation, and that is the most important key to technological development.

On the other hand, values that are directly contrary to our view of progressive values today were often adaptive in the past.

- The technological ability and willingness to slaughter vast numbers of people certainly contributed to the fact that the societies that came from Europe have been dominant during the last several centuries of human history. Germs killed many Native Americans, but European willingness to enslave or slaughter them, and their ability to objectify them as nonhuman, aided their conquest of the Americas.

There are those who argue that this kind of ruthless pursuit of individual or group self-interest is adaptive for American society today as well. As we will see, they are wrong. Many of the values that allowed one society to dominate others in the past are no longer adaptive in the modern world. If they are allowed to dominate the decisions of human societies today, they could give the human story a tragic end.

Fourth, history shows that human beings are very much a product of their histories and their environments. The relative success of various societies had a great deal to do with their geographic and biological environments. Early food production was made possible by the presence of the right combination of domesticated plants and animals in specific geographic areas—plants and animals that simply didn't exist elsewhere. Technological innovations depend entirely on previous developments by past generations.

Fifth, human decisions massively impact our odds of survival and success. We are not just corks bobbing in the stream of history. We make our own futures, from our decisions. For some examples, we turn to Diamond's more recent study, *Collapse: How Societies Choose to Fail or Succeed.* [12]

CHAPTER FORTY-FIVE

The Choices We Make

EASTER ISLAND

The story of Easter Island is particularly compelling.

We are all familiar with Easter Island because of the hundreds of large, stylized statues that had been erected there by people who had no large domesticated animal power. They had nothing but their own muscle to transport and mount stone statues weighing many tons.

Easter Island was occupied about a thousand years ago as part of the great eastward expansion of Polynesian peoples into the Pacific. It is, however, the most remote piece of real estate out there and for that reason, there is no archeological evidence that its people had contact with the inhabitants of any other island—or any other human period—after it was first settled, until Europeans made contact there in the early 1700s.

At its peak, there were apparently about 15,000 people living on an island about nine miles in diameter. When they arrived, the archeological evidence indicates that the colonists found an island loaded with tall trees that were suitable to make large ocean-going canoes, for construction, and to make rope and cloth. The trees also provided various edible fruits, prevented soil erosion from brisk winds, and provided habitat for various land birds. They also found at least 25 nesting seabird species, making it formerly the richest breeding site in all of Polynesia. It was a great place for the seabirds because its isolation kept them free of predators—at least until the humans arrived.

For centuries, as their population grew, Easter Islanders received much of their protein from porpoises that they speared in deep water from the ocean-going canoes. Most fish came from deep-sea fishing, since Easter Island is too far from the equator to support coral reefs that would allow shallow-water fishing.

The Easter Islanders developed agriculture based on many of the crops common to other Polynesian societies. They also brought chickens and developed intensive chicken production. Their agricultural production allowed Eastern Island society to produce adequate food surpluses to feed the large numbers of laborers who were required to transport and erect the statues for which the island is famous. The island itself was divided into 12 pie-shaped zones, each run by a tribe with a chief. These groups apparently engaged in peaceful competition over who could build the largest, most elaborate carvings. Those were placed on even larger platforms and apparently used for religious (ancestor worship) and other communal events.

The Easter Islanders began gradually clearing the forests—both for agriculture and to harvest wood—shortly after they arrived. According to the archeological record, deforestation reached its peak around 1400 and was virtually complete between the 1400s and 1600.

According to Diamond, "The overall picture of Easter Island is the most extreme example of forest destruction in the Pacific and among the most extreme in the world: the whole forest is gone and all of its tree species extinct. Immediate consequences for the islanders were losses of raw materials, losses of wild-caught foods, and decreased crop yields."

Probably most important, without the large tree trunks, they could no longer make large ocean-going canoes. As a result, large ocean-going porpoise and deep-sea fish disappeared from their diet. The islanders had to depend more on birds for protein and on smaller, shallow-water fish. The birds quickly disappeared. Land birds disappeared completely, and sea birds were reduced to relic populations. Wild fruits from trees were dropped from their diet. Deforestation led to soil erosion and decreased crop yields. Wood, the major source of fuel, disappeared. Easter inhabitants were reduced to burning herbs, grasses and sugarcane scraps. Funeral practices changed. Easter Islanders were among the only Polynesian societies to cremate their dead, but this had consumed huge quantities of wood. When the wood was gone, they turned to mummification and bone burial.

The consequences of deforestation and these other human impacts were starvation, population crash, and a descent to cannibalism—the last major remaining source of animal protein besides chickens. The crisis caused the masses to lose faith in the chiefs and priests, and around 1680 they were overthrown by military leaders. Easter Island's formerly complex, integrated society collapsed into an epidemic of civil war.

In the years before the collapse of the old order, the environmental crisis had been exacerbated by attempts to build bigger and bigger statues in an ever more urgent attempt to appeal to ancestors for help. But, of course, the production of bigger statues also consumed huge quantities of wood and bark to construct the wooden "ladders" used to transport the statues across the ground and rope to pull them.

Like many other societies, Easter's collapse swiftly followed the society reaching its peak population, monument construction and environmental impact.

By the time of the first recorded European visit to the Island, in 1722 by Dutch explorer Jacob Roggeveen, most of the great statues had been "thrown down" and broken by competing clans. The Europeans were greeted by tiny canoes that were not ocean-going and a population that had shrunk to between 6,000 and 8,000. The landscape that Roggeveen saw was a wasteland, without a single tree or bush over 10 feet tall.

The contacts between the Europeans and the Easter Islanders resulted in further disaster. Europeans brought smallpox that killed thousands of Islanders who, of course, had no immunity. In 1862-63, two Peruvian ships abducted 1,500 of the remaining Easter Islanders to work as slaves in Peru's guano mines.

By the time Catholic missionaries took up residence on Easter Island in 1872, there were 111 islanders remaining. The society had collapsed. It collapsed as a result of deforestation, the destruction of the bird population and the political and social factors that led to the decisions that made these things happen. This was complicated by the fact that there was no possibility of emigration from the Island—an escape valve that did not present itself because of its isolation.

Collapse was not inevitable, since other island societies faced with potential deforestation developed communal forest management programs that protected their most valuable asset for future generations.

Diamond raises the question: "What did the Easter Islander who cut down the last palm tree say while he was doing it? 'We don't have proof that there aren't more palms somewhere else on Easter? We need more research? Or your proposed ban on logging is premature and driven by fear-mongering?'"

I'll conclude this story with Diamond's summary of why the story of Easter Island is so compelling:

> The Easter Islanders' isolation probably also explains why I have found that their collapse, more than the collapse of any other pre-industrial society, haunts my readers and students. The parallels between Easter Island and the whole modern world are chillingly obvious. Thanks to globalization, international trade, jet planes, and the Internet, all countries on Earth today share resources and affect each other, just as did Easter's dozen clans. Polynesian Easter Island was as isolated in the Pacific Ocean as the Earth is today in space. When Easter Islanders got into difficulties, there was nowhere to which they could flee, nor to which they could turn for help; nor shall we modern Earthlings have recourse elsewhere if our troubles increase. [1]

The Easter Islanders destroyed their environment and society with stone tools and their own muscle power. One of the great challenges of the 21st century is to assure that billions of people with metal tools, machines, nuclear energy and exploding technology do not destroy ours.

The key to the Easter Island story is not just what can happen to a society, but the human *decisions* that created the disaster.

In *Collapse*, Diamond studies the collapse of six ancient societies: Easter Island, Pitcairn and Henderson Island, the Anasazi of North America, the Maya of Mesoamerica and the European society that lived in Norse Greenland for 450 years. He looks at successful decision-making that staved off potential collapse in the New Guinea highlands, Polynesian Tikopia and Tonga, and Japan. Finally, he looks at modern collapse scenarios in Rwanda and Haiti and special challenges facing China, Australia and Montana in the United States.

Why Societies Collapse

Diamond's study identifies five specific reasons that either individually or in combination cause societies to collapse:

1) **Damage that people inflict on their environments that leads to their inability to continue the economic, political and social activities necessary to hold together their society and survive.**
2) **Climate change.**
3) **Acts by hostile neighbors—the impact of intergroup violence and breakdown of security.**
4) **Interruption of relations with friendly neighbors with whom they are interdependent—especially the collapse of trade relations.**
5) **The cultural and political ability of societies to respond to these challenges.**

Diamond writes:

.... problems of deforestation arose for many past societies, among which highland New Guinea, Japan, Tikopia and Tonga, develop successful forest management and continued to prosper, while Easter Island, Mangariva, and Norse Greenland fail to develop successful forest management and collapse resulted. How can we understand such differing outcomes? A society's response depends on its political, economic, and social institutions and on its cultural values. Those institutions and values affect whether a society solves (or even tries to solve) its problems. [2]

In the case of Easter Island, only factor number one, environmental impact—and number five, societal response—were involved in the collapse. The other societies studied involved an interaction of factors.

But the question remains, why don't societies recognize and correct their problems before it's too late? What are they thinking as they cut down the last tree?

Diamond lays out four reasons why societies fail to make the right decisions:

1) Failure to anticipate the problem before it arrives.
Often a society or its decision makers have no prior experience that a particular course of action will lead to a particular outcome. The Norse Greenlanders invested heavily in walrus hunting because there was a major market for ivory from tusks in Europe in the Middle Ages. They had no way of knowing that the Crusades would reopen Europe's access to Asia and Africa and elephant ivory. They also had no way of anticipating that climate change would increase sea ice and impede traffic from Greenland to Europe.

Societies also fail to anticipate because they forget the lessons of history. In the last 15 years, America forgot the impact of the oil price shocks of 1973 and started buying gas-guzzling SUVs. As oil prices rose in 2005 in 2006, we have paid the price for that amnesia.

Other societies fail to anticipate because they rely on false analogies with familiar situations. The French military prepared for World War II by building the famous Maginot Line. It was intended to defend France from the kind of infantry attack that characterized World War I. World War I had involved heavily-defended defensive lines and trench warfare. The German attack, when it actually came, was spearheaded by tanks and armored divisions that passed the Maginot Line through forest formerly thought unsuitable for tanks. Failure to anticipate often results from planning for the last war.

2) Failure to perceive a problem that has actually arrived.
Of course, some problems are very difficult to discern with the naked eye. Without the tools of modern science, there was no way for the first colonists of Mangariva in the Pacific, or the Australians, to know that their activities were causing soil nutrient exhaustion.

The most common reason for the failure to recognize a problem is that it takes the form of a slow trend concealed by wide up-and-down fluctuations. The most salient modern example is global warming.

The scientific community is now unanimous; the average temperatures around the world are rising and human activity and its production of greenhouse gases that trap heat in the atmosphere is a major contributing factor. It took a number of years to recognize this trend, because the increase (currently about .01° per year) is hidden in noisy year-to-year fluctuations. Temperature in a given year might go up or down. You have to back up from the yearly fluctuations to spot the overall upward trend.

Medieval Greenlanders had similar problems in discerning that the climate was getting colder. The Maya and Anasazi had trouble discerning that their climates were becoming drier.

Diamond refers to the problem as "creeping normalcy"—slow trends hidden in noisy fluctuations. If educational performance, the economy, traffic congestion or anything else change gradually, our baseline for evaluating them gradually changes, too. You get "landscape amnesia"—until you see an old picture of the seacoast where a huge glacier once ran into the sea, and suddenly realize that it has shrunken and receded for miles.

To use an old analogy, if you put a frog in a pot of boiling water, it will jump out. You put a frog in a pan of cool water, and *gradually* increase the temperature, and you get a boiled frog.

Part of the answer to the mystery of Easter Island is that every year there were fewer and fewer trees, and fewer people alive who remembered how things used to be. At the point when someone cut down the last fruit-bearing adult palm, the species had ceased to have economic significance.

3) Failure to attempt to solve a problem even when it has been identified.

This turns out to be the most common, and surprising, reason why societies collapse.

The major cause is "rational behavior" by actors—and decision-making elites—that benefits some individual or private self-interest but is harmful to the prospects of the entire society.

This is often complicated because the benefits to a small group that profit from the action is great in the short run, and the resulting damage to everyone else is not very palpable or immediate, except over time.

When hard-rock mining companies pollute the environment, they profit enormously. Those who get scarce jobs may benefit as well. The fact that they are poisoning the rest of us is not as immediately obvious. So the stakes for the small group with a special interest are much higher than they appear for each individual who is negatively impacted. As a result, it's much easier for a big mining company to spend vast amounts of money to protect its profits than to mobilize the resources of millions of people who don't individually perceive great harm. That was a battle we fought every day for the 23 years I was the director of the public interest organization Illinois Public Action. That's why the power of our government must be mobilized to even the odds.

The "tragedy of the commons" also plays a role here. We've seen that it is in the private interest of every fisherman to maximize his catch in the fishery. But it is in the interest of all—including the long-term interest of every fisherman—that the renewable resource of the fishery should be preserved for everyone by limits on catches. The same goes for all potentially renewable resources from trees to soil nutrients to wildlife.

The fact that the first humans to migrate into the Americas apparently exterminated all of the mega fauna (large mammals, birds and reptiles) on the continent had massive negative long-term consequences for their society. But because each private actor pursued his own self-interest, the prospects for the entire society were seriously compromised.

Common action is necessary to address these kinds of problems.

The problem of conflict between private and public interest is intensified when major private economic actors or elites have no apparent stake in long-term protection of resources. Loggers or mining companies with short-term leases who exploit resources, and then desert them, or reorganize themselves by declaring bankruptcy, have no interest in the common good.

When elites think they can insulate themselves from the consequences of communal disaster, they are even less prone to make decisions in the public interest.

For generations, the governing elite in Haiti felt insulated from the effects of deforestation and poverty. As in other societies where rich people believe they can buy their way out of common problems by living in gated communities, buying bottled water and sending their children to private schools, they were simply not as inclined to make decisions in the interests of the entire society.

In *The March of Folly* [2], historian Barbara Tuchman concludes that "chief among the factors affecting political folly is the lust for power, named by Tacitus, 'the most flagrant of all passions'." The drive for status and power led the chiefs of Easter Island to complicate the critical problem of deforestation by their continuing competition over who could build the largest monument. The chief or king who would have put up smaller statues or monuments would have lost his job.

Political systems that allow the leaders to pursue short-term goals that benefit their personal Captain Ahab-like obsession—and have no democratic checks and balances to represent the interests of the entire society—often face disaster.

Conversely, Diamond reminds us that "failures to solve perceived problems because of conflicts of interest between the elite and the masses are much less likely when the elites cannot insulate themselves from the consequences of their actions... the high environmental awareness of the Dutch (including their politicians) goes back to the fact that much of the population—both politicians and masses—live on land lying below sea level, where only the dikes stand between them and drowning...."[4]

The meaning of this scenario was indelibly etched into the consciousness of Americans by Hurricane Katrina.

Other reasons why societies fail to deal with grave problems, even when they have been identified, are more "irrational." In these cases, decision-making elites are unwilling to depart from decisions, investments or values to which they are already deeply committed. Diamond calls this the "sunk cost" effect.

Deeply held religious values are a frequent cause of disastrous behavior. One factor in the deforestation of Easter Island was a religious motivation: to obtain logs to transport and erect the giant statues that were objects of veneration.

The values tied up in people's identity—or perceived meaning of in life—are particularly powerful. Some Montanans, for example, are reluctant to accept the obvious need for government planning to protect wilderness areas because of their commitment to individualism, "individual rights" and self-sufficiency—an idealized cowboy identity.

In Rwanda, the traditional ideal of large families was appropriate in past times of high infant and child mortality, but it has led to a disastrous population explosion today.

The problem is especially severe when societies are committed to "moral law" systems of values that believe entire moral codes of priorities and behaviors come from God or some other higher authority.

Societies with "virtue ethics" systems, where the goal is success and survival of the population (or humanity as a whole), have a far easier time holding fast to core values and abandoning those that may have been appropriate in the past but are no longer appropriate today—like big families, highly differentiated gender roles, or huge cars.

For a time in the late 1970s, many Americans abandoned the notion that gas-guzzling cars were status symbols. The big-car status values of the past returned as gas prices stabilized in the 1990s—and government, pressed by oil companies, refused to put in place tougher emissions standards. American auto values are changing again since inflation adjusted gas prices have been on the rise again in recent years.

Another major reason why societies fail to solve perceived problems is a heavy focus on short-term interest instead of long-term interest. Scarcity tends to exacerbate this tendency. If people are hungry, they'll do anything to get food in the short term; otherwise they wouldn't see the long term anyway.

That's why people use dynamite to catch fish even though it kills the reef upon which future fishing depends. That's why islanders desperate for firewood destroy forests on which the economy of the entire island depends.

As we mentioned in the last section, developments in the modern capital markets have complicated these problems. Formerly, companies often invested in fixed assets and depended on them to produce long-term gains; today they are under massive pressure by financial markets for short-term results. The increasing liquidity these markets allow encourages investors to rapidly move their money out of unprofitable companies or sectors. In other words, financial instruments that were meant to make financial markets more efficient have increased the focus of management on the short term.

Pressure by Wall Street and other financial markets for continuous growth makes it especially difficult for larger companies to focus resources and attention on emerging markets and innovation. Newly-developed products will not solve their basic short-term problem of growth next quarter or next year. By their nature, emerging product markets are small at first. But the bigger a company is, the more it needs bigger and bigger growth numbers to accomplish the same percentage rate of growth each year. Demands for short-term growth take the focus off the long run. [5]

The government, reflecting the long-term interests of society, is the only real counterweight to this tendency in the private sector. But this requires a government that is not dominated by those very vested interests whose interests it must offset.

Diamond presents two final categories of reasons why societies fail to act even when they perceive a problem:

• Crowd psychology
• Denial

As we know, people are pack animals. They get swept up into the goals and activities of the pack. Peer influence has a huge impact in determining what each of us defines as "common sense."

Support for the Crusades became "common sense" in Medieval Europe—even though it caused a massive drain of society's scarce resources. Germans were one of the most highly educated populations in Europe before World War II, but they were swept up by Nazi propaganda.

A key factor that allows these kinds of excesses is the suppression of critical thinking, public debate and the legitimacy of dissent. These all tend to occur in climates of fear. Fear has always been the principal rationale for the suppression of individual rights that are the precursors to "group think." That was as true in George Bush's America as it was in the old Soviet Union, or Nazi Germany.

Denial is yet another factor that paralyzes action. The prospect of an imminent disaster is so terrifying that we simply deny it. Action to solve problems requires hope that the problem can be solved. If the situation appears hopeless, the safest psychological course is to deny it exists or to believe that the problem isn't important. If Easter Islanders didn't believe they could do anything to bring back trees, it was better to deny that the deforestation was a problem in the first place.

My wife and I attended a presentation by former Vice President Al Gore of the slideshow on global warming that was the basis of his book and film *An Inconvenient Truth*. He made a presentation to the House Democratic retreat in 2006. Gore presented a compelling case for the need to act to stop global warming. But he was careful to show that worldwide public policy could actually do something about it. He said he didn't want audiences to slide from denial into despair.

There is of course one final reason that societies collapse.

4) Even after recognizing and attempting to solve the problem, they fail to do so.

They fail either because the solution is beyond their means, or their efforts backfire, or it's simply too late.

Even if the Easter Islanders had done everything they could on their isolated island to reforest, at some point there was a qualitative tipping point, and nothing more could be done. Maybe if they had access to other societies with seedlings, or modern science, the result would have been different. But given the geographic, environmental and historic context of the Easter Island society, there came a point where nothing could be done.

Waiting too long has real consequences.

ADAPTIVE VALUES

Diamond's analysis of the decisions that led to or avoided societal collapse leads us to five key findings that emphasize the importance of progressive values for the prospects of human success and survival.

- **"Virtue Ethics" allow us to focus on the core value of assuring that human beings flourish, and to abandon or adapt other values that may have been appropriate at one time, but are no longer appropriate today.** The "moral law" type of conservative moral system makes it very difficult to adapt value systems to reflect new circumstances.

  Let me reiterate that the need to adapt values does not reflect the view of "moral relativism." It simply means that we should keep our eye on the moral priority—the success and survival of human beings—loving your neighbor. If other subsidiary values get in the way, they must be modified or abandoned.

It's also worth remembering that all "values" do not have religious connotations. Values refer to standards used by a society and its members to determine its priorities for action. The value placed on big cars is not a religious value, but it is a value. Some religions make family size a religious value, most do not—but placing a priority on large families, or having male children, are values.

Survival and success require human societies to adapt the standards they use to set priorities if they are to adapt to changing circumstances.

• **The long-term view is key.** Our decision-making systems have to incentivize consideration of long-term consequences of action—not simply short-term results.

• **It's critical that we maintain our freedoms, civil liberties, and individual rights to allow for creative, critical thinking and action.** Historically, "Groupthink" has led societies to make disastrous decisions.

• **Diamond's analysis makes it obvious that it isn't just actions involving "direct causation" that have moral consequences.** The decisions that led to the collapse on Easter Island were not limited to one person's action that directly affected another. The forces that lead to collapse were complex patterns of events, occurring over many years. They involved complex causation. Since they impacted the success and survival of human societies, they were certainly moral decisions. Yet conservative morality does not impart to them any moral character. Deforestation that leads to collapse obviously has moral consequences. The failure to adapt values and practices in order to avoid starvation definitely involves moral consequences. Overpopulation that creates conflicts resulting in war and genocide has moral consequences.

• **The creation of a democratic society, built on egalitarian principles, is the only real systematic means of assuring that the interests of the entire society are not sacrificed to those of powerful elites.** Most stories of decisions leading to catastrophic collapse involve decision-making elites whose interests diverge from the society at large. Democracy is the only real antidote.

Diamond's study of the decisions that caused or prevented societal collapse makes crystal clear the importance of our battle for progressive values. Their importance will become even clearer as we survey the challenges and possibilities confronting our society at this critical crossroads of history.

CHAPTER FORTY-SIX

The Challenges of the Future

Having considered the historic forces that got us where we are today and having looked at the factors that led to collapse or survival of past societies, we will turn to the future—its challenges and then its possibilities.

We'll consider the challenges through the lens of the five factors the Diamond found related to the collapse of past societies:

- Environmental Damage
- Climate Change
- Acts by Hostile Neighbors—the Impact of Inter-Group Violence and Breakdown of Security
- Interruption of Interdependent Relationships—Especially the Collapse of Trade Relations
- The Cultural and Political Ability of Societies to Respond to these Challenges

Over the last century, three major quantitative changes have tipped and now *qualitatively* impact the world's vulnerability to these factors:

- Globalization
- Technological Development
- Population Growth

GLOBALIZATION

The societies of our planet are increasingly interdependent. Technological advances in communication and transportation have made this interdependence inevitable.

Whereas in the past a society like Japan could remain isolated on its island, that is simply no longer possible.

We now see images of events halfway around the world instantaneously. An epidemic on one continent is a plane flight away from everyone on another. To drive home that fact, consider a study that found the flu season was delayed for two weeks in 2001 by the slowdown in air travel that resulted from the 9/11 attacks.

An angry, hopeless young man in the Middle East is just hours from our shores. A customer service representative can just as easily answer a phone call in Bangalore as Omaha.

Markets are global. The amount of oil pumped from Kuwait affects the pump price in Kansas City.

With every passing day, we are all more and more members of one global community. What happens in Beijing or New Delhi now directly impacts what happens to each of us in Atlanta or San Antonio.

TECHNOLOGICAL DEVELOPMENT

We've already seen that technological development is autocatalytic. It explodes exponentially.

That's true of medical technology, food producing technology, genetic engineering, energy development, communications, manufacturing, data processing.

The world will not experience the same massive technological change over the next hundred years experienced during the last century. It will experience many times that technological change.

With this change will come massively increased power to those who control technology.

That power can be used to solve our problems, or to lead us to disaster. The power of human decisions to impact our ability to survive and succeed will be magnified beyond our imagining.

POPULATION IMPACT AND GROWTH

The thing about population growth is that, like technology, it occurs exponentially, not arithmetically. One hundred couples (200 people), each bearing four children, yield a next generation of 200 couples and 400 people. The next generation has 400 couples and 800 people—and so on. Population grows with the magic of "compound interest."

In *An Inconvenient Truth*, Al Gore says:

> ... *until the time of Jesus Christ and Julius Caesar, human population had grown to a quarter of a billion people. By the time of America's birth in 1776, it had grown to one billion. When the baby boom generation that I'm part of was born at the end of World War II, the population had just crossed 2 billion. In my lifetime, I have watched it go all the way to 6.5 billion. My generation will see it rise to more than 9 billion.... It took 10,000 generations for the human population to reach 2 billion. Then it began to rocket upward from 2*

billion to 9 billion in the course of a single lifetime: ours. We have the moral obligation to take into account the dramatic change in terms of relationship between our species and the planet." [1]

Even though world population increase has slowed in the last several decades, the growth rate in many developing areas greatly exceeds most developed countries—ranging to a high of 4% per year or higher.

But even if couples all restricted themselves to a "replacement rate" of reproduction—about 2.1 children per couple—the world population would continue to increase for about 70 years as the large group of children of past years reaches childbearing age.

And the problem is not simply the size of the population, it is the impact of each person on the resources available from the environment.

Currently, people in the U.S., Japan and Europe consume 32 times more resources and generate 32 times more waste per person than people in the developing world. That ratio will not continue. People in the rest of the world are demanding First World lifestyles.

In many areas development has massively accelerated. China now has 8% to 10% annual increases in gross domestic product and includes one-fourth of all humanity. If China achieves a First World lifestyle that, in and of itself, will double the "human impact" on the planet.

Since 2000, the *emerging* economies have been responsible for 85% of the increase in world oil demand. China alone was responsible for one-third of the increase. China's share of world metal consumption has gone from 10% to 25%. [2] The *Economist* reports:

> *If China follows a similar path to South Korea's as its income rises, then its total oil consumption could increase tenfold in absolute terms over the next three decades, and yet it will still be using 30% less oil per person than the United States does today.* [3]

When you visit eastern China, you can almost see the economy grow. Gleaming skyscrapers dominate the skylines of Schengen, Shanghai, Nanging, and Beijing. Construction cranes sprout like weeds. But of course you also see the unintended environmental impact. At some times of the year the air is so thick with pollution it turns brown. Sixteen of the world's 20 most polluted cities are in China. [4]

It is obviously not possible, nor morally defensible, for First World citizens to continue to enjoy such a disproportionate share of the world's resources while denying them to the rest of the planet.

Even if we wanted to try, an island of prosperity in a sea of poverty is neither stable nor secure.

The problem of populations overtaxing their environments is the main storyline of most historic societal collapses. It represents the central environmental/economic challenge to our future survival and success. Its solution will also have enormous implications for our security. Will hostility between people spin out of control in the next century? Will people from the Third World demand their share of the world's resources through force of arms or terrorism? Will accelerating scarcity cause additional worldwide conflict in the context of ever more powerful technologies of destruction?

Will people in the Third World continue to storm the gates of First World economies through more and more illegal immigration?

Our greatest environmental/economic challenge is to create technologies and make political decisions that allowed economic development for all the people of the world with out unsustainably depleting the Earth's resources.

The current course is unsustainable, and it is complicated by the environmental damage we are currently causing the planet. Let's turn to the first category of factors historically related to collapse for some examples.

CHAPTER FORTY-SEVEN

The Challenges We Face: Massive Environmental Damage

NONRENEWABLE RESOURCES—ESPECIALLY ENERGY

For decades now, we've been depleting nonrenewable resources, such as the fossil fuels coal, oil and natural gas. By definition, these are resources we have no ability to replace. Once they're gone, they're gone. They don't reproduce like fish, forests or wildlife. Some are recyclable in their original form—like metals. But others, like petroleum or coal, are transformed into entirely different substances by their use and are gone forever. When we use the last gallon of natural gas, it will be gone. The hydrocarbon-based economy that depends on fossil fuel will end within the lifetime of most Americans living today. Other energy sources must replace it, or our society as we know it will collapse—it's that simple. Luckily, there are many possible alternatives to fossil fuel, all of which require long-term investment and development.

RENEWABLE RESOURCES

An even bigger problem is the depletion of renewable resources like forests, fish, soil and wildlife. We're using them faster than they are being replaced and renewed.

Deforestation is an especially critical problem for the entire earth, just as it was for Easter Island, and all of the other societies Diamond studied in *Collapse*. Not only do forests provide renewable construction materials and paper, they provide an environment that sustains much of our ecosystem. Of particular importance, they consume the greenhouse gas CO_2 and re-oxygenate the atmosphere. They protect soil moisture and watersheds to provide fresh water, which is in increasingly short supply.

Half of the world's original forests have already been converted to other uses. At present rates, only a quarter of the original forests will remain by 2050.

Fisheries and other sources of wild foods are being depleted as well. Two billion people depend on fish for protein, yet the majority of the world's fisheries have already collapsed or are in steep decline.

Fish species that don't reproduce until several years after they are hatched are a particular problem. Earlier we mentioned the Patagonian Tooth Fish—a deepwater fish from the southern oceans. Since it has been redubbed the Chilean Sea Bass its populations have plummeted. The Chilean Sea Bass is a large fish. It reproduces late and matures slowly. Obviously, if you catch fish before they reproduce, you make the problem of reproducing fish stocks even more difficult.

Another example of the "tragedy of the commons" occurred off the coast of California. *The New York Times* reported that "the very success of the bottom-trawling fleet has been the cause of its failure: the precipitous decline of a variety of bottom-dwelling rockfish and ground fish...." [1]

At a seminar on global resources in the 2003, Dr. Jane Lubchenco of Oregon State University reported on a study of the oceans sponsored by the Pew Charitable Trust. The study found that the ocean ecosystem is in grave danger.

It made a variety of policy proposals including a recommendation that the U.S. ratify the U.N. Law of the Sea Treaty and Convention on Biodiversity. Though 138 countries have done so, the U.S. has yet to act.

A significant fraction of the world's wetlands have already been destroyed. Many saltwater fish depend on mangrove wetlands for breeding grounds. These wetlands are also especially valuable to freshwater fisheries.

To make matters worse, many of the world's coral reefs—home of many fish species—have been damaged or lost. It is estimated that half of the world's remaining reefs will be lost by 2030, if present trends continue.

Many other wild species are also being destroyed—from bird species that pollinate plants, to earth worms that regenerate soil. Predators at the top of the food chain like sharks, bears and wolves are endangered, affecting the entire food chain beneath them.

And soil is being depleted by erosion at rates 10 to 40 times the rates of soil formation. About half of the topsoil in Iowa has been lost in the last 150 years.

This problem is complicated further by salination. Scientists estimate that from 20% to 80% of farmland has been damaged by salination and other factors—even though population increases require more farmland, not less.

This loss is complicated, yet again, by deforestation that contributes to runoff and the erosion.

Remember that these are *renewable* resources. They could be managed at sustainable levels that would assure they could make a contribution to our ability to succeed and survive from now on.

But if we allow the "tragedy of the commons" and the private interest of elites to prevent proper management, their loss will seriously compromise our economic well-being in the 21st Century.

Environmental issues like these are not, as they are sometimes described by Conservatives, simply the esoteric concerns of the "Chablis and brie set." Environmentalists are not being "unrealistic" or proposing that we "sacrifice" economic growth to environmental concerns. These are hard-core resource issues that involve our long-term economic security.

The conflict is not between the economy and the environment—it is between short-term greed and long-term economic well-being for the next generation.

In one form or the other, the "environment" will ultimately survive. Human beings may not—at least in a world of the sort where we want to live.

FRESH WATER

Someone once quipped that the late Senator Paul Simon had written more books than George W. Bush has read. The last of Simon's many books was about the pending shortage of fresh water.

Most of the world's rivers, streams and lakes are already used for irrigation, recreation or drinking water. Underground aquifers, like the one that provides water to Albuquerque, New Mexico, Northwestern Australia, and Iceland, are being depleted. My long-time friend and associate David Zwick has been President of Clean Water Action for several decades. He helped draft the Clean Water Act in the 1970s. He believes that the water crisis is more critical today than ever.

Diamond points out that the Anasazi and Maya were both done in by a shortage of fresh water.

A billion people today do not have easy access to clean fresh water. A 2006 study by the U.N. Food and Agricultural Organization and the Consultative Group on International Agricultural Research concluded that two billion people already live in regions facing a scarcity of water, and without changes in policy that the world will need twice as much water in just 50 years.

The report found that since 1950 the acreage of land under irrigation in Asia has tripled. This has contributed to the increase in worldwide food production. But the report found that Asia's ability to add irrigated farmland is reaching their physical limits. *The New York Times* reported that the study's principal researcher, David Molden, said, "We have to learn how to grow more food with less water... That's imperative, we simply can't just keep expanding land use." [2]

The report also raised fears that global warming would greatly complicate the freshwater problem. The Himalayas provide water for 40% of the world's population. The more rapid glacial melt caused by global warming is increasing the flow of water to India, Nepal, Pakistan and China today, but these depleted glaciers will mean much less water in future years.

CONTAMINATION

Meanwhile, we continue to damage our environment by the harmful things that we introduce.

For many years, Illinois Public Action and its national organization Citizen Action fought to stop toxic pollution and clean up toxic waste. We were heavily involved in campaigns to create the Superfund to clean up toxic chemicals left by polluting industries—and for "community right to know" provisions that allow the people to know what a particular company discharges into the environment. These were helpful, but the chemical industry continues to discharge massive amounts of man-made toxins into the air, water and soil.

Insecticides, pesticides and herbicides are widely used in agriculture and enter the food chain. Some of them contain chemicals that cause cancer, birth defects, brain damage, skin irritation and damage to the immune system. Some also cause reductions in sperm counts.

It's estimated that in the U.S there are at least 130,000 deaths each year from chemicals discharged into our air alone. Oil spills and other toxic discharges also contribute to depletion of wildlife and sea creatures.

ALIEN OR INVASIVE SPECIES

We're also transporting "alien" species or invasive species—intentionally and unintentionally—from place to place. During the colonial period, the most damaging of these species were infectious diseases like smallpox, against which many people had no immunity. They killed millions.

Most recently, we transported the HIV/AIDS virus from Africa around the world.

The dangers of a worldwide flu pandemic could pose a deadly challenge and kill millions. The influenza pandemic of 1918-1919 killed more people than World War I—somewhere between 20 and 40 million people. It was probably the most devastating epidemic in recorded world history. The danger of another flu pandemic could be addressed through more research and a comprehensive standby plan to manufacture and distribute vaccines and as soon as new pathogens have been identified. But while the US is spending billions to defend against rogue country missile attacks that are highly unlikely, it is spending very little to defend against attacks by a new strain of viruses that will almost certainly appear. Worldwide flu epidemics have happened historically every 17 years.

We're also transporting invasive alien species that are larger than microbes—like the zebra mussels that clog power plants, and rabbits that wreaked havoc in Australia because they have no natural predators there, and Asian Carp fish that destroy indigenous species.

This brings us to the second factor that has historically led to collapse: climate change.

CHAPTER FORTY-EIGHT

The Challenges We Face: Climate Change

WHAT GETS YOU INTO TROUBLE

I first became acutely aware of the importance of climate change when I accompanied Jan to a five-day Congressional seminar on the subject conducted by the Aspen Institute in 2003. Scientists presented papers which were then discussed by the bipartisan group in attendance. The facts were eye-opening.

In former Vice President Al Gore's PowerPoint, book and movie on global warming, he displays a quote from Mark Twain: "It ain't what you know that gets into trouble, it's what you know for sure that just ain't so."[1]

A lot of people still believe that the atmosphere is so vast that we humans couldn't possibly affect it. In fact, Gore quotes astronomer Carl Sagan: "If you had a globe covered with a coat of varnish, the thickness of that varnish would be about the same as the thickness of the Earth's atmosphere compared to the Earth itself."[2]

We are indeed affected by the global climate.

Gore points out that, of the 928 peer-reviewed articles in scientific journals on climate change over the last 10 years, 0% doubt that the human discharge of greenhouse gases is causing global warming.

A study by a NASA scientist in September 2006 reported that satellites have detected steady shrinkage of sea ice in the Arctic. They observed more open water in 2005 than any time this century. *The New York Times* reported that "Overall, Dr. (Mark) Serreze said, it was hard to find an explanation for the shifts other than human-caused warming."[3]

The verdict is in on the reality of global warming, but President Bush and the Republicans persist in fiddling while Rome burns—all at the behest of large corporations who are intent on short-term benefit at the expense of our long-term security.

And the stakes are very high.

The U.N. established an Intergovernmental Panel on Climate Change (IPCC) and issued a report in 2001 offering a range of scenarios for predicted temperature increases from 1.4°C to 5.8°C by the end of the century.[4]

Since its publication, observations of what is happening to the environment had tended to confirm and run ahead of the model's predictions. Arctic sea ice is melting unexpectedly fast—at a rate of 9% per decade. [5]

Whereas the ice cap covering Antarctica is 10,000 feet thick, the sea ice covering the Arctic is only 10 feet thick. As a result, the most dramatic impact of global warming is in the Arctic.

Permafrost in the far North has also begun to melt. This will directly threaten much of the human infrastructure that has been built there. Worse, frozen tundra contains 70 billion tons of stored carbon whose release because of melting could further accelerate global warming. In addition, a September 2006 study published in *Nature* finds that methane is bubbling up from the Siberian permafrost at five times the predicted rate. Methane is 23 times more efficient than CO_2 trapping the sun's heat. [6]

Gore quotes Russia's top scientific expert in the field, Sergei Kirpotin from Tomsk State University, as saying: "The permafrost melting is an 'ecological landslide.... connected to global warming'." [7]

Like the melting of the permafrost, the melting of the ice cap itself actually accelerates warming. The ice reflects incoming solar radiation like a mirror. Open seawater absorbs most of the sun's heat. As the water warms, it puts more melting pressure on the ice near it—and we have another autocatalytic process that accelerates on its own. [8]

Climate scientists considered the breakup of the ice shelves on the coasts of Antarctica to be another key leading indicator of global warming. Even with global warming, most scientists thought that the Larsen B Ice Shelf—which was 150 miles long and 30 miles wide—would be stable for at least another century. Beginning January 31, 2002, it completely broke up within 35 days.

Once ice shelves like this are gone, the ice behind them begins to move and fall into the sea. This is especially important because, whereas when the sea-based ice melts it does not appreciably increase sea levels, when land-based ice melts, sea levels rise. [9]

Satellite data indicates the sea levels are currently rising by about 3 mm a year. Land-based data suggests a change from about 2 mm per year over the last century to 4 mm per year in the 1990s. [10]

Sea levels rise for two reasons: when water warms it expands, and the additional land-based ice melting into the sea.

The three great land-based ice masses on the planet are located on the West Antarctic ice shelf, on East Antarctica and on Greenland. The West Antarctic ice shelf and the ice covering Greenland are particularly unstable. If they melted, they would raise sea levels by 20 feet each.

Seasonal melting in Greenland has accelerated dangerously over the last 15 years. In West Antarctica, the ocean flows underneath a significant portion of the shelf, which rests on island moorings, and so does not currently displace seawater. As the ocean has warmed, scientists have documented significant structural changes on the underside of the shelf.[11]

In his book, Gore present maps that show the impact of sea levels increasing by 20 feet. Virtually all of the southeast coast of Florida would be covered by seawater. A substantial portion of the San Francisco Bay area would disappear. The Netherlands would be inundated. More than 20 million people in and around Beijing and 40 million around Shanghai would have to be evacuated. Sixty million around Calcutta and Bangladesh would be displaced. In New York, the World Trade Center site could once again be destroyed, as much of the country's coastal areas would also be flooded. [12]

In 2007, the IPCC issued another report. The panel found that, "warming of the planet is unequivocal, as is now evident from observations of global average air and ocean temperatures, widespread melting of snow and ice, and rising global mean sea level." [13]

It concluded that this increase was caused by human activity with 90% certainty.

Reversing the Gulf Stream

Many scientists believe that the large quantities of Arctic melting will slow or stop the Gulf Stream ocean current. At present, that current carries so much tropical heat to Western Europe that Norway's coastline in winter is 20°C warmer than similar latitudes in Canada. [14]

The Gulf Stream appears to have shut down for several periods over the last 20,000 years. The most recent was around 8,200 years ago when the sudden flow of fresh water from a North American lake tipped into the North Atlantic Ocean. The freshwater diluted the Gulf stream's saltiness and as a consequence weakened its flow, which is dependent on heavier salty water sinking as it cools in the North Atlantic. The action of surface water sinking, in turn, pulls more warm water from the tropics. Melted Arctic ice is likely to have the same effect. [15]

Katrina on Steroids

Warmer oceans will fuel more powerful tropical storms. On July 31, 2005, less than a month before hurricane Katrina hit, a study from MIT supported the scientific consensus that ocean heating arising from global warming is making hurricanes more powerful and destructive. [16]

When Katrina slammed into the Gulf Coast, nature fired a warning shot across humanity's bow. Katrina was the most costly weather-related disaster in recorded history.

In general, global warming leads to more intense weather, and it is not limited to tropical storms. Global warming increases the percentage of precipitation that falls as rain instead of snow. In the last 50 years, the number of major flood events has increased throughout the world each decade. [17]

FLOODING AND DROUGHT

Flooding in Asia has increased dramatically. In July 2005, Mumbai, India received 37 inches of rain in 24 hours. The death toll reached 1,000. But global warming also relocates weather patterns and causes more drought. In Africa, south of the Sahara, these effects have been catastrophic. Since 1963, Lake Chad, formerly the sixth largest in the world, has virtually disappeared. Precipitation has also dramatically decreased in the southern Andes and eastern Mediterranean. [18]

Soil moisture evaporation will increase dramatically with higher temperatures in much of the U.S. A doubling of CO2 in the atmosphere, which at current rates could happen in less than 50 years, would cause up to a 35% loss in soil moisture in the major food-growing areas in the United States. If they quadruple, the figure could go to 65%. The consequences for agriculture would be devastating. [19]

THE CHANGING OCEANS

Coral reefs are the rain forest of the sea. They nurture much of the sea's biodiversity. But global warming stresses corals. In 1998, the second hottest year on record, the world lost 16% of its coral reefs from the combined effect of pollution, dynamite fishing, acidic ocean waters and global warming. In 2005, there was more loss—including some reefs that were healthy when Columbus arrived in the Caribbean in 1492. [20]

CO2 concentration in the atmosphere dissolves in water to increase its acidity, compounding heating effects.

In the ocean, global warming also increases the range of algae blooms which decrease oxygen levels in are vectors for diseases.

CHANGING WILDLIFE

The range of other human disease vectors like mosquitoes, tsetse flies, lice, ticks and fleas is also increased by global warming. Of course, in general, colder winters decrease the threat of microbes to humans. [21]

Climate change is also impacting many of the world's species. Polar bears have now been put on the endangered species list. One long-term study of polar bear populations from Hudson Bay to Manitoba Canada shows the animals are 15% thinner than 30 years ago. The population has dropped 17% over the past 10 years. [22] Another study shows they are drowning in significant numbers, because they had to swim much farther between ice flows. [23]

There are two ways that species adapt to changes in the environment. They change the timing of significant life events, e.g. hibernation, migration or breeding, or they move to other ranges.

Camille Parmesan of the University of Texas and Gary Yoke of Wesleyan University found that of the total of 677 species they studied, two-thirds had brought forward the important events in their life calendar. The Mexican Jay in the Chiricahua Mountains of Arizona was breeding 10 days earlier than 30 years ago. Tree swallows advanced their breeding by nine days between 1959 and 1991.

Of 434 species that move their ranges, four-fifths had moved northward to higher, cooler ground. Of course, many species which can't adapt will die. Chris Thomas, professor of conservation at the University of Leeds in Britain, estimates that if the Intergovernmental Panel on Climate Change's midrange scenario of a 2.3°C increase in world temperature by 2100 is correct, between 15% and 37% of species they modeled will be extinct by 2050. Extinction is forever. [24]

In the United States, hotter temperatures have increased the prevalence of wildfires. Major wildfires in the Americas have increased fivefold since 1950. [25]

SLOWING THE FLOW

Perhaps most devastating is the effect of global warming on the availability of fresh water. As we've seen, the Himalayan glaciers feed rivers that provide water to 40% of the world's population. Within the next 50 years, that 40% may face profound water shortages if world trends in global warming are not abated.

TEMPERATURE AND CO2

How are scientists so certain that greenhouse gases have such an effect on the temperature? To supplement the physics, and data from the recent past, we now have data on temperature and CO2 concentrations for thousands of years in the past.

Ice caps and glaciers built up over tens of thousands of years contain tiny bubbles of air trapped in the snow the year that snow fell. These cores can be read like tree rings, and allow us to understand what was going on in the atmosphere millennia ago. The exact temperature each year can be determined by calculating the ratio of different isotopes of oxygen. Concentrations of CO2 can be calculated directly from the samples. [26]

The results are startling. In the last thousand, years there was one brief warming period during the Middle Ages. Aside from that, the general trend was cooling, until about 50 years ago, when it suddenly turned warmer. From 1950 to 1970, there was a slight moderation of the trend, reflecting the buildup of particulate matter in the air that shrouded the earth that tended to offset the effects of greenhouse gases. Then, as particulate pollution was controlled, and greenhouse gas concentration continued to increase, the warming trend resumed. [27]

In the Antarctic, measurements of CO2 concentration and temperature can go back 650,000 years. The graphical depiction of the temperature and CO2 concentration fit nicely together. While there are complications to the relationship, the bottom line is that when there is more CO2 in the atmosphere, the temperature will increase because more heat from the sun is trapped.

At no point in the last 650,000 years before the industrial era do CO2 concentrations exceed 300 parts per million (ppm). Today, CO2 is about 380 ppm. In 45 years, if there are not dramatic changes in policy, CO2 concentration will exceed 600 ppm—doubling its pre-industrial absolute maximum. [28]

World Bank economist Zmarak Shalzi estimates that based on current policies— and carbon emissions in China and India, the world's fastest-growing emerging economies—will more than double by 2020, though this would still leave China's carbon emissions at one-third the level of those of the United States. [29]

WE HAVE THE WHEREWITHAL, WE NEED THE WILL

I mentioned earlier that Gore is eager to prevent his readers from going from denial and ignorance of this problem, to despair that nothing can be done.

He quotes Robert Socolow and Stephen Pacala of Princeton, who conducted a study of policies that could help solve the climate crisis: "Humanity already possesses the fundamental scientific, technical, and industrial know-how to solve the carbon and climate problems in the next half century." [30]

Gore argues that, together, a number of already-existing, affordable technologies can bring emissions down to a point below 1970 levels. They include:

- More efficient use of electricity and heating and cooling systems, lighting, appliance and electrical equipment.

- End-use efficiency—designing buildings and businesses to use far less energy than they currently do.

- Increased vehicle efficiency by manufacturing cars that run on less gas and putting more hybrid and fuel-cell cars on the roads.

- Making other changes in transportation efficiency, such as designing cities and towns to have better mass transit systems and building heavy trucks with greater fuel efficiency.

- Increasing reliance on renewable energy technologies that already exist, such as wind and bio-fuels.

- Capture and storage of excess carbon from power plants and industrial activities. [31]

Arguments have been advanced by conservative economists that investments in mitigating global warming are not fully justified by the potential returns. But even the conservative *Economist* magazine in a special section dedicated to the subject concluded, "Global warming poses a serious risk and the costs of litigation are manageable." [32]

One hundred and thirty-two nations have signed the Kyoto treaty aimed at beginning to meet the challenge of global warming. Only two advanced nations have not: Australia and the United States. Currently, the U.S. produces 30.3% of worldwide carbon emissions. We emit 5.5 times more *per person* than the world average. [33]

Gore points out that when the danger of the hole in the ozone layer was discovered, the world community acted successfully with American leadership. Now we are well on the way to solving the Stratosphere ozone crisis. [34]

But he cautions that when it comes to global climate change, we are overdue to react. **The tipping point beyond which no full recovery may be possible could occur within the next decade.**

The challenges posed by human environmental damage to the planet and climate change simply will not be met, if priorities are set based on the values of radical conservatives. A value system that places priority on individual personal self-interest alone has not, and will not, come to grips with these problems.

One need only look at the failure of the Bush administration to even recognize that the challenge exists. Jan is on Energy and Commerce Committee of the House that has jurisdiction over climate change issues. When Congress was still in Republican hands in the summer of 2006, the Republican Chairman held a hearing, intended to highlight the views of the few remaining skeptics of global warming. The former Republican leadership failed to take any steps to address the urgent problem. It is critical that the new Democratic majority take the lead.

Energy company executives and other elites have short-term interests that entirely diverge from the long-term interests of the entire society. They completely dominated the decision-making process of the Bush administration and the former Republican leaders of Congress.

Radical conservatives gave no thought that the failure to deal with these issues has a moral dimension. All of these issues involve complex causality, not the action of one person acting directly on another. In a radical conservative view, these are simply not moral questions.

FIDDLING WHILE THE EARTH WARMS

That the radical conservative value system has a ferocious bias against taking long-term interest into account is not surprising. This bias even shows up in the favorite conservative tool of economic decision-making, "cost-benefit analysis."

The Economist magazine recognizes the problem in its special section on global warming:

> *In standard cost-benefit analysis, each pound or dollar spent this year is reckoned to be worth slightly more than one spent next year.... This preference is expressed in a discount rate which, depending on interest rates, is usually said at somewhere between 3% and 6%. So benefits beyond half a century barely count.* [35]

What's more, their system of cost-benefit analysis defies the fundamental principle of equity. Again, *The Economist* on the difficulty of doing economic cost-benefit analysis over borders:

> *Money is worth more in the poor world than in the rich world. The sharpest*

example of that is the implicit value of life; the amount of money spent on healthcare in Britain and India implies that the life of a Britain is worth more than the life of an Indian. Politically, however, this is hard to sustain; indeed, the first meeting of the IPCC nearly fell apart on this question. [36]

Of course, the fundamental flaw is the radical conservative reduction of human beings to commodities, with price tags—a view that is bolstered by their belief that those who are economically successful are more "valuable" and virtuous, since they had the discipline necessary to achieve success.

One of the fundamental precepts of progressive values is that each person is equally valuable because of their innate status as human beings. And of course, this basic precept is central to the mainstream tradition of American values. In the words of the Declaration of Independence, "[T]hat all men are created equal, that they are endowed by their Creator with certain unalienable rights, that among those are life, liberty and the pursuit of happiness."

Finally, the radical conservative view allows its proponents to believe that through their individual actions they can exempt themselves from the dangers we all face as a society. They incorrectly believe that their economic success will allow them to isolate themselves physically and economically from the calamities that affect most of the world.

That is not only immoral; it's incorrect. Everyone is interdependent; the only question is the nature of that interdependence. Marie Antoinette learned that lesson the hard way. The 21st-century economic elite and their radical conservative movement will learn that lesson, too, one way or the other.

In his story of the collapse after 450 years of Greenland Norse society, Jared Diamond writes:

There were many innovations that might have improved the material conditions of the Norse, such as importing more iron and fewer luxuries, allocating more boat time to Markland (Canadian) journeys for obtaining iron and timber, and copying (from the Inuit) or inventing different boats and different hunting techniques. But those innovations could have threatened the power, prestige, and narrow interests of the chiefs....

Thus Norse society created a conflict between the short-term interests of those in power and the long-term interest of the societies are whole. The last right that they obtained for themselves was the privilege of being the last to starve. [37]

Jan sometimes wonders aloud about her conservative congressional colleagues. "They have children that they love. Don't they care about the world they leave to them?" she'll ask.

Radical conservative values, and the heady experience of power, blinds them to the reality that we are all in this together.

WE'RE ALL IN THIS TOGETHER

In An Inconvenient Truth, Gore shows us the first picture ever taken of the Earth as a whole. It was made Christmas Eve 1968 by the Apollo spacecraft as it rose over the lunar horizon. He quotes Archibald McLeish, who after seeing the photo wrote:

> To see the Earth as it truly is, small and blue and beautiful and that eternal silence, where it floats, is to see ourselves as riders on the earth together, brothers. On that bright loneliness in the eternal cold—brothers who know now that they are truly brothers. [38]

At the close of his book, Gore shows another picture of the Earth. This one was taken by a robot spacecraft 4 billion miles beyond our solar system. Earth is a pale blue dot surrounded by the massive blackness of space. Gore writes that the late astronomer Carl Sagan noted that:

> … everything that has ever happened in all of human history has happened on that tiny pixel. All the triumphs and tragedies. All the wars. All the famines. All the major advances. It is our home… and that is what is at stake. Our ability to live on planet Earth—to have a future as a civilization. I believe this is a moral issue. [39]

CHAPTER FORTY-NINE

The Challenges We Face: Acts by Hostile Neighbors—the Impact of Inter-Group Violence and Breakdown of Security

You don't have to do much to convince most people that hostile acts by neighbors can lead to catastrophic collapse. History abounds with examples—often compounded by other factors.

The Roman Empire collapsed partially because of a military defeat by hostile Germanic tribes. The proximate cause of the collapse of most of the Native American societies that existed in 1492 was military conquest by the Europeans.

In fact, wars and the threat of force are sometimes portrayed as the only engines of world history. While, as we've seen, this oversimplified role of military conflict in historic development is far from accurate, it has and continues to be a major factor in the narrative of human development.

As we examine challenges for the future, we should view these issues simultaneously through two prisms. First are the challenges that hostile forces in the world pose directly to the United States. Second, from the standpoint of our worldwide society, we have to think of the conflicts the way we might think about civil wars in our own country. Violent conflict anywhere in the world now almost certainly has consequences, at one level or another, on the success and survival of everyone on the planet.

Our traditional views of conflict between nations and international violence of all types are being qualitatively changed by two of the factors we have already discussed:

- The worldwide explosion of technology, especially military technology, and its diffusion worldwide.

- The massive increase in world population and the per-capita impact on world resources that could turbocharge increased competition for scarce natural resources.

454 · SECTION EIGHT

The Explosion of Military Technology

Technology magnifies its user's power by expanding control over energy and information. As we've seen, technology builds upon itself. It is an autocatalytic process. And it does not expand gradually, but exponentially.

With the development of the nuclear bomb 60 years ago, humans acquired the power to destroy themselves and most life on the planet for the first time in our seven million year evolutionary history.

The knowledge and resources to make nuclear weapons has now spread to at least nine countries: United States, France, Britain, China, Russia, India, Pakistan, North Korea, and most certainly Israel.

Today enough nuclear weapons exist to destroy humanity many times over.

Over the last hundred years, humanity has also developed weaponized biological agents that can infect vast populations with withering efficiency. These weapons could yield results similar to those encountered by Native Americans and Pacific islanders who came in contact with diseases against which they had no immunity. We've also developed chemical weapons that can choke, burn and destroy the nervous systems of millions of victims.

Bioengineering and the new science of synthetic biology will soon allow us to create a whole new living organism. The *Economist* reports that Dr. Craig Venter, "the man who first sequenced the entire genome of a living creature.... is synthesizing genomes, rather than analyzing them. Three years ago he made the first viable synthetic virus from off-the-shelf chemicals.... Now he has a bacterial genome in his sights." [1]

The ability to synthesize organisms gives humans the ability to create many new biological weapons and has awesome implications for our ability to alter the makeup of human beings themselves.

In his book, *Lonely Planets: The Natural Philosophy of Alien Life*, planetary scientist David Grinspoon considers extraterrestrial life. He points out that in fact all life on Earth is directly related, since it is all based on DNA — the only self-copying chemical mechanism in our ecosystem. But he notes that there is no reason to believe that other molecules could not be developed that would self-replicate — creating new life forms that are not based on DNA at all. [2]

There is also no reason to believe that our ability to control and destroy each other will not continue its exponential expansion in the 21st century.

More chilling, it is inconceivable that control of the knowledge that is the basis of this technological explosion can be limited to a few hands. In the years ahead, there will be billions of educated, knowledgeable people in the world who could gain access to the ability to inflict enormous harm.

INCREASES IN WORLD POPULATION AND PER CAPITA IMPACT ON NATURAL RESOURCES—SCARCITY AND CONFLICT

The exponential increase in total human impact on the world's natural resources could greatly increase competition for scarce resources. Of course, the world's most horrific conflicts have historically been fought over control of scarce resources—from land, to water, to oil. The conflict with Japan in World War II was heavily rooted in Japan's desire for secure oil supplies.

Today's conflicts in the Persian Gulf turn heavily on the need for oil.

Resources on Easter Island were overtaxed, and the ultimate result was the collapse of an integrated society, civil war and cannibalism.

When the Norse Greenlanders could no longer support their population, Norse from less productive settlements moved into the "lifeboats" of the more productive settlements. This swamped the more productive settlements. The new mouths to feed completely overtaxed them until they all sank.

The Norse jumped into the "lifeboats" of the most productive settlements the same way immigrants from the Third World have rushed to escape scarcity in the developing world as legal or illegal immigrants to First World countries.

In *Collapse,* Diamond found that population pressures on overtaxed land are one major factor underlying the horrific genocide that killed 800,000 Tutsis in 1994. Rwanda is one of the two most densely populated countries in Africa. It is three times more densely populated than the third most densely populated African country, Nigeria. It is 10 times more densely populated the neighboring Tanzania.

Rwanda's average population was 760 people per square mile. That is higher than Britain (610) and approaches Holland (950). These European countries have highly mechanized, efficient economies and agriculture. Rwandan agriculture is much less efficient and un-mechanized. Farmers depend on hand-held hose, picks, and machetes—and most produce little surplus to feed others.

With more density, and no new land, more young people had to remain at home. Average family size went from 4.9 to 5.3 from 1988 to 1993. By 1993, each person was living off of one seventh of an acre. The percentage of the population living on 1,600 calories per day (below famine level) was 9% in 1982, rising to 40% in 1990.

Violence and theft increased well before 1994, concentrated especially in areas with highest population density and starvation.

The poverty and desperation provided good recruiting grounds for ethnic militias that provided much of the infrastructure that carried out the genocide when ethnic conflict between Hutus and Tutsis exploded.

And when the explosion happened, there were other victims in addition to Tutsis. Hutus that were large landowners were killed. In addition many malnourished and especially poor people with no or very little land died because of starvation–too weak, or not having money to pay the bribes required to buy survival and roadblocks.

Two Belgian economists, Catherine Andre and Jean Philippe Platteau, happened to study an area in northwest Rwanda in the period leading up to the genocide.

They concluded that "the 1994 events provided a unique opportunity to settle scores, or to reshuffle property even among Hutu villagers.... It is not rare, even today, to hear Rwandans argue that a war is necessary to wipe out an excess population and to bring numbers into line with available resources." [3]

Diamond concludes: "I'm accustomed to thinking of population pressure, human environmental impacts and drought as ultimate causes, which make people chronically desperate, and are like the gunpowder inside the powder keg. One also needs a proximate cause: a match to light the keg." [4]

If we do not deal with the problems of increased human impacts and the resulting scarcity of resources like land, and fresh water, massive increases in conflict are inevitable.

Or as Diamond puts it:

Severe problems of overpopulation, environmental impact and climate change cannot persist indefinitely; sooner or later, they're likely to resolve themselves, whether in a manner of Rwanda or in some other manner not of our devising, if we don't succeed in solving them by our own actions. [5]

The problem with scarcity is that it not only promotes conflict and warfare, it also makes societies focus only on the short run. Long-term planning and thinking go out the window if you can't get enough to eat today; just as the long-term impact on the planet is forgotten as an expedient to prevail in war.

It should be obvious then that the massive disparity in the world will be the inevitable cause of great insecurity for us all.

Progressive values of equality and democracy must be extended to the distribution of the world's resources—not simply because it is ethically necessary, but *because it is critical for our own security.*

Just as the desperate young people of Rwanda were prime recruits for ethnic militias, desperate young people throughout the Third World are prime recruits for terrorists and those who would do us harm.

The old Catholic Worker slogan has never been more true: "If you want peace, work for justice."

ROSE-COLORED GLASSES

Radical conservatives, including the Neocons who continue to control America's foreign policy, often accuse Progressives of wearing "rose-colored glasses" when it comes to the nation's security. They claim Progressives just don't understand that the world is full of bad people who want to do us harm; that we want to "unilaterally disarm" or "appease" the forces of evil in the world.

Ironically, they also accuse Progressives of being too pessimistic about the dangers facing the world — of being the "gloom and doom set."

In fact, Progressives are inveterate optimists about human possibility. We believe that human beings are fundamentally good, and when you step back to look at the chart of history, the trend is up. In general, human history is the story of expanding human knowledge and freedom. We have faith that human beings can flourish, that they can succeed and survive; that we *and our children* can live exciting, fulfilling lives, both now and in the future.

But we also possess what the novelist Joseph Conrad referred to as "mature pessimism" about human nature as well. We know that human beings are capable of unspeakable horrors. In Conrad's *The Heart of Darkness,* the protagonist descends into a world with no empathy, where human beings are objectified into objects of slaughter. His story was remade by Francis Ford Coppola as the film *Apocalypse Now,* set in the midst of the Vietnam War.

How else do you explain the tactics of the "Lord's Resistance Army" — a messianic rebel group that conducted a 20-year civil war against Uganda? According to *The New York Times:*

> The Lord's Resistance Army...was exploring a new dimension of violence by building an army of abducted children and forcing them to burn down huts, slice off lips and pound newborn babies to death in wooden mortars, as though they were grinding grain...
>
> "I killed and killed," said Christopher Oyet, an 18-year-old former rebel, who was kidnapped at the age of nine. "Now, I'm scared of myself." [6]

How else to explain the willingness of Rwanda's Hutus to machete 800,000 of their Tutsi neighbors? Remember, most of the Rwandan killing was up close and personal.

How else do we explain the systematic murder of six million Jews in the gas chambers, or the willingness of Europeans to slaughter Native Americans, or the eagerness of terrorists to snuff out the lives of 3,000 innocent people in the 9/11 attacks?

How else is it possible to explain the vicious ethnic violence that spread in Bosnia and Iraq? In the June 15, 2006 *Washington Post,* Nick Rosen reported:

Every morning the streets of Baghdad are littered with dozens of bodies, bruised, torn, beheaded; executed only because they are Sunni, or because they're Shiite. Power drills are an especially popular torture device." [7]

Progressives believe that human beings are fundamentally good, but can perpetrate unthinkable horror—especially if those actions are sanctioned by peer approval.

The Neocons, on the other hand, believe that human beings are innately bad, but that the use of punishment and force as methods of social control can protect us from our own inherent evil.

In a commentary in the Washington Post, Andrew J. Bacevich wrote: "In their book, *Cobra II*, Michael R. Gordon and General Bernard E. Trainor offer this ugly comment from a senior officer in Baghdad, "The only thing these sand niggers understand is force. And I'm about to introduce them to it." [8]

Though they might not use the same language, that pretty much sums up the neocon view of human nature and the Bush foreign policy.

Not only does that view reflect values that we consider morally bankrupt, but the policies and judgments made on the basis of those values fail because they are based on fundamental misunderstandings of human self-interest and motivation. The radical conservative value system is incompatible with our success and survival in the 21st century.

THE FAILURE OF NEOCONSERVATIVE FOREIGN AND MILITARY POLICY

Far from making either the United States or the world safer, neocon foreign and military policies positively endanger our security and that of future generations.

The "strict father" radical conservative values upon which they are based simply don't work to produce the advertised goal of safety and security.

The only good thing to come out of the years of Bush/Neocon foreign policy is that its failure has shown definitively that its underlying assumptions are wrong. Hopefully, this will provide such a clear lesson to America and to the rest of the world that we do not repeat it as we fashion the world of the 21st century.

George W. Bush's foreign policy was designed well before he took office by a group of Neoconservatives who are now household names: Dick Cheney, I. Lewis "Scooter" Libby, Donald Rumsfeld and Paul Wolfowitz. They were part of a group called the Project for a New American Century (PNAC) and published a statement of principles in June 1997. Other signers included Elliott Abrams, Jerry Bauer, Steve Forbes, Midge Decter and Norman Podhoretz—all influential thinkers of the conservative movement.

The PNAC sent a letter to President Clinton in 1998 proposing an invasion of Iraq. It favored the preemptive use of military power to attack other nations even if they did not pose an imminent threat to the United States, and proposed substantial increases in defense spending.

George Lakoff argues that the neocon foreign policy tracks directly with radical conservative "strict father" value metaphor:

> As the strict father is leader of the family, so the president is leader of the country, and America is leader of the world. Being the "leader" means that he 1) is the moral authority, who knows right from wrong, is inherently good, and can be trusted to do what is right; 2) has, and must use, great power to do right; 3) is responsible for protecting us from evil doers, and may have to use preemptive force; 4) has the authority to do whatever is necessary; 5) requires obedience from followers (who he is protecting); 6) may have to fight fire with fire as part of protection; 7) pursues his self-interest, which is the interest of everyone; 8) serves the prosperity and freedom of all. [9]

A few years ago, Jan and I received a holiday card from Vice President Cheney and his wife Lynne. Inside, it said, "And if a sparrow cannot fall to the ground without His notice, is it probable that an empire can rise without His aid?" Our jaws dropped.

Writing just a year after September 11th—but before the Iraq war – veteran *Chicago Tribune* reporter R. C. Longworth wrote an article on the "Cheney doctrine of first strike, world dominion, and preemption." He wrote:

> If Cheney is wrong... America could squander its world leadership in a self-destructive search for empire... This is a prescription for global domination, in essence a worldwide empire. But it emphasizes that this would be a benevolent imperialism, because we would "account sufficiently for the interest" of our allies to keep them from having any reason to challenge us or ever act independently. An undercurrent to this paternalistic doctrine was the idea that Washington would define an ally's interest and expect them to go along.... [10]

It would've been difficult for Bush to enact the neoconservative vision so completely without some precipitating event. The 9/11 attacks provided that event. The country was united by images of the World Trade Center and lined up behind its leader, whose approval ratings for a time neared 90%.

The attacks provided a chance for the Neocons to transfer the entire frame of foreign policy to the "war on terror."

The administration's immediate response to 9/11 was military action to eliminate the Taliban, the regime that had harbored al-Qaeda and Osama bin Laden, who perpetrated the attack. Many Progressives, including Jan and myself, supported military action against the Taliban—a fundamentalist regime that systematically oppressed the people of Afghanistan and especially women. That action came as a direct response to an attack on the United States, was supported by the world community, and conducted by a true coalition of nations.

Not long after the collapse of the Taliban regime and the formation of a new government, the Bush administration began to lose its focus. It failed to capture bin Laden when it had him cornered at Tora Bora mountain, because it outsourced the action to an Afghan warlord instead of using crack American troops in a mission for which they were well-suited and well-trained.

Then, most critically, it failed to make the promised investments in Afghanistan that were necessary to give people a stake in the newly elected regime. As Paul Krugman of the New York Times put it:

> Now, much of Afghanistan has fallen back under the control of the drug-dealing warlords and the Taliban.... During the first 18 months after the Taliban were driven from power, the U.S.-led coalition provided no peacekeeping troops outside of the capital city. Economic aid in a destitute nation shattered by war was minimal in the critical first year, when the new government was trying to build legitimacy. And the result is the floundering and failure we see today. [11]

Of course the greatest blunder of his presidency came next. As everyone now knows, Bush initiated a preemptive war against Iraq under the false pretext that Saddam Hussein had weapons of mass distraction and was somehow implicated in al-Qaeda's attack on America.

The Bush invasion of Iraq was executed over the opposition of most American allies and most of the rest of the world. By the fall of 2007, it had led to the deaths of over 3,900 Americans, as well as almost 28,000 wounded—many seriously damaged for life. The human costs in Iraq itself have been staggering.

In the run-up to the war, Jan worked with several other progressive members of the House to line up Democratic opposition to the resolution proposed by the president to legitimate his invasion. It is not widely remembered that 60% of Democrats in the House voted no on that October 2002 resolution. It seemed a courageous vote at the time. Then, House Democratic Leader Gephardt went to the Rose Garden to sign onto the resolution. After years of war, those who voted no have been completely vindicated by history.

A few months after the invasion, Jan approached Secretary of Defense Rumsfeld after a briefing and asked him how many Iraqi civilians have been killed in the first months of the war. He looked at her and scowled, "How should I know? We're at war. In a couple of years some historian will come up with a number." Jan thought later that it was a short distance from that attitude to the torture of Iraqi prisoners at Abu Ghraib.

As of mid-2007, we still don't know for sure. Of course, Iraqis have died in massive numbers as a result of the insurgency spawned by the invasion and the Civil War that has followed. A study by the Johns Hopkins Bloomberg school of public health surveyed households throughout Iraq, and estimated that as many as 600,000 Iraqi civilians had died from violence from March 2003 to July 2006. [12]

There were horrific incidents like the massacre at Haditha, where "... a squad of Marines, outraged at the loss of a comrade, is said to have run amok, avenging his death by killing two dozen innocent bystanders." [13]

There have been frequent episodes like the one in Samarra, May 30, 2006, where:

> US soldiers manning a checkpoint there opened fire on a speeding vehicle that either did not see or failed to heed the command to stop. Two women in the vehicle were shot dead. One of them, Nahiba Hosayif Jassin, 35, was pregnant. The baby was also killed. The driver, Jassin's brother, had been racing her to the hospital to give birth.... The killing at the Samarra checkpoint was not an atrocity; most likely it was an accident, a mistake. Yet plenty of evidence suggests that in Iraq such mistakes have occurred routinely, with moral and political consequences that have been too long ignored. [14]

Andrew Bacevich wrote in the Washington Post , "Any action resulting in Iraqi civilians' deaths, however inadvertent, undermines the Bush administration's narrative of liberation, and swells the ranks of those resisting the US presence." [15]

Bacevich estimates that the number of innocent Iraqis who died directly at American hands run into the tens of thousands.

These deaths didn't occur because our soldiers were careless or callous. They were the natural result of a US invasion and occupation of another country.

And the death toll is only the tip of the iceberg. The World Health Organization survey of 600 children ages 3 to 10 in Baghdad last year showed 47% said they had been exposed to a traumatic event over the last two years, and 14% currently showed symptoms of post-traumatic stress disorder.[16] Iraqi civilians will be paying the price for this war for decades to come.

THE IRAQI CIVIL WAR

By 2006, American soldiers were being sent into the crosshairs of a
civil war. A September 20, 2006 *Los Angeles Times* article gave a disturbing
flavor of what civil war in Iraq had become. It was written by a middle-
class 54-year-old Iraqi reporter:

> Baghdad—on a recent Sunday, I was buying groceries in my beloved
> Amariya neighborhood in western Baghdad when I heard the sound of an
> AK-47 for about three seconds. It was close, but not very close, so I continued
> shopping.
> As I took a right turn on Munadhama Street, I saw a man lying on the
> ground in a small pool of blood. He wasn't dead.
> The idea of stopping to help or take him to a hospital crossed my mind, but I
> didn't dare. Cars passed without stopping. Pedestrians and shop owners kept
> doing what they were doing, pretending nothing had happened.
> I was still looking at the wounded man and blaming myself for not
> stopping to help. Other shoppers peered at him from a distance, sorrowful
> and compassionate, but did nothing.
> I went on to another grocery store, staying for about five minutes while
> shopping for tomatoes, onions and other vegetables. During that time, the
> man managed to sit up and wave to passing cars. No one stopped. Then, a
> white Volkswagen pulled up. A passenger stepped out with a gun, walked
> steadily to the wounded man and shot him three times. The car took off down
> a side road and vanished.
> No one did anything. No one lifted a finger. The only reaction came from
> a woman in the grocery store. In a low voice, she said, "My God, bless his
> soul."
> I went home and didn't dare tell my wife. I did not want to frighten her...
> After the attack on the Shiite shrine of the Golden Dome in Samarra in
> February, Shiite gunmen tried to raid Sunni mosques in my neighborhood.
> One night, against the backdrop of heavy shooting, we heard the cleric calling
> for help from the mosque's loudspeakers. We stayed up all night, listening as
> they battled for the mosque. It made me feel unsafe. If a Muslim would shoot
> another Muslim, what would they do to a Christian?
> Fear dictates everything we do.
> I see my neighbors less and less. When I go out, I say hello and that's it. I
> fear someone will ask questions about my job working for Americans, which
> could put me in danger. Even if he had no ill will toward me, you might talk
> and reveal an identifying detail. We're afraid of an enemy among us. Someone
> we don't know. It's a cancer.
> In March, assassinations started in our neighborhood. Early one evening,
> I was sitting in my garden with my wife when we heard several gunshots. I
> rushed to the gate to see what was going on, despite my wife's pleas to stay
> inside. My neighbors tell me the gunmen had dropped three men from a car

and shot them in the street before driving off. No one dared approach the victims to find out who they were.

If you'd asked me a year ago whether I would consider leaving Iraq, I would've said maybe, but without enthusiasm. Now it's a definite yes. Things are going from bad to worse, and I can't see any light at the end of the tunnel.

Four weeks ago, I came home from work. As I reached my street, I saw a man lying in a pool of blood. Someone had covered him with bits of cardboard. This was the best they could do. No one dared move him.

I drove on. [17]

By attacking Iraq, Bush kicked open the hornet's nest. The likelihood of the civil conflict that has erupted in Iraq should have been obvious to the Neocon architects of the war, since it is a consequence that often flows from disorder and chaos. It had been predicted by many. Whether it is the power vacuum after the death of Tito in Yugoslavia, or the Killing Fields that resulted from the chaos following the U.S. invasion of Cambodia, the breakdown of social institutions leaves open the very real possibility of civil conflict.

Daniel Byman of Georgetown University and Kenneth Pollack of the Brookings Institution wrote in 2006, "The greatest threat the United States would face from civil war in Iraq is from the spillover—the burdens, the instability, the copycat secession attempts and even follow-on wars that could emerge in neighboring countries. Welcome to the "new Middle East".... [18]

They go on to argue that one of the great problems of any war that unleashes ethnic or regional conflicts is spillover—it's contagious. For instance, the Israeli-Palestinian conflict provoked the civil wars in Jordan in 1970--71, and in Lebanon in 1975-90. The war in Lebanon sparked a civil war in Syria in 1976-82.

Refugee flows from civil wars spill over into surrounding countries. By mid-2007, over 2 million refugees had fled Iraq—mostly to Jordan and Syria. The Rwanda genocide of 1999 was ended by the invasion of the Tutsi-led Rwandan Patriotic Front that was drawn from 500,000 Tutsis who had already fled Rwanda as a result of past pogroms.

As the RPF entered Rwanda a million Hutu refugees fled to Congo:

For two years after 1994, Hutu bands continued to conduct raids in Rwanda and began to work with Congolese dictator Mubuto Sese Seko. The new RPF government in Rwanda responded by attacking not only the Hutu militia camps, but also its much larger neighbor, bolstering a formerly obscure Congolese opposition leader named Laurent Kabila and installing him in power in Kinshasa. A civil war in Congo ensued, killing perhaps four million people. [19]

That's right, *four million* people.

As we've seen in Iraq and Central Africa, violence begets more violence. Wars, especially civil wars, spill over and spin out of control.

LESSONS WE LEARNED FROM NEOCON RULE

Lesson # 1 —War is not just another "tool" of foreign policy. War can spiral out of control. Avoiding war must be one of the key goals of American foreign policy in the 21st century.

It's stating the obvious, that wars result in massive amounts of suffering and death. But the lesson is not that the use of military force is never justified. The use of military power to enforce the results of a legitimate process to resolve human differences is critical—just as the power of the state to resolve disputes through legislatures and courts are ultimately enforced by the use of force.

In Afghanistan and the Balkans, the joint decisions of the international community were enforced successfully by the use of military power. This was not true in Iraq.

Lesson # 2 —If you have them by the "balls," their hearts and minds do not necessarily follow.

The old Vietnam War slogan, "If you have them by the 'balls,' their hearts and minds follow," is just as untrue today as it was forty years ago.

The war in Iraq—and the Bush administration's overall approach to the "war on terror"—has failed in large part because it completely misreads the way people understand their own self-interests—and their own identities.

Did the Neocons really believe that the American troops invading Iraq would be greeted as liberators with rose petals? How would they react if an invading army attacked and occupied the United States, even to replace a detested leader?

By his actions in Iraq, Bush gave credence to bin Laden's charges that America and the West wanted to occupy Muslim lands.

His actions legitimated the Muslim extremist belief that America intended to lead a new crusade against Islam—that what was at stake was nothing less than Muslim identity and culture. This view was helped along by Bush's unfortunate use of the word "crusade" to discuss the War on Terror early on. It was also helped along by Bush's own attempt to tie the war in Iraq to al-Qaeda and Muslim fundamentalism.

In many ways, of course, bin Laden and Bush were very useful to each other when it came to their own home constituencies. Republicans used the specter of bin Laden shamelessly to stay in power in the U.S. While this helped Republicans in the short term, it was disastrous for the safety and security of the United States—and the world community. Of course, it has now become a political albatross for Bush and the Republicans.

At the same time Bush's policies in Iraq recruited thousands, if not millions, to the Islamic fundamentalist cause—exactly the opposite of its advertised intent.

An editorial cartoon printed in the Washington Post in the fall of 2006 hit the nail on the head. Bin Laden is pictured on the phone to Don Rumsfeld. He has a picture on his table of Rumsfeld with the inscription, "Top al-Qaeda recruiter—9/11 Pentagon boss." Bin Laden tells Rumsfeld: "You've been doing a heck of a job, Rummy!" [20]

As the occupation proceeded, the specter of the abuses of Abu Ghraib prison provided Islamic terrorist organizations with the recruiting poster of all time. U.S. troops detained thousands of innocent Iraqis who, once detained, became—along with their families—dedicated opponents of the United States. If your child, or wife or mother were killed or detained by Americans, you probably would join the ranks of those who hated America.

Iraq was just what bin Laden needed. It was just the kind of response he'd hoped for when he attacked America—and the Neocons fell for it hook, line and sinker. It was a response that he could use to show young Muslims that America was at war with Islam and Islamic culture, was challenging their identity, their meaning in life.

We have to remember the rules of politics. People have a wide array of self-interest. But meaning and identity are often more important than anything else. Disrespect is never forgiven. The fear of military force can directly appeal to people's need for physical security, but meaning and identity often trump physical security.

The Center for American Progress and *Foreign Policy* magazine conducted a survey of 100 highly-respected foreign policy and national security experts, among them both Republicans and Democrats; 84% of the respondents said the United States was not winning the War on Terror and 86% said the world was becoming more—not less –dangerous for Americans.

Bob Herbert, reporting on the survey in his New York Times column, summarized, "The war against terror cannot be won by bombing the enemy into submission. The bull in the china shop may be frightening at first, but after awhile it's just enraging." [21]

Lesson # 3—Neocon policy jeopardizes the fundamental interests of the United States.

Every result of Bush's policy in Iraq, and his fundamental approach to the War on Terror, has been inimical to America's national security interests.

• The Bush policy has created thousands of new radicalized Islamists who hate America. It has increased the pool of potential terrorists willing to do damage to America. According to *The New York Times*, "The national intelligence estimate, an assessment by America's 16 intelligence agencies, found that the war in Iraq, rather than stemming the growth of terrorism, had helped fuel its spread across the globe." The report said that Iraq had become "the cause celebre for jihadists, breeding a deep resentment of U.S. involvement in the Muslim world and cultivating supporters for the global jihadist movement." It said that the war was the second most important factor in the spread of terrorism—after "entrenched grievances such as corruption, injustice and fear of Western domination." [22]

• The Bush policy has alienated the people of Iraq whom we came to "liberate." An opinion poll in 2006 suggested that 90% of Iraqis would refuse to live next door to Americans. [23] Another survey asked them the reason for America's invasion of their country. The top three answers were to control Iraq and its oil (76%), to build military bases, and to help Israel. Finally, a poll of 1,150 people in late 2006 found that 78% of Iraqis believed that the American military presence caused more conflict than it prevented; 71% of Iraqis believed that American forces should be withdrawn by the end of 2006. Sixty-one percent said they *approved of attacking Americans—including 92% of Sunnis, 62% of Shiites and 41% of Kurds.*

• The neocon policy caused the global image of the United States to plummet. A BBC poll of 26,000 people in 25 countries, released on the eve of President Bush's 2007 State of the Union message, found that almost three-quarters of those surveyed disapproved of U.S. policy in Iraq and two-thirds said that the U.S. military presence in the Middle East did more harm than good. Only 29% said the U.S. was having a generally positive influence in the world. [24] A summer 2006 international survey by the Pew Research Center also showed that favorable views of the United States had plummeted. In Spain, only 23% held a positive opinion of the United States, down from 41% a year earlier. In Turkey, a NATO ally, support for the United States stood at 12%. [25] This decline was part of a long-term trend that has lasted throughout the Bush Presidency. Another Pew study that interviewed 91,000 people in 50 nations between 2002 and 2005 showed that favorable opinion of the United States has gone from 83% in 2000 (before 9/11, at the end of the Clinton administration) to 56% in 2006. Substantial majorities found the Iraq war had made the world more dangerous.[26]

The trend continued in a spring 2007 Pew study. A majority in 30 of the 46 countries surveyed criticized the United States for what they saw as acting without taking the views of other countries into consideration. Negative feelings were not confined to Muslim countries or the Middle East. Forty-two percent of those in Britain, 60% of those in France and 42% of those in Canada expressed negative feelings about the United States. [27]

• The war has simultaneously benefited two American adversaries who are also enemies of each other—Sunni fundamentalist bin Laden and the Shiite fundamentalist Iranian leadership. While creating potential terrorist recruits for al-Qaeda, the war has also installed a Shiite president and friend of Iran in Baghdad. Bush's policies have strengthened the Iranian surrogate leadership of Hezbollah in Lebanon that emerged as the political winner from the war with Israel in the summer of 2006. In January 2007, Anthony Shadid of *The Washington Post* wrote, "Four years after the United States invaded Iraq, in part to transform the Middle East, Iran is ascendant, many in the region view the Americans in retreat, and Arab countries, their own feelings of weakness accentuated, are awash in sharpening sectarian currents that many blame the United States for exacerbating." [28]

• The war in Iraq has sapped American military forces and communicated the exact opposite of Bush's intended message to the world. It has shown the limits of American power. Paul Krugman summarizes the result:

The most compelling argument against the invasion of Iraq wasn't the suspicion many of us had, which turned out to be correct, that the administration's case was fraudulent. It was the fact that the real reason government officials and many pundits wanted a war—their belief that if the United States used its military might to "hit someone" in the Arab world, never mind exactly who, it would shock and awe Islamic radicals into giving up terrorism—was all too obviously a childish fantasy.

The results of going to war, on the basis of that fantasy, were predictably disastrous: the fiasco in Iraq has ended up demonstrating the limits of US power, strengthening radical Islam—especially the radical Shiites allied with Iran, a group that includes Hezbollah—and losing America the high moral ground. [29]

• *Neo-con policies have cost America the moral high ground in more than just the Arab world.*
Iraq, Abu Ghraib, the Bush secret prisons, Guantanamo and torture, have all cost America the moral high ground: the credibility to lead.

• *Finally, the policy has made Iraq, which formerly was not a base for terrorists aimed at the United States, into a new training and recruiting ground for terrorists bent on our destruction.*

The Bush foreign policy could have been scripted by Osama bin Laden.

THE NEXT POTENTIAL NEOCON DISASTER—IRAN

You'd think that with a track record of total failure, the Neocons would have been tarred, feathered and run out of town. Rumsfeld is gone, but Bush and Cheney have not changed their spots.

In the spring of 2006, I joined Jan and a number of other Democratic members of Congress for dinner with a group of Iran policy scholars and former CIA officials. They believed that the Neocons were planning a military attack on Iran.

They urged the members of Congress to consider two key points:

• The best estimates were that the earliest Iran could develop a nuclear weapon was from four to nine years. They argued America should not once again be stampeded into unnecessary and precipitous use of military power when there was plenty of time to use approaches other than preemptive war.

• Once again a preemptive war would likely spin out of control. Iran is a highly mobilized society with a well-organized and financed military. If the United States tried to take out their nuclear facilities from the air, they would retaliate. They could shut off the straits of Hormuz into the Persian Gulf. They could drive oil prices to record highs. They could send a division of troops in the Shiite areas of Iraq. They could launch a counterstrike at Israel, or Qatar, where the U.S. Central command is located. Our dinner companions warned that a strike against Iran could spin out of control and into a massive region-wide war.

By the middle of 2006 journalist Seymour Hersh confirmed these fears. He reported that senior commanders at the Pentagon had increasingly challenged the president's plans. They warned that an attack on Iran could lead to serious economic, political and military consequences for the United States.

They warned of faulty intelligence, both on Iranian nuclear programs and the location of underground facilities. Hersh quotes a high-ranking general as saying, "The target array is huge, but it's amorphous.... The question we face is, when does innocent infrastructure evolve into something nefarious?... We built this big monster with Iraq, and there was nothing there. This is son of Iraq." [30]

A former senior intelligence official told Hersh, "Bush and Cheney were dead serious about nuclear planning"—using a tactical nuclear weapons in a first strike to destroy the nuclear facility at Natanz. The military, led by the joint Chiefs Chair General Pace, apparently ferociously resisted this option with some success, [31] but it is astounding that the Neocons would seriously consider this possibility—especially since even a tactical nuclear strike would likely involve tens of thousands of civilian casualties.

Of course, the most astounding thing about the neocon drumbeat for war with Iran was their apparent blindness to what has happened in Iraq. Retired Major General William Nash, who commanded the 1st Armored Division, served in Iraq and Bosnia, and worked for the U.N. in Kosovo, told Hersh an American bombing "would be seen not only as an attack on Shiites but as an attack on all Muslims. Throughout the Middle East, it would likely be seen as another example of American imperialism. It would probably cause the war to spread." [32]

In his conclusion, Hersh quotes Muhamed ElBaradei, the Director General of the International Atomic Energy Agency (IAEA), who won the Nobel Peace Prize in 2005. ElBaradei said:

> We should have learned some lessons from Iraq. We should've learned that we should be very careful about assessing our intelligence... We should have learned that we should try to exhaust every possible diplomatic means to solve the problem before thinking of any other enforcement measures... When you push the country into a corner, you are always giving the driver's seat to the hardliners." [33]

Let us recall that in Iraq, ElBaradei was right about the absence of nuclear weapons, and George W. Bush was dead wrong.

By mid-2007, Senator Joe Lieberman, who had many years earlier drunk the neocon Kool-Aid, became the leader of the chorus that continued the drum beat for war with Iran.

THE PROBLEM OF PROLIFERATING WMD

The spread of all forms of Weapons of Mass Destruction—especially nuclear weapons technology—is a massive problem. The current Nuclear Nonproliferation Treaty seeks to limit the spread of nuclear weapons to states that don't currently possess them. This is a critical goal. But the non-nuclear states agreed to this limitation in consideration of the other part of the nuclear nonproliferation regime that is not so well known. The nuclear states agreed to begin the process of reducing their own nuclear weapons stockpiles.

This quid pro quo is obviously central, if we put ourselves in the position of the Iranians, or Indonesians, or South Africans (the only country to abandon nuclear weapons technology once they had it)—or any other non-nuclear state. From their point of view, why should they be considered any less responsible to control nuclear weapons than the Pakistanis or the Israelis—or, for that matter, the Americans? The status quo can last for a while, but ultimately all states must renounce nuclear weapons technology—or many other states, and potentially non-state actors—will gain control of that technology. Mature technology, by its nature, becomes simpler and cheaper. This makes it more accessible.

And the problem is not simply preventing the spread of nuclear weapons to new states. For instance, the U.S. might feel relatively safe today with Pakistan in the nuclear club. Pakistan at the moment is a reliable U.S. ally. But you don't have to stretch your imagination to visualize a Pakistani government controlled by militant Islamists. Remember, Iran, used to be a "reliable" U.S. ally.

A status quo where some states have nuclear weapons and others do not is unsustainable and unstable over the long run. The Neocons have no inkling that this might be true. They are pushing for a next generation of U.S. nuclear weapons modernization, development and deployment. How can the U.S. demand nuclear abstention by other nations while it is planning another nuclear orgy of its own?

In January 2007, former Secretaries of State Henry Kissinger and George Shultz and former Secretaries of Defense William Perry and Sam Nunn wrote an op-ed in *The Wall Street Journal* that called on the Bush administration to take the leadership in reversing reliance on nuclear weapons as a step toward preventing further proliferation. They called on the U.S. to ratify the Comprehensive Test Ban Treaty, take nuclear weapons off alert, make further reductions in nuclear forces and halt production of fissile materials. [34]

Mutual reduction and control of nuclear weapons is critical to the long-term prospects of human survival. This goal will either be reached by our own preemptive action to prevent crisis, or after thousands and perhaps millions have been killed by someone's use of nuclear weapons has horrified the world into action.

JIHADISM AND AMERICAN FOREIGN-POLICY

The rise of Jihadism is a significant threat to the spread of progressive values, especially in the Muslim world. But contrary to some analysts and commentators, it is not our generation's fascism or communism. Writing in *The New Yorker*, George Packer says:

> *Jihadism poses two very different threats to the United States: the danger of catastrophic attack inside the country by a handful of dedicated individuals, and a much broader power to catalyze ideological extremism among vast numbers of people. The Bush administration has waged the war by playing on the fear of the first at home, while failing to address the second abroad, and thereby intensifying it. In the near future, radical Islamism is a greater danger to Muslims and other citizens of foreign countries than to Americans.*[35]

The challenge of Jihadism must be approached in three ways:

- A rigorous defense against terrorist attack—including beefed-up port security and security for chemical plants and other vulnerable commercial institutions. The Bush administration has never focused enough attention on these kinds of security needs because of pushback from big shippers like Wal-Mart, and big chemical and oil companies that are potential commercial targets but don't want the burden of rigorous security.

- We must offer a compelling progressive vision of the world that can compete with fundamentalist fanaticism.

- We must create trade and investment and aid policies that truly foster economic growth in the developing world.

Packard argues that:

> *Ultimately, the Cold War analogy is unhelpful, because it allows Americans to make a virtue out of our ignorance. Islam is far stranger to us than communism. It requires a deeper, subtler knowledge of local realities around the Muslim world, in all their variety, than most American writers and politicians have shown. The policymakers of the Kennedy era overlooked the essentially nationalist nature of Vietnamese communism because they were swept up in binary thinking... how much less to today's policymakers know*

about the Egyptian Muslim Brotherhood, the factions vying within Arab Gulf states, the Muslim minorities in Europe, the configuration of power in Iran, the causes of the Taliban resurgence in Afghanistan... or the rising terrorist threat in Bangladesh? The grand overarching "narrative" of anti-totalitarianism ... can't explain the different kinds of trouble that America faces in a chaotic world. It substitutes will for understanding, which is just as dangerous as the reverse—if the Iraq war has taught us anything, it should be that. [36]

Failure to Address the Security Crisis Caused by Third World Poverty

The Neocons have failed not only because of what they have done, but also because of what they have failed to do: long-term investment in the development of impoverished Third World societies.

The worldwide communications explosion delivers daily images of first world lifestyles to viewers and listeners in slums and villages in every corner of the planet. The gulf that lies between their aspirations and the reality of their daily lives is our most dangerous security risk.

The continuing crisis of poverty in Haiti is emblematic.

Several years ago, Jan accompanied Ethel Kennedy to Haiti. The purpose of the trip was both to learn about the country, and present an award from the Robert Kennedy Foundation to a clinic founded by Dr. Paul Farmer, which was now run by a remarkable woman doctor, Loune Viaud.

Farmer, who subsequently became a good friend, is an extraordinary man. He founded the clinic that now serves a million people a year in the central highlands of Haiti 20 years ago when he was still in Harvard Medical School. He is now on the faculty of Harvard Medical School but spends more than half of the year at the clinic in Haiti—and lately, at a new clinic he and his organization, Partners in Health, have founded in Rwanda. The Rwandan project is funded by former President Clinton's foundation. Farmer is also a trained anthropologist.

In Haiti, he pioneered a model community-based healthcare programs that mobilize local people to prevent and treat HIV/AIDS and other infectious diseases.

The New England Journal of Medicine says: "There are many kinds of gifted physicians: clinicians, researchers, and those who build institutions. Paul Farmer is the rarest of all: a prophet..." [37]

Paul is a tireless advocate for the poor, and for the view that they deserve health care just as much as the rich do.

After Jan met Paul, she became deeply concerned with Haiti. Its recent history is yet another example of the tragic consequences of neocon foreign policy.

HAITI

Haiti was founded 200 years ago as a result of a slave rebellion against French colonial rule. With the exception of Bill Clinton's intervention to reinstate Jean-Bertrand Aristide, the democratically elected president of the country, in the 1990s, the U.S. has traditionally backed the small elite that has dominated the island's economy and politics.

Over much of the last 40 years, the U.S. supported two vicious dictators—"Papa Doc" Duvalier and his son, "Baby Doc." These regimes and the tiny group of elites that constituted their political base systematically exploited and terrorized the island's population.

Much of their power was exercised through the Army—which was created during the U.S. occupation of the country in the early 1900s. In its history, the Haitian Army never fought a foreign foe. It was used exclusively to enforce domestic social control.

In 1990, Jean-Bertrand Aristide, a progressive priest and hero to the country's poor, was elected President by 70% of the vote. Within seven months he had been ousted by a military coup backed by his country's elite and their foreign backers. Aristide was returned to power in 1994 after President Clinton threatened to send American troops to reestablish democracy in Haiti, which is only 600 miles from Florida.

After Aristide returned, he abolished the Haitian army, but economic progress was slow and difficult. Over its history, Haiti has been virtually entirely deforested. The border between Haiti and the Dominican Republic, with which it shares the island of Hispaniola, is a stark line. On one side there are forests. On the other side there are none.

In 1991, international health and population experts created a "human suffering index" that combines measures of human welfare ranging from life expectancy to political freedom. In Paul Farmer's book, Pathologies of Power, he reports that based on this index, 27 of the 141 countries were characterized by "extreme human suffering." Only one of them, Haiti, was in the Western Hemisphere. "In only three countries on earth was suffering judged to be more extreme than that endured in Haiti, each of these countries was in the midst of an internationally-recognized civil war." [38]

Farmer relates that:

Working in contemporary Haiti, where in recent decades political violence has been added to the worst poverty in the hemisphere, one learns a great deal about suffering. In fact, the country has long constituted a sort of laboratory *for the study of affliction, no matter how it is defined. "Life for the Haitian peasant today," observed the anthropologist Jean Weise some 30 years ago, "is the abject misery and a rank familiarity with death." The biggest problem, of course, is unimaginable poverty, and a long succession of dictatorial governments has been more engaged in pillaging than in protecting the rights of workers, even on paper. As Eduardo Galeano noted in 1973, at the height of the Duvalier dictatorship, "The wages in Haiti required by law belong in the Department of Science Fiction: actual wages on coffee plantations vary from $.07 to $.15 a day....*

Today, life expectancy at birth is less than 50 years, in large part because as many as two of every 10 infants die before their first birthday. Tuberculosis and AIDS are the leading causes of death among adults; among children measles and tetanus ravage the undernourished. [39]

Note that all of these afflictions are treatable diseases.

As a result of the abolition of the Army, Aristide became the first president in Haiti's history to peacefully hand over power to another elected civilian, René Préval, in 1996.

Four years later, Aristide was reelected. Unfortunately for Haiti, so was George W. Bush. The Neocons hated Aristide. They used purported election irregularities in the election for the Haitian Senate (and not the President) as the premise for an aid embargo to the fragile government.

Of course, the Bush premise of "election irregularities" was pretty brazen, given the election irregularities that plagued his own election to office; but they used it just the same to block $500 million in aid to the Haitian government.

In 2004, The Boston Globe reported that the aid cutoff ravaged the economy of the nation, already twice as poor as any other in the Western Hemisphere.

The cutoff, intended to pressure the government to adopt political reforms, left Haiti struggling to meet even basic needs and weakened the authority of President Jean-Bertrand Aristide.... Today, Haiti's government, which serves 8 million people, has an annual budget of about $300 million—less than that of Cambridge, Massachusetts, a city of 100,000.... Many of Aristide's supporters, in Haiti and abroad, angrily countered that the international community, particularly the United States, abandoned the fledgling democracy when it needed aid. Many believe that Aristide himself was the target of the de facto economic sanctions just as Haiti was beginning to put its finances back in order. [40]

In fact, the US may have done even more to undermine Aristide. In early 2004, a small group of well-equipped personnel from the former Haitian

Army entered the country and marched on the capital. The exact role of the U.S. is unclear. But the International Republican Institute (IRI) spent $1.2 million of the U.S. taxpayer's money funding Aristide opposition.

In any case, the U.S. was heavily involved in the last chapter of the Aristide government—some of which Jan and I know firsthand.

As the political crisis in Haiti deepened, the Black Caucus in the U.S. Congress demanded a meeting with President George W. Bush to ask him to take the side of the democratically elected regime. The President at that time had not yet met—even once in his term—with the Black Caucus, despite numerous requests. So the leaders of the caucus decided to go to the White House and demand to see the President. They invited Jan to accompany them. The press followed.

They were met by Condoleezza Rice, then the National Security Adviser, Secretary of State Colin Powell and White House Chief of Staff Andrew Card. After some discussion of the issue, Congressman John Conyers said, "Well, I'm not leaving until I see my President." Card then made the mistake of lecturing the members of Congress. He said he was "offended," that they knew that the assembled group had the ear of the President. The group bristled at Card's impertinence and Condoleezza Rice realized that—with the press corps parked outside—she had a "situation."

She told everyone to "relax" and exited to retrieve the President. About 10 minutes later, the President joined the group. He listened quietly as the group made its arguments, and without saying much in response, ended the meeting.

An amusing—potentially apocryphal—interchange happened as members of the delegation put on their coats to leave. Jan had an "Obama" button on her coat. Barack Obama was in the midst of his primary campaign for the United States Senate, which later that year would give control of Illinois' second Senate seat back to the Democrats. Jan had been a big, early backer.

But as Jan went to shake Bush's hand, he jumped back in horror. In a second, she realized that he thought she had an "Osama" button on her coat. So she said, "No, Mr. President, it's Obama—Barack Obama—he's running for the Senate from Illinois." To which he replied, "Well, I don't know him." She answered: "You will, Mr. President, you will."

After the meeting, nothing changed; the rump contingent of the military—including some of the most notorious human-rights abusers— marched on the capital in American-made uniforms, with American-made weapons. The street gangs from the Port-au-Prince slums prepared for a bloody fight to defend the Presidential Palace.

Rather than back the democratically elected government, the US had been pressing Aristide to step down.

LEAVE NOW OR DIE

On her trip to Haiti, Jan had become acquainted with Aristide and especially his wife, Mildred. I was watching the NBC Nightly News on Saturday night when the phone rang at our home in Evanston, Illinois. It was Mildred Aristide calling for Jan from Port-au-Prince. From their chat about the situation, Jan says there was no indication of a woman voluntarily getting ready to pack her bags and move from her home.

A few minutes into the news, NBC reported that Aristide planned to leave the country and go into exile, and that the U.S. was "facilitating" the transition. I walked into the kitchen and told Jan—who was still on the phone with Mildred—what had been reported. Mildred said they had no plans to leave.

The next morning, the Sunday news shows reported that a U.S. government plane was transporting the Aristides to Africa.

From subsequent reports, here's what happened early Sunday morning.

The Aristides were awakened by personnel from the U.S. Embassy early and told that the rump group of soldiers would soon be at the Palace and the U.S. was unable to guarantee the Aristide family's safety. But the U.S. had an aircraft waiting and would transport them out of the country if they left immediately. The message was clear: leave now or die.

On the American aircraft, no one was allowed to raise the window shades for hours. The Aristides were not told where they were being taken. Finally they landed in the Central African Republic (CAR) that had—at U.S. urging—agreed to provide them temporary sanctuary. An interim government with U.S. support was formed in Haiti.

New Haitian presidential elections were finally held in 2005. Renée Préval, the former president and Aristide protégé, was once again elected over the objections of the U.S. and the wealthy elite.

STRUCTURAL VIOLENCE

But Haiti is more than just an example of neocon intervention to oppose a progressive regime. It is a prime example of what Paul Farmer calls "structural violence."

Structural violence influences the nature and distribution of extreme suffering, and tramples the most basic human right of all—the right to survive.

In the forward to Paul Farmer's book on structural violence, Nobel Prize-winning economist Amartya Sen writes:

Human rights violations are not accidents; they are not random in distribution and effect. Rights violations are, rather, systems of deeper pathologies of power and are linked intimately to the social conditions that so often determine who will suffer abuse and who will be shielded from harm. [41]

In *Pathologies of Power*, Farmer analyzes the factors that impose suffering on some people and not others. He finds that sexism and racism are serious negative factors, particularly in developing countries. And he concludes that poverty is the most pervasive and significant factor causing "structural violence."

The World Health Organization, in a 1995 report, concludes that poverty is the world's greatest killer:

Poverty wields its destructive influence at every stage of human life, from the moment of conception to the grave. It conspires with the most deadly and painful diseases to bring a wretched existence to all those who suffer from it. [42]

Farmer says that the poor are not only more likely to suffer, they're less likely to have their suffering noticed. Annually 8.8 million people die of fully preventable diseases — over 25,000 every day. [43]

ACEPHIE'S STORY

Economist Amartya Sen summarizes the story of Acephie, which Farmer uses to illustrate structural violence:

Take the case of Acephie, the comely woman, born in the small village of Kay through which runs Riviere Artiboite, Haiti's largest river. She is lucky to be born into a prosperous peasant family, but her luck does not last for long. When the valley is flooded to make room for a reservoir, the villages are forced up into the stony hills on the sides of the new lake. Their voice does not receive a hearing. The displaced people — the "water refugees" — seek whatever jobs they can get (no longer able to grow the rice, bananas, millet, corn, or sugar cane they grew so abundantly earlier), and Acephie's family ceases to make ends meet. Nevertheless, Acephie — like other young women in families of water refugees — carries the family's agricultural produce (miserable as it is) to the local market. The soldiers, stationed on the way, watch the procession of girls who walk to the market and often flirt with them. The girls feel lucky to get such attention, since the soldiers are powerful and respected men.

When Captain Jacque Honorat woos the tall and fine featured Acephie, with her enormous dark eyes, reciprocation eventually follows (even though

Acephie knows that Honorat is married and has several other partners). The sexual liaison does not last long, but it is enough to disrupt Acephie's life, while Captain Honorat dies of unexplained fevers. After trying to qualify herself as a domestic servant in the neighboring town of Mirebalais, the 22-year-old Acephie moves to Port-au-Prince and finds a servant's job, at a tiny wage. She also began seeing Blanco Nerette, who comes from a similar background (his parents were also water refugees) and now chauffeurs a small bus, and they plan to marry. However, when Acephie becomes pregnant, Blanco does not welcome the news at all. Their relationship founders. Also thanks to her pregnancy, Acephie loses her job. The battle for economic survival turns intense and is now joined by disease. Acephie dies of AIDS—loved still by her own family, but uncared for and unhelped by society. She leaves behind a daughter, also infected by the virus. That is the beginning of another story, but not a long one...

*   The inequities of power that Acephie faced in her brief life involved bureaucracy (beginning with displacements to make room for the new reservoir without adequate rearrangement), class (reflected in Acephie's relations with her employer and with Captain Honorat), gender (related to her standing vis-à-vis the males she encountered—from the soldier to Blanco), and of course the stratified society (with the absence of public facilities for medical attention and care for the poor). Acephie did not encounter any physical violence, but Farmer is persuasive seeing her as a victim of structural violence.* [44]

Acephie died of AIDS, partially because she was a woman—but especially because she was a poor woman who found her best option for economic survival to be a liaison with the soldier and had no access to treatment. This correlation pertains to women in the US as well—the majority of women with AIDS in the US are poor. Globally, half a million women die each year of childbirth. But not all women are equally at risk. In fact, 99.8% of these deaths are in developing countries. [45]

In South Africa, epidemiologists have found that the infant mortality rate among blacks may be as high as 10 times that of whites. Every baby in South Africa is not equally at risk of dying;—poor black children, who have no control whatsoever over their fate, are impacted by structural violence—by a lack of resources necessary to keep them from dying. [46]

A 1986 study in the US, showed that the likelihood of dying from cardiovascular disease, and cerebral vascular disease (strokes or TIAs) was directly related to social class. [47]

Tony Hall, who in 2003 was U.S. ambassador to the world food program, estimated that 825 million people in the world are hungry. [48]

THE EFFECTS OF STRUCTURAL VIOLENCE

- Structural violence is violence. It causes suffering and death just as certainly as the explosion of a bomb. The victim of AIDS who do not have access to retroviral drugs is just as dead as he would be if he were shot.

- Structural violence leads to political violence—domestic violence, civil wars and international violence. The structural violence caused by poverty is not always endured in silence and passivity. It is a fundamental cause of civil wars, revolutions, guerrilla movements, terrorist acts and genocide that threaten the stability and survival of societies. And we've seen that what happens in any society now threatens every other society. Haiti's refugees have flooded the U.S. and neighboring Dominican Republic. Haiti is also one of the major platforms for drug trafficking in the United States.

Farmer writes:

In rural Haiti, both violence and disease have always appeared as pathologies of power. Structural violence was at the heart of Haiti's creation, and this former slave colony is as good a reminder as any of the intimate ties between those who are the victims of violence and those who are shielded from it. More guns and more repression may well be the time honored prescription for policing poverty, but violence and chaos will not go away if the hunger, illness and racism that are the lot of so many are not addressed in any meaningful and durable fashion. [49]

- The same forms of structural violence impact large numbers of people in our own society. Poverty in the U.S. has risen consistently since George W. Bush took office—37 million Americans now live in poverty and 43% of those live on less than $7,800 per year for a family of three. In 2005, 1.3 million people were added to the record 46.6 million people (15.9% of the population) with no health coverage. [50]

- If we broaden our focus for the challenges that affect our society in the 21st century to include everyone on the planet, the problem of structural violence affects huge percentages of the world population. Remember that 80% of the world's population lives in a developing country. "Our society" includes all of them, too. Their children are all of humanity's children.

- The moral importance of structural violence is staggering. We can't blame forces "beyond our control." We can't blame "mother nature." Structural violence is caused by human decisions—particularly with the rise of technology and affluence that could abate so much of the human suffering it causes.

AIDS, malaria, diarrhea, tuberculosis—the big killers of the Third World are *all* treatable. Many are preventable. That so many people suffer and die from them results from a decision—made by human decision makers—not to allocate the resources to prevent them. A "Manhattan Project" to provide clean water to everyone in the world would prevent the deaths of 6,000 people per day—and 1.4 million children under five each year.

Instead, radical conservatives reallocate those resources to the very rich. While millions die from treatable diseases, the Republicans attempt to eliminate the Estate Tax and redirect $1 trillion over the next 10 years to the heirs of multimillionaires. That is a human decision to perpetrate systematic violence and suffering on millions of their fellow human beings.

It is a direct assault on the progressive values that have defined the progress of human civilization. It violates the first moral obligation to do unto others as we would have them do unto us.

It is also an active violation of human rights. The most basic human right, after all, is the right to survive.

Article 25 of the Universal Declaration of Human Rights of the UN reads:

> *Everyone has the right to a standard of living adequate for the health and well-being of himself and his family, including food, clothing, housing and medical care and necessary social services, and the right to security in the event of unemployment, sickness, disability, widowhood, old age or other lack of livelihood in circumstances beyond his control.*

Article 27 says that everyone has the right "to share in scientific advancement and its benefits."

These statements are the reflection of the commitment to progressive values by the world community. They are the antithesis of radical conservative Republican values.

PROGRESSIVE VALUES AND SECURITY

The Bush years have provided a stark demonstration that the "tough," macho bluster of radical conservative values does not provide us with more security. In fact, their application in the modern world provides just the opposite. They are formula for war, death and human suffering.

Radical conservative values are not adapted for our survival and success today, or in the world of the future.

1) Neoconservative policy ignores the core progressive value of empathy.
This represents a moral failure. But it also prevents neoconservative policymakers from correctly predicting the consequences of their own actions. It prevents them from understanding the responses of the people whose behavior they are trying to change. Neoconservatives have a very difficult time putting themselves in the position of the average citizens of Baghdad, or the peasants in Mexico, or terrorist recruits—and then imagining how they *themselves* would react.

They find it impossible to imagine how they would react as the subject of an occupation by a foreign power, or if NAFTA cut the price of the corn on which they depend to feed their families, or as a young Muslim looking for meaning in life. They don't ask the question: how would I behave if my wife were killed by mistake at an American checkpoint, or if I were forced to be part of the naked pile of bodies in Abu Ghraib? How would I feel if every day I had to make do with little electric power and constant physical insecurity?

From a progressive point of view, decision-making based on empathy for others is morally right. But it is also necessary to understand other people's self-interest and predict how they will respond to your actions. Empathy is necessary to effectively execute any political action. Lack of empathy has led the Neocons to take actions that *create* more terrorists every day than they could possibly kill.

As we saw when it comes to managing organizations, empathy is necessary to understand that—positive reinforcement works empirically better to get people to change their behavior than negative sanctions. The evidence shows that the results of negative sanctions tend to come out "sideways"; they just don't work as well as positive incentives.

The core progressive value of empathy is especially important for the most powerful nation in the world. It is all that prevents the powerful from acting like a bull in a china shop. It defines the difference between arrogant, ignorant action and wise, effective action.

Neocons like to portray themselves as worldly, hardened realists. In fact, they are naïve and parochial. Their failure to empathize and understand others means that their pretensions to being tough and world-wise are completely baseless. Being cosmopolitan and sophisticated about the world requires empathy, not arrogance and self-righteousness.

2) The radical conservatives' failure to acknowledge that complex causation has moral consequences makes it impossible to address the problems of the modern world.
The world is not a gunfight at the OK Corral between George W. Bush and Saddam Hussein. It is the product of past decisions about our environment, our resources, and our complex self-interests. The notion that the values we use to set our priorities for action should be limited to those that involve direct action of one actor on another simply doesn't reflect the real-world. Actions taken with that assumption fail to achieve their desired goals.

People and cultures are the products of past decisions that have impacted their physical and social environments. Al-Qaeda was a product of the Cold War battle by the old Soviet Union to continue its dominance of Afghanistan. The U.S. supplied bin Laden and his Mujahideen fighters with millions of dollars of weapons. And before the successful policy of the U.N. inspectors in the Clinton administration that rid Iraq of weapons of mass destruction, Saddam Hussein did have chemical weapons. We know, because the U.S. sold him the chemicals and did nothing to protest his use of them in Iraq's long war with Iran. We had the receipts.

Action has consequences beyond the direct, immediate impact.

The United States helped set the stage for the fundamentalist resurgence of Islam in Iran. The CIA helped the Shah (a King) return to absolute power by overthrowing the democratically elected left-leaning government of Mossadegh in 1953. Our support for the Shah's regime—with its increasing economic inequality and draconian political oppression—created the conditions for the triumph of the Islamic "revolution" in the late 1970s.

And priorities based only on direct causation have no chance of addressing poverty and structural violence. In fact, by ignoring complex causation, conservatives deny the existence of structural violence. In their view, people either take responsible action, or they don't. People have the discipline and the drive to escape poverty, or they don't. From their point of view, life is all a matter of individual action—the structure of the world economy, or the stratification of society, or availability of education or health care, have nothing to do with it. That view does not describe the real world, and action based on it will fail.

3) The failure of radical conservative values to take a long-term view is heavily related to its rejection of moral importance of complex causation.
Radical conservative values result in action intended to "win the battle," but end up losing the war. It may feel good—or even seem effective—to round up every likely "suspect" in Baghdad and put them in Abu Ghraib in the short term. But in the long run that radicalizes the entire population to hate you.

It may feel "good" to torture "terrorist" suspects. But—aside from the fact that intelligence experts say it doesn't yield accurate information—it also places our soldiers, CIA employees, government officials and other citizens at risk of similar treatment. And it endangers our troops on the battlefield. There was a time when combatants from other nations were quicker to surrender to U.S. forces because they knew they would be treated according to the Geneva Conventions. No longer.

Finally, it obliterates our moral authority to stand for human rights everywhere else in the world.

4) The "Exceptionalism" that flows from radical conservative "moral law" values is dysfunctional in the modern integrated world.

One of the biggest reasons people in other countries hate George Bush is that he acts with double standards. He assumes that everyone ought to realize that he and his government have moral superiority to do whatever he thinks is necessary to advance his goals—because his goals are the one true set of moral goals.

The "moral law" approach to morality is the basis of all fundamentalism. Fundamentalists believe that they alone have received revelation from God; that they are the only chosen people; that if you don't see it their way, you're wrong—not just intellectually wrong, *morally* wrong. That results in moral and intellectual arrogance—in American "exceptionalism."

Progressive values prioritize the success and survival of *all* human beings. Our values require us to be passionate about the pursuit of that goal. But they also require us to be realistic about our own intellectual limitations. That realism, or intellectual modesty, prevents us from falling into the incorrect view that we alone have the answer to all of life's problems—that our beliefs or culture are the highest expressions of immutable laws of nature.

Progressive values enable us to keep our eyes on the ball—human success and survival—and not mistakenly assume that one culture or religion has a lock on insight as to how that goal should be achieved.

Politically, this radical conservative exceptionalism increasingly leads to failure:

> • It sends a message to others that we don't respect them, their culture or their religion.

> • It denies the fact that the United States is not the only center of power in the world. There will be more and more centers of power as the world evolves over the next century. Europe, China, India, Japan, the Muslim world, and soon a South American bloc. Effective foreign and security policy in the 21st century requires

highly developed skills at multilateralism—not the arrogant assumption that only American leaders know what is right.

• To everyone else, it makes Americans look like hypocrites. Under George Bush, the U.S. has pressed other governments to pledge that they will exempt the U.S. from the jurisdiction of the International Criminal Court (ICC). The rest of the world's view has been, "who the hell do they think they are?" Of course, the Bush administration's willingness to torture suspects, open secret prisons, hold prisoners without trial and flout the Geneva conventions gives us a deeper understanding of why they are so concerned about the ICC. To most people in the world, it's common sense and "what's good for the goose is good for the gander."

•Exceptionalism completely undercuts our ability to exert moral leadership. How can America demand others be denied nuclear weapons, if we refuse to abide by our treaty commitments to reduce nuclear stockpiles—and instead develop a new generation of nuclear weapons? How can America ask others to reduce the production of greenhouse gases if we refuse to do so?

•This kind of exceptionalism endangers Americans abroad. Imagine this: The President of Sudan arrests American journalists and human-rights workers involved in trying to prevent the Khartoum government from continuing to commit genocide in Darfur. He holds them incommunicado, and tortures them in secret prisons. If asked, he says he believes they are likely terrorists. Some are sent to other countries for further interrogation using "alternative" techniques. He finally puts them on trial before military tribunals set up exactly like those President Bush wants to use on prisoners at Guantanamo. The prisoners can be convicted based on classified evidence against them, but they may not see the evidence. How would Americans react? Unfair show trials? Totalitarian tactics?

When Jan went with a delegation to inspect the prisons at Guantanamo in 2002, she asked the commander, Major General Geoffrey Miller (subsequently, the commander who presided over Abu Ghraib in Iraq) how the prisoners could be entirely denied their rights to due process. "How can we say they are neither prisoners of war, who are subject to the Geneva conventions, nor charge them as criminals in the courts?" she asked.

"Trust me, ma'am," came the reply. "These are all bad guys."

Of course, this turned out not to be true. Hundreds have been released without charge. Just as it wasn't true of Maher Arar, a

Canadian who was arrested at Kennedy Airport on his way back from a vacation in Tunisia. The U.S. was acting on bad intelligence from the Canadians. But that didn't matter. Without any due process, he was subject to "extraordinary rendition." He was sent to Syria by way of Jordan, where he was held and tortured for a year.

He spent most of his time in a tiny underground cell about the size of a grave.

He was finally released when the Syrians could find no evidence that he was a terrorist. The Canadian government commission confirmed this in a fall 2006 report. As New York Times columnist Bob Herbert reports, "He was nothing more than a quiet family man when he found himself socked into a vortex of incompetence, hysteria and a so-called war on terrorism that had gone completely haywire." [51]

That's why traditional progressive values—and the U.S. Bill of Rights—give suspects a right to due process. We don't just trust the government that "they're all bad guys." We've learned from history that that attitude is the surest route to tyranny.

If we try to exempt ourselves from these values—if we contend we can violate their rights—others will do the same thing to Americans.

• That will not only be a tragedy for Americans, it will undermine the development of an international rule of law that is critical to assure that nonviolent resolution of conflict in the future. Exceptionalism makes it easy to objectify other people—to make them less than human. That is just the opposite of what's needed to assure that the people on our small planet live in peace. It polarizes the world between us and them. It fans the flames of division and sectarianism. The Neocons view themselves and America as morally superior—as the "good guys" in a "good guy-bad guy" drama. It challenges other nations as "evil." It seeks to create an "American Century." Think about what the rest of the world thinks about an "American Century."

5) Radical conservative values place a priority on unrestrained pursuit of individual self-interest. When that is combined with conservative exceptionalism, it plays out in unilateral action that is dangerous to peace in the modern world.

In the case of Iraq, the unilateralist approach went to the extent of "preemptive war." As it turned out, of course, the "weapons of mass destruction" which the war was intended to "preempt" did not exist. Our use of preemptive war undercuts the emerging institution of non-violent conflict resolution and legitimates the use of preemptive war by others. If we can engage in preemptive war, why not everyone else?

To prevent the massive increase in military technological power from destroying us—or a large portion of us—we must develop methods of worldwide nonviolent conflict resolution. Humanity has invested its greatest hopes in this regard in the United Nations. Unilateral, preemptive war completely undermines the development of these procedures. And of course, the neo-cons would like to destroy or radically limit the U.N. and other international institutions as well.

DANGEROUS VALUES

In short, radical conservative values are not tough, realistic approaches to a dangerous world. They are themselves a danger to peace and security. In many respects, they represent the antithesis of the priorities needed to prevent our burgeoning technology and exploding population and growing interdependence from combining to form an explosive brew that endangers our survival.

CHAPTER FIFTY

The Challenges We Face: Interruption of Interdependent Relationships—Especially the Collapse of Trade Relations

PITCAIRN AND HENDERSON

In *Collapse*, Diamond presents several case studies where the collapse of trade relationships contributed directly to a society's decline and collapse. The most graphic was the case at Pitcairn and Henderson Islands in southeast Polynesia. These two islands supported societies that depended heavily for many goods on trade with Mangareva—a larger island. It was the geographic hub of a much larger trading network, of which the ocean journey to Pitcairn and Henderson was the shortest spoke. For many years, Mangareva had most of the resources it needed to sustain its society. It did however have inferior stone. Pitcairn had great stone and traded with Mangareva for many of the necessities its small land area lacked.

Henderson had abundant seafood, bird populations and turtles. Henderson apparently traded sea turtles—a luxury food—and ceremonial bird feathers used for ornaments and feathered cloaks in Polynesia. These would be analogous to gold and sable for us today.

Pitcairn traded its stone both to Henderson and, more importantly, to the "mother island" of Mangareva in exchange for manufactured goods, crops, pigs, tools and oyster shells.

The trade between them also provided the smaller societies with exchanges of marriage partners, technical skills and the opportunity to re-import crops that by chance had died out.

The trade continued for 450 years—from A.D 1000 to 1450. But by 1500, the trade stopped.

The reason appears to have stemmed from disastrous environmental changes in Mangareva—and to a lesser extent of Pitcairn.

Mangareva was especially susceptible to deforestation, which led directly to many of the consequences we saw on Easter Island. In particular, deforestation led to reduced fishing yields because there were no trees large enough to build canoes. In addition, it led to massive soil erosion. Diamond writes:

With too many people and too little food, Mangareva society slid into a nightmare of civil war and chronic hunger.... All that political chaos alone would have made it difficult to muster the manpower and supplies necessary for oceangoing canoe travel, and to go off for a month and leave one's garden untended, even if trees for canoes themselves did not become unavailable. [1]

With the collapse of Mangareva, the entire southeast Polynesian trade network collapsed as well. Henderson and Pitcairn could not survive on their own. Henderson, in particular, needed volcanic stone to make tools. Both societies overtaxed their resources to survive. Five of nine species of land birds were exterminated. They over-exploited their shellfish.

In the end, no one was left alive on Henderson or Pitcairn. Neither had trees large enough to make ocean-going canoes. When the canoes stopped coming from Mangareva, each of the small societies was effectively isolated.

As populations shrunk on each it would have become impossible to consummate marriages not in violation of incest taboos—or alternatively resulting in inbreeding, causing congenital deformity to proliferate.

We don't know how human life ended on Henderson or Pitcairn. Diamond asks, Did the last Henderson Islanders spend much time on the beaches, for generation after generation, staring out to sea in hopes of sighting the canoes that stopped coming, until even the memory of what a canoes looked like grew dim? [2]

Diamond concludes his study of the collapse of Henderson and Pitcairn this way:

Lest these islands still seem to you to remote in space and time to be relevant to our modern societies, just think about the risks (as well as the benefits) of an increasing globalization and increasing worldwide economic interdependence. Many economically important but ecologically fragile areas (think oil) already affect the rest of us, just as Mangareva affected Pitcairn and Henderson.[3]

We don't have to go far to remember the impact of our dependence on other societies for resources. The 1973 oil shock triggered the end of the post-World War II expansion. Median incomes for Americans have increased only modestly since.

There are at least four major aspects of the worldwide increase in economic interdependence that will provide major challenges in the future:

• Dependence of developed economies on others for critical resources that may become exhausted.

- Collapse in the financial markets or the trading system.

- Political interruptions in trade relationships.

- The effect of globalization on the distribution of world economic resources between countries and within them.

1) Dependence of developed economies on others for critical resources that may become exhausted.

At the current pace, oil resources will become exhausted during the first half of the 21st century. Serious programs for efficient oil use could extend our supplies. But in the end oil is, after all, a nonrenewable resource.

One of the most critical challenges facing human civilization will be to husband this and other energy resources and to create new sustainable resources to replace it. Whether they include wind, solar, biomass (ethanol), cellulosic ethanol (made of switch grass and other very high-fiber crops), fusion power—or some yet undiscovered technology—available sustainable energy is critical to our success and survival. It's certainly critical to the ability of the massive population in the developing world to have a First World lifestyle without exhausting the resources of the planet.

In the meantime, the more that control of energy resources is concentrated, the more vulnerable they are to disruption.

Of course, it isn't just nonrenewable resources for which countries depend on each other. Fish stocks, forests and wildlife are managed today by nation states—separately and working together through treaties and international organizations—to manage the "tragedy of the commons" and assure that the resources are available to future generations. As we've seen, these efforts have been only partially successful. By 2050, half of the remaining forest will have disappeared at current rates. For all of the failed societies Diamond studied, deforestation was a major factor. Yet we are dependent on many different governments to protect this common resource. And many of them are poor, fragile governments. The same goes for ocean resources. A major priority has to be placed on protecting all of these resources through international agreement and economic development that will assure that people in the developing world avoid their destruction. Policies that actually encourage clearing of forestland (like the fumigation of coca by U.S. agents in Colombia) must be stopped.

The disappearance of the world's forests, fish and other wildlife could devastate economies worldwide—including our own in the United States.

2) COLLAPSE OF FINANCIAL MARKETS OR TRADING SYSTEMS.

In the last 50 years, trading system and financial markets have truly globalized. But they are still subject to potential catastrophic disruptions. The Asian financial crisis of 1997-98 devastated the standard of living of many Asians, and seriously disrupted economic activity worldwide. Similar disruptions in Mexico and Latin America have also taken their toll.

The International Monetary Fund (IMF) was set up to stabilize the international economy and help bail out states that became fiscal "basket cases." But the IMF's economic philosophy—its emphasis on public-sector austerity and market-based solutions—has often left low-income peasants and workers to pay the price of the "irrational exuberance" of the wealthy.

What's more, the virtually unregulated nature of international currency trading still leaves the world vulnerable to the kinds of financial problems that we ended in the United States with the regulatory reforms of the New Deal 70 years ago.

As we've seen, capital markets have become much more liquid over the years. Whereas before much international investment would take the form of fixed investment in plants and equipment, increasing amounts take the form of securitized financial investments—stocks, bonds, units in partnerships, etc. These kinds of assets can be dumped very rapidly in the world's increasingly speedy financial markets, making them susceptible to boom and bust cycles—and making countries susceptible to rapid disinvestment.

Capital can rush out of countries like water when a dam bursts—as it did in the Asian financial crisis of the 1990s.

International capital flows, and currency markets in particular, are in great need of more regulation—as are multinational corporations in general. Market-based self-interest acting by itself can lead to panics and financial crashes—that's why at the national level we have the Commodity Futures Trading Commission, the Federal Trade Commission, the Security and Exchange Commission, bank regulators and the lot. The same structures are needed to protect against international market crises that can disrupt international trade and lead to economic meltdowns of vulnerable economies.

Given a new level of economic integration, when a portion of the economy sneezes in China, we get a cold in the United States.

THE TRADE DEFICIT AND YOU

The U.S. economy itself could someday be vulnerable directly to a financial meltdown, if its trade deficit continues to grow.

In 2006, the U.S. trade deficit climbed to a record high for the fifth straight year—$764 billion, according to the Commerce Department.[4] The U.S. needs to borrow almost $2 billion a day of foreign capital to fund its trade gap—which represents the excess of what the US consumers and corporations buy abroad over what we sell. This kind of imbalance obviously can't go on forever. The trade deficit is mainly limited by the willingness of foreign investors to provide the needed capital. Much of the U.S. foreign debt over the last few years has been purchased by Japan and China.

Regardless of short-term fluctuations, over the next decades, oil prices will almost certainly increase as oil becomes scarcer. This will drive the U.S. trade deficit higher as well.

LENDING IN THE SHADOWS

The fragility of financial system is exacerbated by one other important factor. Many lenders are forsaking the transparent global financial markets for the shadows of private financial deals. *The Economist* reports that syndicated loans vaulted to $3.5 trillion in 2005 from 2.3 trillion in 2000. [5]

> *Thanks to the low cost of debt, private lenders, such as hedge funds, are extending vast amounts of credit to leverage buyout firms and other private borrowers. Forsaking the sunlit uplands of global finance, the market for capital is plunging into the shadows.*
>
> *For financiers, this is an irresistibly lucrative place to be. In thinly traded, lightly regulated and under reported markets, the bold can make an awful lot of money—and they can lose it on an even more extravagant scale....*
>
> *The shadows are scary, because nobody quite knows what secrets they hold. That has regulators worried—and rightly so.* [6]

This trend toward private financing is complicated further because of the creation of many new financial products:

> *A barely regulated private-equity group could very well borrow money from syndicates of private lenders, including hedge funds, to spend on taking a public company private. At each stage, risk can be converted into securities, sliced up, repackaged, sold and sliced up again. The endless opportunities to write contracts on underlying debt instruments explains why the outstanding value of credit derivative contracts has rocketed to $26 trillion—$9 trillion more than six months ago, and seven times as much as in 2003.* [7]

The Economist quotes Timothy Geithner, the Federal Reserve's man on Wall Street, as warning that all this might, "make financial crises less common, but more severe." [8] The increased use of derivatives and private financing contributed to the sense of uncertainty in financial system surrounding the collapse of the sub-prime lending market in the summer of 2007. As this book goes to press, central banks around the world have infused hundreds of billions of dollars of liquidity to the banking system to stabilize these markets and help ally fears. So far this has avoided a serious market collapse. But the future impact of "lending in the shadows" may be far more difficult to contain.

3) POLITICAL INTERRUPTION OF TRADE RELATIONSHIPS.

We—and other societies—are also vulnerable to non-economic interruptions in trade relationships that can endanger our economies. An attack by the U.S. on Iran could, for instance, substantially increase our oil prices.

Economic sanctions played a major role in forcing an end to apartheid in South Africa by threatening its economic elite.

CUBA

Sometimes these political interruptions are entirely irrational and serve only the interest of a small group at the expense of the entire society. Take the Cuban trade embargo and travel ban.

The U.S. now trades with all former or current communist countries except Cuba and North Korea. China is one of our biggest trading partners. In the last 65 years, we have had a major shooting war with Germany, Japan, Italy and Vietnam. All are major trading partners.

Cuba, which is 90 miles from the United States mainland, has never been at war with the United States. But the small group of Cuban exiles in South Florida have held American policy hostage for 48 years attempting to overthrow the regime of Fidel Castro and the Cuban government.

Jan and I visited Cuba several years ago with a delegation organized by Washington's Center for International Policy. The trip was led by Cuba experts Bill Goodfellow and Sarah Stephens. We met with a wide array of Cubans ranging from dissidents to Fidel Castro, as well as Ricardo Alarcon, the president of the National Assembly, and others who would likely be part of a post-Castro Cuban leadership.

Trade and travel between the U.S. and Cuba would be enormously beneficial to both countries. It would open up Cuban society, at the same time it would provide lucrative markets for U.S. goods.

Polling shows that most Americans agree with this common-sense position—including many Republicans and American farm and business interests. On several occasions, both houses of the formerly Republican Congress passed bills opening travel to Cuba—passing them with substantial bipartisan majorities. But in each case, these bills have been tied up at White House insistence, since the Cuban exile community in South Florida is a key Republican base constituency in a key swing electoral state.

Cuba policy is just one more example of a small vested interest controlling national decisions to the detriment of the interests of the entire society. The U.S. has spent hundreds of millions of dollars over almost half a century to bring down Fidel Castro. We have foregone untold billions in trade and investment opportunities in Cuba. In fact, our original anti-Castro policy helped precipitate the Cuban missile crisis that almost resulted in a nuclear war in the 1960s.

4) THE EFFECTS OF GLOBALIZATION ON THE DISTRIBUTION OF WORLDWIDE ECONOMIC RESOURCES BETWEEN COUNTRIES, AND WITHIN THEM.

We've already discussed the impact of international trade on wages in the United States. For the United States, the challenge of the early part of the 21st century is to prevent US wages from being dragged downward by trade policies that allow them to be set as if human beings are nothing but commodities.

There is no reason why trade agreements that set international standards for investors, capital ownership and intellectual property, should not also set international standards for labor rights, working conditions and environmental impacts. This is a must if we are to avoid being forced by competitive pressure to lower our standards to the lowest common denominator.

The Europeans did it to integrate much of Europe's economy. We can use the same approach worldwide.

These considerations pertain to another set of challenges as well— challenges the trade policies present to the distribution of resources and spread of structural violence in the developing world.

CIUDAD JUÁREZ—THE INVISIBLE HAND IS A FIST

Jan and I went to Ciudad Juarez in Mexico with a congressional delegation investigating the effects of NAFTA on low-income Mexican workers. Ciudad Juarez is a city of 1.3 million souls. It lies directly across the Rio Grande from El Paso, Texas. The city shares a TV market with El Paso. It lies in the same valley. It is surrounded by the same mountains. Yet on one side of the river (the U.S. side), a worker can make $10-$15 per hour doing the same job, for the same company, that will pay the same worker on the other side of the river one dollar an hour. The only difference is that 100 yards of river.

Corporations say they should not be expected to pay as much for labor in the developing world as they do in countries like the U.S. The cost of living is less than developing countries, they say. What about Ciudad Juarez? In many ways, it lies in the same economic market, the same metro area as El Paso, yet the pay differential is 10 or 15 to one.

We saw workers in Mexico who lived in hovels with no running water who worked for U.S. companies. Some of them lived in crates used to ship the products they make. Many of these workers had been drawn to the city to look for work after NAFTA lowered the price of agriculture produce—and especially corn—from which they had formerly earned their livelihoods as peasants.

In the same way, NAFTA has contributed mightily to the influx of undocumented immigrants seeking work in the United States.

Globalization will heavily impact the vast majority of people in developing countries who live off the land. If competitive market forces are allowed to have free reign in global trade, the transition to more globalized markets will exact a mighty cost from peasants. When their already marginalized lives collapse in the face of lower commodity prices, structural violence will soar.

Coffee farmers in Central America and corn farmers in Mexico have already had their livelihoods shattered by this kind of trade. The ever-increasing resistance of new center-left Latin American governments to these global trade arrangements and the IMF's "austerity" policies reflect the reality that the prescription of "unrestrained competitive markets" has not worked to improve the livelihood of most people.

The "invisible hand" of unrestrained markets turned out to be a fist when it came to most of their countries' population. These policies benefited the biggest corporations and the wealthiest classes in society, not most people.

Jan and I attended an Aspen Institute congressional seminar in Mexico on Latin American policy in 2006. It included presentations from a wide range of Latin American scholars, who confirmed the growing rejection of unregulated competitive market policies in Latin America. In fact, by 2007 center-left governments had been elected in virtually all of Latin America except Colombia and Mexico.

In the spring of 2006, Jan attended the inaugural in Santiago of the first woman president of Chile, Michele Bachellet. Jan subsequently hosted a dinner in her honor for women "movers and shakers" in Washington. Bachellet is an example of the new generation of Latin American leader.

Her father was a Chilean Air Force General who was killed by Augusto Pinochet, the dictator who led the US-backed military coup against democratically elected left-wing President Salvador Allende in the early 1970s.

She and her mother were both imprisoned and tortured by Pinochet's government. Of course, it is now clear that Pinochet killed, and "disappeared," tens of thousands of progressive Chileans after the coup.

While he ran the Chilean government, Pinochet, with the help of economists from the "Chicago school," led by Milton Friedman and his group of "free marketers," transformed the Chilean economy into a "free-market paradise." They privatized the Social Security system and allowed free rein for big corporations. The economy grew—but just as in the U.S. under Bush, not for most Chileans.

Once Chile was finally returned to democracy, the electorate rejected the right's policies—as they have throughout Latin America. Bachelet succeeded another center-left president. One of her early challenges will be to clean up the mess caused by the privatization of Chile's Social Security system. It left many Chileans without guaranteed Social Security benefits. In many respects, it resembles the system Bush and the right want to use in the U.S. to replace our current system of guaranteed Social Security benefits.

CHAPTER FIFTY-ONE

The Challenges We Face:
The Cultural and Political Ability
of Our Society to Respond

WE CAN DECIDE

None of the major 21st-century challenges to our success and survival involves outside threats that are beyond human control. They do not involve an inevitable degeneration of our environment that results from natural processes, or climatic changes brought on—like the Ice Age—by changes in the Earth's orientation in space. While hostile human beings may attack each other, we don't face an invading army from another planet, à la "The War of the Worlds."

No society on some other planet will cut off trade relations and leave us stranded like Henderson or Pitcairn Island. The sole exception may be the development and spread of microbial pathogens that infect large populations before we learn how to immunize ourselves, control their spread or cure those who are stricken. Even there, our ability to take action can head off potential threat.

In our case, these challenges all involve human decisions and human action. We control our destiny.

The real question facing us in the 21st century is: are we up to the challenge?

When it comes to the principal factors that have caused the collapse of societies in the past, we've seen how radical conservative values fail to meet those challenges.

This is true whether the problem is environmental damage, climate change, inter-group violence and security (including structural violence), or problems related to dependence on other societies through trade.

Traditional progressive values result in priorities for action that allow us the best opportunity to cope with the challenges.

But while our future may in fact be in our hands—subject to human decision—we've seen that when many past societies were faced with similar challenges, they made the wrong choices.

And the difference today is that the society in question is not a small portion of the human family—it's the whole of humanity. The stakes are now incredibly high.

Overriding Factors—Special Interests, Short-Term Focus, Failure to Adapt

Analyzing why past societies failed to make the right choices, Diamond's study identified several overriding factors. One is the dominant decision-making elite whose short-term self-interest does not correspond with the long-term interest of society. We'll discuss how to deal with that problem in more detail in Section Nine.

The other is the failure to adapt society's values, its priorities for action and its resource allocation to new conditions.

For each of the major challenges we've discussed, we've seen how our society must adapt and expand on the traditional progressive values that have defined human progress, precisely because they're best suited to allow our survival and success over the long run. For example, on a small, fragile, interconnected planet, where people have expanding technological power to do each other harm, war simply doesn't make sense as a means for resolving international differences. It's just too dangerous. It's like allowing a gunfight on airplane. Doctrines like the neoconservative "preemptive" war threaten us all.

But there is another set of progressive values that directly affect our ability to adapt and deal with problems and challenges in the future.

Critical Thinking and Open Societies

It's necessary for world society to foster values and protect critical thinking, curiosity, scientific inquiry, research and education, diversity and tolerance, and free expression.

Radical conservative fundamentalist values fail to meet this test. All you need to do is look at the debate over evolution and "intelligent design," or the attempts to limit stem cell research, or see the massive anti-scientific bias in radical conservative thought.

Of course, in fact, any value system that believes it is the sole possessor of "revealed truth" or "moral law" discourages critical thinking and encourages intolerance.

The intolerance that results from believing that you are the sole possessor of "revealed truth" discourages discovery and critical debate. It discourages the constant critical re-examination of the assumptions that lie at the core of scientific progress.

Tolerance for diversity—in ideas, culture, race, and religion—underlies critical thinking and the ability to adapt our values and priorities to meet our challenges.

Because repetition is necessary to drive home a point, let me once again make this perfectly clear: the ability to adapt one's values and priorities to do conditions does not equal "moral relativism." Progressives are passionately committed to one core moral principle—the survival and success of all human beings—"love thy neighbor as thyself." All other values and priorities are instrumental to the principal value. That is not relativism at all. One key priority never changes.

In fact, the concept of "integrity" has as its foundation this progressive view of values and morality. Someone has integrity when he acts with one unified standard for moral behavior that never wavers—that applies equally to all of his interactions and all of his decisions. The values we place on big cars, or country club memberships, or sexual ethics, or same-sex marriage all must reflect the consequences for the one central integrating value—the survival and success of all humanity. They must respond to the question: what is loving my neighbor?

Protecting a tolerant, diverse society—protecting critical thinking and free expression—requires a progressive understanding of human rights— the understandings that are implicit in our own Bill of Rights and the U.N.'s Universal Declaration of Human Rights.

That is why Progressives are so committed to the concept of the right to privacy. The state should not be encroaching on individual action, or thought or speech unless it substantially encroaches on the freedoms of others. That's why the right to due process and independent judicial systems are important in free societies.

It's Always Done in the Name of Security

Historically, national security is always the rationale used by governments to restrict these rights. The Germans used the burning of the Reichstag as a premise to pass laws against the Jews, leftists and other "enemies of National Socialism." Stalin used national security as the rationale to send tens of thousands of Russians to gulags. National security was the premise for military dictatorships in Latin America; it was the rationale for murdering and "disappearing" thousands, with support from conservative U.S., governments throughout the 1950s, '60s and '70s.

The argument that these rights must be suspended in order to guarantee our safety against "terrorists" or "communists" or "drug lords" is the same argument that has always led societies down the road to tyranny.

These rights are only tested precisely at times of concern for national security. The passage of the Patriot Act that gave government access to records of the books you check out a library. September 11th was used as pretext for passing laws, like the Patriot Act, that had long been on the conservative agenda and had previously been defeated. It was used as an excuse for warrantless wiretaps conducted by the NSA, indefinite detention of prisoners without charge, and other draconian encroachments on progressive values.

In the end, attempts to undermine the values that allow us to have a society that fosters critical thought, free speech, diversity, tolerance and all the rest, are dangerous to our long-term security as a society. It is the attempts to undermine these values in the name of national security, that are themselves the danger to national security because it will lead to the kinds of stultified, unimaginative culture that in the past have failed.

During Francisco Franco's right-wing dictatorship in Spain, Spanish culture, inquiry, innovation and creativity were suffocated. Jan and I visited Spain a few years after Franco's death, when Democratic rights were restored under the leadership of the center-left government. It's as if the society's pent-up creativity exploded in excitement, creativity and vitality. Spain's economy was once again growing. Cultural life was reawakened; youthful energy was everywhere.

When a state violates someone's civil liberties or human rights, the price is not paid exclusively by the individual whose rights are deprived; everyone in the society suffers.

Because if they can come for someone else, they can come for you as well.

But in a larger sense, we suffer because the creativity and vitality of curiosity are sapped from society—and that drastically limits our long term ability to succeed and survive in the modern world.

The priority of protecting individual rights has grown all the more important in the world of exploding technological capability. Technological power gives those who possess it the ability to dominate and control others. Guns and steel gave Europeans the ability to dominate the people of the New World. That is even truer of the next-generation technology that can give scientists the ability to create new species out of building blocks from off-the-shelf DNA segments. Synthetic biology may give some humans the ability to completely reprogram others. Our understanding of the human brain will give us increasing ability to control people's minds.

Massive improvements in communication technology, and the ability to track people using global positioning systems, give governments the ability to exercise levels of control over its citizens that were previously unthinkable. The world described by George Orwell in the book *1984* may not have arrived as advertised two decades ago, but it is still a very real possibility.

A major challenge to all of us in the 21st century is to jealously guard our human rights and due process of law to protect us all from Orwell's vision of the future.

CLEARING THE GAUNTLET

Earlier I mentioned planetary scientist David Grinspoon's book, *Lonely Planets,* that explores the question of extraterrestrial life—both basic biological life and intelligent sentient life.

Toward the end of his book, Grinspoon speculates on the chances of survival for intelligent life in the universe. He argues that every civilization of intelligent creatures must pass through a gauntlet that tests whether the values and political structures of the society are capable of keeping pace with the exponentially increasing power of the society's technology. If its values and political structures can keep pace with technological change, the society may pass into a phase of enormous freedom and possibility. If it does not, the power of its own technology will destroy it. Perhaps, he postulates, civilizations are like seahorses. Many are born, but only a few survive.

For the first time, a little more than half a century ago, human society entered that gauntlet. The autocatalytic nature of technological growth reached a point of takeoff that for the first time gave us the power to destroy ourselves and all life on our tiny, fragile planet. From that moment on, the race began.

The next several generations of humans will decide how that race turns out. They won't simply observe it, or describe it; *they will decide it.* Whatever the future holds will be a result of human decision for which we are all responsible.

We will decide if we pass through that gauntlet or—like our cousins the Neanderthals—become evolutionary dead ends. We will decide if humanity passes into a new era of possibility and freedom—or the human story simply ends.

Much is at stake. That's why the struggle for progressive values matters.

CHAPTER FIFTY-TWO

The Progressive Vision—The Kind of Society We Want to Create

THE FOUNDATION IS PROGRESSIVE VALUES

The progressive vision of our future is about making it through that gauntlet. It's about successfully meeting the 21st century challenges to our success and survival.

Explaining our vision is first and foremost about reaffirming our faith in progressive values as the standards we use to craft the future.

That faith can be expressed both in symbols of our progressive religious traditions, and in the language of our civic tradition—the Bill of Rights, the Universal Declaration of Human Rights, the progressive tradition of our political history.

Most people—most Americans—most swing voters—have a frame embedded in their consciousness that affirms as "common sense" that unity and brotherhood are superior to division and hatred; that loving your neighbor is in fact, the highest expression of human values; that the values of empathy, responsibility and competence are superior to the unbridled pursuit of individual interest; that sacrifice and commitment give life meaning, not greed and selfishness.

They know instinctively that people can accomplish more together than they can if they are divided. They know better than to believe Big Brother in Orwell's 1984 when he says that war is peace, that slavery—and the sacrifice of individual human rights—is freedom; or that the selfishness of a few will somehow forge a common good.

But there is a competing frame embedded in the unconscious that denies that common sense and calls up another darker set of inclinations. Some of those inclinations are deeply rooted in our evolution and history. In presenting our vision for the future, progressives must first and foremost activate and affirm the progressive frame of common sense values. Humans are pack animals—they need to have their instincts affirmed by others. It's our job to offer those values every time we communicate—to remorselessly appeal to them—to make them all-pervasive.

WHAT KIND OF A SOCIETY DO WE REJECT?

First, of course, we want a society that avoids the potential catastrophes implicit in the challenges we've just discussed.

We reject a future where environmental damage, or over-taxation of our Earth's resources, or global climate change lead to violence, genocide, or to a standard of living that prevents the next-generation from being better off than our own.

We reject a future of massive inequality that turns America into an armed camp—where the "haves" protect a greater and greater share of the world's resources from the have-nots of the world and our own country.

We reject a future of global conflict between religions and ethnic groups that leads to more death and suffering.

We reject a future where structural violence inflicts unnecessary suffering on people worldwide.

We reject a future that requires us to sacrifice our liberty to our fear— or where our culture is suffocated and our inquiry is limited by dogma and stifling ideology.

We reject a future where we allow the institutions we have created to take on lives of their own, and prevent us from making the decisions that will allow us to control our technology and shape our history.

Most importantly, failure is not an option. We reject the future that ends in a mushroom cloud or the catastrophic collapse of our environment.

THE FUTURE'S POSSIBILITY

There is another side to our increasing technological power—the power to fashion a society that allows the fulfillment of human possibility like never before.

Put simply, our technology could allow us to create a society where everyone can satisfy their physical needs, where everyone can expand their ability to exert control and find structure in their lives; a society that nurtures and encourages genuine, mutually respectful human relationships; a society where everyone has access to intellectual stimulation and creative work; a society where everyone is free to make his own commitments, and find his own path to meaning and fulfillment. We can create a society that can exponentially expand the ability of the *entire human family* to fulfill the six categories of self-interest we identified at the beginning of this book.

ESCAPE FROM ECONOMIC NECESSITY— A NEW WORLD OF CREATIVE WORK

Throughout our history, most human beings have been plagued by economic necessity. The creation of complex societies and economic differentiation allowed a small percentage of humanity to escape the daily task of finding or producing enough food. That allowed for the takeoff of human civilization, since those people were freed to invent writing, art, technology and to manage large human organizations.

But still, today, huge percentages of humanity live precariously—forced to do routine, stifling, backbreaking, mind-numbing work. People spend entire days doing stoop labor in fields, or repeating the same motions on assembly lines, or sewing pair after pair of trousers.

This is especially true in the developing world, but it's still true for many in the U.S. as well. Our computers and other technology can finally free all of us to be part of the world of creative, challenging work.

Ending economic necessity doesn't require the end of scarcity of all types. It does mean an end to the million-year-old struggle to fulfill the needs that are required for survival and basic comfort—the core physical needs—food, shelter, warmth and physical security.

The invention of food production 13,000 years ago freed a portion of humanity from economic necessity. By creating surpluses of food, it enabled a portion of society to study, invent, write and build. The future will allow everyone to be freed of backbreaking, repetitive toil.

Over the last two decades, we've all seen the potential of computers to do routine tasks that humans were once forced to perform. We've just begun to experience a fraction of what's possible. Like other technology, computer technology is autocatalytic—it catalyzes itself to create new innovation that builds on the foundation of past discovery. It expands exponentially.

Gordon Moore, a computer scientist, predicted in 1965 that chip speed would double every twenty-four months. Since that time, what's come to be known as Moore's Law has come to pass. There's been an exponential expansion in computers speed.

When I was 15 years old my dad, a lieutenant colonel and pilot in the U.S. Air Force Reserve, arranged for me to go with him to "fly" a B-52 simulator at Carswell Air Force Base in Fort Worth, Texas. I remember how massive the computer appeared to be that ran the simulator. There were rooms of computers powered by vacuum tubes. Today that computing power would fit on a small chip.

The first computer system I bought for my office just 25 years ago had a 40 MB hard drive. Today an average laptop has 60 GB or more on a tiny storage device. That's 1,500 times more storage—and you can carry it around. The other day I bought a new "flash drive" that attaches to my key chain. I can plug it into my computer and copy up to 4 GB of data to a device that fits in my pocket.

Computers and automated systems do thousands of tasks humans once labored for days, weeks and years to accomplish—in seconds. More importantly, computers and automated systems free us from the routine, mindless work.

Before you say, "But doesn't that just throw good people out of work?"—it doesn't have to. All of us could share in the bounty of increased productivity resulting from technology's growth. In the U.S. since 1973, most of the benefit has flowed to the richest among us. But no law of nature says that has to be so.

I know some Progressives who bemoan the elimination of the kinds of low-wage jobs that are being replaced by automation. None of them has been a migrant worker or has worked in a sweatshop. There is nothing noble about backbreaking, spirit-crushing work from dawn till dusk. It is virtual slavery.

There are three ways people experience their work lives. For some people, work is simply a job—a way to generate the income necessary to allow their survival—or, if you're lucky—the time to get fulfillment in some other area of your life.

The second is as a career. Work contributes directly to the status, power and identity of the worker.

The third is as a calling. You would do the work even if you were never paid. You do it because of its intrinsic value. There are many people today—I'm one of them, for whom this is true. We love our work. We love the activities we are called upon to do. We love the people we work with. We love the challenge the work presents.

In the new world of the future, it is possible for everyone to have the opportunity to do work that is a calling—where the work of everyone in the society is creative and challenging and interesting.

Such a world would be made possible by the wise use of our technology, and by overcoming the challenges we have discussed—especially the challenge of overpopulation and over-taxation of the world's natural resources.

To create such a world requires the elimination of economic necessity—an element that has been a constant until now—throughout human history. But the elimination of economic necessity is a necessary, but not sufficient, condition for this kind of society. The second necessary ingredient is the elimination of structural inequality and exploitation—a society that fairly distributes the fruits of our growing technological progress.

A SECURE FUTURE

Eliminating economic necessity would have monumental consequences for our physical security. Economic necessity causes fear. Fear leads to hatred, division and war. The scarcity of the necessities of life cause heightened competition for those resources. Historically, that leads to crime, war, civil war, structural violence and genocide.

Ending economic necessity could provide the economic basis for a peaceful society. But once again, it's a necessary but not sufficient condition. At least three more elements are required:

- The conscious creation and nurture of institutions to peacefully resolve disputes.

- The systematic inculcation in our children of progressive values of empathy, responsibility, competency, and mutual respect, and also through the political dialogue that diffuses "common sense."

- The fair distribution of the bounty of our economic and technological growth.

A TRULY DEMOCRATIC SOCIETY

The end of economic necessity would provide the economic basis for a truly democratic society—for the first time in human history.

Primitive hunter-gatherer bands had egalitarian social structures—but that simply meant that people were bound together in common bondage to economic necessity. The daily drill was finding or hunting down enough food to sustain the band. That was about all humans could accomplish. No one was free to explore the nature of the universe, or invent writing, or learn how to harness nonhuman energy, or a write a great opera.

Those possibilities presented themselves only when humans invented food production, and could produce a surplus so that some members of the society were no longer engaged in daily food gathering.

But the other consequence of economic differentiation was a division of society into classes—early on, as rulers and commoners—and later on as landowners, peasants, owners and workers, professionals and blue collar. That left some people freed from economic necessity, but very few.

The promise of our technology brings us full circle, to a point where the economic freedom that was first made possible by food production for part of society, will become available to everyone. And that allows the possibility of a truly democratic society for the first time in human history. Egalitarianism will be back—but on a completely different basis. It creates an egalitarian option that does not level economic well-being *down*—but levels it *up*.

This continues the gradual trend toward wider and wider distribution of the benefits of economic growth that has proceeded in fits and starts for centuries. But now the qualitative change of technology can transform this gradual, quantitative change in society into *qualitative* change as well.

Once again, there's no guarantee that the technological explosion will lead to a truly democratic society. Just as with security, true democracy depends on our ability to:

- Overcome challenges that could overtax our planet's resources.

- Imbue the value of equality into our political dialogue and culture.

- Create structural change in the power relations of society to guarantee equality. Frederick Douglass said it best—"power surrenders nothing without a struggle—it never has, it never will." Society becomes more democratic only when those without power demand it.

Personal freedom to select and achieve goals and structure life

The end of economic necessity can do more than any other single factor to broaden personal freedom to select goals and structure one's life. Economic necessity is the foundation of structural violence. Its end would allow hundreds of millions of people to massively broaden their personal freedom.

And once again another element is critical. Technology in the hands of despots can be used to bring the opposite of freedom—control and tyranny. To create freedom, technology must do its magic in a society with broad distribution of power, and many centers of influence—a democratic society with strong protections for individual rights. As technological power intensifies, it also magnifies the power of those who possess it. Technology could make possible the broad distribution of power by eliminating economic necessity and turbocharging the diffusion of information throughout the society.

But if its control is concentrated, it could facilitate unheard-of levels of tyranny and domination.

In other words, technology imparts to the distribution of power some of its own autocatalytic properties. In a society that has substantial democratic distribution of power and strong protections for individual rights to begin with, qualitative technological expansion can strengthen and broaden the distribution of power by providing everyone with unprecedented ability to communicate unprecedented levels of information.

But if it's made available only to the elites of highly hierarchical societies, it will allow the unprecedented power to control its citizenry for providing them with a mechanism to control the minds and know the whereabouts of its people. Big Brother can either be empowered or vanquished by exploding technology—the distribution of power and resources in society over the next few decades will help determine his fate.

UNPRECEDENTED LEVELS OF INTELLECTUAL STIMULATION AND FULFILLMENT

The technological explosion can also create a basis for a society where everyone has an unprecedented ability to satisfy the hardwired drive to know to satisfy our intellectual curiosity.

Those of us with the economic means already have the capacity to access more information about the world—personally—than the greatest scholars could imagine just 50 years ago.

The end of economic necessity would allow the deployment of the brainpower and ingenuity of all of humankind to address the issues, problems and mysteries that today are addressed only by the educated minority of the world's population.

Every time a person is sentenced by economic circumstances to receive little education, and spend her life in physically difficult, repetitive menial work, the rest of us may be deprived of a brain surgeon, or poet, or actor, or the person who will cure cancer. A mind is a terrible thing to waste. The end of economic necessity would allow for yet another qualitative explosion in human knowledge of the same sort that happened when food production first allowed some of us to focus on pursuits other than feeding ourselves.

Again, however, a democratic society is critical—since technological innovation could also be used to create a race of fully controlled "worker bees" with limited intellectual capacity for curiosity.

A SOCIETY WITH NEW POSSIBILITIES FOR RICH, STIMULATING, MUTUALLY RESPECTFUL SOCIAL RELATIONSHIPS

There's been a great deal of commentary about the increasing social alienation—or atomization—of American society. The book *Bowling Alone: The Collapse and Revival of American Community,* by Robert Putnam, documents this trend. But the end of economic necessity and the globalization of communication and transportation could provide the basis for a new world society that allows and encourages rich, stimulating, mutually respectful social relationships that are available to more people than ever before.

The future could provide us much more leisure time that could be devoted to family and friends. It could allow us to control more of our own time. It could provide us with the opportunity to know and relate to a wide variety of people from many different cultures and traditions.

The end of economic necessity would eliminate the principle underlying cause of communal and ethnic conflict that has characterized human society since the dawn of history, and continues to serve as the major engine of conflict in the world today.

The universality of progressive values provides the standard that can allow us to move from our particular history into the culturally heterogeneous, but mutually respectful, future. And the United States could serve as the model for the new culturally integrated world.

But in many respects, that can already be said of America. Within a very few years, America will be a majority minority country. Some people think that kind of cultural heterogeneity is a problem. In fact, it's our greatest strength.

A few years ago, I attended a speech by the Deputy Ambassador from Pakistan. He said something quite striking. He said he'd been posted in many countries, but that America was the only country in the world were no matter how you look, no matter what your accent, most people assume you are an American.

America is increasingly coming to reflect the world community. That gives us an enormous competitive advantage in understanding and relating to the rest of the world. It also allows us to serve as an example of how to craft a society where people from many cultures can each flourish, maintain mutual respect and simultaneously share a common vision for the future.

Mutually respectful cultural diversity is more stimulating and interesting than a world in which each person spends his entire life in an isolated cultural enclave. But it also reinforces the ability of its members to empathize with each other and strengthens the foundation for mutual respect and tolerance of diversity. That is critical to allowing diversity to sustain itself.

That's the progressive vision of human social relationship—but it's not the inevitable consequence of the explosion of technological capacity. Absent a broadly democratic diffusion of power in society, exploding technology could provide the basis for the Nazi nightmare of racial domination that plagued the Earth only six decades ago.

A SOCIETY WHERE EACH PERSON IS EMPOWERED TO SEEK HIS
OWN MEANING IN LIFE, TO MAKE COMMITMENTS OF HIS OWN
CHOOSING, TO LIVE OUT HIS OWN DREAMS AND TO DEVELOP HIS
OWN INTELLECTUAL, PHYSICAL AND SPIRITUAL CAPABILITIES TO THE
MAXIMUM EXTENT HE DESIRES.

That, after all, is the progressive concept of human freedom—a society where each person is empowered to create his own meaning, his own identity—through commitments of his own choosing. It's a society where each person is allowed and encouraged to live a fulfilling life by committing his life to something other than himself—to helping each other, to the pursuit of knowledge, to his family, to his art, to his religion— to goals of his own choosing; with the only limitation being that he does not prevent others from doing the same.

The progressive vision is a society where each person, everywhere, has the freedom to define himself and achieve a fulfilling life. The progressive vision is a society where each person feels that his life is meaningful and has the power to select the commitments that make it so.

The end of economic necessity and the creation of a democratic society are prerequisites to make such a vision possible.

Progressives believe that we are only capable of achieving this goal together—not separately. We believe that we are in this together, and that a society based entirely on the pursuit of individual interests can't realize our aspirations for human success and survival.

And Progressives believe that in working together we have the best chance of benefit—not only for the entire society—but for each of us individually. Society is not a zero-sum game—rather, we believe that helping everyone to be proud of who he is, to be more productive, better educated, and healthy, gives us all the ability to live richer, smarter, healthier, more secure and more meaningful lives.

THE NEXT GREAT LEAP FORWARD

Twice before, since human beings differentiated from a line of African apes, quantitative change has tipped into major qualitative transformation. The first was 50,000 years ago when changes in the brain and voice box resulted in creatures there were anatomically and behaviorally modern humans. The second—the invention of food production about 13,000 years ago—set in motion the changes in our society and technology that have powered our development since.

The autocatalytic explosion of technology has set in motion forces that may result in a third great leap forward for human beings—the escape from economic necessity. It would be the logical conclusion of the process that began when people stopped being hunter-gatherers and began producing their own crops and herds. If it happens, it will provide a qualitative turning point in human history.

But first we have to make it through Grinspoon's gauntlet. We have to prove that our values and political structures can manage and control our exponentially expanding technological capacity.

To do that, we have to beat the right, here and now, in modern America. And that requires us to provide the voters with a clear understanding of what's at stake in this battle—and our vision of the future.

Describing the Progressive Vision and the Struggle to Make It Reality: Vision is Critical to Victory

Our eloquence at describing the progressive vision is critical to our ability to make it reality.

The voters instinctively want to know where leaders want to take them. More importantly, vision inspires. By inspiring swing voters with our vision for the future we persuade them. By inspiring mobilizable voters, we motivate them.

Vision *inspires* because it calls on the listener to commit himself to bring that vision into being—to make it reality. It addresses the most critical human self-interest—the need for meaning.

The great political leaders and movements of history have all called on their followers to turn a vision into reality. More than anything else people are searching for meaning. Political movements that hold out a vision of the future and ask for commitment to help make it real provide that sense of meaning.

Voters have to be reminded that politics is not just about who gets contracts or goes on trips. It is not mainly about perks and petty rivalries. It is not mainly about negative ads or character assassination.

By describing our vision for the future we reminded voters that politics is not a game; it's not a drill. It's the real thing—the real process through which we will successfully shape our common future or fail to do so. All the rest is part of the process, but inconsequential by contrast.

The right understands just how critical vision is to victory. Most recently, they've attempted to frame the foreign-policy debate by presenting the war to stop Muslim radicals as the defining battle of "civilization" versus the forces of "evil."

Progressives believe that defending America from any form of terrorism is critically important, but it is only part of a larger historic challenge to determine if our political and spiritual abilities can keep pace with our technological prowess. It is part of—and a product of—the broad package of challenges facing the world in the 21st Century.

What Describing the Progressive Vision Does Not Involve

Very often Progressives make the mistake of confusing a statement of progressive vision with two things that it definitely is not:

1) A list of policies and programs that we support. Policies and programs are not a vision. We lost the 2006 presidential election, in part, because our candidate talked about policy and programs while they talked about right and wrong and their vision for the world.

It was a good thing for the Democratic congressional leadership to lay out a list of initiatives that Democrats would pass on our first hundred hours in power. That list was a down payment on a progressive program—and provided symbols for our values.

But even that is not a statement of vision for the future.

2) A slogan. A slogan is not a statement of our vision either—although a metaphoric slogan can become a shorthand symbol for a vision that is painted in broader strokes elsewhere.

Some of those stand-in slogans are familiar to us all:

* The New Deal
* The New Frontier
* The Great Society
* The Blessed Community
* I Have a Dream
* The Bridge to the 21st Century

All the slogans have two things in common. They all paint a picture in our minds with inspirational language. And they all involve progressive struggles that Progressives won.

Regardless, slogans by themselves do not describe our vision for America or the world. To be useful, they must refer back to a broader understanding of that vision that is regularly repeated elsewhere.

Rules for Communicating Our Vision of the Future

Rule # 1—The vision must be placed in the progressive value frame and set up a contrast between progressive and conservative values.

We have to activate the unconscious progressive value frame that is present in everyone. We must be self-confident and assertive.

In particular, we must contrast the right wing's belief in unbridled pursuit of individual interest with commitment to the common good; selfishness versus commitment to others; hope versus fear; division versus unity.

RULE # 2—THE VISION MUST BE PLACED IN AN HISTORIC CONTEXT.

A progressive vision applies our values to our historic moment and to the future.

We have to give the voters a sense of important historical consequence—a sense that we are at a crossroads of history—a sense of the challenges we face and the possibilities we might realize.

RULE # 3—LIKE ALL POLITICAL COMMUNICATION WE NEED TO USE SYMBOLS.

Visions are about seeing things—not thinking about them. These symbols must make the voter feel and visualize our vision of the future. We need to use stories, metaphors, language that paints pictures; those appeal to the emotions.

RULE # 4—MOST IMPORTANT, THE STATEMENT OF OUR VISION MUST INSPIRE VOTERS AND CALL ON THEM TO MAKE A COMMITMENT TO THE TASK OF MAKING THE VISION INTO REALITY.

And that requires that its description have five characteristics:

- Its achievement must require that we overcome obstacles that we must achieve at a new level of proficiency.

- Overcoming those obstacles requires courage. It must call on us to overcome fear.

- In doing so it must make us feel *empowered.*

- It must call on the voter to sacrifice to make the vision a reality—to make a commitment. Remember we are not talking about the kind of sacrifice that involves lowered expectations. We're talking about sacrifice for a better future. It is from commitment that the voter will receive a sense of meaning—a sense that he is part of something important.

- It must appeal to hope. To inspire requires a faith in what Barack Obama calls the "audacity of hope." It requires faith that we can overcome.

In a Labor Day 2006 poll of non-supervisory workers sponsored by the labor federation Change to Win, Lake Research Partners found that, in a major change from past generations, a majority of Americans does not believe that the next generation of Americans will be better off than the current generation. Only 18% believe the next generation will be better off economically than the current generation, while 51% feel they will be worse off.

However, the poll also found:

"Working Americans believe the American Dream is still attainable, and that our country can and should do better."

By the "American Dream," workers do not mean getting rich or winning the lottery. For most working Americans, the survey found: "It is about achieving the basis of middle-class comfort and security: a good job, owning a home, a secure retirement, quality and affordable health care and a better life for their children." [2]

Progressives need to rekindle hope that the next generation will live better than our own.

If we call on Americans to sacrifice for a better future, they will respond (e.g., John F. Kennedy). If we call on them to sacrifice—to tighten their belts—because they must lower their expectations (e.g., Jimmy Carter), we will not inspire them, and they will turn elsewhere for leadership.

RULE # 5—WE MUST EXPLAIN AMERICA'S LEADERSHIP ROLE IN ACHIEVING OUR MISSION—HOW AMERICA CAN BE THE "CITY ON THE HILL"—AN EXAMPLE OF THOSE VALUES THAT DEFINE OUR VISION OF THE FUTURE.

RULE # 6—THE BEST POSSIBLE SYMBOL FOR THE PROGRESSIVE VISION IS A PERSON—A LEADER OR CANDIDATE OR ROLE MODEL THAT DEFINES OUR HOPE FOR THE FUTURE; A TRANSFORMING LEADER.

We all know examples who defined that hope for their generation: Franklin and Eleanor Roosevelt, John and Robert Kennedy, Martin Luther King, Nelson Mandela.

EXAMPLES:
SPEECHES THAT DESCRIBE
THE PROGRESSIVE VISION OF THE FUTURE

Each of the five speeches reproduced below describes the speaker's progressive vision. Each takes traditional American progressive values and applies them to a particular historic moment. Each uses the progressive value frame and an understanding of history to frame the debate. Each uses powerful, visual symbols that engage the listener's emotions. Each enlists and inspires the listener to join the struggle to make his vision a reality by asking commitment and sacrifice.

The first example is John F. Kennedy's inaugural address delivered January 20, 1961. Kennedy's campaign had relied heavily on projecting his vision. His slogans in the campaign had been, "A Time for Greatness" and "Leadership for the '60s."

The speech was delivered at the height of the Cold War, so some of its references seen out of date or irrelevant today. But much in the vision remains remarkably relevant, even after 45 years. Its 27 paragraphs appear below:

JOHN F. KENNEDY, INAUGURAL ADDRESS
DELIVERED FRIDAY, JANUARY 20, 1961

Vice President Johnson, Mr. Speaker, Mr. Chief Justice, President Eisenhower, Vice President Nixon, President Truman, reverend clergy, fellow citizens, we observe today not a victory of party, but a celebration of freedom—symbolizing an end, as well as a beginning—signifying renewal, as well as change. For I have sworn before you and Almighty God the same solemn oath our forebears prescribed nearly a century and three quarters ago.

The world is very different now. For man holds in his mortal hands the power to abolish all forms of human poverty and all forms of human life. And yet the same revolutionary beliefs for which our forebears fought are still at issue around the globe—the belief that the rights of man come not from the generosity of the state, but from the hand of God.

We dare not forget today that we are the heirs of that first revolution. Let the word go forth from this time and place, to friend and foe alike, that the torch has been passed to a new generation of Americans—born in this century, tempered by war, disciplined by a hard and bitter peace, proud of our ancient heritage—and unwilling to witness or permit the slow undoing of those human rights to which this Nation has always been committed, and to which we are committed today at home and around the world.

Let every nation know, whether it wishes us well or ill, that we shall pay any price, bear any burden, meet any hardship, support any friend, oppose any foe, in order to assure the survival and the success of liberty.

This much we pledge—and more.

To those old allies whose cultural and spiritual origins we share, we pledge the loyalty of faithful friends. United, there is little we cannot do in a host of cooperative ventures. Divided, there is little we can do—for we dare not meet a powerful challenge at odds and split asunder.

To those new States whom we welcome to the ranks of the free, we pledge our word that one form of colonial control shall not have passed away merely to be replaced by a far more iron tyranny. We shall not always expect to find them supporting our view. But we shall always hope to find them strongly supporting their own freedom—and to remember that, in the past, those who foolishly sought power by riding the back of the tiger ended up inside.

To those peoples in the huts and villages across the globe struggling to break the bonds of mass misery, we pledge our best efforts to help them help themselves, for whatever period is required—not because the Communists may be doing it, not because we seek their votes, but because it is right. If a free society cannot help the many who are poor, it cannot save the few who are rich.

To our sister republics south of our border, we offer a special pledge—to convert our good words into good deeds—in a new alliance for progress—to assist free men and free governments in casting off the chains of poverty. But this peaceful revolution of hope cannot become the prey of hostile powers. Let all our neighbors know that we shall join with them to oppose aggression or subversion anywhere in the Americas. And let every other power know that this Hemisphere intends to remain the master of its own house.

To that world assembly of sovereign states, the United Nations, our last best hope in an age where the instruments of war have far outpaced the instruments of peace, we renew our pledge of support—to prevent it from becoming merely a forum for invective—to strengthen its shield of the new and the weak—and to enlarge the area in which its writ may run.

Finally, to those nations who would make themselves our adversary, we offer not a pledge but a request: that both sides begin anew the quest for peace, before the dark powers of destruction unleashed by science engulf all humanity in planned or accidental self-destruction.

We dare not tempt them with weakness. For only when our arms are sufficient beyond doubt can we be certain beyond doubt that they will never be employed.

But neither can two great and powerful groups of nations take comfort from our present course—both sides overburdened by the cost of modern weapons, both rightly alarmed by the steady spread of the deadly atom, yet both racing to alter that uncertain balance of terror that stays the hand of mankind's final war.

So let us begin anew—remembering on both sides that civility is not a sign of weakness, and sincerity is always subject to proof. Let us never negotiate out of fear. But let us never fear to negotiate.

Let both sides explore what problems unite us instead of belaboring those problems which divide us.

Let both sides, for the first time, formulate serious and precise proposals for the inspection and control of arms—and bring the absolute power to destroy other nations under the absolute control of all nations.

Let both sides seek to invoke the wonders of science instead of its terrors. Together let us explore the stars, conquer the deserts, eradicate disease, tap the ocean depths, and encourage the arts and commerce.

Let both sides unite to heed in all corners of the earth the command of Isaiah—to "undo the heavy burdens ... and to let the oppressed go free."

And if a beachhead of cooperation may push back the jungle of suspicion, let both sides join in creating a new endeavor, not a new balance of power, but a new world of law, where the strong are just and the weak secure and the peace preserved.

All this will not be finished in the first 100 days. Nor will it be finished in the first 1,000 days, nor in the life of this Administration, nor even perhaps in our lifetime on this planet. But let us begin.

In your hands, my fellow citizens, more than in mine, will rest the final success or failure of our course. Since this country was founded, each generation of Americans has been summoned to give testimony to its national loyalty. The graves of young Americans who answered the call to service surround the globe.

Now the trumpet summons us again—not as a call to bear arms, though arms we need; not as a call to battle, though embattled we are—but a call to bear the burden of a long twilight struggle, year in and year out, "rejoicing in hope, patient in tribulation"—a struggle against the common enemies of man: tyranny, poverty, disease, and war itself.

Can we forge against these enemies a grand and global alliance, North and South, East and West, that can assure a more fruitful life for all mankind? Will you join in that historic effort?

In the long history of the world, only a few generations have been granted the role of defending freedom in its hour of maximum danger. I do not shrink from this responsibility—I welcome it. I do not believe that any of us would exchange places with any other people or any other generation. The energy, the faith, the devotion which we bring to this endeavor will light our country and all who serve it—and the glow from that fire can truly light the world.

And so, my fellow Americans: ask not what your country can do for you— ask what you can do for your country.

My fellow citizens of the world: ask not what America will do for you, but what together we can do for the freedom of man.

Finally, whether you are citizens of America or citizens of the world, ask of us the same high standards of strength and sacrifice which we ask of you. With a good conscience our only sure reward, with history the final judge of our deeds, let us go forth to lead the land we love, asking His blessing and His help, but knowing that here on earth God's work must truly be our own.

★

When George W. Bush was first elected, my wife Jan told me that as a member of Congress, as much as she hated to, she thought she should go to his Inaugural. But if she were going to go, she insisted that I go, too.

I sat with the other congressional spouses. Most were Republicans, decked out in their furs and ready to have a great time. Bush's speech was uninspired. Toward the end, he came to the part where he called for "tax cuts." For the first time, the fur-bedecked spouses surrounding me leapt to their feet in thunderous applause.

It was shocking, how far we'd come. Bush's inaugural address could not have contrasted more sharply with John Kennedy's call to, "Ask not what your country can do for you, but what you can do for your country."

That contrast, as much as anything, symbolized to me the difference between Conservatives and Progressives. It will be Kennedy's words that will be remembered by history.

Second are excerpts from Lyndon Johnson 1965 inaugural.

Progressives often think of Johnson today entirely in terms of the Vietnam War. Johnson was also the President of the Great Society.

LYNDON B. JOHNSON, INAUGURAL ADDRESS, EXCERPTS
DELIVERED WEDNESDAY, JANUARY 20, 1965

Think of our world as it looks from the rocket that is heading toward Mars. It is like a child's globe, hanging in space, the continents stuck to its side like colored maps. We are all fellow passengers on a dot of earth. And each of us, in the span of time, has really only a moment among our companions.

How incredible it is that in this fragile existence, we should hate and destroy one another. There are possibilities enough for all who will abandon mastery over others to pursue mastery over nature. There is world enough for all to seek their happiness in their own way.

Our Nation's course is abundantly clear. We aspire to nothing that belongs to others. We seek no dominion over our fellow man, but man's dominion over tyranny and misery.

But more is required. Men want to be a part of a common enterprise — a cause greater than themselves. Each of us must find a way to advance the purpose of the Nation, thus finding new purpose for ourselves. Without this, we shall become a nation of strangers.

By working shoulder to shoulder, together we can increase the bounty of all. We have discovered that every child who learns, every man who finds work, every sick body that is made whole—like a candle added to an altar— brightens the hope of all the faithful.

So let us reject any among us who seek to reopen old wounds and to rekindle old hatreds. They stand in the way of a seeking nation.

Third are excerpted sections of Franklin Roosevelt's first inaugural address. It was delivered on March 4, 1933, at the height of the Great Depression.

FRANKLIN D. ROOSEVELT, FIRST INAUGURAL ADDRESS, EXCERPTS DELIVERED SATURDAY, MARCH 4, 1933

I am certain that my fellow Americans expect that on my induction into the Presidency I will address them with a candor and a decision which the present situation of our Nation impels. This is preeminently the time to speak the truth, the whole truth, frankly and boldly. Nor need we shrink from honestly facing conditions in our country today. This great Nation will endure as it has endured, will revive and will prosper. So, first of all, let me assert my firm belief that the only thing we have to fear is fear itself—nameless, unreasoning, unjustified terror which paralyzes needed efforts to convert retreat into advance. In every dark hour of our national life a leadership of frankness and vigor has met with that understanding and support of the people themselves which is essential to victory. I am convinced that you will again give that support to leadership in these critical days.

In such a spirit on my part and on yours we face our common difficulties. They concern, thank God, only material things. Values have shrunken to fantastic levels; taxes have risen; our ability to pay has fallen; government of all kinds is faced by serious curtailment of income; the means of exchange are frozen in the currents of trade; the withered leaves of industrial enterprise lie on every side; farmers find no markets for their produce; the savings of many years in thousands of families are gone.

More important, a host of unemployed citizens face the grim problem of existence, and an equally great number toil with little return. Only a foolish optimist can deny the dark realities of the moment.

Yet our distress comes from no failure of substance. We are stricken by no plague of locusts. Compared with the perils which our forefathers conquered because they believed and were not afraid, we have still much to be thankful for. Nature still offers her bounty and human efforts have multiplied it. Plenty is at our doorstep, but a generous use of it languishes in the very sight of the supply. Primarily this is because the rulers of the exchange of mankind's goods have failed, through their own stubbornness and their own incompetence, have admitted their failure, and abdicated. Practices of the unscrupulous moneychangers stand indicted in the court of public opinion, rejected by the hearts and minds of men.

True they have tried, but their efforts have been cast in the pattern of an outworn tradition. Faced by failure of credit they have proposed only the lending of more money. Stripped of the lure of profit by which to induce our people to follow their false leadership, they have resorted to exhortations, pleading tearfully for restored confidence. They know only the rules of a generation of self-seekers. They have no vision, and when there is no vision the people perish.

The moneychangers have fled from their high seats in the temple of our civilization. We may now restore that temple to the ancient truths. The measure of the restoration lies in the extent to which we apply social values more noble than mere monetary profit.

Happiness lies not in the mere possession of money; it lies in the joy of achievement, in the thrill of creative effort. The joy and moral stimulation of work no longer must be forgotten in the mad chase of evanescent profits. These dark days will be worth all they cost us if they teach us that our true destiny is not to be ministered unto but to minister to ourselves and to our fellow men.

Recognition of the falsity of material wealth as the standard of success goes hand in hand with the abandonment of the false belief that public office and high political position are to be valued only by the standards of pride of place and personal profit; and there must be an end to a conduct in banking and in business which too often has given to a sacred trust the likeness of callous and selfish wrongdoing. Small wonder that confidence languishes, for it thrives only on honesty, on honor, on the sacredness of obligations, on faithful protection, on unselfish performance; without them it cannot live.

Restoration calls, however, not for changes in ethics alone. This Nation asks for action, and action now.

Our greatest primary task is to put people to work. This is no unsolvable problem if we face it wisely and courageously. It can be accomplished in part by direct recruiting by the Government itself, treating the task as we would treat the emergency of a war, but at the same time, through this employment, accomplishing greatly needed projects to stimulate and reorganize the use of our natural resources.

Hand in hand with this we must frankly recognize the overbalance of population in our industrial centers and, by engaging on a national scale in a redistribution, endeavor to provide a better use of the land for those best fitted for the land. The task can be helped by definite efforts to raise the values of agricultural products and with this the power to purchase the output of our cities. It can be helped by preventing realistically the tragedy of the growing loss through foreclosure of our small homes and our farms. It can be helped by insistence that the Federal, State, and local governments act forthwith on the demand that their cost be drastically reduced. It can be helped by the unifying of relief activities which today are often scattered, uneconomical, and unequal. It can be helped by national planning for and supervision of all forms of transportation and of communications and other utilities which have a definitely public character. There are many ways in which it can be helped, but it can never be helped merely by talking about it. We must act and act quickly.

Finally, in our progress toward a resumption of work we require two safeguards against a return of the evils of the old order; there must be a strict supervision of all banking and credits and investments; there must be an end to speculation with other people's money, and there must be provision for an adequate but sound currency....

The basic thought that guides these specific means of national recovery is not narrowly nationalistic. It is the insistence, as a first consideration, upon the interdependence of the various elements in all parts of the United States—a recognition of the old and permanently important manifestation of the American spirit of the pioneer. It is the way to recovery. It is the immediate way. It is the strongest assurance that the recovery will endure.

In the field of world policy I would dedicate this Nation to the policy of the good neighbor—the neighbor who resolutely respects himself and, because he does so, respects the rights of others—the neighbor who respects his obligations and respects the sanctity of his agreements in and with a world of neighbors.

If I read the temper of our people correctly, we now realize as we have never realized before our interdependence on each other; that we can not merely take but we must give as well; that if we are to go forward, we must move as a trained and loyal army willing to sacrifice for the good of a common discipline, because without such discipline no progress is made, no leadership becomes effective. We are, I know, ready and willing to submit our lives and property to such discipline, because it makes possible a leadership which aims at a larger good. This I propose to offer, pledging that the larger purposes will bind upon us all as a sacred obligation with a unity of duty hitherto evoked only in time of armed strife.

With this pledge taken, I assume unhesitatingly the leadership of this great army of our people dedicated to a disciplined attack upon our common problems....

We face the arduous days that lie before us in the warm courage of the national unity; with the clear consciousness of seeking old and precious moral values; with the clean satisfaction that comes from the stern performance of duty by old and young alike. We aim at the assurance of a rounded and permanent national life.

We do not distrust the future of essential democracy. The people of the United States have not failed. In their need they have registered a mandate that they want direct, vigorous action. They have asked for discipline and direction under leadership. They have made me the present instrument of their wishes. In the spirit of the gift I take it.

In this dedication of a Nation we humbly ask the blessing of God. May He protect each and every one of us. May He guide me in the days to come.

Fourth is the famous "I Have a Dream" speech by Dr. Martin Luther King Jr. It was delivered August 28, 1963 at the great civil rights march on Washington in the shadow of the Lincoln Memorial.

Dr. Martin Luther King Jr.,
"I Have a Dream"
Delivered Wednesday, August 28, 1963

I am happy to join with you today in what will go down in history as the greatest demonstration for freedom in the history of our nation.

Five score years ago, a great American, in whose symbolic shadow we stand today, signed the Emancipation Proclamation. This momentous decree came as a great beacon light of hope to millions of Negro slaves who had been seared in the flames of withering injustice. It came as a joyous daybreak to end the long night of their captivity.

But one hundred years later, the Negro still is not free. One hundred years later, the life of the Negro is still sadly crippled by the manacles of segregation and the chains of discrimination. One hundred years later, the Negro lives on a lonely island of poverty in the midst of a vast ocean of material prosperity. One hundred years later, the Negro is still languished in the corners of American society and finds himself an exile in his own land. And so we've come here today to dramatize a shameful condition.

In a sense we've come to our nation's capital to cash a check. When the architects of our republic wrote the magnificent words of the Constitution and the Declaration of Independence, they were signing a promissory note to which every American was to fall heir. This note was a promise that all men, yes, black men as well as white men, would be guaranteed the "unalienable Rights" of "Life, Liberty and the pursuit of happiness." It is obvious today that America has defaulted on this promissory note, insofar as her citizens of color are concerned. Instead of honoring this sacred obligation, America has given the Negro people a bad check, a check which has come back marked "insufficient funds."

But we refuse to believe that the bank of justice is bankrupt. We refuse to believe that there are insufficient funds in the great vaults of opportunity of this nation. And so, we've come to cash this check, a check that will give us upon demand the riches of freedom and the security of justice.

We have also come to this hallowed spot to remind America of the fierce urgency of Now. This is no time to engage in the luxury of cooling off or to take the tranquilizing drug of gradualism. Now is the time to make real the promises of democracy. Now is the time to rise from the dark and desolate valley of segregation to the sunlit path of racial justice. Now is the time to lift our nation from the quicksand's of racial injustice to the solid rock of brotherhood. Now is the time to make justice a reality for all of God's children.

It would be fatal for the nation to overlook the urgency of the moment. This sweltering summer of the Negro's legitimate discontent will not pass until there is an invigorating autumn of freedom and equality. Nineteen sixty-three is not an end, but a beginning. And those who hope that the Negro needed to blow off steam and will now be content will have a rude awakening if the nation returns to business as usual. And there will be neither rest nor tranquility in America until the Negro is granted his citizenship rights. The whirlwinds of revolt will continue to shake the foundations of our nation until the bright day of justice emerges.

But there is something that I must say to my people, who stand on the warm threshold which leads into the palace of justice: In the process of gaining our rightful place, we must not be guilty of wrongful deeds. Let us not seek to satisfy our thirst for freedom by drinking from the cup of bitterness and hatred. We must forever conduct our struggle on the high plane of dignity and discipline. We must not allow our creative protest to degenerate into physical violence. Again and again, we must rise to the majestic heights of meeting physical force with soul force.

The marvelous new militancy which has engulfed the Negro community must not lead us to a distrust of all white people, for many of our white brothers, as evidenced by their presence here today, have come to realize that their destiny is tied up with our destiny. And they have come to realize that their freedom is inextricably bound to our freedom.

We cannot walk alone.

And as we walk, we must make the pledge that we shall always march ahead.

We cannot turn back.

There are those who are asking the devotees of civil rights, "When will you be satisfied?" We can never be satisfied as long as the Negro is the victim of the unspeakable horrors of police brutality. We can never be satisfied as long as our bodies, heavy with the fatigue of travel, cannot gain lodging in the motels of the highways and the hotels of the cities. We cannot be satisfied as long as the Negro's basic mobility is from a smaller ghetto to a larger one. We can never be satisfied as long as our children are stripped of their self-hood and robbed of their dignity by a sign stating: "For Whites Only." We cannot be satisfied as long as a Negro in Mississippi cannot vote and a Negro in New York believes he has nothing for which to vote. No, no, we are not satisfied, and we will not be satisfied until "justice rolls down like waters, and righteousness like a mighty stream."

I am not unmindful that some of you have come here out of great trials and tribulations. Some of you have come fresh from narrow jail cells. And some of you have come from areas where your quest—quest for freedom left you battered by the storms of persecution and staggered by the winds of police brutality. You have been the veterans of creative suffering. Continue to work with the faith that unearned suffering is redemptive. Go back to Mississippi, go back to Alabama, go back to South Carolina, go back to Georgia, go back to Louisiana, go back to the slums and ghettos of our northern cities, knowing that somehow this situation can and will be changed.

Let us not wallow in the valley of despair, I say to you today, my friends.

And so even though we face the difficulties of today and tomorrow, I still have a dream. It is a dream deeply rooted in the American dream.

I have a dream that one day this nation will rise up and live out the true meaning of its creed: "We hold these truths to be self-evident, that all men are created equal."

I have a dream that one day on the red hills of Georgia, the sons of former slaves and the sons of former slave owners will be able to sit down together at the table of brotherhood.

I have a dream that one day even the state of Mississippi, a state sweltering with the heat of injustice, sweltering with the heat of oppression, will be transformed into an oasis of freedom and justice.

I have a dream that my four little children will one day live in a nation where they will not be judged by the color of their skin but by the content of their character.

I have a dream today!

I have a dream that one day, down in Alabama, with its vicious racists, with its governor having his lips dripping with the words of "interposition" and "nullification"—one day right there in Alabama little black boys and black girls will be able to join hands with little white boys and white girls as sisters and brothers.

I have a dream today!

I have a dream that one day every valley shall be exalted, and every hill and mountain shall be made low, the rough places will be made plain, and the crooked places will be made straight; "and the glory of the Lord shall be revealed and all flesh shall see it together."

This is our hope, and this is the faith that I go back to the South with.

With this faith, we will be able to hew out of the mountain of despair a stone of hope. With this faith, we will be able to transform the jangling discords of our nation into a beautiful symphony of brotherhood. With this faith, we will be able to work together, to pray together, to struggle together, to go to jail together, to stand up for freedom together, knowing that we will be free one day.

And this will be the day — this will be the day when all of God's children will be able to sing with new meaning:

My country 'tis of thee, sweet land of liberty, of thee I sing.
Land where my fathers died, land of the Pilgrim's pride,
From every mountainside, let freedom ring!
And if America is to be a great nation, this must become true.
And so let freedom ring from the prodigious hilltops of New Hampshire.
Let freedom ring from the mighty mountains of New York.
Let freedom ring from the heightening Alleghenies of Pennsylvania.
Let freedom ring from the snow-capped Rockies of Colorado.
Let freedom ring from the curvaceous slopes of California.
But not only that:
Let freedom ring from Stone Mountain of Georgia.
Let freedom ring from Lookout Mountain of Tennessee.
Let freedom ring from every hill and molehill of Mississippi.
From every mountainside, let freedom ring.

And when this happens, when we allow freedom ring, when we let it ring from every village and every hamlet, from every state and every city, we will be able to speed up that day when all of God's children, black men and white men, Jews and Gentiles, Protestants and Catholics, will be able to join hands and sing in the words of the old Negro spiritual:

Free at last! Free at last!
Thank God Almighty, we are free at last!

Finally, Barack Obama's keynote address to the 2004 National Democratic Convention. Obama has shown himself capable of vividly communicating the progressive vision and inspiring his listeners. His life story itself is a powerful symbol of that vision.

Barack Obama,
2004 Democratic National Convention Keynote Address
Delivered Tuesday, July 27, 2004

Thank you so much. Thank you. Thank you. Thank you so much. Thank you so much. Thank you. Thank you. Thank you, Dick Durbin. You make us all proud.

On behalf of the great state of Illinois, crossroads of a nation, Land of Lincoln, let me express my deepest gratitude for the privilege of addressing this convention.

Tonight is a particular honor for me because, let's face it, my presence on this stage is pretty unlikely. My father was a foreign student, born and raised in a small village in Kenya. He grew up herding goats, went to school in a tin-roof shack. His father—my grandfather—was a cook, a domestic servant to the British.

But my grandfather had larger dreams for his son. Through hard work and perseverance, my father got a scholarship to study in a magical place, America, that shone as a beacon of freedom and opportunity to so many who had come before.

While studying here, my father met my mother. She was born in a town on the other side of the world, in Kansas. Her father worked on oil rigs and farms through most of the Depression. The day after Pearl Harbor, my grandfather signed up for duty; joined Patton's army, marched across Europe. Back home, my grandmother raised a baby and went to work on a bomber assembly line. After the war, they studied on the G.I. Bill, bought a house through F.H.A., and later moved west all the way to Hawaii in search of opportunity.

And they, too, had big dreams for their daughter. A common dream, born of two continents.

My parents shared not only an improbable love, they shared an abiding faith in the possibilities of this nation. They would give me an African name, Barack, or "blessed," believing that in a tolerant America your name is no barrier to success. They imagined—They imagined me going to the best schools in the land, even though they weren't rich, because in a generous America you don't have to be rich to achieve your potential.

They're both passed away now. And yet, I know that on this night they look down on me with great pride.

They stand here—And I stand here today, grateful for the diversity of my heritage, aware that my parents' dreams live on in my two precious daughters. I stand here knowing that my story is part of the larger American story, that I owe a debt to all of those who came before me, and that, in no other country on earth, is my story even possible.

Tonight, we gather to affirm the greatness of our Nation — not because of the height of our skyscrapers, or the power of our military, or the size of our economy. Our pride is based on a very simple premise, summed up in a declaration made over two hundred years ago:

> *We hold these truths to be self-evident, that all men are created equal, that they are endowed by their Creator with certain inalienable rights, that among these are Life, Liberty and the pursuit of Happiness.*

That is the true genius of America, a faith—a faith in simple dreams, an insistence on small miracles; that we can tuck in our children at night and know that they are fed and clothed and safe from harm; that we can say what we think, write what we think, without hearing a sudden knock on the door; that we can have an idea and start our own business without paying a bribe; that we can participate in the political process without fear of retribution, and that our votes will be counted—at least most of the time.

This year, in this election we are called to reaffirm our values and our commitments, to hold them against a hard reality and see how we're measuring up to the legacy of our forbearers and the promise of future generations.

And fellow Americans, Democrats, Republicans, Independents, I say to you tonight: We have more work to do—more work to do for the workers I met in Galesburg, Illinois, who are losing their union jobs at the Maytag plant that's moving to Mexico, and now are having to compete with their own children for jobs that pay seven bucks an hour; more to do for the father that I met who was losing his job and choking back the tears, wondering how he would pay 4,500 dollars a month for the drugs his son needs without the health benefits that he counted on; more to do for the young woman in East St. Louis, and thousands more like her, who has the grades, has the drive, has the will, but doesn't have the money to go to college.

Now, don't get me wrong. The people I meet—in small towns and big cities, in diners and office parks—they don't expect government to solve all their problems. They know they have to work hard to get ahead, and they want to. Go into the collar counties around Chicago, and people will tell you they don't want their tax money wasted, by a welfare agency or by the Pentagon. Go in—Go into any inner city neighborhood, and folks will tell you that government alone can't teach our kids to learn; they know that parents have to teach, that children can't achieve unless we raise their expectations and turn off the television sets and eradicate the slander that says a black youth with a book is acting white. They know those things.

People don't expect—People don't expect government to solve all their problems. But they sense, deep in their bones, that with just a slight change in priorities, we can make sure that every child in America has a decent shot at life, and that the doors of opportunity remain open to all.

They know we can do better. And they want that choice.

In this election, we offer that choice. Our Party has chosen a man to lead us who embodies the best this country has to offer. And that man is John Kerry.

John Kerry understands the ideals of community, faith, and service because they've defined his life. From his heroic service to Vietnam, to his years as a prosecutor and lieutenant governor, through two decades in the United States Senate, he's devoted himself to this country. Again and again, we've seen him make tough choices when easier ones were available.

His values and his record and affirm what is best in us. John Kerry believes in an America where hard work is rewarded; so instead of offering tax breaks to companies shipping jobs overseas, he offers them to companies creating jobs here at home.

John Kerry believes in an America where all Americans can afford the same health coverage our politicians in Washington have for themselves.

John Kerry believes in energy independence, so we aren't held hostage to the profits of oil companies, or the sabotage of foreign oil fields.

John Kerry believes in the Constitutional freedoms that have made our country the envy of the world, and he will never sacrifice our basic liberties, nor use faith as a wedge to divide us.

And John Kerry believes that in a dangerous world war must be an option sometimes, but it should never be the first option.

You know, a while back—a while back I met a young man named Shamus in a V.F.W. Hall in East Moline, Illinois. He was a good-looking kid—six-two, six-three, clear-eyed, with an easy smile. He told me he'd joined the Marines and was heading to Iraq the following week. And as I listened to him explain why he'd enlisted, the absolute faith he had in our country and its leaders, his devotion to duty and service, I thought this young man was all that any of us might ever hope for in a child.

But then I asked myself, "Are we serving Shamus as well as he is serving us?"

I thought of the 900 men and women—sons and daughters, husbands and wives, friends and neighbors, who won't be returning to their own hometowns. I thought of the families I've met who were struggling to get by without a loved one's full income, or whose loved ones had returned with a limb missing or nerves shattered, but still lacked long-term health benefits because they were Reservists.

When we send our young men and women into harm's way, we have a solemn obligation not to fudge the numbers or shade the truth about why they're going, to care for their families while they're gone, to tend to the soldiers upon their return, and to never ever go to war without enough troops to win the war, secure the peace, and earn the respect of the world.

Now—Now let me be clear. Let me be clear. We have real enemies in the world. These enemies must be found. They must be pursued. And they must be defeated. John Kerry knows this. And just as Lieutenant Kerry did not hesitate to risk his life to protect the men who served with him in Vietnam, President Kerry will not hesitate one moment to use our military might to keep America safe and secure.

John Kerry believes in America. And he knows that it's not enough for just some of us to prosper—for alongside our famous individualism, there's another ingredient in the American saga, a belief that we're all connected as one people. If there is a child on the south side of Chicago who can't read, that matters to me, even if it's not my child. If there is a senior citizen somewhere who can't pay for their prescription drugs, and having to choose between medicine and the rent, that makes my life poorer, even if it's not my grandparent. If there's an Arab-American family being rounded up without benefit of an attorney or due process, that threatens my civil liberties.

It is that fundamental belief—It is that fundamental belief: I am my brother's keeper, I am my sister's keeper, that makes this country work. It's what allows us to pursue our individual dreams and yet still come together as one American family.

E pluribus unum: "Out of many, one."

Now even as we speak, there are those who are preparing to divide us—the spin masters, the negative ad peddlers who embrace the politics of "anything goes." Well, I say to them tonight, there is not a liberal America and a conservative America—there is the United States of America. There is not a Black America and a White America and Latino America and Asian America—there's the United States of America.

The pundits, the pundits like to slice-and-dice our country into Red States and Blue States; Red States for Republicans, Blue States for Democrats. But I've got news for them, too. We worship an "awesome God" in the Blue States, and we don't like federal agents poking around in our libraries in the Red States. We coach Little League in the Blue States and yes, we've got some gay friends in the Red States. There are patriots who opposed the war in Iraq and there are patriots who supported the war in Iraq. We are one people, all of us pledging allegiance to the stars and stripes, all of us defending the United States of America.

In the end—In the end—In the end, that's what this election is about. Do we participate in a politics of cynicism or do we participate in a politics of hope?

John Kerry calls on us to hope. John Edwards calls on us to hope.

I'm not talking about blind optimism here—the almost willful ignorance that thinks unemployment will go away if we just don't think about it, or the health care crisis will solve itself if we just ignore it. That's not what I'm talking about. I'm talking about something more substantial. It's the hope of slaves sitting around a fire singing freedom songs; the hope of immigrants setting out for distant shores; the hope of a young naval lieutenant bravely patrolling the Mekong Delta; the hope of a millworker's son who dares to defy the odds; the hope of a skinny kid with a funny name who believes that America has a place for him, too.

Hope—Hope in the face of difficulty. Hope in the face of uncertainty. The audacity of hope!

In the end, that is God's greatest gift to us, the bedrock of this nation. A belief in things not seen. A belief that there are better days ahead.

I believe that we can give our middle class relief and provide working families with a road to opportunity.

I believe we can provide jobs to the jobless, homes to the homeless, and reclaim young people in cities across America from violence and despair.

I believe that we have a righteous wind at our backs and that as we stand on the crossroads of history, we can make the right choices, and meet the challenges that face us.

America! Tonight, if you feel the same energy that I do, if you feel the same urgency that I do, if you feel the same passion that I do, if you feel the same hopefulness that I do—if we do what we must do, then I have no doubt that all across the country, from Florida to Oregon, from Washington to Maine, the people will rise up in November, and John Kerry will be sworn in as President, and John Edwards will be sworn in as Vice President, and this country will reclaim its promise, and out of this long political darkness a brighter day will come.

Thank you very much everybody. God bless you. Thank you.

Throughout our history, American leaders have proudly, clearly and self-confidently invoked the progressive values that define America's greatness.

They called upon its citizens to sacrifice—not because of their failure, but in order to create a better life for our children.

They called upon Americans to commit themselves to the common good—to each other and the next generation.

We know how to inspire. We know how to call on people to hope.

If we do what we know how to do, we can awaken America to lead the world to overcome the challenges of the 21st Century and realize the great promise of a truly democratic society.

SECTION NINE

BUILDING A DEMOCRATIC SOCIETY

CHAPTER FIFTY-THREE

Structural Change

When we talk about a democratic society were not just talking about voting—though that is a critical aspect of a democratic society.

We're not just talking about due process and protection of minority rights—though that's critical to a democratic society as well.

By a democratic society, I mean a society where power is widely diffused to everyone.

That is not just some utopian ideal. Complex societies necessarily include elites who make decisions. But in a democratic society:

- The power to select these elites and hold them accountable is spread equally throughout the society.

- That society includes many different elites and centers of power that can provide checks and balances on each other—to assure individual freedom, and the protection of minority rights, and to prevent tyranny.

WHAT IS POWER?

Political scientists and philosophers have offered various definitions of power for centuries.

For the purpose of the discussion here, our working definition is that power is the ability to select and achieve goals.

In a social context that often requires the ability to change the behavior of others; power is getting other people to do things that they would not otherwise do.

Social power can be exercised in a variety of ways—through persuasion, intimidation, coercion, the exercise of physical force, by providing incentives. In general, it can be achieved by addressing and engaging any of the six categories of self-interests.

But let's also remember that individual power can be exercised and enhanced without any reference to others at all. The Internet enhances the personal power of individuals to rapidly access information. Education enhances individual power to manipulate nature. When you set a goal to lose 10 pounds, you can achieve that goal yourself—without changing anyone else's behavior.

Power is about being able to select and achieve goals, either individually or as a group. Alexander the Great exercised power by conquering societies from Greece to India using armies and physical violence. Robert Oppenheimer exercised power by harnessing the energy of the atom bomb using the intellectual resources of his team of scientists. Bill Gates exercises his power by organizing the talent of software designers and marketers. Bill Clinton exercised power by persuading the voters to elect him President and then by exercising control over the apparatus of the federal government.

Virtually every middle-class American is a great deal more powerful than a poor peasant in Sudan because he has more individual and social resources that allow him to select and achieve a wider array of goals—both individually and socially.

People use power to select and achieve goals that are associated with the six categories of self-interest. As a result, someone who has more power is generally—on average—more likely to live a fulfilling life, to flourish, to succeed and survive.

WHY A DEMOCRATIC SOCIETY IS SO IMPORTANT IN THE MODERN WORLD—THE IMPORTANCE OF STRUCTURAL CHANGE

Why is it so critical that Progressives focus on the creation of a democratic society, where power is widely diffused?

• Our fundamental goal as Progressives is the success and survival of all human beings, and it's more likely that people with more power can succeed and survive. It obviously follows that the creation of a democratic society—that diffuses power to everyone—is a baseline progressive goal. The diffusion of power gives more people the opportunity to flourish. It's that simple.

• We've seen that the exponential explosion of technology infects the distribution of power with the same autocatalytic quality that is characteristic of technological innovation. Technology gives power to its possessor. Its rapid expansion gives small elites exponentially increased ability to control and oppress others. If, on the other hand, the power of technology is widely distributed in a more democratic society, its exponential expansion tends to accelerate the process of further democratization.

As the speed of technological innovation accelerates, our long-term ability to create a democratic society—and avoid its Orwellian counterpart—depends heavily on the level of democratization into which technology is inserted over the next several decades. That obviously goes for technologies like nuclear weapons, and technologies for surveillance. But it also goes for most other forms of technology as well—technology of all sorts imparts power.

• We've seen that one of the chief reasons that past societies have failed to take the actions that would prevent their collapse is that decision-making elites had individual interests that were not compatible with the long-term interest of the society as a whole.

This is particularly true when they their greater power gives them the illusion that they are immune to the negative consequences of their own actions –if they believe that their private schools, gated communities and huge incomes will allow them to escape the consequences of poor public schools, climate change, poverty and all the rest.

The principal line of defense against the incongruity of interest between decision-making elites and the entire society is to assure that the power held by decision-makers is accountable to a democratic society.

• How we change the structures of our economic and political systems today has a major impact on future prospects for progressive political success.

By cutting taxes as their first order of business, the Republicans changed the economic possibilities of government—at least for the near term. They won a major battle in their war to remove power from the public sector and strengthen corporate-sector decision-making. On the other hand, one of our strongest political cards is the existence of Social Security and Medicare. The fact that they exist, and that many Americans have a clear vested interest in them, makes it much more difficult for the right to *dismantle* them, than it would be for them to defeat the "idea" of Social Security or Medicare. *Facts on the ground trump ideas.*

On occasion you hear the notion that we should allow things to get worse so they can get bad enough that people will call for radical change. That notion is simply wrong. In fact, it rarely ever happens in human history.

Change occurs when there is a problem—call it a self-interest deficit—for a group of people in society who have adequate power to force a change in the way society's resources are distributed or the way decisions are made. Change does not occur simply because things get "bad enough" for a large section of the population. It requires that the affected group have enough power to do something about it.

Is there any question that things are "bad enough" for the great mass of people in the Third World? If all it took were unhappiness, many things would have changed in the world. In reality it takes unhappiness, coupled with the power to do something about it.

Long-lasting, fundamental change in society requires that we must focus on *structural change*—change in the structures that allocate wealth and power. Election reform, labor law reform, campaign finance reform, universal healthcare, changes in the basic rules of international trade—these have a fundamental effect of on the power of our constituencies. They create the material bases that allow those constituencies to exercise political power to create future progressive change.

Obviously, we also have to prevent regressive structural reform—packing the courts with conservative jurists, reallocating wealth through "tax reform," privatizing Social Security. Not only are these bad policies in and of themselves, but their enactment would weaken the power of our constituencies and lessen the ability of Progressives to define the future.

POWER AND STRUGGLE

We don't believe that for me to have a more fulfilling life, you have to have a less fulfilling life. That goes for power as well. Understood as the ability to select and achieve goals, there is not a fixed quantity of power over which everyone in human society must compete. The total quantity of power in human society can be expanded—and technology is doing that every day.

Of course, where two people want to achieve the same goal—or to compete over a resource that is truly scarce—there *is* a zero-sum game. If we both want to be president, only one of us can win.

But if we work to assure there is enough food to satisfy everyone's hunger, there doesn't have to be competition over who can eat. Everyone can eat—there needn't be a zero-sum game over who eats and who starves.

Regardless, those who possess more power than others have historically been resistant to give it up. That's why it's again worth quoting Frederick Douglass, who said, "Power surrenders nothing without a struggle. It never has, it never will."

Progressives need to understand that building a democratic society—at home and around the world—is not just about good ideas, or civil conversation. *It's about political struggle.*

CHAPTER FIFTY-FOUR

The Progressive Agenda
for Structural Change

All this means that the progressive agenda for action should focus heavily on political struggle that affects the distribution of power in society. We need to focus on structural change that democratizes and diffuses power in society, and empowers everyday people. We have to struggle against right wing assaults that would make society less democratic—concentrating power in the hands of a few.

That implies that while it is a fine thing for people to devote time and energy to a wide array of issues and interests, the principal focus for progressive energy should be the battles that directly affect the distribution of power—both in America and around the world.

I would argue that in the near term, the major battles in that struggle for structural change will be fought on 13 fronts.

THE BATTLE OVER THE DISTRIBUTION OF INCOME, AND THE CONTROL OF WEALTH IN THE UNITED STATES

More than any other factor, the possession of wealth and income impacts your power—your ability to select and achieve goals—in modern society. As we've seen, over the last 50 years a smaller and smaller percentage of the population has come to control a larger and larger percentage of America's income and wealth. The top tier of the population—and especially the top 1%—siphoned off almost all the economic growth our economy has created from 2003 to 2007.

In Congress, the drive for more wealth and income concentration continued throughout the Republican era. Even now, it's embodied in the Republicans' continued attempts to make their tax cuts permanent, repeal the estate tax, destroy unions and create trade policies that benefit the wealthy.

We've seen that the increasing inequity in the distribution of income and wealth underlies the partisan polarization of politics. Most important, it decreases the democratization of American society and concentrates power in the hands of a smaller and smaller percentage of our citizens. And this group often believes—incorrectly—that they are protected from the consequences of their decisions, consequences that are dangerous to everyone else.

In Section Seven we discussed several direct means to end income and wealth inequality:

- Strong unions;

- Trade policies and aimed at maintaining higher wages, safe working conditions, and the protection of the environment;

- Policies that shift the tax burden away from the poor and middle class to the wealthy;

- Living wages and a high-wage, bottom-up economy.

Several other factors can indirectly affect the democratization of wealth and income as well.

- *Maintaining strong pensions for retirees.*

The US pension system is in serious jeopardy, and the radical conservatives spent most of their political capital after the 2004 presidential election attempting to make matters worse.

The strength of pensions is obviously central to maintaining a standard a living for retirees. One of the chief reasons why the distribution of income compressed between the Great Depression and 1973 was the creation of Social Security and the pension system. Coupled with Medicare, these programs massively reduced poverty among the elderly.

Of course, President Bush and the right want to abandon the system of guaranteed benefits provided by Social Security and put in its place a system of risky private accounts. American voters have correctly rejected this attempt.

But the problem goes further than Social Security. Over the last two decades, the system of guaranteed private pensions provided by corporations in addition to Social Security has been jettisoned for a system of employee investment accounts (401(k)'s and the like) that shift the financial burden of pensions from corporations to individual investments. This leaves employees much less secure than the earlier system.

For example, consider the situation of Sean Schuback, a 15-year veteran of Verizon. He arrived at work one morning to the unsettling news that the telecommunications giant was freezing its pensions plan. "In an instant, Schuback, 33, who joined the company as a phone operator right out of high school, saw the $469,286 pension payout he was told he could receive by working another 15 years sliced to $245,494, where it would stay no matter how many more years he put in. [1]

An apocryphal story from Malcolm Gladwell will explain why corporations are so keen on changing the pension system.

In a piece he wrote for *The New Yorker*, Gladwell explains:

The years just after the Second World War were a time of great industrial upheaval in the United States. Strikes were commonplace. Workers moved from one company to another. Runaway inflation was eroding the values of wages. In the uncertain 1940s, in the wake of the Depression and the war, workers wanted security, and in 1949, the head of the Toledo, Ohio, local of the United Auto Workers, Richard Grosser, came up with the a proposal. The workers of Toledo needed pensions. But, he said, the pension plan should be regional, spread among many small auto parts makers, electrical appliance manufacturers, and plastic shops in the Toledo area. That way, if workers switched jobs they could take their pension credits with them, and if a company went bankrupt its workers retirement would be safe. Every company in the area, Grosser proposed, should pay $.10 an hour, per worker, into a centralized fund.

The business owners of Toledo reacted immediately. "They were terrified," says Jennifer Klein, a labor historian at Yale University, who has written about the Toledo case. "They organized a trade association to stop the plan. In the business press, they actually said, "This idea might be efficient and rational. But it's too dangerous." Some of the larger employers stepped forward and said, "We'll offer you a company pension. Forget about the whole other idea." They took on the cost of setting up an individual company pension, at great expense, in order to head off what they saw as too much organized power for workers in the region."

A year later, the same issue came up in Detroit. The president of General Motors at the time was Charles E. Wilson, known as Engine Charlie. Wilson was one of the highest-paid corporate executives in America, earning $586,100 (and paying, incidentally, $430,350 in taxes). He was in contract talks with Walter Reuther, the national president of the UAW. The two men had already agreed on a cost-of-living allowance. Now, Wilson went one step further, and, for the first time, offered every GM employee health-care benefits and a pension.

Reuther had his doubts. He lived in a northwest Detroit bungalow, and drove a 1940 Chevrolet. His salary was $10,000 a year. He was the son of a Debsian Socialist, worked for the Socialist Party during his college days, and went to the Soviet Union in the 1930s to teach peasants how to be auto machinists. His inclination was to fight for change that benefited every *worker, not just those lucky enough to be employed by General Motors. In the 1930s, unions had launched a number of health care plans, many of which cut across individual companies and industry lines. In the 1940s, they argued for expanding Social Security. In 1945, when President Truman first proposed national health insurance, they cheered. In 1947, when Ford offered its workers a pension, the union voted it down. The labor movement believed that the safest and most efficient way to provide insurance against ill health and old age was to spread the cost and risk of benefits over the biggest and most diverse group possible. Walter Reuther, as Nelson Lichtenstein argues in his definitive biography, believed that risk ought to be broadly collectivized. Charlie Wilson, on the other hand, felt the way the business leaders of Toledo did: the collectivization was a threat to the free market and to the autonomy of business owners. In his view, companies themselves ought to be assuming the risk of providing insurance.*

America's private pension system is now in crisis. Over the past few years, American taxpayers have been put at risk by assuming tens of billions of dollars of pension liabilities from once profitable companies. Hundreds of thousands of retired steelworkers and airline employees have seen health-care benefits that were promised to them by their employers vanish. General Motors, the country's largest automaker, is between $40 and $50 billion behind in the money it needs to fulfill health-care and pension promises. This crisis is sometimes portrayed as a result of corporate America's excessive generosity and making promises to its workers. But when it comes to retirement, health, disability, and unemployment benefits there is nothing exceptional about the United States: it is average among industrialized countries—more generous than in Australia, Canada, Ireland and Italy, just behind Finland and the United Kingdom, and on par with the Netherlands and Denmark. The difference is that in most countries, the government, or large groups of companies, provides pensions and health insurance. The United States, by contrast, has over the past 50 years followed the lead of Charlie Wilson and the bosses of Toledo and made individual companies responsible for the care of their retirees. It is this fact, as much as any other, that explains the current crisis. In 1950, Charlie Wilson was wrong, and Walter Reuther was right. [2]

Gladwell concludes, "If the risk of providing health care and old age pensions are shared by all of us, then companies can succeed or fail based on what they do and not the number of retirees." [3] Yet another example where the "private market" doesn't do the job.

Gladwell goes on in his article to explain that the key to this problem is "the dependency ratio"—the number of people working to support each retiree. As these companies have become more efficient and productivity has increased, they have fewer workers per retiree. In 2001, when Bethlehem Steel declared bankruptcy, it had 12,000 active employees and 95,000 retirees. [4]

The problem is that pensions should be underwritten by the largest possible risk pool; that means government action, not just private employer action. Fixing this problem has to be a key focus for Progressives. It directly affects the distribution of wealth and income in America.

The right will continue its attacks on Social Security. We must defend it.

We should also propose nationally managed investment programs for all Americans and for all companies that could accommodate different levels of risk and contributions by individuals and companies. The system could be similar to the retirement investment system available to federal employees, but must provide a national structure for pensions that would allow employees to move between jobs and spread the risk among many employers and employees.

But this program is no substitute for Social Security—it should supplement the rock-solid guaranteed benefit provided the Social Security program.

• *The critical need for universal health care.*
We've already discussed the enormous importance of universal health care, to the economy and to our citizens. But it's also important to remember that healthcare costs are a crucial element affecting the distribution of income and wealth. An increasing percentage of nongovernmental health-care cost is borne by individuals—not employers. It comes in the form of payments made by the increasing number of uninsured, higher co-pays and deductibles. It comes right off the top of middle-class disposable income and obviously represents a much greater portion of their incomes than that of high-income people.

Catastrophic health-care costs are the leading cause of personal bankruptcy in United States.

What's more, the overall inefficiency in the American healthcare system takes a huge bite out of America's overall GDP—leaving less and less for increases in workers' real income. Americans pay 40% more per capita than the countries with the next highest expenditure per person; yet health care outcomes are down in the middle of the pack of industrialized countries. Life expectancy in the United States is 41st among the world's nations. Countries with longer life expectancy include Japan, most of Europe, Guam, Jordan and the Cayman Islands.

According to a study published by the Organization for Economic Cooperation and Development in 2003, the United States had fewer practicing physicians, practicing nurses, and acute-care bed days per capita than the median country in the Organization for Economic

Cooperation and Development (OECD). Nevertheless, U.S. health spending per capita was almost two and a half times the per capita health spending of the median OECD country. [5]

According to the Kaiser Family Foundation, the cost of family coverage has risen 87% since 2000, while consumer prices are up only 18% and workers' incomes up 20%. And that's without considering the effect of deductibles and other out-of-pocket payments. [6]

Guaranteed health care for all is at the top of the progressive agenda.

My preference is simple; everyone should have a choice of a Medicare-type plan—either individually or at their work place.

Medicare is as American as apple pie, and it is massively more efficient than private insurance companies.

In state legislatures, we used to propose that regulators require private health insurance companies to keep the percentage of their administrative costs as low as Medicare. Insurers used to question how that would be possible: Medicare has a massive number of clients over which to spread the cost, and no advertising expense. How can we compete with that? We would say *precisely*—that's one of the main reasons why America's private health care system generates 40% higher health care costs per person than any other country.

Michael Moore's movie, "Sicko," documents the armies of people that insurance companies pay full-time *to deny claims*. They don't add any value to the health care system, just to the health insurance company.

The Guaranteed Affordable Choice Plan would allow individuals to keep their current insurance or to opt into a public plan. Companies would be required to offer employees an option of a private plan or the public plan as well. Medicaid would be rolled into the plan, and much of the cost would be paid by taxes and not direct premiums.

The plan would cover everyone who was not covered by another plan, and above a certain income they would be required to make contributions to the plan in the same way they pay payroll taxes today. But many businesses would opt into the plan as well, because its administrative costs would be so low and its bargaining power for health care price reductions would be so high.

A March 2007 *New York Times* poll found that 60% of voters— including 62% of independents and 46% of Republicans—said they would be willing to pay more in taxes to pay for guaranteed health care for all. [7]

THE UPCOMING HEALTH-CARE BATTLE—THE STAGE IS SET

Once again, almost a decade and a half after the defeat of the Clinton health care proposal, the stage is again set for another monumental battle over the future of the American health care system in 2009.

If it occurs, it will be the most significant domestic political battle since the passage of Medicare—affecting one sixth of the U.S. gross domestic product.

In many respects, the strategic situation with respect to health care is similar to 1991—the year before Clinton was elected President. Then the health care crisis was widely acknowledged as a major national problem. The issue was widely discussed in the 1992 Presidential election. By 1993, there was near unanimous consensus that some major overhaul of the nation's health care system was inevitable.

Yet a Democratic President made a comprehensive proposal for change to a heavily Democratic Congress—and lost.

Our task—two years before the battle will likely be joined—is to plan a strategy, create the political environment, and assemble the political and organizational resources that will overcome the formidable array of forces that will once again oppose fundamental change.

That task is informed by the failure of the Clinton health care plan, and by our successful battle to prevent the privatization of Social Security—a defensive fight that was in many ways modeled on the right's strategy in 1993-94.

TASKS THAT MUST BE DONE TO ASSURE VICTORY IN THE BATTLE FOR HEALTH CARE FOR ALL

Mounting a successful campaign to reshape the structure of one-sixth of the American political economy is a tall order. It is far more daunting than any domestic policy campaign undertaken by Progressives in the last half century—obviously including the 1993-94 campaign for the Clinton plan.

It is daunting. But it can be done.

Victory in this battle is possible only if:

• A progressive Democrat is elected President.

• Democrats increase their margins in the House—and especially the Senate. We will need 60 votes to win in the Senate and must expect to loose at least a handful of Democrats. While we will pick up a handful of Republicans, their number will be very limited.

Even with these preconditions in place, to win we must accomplish the following tasks in the period leading up to 2009:

• **We must create a national consensus that health care is a right, not a commodity; and that government must guarantee that**

right. This requires that the public strongly support a materially increased role for the public sector as a provider of health care and health insurance; as a regulator of private sector providers; and by using its buying power to control costs.

- **We must create a national consensus that the health care system is in crisis.** This does not simply mean agreement that everyone should have health care, or that health care is a right. It means that there must be widespread consensus that many Americans can't pay for the health care they need without sacrificing their standard of living; and/or anger (or revulsion) that some people can't access health care. To win we must not just generate understanding, but emotion–anger, revulsion, disgust. Over the next two years, we must generate a depth of passion on the part of large segments of the population—passion that will no longer accept the status quo. *This will require an ongoing highly integrated earned-media messaging program that brings the growing crisis into relief over the next two years.*

- **Our messaging program over the next two years should focus heavily on reducing the credibility of the health insurance industry and focusing on the failure of private health insurance.** Our principal foe in this battle will inevitably be the private health insurance industry. It must be discredited.

- **We need to systematically forge relationships with large sectors of the business/employer community.** We need their economic power to have any chance of offsetting the power of the insurance and pharmaceutical companies. The principal targets for this buy-in are the large manufacturing industries that have massive legacy costs—firms where the ratio of their retirees to the current work force is often a greater factor in determining their competitive position, than the price or quality of their products. Any sector that is pressed by strong international competition is also a prime target because the U.S. healthcare system forces them to internalize health care costs that are spread over the entire population in all other industrial societies.

- **We need to convince political leaders that they owe their elections, at least in part, to the groundswell of support of universal health care, and that they face political peril if they fail to deliver on universal health care in 2009.**

- **We need not agree in advance on the components of a plan, but we must foster a process that can ultimately yield consensus.** In the end our proposal must *not be frightening*. It must sound *familiar*. It must sound *American*. It must sound simple and elegant (if it is confusing, it will feel dangerous and hard to understand). It must make people feel that it will *empower them* to have *more control* over their lives (more choice of things like doctors and hospitals), not less. It must appear to improve people's individual health care coverage.

- **Over the next two years, we must design and organize a massive national field program.** A successful strategy requires that we lay the groundwork for a major mass mobilization across the country. It will require the creation of a field apparatus that can simultaneously light the fire and focus its energy on critical targets. It will require mobilization of a size and scope we have not organized for a domestic, economic issue since the Great Depression.

- **We must focus especially on the mobilization of the labor movement and the faith community.** A successful mass mobilization must have both an economic populist and moral component. It will require that large numbers of Americans believe they have a lot personally on the line. But it also requires that we raise the question of universal health care to a moral level—not just a cause people support—but one to which they become *committed.* In our recent history, the civil rights movement and anti-war movements have taken on this moral dimension. This movement will be different, but if we cannot generate a moral, as well as populist dimension, it will not succeed. The base of the populist mobilization will most certainly be *organized labor.* The base of the moral component must be a large infrastructure in the *faith community.*

- **We must systematically leverage the connections and resources of a massive array of institutions and organizations of all types.** These must be forged into some kind of network over the next two years and have practice working with each other before the gun goes off in 2009.

- **To be successful, we must put in place commitments for hundreds of millions of dollars to be used to finance paid communications and mobilization once the battle is joined.** In 1993, the other side completely out-communicated the proponents of universal health care—even though we had the advantage of the bully pulpit of the Presidency.

These are major tasks. But they can be done.

DISTRIBUTION OF QUALITY EDUCATIONAL OPPORTUNITY

A huge factor affecting long-term income distribution is educational attainment. After World War II, someone with a high-school education could aspire to a middle-class lifestyle based on the union wages negotiated by the increasingly powerful labor movement—especially in heavy industry.

Today, a middle-class income requires at least a college degree. Yet access to higher education is far from universal. Unlike high-school education, Americans are not guaranteed free college education. In fact, the percentage of college costs borne directly by the public sector has plummeted at the same time that the cost of college has escalated far faster than the cost of living.

It now costs $40,000 per year to go to a selective private college and $15,000 per year for an in-state student to attend a public university.

In 2005, Federal Pell Grants top out at $4,050. The Bush administration's 2006 budget—which we fought through the Emergency Campaign for America's priorities—slashed student tuition assistance by $16 billion, to help pay for more tax breaks for millionaires. [8]

State legislatures have also cut subsidies to public universities.

A new report by a committee advising Congress and the Department of Education found that during this decade, 2.5 million students will either drop out or fail to enroll in college, because of costs.

Add that to the terrific drain that the cost of sending kids to college puts on the incomes of middle-class families, and you have a massive impact on the distribution of income. After all, the cost of college represents a much smaller percentage of income for the wealthy than for middle-class Americans.

But that's not all. According to a study by the Century Foundation, only 3% of students at the 146 most competitive colleges come from families whose income puts them in the bottom socioeconomic quarter. Seventy-four percent come from the top quarter. [9]

Most of the inequity results from the differential level of preparation offered by the wealthy to its children: better schools, better preschools, more highly educated parents. Part of the inequity results from "affirmative action" programs for the wealthy. These include preferences for "legacies"—kids of alums; and "development cases"—the children of celebrities, wealthy executives and professional politicians.

And educational inequity isn't limited to higher education. The public and private schools available to the wealthy are almost uniformly superior to those available to children from average-income families. This is particularly true where property taxes are used to fund education on a district-by-district basis. High-property-tax-base districts have substantially more money to spend—four to five times as much per student—than other districts.

The Federal Head Start Program was established in the 1960s to help offset some of these educational hurdles for children of low-income families. It has proven very effective, but too limited in size and duration. A study by the Institute of Early Education Research showed that for every dollar spent on pre-kindergarten, there is an estimated return of seven dollars in future savings due to higher earnings, as well as reduced crime and less need for remedial education. [10]

Part of a progressive agenda to democratize society has to include universal free preschool; free universal higher education; increased access of children from average income families to elite universities—based on achievement as well as racial and economic social hardship; and equal funding for every child's public education at the same high levels that wealthy kids have today.

All of this will cost money. But education is not an expenditure, it's an investment. Study after study has shown that huge portions of America's economic growth have been directly attributable to education. Progressives have to make full access to public education at all levels a central priority.

ECONOMIC DEVELOPMENT

A final means of indirectly decreasing income and wealth inequality is economic development in poor neighborhoods. The issues involved here relate fundamentally to the availability of investment dollars of all sorts— from mortgages, to venture capital, to bank loans.

As I mentioned, in the 1970s, when I was at the Citizens Action Program (CAP), we were very involved in developing the issue of "redlining," where banks and insurance companies drew "red lines" around some communities and refused to invest there. The work of the late Gail Cincotta, National Peoples Action and the National Training and Information Center helped pass the Community Reinvestment Act (CRA) that has been crucial in channeling investment to many low-income areas. Much more should be done. These issues directly impact the disparity of wealth and income.

THE BATTLE TO DEFEND THE PUBLIC SECTOR—THE PUBLIC SECTOR MUST BE EXPANDED TO PROVIDE GOODS AND SERVICES THAT ARE NOT PROVIDED EFFICIENTLY BY THE PRIVATE MARKET.

In other words, Progressives need to stand up for the public sector and work to expand the mandate of the democratic decision-making structures of government to provide for the common good.

The last 20 years our defensive crouch has been particularly pronounced when it comes to the public sector. Bush's Social Security proposals collapsed in 2005. He was unable to pass a budget for fiscal 2007 that would further cut nutritional programs, health care and education in order to get even more tax breaks for millionaires. And now Democrats control Congress.

The reason he failed in both of these initiatives is that public opinion has turned against them.

Now we have to take the offensive. **That involves many future battles—four major battles in the near term. We've just talked about three:**

- *Quality Health Care for all.*
- *Universal higher education and preschool.*
- *The battle to defend Social Security and restructure pensions to protect average American retirees.*
- *A fourth will be the battle to expand public revenues to fully fund key governmental functions—especially critical social priorities and public infrastructure.*

Over the last 20 years, key government services have been starved for resources—both at the federal and state levels. Federal budget cuts have gutted funding for student loans, health care, child care, child-support collection, child nutrition—the list goes on and on—all to give tax breaks to millionaires. Many of these cuts have gone to the bone. In Illinois, for example, the prison population has increased 20% over the last five years, but staff has dropped 30%—to dangerous levels. The right has shortchanged long-term economic growth by neglecting investments in education and infrastructure.

It's time for Progressives to turn the tide on funding for the public sector. The tide was turned once during the Clinton administration. On Inauguration Day 2001, outgoing President Bill Clinton turned a $5 trillion five-year projected surplus over to George W. Bush. The radical right turned that into the largest deficit in American history—a deficit that not only retards the growth of critical public sector spending, but also passes along thousands of dollars in debt to *each* of our kids.

Clinton already showed how to proceed. In 1993, he got Congress to pass a tax bill that rolled back tax breaks for America's wealthiest families. The right predicted economic disaster. Instead, Americans experienced the most prosperous period in human history. We can do it again. Roll back tax cuts for the wealthiest Americans and stop the repeal of the estate tax that would cost an additional trillion dollars.

THE BATTLE TO RESTRICT THE POWER OF CORPORATIONS TO DAMAGE THE ENVIRONMENT AND DISCHARGE GREENHOUSE GASES THAT CAUSE CLIMATE CHANGE

Progressives must once again take the environmental offensive. We can't afford to cede the power to make environmental decisions to corporations that have an interest in short-term return rather than the long-term good of society. Corporations won't look out for the long haul if they're not required to by all of us acting through government. It's not because they're bad people. Corporate managers have been hired to maximize short-term returns, and that conflicts with what's best for our environment and the climate. It's that simple.

This is a question of who has the power to make decisions.

And we have to reframe the battle. The fight for the environment is not a contest between the ecosystem and the economy. It's a struggle between shortsighted, short-term benefit for a few and the long-term economic security for our children.

THE BATTLE TO UNIONIZE THE WORK FORCE

We've seen how collective bargaining is indispensable to build a high-wage economy and end economic inequality. Unionized workers make around 30% more than their counterparts in comparable jobs. It's no accident that today the share of our national income going to the wages of working people is at a 50-year low—and the share going to corporate profits is higher than ever.

More than anything else, that's because of a two-decade long attack on the rights of working people to join unions orchestrated by Big Business, and right-wing Republicans like President Bush.

As a result, middle-class wages have plummeted, and health-care benefits and pensions are evaporating—all while the percentage of income going to the richest Americans has skyrocketed. And at the bottom of the income ladder, the number of people in poverty or and with no health care has exploded.

Contract negotiations by a democratic labor movement distribute more of the goods and services produced by our society to its makers and empower them economically.

Unions also empower workers politically and inoculate their members from the siren song of right-wing snake oil salesmen. They give an organizational context that puts society into perspective. While white non-union men typically vote 80% Republican, white labor union members vote two-thirds Democratic. Additionally, union members turn out to vote at rates far in excess of other voters.

Just as important, they provide financial and organizational muscle to take on Big Business and the forces of the right—in many arenas. A stronger labor movement will change the overall balance of power in society. That will benefit every progressive constituency—from senior citizens to the gay community.

Labor was the driving force for the movement to stop the privatization of Social Security, battle the Bush tax cuts and oppose right-wing court appointees. Labor has supported a wide array of public interest organizations. And labor has provided the backbone of Democratic Get-Out-the-Vote efforts.

The labor movement is the foundation of the progressive movement in America. No wonder, then, that the labor movement has been under assault. In the U.S. the percentage of American workers with union cards has plummeted from 20% in 1980 to only 13% today. Though outside of the U.S. the decline has not been so severe, union density has fallen throughout the industrial countries.

Part of the reason stems from the migration of heavily unionized manufacturing jobs to developing countries and the overall reduction of workers in manufacturing due to increases in productivity.

But union membership has also declined because of a concentrated attack by Big Business and the right, which prefer to operate in a "union free environment." The assault began in earnest when Ronald Reagan fired striking air-traffic controllers in the early 1980s. That sent a signal throughout the economy that the era of "accommodation" between labor and management that had continued since World War II was over.

In the George W. Bush years, the assault has been intensified. He appointed anti-labor members to the National Labor Relations Board and the courts. The business attack on unions is dependent upon routine violation of the laws passed during the New Deal to protect the right to organize.

Paul Krugman of the *New York Times* reports that "experts estimate that by 1980, employers were illegally firing at least one out of every 20 workers who voted for a union. But employers rarely faced serious consequences for their lawbreaking, and that's due to America's political shift to the right." [11]

There is no doubt that left to their own devices, workers still believe in unions. A Labor Day 2006 Lake Research poll of workers found that "more than two-thirds (68%) believe that if more working people join together in unions, things could be better for working people." [12]

The assault on labor is symbolized by Wal-Mart which, in an internal memo written in 2005, conceded that 46% of its workers' children were either on Medicaid or lacked health insurance. Regardless, the memo expressed concern that their wages and benefits were rising, "because we pay an associate more in salary and benefits as his or her tenure increases."

So, Wal-Mart announced in the fall of 2006 that it wanted to transform its workforce to 40% part-time from 20%, so that long-term employees won't get wage and benefit increases.

Krugman writes:

> So what is keeping paychecks down? Major employers like Wal-Mart have decided that their interests are best served by treating workers as a disposable commodity, paid as little as possible and encouraged to leave after a year or two. And their employers don't worry that angry workers will respond to their war on wages by forming unions, because they know that government officials, who are supposed to protect workers rights, will do everything they can to come down on the side of the wage cutters." [13]

The right has challenged the labor movement's right to use union dues for political advocacy without explicit positive approval by each individual member (as if corporations get explicit permission to use their money to achieve political goals from each investor or customer). In general, the right understands that its key organizational target is organized labor.

Democratization of power in America requires us to revitalize the labor movement. This requires:

- Increasingly imaginative and intensive organizing programs and corporate campaigns to recruit a larger percentage of the workforce.

- Action by progressive Democrats to reform and enforce labor laws and prevent corporations from coercing workers not to join unions. In early 2007, the House passed the Employee Free Choice Act that would be a major step in that direction. But that kind of legislation will never become law until George W. Bush is no longer President. Progressives need to prepare a massive campaign to pass EFCA the moment that a new Democratic President is sworn into office.

- Reframe the public's understanding of unions as a critical and necessary part of the world economy. The right has done quite a job over the last quarter-century of marginalizing Unionism and creating a commonsense frame in public discourse that any interference in the "free" market in setting wages is somehow a violation of the laws of nature. We need to repeatedly, and confidently, refute that assumption. In particular, we need to frame the battle for EFCA as a fight to give middle-class Americans the tools to organize to defend their standard of living.

- Promote the development of a strong labor movement in other countries, and promote close cooperation of unions worldwide—especially in developing countries. The World Trade Organization agreements explicitly protect the flow of capital, protection of patents, and other corporate interests. It does not protect the right to organize—nor the right for international unions to function across borders. The biggest corporations are all multinational. To compete, the labor movement must be international as well.
We'll never stop the "race to the bottom" in wages and benefits in America if corporations can exploit workers in other countries with impunity.
The American middle class has a huge vested interest in the ability of workers in China, Burma and Mexico to organize unions and bargain collectively. In many ways, the "American Dream" depends on workers' right to organize in the developing world.

THE BATTLE TO PREVENT CONSOLIDATION OF AMERICA'S MEDIA IN THE HANDS OF A FEW

Politicians and the punditry were flabbergasted when the grassroots buzz-saw chewed up a 2003 move by the Federal Communications Commission (FCC) to allow even greater concentration of media ownership. In retrospect, it shouldn't be surprising that a public that spends so much of its time tuned in to TV and radio outlets would have strong feelings about its concentration in ownership—and they did. The Bush-appointed FCC chair, Michael Powell, son of Colin Powell, was prevented from promulgating his plan to concentrate media ownership by a bi-partisan cascade of opposition in Congress that reflected the grassroots firestorm.

The reason for people's strong feelings are evident from several reports that the FCC had suppressed since 2003 that dramatically demonstrated the dangers of concentrating the power of media ownership in a few hands.

According to *The Nation*:

One report found locally owned television stations provide 20% more local news than stations owned by broadcasting behemoths. Another detailed a 35% drop in the number of independently owned radio stations following the removal of most ownership caps by the 1996 Telecommunications Act.

The Nation continued that the new FCC Chairman, Kevin Martin, is still rushing to "promote further consolidation with a new round of rule changes that were expected to include an attempt to eliminate the ban on cross-ownership of newspapers and broadcast outlets. Such a shift would allow one corporation to own newspapers, television and radio stations, the cable system and the busiest Internet sites in one community. This would create media "company towns" where the discourse is defined by a single newsroom. That means big profits for firms that own "the news," but big democracy deficits for citizens—which is why 3 million Americans opposed an FCC move to ease ownership limits when the issue arose in 2003." [14]

The effort to prevent concentration needs to be supplemented by support for progressive media outlets like Air America, which in early 2007 was purchased out of bankruptcy by a new group of backers—or Nova M Radio, a new progressive talk radio network founded by original Air America founders Sheldon and Anita Drobny. Progressive cable, radio, newspapers and media outlets are critical.

After all, the guy who said, "The press is free, to those who own them," was right.

And this extends to the new media as well. In a speech at the National Press Club, Charles Benton, an expert in issues concerning access to the media, argued that universal access to broadband technology is "now as important to the advancement of the American ideal of equal opportunity in the 21st century as universal access to education and universal phone service was in the last...

"This principle is simple, powerful, and fundamentally important to our nation's future competitiveness and consumers' future opportunities. We must unleash the rivers of data and opportunity that broadband can enable..." [15]

THE BATTLE FOR IMMIGRATION REFORM AND NATURALIZATION OF IMMIGRANTS

Immigration reform is a major issue on many levels. It is a critical human issue about families that are split apart, about millions of people who live in the shadows with no legal status and who are subject to exploitation that damages them and drives down wages for everyone else. An estimated four million children of undocumented aliens were born in the U.S. and as a result are U.S. citizens, yet they are separated—or are at risk of being separated—from their parents by the current U.S. immigration laws.

Some Progressives oppose allowing a "future flow" of workers—especially from Mexico—once an immigration bill is passed. But the problem is that so long as there is a massive inequity in wages in Mexico and the United States, no fence or other barrier is going to eliminate the flow of Mexican immigrants. So long as they remain undocumented, their illegal status will allow them to be exploited by employers and that in turn will drag down the wages of all workers in the United States. Comprehensive immigration reform will help increase the bargaining power of American workers across the board.

But the immigration battle is also important because it will have an enormous impact on the battle for power between the progressive and conservative forces in American society. As of 2007, there are 12 million undocumented immigrants in the United States. If they are placed on an earned pathway to citizenship through immigration reform, they will be eligible for citizenship and voting rights by 2012 and 2016.

They will join the nearly 30 million immigrants who are legal residents and could apply today for citizenship, or are citizens yet not registered to vote, or immigrant voters who never go to the polls, or immigrants who will turn 18 years old this year and could register to vote.

If Democrats continue to stand firmly for immigrant rights, the issue will define immigrants' voting loyalties for a generation. If we are successful, a gigantic block of progressive voters will enter the electorate over the next 15 years—a block that could be decisive in the battle for the future.

THE BATTLE FOR ELECTORAL REFORM AND PUBLIC FINANCING OF ELECTIONS

America will never be a truly democratic society if the wealthy have disproportionate influence over elections through large campaign contributions. Someone's going to pay for the political communication. If political leaders are dependent on big donors for financing, these donors will wield disproportionate power—it's as simple as that.

Proposals such as a fund to match contributions of $200 or less at a seven- or eight–to-one ratio would go a long way to democratize our electoral process.

America also needs federal standards for federal elections. These need to go beyond the current Help Americans Vote Act (HAVA) provisions. They should provide that ex-felons be allowed to vote after serving their sentences, and provide minimum ratios of voting equipment per voter.

The Republicans have promoted a variety of laws that have actually discouraged voting—especially voting by poor and older voters. Twenty-four states now have laws requiring IDs for voting at the polls—some, picture IDs. Older and poorer voters are much less prone to have picture IDs. Many don't drive. The cost of non-driver's license state IDs—though generally minimal—is the equivalent of a "poll tax" on the poor. It creates one more hurdle to vote—and generally that is the idea, as there is little evidence of voter fraud on the part of individual voters in most elections.

Recent history shows that attempts to manipulate results are much more prone to come from election authorities themselves.

The redistricting process is also a critical factor. Through their control of state legislatures, the Republicans gained substantial advantage when it came to drawing Congressional districts after the 2000 census. Tom DeLay's notorious Texas redistricting project is symbolic of the importance of *who* gets to draw congressional district lines. In some states redistricting has been taken over by non-partisan commissions. Many believe it should be taken out of "politics."

But in the near term, the Democratic legislative victories in 2006 have already improved our positioning for the redistricting battles that will follow the 2010 census, and we must have a laser-like focus on key legislative races in the 2008 and 2010 elections to set the parameters of political debate in 2012 and beyond.

THE BATTLE TO CONTROL THE WORLD'S EXPLODING POPULATION— AND EACH PERSON'S IMPACT ON GLOBAL RESOURCES.

Technology provides the underlying economic basis to eliminate poverty—to eliminate necessity in the world. And that in turn provides an economic basis for a truly democratic society—the economic ability for everyone to escape necessity.

But as we've seen, this extraordinary leap in human social evolution could be threatened by the twin problems of population growth and the growing per-person impact on world resources.

The first public act of the new Bush administration in 2001 was to cut off funds for family planning in the developing world if the option of abortion was even discussed at the clinic. The radical right has essentially ended U.S. support for population control.

And its support for the auto and oil industry has prevented it from increasing the efficiency of cars and decreasing the reliance on unsustainable energy sources.

In fact, as we've seen, as a society we have an energy emergency. Within several decades, the hydrocarbon era will end. We need a sustainable alternative ready to replace it that doesn't squeeze our global resources to the point of collapse.

The right's dogmatic commitment to "free markets" at all costs makes them blind to the need to husband renewable natural resources like fishes and forests; because of the "tragedy of the commons," the markets won't do it.

The 300 millionth American was born in the fall of 2006. That child was born in the same year that the 200 millionth American turned 38. And remember, population growth in the United States is much smaller than most of the developing world.

There are at least four priority fronts in this battle:

- We need a huge increase of funds to support family planning in the developing world and in the United States.
- The world needs an emergency campaign to provide education to women worldwide. Study after study shows that the most effective form of birth control is the education of women. Educated women—in developing emerging economies—simply did not have as many children.
- Progressives should fight for an emergency initiative to find sustainable alternatives to hydrocarbon fuels, and dramatically reduce the waste of the planet's resources—both in production and use.
- Governments around the world must ensure that renewable resources are harvested by methods—and at rates—that allow them to renew themselves at sustainable levels. This is especially critical for the planet's supply of fish, forests and soil.

THE BATTLE TO REDUCE STRUCTURAL VIOLENCE— ESPECIALLY IN DEVELOPING COUNTRIES

The diversion of small amounts of the world's resources to end structural violence would yield enormous returns when it comes to reducing suffering and increasing the power of people worldwide.

Remember that the medicines that cure malaria cost only $.55 per dose, the nets to shield children from malaria carrying mosquitoes are only a dollar each and the annual cost of indoor insecticide spraying is $10—yet 800,000 African children die of malaria each year.

One of the great tragedies of the Bush years is not simply the damage done by his policies, but the missed opportunities. Money invested in public health, HIV treatment, health care clinics, fresh water, education for women, etc. would yield such massive results. Think what could have been done with the hundreds of billions of dollars spent on the Iraq war alone.

But an end to structural violence and acceleration of economic development in much of the world requires other major changes.

- Large-scale investments in public infrastructure that make economic development possible—especially roads, water, sewer and communication systems. The value of business investment— public and private—is greatly magnified by public infrastructure and the private market will not provide it.
- Serious investment in education—especially for women.

- Trade policies that allow for integration of the world economy, while they protect the well-being of the vast number of developing world peasants. When developing world economies are open to imports of agricultural products that have been produced by highly mechanized and subsidized First World agriculture, prices of peasant-produced commodities collapse. Those subsidies have become a major hurdle in further trade liberalization, and for good reason.

Progressives must favor trade arrangements that simultaneously boost economic efficiency *and* protect the incomes of peasants in Third World countries while their economies develop. When we don't consider the consequences of our policies on the welfare of peasants, it is not without cost to us.

To democratize the world means increasing the income of people in the developing world. Trade deals need to reflect that priority, not simply the interests of large multinational corporations.

THE BATTLE TO EMPOWER MULTINATIONAL ORGANIZATIONS— ESPECIALLY THE UNITED NATIONS—TO BRING PEACEFUL RESOLUTION TO INTERNATIONAL DISPUTES, PROMOTE HUMAN RIGHTS, AND FOSTER ECONOMIC DEVELOPMENT

The Neocons do not share this goal. The fact is that Progressives are not about an American empire. We are about a world community—a stable, peaceful, prosperous, democratic world community.

Progressives do not look forward to a century of American domination of the world—but to a century of American *leadership* in creating a world that embodies progressive principles.

Progressives reject unilateralist, preemptive action. That doesn't mean abandoning America's right to take unilateral action in the world, where it's necessary and appropriate. But our first course should always be to take international action through multinational institutions and to strengthen them.

The campaign to end the war in Iraq is so critical not only because it will end a tragic and misguided war. Its success will also assure that America learns the central lesson of the Iraq tragedy: that the unilateralist, neocon values and assumptions upon which it was premised endanger our security and the security of the entire planet.

It's in our own interest to create a multi-polar world where all countries and cultures have a stake in peace and economic progress. The worldwide society is ultimately no different from a national or regional society.

STAND UP STRAIGHT: HOW PROGRESSIVES CAN WIN

Take the example of Europe. After World War II, it gradually became clear that the best way to assure that there was not a repeat of the European wars that have persisted for generations was to build a Europe in which each country had a stake in the economic and political success of the others.

The Marshall Plan to rebuild Europe, the European Common Market, then the European Union were visionary steps that have successfully created an integrated, largely peaceful, largely prosperous Europe—just 60 years after World War II.

European integration was undertaken with a clear understanding that each country had to put aside its imperial designs; that the rich countries would invest substantial sums in developing the economies of the poor countries; and that the rich countries would maintain high wages and social safety nets. They would raise the wages and social policy and standards of the less developed economies rather than let competitive forces from low-wage countries drag down the standards of living in higher-wage countries.

That's a very different approach to trade and economic integration than NAFTA.

The success of Europe demonstrates the importance of creating strong international institutions that allow all players to have a common stake in stability, prosperity and—in Europe's case—a new continent-wide culture.

In the midst of World War II, the idea of a peaceful, integrated Europe would have seemed absurd.

Strong multinational institutions are even more essential in the face of the growth of multinational corporations. Many have more gross revenue than some countries have gross domestic product. Without democratically accountable structures of comparable size to regulate these enterprises, they become governments unto themselves—with power that is unchecked and unaccountable.

One of the chief challenges of the 21st century will be the race to develop democratically based international institutions to regulate multinational corporations.

You can't have a democratic society in a world where multinational corporations are allowed to function as free agents that are unaccountable to democratic governments through international bodies of worldwide scale.

It's the technological forces that are unleashed by innate human curiosity that provide the energy underlying the necessity for larger and larger structures of human relationships.

The poet Robert Frost wrote, in "Mending Wall": "Something there is that doesn't love a wall, That wants it down." [16] One of those things is human technology: the forces that fly us faster, allow instantaneous, person-to-person communication; and bring us to rely on each other in ever more aspects of our lives. The other is the evolving recognition that at their core, all human beings share a common humanity, the same desires for meaning, relationship and the possibility of being all they can be.

Fundamentally, the political process that will ultimately forge a democratic and secure world culture are the same processes that forced the fiefdoms in the British Isles to be forged into England, or that melded European cultures that have had periodic wars for centuries into the new Europe. To date, the U.N., even with its many flaws, is the greatest single expression of the movement toward the creation of democratic political structures that will allow human beings to resolve their differences without resorting to organized violence, and fulfill their dreams without shattering those of their fellow men and women.

It will not be many decades before the notion that human-sanctioned violence of war will be just as unfathomable as the concept—common just 150 years ago—that we should systematically enslave other men and women right here in America. Today we view street gangs who defend turf as atavistic throwbacks to an earlier stage in human development. One day we will feel the same about the use of war.

Progressives can't slacken from our commitment to build a common, multinational future for the entire planet. It is indispensable for a worldwide democratic society.

THE BATTLE FOR MUSCULAR MULTILATERALISM — THE UNITED STATES NEEDS TO MAINTAIN A STRONG, FLEXIBLE MILITARY. U.S. MILITARY POWER SHOULD BE USED TO PROMOTE A PROGRESSIVE AGENDA, AS OFTEN AS POSSIBLE IN MULTINATIONAL CONTEXT.

In all societies, force or the threat of force is used to guarantee the peaceful resolution of disputes and enforce the society's laws. The same is true in the international context. The question is not whether the threat of force will be used. It is how it will be controlled and to what ends.

Progressives need to fight to ensure that U.S. military power is used to enforce a developing body of international law, using processes of legitimate international institutions.

Though this approach to the projection and use of military power is very different than the current neocon-dominated U.S. policy, it is not radical or new. In most cases, President Clinton's administration embodied this approach. Under Clinton, the U.S. acted militarily to support the U.N./

NATO initiative to prevent "ethnic cleansing" in Kosovo, and to support the resolution of the Balkan wars.

The US *should have* acted more forcefully to catalyze military action from the international community to stop the Rwandan genocide. In retrospect, even a small international military contingent could have prevented hundreds of thousands of deaths.

The enmity that Bush's unilateral approach has earned worldwide, its inability to exert moral leadership, and the depletion of military assets, have prevented it from playing a leading role in preventing another genocide in Darfur. The situation there clearly requires military intervention by the international community. The U.S. is better equipped than any other nation to contribute logistical support to such an effort—which should be spearheaded by non-Western forces from the African Union and the UN on the ground.

The situation on the Korean peninsula is another where international action is critical.

North Korea's entry into the nuclear club signaled yet another major failure of the Bush foreign policy. Former Secretary of State Madeleine Albright put it clearly: "During the two terms in the Clinton administration, there were no nuclear weapons tested by North Korea, no new plutonium production, and no new nuclear weapons developed by Pyongyang. Through our policy of constructive engagement, the world was safer. President Bush chose a different path, and the results are evident for all to see." [17]

Gary Samre, a North Korea expert who helped negotiate the original 1994 agreement, added, " The Clinton administration was prepared to accept an imperfect agreement in the interest of orchestrating limits. The Bush administration is not prepared to accept an imperfect agreement, and the result is that we have none." [18]

Selig Harrison of the Center for International Policy in Washington had just returned from meetings with North Korean leaders before the nuclear tests in the fall of 2006. In an article in *The Washington Post*, he said:

> *Paradoxical as it may seem, Pyongyang staged the test as a last-ditch effort to jumpstart a bilateral dialogue on the normalization of relations that the United States has so far spurned. Over and over, I was told that Pyongyang wants bilateral negotiations to set the stage for implementation of the denuclearization agreement it concluded in Beijing in September 19, 2005 with the United States, China, Russia and Japan and South Korea.*
>
> *Washington focused on Article 1 of the accord, in which North Korea agreed to "abandon all nuclear weapons and existing nuclear programs." But what made the agreement acceptable to Pyongyang was the pledge in Article Two that the United States and North Korea would "respect each other's*

sovereignty, exist peacefully together and take steps to normalize relations."
*In North Korean eyes, it was a flagrant violation when, four days after
the agreement was signed, the United States in effect declared economic
war on the Kim Jong Il regime. The Treasury Department imposed financial
sanctions designed to cut off North Korean access to the international banking
system, branding it a "criminal state" guilty of counterfeiting and money-
laundering.*

*The sanctions issue has given the initiative to hard-liners in Pyongyang,
who can plausibly argue that the sanctions are the cutting edge of a calculated
effort by dominant elements in the Bush administration to undercut the
Beijing agreement, squeeze the Kim regime and eventually force its collapse.*

*To advance U.S. security interests, the United States should agree to bilateral
negotiations. It should press North Korea to suspend further nuclear and
missile tests while negotiations on normalization proceed, freeze plutonium
production and make a firm, time-bound commitment to return to the six-
party talks. In return, the administration should negotiate compromise on
the financial sanctions to reopen North Korean access to the international
banking system, offer large-scale the energy cooperation, and remove North
Korea from the State Department's list of terrorist states, thus opening the
way for multilateral aid from the World Bank, the International Monetary
Fund and the Asian Development Bank, all of which North Korea is actively
seeking to join.*

*Playing games with "regime change" has become much too dangerous
and should now give way to a sustained diplomatic effort to roll back North
Korea's nuclear weapons programs, while it is still in its early stages.* [19]

In February 2007, four months after the North Korean nuclear test, the
parties to the Six-Nation talks signed onto a plan to "freeze" North Korea's
Yongbyon nuclear facility and required the U.S. to begin unfreezing North
Korean bank assets as well as provide energy assistance. In July 2007, the
North Koreans shut down its nuclear reactor, after the completion of the
first delivery of oil under the agreement. The next step is supposed to be
the disabling of the reactor under international supervision.

Conservatives attacked the agreement as a betrayal. In fact, by
abandoning the Clinton Administration's nuclear agreement for six years,
Bush had allowed North Korea to become a nuclear weapons state before
Bush was forced by reality to reenter a similar agreement.

Part of the reason appears to be another great "intelligence failure." In
2003, intelligence reports indicated that North Korea had begun a program
to enrich uranium in violation of the 1994 accords. But it turns out that
that "intelligence" may not have been accurate—that North Korea never
had a uranium enrichment program. But by abandoning the 1994 Agreed
Framework, and international inspections, the Bush Administration

allowed North Korea to harvest plutonium from the Yongbyon nuclear facility. Its confrontational posture encouraged North Korea to do so in order to increase its bargaining leverage– another astounding neocon foreign policy failure.

But in many respects the most dangerous scenario on the Korean Peninsula would be precisely the "collapse" that the Neocons seek.

In a fall 2006 article in *The Atlantic Monthly,* author Robert Kaplan points out that:

> *In other divided countries in the 20th century—Vietnam, Germany, and Yemen—the forces of unity ultimately triumphed. But history suggests the unification does not happen through a calibrated political process in which the interests of all sides are respected. Rather, it tends to happen through a cataclysm of events that, piles of white papers and war gaming exercises notwithstanding, catches experts by surprise.*

Kaplan summarizes the situation in North Korea:

> *The threat from the north of the DMZ is formidable. North Korea boasts 100,000 well-trained special operations forces and one of the world's largest biological and chemical arsenals. It has stockpiles of anthrax, cholera, and plague, as well as eight industrial facilities for producing chemical agents— any of which could be launched at Seoul by the Army's conventional artillery. If the governing infrastructure in Pyongyang were to unravel, the result would be widespread lawlessness (compounded by the guerrilla mentality of the Kim Family Regime's armed forces), as well as a mass migration out of and within North Korea. In short, North Korea's potential for anarchy is equal to that of Iraq, and the potential for the deployment of weapons of mass destruction—either during or after pre-collapse fighting—is far greater.*

Kaplan quotes Colonel Maxwell, the Chief of Staff of U.S .Special Operations in South Korea, that in the event the regime were to collapse:

> *"The situation in the North could become so messy and ambiguous," Maxwell says, "that the collapse of the chain of command of the KFR could be more dangerous than the preservation of it, particularly when one considers control over WMD."*
>
> *In order to prevent a debacle of the sort that occurred in Iraq—but with potentially deadlier consequences, because of the free-floating WMD—a successful relief operation would require making contacts with KFR generals and various factions of the former North Korean military, who would be vying for control in different regions. If the generals were not absorbed into the operational command structure of the occupying force, Maxwell says, they might form the basis for an insurgency. The Chinese, who have connections inside the North Korean military, would be best positioned to make these contacts—but the role of U.S. Army Special Forces in this effort might be*

substantial. Green Berets and the CIA would be among the first in, much like in Afghanistan in 2001.

Obviously, the United States could not unilaterally insert troops into a dissolved North Korea. It would likely be a four-powered intervention force — the United States, China, South Korea, and Russia — officially sanctioned by the United Nations. [20]

The situation in Korea brings us to the next major battleground for creating a democratic world.

PREVENTING THE PROLIFERATION OF WEAPONS OF MASS DESTRUCTION IN GENERAL AND NUCLEAR WEAPONS IN PARTICULAR

On the international scale, no subject could be more relevant to the creation of a democratic world. WMD — and especially nuclear weapons — are all about power. Nuclear weapons give massive power to those who possess them — power to defend, or coerce — the power brought by the status of being a member of the nuclear club.

But one thing is certain, the more nuclear weapons there are and the more broadly their control is spread, the more likely they are to be used and spread further.

That premise underlies the nuclear nonproliferation treaty to which the U.S. is a signatory. But bogged down in Iraq, the Bush administration has given little real priority to dealing with a new era of proliferation.

Of course, the central problem of trying to prevent emerging countries from obtaining nuclear weapons is that, from their point of view, it's hard to argue why the countries currently in the club should have nuclear weapons and they should not. Nuclear weapons equate to power in the world. They also provide a deterrent to attack. It's not lost on other countries that the U.S. is much less likely to take military action against North Korea because it has nuclear weapons. As long as some countries have nuclear weapons, other countries are going to want to try to get them.

Of course, the Nuclear Nonproliferation Treaty addresses the problem. At the same time it restricts nuclear proliferation to states, it also calls for reductions in nuclear stockpiles of current nuclear powers.

Unfortunately, we've seen that the Neocons plan to do just the opposite — to develop a whole new generation of nuclear weapons in the United States.

The fight for a serious, effective approach to nuclear nonproliferation, which includes new incentives to eliminate nuclear weapons from every country of the world, has to be at the top of the progressive agenda. Nuclear weapons should be treated the same way as chemical and biological weapons — they're simply too dangerous to use and should ultimately be eliminated. Obviously, that would also require tight international controls on available supplies of weapon grade plutonium and strengthened regulations on the enrichment of uranium for non-weapon uses.

THE BATTLE TO DEFEND HUMAN RIGHTS — AT HOME AND ABROAD

In an op-ed in the *Chicago Tribune* following congressional passage of the Republican plan for dealing with "enemy combatants," humorist and writer Garrison Keillor wrote:

> *I would not send my college kid off for a semester abroad, if I were you. Last week, we suspended human rights in America, and what goes around comes around. Ixnay habeas corpus.*
>
> *The U.S. Senate, in all its splendor and majesty, decided that an "enemy combatant" is a non-citizen, whom the president says is an enemy combatant, including your Korean greengrocer or your Swedish grandmother or your Czech au pair, and can be arrested and held for as long as the authorities wish without any right of appeal to a court of law to examine the matter. If your college kids were to be arrested in Bangkok or Cairo, suspected of "crimes against the state" and held in prison, you'd assume that the American Foreign Service officer would be able to speak to your kids and arrange for a lawyer, but this may not be true anymore. Be forewarned...*
>
> *None of the men and women who voted for this bill has any right to speak in public about the rule of law anymore, or take a high moral view of the Third Reich, or to wax poetic about the American Ideal.* [21]

Ariel Dorfman is a Chilean American writer and professor at Duke University. He is also author of *Death and the Maiden*. In the fall of 2006 he published a remarkable op-ed in the *Washington Post*:

> *It still haunts me, the first time — it was in Chile, in October 1973 — that I met someone who'd been tortured. To save my life, I had sought refuge in the Argentine Embassy some weeks after the coup that toppled the democratically elected government of Salvador Allende, a government for which I had worked. And then, suddenly, one afternoon, there he was. A large-boned man, gaunt and yet strangely flabby, with eyes like a child, eyes that could not stop blinking and a body that could not stop shivering.*
>
> *That is what stays with me — that he was cold under the balmy afternoon sun of Santiago de Chile, trembling as though he would never be warm again, as though the electric current was still coursing through him. Still possessed, somehow still inhabited by his captors, still imprisoned in that cell and the National Stadium, his hands disobeying the orders from his brain to quell the shuddering, his body unable to forget what had been done to it just as, nearly 33 years later, I, too, cannot banish that devastated life from my memory.*

It was his image, in fact, that swirled up from the past as I pondered the current political debate in the United States about the practicality of torture. Something in me must have needed to resurrect the victim, force my fellow citizens here to spend a few minutes with the eternal iciness that had settled into the man's heart and flesh, and demand that they take a good hard look at him before anyone dare maintain that, to save lives, it might be necessary to inflict unbearable pain on a fellow human being. Perhaps the optimist in me hoped that this damaged Argentine man could, all these decades later, help shatter the perverse innocence of contemporary Americans, just as he had burst the bubble of ignorance protecting the young Chilean I used to be, someone who back then had encountered torture mainly through books and movies and newspaper reports.

That is not, however, the only lesson that today's ruthless world can teach from the distant man condemned to shiver forever.

All those years ago, that torture victim kept moving his lips, trying to articulate an explanation, muttering the same words over and over. "It was a mistake," he repeated, and in the next few days I pieced together his sad and foolish tale. He was an Argentine revolutionary who fled his homeland and, as soon as he crossed the mountains into Chile, had begun to boast about what he would do to the military there if it staged a coup, about his expertise with arms of every sort, about his colossal stash of weapons. Bluster and braggadocio—and every word of it false.

But how could he convince those men who were beating him, hooking his penis to electric wires and waterboarding him? How could he prove to them that he had been lying, prancing in front of his Chilean comrades, just trying to impress the ladies with his fraudulent insurgent persona?

Of course, he couldn't. He confessed to anything and everything they wanted to drag from his hoarse, howling throat; he invented accomplices and addresses and culprits; and then, when it became apparent that all this was imaginary, he said he was subjected to further ordeals.

There was no escape.

That is the hideous predicament of the torture victim. It was always the same story, what I discovered in the ensuing years, as I became an unwilling expert on all manner of torments and degradations; my life and my writing overflowing with grief from every continent. Each of those mutilated spines and fractured lives—Chinese, Guatemalan, Egyptian, Indonesian, Iranian, Uzbek, need I go on?—all of them, men and women alike, surrendered the same story of essential asymmetry, where one man has all the power in the world and the other has nothing but pain, where one man can decree death at the flick of a wrist and the other can only pray that the wrist will be flicked soon.

It is a story that our species has listened to with mounting revulsion, a horror that has led almost every nation to sign treaties over the past decades declaring these abominations as crimes against humanity, transgressions interdicted all across the earth. That is the wisdom, national and international, it has taken us thousands of years of tribulation and shame to achieve. That is the wisdom we are being asked to throw away when we formulate the question—does torture work?—when we allow ourselves to ask whether we can afford to outlaw torture if we want to defeat terrorism.

I will leave others to claim that torture, in fact, does not work, that confessions obtained under duress—such as that extracted from the heaving body of that poor Argentine braggart in some Santiago cesspool in 1973—are useless. Or to contend that the United States had better not do that to anyone in our custody lest someday another nation or entity or group decides to treat our prisoners the same way.

I find these arguments—and there are many more—to be irrefutable. But I cannot bring myself to use them, for fear of honoring the debate by participating in it.

Can't the United States see that when we allow someone to be tortured by our agents, it is not only the victim and perpetrator who are corrupted, not only the "intelligence" that is contaminated, but also everyone who looked away and said they did not know, everyone who consented tacitly to that outrage so they could sleep a little safer at night, all the citizens who did not march in the streets by the millions to demand the resignation of whoever suggested, even whispered, that torture is inevitable in our day and age, that we must embrace its darkness?

Are we so morally sick, so deaf and dumb and blind, that we do not understand this? Are we so fearful, so in love with our own security and steeped in our own pain, that we are really willing to let people be tortured in the name of America? Have we so lost our bearings that we do not realize that each of us could be the hapless Argentine who sat under the Santiago's sun, so possessed by the evil done to him that he could not stop shivering ? [22]

That is the tone Progressives must take when defending human rights—uncompromising, morally clear assertiveness. We must defend human rights with this tone, both because there can be no compromise— and because it is most effective. When we discuss our values we win, since we appeal to the highest nature of humanity. When we debate simple policy, we may or may not win.

The right to be free from torture, and to have access to an independent court to prove that you are wrongfully imprisoned, or the right to free speech and thought—are universal human rights. They are inalienable rights—and they are essential to the creation of a democratic society in the world.

In addition to the battles to deal with broad human rights and due process there are additional specific battlegrounds that are also very important.

CONTINUING THE FIGHT TO END DISCRIMINATION.

For the last half-century, Progressives have fought with increasing success to eliminate discrimination based on race, gender, sexual orientation and ethnicity. The battlegrounds will continue to include the struggle against legal, social and particularly economic barriers and they will continue to occupy a central place in the fight for a democratic society.

These causes must not, cannot, and need not be abandoned or shortchanged in order to attract swing voters to the progressive cause— assuming Progressives take the bull by the horns and control the frame and terms of debate.

APPOINTMENTS TO THE JUDICIARY.

The values of the judges given lifetime appointments to the federal bench are critical to the prospects for a democratic America. People for the American Way and the Alliance for Justice have led the way in these battles. As I write this book, we stand one heartbeat away from a Supreme Court dominated by Justices committed to the radical conservative value system. Already, Justice Kennedy's "swing" vote is too often is cast with the radical conservative, Roberts faction of the Court. If there were no other reason to elect a Democratic president in 2008, that fact would be reason enough.

If necessary, Democrats should expend every ounce of energy to prevent a solid radical conservative majority on the Supreme Court that might last for decades. There's just too much at stake.

Human rights, due process and the ability of new progressive government to achieve progressive goals all hang in the balance.

PROTECTION OF THE CIVIL JUSTICE SYSTEM.

For the last two decades, Big Business has continued a sustained assault to limit the ability of negligence victims to recover damages in court.

When its own research found that the Ford Pinto had defects in its fuel system that caused it to occasionally explode when rear-ended, the company calculated the cost of the fix. It turned out it would only cost a couple of dollars a car to fix the problem, but the company decided that it would likely pay out less in wrongful death suits than it would cost to do the fix.

People would have continued to die in fiery crashes if a plaintiff's lawyer had not filed a suit against Ford, asking punitive damages for this kind of irresponsible behavior. The lawyers turned up internal Ford memos that laid out its callous calculus.

A jury of average Americans awarded the plaintiff punitive damages large enough to change Ford's economic calculation. It also sent a message to other businesses that reckless and irresponsible decisions which damage other people do have a cost.

Of course, that wouldn't have happened if the victim who was injured couldn't have afforded a lawyer. Most normal people don't have the wherewithal to take on a large company. That's why it's so important that there are plaintiffs' lawyers who are willing to bear the costs of the suit in exchange for a percentage of the award. Needless to say, Big Business doesn't like this system and wants it changed.

The tort system has also been a favorite target of the medical profession. Over 40,000 people are killed by medical negligence each year. That's more than die in auto accidents or because of handgun violence. But rather than attack the causes of medical negligence and improve the quality of care, the Republican response has been to propose reducing the liability of those who are negligent.

A few years ago there was a hearing in the Kentucky legislature on a bill to limit the rights of victims in cases of medical malpractice. After various witnesses from the hospitals and medical profession had testified at length about the need to limit "non-economic" damages, a citizen testified that the doctor had mistakenly cut off his penis. That was a showstopper for the mostly male legislators.

Jan says the next time a member of Congress makes an argument for a $250,000 cap on "non-economic" damages, she'll tell the Kentucky story and say, "Well, Congressman, I wouldn't give you five cents for it, but I'll bet it's worth more than $250,000 to you."

In fact, the number of medical malpractice lawsuits has not increased in recent years, but there has been an increase in instances of medical negligence.

And there is no clear relationship between tort claim payouts and medical malpractice insurance costs to doctors. That's because insurance companies mainly make money in the earnings off their investments, not insurance underwriting. Insurance companies sell insurance to get clients to give them money so they can invest it.

History has shown that so-called "hard" insurance markets—where rates for liability insurance increased, and coverage is harder to get—occur when the earnings on insurance company investment portfolios are down. This, of course, has nothing at all to do with claims.

In a hearing on medical malpractice caps before Jan's House Government Reform Subcommittee a few years ago, she grilled the insurance company witnesses—challenging them to pledge that rates would drop if their liability was capped.

"Can you guarantee that rates will drop 25% if liability is capped?" She asked. "No" was the answer. "How about 10%?" — "No" again. "How about 5%?" — "No" again.

"Can you guarantee that rates will drop at all?" she asked. "Well, no," said the witness.

"Then why are we here?" she asked.

In the civil justice system, ordinary Americans with no ax to grind, who don't receive campaign contributions, sit on juries. They look at both sides of the dispute and make a decision to hold huge corporations accountable. Juries are one of the most democratic institutions in America, and the progressive agenda has to include their vigorous defense.

PRISON AND SENTENCING REFORM

Ask which country imprisons the highest percentage of its population, and most people will tell you it's some totalitarian regime or military dictatorship. They would be wrong.

The U.S.—home of the free—incarcerates more of its citizens than any other country, a lot more. America locks up five times more of their citizens than the average for the rest of the world. A shocking 25% of all of the world's prisoners are in US prisons and jails—even though we have only 5% of the world's population.

The U.S. is a high-incarceration-rate society—and that has big consequences.

When I spent five months as an inmate at the Federal Prison Camp at Terre Haute, I learned from prisoners firsthand the impact of incarceration on their lives and families.

Like Martha Stewart, I was in a minimum security facility, with nothing but nonviolent offenders. Yet I met inmates were serving 20- and 25-year sentences.

It wasn't always so. The number of inmates and length of sentences have skyrocketed over the last 20 years in response to mandatory minimum drug sentences, and the war on drugs in general. These laws were passed as part of a national conservative push for "tough" sentences—even though study after study shows that drug addition is an illness that can be combated much more effectively by treatment and education than by law enforcement and interdiction.

The cost of the prison system has soared to a staggering $90 billion a year and prisons are bursting at the seams.

In the end, 95% of inmates are released back into our communities. And two thirds of them—67%—are released prisoners who return to jail.

In other words, the American prison system is failing at its key mission—making our society safer.

Here are some reasons why:

- The very long sentences destroy the inmate's connections with the outside world. Long sentences make it less and less likely that an inmate can successfully reenter society. Spouses divorce; families and old friends drift away. When they return to society, their life is gone—so they fall back on what they know, criminal activity. The longer someone is incarcerated, the harder it is for him to once again get a sound foothold in life.

- Inmates receive little in the way of education and training. Prisons in the United States are basically warehouses. The corrections system does not view its mission as preparing inmates to succeed without crime—to prevent criminal activity and a return to society. There is no reason a young man without a high school diploma shouldn't get a GED and bachelor's degree if he spends five years behind bars. Then, when he leaves prison he'd have the educational tools to help him succeed.

- Study after study shows the likelihood of recidivism is heavily related to the strength of an inmate's family. Yet in my experience, prisons make it tough to maintain families. They are generally located far from major population centers from which they draw their inmates. Phone charges in the federal system are $.23 a minute—five times the going rate. That's tough on prisoners with no income. And phone calls are limited to 300 minutes per month. Finally, there are often no opportunities for social contact with spouses except for crowded visiting rooms—and certainly no conjugal visits. It is very hard for a young family to stay together for years under those circumstances.

These are not just "pro-prisoner" issues. Prisoners should return to the community equipped to make a contribution to society and avoid further criminal activity. America's approach to prisons today doesn't produce that result. There is also the question of how the rest of the world's societies deal with their needs to stop crime, while managing to incarcerate only one-fifth as many of its citizens as we do.

How can Progressives talk about an issue like prison reform and sentencing in a way that will appeal to most ordinary Americans?

First, the issue needs to be framed as a question of what works to prevent inmates from re-offending when they reenter society. When 95% of inmates do reenter society, and two-thirds of them commit another crime, the current system obviously isn't working, especially given the fortune we are spending on it.

Second, when we talk about education programs, we'll have a lot more success if we talk about "requiring" prisoners to upgrade their skills so they can make a contribution to society than if we talk about "giving" inmates educational opportunity.

At Terre Haute, I knew a high-school dropout who made thousands of dollars a week on the street selling drugs at the age of 18 and is serving five years in prison. He's likely to go right back to what he knows if he hasn't acquired marketable skills before he gets out. We need to insist that prisoners should not be allowed to "sit around" while they're incarcerated. They should be *required* to upgrade their education or get a trade, as though it were part of their punishment. And the fact is that most inmates would love to do just that, but the opportunities just do not exist.

Third, we should propose "earned good time" to shorten total prison time. Inmates would earn additional time off their sentences for activities that research shows cut the odds of recidivism. These would include postsecondary education, getting a certified trade, drug rehabilitation programs, and activities aimed at improving the success of other inmates like teaching Adult Education Classes.

The other key question that bears directly on the creation of a democratic society is the disenfranchisement of former felons in many states. Some states like Illinois reinstate the voting rights of felons immediately after they serve their time. Others do not.

Although only 12% of the U.S. population is African-American, they constitute 40% of America's inmates. In fact, one in three African-American males can expect to serve time. Until an executive order by the new Governor, Florida disenfranchised 600,000 ex-felons—many of them African-American. That substantially affected the outcome of elections and benefited Republicans. In fact, were it not for the disenfranchisement of former felons in Florida, George W. Bush would never have been President of the United States.

Several states still deprive ex-convicts of the right to vote for the rest of their lives. Seven more disenfranchise some felons and impose a waiting period before they can regain their right to vote. In some parts of the country, up to 7% of the adult population is legally prohibited from voting. No other country that calls itself a democracy disenfranchises former felons. Many allow them to vote while serving their sentences.[23]

Progressives should demand a uniform national policy of reinstating the voting rights of felons once they've served their time.

THE BATTLE FOR PROGRESSIVE CONTROL OF GOVERNMENT
AT ALL LEVELS IN THE UNITED STATES

The outcome of the public policy battles we've just described hinges on progressive control of government at the local, state and federal levels throughout the United States.

Control of the federal government is crucial, since federal policy has the most impact on creating a democratic society in the U.S. and around the world. But state and local governments have an enormous impact too. That's why we have to build strong progressive organizations—and a strong Democratic Party structure—in every state and locale. The past practice of writing off huge sections of America because they are unlikely to elect Democrats to Congress, or are not swing presidential states, greatly weakens our ability to achieve our goals.

On the other hand, it's also important to target resources strategically around elections to win control of Congress and the presidency. The federal government controls the national, and to some degree, the worldwide political debate. It won't do much good to have a "strong" local Democratic party in an America dominated by the right.

And let's be clear. The progressive movement cannot be successful without control of government.

Too much is at stake. We can't be satisfied to be losers who take solace in sitting on the sidelines arguing that we were "right." Politics is not a drill. It's the real thing that affects everyday people– and the future of humanity—every day. It's our job to *win.*

THE BATTLE FOR PROGRESSIVE CONTROL
OF GOVERNMENTS AROUND THE WORLD

American Progressives have a stake in the progressive control of governments throughout the world in just the same way that the outcome of a Senate election in Montana matters to someone who lives in Georgia.

You might argue that there is a big difference, that the Senator from Montana makes policy for all of us in the U.S. That's true. But the kinds of decisions made by governments in other areas in the world have a big impact on American interests and on the struggle for a democratic society— worldwide. Their actions directly impact Americans economically, environmentally and militarily everyday. No unions in Singapore means lower wages in Sacramento.

So Progressives are anything but isolationists.

We believe that the creation of a democratic society throughout the world is critical to the long-term interests of the United States—and every one of our families. It's important for the government of the United States to support progressive regimes around the world. For instance, the U.S. government should applaud the resurgence of social democratic, center-left governments in Latin America that were once run by right-wing governments dominated by the economic elite.

The U.S. should encourage regimes to promote institutions that protect workers' rights. It should encourage actions to control the power of corporations to destroy the environment. It should encourage free universal education and healthcare. It should stand for trade agreements that create international standards for labor and environment rights. America always should be a leader of the struggle for freedom and progressive governments—not military dictatorships, or the world's most powerful corporations and moguls.

George W. Bush talks about bringing "democracy" to the Middle East. He uses the right word. But he's only talking about elections—not the creation of a democratic society, where power is diffused to everyone.

That brings us to our last battleground.

PROGRESSIVES MUST ORGANIZE AND SUPPORT MASS MOVEMENTS THAT EMPOWER THE POWERLESS — BOTH HERE AND ABROAD

The anti-slave freedom fighter Frederick Douglass used to say, "You can't have the rain without thunder and lightning."

Apartheid did not end in South Africa without a mass movement spearheaded by the African National Congress—and an international economic boycott.

America did not win its independence without the Revolutionary War. African-Americans didn't get the right to vote without sit-ins, freedom rides and marches.

Freedom and democracy do not just happen, they are born of struggle.

Organizing and struggle are necessary to victory. But they do more as well. Struggle empowers its participants in and of itself. From the Des Moines housewife who joins a community organization, to the worker in a chicken processing plant who joins a union, to the college student who knocks on doors in a political campaign, to the immigrant who joins millions to march in Los Angeles, to the Third World workers who join a general strike—*organizing empowers*. It empowers very directly—and independently of its ultimate success.

When someone joins an organized struggle, they make the decision to make their own history—to become centers of creativity and action. They reject the role of passive victim and take action to shape their own future. Organizing very directly satisfies people's need for meaning. It makes them significant actors.

The battle for a progressive future is not solely about policy choices, or values or vision. It's not just about nuts-and-bolts execution, or effective messaging. It's about involving millions of everyday people in the battle for the future—the battle to create a democratic society.

Conclusion

Priorities for Action

I've argued throughout this book that once people's basic biological needs are satisfied, meaning is the greatest motivator. That goes for everyone, and it definitely is true for people who are involved at one level or the other in progressive political action. Whether they are defining strategy, walking precincts, or cheering at a rally, they care about the two things that impart meaning to action: they want to be part of a movement that can really make an historic difference, and they want to find a personal role that will allow them to make a significant contribution.

So the question of our priorities for action is at once both strategic and personal. As a movement, we need to decide on priorities that will maximize our chances of creating a society built on progressive values. In the near term, we need priorities that will give us the best chance of turning this historic opportunity into a long-term progressive realignment of American politics. And individually, each of us needs to decide how we can personally contribute.

Remember that a long-term realignment requires both a sustainable electoral majority, and the reframing of American political dialogue.

After considering all of the things we've discussed in this book, I believe that there are 18 particularly important priorities for Progressives in the months and years ahead.

PRIORITY FOR ACTION # 1

FRAMING THE DEBATE. PROGRESSIVES NEED TO CONSISTENTLY FRAME THE POLITICAL DIALOGUE IN TERMS OF PROGRESSIVE VALUES AND A PROGRESSIVE VISION FOR THE FUTURE

That is critical both to our ability to win the battle for the hearts and minds of persuadable voters and to our ability to inspire and motivate mobilize voters.

We are certainly making progress. Even before the 2006 midterm elections, in October 2006, the New York Times/CBS news poll asked, "Does the Republican Party or the Democratic Party come closer to sharing your moral values?" Forty-seven percent said Democrats, 28% said Republicans. [1]

Progressives must call America to purpose, to possibility, and to hope once again. We must assert our values, proudly and self-confidently. We have to listen to our mothers and stand up straight.

In their 2006 paper, the "The Politics of Definition," John Halpin and Ruy Teixeira argued that Democrats and Progressives suffered from an identity gap. That gap resulted both from Republican domination of the political terms of debate, and from progressive unwillingness to stand firmly for our own vision and values.

They pointed to a Democracy Corps poll in early 2006 that showed a double-digit identity gap even among voters residing in strongly Democratic areas. Eighty-four percent of Republican voters surveyed said they knew what the Republican Party stands for, exactly double the 42% margin for Democrats. [2]

Halpin and Teixeira argued, correctly, that "no identity translates into no character, no integrity, no vision worth fighting for, no domestic agenda, no national security agenda, no basic understanding of the problems facing everyday citizens, no contrast with the other side, no reason to vote for progressive candidates."

Many things have changed in the last year, but it still remains true that many more people know what Democrats are *against* than what we're *for*. And of course that's makes perfect sense. For the last 12 years, we've been battling horrible right-wing initiatives. House Speaker Nancy Pelosi passed her "100 Hour" program as a down payment on a broad progressive program, in considerable measure to help brand the Democratic agenda and give voters a sense of what we are *for*. At Americans United for Change, we helped organize the Change America Now (CAN) Campaign to pass that agenda through the House and Senate with big bipartisan majorities.

But policies by themselves won't do the trick. An essential truth of human nature is that *frames* trump facts. When presented with facts that are inconsistent with the frame through which people view the world, the frame will generally win, and inconsistent facts will be discarded or discounted.

That's why our top priority has to be the relentless, proud, self-confident repetition of our frame, our values, and our vision for the future. We have to activate the progressive value frame that exists in the minds of swing voters. We have to set the frame for political debate in America. It's our job to shape the voters' unconscious understanding of what constitutes political "common sense."

PRIORITY FOR ACTION # 2
VICTORY REQUIRES THAT WE GIVE EQUAL ATTENTION TO OUR STRATEGY, VALUES AND VISION ON THE ONE HAND, AND THE NUTS AND BOLTS OF EXECUTION ON THE OTHER.

Discussion of great political strategy, profession of deeply held values, and clarity of vision are essentially irrelevant academic exercises if they are not an integral part of effective political action.

In fact, political success generally hinges much more heavily on solid nuts and bolts execution than it does on great thinkers and political visionaries.

At the same time, the most competent execution, by the best political operatives, will not succeed in creating long-term progressive political realignment in America in the absence of clearly articulated strategy, values and vision.

We have to have them both. They are inextricably linked.

We need to focus on everything from nuts and bolts, to the meaning of life.

PRIORITY FOR ACTION # 3
PERSUADABLES AND MOBILIZABLES. THE TWO DECISIVE GROUPS WHO ARE THE PRIMARY TARGET FOR OUR COMMUNICATION ARE THE PERSUADABLE AND MOBILIZABLE VOTERS WHO DECIDE THE OUTCOME OF ELECTIONS.

Remember, persuadable voters are the relatively small group that regularly votes, but switches back and forth between political parties. Mobilizable voters are the group that would vote Democratic, but will not go to the polls unless they are mobilized.

They are the only two groups whose behavior can be changed by a political campaign.

PRIORITY FOR ACTION # 4
THE BASE VOTERS VS. SWING VOTERS CONFLICT IS A MYTH. WHILE THE MESSAGES THAT PERSUADE SWING VOTERS AND MOTIVATE MOBILIZABLE VOTERS ARE DIFFERENT, THEY NEED NOT CONFLICT.

The candidate qualities that are most effective for persuasion are also the ones that most effectively motivate and inspire our base voters as well.

Candidates who self-confidently communicate a progressive vision, demonstrate their commitment to progressive values and inspire voters with passion and commitment are the most effective at persuasion *and* mobilization.

Those who argue that to win, progressive candidates have to hide their values, moderate their positions or avoid battles are generally *wrong*.

Priority for Action # 5
We need to remember that people vote for people — not ideas, or issues.

In the end, persuadable voters are convinced by the personal qualities of a candidate. And candidates can motivate mobilizable voters if they can inspire them—if they can give them a sense of excitement and empowerment. Mobilizable voters are not motivated by position papers or resumes. They're motivated by inspiration that makes them feel that their vote can impart some level of meaning to their lives.

In the presidential contest of 2008, Democrats need to search first and foremost for a candidate who embodies our vision and our values—one who can inspire and motivate.

That will count more than experience, or the issue agenda, or voting records. More than anything else, we need a candidate who has the vision to lead America to meet the challenges and fulfill the promise of this critical crossroads in human history. We need a candidate who can inspire us to be more than we are—who calls on us to rise to the challenge.

We need a candidate who can appeal to the best of our hopes rather than the worst of our fears—a candidate who renews John Kennedy's call to "ask not what your country can do for you, ask what you can do for your country"—who convinces us we're all in this together, and that together we can succeed.

Priority for Action # 6
Organizing for victory. We need to focus our resources on building lasting, mass-based organizations – for electoral and issue campaigns.

Some people think that TV, great PR, and the Internet have made mass-based organizations obsolete. Wrong. Serious mass-based organization is the future.

In elections, field operations give us the means to focus as much attention on mobilizable voters as we do on persuadables. The principal field vehicle for elections should be the renewal of the volunteer structure of the Democratic Party. In 2004, Democrats and our progressive allies spent about the same number of dollars as Republicans and their conservative supporters. The difference was that a much greater portion of Republican activity was conducted and coordinated through the party itself.

There's no reason why we should have to reinvent the wheel every election. Democrats need to create nationwide, permanent, precinct-based, door-to-door organizations that develop indigenous local leaders to manage the precinct, do voter I.D. and GOTV operations, and build support between elections.

In individual races, and certainly in primary campaigns, we need to supplement the party structure with candidate-focused field operations. But we should seek to make the Democratic Party the progressive field structure for General Elections.

This emphasis runs contrary to the priority placed by most campaigns on paid-TV advertising—a priority that results partially from the economic incentives of many political consultants who make more from TV than from field operations. The fact is that over the long run—especially for mobilizable voters, and even for persuadables—there is nothing more important than repeated personal communication from a neighbor at the door or on the phone.

As we've seen, mobilization contributes just as many new voters to margins of victory as does persuasion. It often receives far fewer resources. That priority loses elections. The Republicans learned how to do field operations *from* Democrats. In 2004 they actually did a better job.

The Internet can help us find and nurture activists, and with millions of dollars being spent on major elections there is no excuse for our failure to develop strong permanent Democratic Party field organizations across America.

In addition, progressive organizations of all sorts have to concentrate their energy on developing strong mobilizable activist bases. To hold political officials accountable to progressive values, nothing beats dozens, thousands or millions of phone calls, packed townhall meetings, and press events involving local people in every corner of America. "Letterhead" organizations are a fine thing, but what is needed most is real grassroots mobilization. The Internet and the blogs open more and more opportunities for engaging and mobilizing grass roots constituencies.

Organizations like MoveOn, USAction, and Americans United for Change are models. And the campaign to stop the privatization of Social

Security showed how it can be done—a combination of aggressive press and messaging, with well-organized field operations that involve mobilizing hundreds of thousands of rank-and-file Americans.

PRIORITY FOR ACTION # 7
WE MUST REDEFINE "COMMON SENSE" BY REPEATEDLY COMMUNICATING PROGRESSIVE MESSAGE FRAMES DAY IN AND DAY OUT.

We have to surround voters with progressive message frames. Concretely, that means:

*   Battling to prevent media concentration that allows corporate domination of major mass media and entertainment outlets.

*   Building and supporting successful progressive media outlets like Air America, Nova M Radio, *The American Prospect*, *The Nation* and other new national progressive outlets.

*   Nurturing a robust progressive "blogosphere."

*   Publishing a blizzard of books and articles with progressive points of view—in the popular, scholarly, and trade media.

*   Producing fiction books, films and TV shows that develop progressive themes. The best metaphors are stories.

*   Conducting high-energy, campaign-style press operations year-round to frame the progressive message in the earned media using the model of organizations like Americans United for Change.

*   Tracking and responding to right wing media using techniques pioneered by groups like Media Matters.

*   Producing studies and position papers for major issue battles from a progressive point of view using the approach used by many right wing think tanks, and by progressive organizations like the Center for American Progress (CAP), Campaign for America's Future (CAF), Demos, and the Economic Policy Institute (EPI).

PRIORITY FOR ACTION # 8
CHANGING THE RELATIONS OF POWER. WE NEED TO FOCUS ON MAKING STRUCTURAL CHANGE—ON CHANGING THE RELATIONS OF POWER IN ORDER TO CREATE A TRULY DEMOCRATIC SOCIETY AROUND THE WORLD.

This priority includes all of the fronts we discussed in Section Nine:

- The battle over the distribution of income and wealth in the U.S.

- Expanding the power of Americans, acting through their government, to provide goods and services that are not provided efficiently through the private market.

- Restricting the power of companies to damage the environment and discharge greenhouse gases that cause climate change.

- Supporting the unionization of the workforce.

- Controlling the world's growing population—and per-person impact on global resources.

- Preventing the consolidation of America's media.

- Allocating resources to reduce structural violence—especially in developing countries.

- Empowering multinational organizations—especially the United Nations—to bring peaceful resolutions to international disputes; and ending the domination of neocon values and assumptions in American foreign policy.

- Maintaining a strong, flexible U.S. military—using military power to promote self-determination and a *progressive* agenda—as often as possible in a multinational context.

- Preventing the proliferation of weapons of mass destruction in general, and nuclear weapons in particular.

- Defending human rights, and due process of law and independent judiciary, in the U.S. and around the world.

- Promoting progressive control of government at all levels in the United States.

- Promoting progressive control of governments around the world.

- Organizing and supporting mass movements that empower the powerless—both here and abroad.

PRIORITY FOR ACTION # 9
IT'S THE STEAK, NOT JUST THE SIZZLE. SUBSTANCE MATTERS TO POLITICAL OUTCOMES.

As the Bush poll numbers began to plummet in the spring of 2006, there was a great deal of talk among the "chattering class" that his message and spin operations needed to be reorganized. Of course, that was not the problem at all. They were brilliant at spin.

The problem was with the substance of his policies. Frames trump facts, but at some point frames can be strained to the breaking point by events in the real world.

The problem with the neocon Iraq policy was not how it was spun. It was a disaster on the ground.

The problem with Katrina was not the spin. It was the massive incompetence coupled with an ideology that left Bush unprepared to cope with the greatest natural disaster in U.S. history.

For months the Bush people kept insisting that the economy was growing, and the voters were being told that things were getting better. In fact the economy was better—for the small segment of the wealthiest individuals and corporations—but not for most Americans, where incomes were stagnant. The Bush crowd did everything they could to divert wealth and income to high-income people and away from the middle class, and were surprised when the voters noticed.

The decline in Republican fortunes is directly related to the failure of their ideology and policies. There has been only one benefit of the right's near-total domination of our politics for so many years. They had a free hand to apply and test out their neocon foreign policies and trickle-down economic theories—and their failure is no longer theoretical but an empirical fact.

The Republicans learned that policies can be spun for a while but in the end, substance and results do matter. We have to remember that lesson as well.

PRIORITY FOR ACTION # 10
BIG IDEAS. RECLAIMING THE AMERICAN DREAM.

We should develop grassroots and message-based campaigns to support the passage of major congressional initiatives to deal boldly with the new issues facing America.

I'm not talking here about down payments on the progressive program, as important as they are. I'm talking about major overhauls that will truly address fundamental needs that face the country.

These include:

• **A Plan for Quality Health Care for All.** The health-care crisis intensifies on every front—the number of uninsured, skyrocketing costs, differential access. Polls show popular support for universal health care at massive levels. Time to take the bull by the horns, and take on the special interests.

The proposal should be clear and elegant. It should be uncomplicated and sound familiar. I believe that providing a Guaranteed, Affordable Choice plan that gave Americans the option to keep their private insurance or be part of a public plan is a winner.

• **Universal Access to Higher Education and Preschool.** Today, even a middle-class income requires a college degree. Access to college is far from universal. Remember that it now costs $40,000 a year to go to a selective private college, and $15,000 a year for an in-state student to attend a public university.

Yet in 2005, Federal Pell grants totaled only $4,050 per student per year.

We should propose increasing grants adequately to allow anyone to attend a public university at no cost; and sufficiently increase affordable student loans to cover the cost of access to the best elite universities.

In addition, we need to fund Head Start and other preschool programs adequately to assure that every child has access to quality preschool.

• **Energy Independence and Global Warming.** Progressives should propose a comprehensive energy-independence initiative to develop alternative fuels, lower fuel costs, cut carbon emissions, and address the critical problem of global warming.

Whatever gas prices are doing month-to-month, the price of hydrocarbons will increase as they become more and more scarce. And our dependence on the Middle East for oil also carries with it critical implications for foreign policy.

I'm not talking about incremental energy legislation. We need to do with energy what President Kennedy did with the space program. We need to challenge ourselves to achieve energy independence by a date certain—say, the end of the next decade.

For us, energy independence should have three meanings:

1. That we no longer are dependent on nonrenewable sources of energy such as oil;
2. That America itself can produce enough energy to meet our core needs;
3. That we are no longer dependent on energy sources that will destroy our climate and environment.

Taken together, these three initiatives address many of the core economic factors that are destroying America's middle class. For the first time since the Depression, more than half of workers believe that their children will not have better lives than they themselves do. That lack of hope results from major economic and social forces that we can address by "tinkering" around the edges.

Each of these elements of the "Agenda to Reclaim the American Dream" has broad, intense support in polling. What we need is the political will to turn that support into the centerpiece of American political dialogue.

PRIORITY FOR ACTION # 11
WE MUST PRESS CONGRESS TO DO WHATEVER IS NECESSARY TO FORCE THE REDEPLOYMENT OF AMERICAN TROOPS OUT OF IRAQ— AND ABANDON THE PRECEPTS OF NEOCON FOREIGN POLICY.

This is a must. Democrats won the 2006 Midterms largely because the war in Iraq convinced many Americans that Republicans were no longer fit to govern. Democrats can't muddle their way through on this one. We have to be decisive, tough-minded and fearless in making the decisions that need to be made.

When people ask Democrats for our plan in Iraq we have to be clear— our plan was not to go in the first place. Now, it is up to us to do the best we can to limit the damage. Once Bush invaded Iraq, in reality no good outcome was possible. The bottom has fallen out and support for the Iraq War. Congress must do everything in its power to force the issue and require a phased withdrawal by a date certain.

To force Bush to reverse course—or to begin the redeployment of troops from Iraq—before the next election requires that we put enough pressure on Republicans to force their support for the war to collapse.

PRIORITY FOR ACTION # 12
AGENTS OF CHANGE. TO BE SUCCESSFUL, DEMOCRATS AND PROGRESSIVES MUST CONSTANTLY POSITION OURSELVES AS POPULISTS—AS AGENTS OF CHANGE.

Of course, as Progressives, we are agents of change. But that's not how many people have historically seen us. Many conservatives believe that we represent the "cultural" status quo—the Hollywood, professional, bureaucratic, social-engineering, latte-drinking liberals who smugly looked down on them and wanted to control their lives.

While many conservatives will never be convinced to the contrary, there are also many persuadable voters who can be swayed when we demonstrate that we favor change, we challenge entrenched power, and we truly believe in democracy—that we battle *for* average people because we are average people.

The Democratic leadership in the House and Senate needs to communicate that Democrats can govern, that they are strong effective leaders. But we must never forget that it is even more important that people be reminded that we are *on their side.*

Whether or not we appear as populist agents of change on the one hand or defenders of elites on the other depends on three factors:

- We must constantly assert our value frame and vision for the future—a vision that calls for change and hope.

- We need to focus heavily on questions that involve who has the power—especially economic power. Progressives want to democratize power—to take power from elites and give it to average people. Many, many of the people attracted to the right's version of populism simply feel powerless.

- When we present positions on cultural issues on which we disagree, we need to do it with respect, and appeal to the values of tolerance. If we treat groups of average people with disdain and disrespect, and without regard for the tolerance we ourselves espouse, that disrespect goes right to the heart of their need for meaning—right to their identity. Disrespect will never be forgiven, and more than anything else, it will validate their view that we ourselves are the elite—not agents of change.

In his book, *Wealth and Democracy: A Political History of the American Rich,* Kevin Phillips points out that the Democratic administrations that have been successful historic watersheds have always presented themselves in populist terms—in opposition to entrenched elites. [3]

PRIORITY FOR ACTION # 13
PROJECTING A WINNING ATTITUDE.

People don't want to follow losers or whiners; they want to spend time with winners. If we don't think we are winners, we will never win the long-term battle for the hearts and minds of Americans.

Progressives and progressive values *will* define the future, and human progress. We have to believe that—and always act as if it is true.

And that means that Progressives need to stop spending half their time criticizing fellow Democrats.

PRIORITY FOR ACTION # 14
BUILDING A PROGRESSIVE MOVEMENT.

In his book, *Being Right Is Not Enough: What Progressives Must Learn from Conservative Success,* Paul Waldman quotes a 1971 memo by Lewis Powell, who would later be nominated by Richard Nixon to the Supreme Court. The memo was written to the U.S. Chamber of Commerce and provided an action plan for the men who would found the Conservative Movement of the coming decades. Waldman says:

> In what could stand as a motto for the conservative movement he helped spawn, Powell wrote, "Strength lies in organization, and careful long-range planning and implementation, in consistency of action over an indefinite period of years, and the scale of financing available only through joint effort, and in the political power available only from united action and national organizations." [4]

The Right created a coherent political movement. It was comprised of many factions and organizations, but it had a distinct set of processes and values—and organizational culture—that gave it coherence and made it much more than the sum of its parts.

By that definition, there is also a Progressive Movement in America, but it needs to be dramatically strengthened to effectively compete with the conservative movement over the long run.

Several steps are necessary:

•Funders should focus resources with conscious concern as to how each organization's efforts contribute to the Progressive Movement as a whole—not just to achieving some isolated single-issue goal.

Historically liberal foundations have assiduously avoided precisely this kind of political concern in making grants to single issue organizations of all types. Their right-wing counterparts—

the Adolph Coors Foundation, the Koch Family Foundation, The Scaife Foundation and the like—are in the business of funding movement organizations to advance the conservative cause. The Democracy Alliance, a consortium of major progressive donors, may be a step in this direction.

•Funders and large progressive institutional players need to invest in multi-issue progressive organizations that have the single goal of advancing the progressive agenda and defeating the Right. Organizations like USAction, Americans United for Change, the Campaign for America's Future, the Midwest Academy, MoveOn. org, People For the American Way, and think tanks like the Center for American Progress and Demos are prime examples. These organizations are not in business simply to advance the interests of a particular constituency, or to win a specific issue battle—but to organize for progressive ideas and progressive political power.

•Progressives from every type of organization should build on the working relationships forged through the coalitions that have been formed to fight the Bush tax cuts, the privatization of Social Security, right-wing Supreme Court nominations, the Iraq War— and the fight for children's health insurance.

We've done a good deal over the last few years to develop regular procedures for communication, mobilization and decision-making. We have to self-consciously create opportunities for each institution to become invested in the success of the entire movement—a real sense that the whole is greater than the sum of its parts.

Priority for Action # 15
Progressives in America need to work closely with Progressives around the world.

Preventing a wage race to the bottom depends not only on what we do in the U.S., but the ability of labor unions to organize around the world.

Preventing environmental catastrophe or global warming depends as much on what happens in China and India as what happens in California or Montana.

Protecting fishing stocks in the Pacific depends as much on what happens in Tokyo and Santiago as it does on what happens in Washington, D.C.

Fulfilling the promise of a democratic society depends as much on educating women in Africa, as it does on our work in Tennessee.

Preventing terrorism in our cities requires that people have economic opportunity in Yemen.

In an increasingly integrated world, Progressives must coordinate our strategies, and provide mutual assistance to each other around the globe. Multinational corporations don't have any problem developing worldwide networks. We must do the same.

That means that American progressives need to get to know progressive leaders from around the world.

We can build a worldwide vision for the future of the planet that is rooted in internationally recognized progressive values.

PRIORITY FOR ACTION # 16
HOPE TRUMPS FEAR.

In the end, unvarnished fear is a destructive emotion. It doesn't lead to action, but to paralysis. It doesn't inspire sacrifice for the common good; it either fosters a malaise of hopelessness or a "save yourself" desperation.

For years, Bush and the radical conservatives have used fear as their chief weapon to maintain support and justify their attempts to aggregate unconstrained power. Fear makes people cower. It is the weapon used by tyrants to control and dominate.

Roosevelt was right: "The only thing we have to fear is fear itself."

The antidote to fear is hope. Progressives must be realistic about the many challenges that face America, and all of human society; but we must always offer hope for success. Human beings respond instinctively to a call to sacrifice for hope and possibility. While they can be immobilized by fear, hope makes them stand tall and fight.

In Barack Obama's words, the key to progressive success is "the audacity of hope."

PRIORITY FOR ACTION # 17
POLITICS IS NOT JUST ANOTHER GAME—WE HAVE TO FIGHT LIKE THE FUTURE OF HUMAN SOCIETY IS AT STAKE—BECAUSE IT IS.

Human beings have never been forced to make decisions with more consequences than we will be called upon to make in the 21st century.

The political decisions of this generation—and the few to follow—will determine if humanity makes it through that gauntlet; whether our values and political structures can keep pace with our exploding technological capacity; whether we create a truly democratic society, or become an evolutionary dead-end.

Thirteen thousand years ago human beings made the pivotal decision to begin food production—a decision that qualitatively transformed human society, technology and possibility. We are only 650 generations removed from our forebears who made that momentous decision. The hunter-gatherer lifestyle had sustained human life for millions of years. Our forebears had the luxury of taking thousands of years to make these decisions to switch from hunter-gathering to farming and herding. The decisions we are required to make are equally momentous, but they must be made in decades, years and sometimes minutes.

Every winter the Democratic Caucus of the House has a retreat attended by members and their spouses. In the winter of 2001, following the Bush election, it was held at a resort in southeastern Pennsylvania. George W. Bush had just been elected and attended the retreat to address Congressional Democrats for the first time. My personal impression of the new President was frightening. I realized just how frightening on the drive home, when the movie on the bus was "Thirteen Days"—the story of the Cuban Missile Crisis.

In October 1963, the Soviet Union began installing nuclear-tipped missiles in Cuba, 90 miles from the U.S. mainland. President Kennedy and his Russian counterparts made decisions over a period of 13 days that could have led the world over the cliff to nuclear catastrophe. I for one am thankful that John Kennedy was there to use the progressive values he expressed in his Inaugural Address to make those decisions. What if George W. Bush, Dick Cheney and Don Rumsfeld had been making those decisions, using the values implicit in the neocon worldview?

The decisions our society faces today are no less momentous than those made by Kennedy 40 years ago. It's up to us to determine who is in the room when those decisions are made, and to assure that progressive values are used in making them.

PRIORITY FOR ACTION # 18
DON'T STAND ON THE SIDELINES.

Meaning in life involves making commitments to something outside yourself. Forty years ago, the events of the 1960s convinced me that nothing would be more rewarding—nothing was more important—than the struggle for social and economic justice. After four decades, I still feel exactly the same way.

I've already mentioned Jan's spring 2006 trips to Africa and Chile. In South Africa, her delegation visited Robben Island, where Nelson Mandela was imprisoned with other African National Congress leaders for part of his 27-year incarceration by the Apartheid regime. Mandela had managed to convince his guards to provide the prisoners a library. He had instructed his fellow inmates that they must use the time—against all hope—"to prepare to govern." With much of the world, I remember watching the television on a Sunday morning as Mandela walked from that prison— and later as he presided over South Africa's first democratically elected government. Change happens.

On the same trip, Jan's delegation also visited Liberia, where newly elected President Ellen Johnson had just taken the helm of a battered and war-torn country. Johnson, too, had been imprisoned in the course of her struggle for an end to the ethnic strife in Liberia. Now she's Liberia's President. Change happens.

On Jan's trip to newly elected Chilean President Michelle Bachellet's inaugural, she visited the Villa Grimaldi where Bachellet and her mother had been held and tortured 30 years earlier by the dictatorship of Augusto Pinochet. Her father, an Air Force general, had already been tortured and died in prison. Now she is President of Chile. Change happens.

We can make the future.

Human beings are about six decades along into that gauntlet that will decide if our values and politics can keep pace with our exploding technological capacity. The next few generations will determine whether that gauntlet becomes a dark dead-end tunnel that extinguishes human history or whether we emerge to create the first truly democratic society.

Our challenge is to construct a future based on the progressive values that have always been the most precious creation of human society—now more than ever.

However you can contribute, I believe there is no more important work—nothing more meaningful to which you can commit your life.

And I can promise you greatness.

I guarantee it.

Martin Luther King said:

> Everyone can be great. Because anybody can serve. You don't have to have a college degree to serve. You don't have to make your subject and verb agree to serve. You don't have to know about Plato and Aristotle to serve. You don't have to know Einstein's theory of relativity to serve. You don't have to know the second law of thermodynamics in physics to serve. You only need a heart full of grace. A soul generated by love.

King continued:

> As long as there is poverty in the world I can never be rich, even if I have $1 billion. As long as diseases are rampant and millions of people in this world

cannot expect to live more than 28 or 30 years, I can never be totally healthy, even if I just got a good checkup at the Mayo Clinic. I can never be what I want to be until you are what you ought to be. This is the way our world is made. No individual or nation can stand our boasting of being independent. We are inter-dependent.

The ultimate measure of a man or woman is not where he stands in moments of comfort and convenience, but where he stands at times of challenge and controversy. The true neighbor will risk his position, his prestige, and even his life for the welfare of others. In dangerous valleys and hazardous pathways, he will lift some bruised and beaten brother or sister to a higher and more noble life. [5]

You can do that as:

- A community organizer empowering people to stand for themselves;

- At the U.N. working to create the architecture of a peaceful world;

- A congressional staffer, providing expertise and political savvy to make the forces of justice victorious in the everyday battles with the thousands of special interest lobbyists and contributors;

- A leader of a nongovernmental organization battling to protect our environment;

- Organizing to end an unjust war;

- Working with refugees of war and terror in Colombia;

- Helping to reduce the spread of AIDS in Africa;

- Organizing minimum-wage workers to fight for economic justice and a better life on the west side of Chicago;

- A scientist;

- A doctor;

- A lawyer who takes on the wealthiest corporations, or defends the rights of the powerless;

- Campaigning for progressive candidates for public office;

- Running for office yourself so you can provide the kind of committed leadership that can make all of us great.

If the struggle to create a progressive future—the fight for justice—becomes your life's work, you may never get rich, but you will be able to look yourself in the mirror each morning and know that you are devoting your life to bringing to birth a just world where every child can reach out and fulfill his or her potential, can be what he or she ought to be.

And never be discouraged or believe for a minute that you can't be successful because there are not enough of you out there who are devoted to the struggle.

To paraphrase Margaret Mead: "Never think that a small group of committed people can't change the world. No one else ever has."

END NOTES

SECTION ONE

Chapter One:

[1] Robert Kennedy, Jr., "Was the 2004 Election Stolen?," *Rolling Stone*, June 1, 2006.

Chapter Two:

[1] House data summarized in a November 13, 2006 memo by Congressman Rahm Emanuel.

Chapter Three:

[1] E.J. Dionne, *The Washington Post*, April 21, 2006

[2] Rick Klein, *The Boston Globe*, November 12, 2006

SECTION TWO

CHAPTER FOUR:

[1] Thomas Franks, *What's the Matter With Kansas?: How Conservatives Won the Heart of America* (New York: Owl Books, 2004)

[2] Paul Krugman, "Class War Politics," *The New York Times*, June 19, 2006, p. 19

[3] Michael Shaara, *The Killer Angels* (New York: Random House, 1975), pp. 324-327

[4] Vera Foundation, "Confronting Confinement," p. 58

CHAPTER FIVE:

[1] Nolan McCarty, Keith T. Poole, Howard Rosenthal, *Polarized America: The Dance of Ideology and Unequal Riches* (Cambridge: MIT Press, 2006), pp. 75-76

[2] Center on Budget and Policy Priorities, 2006

[3] Jared Diamond, *Guns, Germs, and Steel: The Fates of Human Societies* (New York: W.W. Norton and Co, 1997), p. 213

[4] Diamond, *Guns, Germs, and Steel*, p. 202

CHAPTER SIX:

[1] Thomas A. Peters and Robert J. Waterman, Jr., *In Search of Excellence* (New York: Harper Collins, 1984), pp. xxi-xxii

[2] Ibid, p. 81

Chapter Seven:

[1] George Lakoff, *Whose Freedom? The Battle Over America's Most Important Idea* (New York: Farrar, Strauss and Giroux, 2006), p. 10

[2] Dr. Daoyun Ji and Dr. Matthew Wilson, "Coordinated Memory Replay in the Visual Cortex and Hippocampus During Sleep," Nature Neuroscience, December 17, 2006, pp. 100-107

[3] Lakoff, *Whose Freedom?*, p. 12

[4] Ibid, p. 12

[5] Ibid, p. 12

[6] Ibid, p. 28

[7] Ibid, p. 13

Chapter Eight:

[1] David Brown, "Why Do Cats Hang Around Us? (Hint: They Can't Open Cans)," *The Washington Post*, June 29, 2007, p. A03

Chapter Ten:

[1] Celia W. Dugger, "Push for New Tactics as War on Malaria Falters," *The New York Times*, June 28, 2006, p. A01

SECTION THREE

Chapter Fourteen:

[1] Thomas J. Peters and Robert H. Waterman, *In Search of Excellence* (New York: Warner Books, 1984), p. 73

[2] Ibid, p. 74

[3] Ibid, p. 74

[4] E. J. Dionne, "'The Real America', Redefined," *The Washington Post*, December 19, 2006, p. A29

[5] Briefing by Anna Greenberg, August 14, 2007.

Chapter Sixteen:

[1] Malcolm Gladwell, *Blink* (New York: Little, Brown and Co., 2005)

[2] Malcolm Gladwell, *The Tipping Point* (Boston: Little, Brown and Co. Back Bay, 2002), p. 35

[3] Gladwell, *The Tipping Point*, p. 48

[4] Ibid, p. 48

[5] Ibid, p. 70

[6] Ibid, pp. 77-78

[7] Ibid, p. 83

[8] Gladwell, *Blink*, p. 205

[9] Gladwell, *The Tipping Point*, p. 196-197

[10] Neil Smelser, *The Theory of Collective Behavior*, (Glencoe: The Free Press of Glencoe, 1963)

CHAPTER SEVENTEEN:

[1] Gladwell, *Blink*, p. 11-12

[2] Peters and Waterman, *In Search of Excellence*, p. 59

[3] Ibid, pp. 66-67

[4] Ibid, p. 67

[5] Gregory Bateson, *Mind and Nature: A Necessary Unity* (New York: Bantam, 1980), p. 14

CHAPTER EIGHTEEN:

[1] *Chicago Tribune* poll, November 22, 2006, p. 17

[2] *The Washington Post*, "Democrats Look Beyond City Limits," July 2, 2006, p. A5

[3] Jim Wallis, *God's Politics* (New York: HarperOne, 2006)

[4] Faithful Democrats, PowerPoint, June 10, 2006

SECTION FOUR

CHAPTER TWENTY-ONE:

[1] Tucker Carlson, "Memo to the Democrats: Quit Being Losers!", *New York Times Magazine*, January 19, 2003, Section 6, p. 36

[2] David S. Broder, "The GOP Lag Among Latinos," *Washington Post Weekly Edition*, July 31, 2006, p. 4

[3] Malcolm Gladwell, *Blink* (New York: Little, Brown and Co., 2005), p. 33

[4] Donald T. Phillips, *Lincoln on Leadership* (New York: Warner Books, 1993), p. 40

[5] Joe Klein, *Primary Colors* (New York: Grand Central Publishing, 1996), pp. 1-2

[6] Thomas J. Peters and Robert H. Waterman, *In Search of Excellence (New York: Warner Books, 1982), pp. 58-59*

[7] Ibid.

[8] Ibid., p. 83

CHAPTER TWENTY-TWO:

[1] U.S. Census Bureau, reported in *The Washington Post*, May 26, 2005

CHAPTER TWENTY-THREE:

[1] Phillips, Lincoln on Leadership, p. 158

[2] Peters and Austin, *A Passion for Excellence* (New York: Harper & Row, 1985), pp. 278, 281

[3] Phillips, *Lincoln on Leadership*, p. 159

CHAPTER TWENTY-FOUR:

Daniel Goleman, *Social Intelligence* (New York: Bantam Books, 2006), pp. 15-16

[2] Clive Thompson, "There's a Sucker Born in Every Medial Prefrontal Cortex," *The New York Times Magazine*, October 26, 2003

[3] Gladwell, *Blink*, p. 12

[4] Ibid, p. 12

[5] Ibid, p. 12

[6] Ibid, p. 27

[7] Ibid, p. 85

CHAPTER TWENTY-EIGHT:

[1] Malcolm Gladwell, *The Tipping Point* (New York: Little, Brown and Co., 2002), p. 98

[2] Ibid, p.22

[3] Ibid, p. 98

CHAPTER TWENTY-NINE:

[1] Ibid, p.142

[2] Ibid, pp. 153-154

[3] Ibid, pp. 165-168

SECTION FIVE

CHAPTER THIRTY-THREE:

[1] Saul Alinsky, *Rules for Radicals* (New York: Vintage Books, 1989)

[2] Paraphrased from the original quote from California Assembly Speaker Jesse Unruh, "If you can't take their money, drink their booze, screw their women and look them in the eye and vote against them, you don't belong here," "The New Jesse Unruh," *Time* Magazine, September 14, 1970

CHAPTER THIRTY-FIVE:

[1] Clayton M. Christensen, *The Innovator's Dilemma* (New York: Harper Collins, 2000), p. xxiii.

[2] Ibid, p. 105

SECTION SIX

CHAPTER THIRTY-SEVEN:

[1] Clayton M. Christensen, *The Innovator's Dilemma* (New York: Harper Collins 2000), pp. 184-200

[2] Thomas J. Peters and Robert H. Waterman, *In Search of Excellence* (New York: Warner Books,1984), p.75

CHAPTER THIRTY-EIGHT:

[1] *Chicago Tribune*, August 10, 2006

[2] Thomas J. Peters and Robert H. Waterman, *In Search of Excellence* (New York: Warner Books,1984), p.68

[3] Ibid, p. 68

[4] John Keegan, *The Mask of Command* (New York: Penguin Group, 1988)

[5] Peters and Waterman, pp. 84-85

CHAPTER THIRTY-NINE:

[1] Alan Gerber and Donald Green, "Does Canvassing Increase Voter Turnout? A Field Experiment," *Proceedings of the National Academy of Sciences of the United States*, Vol 96, Issue 19, 10939-10942, September 14, 1999.

[2] Robert Kennedy, Jr., "Was the 2004 Election Stolen?", *Rolling Stone*, June 1, 2006

SECTION SEVEN

CHAPTER FORTY:

[1] George Lakoff, *Whose Freedom?* (New York: Farrar, Straus and Giroux, 2006), pp. 74-76 and pp. 97-99

[2] Ibid, pp. 76-77

[3] Ibid, p. 77

CHAPTER FORTY-ONE:

[1] Jared Diamond, *Guns, Germs, and Steel: The Fates of Human Societies* (New York: W. W. Norton & Co., 1999), p. 272

[2] Daniel Goleman, *Social Intelligence: The New Science of Human Relationships* (New York: Bantam, 2006), p. 18

[3] *Washington Post National Weekly*, October 28, 2006, p. 35

[4] *Washington Post National Weekly*, October 28, 2006, p. 35

[5] Lakoff, *Whose Freedom?*, p. 86

[6] *The Economist*, October 14, 2006, p.86

[7] Diamond, *Guns, Germs, and Steel*, 1999

[8] Adam Smith, *An Inquiry into the Nature and Causes of the Wealth of Nations* (London: Methuen & Co., 1904)

[9] *The Washington Post*, March 5, 2007

[10] *The Economist*, September 30, 2006, p. 100

CHAPTER FORTY-TWO:

[1] *The New York Times,* August 28, 2006

[2] *The Washington Post,* January 24, 2007, p. A13

[3] Paul Krugman, "Left Behind Economics," *The New York Times,* July 14, 2006

[4] Nolan McCarty, Keith T. Poole and Howard Rosenthal, *Polarized America: The Dance of Ideology and Unequal Riches* (Cambridge, MA: The MIT Press, 2006)

[5] Citizens for Tax Justice, Report, May 12, 2006

[6] *New York Times,* editorial page, August 30, 2006

[7] Kevin Phillips, *Wealth and Democracy: A Political History of the American Rich* (New York: Broadway, 2003)

[8] Ibid

[9] Ibid

SECTION EIGHT

CHAPTER FORTY-FOUR:

[1] Jared Diamond, *Guns, Germs, and Steel* (New York: W. W. Norton & Co., 1999), p. 36

[2] Ibid, p. 50

[3] Ibid, p. 86

[4] Ibid, p. 92

[5] Ibid, p. 266

[6] Ibid, p. 276

[7] Ibid, p. 281

[8] Ibid, p. 282

[9] Ibid, pp. 288-289

[10] Clayton M. Christensen, *The Innovator's Dilemma* (Harper Business Essentials, 2003)

[11] Diamond, *Guns, Germs, and Steel, pp. 258-259*

[12] Jared Diamond, *Collapse* (New York: Viking Penguin, 2005)

CHAPTER FORTY-FIVE:

[1] Diamond, *Collapse,* p. 119

[2] Ibid, p. 15

[3] Barbara W. Tuchman, *The March of Folly* (New York: Ballantine, 1985)

[4] Diamond, *Collapse,* p. 431

[5] Christensen, *The Innovator's Dilemma*

CHAPTER FORTY-SIX:

[1] Al Gore, *An Inconvenient Truth* (New York: Rodale Books, 2006)

[2] *The Economist*, November 16, 2006, p. 18

[3] *The Economist*, November 16, 2006, p. 18

[4] *The Economist*, September 16, 2006, p. 70

CHAPTER FORTY-SEVEN:

[1] Jon Christensen, "Unlikely Partners Create Plan to Save Ocean Habitat Along with Fishing," *The New York Times*, August 8, 2006, p. 3

[2] Celia Dugger, "Need for Water Could Double in 50 Years, U.N. Study Finds," *The New York Times*, August 22, 2006

CHAPTER FORTY-EIGHT:

[1] Gore, *An Inconvenient Truth*, p. 20

[2] Ibid, p. 22

[3] Andrew C. Revkin, "NASA Scientists See New Signs of Global Warming," *The New York Times*, September 9, 2006

[4] *The Economist*, September 9, 2006

[5] Ibid

[6] "Methane a New Climate Threat: Methane Escaping Five Times Faster Than Previously Thought," Associated Press, September 7, 2006

[7] Gore, *An Inconvenient Truth*, p. 33

[8] Ibid, p. 144

[9] Ibid, pp. 182-184

[10] *The Economist*, September 9, 2006

[11] Gore, *An Inconvenient Truth*, p. 190

[12] Ibid, p. 196-200

[13] William Neikirk, "UN Report Predicts Global Warming Effects in U.S.," *Chicago Tribune*, February 2, 2007

[14] *The Economist*, September 9, 2006

[15] Ibid

[16] Gore, *An Inconvenient Truth*, p. 92

[17] Ibid, p. 106

[18] Ibid, pp. 114-115

[19] Ibid, p. 121

[20] Ibid, p. 164

[21] Ibid, p. 172

[22] *The Economist*, September 9, 2006

[23] Gore, *An Inconvenient Truth*, p. 147

[24] *The Economist*, September 9, 2006, p. 13

[25] Gore, *An Inconvenient Truth*, p. 229

[26] Ibid, p. 63

[27] *The Economist*, September 9, 2006

[28] Gore, *An Inconvenient Truth*, p. 67

[29] *The Economist*, September 16, 2006, p. 20

[30] Gore, *An Inconvenient Truth*, p. 280

[31] Ibid, p. 281

[32] *The Economist*, September 9, 2006, p. 17

[33] Gore, *An Inconvenient Truth*, p. 253

[34] Ibid, p. 294

[35] *The Economist*, September 9, 2006, p. 16

[36] Ibid, p.16

[37] Diamond, *Collapse*, p. 276

[38] Gore, *An Inconvenient Truth*, p. 12

[39] Ibid, p. 298

CHAPTER FORTY-NINE:

[1] *The Economist*, September 2, 2006, p. 70

[2] David Grinspoon, *Lonely Planets: The Natural Philosophy of Alien Life* (New York: HarperCollins, 2003)

[3] Diamond, *Collapse*, pp. 325-326

[4] Ibid, p. 226

[5] Ibid, p. 378

[6] *The New York Times*, September 15, 2006

[7] Nick Rosen, *Washington Post Weekly Edition*, June 15, 2006, p. 21

[8] Andrew J. Bacevich, *The Washington Post Weekly Edition*, September 17, 2006, p. 21

[9] George Lakoff, *Whose Freedom? The Battle over America's Most Important Idea* (New York: Farrar, Straus and Giroux, 2006), p. 218

[10] R. C. Longworth, "Cheney doctrine of first strike, world dominion, and preemption," Chicago Tribune, September 29, 2002

[11] Paul Krugman, *The New York Times*, September 11, 2006

[12] *The New York Times*, October 11, 2006

[13] *The Washington Post Weekly Edition*, September 17, 2006, p. 21

[14] Ibid, p.21

[15] Ibid, p. 21

[16] *The Washington Post*, June 22, 2007

[17] *The Los Angeles Times*, September 20, 2006

[18] *Washington Post Weekly Edition*, August 28, 2006, p. 21

[19] *Washington Post Weekend Magazine*, August 23, 2006, p. 21

[20] *Washington Post Weekly Edition*, September 11, 2006, p. 3

21 *The New York Times*, August 14, 2006

22 *The New York Times*, September 27, 2006, p. A30

23 *The Economist*, September 2, 2006, p. 25

24 *The Washington Post*, January 23, 2007

25 *The New York Times*, June 14, 2006

26 *The New York Times*, September 11, 2006, p. 30

27 Pew Global Attitudes Project, reported in *The Washington Post*, June 27, 2007

28 *The Washington Post*, January 30, 2007, p. A1

29 Paul Krugman, "Shock and Awe," *The New York Times*, July 31, 2006

30 Seymour M. Hersh, *The New Yorker*, July 10, 2006

31 Ibid

32 Ibid

33 Ibid

34 *The Washington Post*, February 7, 2007

35 *The New Yorker*, July 10, 2006

36 George Packer, The New Yorker, July 10, 2006, p.96

37 Paul Farmer, *Pathologies of Power*, forward by Amartya Sen.

38 Farmer, *Pathologies of Power* (Berkeley: University of California, 2005), p. 30

39 Ibid, pp. 30-31

40 Farah Stockman and Susan Milligan, The Boston Globe, March 7, 2004

41 Farmer, *Pathologies of Power*, forward by Amartya Sen, p. xxvii

42 The World Health Organization, 1995, p. 5, reported in Farmer, *Pathologies of Power*, p. 50

43 *The Boston Globe*, January 26, 2003

44 Farmer, forward by Amartya Sen, Pathologies of Power, 2005, pp. xv-xvi

45 Ibid, p. 44

46 Ibid, p. 45

47 Ibid, p. 45

48 Meeting in Rome with Tony Hall, U.S. Ambassador to the U.N. food program, June 2003.

49 Ibid, p. xxvii

50 *The New York Times*, August 30, 2006, p. 20

51 *The New York Times*, September 21, 2006

CHAPTER FIFTY:

1 Diamond, *Collapse*, pp. 132-133

2 Ibid, pp. 133-134

3 Ibid, p. 135

4 *The Washington Post*, February 14, 2007

[5] *The Economist,* September 23, 2006, p. 11

[6] Ibid, p. 11

[7] Ibid, p. 11

[8] Ibid, p. 11

CHAPTER FIFTY-TWO:

[1] Robert Putnam, *Bowling Alone: The Collapse and Revival of American Community* (New York: Simon & Schuster, 2000)

[2] Lake Research Partners, "American Dream Survey: Hope and Fear in Working America," August 28, 2006

SECTION NINE

CHAPTER FIFTY-FOUR:

[1] *The Washington Post Weekly,* September 25, 2006

[2] Gladwell, "The Risk Pool," The New Yorker, August 28, 2006

[3] Gladwell, "The Risk Pool," *The New Yorker,* August 28, 2006

[4] Gladwell, "The Risk Pool," *The New Yorker,* August 28, 2006

[5] Health Affairs, 25, no. 3 (2006): 819-831 doi: 10.1377/hlthaff.25.3.819, "Health Care Spending And Use Of Information Technology In OECD Countries," Gerard F. Anderson, Bianca K. Frogner, Roger A. Johns and Uwe E. Reinhardt

[6] *The New York Times,* September 27, 2006

[7] *The New York Times,* March 2, 2007

[8] *The New Yorker,* October 2, 2006, p.76

[9] Dorothy Wickenden, *The New Yorker,* October 2, 2006

[10] National Institute for Early Education, research paper, December 2003

[11] Paul Krugman, *The New York Times,* October 6, 2006

[12] Lake Research Partners, in "American Dream Survey: Hope and Fear in Working America 2006"

[13] Paul Krugman, "A Brutal Way with Wages," *The New York Times,* October 6, 2006

[14] *The Nation,* October 16, 2006, p. 6

[15] Charles Benton, Speech at the National Press Club, February 9, 2007

[16] Robert Frost, "Mending Wall," *The Poems of Robert Frost* (New York: Holt, Rinehart & Winston, 1969)

[17] Kate Zernike, "Political Action: The Ad Campaign; A Nuclear Drama," *The New York Times,* October 12, 2006

[18] *The New York Times,* October 12, 2006

[19] Selig S. Harrison, "In a Test, a Reason to Talk," *The Washington Post,* October 10, 2006, p. A21

[20] Robert Kaplan, *The Atlantic Monthly,* October 2006

[21] Garrison Keillor, "Congress' Shameful Retreat from American Values," *Chicago Tribune*, October 1, 2006

[22] Ariel Dorfman, *Washington Post National Weekly Edition*, October 28, 2006

[23] Sasha Abramsky, Senior Fellow at the Demos Foundation, *The Rocky Mountain News*, August 4, 2006

CONCLUSION

[1] *The New York Times*, October 10, 2006

[2] John Halpin and Ruy Teixeira, "The Politics of Definition," *The American Prospect*, May 2006, p. 2

[3] Kevin Phillips, *Wealth and Democracy: A Political History of the American Rich* (New York: Broadway, 2003), p. 341

[4] Paul Waldman, Being Right Is Not Enough: What Progressives Must Learn from Conservative Success (Hoboken, NJ: Wiley, 2006), p. 13

[5] Coretta Scott King, *The Words of Martin Luther King, Jr.*, (New York, Newmarket Press, 1987)

INDEX

April 1968, 69–70
Aristide, Jean-Bertrand, 473–476
Aspen Institute, 443, 494
Atlantic Monthly, 546
attacks, using as an occasion to deliver negatives, 243–244
Austin, Nancy, 183
Axelrod, David, 158

B

Bacevich, Andrew J., 461
Bachellet, Michelle, 494, 592
Baker, Jim, 111
bands, 407–408
baseline poll, 214–225
Bateson, Gregory, 102
Begala, Paul, 142–143
belief, acting yourself into, 203
believability, 325–326
Benton, Charles, 554
Benton, William, 327
Bergman, Saul, 114
Black Caucus, 475
Blackwell, Ken, Ohio Secretary of State, 12
blue demographics, 112–118, 209
Blum, Jeff, 14
Bonilla, Henry, 10
Booth, Heather, 56–57, 273
Booth, Paul, 57
Brady, Jim and Sarah, 243
Bright House Institute, 190–191
Brock, David, 72
Brown, Sherrod, 4, 124
Brown University, 103
budgets, protecting, 291
Burns, Conrad, 10
Burns, George MacGregor, 173-174
Bush, George H.W., 246
Bush, George W., 149, 152, 154-160,171,191, 226-227, 230, 232–233, 239, 270, 280, 371, 430, 458, 463–464, 469, 475, 482–484, 517, 532–535, 539, 544, 574, 584, 591
Butz, Earl, 137–138
Byman, Daniel, 463

I

T

winning, attitude of, 314
winning number, 259
Wolfowitz, Paul, 458
Working Assets, 280
World Health Organization, 477
World Trade Organization, 536, 553

Y
Yoke, Gary, 447

Z
Zimbardo, Phillip, 235–236
Zwick, David, 440